Practical Art of
Motion Picture Sound
Second Edition

David Lewis Yewdall M.P.S.E.

Focal Press

An Imprint of Elsevier Science
AMSTERDAM   BOSTON   LONDON   NEW YORK   OXFORD   P
SAN DIEGO   SAN FRANCISCO   SINGAPORE   SYDNEY   TOKY

Focal Press is an imprint of Elsevier

Library of Congress Cataloging-in-Publication Data
A catalog record for this book is available from the Library of Congress.

ISBN: 0-240-80525-9

British Library Cataloguing-in-Publication Data
A catalogue record for this book is available from the British Library.

The publisher offers special discounts on bulk orders of this book.
For information, please contact:
Manager of Special Sales
Elsevier Science
200 Wheeler Road
Burlington, MA 01803
Tel: 781-313-4700
Fax: 781-313-4880

For information on all Focal Press publications available, contact our World Wide Web home page at: http://www.focalpress.com

10 9 8 7 6 5 4 3 2

Printed in the United States of America

To my wife
Lisa
Her patience, hard work and support made it possible.

Special Thanks and Acknowledgments

Roger Corman

Bruce Campbell

André Perreault
Lead Mixer

Ethan Bush
Operations Manager—Enterprise Post

Catherine Clark and the Jack Poley Estate

Uila-Maija Parikka
Helsinki, Finland

Coffey Sound
Special thanks for supplying the Deva and marching microphones to make the comparison recording test possible

Jim Webb
Production Film Mixer

Brenda Hollingsworth
Manager—Goldwyn Sound Facility

Richard L. Anderson M.P.S.E.

The John A. Bonner Family

Dwayne E. Avery M.P.S.E.

Donald S. Flick M.P.S.E.

Stephen Hunter Flick

John A. Larsen

Rick Mirchell

Joseph John Sikorski

James Troutman

Robert Wise
Director

Night Technologies International

N.T. Audio

Dan O'Connell
One Step Up—Foley Stage

The John deSosa Mosely Family

and the thousands of sound craftsmen and women who strive daily to improve the audio art form.

Table of Contents

A Memorial to Excellence

John Bonner

Before we commence, I wish to remember these two gentlemen to you. Without question, John Bonner and John Mosely had the greatest influence on my personal education in the audio arts as well as the development of my own professional disciplines to serve that art form.

John Bonner worked within the studio environment, serving both studio and professional alike, always placing the good of the art form above the short-term and often artificial profit gain.

John Mosely was the classic independent maverick, willing to lay his job and reputation on the line for those things he believed in. When it came to his craft he was unwavering and uncompromising, but also extremely inventive as well as innovative.

From John Mosely I learned the physics and disciplines along with his personal theology on how the ideal presentation of sound *should* be. We did not always agree on the creative applications, but one could not dispute his expertise or mastery of audio engineering.

From John Bonner I had the infusion of *practical* application, the realities of working within an industry that is forever changing, forever reinventing itself. He taught me how to

John Mosely

hold onto my own principles and creative applications in the ever-present factory-style grind which often suffers the unfortunate effects of artistic mediocrity. This *practical* approach is where the title of this book is derived.

To both of these men, who provided me with a benchmark standard to strive for, I owe the success of my career and my own reputation for professional excellence that has never failed me. For this reason, I hope you will always remember their names as well as their contribution to the motion picture and television industry and to our craft.

Chapter 1
The Empowerment
of Sound

"It's probably not a good idea to come into this room and hear this demo—because, after I finish, you will belong to me."

David Lewis Yewdall, teasing clients unschooled in the art of sound before a demonstration at the author's facility

This book is for everyone interested in sound. It does not matter if you are in the sound business. It does not matter if you aspire to personally design and prepare your own soundtracks for the silver screen, for television broadcast, or for live theatre performances. This book is just as important to those not involved in the actual hands-on creative efforts, but just as responsible for the ultimate success of the soundtrack through the misunderstood and seldom considered phases of preplanning, budgeting, and scheduling. This book has been written with one objective in mind—to empower you, the reader, in ways seldom offered or available. Many years ago, and I hesitate to admit just how many, I produced numerous amateur "home-movie" productions, dreaming of the day when I would set off for Hollywood and work on feature films.

I scoured libraries, bookstores, and technical periodicals looking for any information about the skills and techniques I would need to make more exciting and interesting films. I am not referring to the "technodata" books of engineering or the idealistic platitudes that so often fill such texts. I was starved for the real thing—the practical and experienced craftsperson who had set down his or her thoughts and advice from which others could learn. Such books were, and still are, rare. Many talk *at* their subject—few talk *about* it with substance and experience. It is for that very reason this book has been written—for the accurate compilation of the experiences and expertise of dozens of men and women who bring some of the most exciting audio achievements to the screen, regardless of the media format.

Figure 1.1 The author is developing direct-to-picture vari-speed sound effects by interlocking his 35 mm Moviola to the Magna-Tech in his transfer bay. It was the most effective way to create the hydrogen car sound effects for the New World picture *Black Moon Rising*, 1984. (Photo by David Yewdall)

Our world is filled with a vast amount of misinformation. The most damaging is the misinformation that we hear or see written by those we respect or hold in high esteem, or by those who have initials following their names that lend the perception that they should know what they are talking about—particularly books and papers written by people with PhD initials after their names. Most misinformation is born out of ignorance, drawing the wrong conclusions, or having knowledge of the front end and knowledge of the back end and then guessing or extrapolating what the middle is, and erring in the process.

For instance, I have great respect for Ted Turner's Turner Classic Movies cable channel. I consider it the last bastion of commercial-free presentations of great film. But then they run an occasional blurb about their publication and the voice says, "Turner Classic Movies, thirty frames a second . . ." I heave a sigh of disappointment every time I hear that. Thirty frames a second is a video standard. Motion pictures are shot at twenty-four frames per second. The extra six frames are made up by using a "drop-frame" video transfer technique in which every fourth frame of the film is repeated, thus making twenty-four frames per second view at thirty frames (video) per second.

This is how misinformation spreads throughout your daily life. Reading something as printed text or hearing it spoken by a voice that represents a standard of respected quality blurs the truth and confuses those who read and listen to it. I have, therefore, striven to present the material in this book as straightforwardly as possible. You will not find a bibliography note anywhere, because I do not draw on other people's works to build my own. I will tell it like it is—as straight and honestly as I can.

Back to the issue of the audio art form. Sound is sound—whether you are working on amateur film productions, commercials, student films, documentaries, multimedia presentations, CD-ROM games, interactive virtual reality, episodic or long-form television, or even multimillion dollar theatrical motion picture events. The recording of dialog and sound effects, the style of editing, and the preparation of these sounds, as well as the philosophical taste and manner of mixing the sounds together are all virtually the same.

Read this paragraph very carefully. Whether you record with an analog tape recorder, a digital DAT machine, straight to hard disk, or to liquid-helium molecular storage; whether you cut on film with a Moviola and a synchronizer; or whether you spin a trackball with a nonlinear computer platform, the techniques, procedures, technical disciplines, and creative craftsmanship of creating an acoustical event are the same. Only the tools change—the artistic and scientific principles remain the same. Whether I cut the sound cue with a Rivas splicer and scrape the magnetic soundtrack from the edge with a degaussed razor blade, or whether I use a mouse to manipulate a digital cut on a computer screen and encode a fade-in, the artistic reasons for doing it and the net results are identical. Of course, unique applications differ from one medium to another, but the art form and techniques of sound recording, sound design, dialog preparation, and sound effect editing are identical.

The reason I have taken this moment to stress the art form so vehemently is that not enough people understand this, especially those perhaps most responsible for ensuring the success of the final audiotrack by planning for it long before the cameras even roll.

I will refer to the "technical disciplines" many times throughout this book, and I want you to understand why. Many of us are rather puzzled by the educational institutions that now offer film and television courses. Most of these schools are caught up in theory and raw creativity style instruction, something they call "critical studies." Many are literally discarding and openly discounting the need for the film student to develop the technical skills and discipline necessary to create a successful project. This style of instruction is akin to a mechanic putting an engine into your car, offering creative ideas about where to go, but not giving you a steering wheel, transmission, or brakes to drive it. What good is theory and creativity when you are frustrated and floundering with the very tools that you need to bring your creative vision to fruition?

Even more important than knowing how to use the physical tools of production is knowing what is possible. I wish I had a nickel for every time I heard producers or directors say they did not know they actually had to do something or preplan the shot or action so that they could achieve something creatively that they assumed could only be achieved months later in post-production. They were not empowered by their educational background to release their full potential and creative desires.

I served as the supervising sound editor on an unremarkable kickboxing picture several years ago. After the final mix, the director and producer both displayed little enthusiasm about what they had just heard during the final continuity playback. I noticed this and asked what was troubling them. The director's brow furrowed as he struggled to articulate his feelings. "I don't know, I guess I thought it would just sound—bigger."

I knew exactly what the problem was, and what it had always been—but seldom did I have such a receptive audience as I had right then and there. "I want you both to listen to me very carefully. We gave you the soundtrack for the movie that you made." The two men sat there waiting, as if I had not made my point yet. The director shook his head. "I don't understand." I knew he did not.

"What did you expect to hear?" I asked.

"I thought we would have stereo pan-by stuff, you know, big—broad."

"Absolutely, we can do all of that. But you first have to make the movie in such a way that we can do those kinds of things. For instance, you want all these stereo pan-by effects, but you didn't give us the cinematic opportunities to do it—because you didn't plan for it."

"Plan for it? What do you call those car-by shots?"

"A perfect example. Your film was photographed monophonically."

The producer leaned forward. "Mono-what?"

"When the car races by, your cameraman panned with the car, keeping the image in the center. If we put the sound of the car into a pan-pot joystick, where do you expect us to pan it when the action remains in the center of the screen? What your cinematographer should have done was to keep the camera anchored down, filming the car going past him, whooshing close by to the left off-screen. While the stunt driver set up the action again, you set up the second shot, turning the camera around to catch the car whooshing past, only this time from the right of the screen and throttling down the road away from the camera."

The producer started to understand. "This way they can pan the car from center to hard left and then come by hard right and go away into the center of the screen."

I smiled. "That's right—except you have to continue to plan for it when you cut the picture. Many picture editors do not understand the difference between cutting for television and cutting for theatrical release, between cutting monophonically and cutting for stereo. Many picture editors would cut the first shot just as the car disappeared screen left and then a frame before it appeared on the right. That's monophonic thinking. Your picture editor should give a full beat once it has disappeared screen left, and a full beat before it appears screen right, knowing that the follow-through stereo panning effect the mixer makes will yield the fullest stereophonic result, making it big and full."

I'm sure it was a bitter revelation for the two men, but judging from their subsequent pictures I would say they learned much from that enlightenment. From that moment, they became empowered—the proverbial light bulb had gone on—and their creative planning and preparations would be forever different.

The sharing of actual "war" stories and examples like this is a vital part of this book. It is the glue that bonds the information and techniques in such a way as to give a certain vicarious experience that will serve you well in the future. Of course you will make mistakes of your own along the way; we all do. Hopefully, though, you will learn from the mistakes described herein, and avoid making them yourself.

This book is written with real industry terms—not just technical words, but the jargon and nomenclature that is part of the language and understanding of motion picture crafts-people. For instance, one simple example that often appears is the word "sync." By proper dictionary spelling, the word is "synch," as it would be outside of post-production industry usage. In the professional industry jargon, however, this word is spelled without the "h." Rather than write this book with a literary correctness, I have decided to spell the words as they have come to be known in their professional applications. On occasion I may pause with a definition or an explanation, but for a fluid flow I have decided to spell the words as they have come to be known in their professional applications. You will find that if you read this book in sequential order, both your vocabulary and your technical understanding of the process will grow exponentially. As you learn more terms, you will not only understand them individually, you also will quickly develop a rhythm and an ability to assimilate and comprehend. By the time you finish this book you should not only be enriched with detailed explanations of techniques and practical applications, but through the various examples and actual experiences you should begin to understand why the industry works the way it does.

One more ingredient is vital to any kind of work you do, whether creative or mechanical. You must have passion for what you are doing. Frankly, most craftspeople today are working in jobs other than those they dreamed of doing. This is not necessarily a bad thing; in fact, it can often lead to even more interesting and fulfilling opportunities—as long as you fuel your working gas tank with passion.

Many newcomers to the industry confuse the concept of loving the idea of doing something with being passionate about actually doing it. It reflects in their work; it reflects in their attitude of how to work. Many lose their way, spending untold fruitless hours trying to develop shortcuts rather than rolling up their sleeves and simply doing the work. For those of us endowed with the love of and passion for our work, there is only the craft, the yearning to achieve a greater level of quality and meaning. The secret to real success and personal satisfaction is knowing that you must have passion for everything you do, even for jobs for which you have disdain. You cannot work in this industry by doing only what you want to do, and you probably cannot start right away working at the job of your dreams. The quickest way to achieve promotion and advancement toward your dream career is to approach each job assignment and task with as much passion and enthusiasm as if it were your dream job.

During a spirited argument with a colleague over the creative abstractness of the sound design of a picture on which we were working, he became flustered and suddenly blurted out, "Yewdall, you know what your problem is? You have a passion for what you do, and you think it makes a difference!"

I nodded. "You're right, I do have a passion for what I do, and I know it makes a difference."

The passion you have for your work will be a double-edged sword. It will energize you and empower you to stretch, to go that extra distance to create and achieve. Unfortunately, it will also lay you open and expose you to those who would ridicule and destroy rather than inspire and challenge. You cannot have one without the other. You must choose. Are you going to be a photocopy drone of a thousand others and mindlessly turn out formula products that everyone has seen and heard over and over again, or are you going to stretch and do something new and different? Therein lies the challenge; therein lies the passion.

You will also notice that very often I present ideas or examples in military terms. I do this for a good reason. Making a motion picture is almost identical to a military operation. No two films are the same—you must alter and adjust your tactics for the new material and problems that arise. Good filmmaking is five percent creativity and ninety-five percent problem solving. Keep this simple axiom in the forefront of your mind, and you will become one of the Navy Seal commandos of your craft.

Chapter 2
Our Amateur Beginnings

When I was in junior high school, I had to stay home for several weeks because of a contagious illness. My father had an old office 1/4" audiotape machine with a simple omnidirectional microphone that was really intended for recording close-proximity voices. In a matter of days I was swept into a fantasy world of writing and recording my own performances like ones I had heard on the radio plays. I played all the parts—moving about the room to simulate perspective, making a wide variety of sound effects and movements to conjure up mental images of Detective Ajax as he sought out the bad dealings of John J. Ellis and his henchmen.

I opened and closed doors, shuffled papers, moved chairs about. My parents had an antique rocking chair that had a great wooden creak when you sat in it. I ignited a firecracker to make gunshots and threw a canvas sack of potatoes on the floor for body falls. It wasn't until the recording tape broke, however, and I took up scissors and tape to splice it back together that I got the shock of my life. After I repaired the break, I wondered if I could cut and move around prerecorded sounds at will. This could remove the unwanted movement sounds—trim the mistakes and better tighten up the sound effects. Years later I came to appreciate how the early craftspeople in the infancy of motion pictures must have felt when they first tried moving shots and cutting for effect rather than repair. The power of editing had sunk in.

Late at night I would crawl under the covers, hiding the audiotape machine under the blankets, and play the sequence over and over. Though I would be embarrassed by its crudeness today, it was the germination and the empowerment of sound and storytelling for me. I had made a greater audio illusion than I ever thought possible.

Several years later I joined the high school photography club. That was when I became visually oriented. The exciting homemade radio shows became just fond memories after I found a fateful twenty-dollar bill hidden in a roll-top desk at a thrift shop. I had been looking at a black plastic Eastman Kodak 8 mm spring-wound camera that could be ordered from the Sears catalog for $19.95. Guess how I spent the twenty-dollar bill?

The camera did not even have a lens, only a series of holes in a rotatable disk that acted as f-stops. The spring-wind motor lasted only twenty-two seconds, so I carefully had to plan

Figure 2.1 Amateur high school film *The Nuremberg Affair*. Warren Wheymeyer and Chris Callow act as German soldiers in a firefight scene with French resistance fighters. (Photo by David Yewdall)

how long the shots could be—but with it my life changed forever. The visual image now moved, and with a little imagination I quickly made the camera do dozens of things I'm sure the designer and manufacturer never intended for it to do.

Later that year I was projecting some 8 mm film on the bedroom wall for some of my high school friends who had been a part of the wild and frenzied film shoot the previous weekend. We had performed the action on an ambitious scale—at least for small-town high school students. We were shooting an action film about the French Resistance ambushing a German patrol in a canyon, entitled *The Nuremberg Affair*. We carefully buried several pounds of black powder in numerous soft-drink paper cups around the narrow flatland between two canyon walls of a friend's California ranch as a couple of dozen of us dressed in military uniforms.

A hulk of a car had been hauled up from the junkyard, a vehicle identical to the operating one serving as the stunt car. We carefully filmed a sequence that gave the illusion of a French Resistance mortar shell hitting the staff vehicle, blowing it up, and sending a dozen soldiers sprawling into the dirt and shrubs of the wash. In the next set-up, they rose and charged the camera. My special-effects man, sitting just off-camera, ignited each soft-drink "mortar-cup" charge, sending a geyser of dirt and debris into the air. The high school stunt actors had fun as they jumped and flung themselves about—being invisibly ambushed by the off-screen French underground.

A week later we huddled together to watch the crudely edited sequence. It happened that my radio was sitting on the windowsill of my bedroom. An audio commercial advertising *The Guns of Navarone* burst forth. Action-combat sound effects and stirring music was playing while the segment of our amateur mortar attack flickered on the bedroom wall. Several of us reacted to the sudden sensation—the home movie suddenly came alive, as many of the sound effects seemed to work quite well with the visual action. That year I won an Eastman Kodak Teenage Award for *The Nuremberg Affair*. The bug had really bitten hard.

Up until that time, I had just been making silent films—with an eye toward the visual. Now my visual eye grew a pair of ears. Of course, sound did not just appear on the film from then on. We quickly learned that there seemed to be a whole lot more to sound than simply having the desire to include it as part of the performance package. It also did not help much that back in the 1960s no such thing existed as home video cameras with miniature microphones attached. Super 8mm was offering a magnetic striped film, but any kind of additional sound editing and mixing was very crude and difficult.

We did make two amateur short films that had separate 1/4" soundtracks. Of course, no interlocking sync mechanism existed, and the only way to even come close was to use a 1/4" tape recorder that had a sensitive pause switch. I would sit and carefully monitor the sound, and when it started to run a little faster than the film being projected, I would give the machine little pauses every so often, helping the soundtrack jog closer to its intended sync. All of this seemed very amateurish and frustrating. Yet as difficult as noninterlocking sound gear was to deal with, it had become essential to have a soundtrack with the picture.

EARLY APPLICATIONS

My first real application of custom sound recording for public entertainment occurred when I was given the sound effects job for Coalinga's West Hills College presentation of the play *Picnic*. Sound effect records of the day were pretty dreadful, and only the audiophiles building their own Heathkit high-fidelity systems were interested more in authentic realism and speaker replication than in entertainment expression.

As you work more in sound, you will quickly learn the difference between reality sound and entertainment sound. I can play you a recording of a rifle butt hitting the chin of a man's skull. It is an absolutely authentic recording, yet it sounds flat and lifeless. On the other hand, I can edit three carefully chosen sound cues together in parallel and play them as one, and I promise that you will cringe and double over in empathetic pain. Therein lies the essential difference between realism, which is an actual recording of an event, and a sound designer's version of the same event, which is a combination brew that evokes emotion and pathos.

I soon gave up trying to find prerecorded sound effects and set out to record my own. I did not know much about how to record good sound, but I was fortunate to have acquired a monaural Uher model 1000 1/4" tape deck that I used for my amateur 16mm filmmaking. I talked a local policeman into driving his squad car out of town and, from a couple of miles out, drive toward me at high speed with his siren wailing away. I recorded doorbells and dogs barking, as well as evening cricket backgrounds. At that time I was not at all interested in pursuing a career in sound, and actually would not take it seriously for another ten years, yet there I was practicing the basic techniques I still use today.

While making a documentary film about my hometown, we had gotten permission to blow up an oil derrick on Kettleman Hills. We had shot the sequence MOS (without sound) and decided later we needed an explosion sound effect. I did not know how to record an explosion, nor did I think the explosions we made for our films would sound very good; how they looked and how they sounded in reality were two entirely different things.

I decided to experiment. I discovered that by wrapping the microphone in a face towel and holding it right up to my mouth I could mimic a concussionary explosion with my lips and tongue, forcing air through my clenched teeth. The audio illusion was magnificent!

A few years later a couple of friends and my father joined me in making a fundraising film for Calvin Crest, a Presbyterian church camp in the Sierra Nevada mountains. It was our first serious attempt at shooting synchronous sound while we filmed. We had built a homemade camera crane to replicate Hollywood-style sweeping camera moves in and among the pine trees. The eighteen-foot reach crane was made of wood and used precision ball-bearing pillow-blocks for rotation pivots.

We never actually had a synchronous motor on the camera, so during the post-production editorial phase of the project I learned how to eyeball sync. I discovered that a non-sync motor means that the sound recording drifts. I painstakingly resynced the sound every few seconds as the drift increased. Becoming extremely observant, I looked for the slightest movement and identified the particular sounds that must have come from that movement. I then listened to the track, found such audible movements, and lined the sound and action into sync. Conversely, I learned to take sound with no synchronous relationship at all with the image that I had, and, through clever cuts and manipulation, make the sound work for moments when we had no original sound recording at all.

I am the first to admit how bizarre and out of place the camera set-up in Figure 2.2 appears. Most filmmakers starting out will tell you (especially if you have no money and must work "poor-boy" style) that you must learn how to mix and match various kinds of equipment together—to make do when money to rent modern camera and sound equipment is scarce. In the photo, I am standing just to the side of the lens of the 16 mm Arriflex as I direct the action. My partner, Larry Yarbrough, is standing just behind me, coordinating the lighting and handling the audio playback of prerecorded dialog, as we did not record very much sync sound back then. Our actors listened to a prerecorded tape played back through a speaker off-screen as they mouthed the dialog—much the same way musicals are filmed to playback. As I said, you have to make do with what you have. It certainly was not a convenient camera platform, but boy was it rock-steady!

Of course, our soundtrack was crude by professional audio standards today, but for its day and for where I was on the evolutionary scale of experience, Calvin Crest had opened a multitude of doors and possibilities—it allowed me to develop different ideas because of new, empowering, creative tools then in hand. With what I had learned through the "baptism by fire" of doing, I could take a simple 35 mm combat Eymo camera with a spring-wound motor and an unremarkable 1/4" tape recorder with absolutely no sound sync relationship between them and, if I had the will to do so, I could make a full-length motion picture with both perfectly synchronized sound, and depth and breadth of entertainment value. I was—and still am—only limited by my own imagination—just as you are.

INTERVIEW WITH BRUCE CAMPBELL

Bruce Campbell is probably best known and recognized both for his starring role in the television series "Briscoe County, Jr.," in which he portrays the title character, and for his portrayal of the hero in the *Evil Dead* film trilogy. When it comes to sound, Bruce is one of

Figure 2.2 I'm standing just behind the lens of a 16 mm Arriflex sitting atop the giant 100 Moey gear head specially designed for the giant MGM 65 mm cameras. This particular gear head was one of the set used in William Wyler's *Ben-Hur*. (Photo by David Yewdall)

the most passionate and audio-involved actor-director-producers I have ever met and had the great pleasure to work alongside.

Bruce began making amateur movies with his high school buddies Sam Raimi (who went on to direct pictures such as *Crimewave* and *Darkman*, and the cult classics *Evil Dead*, *Evil Dead 2*, and the ultimate sequel, *Army of Darkness*) and Rob Tapert (producer of movies and television shows). They grew up just outside Detroit, where they spent increasingly more time creating their first amateur efforts.

"Originally, we worked with regular 8 mm film and a little wind-up camera. The film was 16 mm in width. You would shoot one side, which was fifty feet long, then flip the roll over and expose the other side. You sent it to the lab and they developed it and slit it in half for you," remembers Bruce.

"Of course, we shot those films silent; at least, as we know and understand synchronous sound recording today. Our friend, Scott Spiegel, had a cassette recorder, and he had recorded our dialog as we shot the film. Of course, there was nothing like what we have today with crystal sync and time code. We just recorded it to the cassette, and Scott would keep careful track of the various angles and takes and rerecord/transfer them later as close as he could to the final-cut 8 mm film.

"Scott would also record sound effects and backgrounds, many of them from television broadcasts of Three Stooges films. The nice thing about the Stooges was that they didn't have any music during the action scenes, just dialog and loud sound effects. Scott would have all the sound effects he intended to use lined up on one cassette tape like a radio man would set up his cue list and have his sound effect source material at the ready.

"We would get in a room and watch the cut 8 mm picture, then Scott would roll the original dialog cassette, playing the sound through a speaker. Scott would play the second cassette of sound effects at precise moments in the action against the dialog cassette, and we would stand around and add extra dialog lines that we had not previously recorded when we shot the film to begin with. All this time, Scott was rerecording the collage of speaker playback sound and our new live dialog performances onto a new cassette in a crude but effective sound mix.

"It was kind of like doing live radio as we were injecting sound effects, looping dialog and mixing it all at once, the difference being that we had to keep in sync to the picture. The real trick was Scott Spiegel mastering the pause button to keep on top of the sync issues.

"Scott was the master of this, so we let him do it. We had a varispeed projector, and Scott had made marks on the edges of the film that only he could see during a presentation so that he could tell how out-of-sync the cassette playback was going to be; then he would adjust the projector a little faster or a little slower to correct the sync. Sometimes Scott would have to fast-forward or rewind the cassette real quick in order for the playback to be right. You could hear the on and off clicks in the track, but we didn't care—after all, we had sound!

"We would test our films at parties. If [we] could get people to stop partying and watch the movie, then we knew we had a good one. We made about fifty of these short movies, both comedies and dramas.

"Then we moved up to Super 8 mm, which had a magnetic sound stripe on it so you could record sound as you filmed the action. The quality of the sound was very poor by today's standards, but at the time it was a miracle! You could either send your Super 8 film out for sound striping [having a thin ribbon of magnetic emulsion applied to the edge of the film for the purposes of adding a soundtrack later], or you could buy Super 8 film with a magnetic sound stripe on it.

"There were projectors that had sound-on-sound, where you had the ability for one attempt to dub something in over the soundtrack that was already on the film. Say the action in your Super 8 mm film has two guys acting out a shootout scene, and the first actor's line, 'Stick 'em up!' was already on the film. Reacting to the first guy, the second actor turned, drew his pistol, and fired, which of course is a cap gun or a quarter-load blank. If you wanted a big sound effect for the gunshot, using the sound-on-sound technique, you would only have one chance to lay a gunshot in. If you did not record it in correctly or close enough sync, then you wiped out the actor's voice and you would have to then loop the actor saying 'Stick 'em up!' all over again, which on Super 8 mm film was going to be extremely difficult at best.

"On the original Super 8 mm projectors you could only record on the main magnetic stripe, but when the new generation of projectors came out, you could record on the balance stripe [a thin layer of magnetic emulsion on the opposite side of the film from the primary magnetic soundtrack to maintain an even thickness for stability in film transport and winding or rewinding onto a film reel]. This allowed us to record music and sound effects much easier by utilizing the balance stripe as a second track instead of messing up the original recorded track that had been recorded in sync when we originally filmed the sequence.

"Our post-production supervisor was the lady behind the counter at K-Mart. She would see us coming and say, 'Okay fellas, whad'ya got now?' Whether it was developing or sending our cut film back to have a new balance stripe applied to the edge so we could record a smoother music track, she was our lab.

"Sam Raimi did a fifty-minute film called *The Happy Valley Kid,* the story of a college student driven insane, that he shot on the Michigan State University campus with real professors and real students, and Rob Tapert portrayed the Happy Valley Kid. The film cost about seven hundred dollars to make, and they showed it at midnight showings to students. The kids loved to see the film because they got to see *The Happy Valley Kid* blow away all the evil professors. Sam actually got the professors to allow themselves to be shot and gunned down on film. They made about thirty-five hundred bucks on it—probably some of the best vicarious therapy that frustrated students could sit down and enjoy without going postal themselves.

"We actually raised the money to make a movie based on a Super 8mm film that we had shot as a pilot, as a device to show investors the kind of motion picture that we were going to make and convince them to invest money in us. Sam Raimi had been studying some occult history in humanities class when his prolific and overactive imagination gave him a middle-of-the-night vision. I personally think it stemmed from something he had eaten for dinner earlier in the evening, but a lot of Sam's subsequent script was based on the Necronomicon stuff that came up in class.

"We made our best Super 8mm double-system sound film yet. We had acquired much better sound effects, using a 1/4" reel-to-reel deck whenever we could get our hands on one. We would carefully patch directly in from a stereo system so we could control the quality of the sound transfer for music or sound effects. By this time we had gotten much better about understanding recording levels, even the concept of distortion and how to avoid it as much as possible. By the time we raised the money to make the first *Evil Dead* film, we were much better prepared, at least knowing that we wanted a really good and interesting sound, and we knew that before we went out to film the picture.

"When we finished cutting the picture of *Evil Dead* and were ready for the post-production sound process, we went to Sound One in New York City with Elisha Birnbaum. We immediately discovered that, from an audio point-of-view, it was a whole new ball game and that we weren't in Kansas anymore. We had a lot of bones and blood and carnage in the film, so Sam and I would go to a market and we would buy chickens and celery and carrots and meat cleavers and that sort of stuff to use for recording. Elisha was a one-man show. He would roll the picture, then run in and perform Foley cues on the stage; then he would run back into the back booth to stop the system.

"Our supervising sound editor was Joe Masefield. Joe was extremely detail oriented. Each sound effect had a number, based on the reel it belonged to, whether it was a cue of Foley or a sound effect or dialog or whatever. He sat there in the recording booth and told us what we needed to perform. For Sam and I, we were still kind of lagging from our amateur days of how to make sounds, because we would argue who could make the best gravy-sucking sound and who would twist and cut the celery while the other guy was making awful slurping noises. We heard later that it took weeks for them to get the smell of rotting cabbage and chicken out of their Foley stage.

"Mel Zelniker was the mixer. He was really good for us, as he brought us up out of our amateur beginnings and helped to point us into a more professional way of doing things. Mel would teach us stage protocol and procedure through example. Sam stepped off the stage for a drink of water and returned just as Mel mixed the sound of a body being flopped into a grave. Sam asked Mel if he could mix the bodyfall a little hotter. Mel played the game of not touching the fader pot to see if we noticed—you know, the way mixers can do. It was so embarrassing because then he would ask Sam what he thought after he supposedly mixed it hotter, and Sam would say he liked it, and Mel would huff and reply, 'I didn't touch it.'

"Then Mel would run it again, only this time he would push the volume until it was obviously over the top. He'd ask us, 'How was that?' We'd nod our heads, 'That was fine, just fine.' Mel snapped back at us, 'It's too loud!' and he would run it again and bring the volume back down. Mel knew we were a couple of hicks from Detroit, but in his own way he was trying to teach us at the same time.

"At one point I asked him if he could lower one of my loop lines. Mel turned on me, 'What's the matter, you embarrassed?!'

"I didn't know what to say. 'Yeah, I am actually.'

"Mel shrugged, 'Okay, I just wanted to clear that up,' and he would continue mixing. He would mix one long pass at a time, and we actually got a weird effect out of it. Their equipment had an odd, funky problem with one of the fader pots; it left an open chamber, which created a strange airy-like sound that, if he just moved that pot up a little, created the best eerie ambiance for us. It was not a wind; it was almost like you were in a hollow room. That was our gift. Every so often either Sam or I would say, 'Hey, stick that ambiance in there!' Mel would frown, 'You guys! You're usin' it too much!'

"It wasn't until after the mix that Mel and his engineer discovered that a rotating fan motor vibration was being conducted through hard point contact that was leaking into the echo chamber, a clever technique that Mel quietly tucked away for future use.

"For our first real movie we got several gifts. Another one happened in the middle of the night when we were shooting the film in Tennessee. Sam was awakened by a ghostly wind that was coming through the broken glass window in his room. He ran down the hall and dragged the sound guy out of bed to fire up the Nagra to record it. That airy tonal wind became the signature for the film. The fact is, there are gifts around you all of the time, whether you are shooting or not—the trick is for you to recognize the gifts when they happen and be versatile enough to take advantage of them. That's when the magic really happens."

Several years later, the trio made the sequel, *Evil Dead 2*. It was their first opportunity to work with the sound to prebuild entire segments before they got to the rerecording dubbing stage. They had progressed from the Moviola, in which their sound had been cut on 35 mm mag-stripe and fullcoat to 24-track using videotape and time code to interlock the sync between picture (on videotape) and soundtrack (being assembled on 24-track 2" tape). Bruce Campbell not only reprised his character of Ash from the original *Evil Dead*, but he also handled the post-production sound chores. He started by insisting on walking his own footsteps in the film, and one thing lead to another. The attention to detail became an obsession.

"We cut the picture for *Evil Dead 2* in Ferndale, Michigan, in a dentist's office. I asked the manager of the building to give me one of the offices for a month that was in the center of the building, not near the front and not near the back. I didn't want to contend with traffic noise. We got the deepest part of an office that was well insulated by the old building's thick walls. I asked a sound engineer by the name of Ed Wolfman, who I would describe in radio terms as a *tonemeister*, a German term for a master craftsman mixer or recordist, to come look at this huge plaster room we had. I told him that I wanted to record wild sound effects in this room, and how could I best go about utilizing the space acoustically?

"We built a wooden section of the floor, then built a downscaled replica of the original cabin set from the film. We needed the floor to replicate the correct hollowness that we had from the original cabin because we had a lot of scuffling, props falling, footsteps—a lot of movement that would have to fold in seamlessly into the production recording. Ed told us to build one of the walls nonsymmetrical—angle it off ten percent, twenty percent—so we put in a dummy wall that angled in, so that the sound would not reflect back and forth and build up slap and reverb. We did the foam-and-egg-carton routine by attaching them in regimented sheets around on sections of the wall for trapping and controlling sound waves.

"While Sam [Raimi] was in a different part of the office building picture-cutting the film, I cranked up my word processor and built an audio event list—a chronological list of sounds that were going to be needed for the picture that we could replicate in our down-sized cabin stage and custom record them. I guess you would consider this wild Foley. These sound cues were not performed while we watched picture or anything. We would review the list and see 'things rattle on a table.' Okay, let's record a bunch of things rattling on a table, and we'll record a number of variations. 'Table falls over'—we recorded several variations of a table falling over, etc.

"This one office of the dentist building had water damage from the radiators, and we thought, 'Let's help 'em out just a little bit more.' So I took an axe and recorded some really good chops and scrapes. It is so hard to find that kind of material in just that kind of condition to record. It was so crunchy, and it had these old dried wood slats from the 1920s—it was perfectly brittle. One little chop led to another. 'Keep that recorder rolling!' I'd swing the axe, smashing and bashing. I felt guilty about what I was doing to the ceiling, but the recordings were priceless. It is just impossible to simulate that kind of sound any other way!"

The result of all this was Bruce and Sam returning to Los Angeles for formal post-production sound-editorial work with a wealth of custom-recorded material under their arms, meticulously developed over weeks of study and experimentation.

Bruce Campbell continued his acting and directing career both here and abroad, spending much of his time in New Zealand, writing, directing, and even appearing in the "Xena" and "Hercules" television series, as well as developing theatrical motion picture projects of his own.

Bruce admits that sound has had a tremendous effect on his professional career. It has made him a better storyteller and a more creative filmmaker, but he admits that he misses having the luxury of the hands-on participation in custom-recording and developing sound-tracks. Listen to the "Xena" and "Hercules" television shows. The roots of their sound design go all the way back to those early days in Detroit when Bruce and his friends struggled not only to keep an audiotrack in sync with the visual image but also to create something extraordinary.

DEVELOP YOUR EYES AND EARS TO OBSERVE

I do not mean for this to sound egotistical or pompous, but shortly after you finish reading this book, most of you will notice that you see and hear things differently than you did before. The fact is, you have always seen and heard them—you have just not been as aware of them as you now are going to become. This transition does not happen all at once. It does not go "flomp" like a heavy curtain, and suddenly you have visual and audio awareness. You probably will not be aware that the change is taking place, but, several weeks or a few months from now, you will suddenly stop and recognize that your sensory perceptions have been changing. Some of you will thank me, and others will curse me. Some people become so aware, that they find it incredibly hard to watch movies or television again. This is a common side effect. It is really nothing more than your awareness kicking in, along with a growing knowledge of how things work. Be comforted by knowing that this hyperawareness appears to wear off over time. In fact, it actually does not.

Your subconscious learns to separate awareness of technique and disciplines from the assimilation of form and storytelling, the division between left-brain and right-brain jurisdictions. Regardless of whether you are aware of it, you learn how to watch a motion picture or television program and disregard its warts and imperfections. If you did not learn this ability, you probably would be driven to the point of insanity (of course, that might explain a few things in our industry these days).

As for myself, I remember the exact moment the figurative light bulb went on for me. I was sitting in my folks' camper, parked amid the tall redwood trees near the Russian River in northern California, reading Spottiswood's book *Film and Its Techniques.* I was slowly making my way through the chapter dealing with the film synchronizer and how film is synced together when *Kapow*! Suddenly everything I had read before, most of which I was struggling to understand conceptually, came together and made perfect sense. Those of you who have gone through this transition, this piercing of the concept membrane, know exactly to what I'm referring. Those of you who have not experienced it are in for a wonderful moment filled with a special excitement.

PROTECT YOUR MOST PRECIOUS POSSESSIONS

The world has become a combat zone for one of your most precious possessions, your ability to hear. During everyday activities, you are constantly in close proximity with audio sources with the potential to permanently impair your future ability to hear. Unfortunately, you probably give none of these sources a passing consideration.

If you hope to continue to see and hear the world around you clearly for a long time, then let go of any naive misperception that those senses will always perfectly be with you. This book does not address the everyday dangers and potentially harmful situations regarding loss of or impairment to your eyesight because it was not written with authority on that topic. As for protecting your ability to hear clearly, one of the most common and sensory-damaging dangers is distortion. This is not the same as volume. Your ears can handle a considerable amount of clearly produced volume; however, if the audio source is filled with distortion, the human ear soon fatigues and starts to degenerate. A common source of distortion is the device known as the "boom box." Car radios are another source of overdriven audio sources, played through underqualified amplifiers and reproduced by speakers setting up a much higher distortion-noise-to-clear-signal ratio, which begins to break down the sensitivity of your audio sensors.

In another scenario, you attend a rock concert. After a few minutes, you start to feel buzzing or tingling in your ears. This is the first sign that your ears have become overloaded and are in danger of suffering permanent and irreparable damage.

The audio signal in question does not have to be loud, however. Many television engineers and craftspeople who work in close proximity to a bank of television monitors for long periods of time discover that they have either lost or are losing their high-end sensitivity. Many of these individuals cannot hear 10 kHz and above.

Sometimes I had groups of students from either a high school or college come to the studio to tour the facility and receive an audio demonstration. During the demos, I would put a specially made test-tone tape on a DAT machine and play a 1 kHz tone, which everyone could hear. They would see the signal register accordingly on the VU meter. I would then play them 17 kHz. Only about half could hear that, but they could all see the signal on the VU meter. I would then play them 10 kHz with the same strength on the VU meter. By this time, several students inevitably would be in tears; they had lost the ability to hear a 10-kHz tone so early in life. After asking one or two poignant questions regarding their daily habits of audio exposure, I knew the exact culprit. Almost no demonstration strikes home more dramatically than this, forcing a personal self-awareness and disallowing denial. The students could fib to me about whether they could hear the signal, but they themselves knew they could not hear it; the proof was in front of them, the visual affirmation of the strong and stable volume on the VU meter for all to see. I plead with you, before it is too late: become aware of the dangers that surround you every day, understand what audio fatigue is, realize that length of duration to high decibels and audio distortion results in permanent hearing loss, either select frequency or total.

Someone asked me once, "If you had to choose between being blind or deaf, which would you choose?" I did not hesitate. I chose blind. As visual a person as I am, I could not imagine living in a world where I could not enjoy the sweet vibrant sound of the cello, the wind as it moves through the pine trees with the blue jays and mourning doves, or the sensual caress of the whispered words from my wife as we cuddle together and share the day's events. So protect your most precious of personal possessions—your eyes and ears.

Chapter 3
The First Tuesday Night
in February

The chilly evening breeze buffets the men and women who crowd the smoked-glass doors of the masonry building at Wilshire Boulevard and Almont in Los Angeles—the head-quarters of the Academy of Motion Picture Arts and Sciences. The first Tuesday night of each February, many of the top sound craftspeople in the motion picture industry gather, members of the Sound Branch of the Academy as well as several hundred associate observers, to review those films competing for the honor of being nominated for the Academy Award for Best Sound Effects Editing.

Six weeks before, the sound-editor members of the sound branch voted by written ballot for five of their top choices from that year's nearly 400 qualifying motion pictures. Those ballots had been mailed to PricewaterhouseCoopers LLP, at which point the seven semifinalists had been determined—those garnishing the highest number of votes by their first-through-fifth-choice ranking. Over the last few weeks, the producers of the "anxious seven" had been notified so that they could prepare a sample reel for the first Tuesday evening in February—an event affectionately known as the "bake-off," a term coined by Richard Anderson, supervising sound editor and co-sharer of the Academy Award for Best Sound Effects Editing in 1981 (along with Ben Burtt for the action-adventure sensation *Raiders of the Lost Ark*).

The sample reel must contain actual clips from a release print of the picture. The sound-track cannot be enhanced, remixed, or reprinted: it must be identical to what was exhibited in the theatres. The task of choosing the clips that comprise the allotted ten minutes in the bake-off is left to the supervising sound editor, because it is he or she who honchoed the preparation of the soundtrack for the rerecording mixing stage in the first place.

In the lobby, representatives from PricewaterhouseCoopers LLP check off the names of the voting sound-branch members as they step up to identify themselves. One representa-tive checks the names on the list as the other issues each voter a ballot, each assigned with a designated number for identification. The members are also given an information sheet regarding the seven pertinent feature films.

The voters head up the staircase to the legendary Samuel Goldwyn Academy Theatre on the second floor to see and schmooze with hundreds of colleagues, many of whom have not been seen since the sound bake-off the previous year. The center quadrant of seats is roped off and reserved for the award-nominating committee members, so that they can listen to and judge the sound presentation of each sample reel in that acoustically ideal section.

As everybody settles down at the appointed hour, the chairman of the Sound effects Editing Award Rules Committee steps to the podium to review the year's rules and to lend a personal word of wisdom to those of us about to sit in judgment of our fellow craftspeople. This forum is not supposed to be about politics, although politics definitely deals a few wildcards from time to time. Additionally, this forum is not supposed to be about personalities, about whom we like or dislike as individuals, although it can be sorely difficult to separate one's personal feelings and biases from the task at hand. I gaze up to see two massive statues of Oscar® standing vigil over this presentation, here in the greatest of all theatres in the world, and I know that as an Academy member I must rise above politics and personal favor. We are here not only to judge our colleagues but also to celebrate our art form and to be challenged throughout the coming year to raise our professional standards and artistic achievements accordingly.

During a lighter moment, the chairman pokes a jab at the ever-rising volume of motion picture soundtracks as he thanks all the sound craftspeople over at Warner Brothers (some 14 miles away) who could not be here tonight, but who will hear the playback of the sample reels anyway!

After seventy minutes of high-octane audio playback from SDDS, DTS, and Dolby SR-D mastered soundtracks, the audience experiences a good dose of audio fatigue. If ever there was a litmus test for considering the responsibility to monitor more reasonable volume levels, especially through sustained sequences that truly leave your ears ringing, this Tuesday night bake-off is it. Just because sound is mixed loud does not mean that it sounds better. Just because digital and the new achievements in speaker design and amplifier clarity allow sound to be brought into the theatre at ever-increasing decibel levels does not mean that it should be.

As you read this book, consider well the power of silence. Years ago, when I walked onto Stage "D" at Goldwyn for the rerecording process of *Escape from New York,* Bill Varney, the lead mixer, turned and announced to everyone that we would build dynamics into the mix. We all agreed enthusiastically. Of course, at the time I did not have a clue what he meant or what he was talking about, but over the next four years and eleven pictures for which I supervised the sound editorial that mixed on Stage "D" I came to understand and appreciate exactly what Bill meant.

One must bring the soundtrack down; the levels should be lowered and relaxed between the high-energy action peaks. Not only does this give the audience a chance to recover from the strength and power of the action sequences, but coming down also allows the sound to go back up again. The power and volume seem bigger and louder than they really are if time is taken to come down and the audience's ears are allowed to rest.

If the soundtrack constantly is active and loud, the sound has nowhere to go when it must go up for the action moments. It is exactly like riding a roller coaster: you cannot enjoy the thrill of the high-drop runs unless you have come down to the bottom, paused, and anticipated the climb back up to the top again. A great classical composer also understood this principle extremely well. Beethoven, the master of mood and drama, composed a passage with notations of *adagio* or *largo* with a *pianissimo* delicacy, followed by a sudden explosion of power and glory at double *fortissimo* with a *presto* urgency. Those who have listened to Beethoven's legendary "Moonlight Sonata" probably know only its melodious and moody opening movement. Those who have played this seemingly passive piece on the piano, however, surely understand my point when they dash through the third movement! Seldom is the strength and precise dexterity of the pianist's hands and fingers more greatly challenged.

So too with the motion picture soundtrack. While conceptualizing, designing, and executing a final soundtrack of dialog, music, and sound effects into one interwoven yet fluid and continuous audio event, the entire team of audio craftspeople does well to think in terms of dynamics—the entire roller-coaster ride.

Unfortunately, the entire sound team can design and execute the most amazing soundtrack ever, but if the director and producer do not understand the philosophy of dynamics and audio dramatization, then all the skill and effort of the entire sound collaboration are for naught. Dynamics. It seems so obvious, so simple and basic, yet so many filmmakers fall into this trap. I discuss this and other audio philosophies more closely throughout this book, especially in Chapter 19, but you may be wondering why I took this moment to bring up the philosophy of dynamics at this time, in this chapter.

The answer is simple—presentation. Year after year, we convene at the Samuel Goldwyn Theatre to judge the last seven challengers for the final nominations. As described earlier, the supervising sound editors of these seven motion pictures are called on to prepare a ten-minute presentation for our consideration. The smart supervising sound editor must assume that the members of the sound branch in the audience who are listening to and voting on these final seven have not seen the entire picture, either in a commercial theatre or at any of the consideration screenings. The smart supervising sound editor, like a cunning field commander, selects and deploys the best representation of the creative work in a way that affects the professional audience enough to garner one of the potential three nomination slots. The ten-minute presentation reel is not meant to be a ten-minute encapsulation of the film's story. It is a short piece to best present the film's unique sound effect qualities and craftsmanship to earn consideration for an Academy Award nomination.

Not too long ago, a big Harrison Ford action picture was one of the seven bake-off contenders. The supervising sound editors rolled the dice of their presentation reel mainly on their powerful jet sound effects. Yes, the sound was huge; yes, the gigantic low-end sound reached out of the subwoofer speakers and gripped us in our seats. But we were not impressed. Sound editors know that jets are easy to design and cut. Low-end power is as common and overused as a worn-out cliché. Sound editors know that the precision of frame-accurate sync does not exist with jets. It was the wrong thing on which to risk an Academy Award nomination. Consequently, the film was not nominated. I felt bad for those editors, though, because many excellent and well-developed audio passages could be found in the picture, a number of them during subtle and quiet sequences.

On the other hand, Richard Anderson and David Whittaker tackled the job of putting together a ten-minute reel for *Daylight*, with the concept of presentation as the focal point. I happened to be cutting sound on *The Fifth Element* at Weddington Productions, the sound-editorial facility where *Daylight* had been produced, so I was very interested in watching Richard and David as they set up a KEM across the hall from my room and painstakingly broke down the entire picture. They isolated various moments in the movie and discussed whether they thought each one presented an audio performance or technique that would capture respect and interest by the sound-branch members, hopefully making *Daylight* worthy of an Academy Award nomination.

Richard and David wrote down important scene descriptions with notes outlining the audio moments they felt strong about showing. They listed each segment on a separate index card, and then taped them to the wall opposite the 35 mm KEM. As they moved the index cards around and slowly discarded the lesser-priority sequences, they systematically rearranged the segments in a different order to achieve a tactical positioning balance, not only to tell a story about the movie, but also to tell a story about the sound effects. In essence, they devised a miniature roller coaster of their own, building in dynamics to allow the sound-branch viewers the ups and downs, showing off both big and subtle sounds that set their work apart. Consequently, *Daylight* became one of the three pictures nominated for that year's Academy Award.

As the chairman finishes his review of the rules and regulations and his duty of describing how the theatre speakers have been swept and balanced for tonight's presentation, we sit and think about literally thousands of the world's foremost theatrical sound craftspeople, most of whom are unsung heroes, who make it possible for the supervising sound editor to step to the podium on Academy Award night and accept the golden statuette for Best Sound Effects Editing.

How many production sound mixers, boom operators, cable men, audio engineers, sound effects and dialog editors, sound assistants, sound designers, sound librarians, equipment and acoustical engineers, ADR and Foley mixers and recordists, Foley artists, Walla Group and vocal mimic performers, and many others are literally wrapped in an embryonic envelope of this left, center, right, and split surround-sound experience? How many long and overworked hours went into moments of the picture that we probably never completely appreciate?

The lights of the theatre dim as the first sample reel is about to be projected. I glance up to one of the giant statues of Oscar®. He has stood vigilant for many years, holding his golden sword as he watches over the audience. I can almost imagine he is looking at me. His smooth face has an almost omnipotent presence, silently reminding me to put any personal tendentious susceptibilities aside and to view these seven presentation reels with an objectivity worthy of the fair and idealistic judgment that Oscar® represents.

But how did these soundtracks get here? How did they survive the challenges and the often stormy path to fruition? Let us go back, all the way back, even before the cameras start to roll. It all begins with the vision and dedication to achieve a work of audio art, an acoustical experience that stays with the audience. It starts with careful and realistic planning—a plan for success.

Chapter 4
Success or Failure: Before
the Camera Even Rolls

The success or failure of your final soundtrack is decided by you, before the cameras even roll—even before you commence preproduction!

The above twenty-two words constitute perhaps the most important single truth in this book. It is so important that I want you to read it again. The success or failure of your final soundtrack is decided by you, before the cameras even roll—even before you commence preproduction!

You not only must hire a good production sound mixer along with a supreme boom person, you must know the pitfalls and traditional clash of production's form and function to "get it in the can" and on its way to the cutting room. You must know how to convey the parameters and needs to the non-sound departments, which have such a major impact on the ability of the sound-recording team to capture a great production dialog track. If you do not allow enough money in the lighting budget to rent enough cable, you do not get the generators far enough away from the set, resulting in continuous intrusion of background generator noise. This isn't so bad if you are filming in bustling city streets, but it certainly does not bode well if you are filming medieval knights and fair maidens prancing around in a Middle Ages atmosphere. Regardless of the period or setting of the film, unwanted ambient noises only intrude on the magic of production performances.

In addition, you must know about the dangers and intrusions of cellular phones and radio-control equipment when working with wireless microphones. You must know how to budget for multiple microphone set-ups using multiple boom persons and multiple cameras. You must understand the ramifications of inclement weather and the daily cycle of atmospheric inversions that can cause unpredictable wind-buffet problems during an exterior shoot.

With today's advancements in wind-control devices and numerous new mounts and shock absorbers, production mixers capture recordings with greater clarity and dynamic

Figure 4.1 Sound boom operators must get into the middle of any action being created on the screen: from hurricane-driven rain, to car-chase sequences, to dangerously moving equipment. Here, two boom operators bundle up in padded-body wraps, gauntlets, and machinist masks to protect themselves from flying bits of rock and debris, while still striving to capture the best microphone placement possible. (Photo by Ulla-Maija Parikka)

range than ever before, but they can't do it alone. Such tools in the recording equipment package do not come free as part of the daily rate of the sound mixer. You must allow enough money in the equipment rental package, whether it is rented from an audio facility or whether it is the property of the sound person utilizing his or her own gear.

It is important that you consult with your director of photography. After careful consideration of the photographic challenges you must overcome, you will soon know what kind of cameras you should rent. Three unblimped Arri-III cameras grinding away as they shoot the coverage of three men lounging in a steam room speaking their lines poses some awful sound problems—that is, if you hope to have a production track to use in the final mix! The motors of three unblimped cameras reverberating off hard tile walls will not yield a usable soundtrack. Do you throw up your hands and tell the sound mixer to just get a guide track, conceding that you will have to loop it later in post-production? You can—but why should you?

Of all the films I have contracted and supervised, I remember only three pictures on which I was brought in before the producer commenced preproduction to advise and counsel during the budgeting and tactical planning, the desired result being a successful final track.

John Carpenter set me as the supervising sound editor for *The Thing* a year before he started shooting. I helped advise and consult with both John Carpenter and his production mixer, Tommy Causey, before they even left for Alaska, where they shot the "Antarctica" location sequences. By this time, I had already done two of John's pictures, for both of which Tommy had served as production mixer. Tommy used to call me and ask if we could get together to have coffee and discuss the upcoming shoot. It gave me a great opportunity to ask him to record certain wild tracks while he was there. He would tell me how he intended to cover the action and what kind of microphones he intended to use. After every cast-and-crew screening Tommy always told me that he really appreciated the coffee and conversation, as he would not have thought of something that I had added, or that I had said something that stimulated his thinking, which led to ingenious problem solving.

While John and his team shot up north in the snow, I saw dailies at Universal and went out into the countryside on custom-recording stints to begin developing the inventory of specialty sounds that were needed, months before sound teams were usually brought onto a picture. This preparation and creative foreplay gave us the extra edge in making an exciting and memorable soundtrack. (Oddly enough, the cold, bone-chilling winds of *The Thing* actually were recorded in hot desert country just a few miles northwest of Palm Springs.) To this day, I have been set for other film projects because I did the sound for *The Thing*.

A couple of years later, Lawrence Kubik and Terry Leonard sat down with us before they commenced preproduction on their action-packed antiterrorist picture *Death Before Dishonor*. They needed the kind of sound of *Raiders of the Lost Ark*, but on a very tight budget. Intrigued by the challenge to achieve a soundtrack under such tight restrictions, coupled with Terry Leonard's reputation for bringing to the screen some of the most exciting action sequences captured on film today—sequences that always allowed a creative sound designer to really show off—I decided to take it on.

To avert any misunderstandings (and especially any convenient memory loss months later, during post-production), we insisted that the sound-mixing facility be located where we would ultimately rerecord the final soundtrack. We further insisted that the final rerecording mixers be set and that all personnel with any kind of financial, tactical, or logistical impact on the sound process for which I was being held singularly responsible meet with me and my team, along with the film's producers. Using a felt-tip marker and big sheets of paper pinned to the wall, we charted out a battle plan for success.

Because we could not afford to waste precious budget dollars, we focused on what the production recording team must come back with from location. We gave the producers a wish list of sounds to record in addition to the style of production recording. Because of certain sequences in the script where we knew the dialog would later be looped in post-production for talent and/or performance reasons, we suggested they merely record a guide track of the talent speaking their lines for those specific sequences. The production sound mixer should concentrate on the nearly impossible production sound effect actions taking place in nearly every action set-up—getting the actors to speak their lines as individual wild tracks (WT) whenever he could.

Hundreds of valuable cues of audio track came back, authentic to the Middle Eastern setting and precisely accurate to the action. This saved thousands of dollars of post-production sound redevelopment work, allowing the sound-design chores to concentrate on high-profile needs, rather than track-building from scratch.

Because we could not afford nearly as much Foley stage time as would have been preferred, we all agreed as to what kind of Foley cues we would key on and what kind of Foley we would not detail but could handle as hard-cut effects. We placed the few dollars available at the heart of the audio experience. This included making the producers select and contract with the rerecording facility and involving the rerecording mixers and facility executive staff in the planning and decision-making process. Each mixer listened to and signed off on the style and procedure of how we would mount the sound job, starting with the production recordings and following through to delivering the final-cut units to the stage to be mixed into a final track. We charted out the precise number of days, sometimes even to the hour, that would be devoted to individual processes. Also, we set an exact limit to the number of channels that would be used to perform the Foley cues, which mathematically yielded a precise amount of 35mm stripe stock to be consumed. With this information, we confidently built in cap guarantees not to be exceeded, which in turn built comfort levels for the producers. We laid out what kind of predubbing strategy would be expected, complete and proper coverage without undue separations, specifying a precise number of 35mm fullcoats needed for each pass. Mathematically and tactically, both the facility budget and dubbing schedule unfolded forthwith. It was up to us to do our part, but we could not, and would not be able to, guarantee that we could accomplish the mission unless everyone along the way agreed and signed off on his or her own contribution and performance warranty as outlined by the various teams involved. Everyone agreed, and fourteen months later the Cary Grant Theatre at MGM rocked with a glorious acoustical experience, made possible by the thorough collaboration of problem-solving professionals able to lead the producers and director into the sound mix of their dreams.

In a completely different situation, I handled the sound-editorial chores on a South-Central action picture. We had not been part of any preplanning process, nor had we any say on style and procedure. As with most jobs, my sound team and I were brought onboard as an afterthought, only as the completion of picture editorial neared. We inherited a production track that was poorly recorded, with a great deal of hiss, and without thought of wild track coverage. To further aggravate the problem, the producer did not take our advice and loop what was considered to be a minimum requirement to reconstruct the track. The excuse was that the money was not in the budget for that much ADR. (This is a typical statement, heard quite often, almost always followed several months later by a much greater expenditure than would have been needed had the producers listened to and taken the advice of the supervising sound editor.)

The producer walked onto Stage 2 of Ryder Sound as we commenced rehearsing for a final pass of Reel 1. He listened a moment, then turned and asked, "Why are the sound effects so hissy?" The effects mixer cringed, as he was sure I would pop my cork, but I smiled and calmly turned to the head mixer (who incidentally had just recently won an Academy Award for Best Sound). "Could you mute the dialog predub please?" I asked.

"Sure," he replied as his agile fingers flicked the mute button. The entire dialog predub vanished from the speakers. Now the music and sound effects played fully and pristinely, devoid of any hiss or other audio blemishes. The producer nodded approval, then noticed the absence of dialog from the flapping lips. "What happened to the dialog track?"

I gestured to the head mixer once more. "Could you please unmute the dialog predub?"

He flipped off the mute button, and the dialog returned, along with the obnoxious hiss. The producer stood silently, listening intently, then understood the problem. "Oh, the hiss is in the dialog tracks." He turned to the head mixer. "Can you fix that?"

The mixer glanced up at him, expressionless. "That *is* fixed."

This made for more than one inevitable return to the ADR stage as we replaced increasingly more dialog cues—dialog we had counseled the producer to let us ADR weeks earlier. Additionally, more time was needed to remix and update numerous sequences. This experience did much to chisel a permanent understanding between producer and sound supervisor—and a commitment not to repeat such a fiasco on future films. Much to my surprise, the producer called me in for his next picture, which was a vast improvement—but it wasn't until the following picture that the producer and I bonded and truly collaborated in mounting a supreme action soundtrack.

The producer called me in as he was finishing the budget. "Okay, Yewdall, you keep busting my chops every time we do a picture together, so this time you are in it alongside me. No excuses!"

He made it clear that he wanted a giant soundtrack, but did not have a giant budget. After listening to him explain all about the production special-effects work to be done on the set, I told him that we should only record a guide track. We decided that we would ultimately ADR every syllable in the picture. It would not only give us a chance to concentrate on diction, delivery, and acting at a later time, but also it would eliminate the continual ambiance from the center speaker, which often subdues stereophonic dynamics, allowing us to design a much bigger soundtrack. In fact, the final mix was so alive and full that clients viewing dailies in the laboratory's screening facility were said to have rushed out of the theatre and out the back door, convinced a terrorist take over was in progress. To this day, the producer calls that picture his monster soundtrack—and rightfully so.

UNDERSTANDING THE ART FORM OF SOUND

First, you must know the techniques available to you; many filmmakers today do not. They don't have a background in the technical disciplines, hence they have no knowledge of what is possible or how to realize the vision trapped inside their heads. This stifles their ability to articulate to their department heads clear, meaningful guidance, so they suffocate their craftspeople in abstract terminology that makes for so much artsy-sounding double-talk. They use excuse terms such as "Oh, we'll loop it later," or "We'll fix it in post," or the one I really detest, "We'll fix it when we mix it." These are, more often than not, lazy excuses that really say "I don't know how to handle this," "Oops, we didn't consider that," or "This isn't important to me right now."

Sometimes you must step back, take a moment, and do everything you can do to capture a pristine dialog recording. The vast majority of filmmakers will tell you they demand as much of the original recording as possible; they want the magic of the moment. Many times you know that post-sound can and will handle the moment as well as if not better than a live recording—so you either shoot MOS (without sound) or you stick a microphone in there to get a guide track. You must know your options.

THE "COLLATERAL" TERROR LURKS AT EVERY TURN

If you are making an independent film, you must have a firm grip on understanding the process and costs involved, both direct and collateral. Most production accountants can recite the direct costs like the litany of doctrine, but few understand the process well enough to judge the collateral impact and monetary waste beyond the budget line items.

For example, on an animated feature, the post-production supervisor had called around to get price quotes from sound facilities to layback our completed Pro Tools sessions to 24-track tape. The post-production supervisor had chosen a facility across town because its rate was the lowest and the facility did a lot of animation. When making the inquiry, he had been given a very low rate and had been told that the average time to transfer a reel to 24-track was no more than 30 minutes.

The post-production supervisor was delighted, and on his scratch-pad he scribbled the hourly rate, divided it in half, multiplied it by 4 (the number of reels in the show), and then by 3 (the number of 24-track tapes the supervising sound editor estimated would be needed). That was the extent of the diligence used when the decision was made to use this particular facility to do the layback work.

The first layback booking was made for Thursday afternoon at one o'clock. Based on the scanty research (due to the post-production supervisor's ignorance about the process) and the decision made forthwith, it was decided that, since it would take only 30 minutes per reel to layback, I would not be without my hard drives long enough to justify the rental of what we call a *layback* or *transport* drive. A layback or transport drive is a hard drive dedicated to the job of transferring the edited sessions and all the sound files needed for a successful layback; this way, an editor does not need to give up the hard drive and can continue cutting on other reels.

The first error was a lack of communication from the post-production supervisor and the facility manager in defining what each person meant by a "reel" (in terms of length) and how many channels of sounds each person was talking about regarding the scope of work to be transferred. Each had assumed they were both talking about the same parameters. Sadly, they were not. In traditional film editing terms, a theatrical project is broken down into reels of one thousand feet or less. This means that the average 90- to 100-minute feature will be Picture Cut on nine-to-ten reels, each running an average of 8 to 10 minutes in length. After the final sound mix is complete, these reels are assembled into "AB" projection reels (wherein edit reels 1 and 2 are combined to create a projection reel 1AB, edit reels 3 and 4 are combined to create projection reel 2AB, and so forth). Projection reels are shipped all over the world for theatrical presentation. Whether they are projected using two projectors that switch back and forth at the end of reel changeovers, or whether the projectionist mounts the reels together into one big 10,000-foot platter for automated projection—they are still shipped out on 2,000-foot "AB" projection reels.

When the facility manager heard the post-production supervisor say that our project was four reels long, he assumed that the reels would run approximately 8 to 10 minutes in length, like the reels they cut in their own facility. We were really cutting preassembled AB-style, just like projection reels in length, as the studio had already determined that the animated feature we were doing was a direct-to-video product. Therefore our reels were running an average of 20 to 21 minutes in length—over twice as long as what the facility manager expected.

Second, the facility manager was accustomed to dealing with his own in-house product, which was simple television cartoon work that needed only four to eight sound effect tracks for each reel. For him this was a single-pass transfer. Our post-production supervisor had not made it clear that the sound-editorial team was preparing the work in a theatrical design, utilizing all twenty-two channels for every reel to be transferred.

Since the facility only had a Pro Tools unit that could only play back eight dedicated channels at once, the transfer person transferred channels 1 through 8 all the way through 20 to 22 minutes of an A-B reel, not 8 to 10 minutes of a traditional cut reel. Then he rewound back to heads, reassigned the eight playback outputs to channels 9 through 16, transferred that 20- to 22-minute pass, then rewound back to heads and reassigned the eight playback outputs to channels 17 through 22 to finish the reel. Instead of taking an average of half an hour per reel, each reel took an average of two hours. Add to that a two-hour delay because they could not figure out why the time code from the 24-track was not driving the Pro Tools session.

The crew finally discovered that the reason the time code was not getting through to the computer was that the facility transfer technician had put the patch cord into the wrong assignment in the patch bay and had not thought to double-check the signal path. To add more woes to the hemorrhaging problem, the facility was running its Pro Tools sessions on an old Macintosh Quadra 800. It was accustomed to a handful of sound effects channels with sprinklings of little cartoon effects that it could easily handle. On the other hand, we ran extremely complex theatrical-designed sound with gigantic sound files, many in excess of 50 megabytes apiece. One background pass alone managed 8 gigabytes of audio files in a single session—a session twice as long as traditional cut reels. At the time, I used a Macintosh PowerMac 9600 at my workstation, and they tried to get by with only a Quadra 800. The session froze up on the transfer person, and he didn't know what was wrong. The editor upstairs kept saying the drive was too fragmented, and so they wasted hours re-defragmenting a drive that had just been defragmented the previous day.

I received an urgent call and drove over to help get things rolling again. I asked them if they had tried opening the computer's system folder and throwing out the Digidesign set-up document—on the suspicion that it had become corrupted and needed to be rebuilt. They didn't even know what I was talking about. Once I opened the system folder and showed them the set-up document, I threw it in the trash and rebooted the computer, then reset the hardware commands. The Pro Tools session came up and proceeded to work again.

Part of the reason the facility offered such an apparently great transfer deal was that it did not have to pay a transfer technician very high wages, as he was barely an apprentice, just learning the business. He transferred sound by a monkey-see, monkey-do approach; he had been shown to put this cord here, push this button, turn this knob, and it should work. The apprentice was shoved into a job way beyond his skill level and was not instructed in the art of precise digital-to-analog transfer—nor had he been taught how to follow a signal path, how to detect distortion, how to properly monitor playback, how to tone up stock (and why), or how to problem-solve.

The facility did not have an engineer on staff—someone who could have intervened with expert assistance to ferret out the problem and get the transfer bay running again. Instead, a sound editor was called down from the cutting rooms upstairs, someone who had barely gotten his own feet wet with Pro Tools, someone only a few steps ahead of the transfer person. Not only was the layback session of Thursday blown completely out, but a second session was necessary for the following day, which ended up taking nine hours more. As a consequence, I was without my drive and unable to do any further cutting for nearly two days because of this collateral oversight. In addition to nearly a thousand dollars of lost editorial talent, the layback schedule that on paper looked like it would take two simple hours actually took fourteen, wiping out the entire allocated monies for all the laybacks—and we had just started the process!

These collateral pitfalls cause many horror stories in the world of filmmaking. Filmmakers' ignorance of the process is compounded by the failure to ask questions or to admit lack of knowledge; the most common mistake is accepting the lowest bid because the client erroneously thinks money will be saved. Much of the ignorance factor is due not only to the ever-widening gap of technical understanding by the producers and unit production managers, but by the very person producers hire to look after this phase of production—the post-production supervisor. The old studio system used to train producers and directors, through a working infrastructure in which form and function had a tight, continuous flow, and the production unit had a clearer understanding of how film was made, articulating its vision and design accordingly. Today many producers and directors enter the arena "cowboy"-style, shooting from the hip, flashing "sexy" terms and glitzy fads during their pitch sessions to launch the deal—yet they seldom understand that which their tongues brandish like a rapier.

Many executive-level decision-makers in the studios today rose from the ranks of number-crunching accountants, attorneys, and talent agent "packagers"—with little or no background in the art of storytelling and technical filmmaking, without having spent any time working in a craft that would teach production disciplines. They continue to compress schedules and to structure inadequate budgets.

A point of diminishing returns arrives at which the studios (producers) shoot themselves in the foot, both creatively and financially, because they don't understand the process or properly consult supervisors and contractors of the technical crafts who can structure a plan to ensure the project's fruition.

PENNY-WISE AND POUND-FOOLISH

A frequent blunder is not adopting a procedural protocol to make protection back-ups of original recorded dailies or masters before shipping from one site to another. The extra dollars added to the line-item budget are minuscule indeed compared to the ramifications of no back-up protection and the consequent loss of one or more tapes along the way.

I had a robust discussion with a producer over the practice of striking a back-up set of production DATs each day before shipping the dailies overseas to Los Angeles. For a mere $250, all the daily DATs would have been copied just prior to shipment. He argued with me that it was an unnecessary redundancy and that he would not line anybody's pockets. Sure enough, two months later, the post-production supervisor of the studio called me up. "Dave—we've got a problem."

The overseas courier had lost the previous day's shipment. The film negative had made it, but not the corresponding DAT. They had filmed a sequence at night on the docks of Hong Kong. An additional complication arose in that the scene was not even scripted, but had been made up on the spur of the moment and shot impromptu. There were no script notes and only the barest of directions and intentions from the script supervisor.

Consultation with the director and actors shed little light on the dialog and dramatic intent. After due consideration and discussion with the post-production supervisor, we set upon an expensive and complex procedure, necessary because the producer had not spent that paltry $250 for a back-up DAT copy before lab shipments.

Two lip-readers were hired to try to determine what the actors were saying. The television monitors were too small for the lip-readers to see anything adequately because the footage was shot at night with moody lighting. This meant we had to use an ADR room where the film image projected much larger. Naturally, the work could not be done in real time. It took the lip-readers two full days of work to glean as much as they could. Remember, these were raw dailies, not finished and polished cut scenes. The lip-readers had to figure out each take of every angle because the sequence was unscripted and the dialog varied from take to take.

Then we brought in the actors to ADR their lines as best as they could to each and every daily take. After all, the picture editor could cut the sequence only after he had the dialog in the mouths of the actors.

After the preliminary ADR session, my dialog editor cut the rough dialog in sync to the daily footage as best she could. This session was then sent out to have the cut ADR transferred onto a Beta SP videotape that the picture assistant could then digitize into the Avid (a nonlinear picture editing system).

It should go without saying that once the picture editor finished cutting the sequence, the entire dock sequence had to be reperformed by the actors on the ADR stage for a final and more polished performance.

All in all, the costs of this disaster ran upward of $40,000, if you include all collateral costs that would not have been expended if a duplicate DAT back-up had been made in the first place. To make matters worse, they had not secured a completion bond nor had they opted for the errors-and-omissions clause in the insurance policy.

DEVELOPING GRASS-ROOTS COMMON SENSE

Budget properly, but not exorbitantly, for sound. Make sure that you are current on the costs and techniques of creating what you need. Most important, even if you do not want to reveal the amount of money budgeted for certain line items, at least go over the line items you have in the budget with the department heads and vendors with whom you intend to work. I have yet to go over a budget that was not missing one or more items—items the producer had either not considered or did not realize had to be included in the process: everything from giving the electrical department enough allowance for extra cable to control generator noise, to providing wardrobe with funds for the soft booties actors wear for all but full-length shots, to allowing enough time for a proper Foley job and enough lead time for the supervising sound editor and/or sound designer to create and record the special sound effects unique to the visuals of the film.

The technicians, equipment, and processes change so quickly, and are still evolving and changing so quickly, that you must take constant pulse-checks to see how the industry's technical protocol is shooting and delivering film—otherwise you will find yourself budgeting and scheduling unrealistically for the new generation of post-production processes. Since 1989 the most revolutionary aspects of production have been in the mechanics of how technicians record, edit, and mix the final soundtrack—namely, digital technology. This has changed the sound process more profoundly than nearly any other innovation in the past fifty years.

Costs have come down in some areas, and have risen dramatically in others. Budget what is necessary for your film—and allow enough time to properly finish the sound processes of the picture. A sad but true axiom in this business is: There is never enough time or money to do it right, but they always seem to find more time and money to do it over!

Half the time, I don't feel like a sound craftsman. I feel like the guy in that old Midas muffler commercial who shrugs at the camera and says, "You can pay me now—or pay me later." The truly sad thing is that it is not really very funny. My colleagues and I often shake our heads in disbelief at the millions of dollars of waste and inefficient use of budget funds. We see clients and executives caught up in repeating clichés or buzzwords—the latest "hip" phrase or technical nickname. They want to be on the cutting edge, they want to have the new hot-rod technologies in their pictures, but they rarely understand what they are saying or how it works. It becomes the slickest recital of technical double-talk, not because they truly understand the neat new words, but because they think it will make their picture better.

While working on a low-budget action robot picture, I entered the rerecording mix stage to commence predubbing sound effects when the director called out to me. "Hey, Dave, you did prepare the sound effects in THX, didn't you?" I smiled and started to laugh at his jest, when the rerecording mixer caught my eye. He was earnestly trying to get my attention and warn me not to react. It was then that I realized the director was not jesting—he was serious! I stood stunned. I could not believe he would have made such a statement in front of everybody. Rather than expose his ignorance to his producer and staff, I simply let it slide, and offered an off-handed affirmation. "THX—absolutely."

An old and tired cliché I really detest unfortunately is very true: "(1) You can have good quality. (2) You can have it fast. (3) You can have it cheap. You may pick only two of the three." When potential clients tell me they want all three options, I know what kind of person I am dealing with—so I recommend another sound-editorial firm. No genuine collaboration can happen with people who expect and demand all three.

One False Move is a classic example of this cliché in action. When Carl Franklin and Jesse Beaton interviewed me, we came to an impasse in the budget restrictions. I rose, shook their hands, bid them well, and left. Carl followed me down the hall and blocked my exit. "I'm really disappointed with you, Yewdall."

"You're disappointed with me?" I sighed. "You're the ones with no money."

"Yeah, well, I thought one Cormanite would help out another Cormanite," snapped Carl.

I grinned. "You worked with Roger Corman? Why didn't you say that to begin with? Cormanites can always work things out."

And with that, we returned to the office to work things out. "All right," I said, "if you don't have much money, you must give me a lot more time." Carl and Jesse were able to give me six extra weeks. This allowed me to do more work personally, rather than paying for a larger editorial staff. That the picture came at a slow time in the traditional industry schedule also helped.

Here is another point to note: In peak season, financial concessions are rare. If you hope to cut special rates or deals, aim for the dead period during the Cannes Film Festival.

THE TEMP DUB

A new cut version of a picture is seen as counterproductive by studio executives, as they usually are not trained to view cut picture with only the raw cut production sound. They don't fully understand the clipped words and the shifts in background presences behind the various angles of actors delivering their lines. They watch a fight scene and have difficulty understanding how well it is working without the sounds of face impacts and body punches. This has caused an epidemic of temp dubbing on a scale never before seen or imagined in the industry.

Ten years ago we called temp dubs the process of sticking $50,000 in the toilet and flushing it away. Today, we accept it as a necessary evil. Entire procedures and tactical battle plans are developed to survive the inevitable temp dub—and they don't come as a single event. Where there is one, there will be more. How many times has a producer assured me not to worry about a temp dub? Either there will not be one because no money is in the budget for one, the producer insists, or there will be one temp dub and that is it!

A ghoulish comedy for which I supervised the sound a few years back is an excellent example of this. Two gentlemen, with whom I had had very good experience on an aviation action film the previous year, were its producers. I was assured there would be no temp dub; certainly no money was in the budget for one. But the project had a first-time director, a respected comedy writer on major films now looking to cross over and sit in the director's chair. Being a talented writer, however, did not suddenly infuse him with the knowledge of the technical disciplines with which motion pictures were made, especially the post-production processes.

We had no sooner looked at the director's cut of the picture than the director ordered up a temp dub. I decided not to cut my wrists just then, as I picked up the phone and called the producer for an explanation. He was as surprised as I was, and he told me to forget about it. I instructed my crew to continue preparing for the final. Within an hour, I received a call from the producer, apologizing and explaining that he could do nothing about it. If the director wanted a temp dub, then we needed to prepare one. I reminded the producer that no allowance had been made for the temp dub in the budget. He knew that. He had to figure things out, but for now, he said, just use budget monies to prepare the temp dub. He would figure out how to cover the overage costs. I asked the producer why he could not block the director's request. After all, I had been trained that the pecking order of command gave producers the veto power to overrule directors, especially when issues of budget hemorrhaging were the topic of conversation. The producer explained that the hierarchy was not typical on this picture—the director was granted a separate deal with the studio that effectively transcended the producer's authority over him. I reluctantly agreed to the temp dub, but reminded the producer that it would seriously eat into the dollars budgeted for the final cutting costs until he could fortify the overage.

After the first temp dub we had resumed preparations for the final when we received a second phone call from the producer. The director had ordered up a second temp dub for another series of screenings. No compensation had been made for the first temp, and now a second temp dub was being ordered? The producer sighed and told us to just continue to use budget dollars until he could figure it out. This would definitely be the last temp dub, and the nightmare would be over.

The nightmare continued for four weeks. Each week the director ordered up yet another temp dub. Each week the producer was unable to deal with studio executives and was dismissed from acquiring additional budget dollars to offset the temp dub costs.

After the fourth temp dub, the producer asked how much longer it would take us to prepare the final mix. I shrugged and said that as far as I was concerned we were already prepared. His eyes widened in disbelief as he asked how that was possible. I told him that the four temp dubs had burned up the entire sound editorial budget due to the director's dictates. Nothing was left to pay the editors to prepare the final soundtrack unless compensation was forthcoming—therefore the fourth temp dub would have to serve as the final mix! The producer did not believe we would really do that. To this day, the film is shown on television and viewed on videocassettes with the fourth temp dub as its ultimate soundtrack.

You can easily see how a judgment error in the director/producer jurisdiction can have calamitous collateral effects on the end product. Someone, either at the studio or over at the attorney's offices, had been allowed to structure a serious anomaly into the traditional chain-of-command hierarchy. This unwise decision, made long before the cameras ever rolled, laid the groundwork for financial and quality control disasters.

Remember this one truth. No one gives you anything free. *Someone* pays for it—most of the time, you. If producers only knew what really goes on behind the scenes to offset the fast-talking promises given a client to secure the deal, they would be quicker to negotiate fairly structured relationships and play the game right.

READ THE FINE PRINT

Several years ago a friend brought me a contract from another sound editorial firm. He told me the director and producer were still fighting with the editorial firm regarding the overages on their last picture. This contract was for a major motion picture, and they did not want to end up suffering a big overage bill after the final sound mix was completed. Would I read through the contract and highlight potential land mines that could blow up as extra "hidden" costs? I read through the contract.

The editorial firm guaranteed, for a flat fee, a Foley track for each reel of the picture. The cost seemed suspiciously low. When I reread it, I discovered it would bill a flat guaranteed price of "a Foley track"—in other words, Foley-1 of each reel. Foley tracks 2 through (heaven knows how many) 30 or 40 would obviously be billed out as extra costs above and beyond the bounds of the contract.

All the Dolby "A" noise-reduction channels would be thrown into the deal free. Sounds good—except that by this time nobody of consequence used Dolby "A" channels, and those who were using them had already amortized their cost and threw them into every deal free. Of course, nowhere in the contract did it specify about the free use of Dolby "SR" channels— the accepted and required noise-reduction system at the time. This would, of course, appear as extra costs above and beyond the bounds of the contract.

To help cut costs, the contract specified that all 35 mm fullcoat rolls (with the exception of final mix rolls) would be rental stock—costing a flat five dollars each. It was estimated, based on the director's last project and the style of sound post-production tactics that this project would use at least 750,000 feet of 35 mm fullcoat. That would cost the budget an estimated $3,750 in stock rental.

Since the picture and client were of major importance, the sound-editorial firm wrote into the contract that it would purchase all brand-new stock and guarantee to the client that the first use of this new rental stock would be on this picture. This must have sounded delicious to the producer and director. However, in a different part of the contract, near the back, appeared a disclaimer that if any fullcoat rental stock was physically cut for any reason, it would revert from rental to purchase—the purchase price in keeping with the going rates of the studio at the time. A purchase price was not specified or quoted anywhere in the contract. I happened to know that the current purchase price of one roll of fullcoat at the studios

Figure 4.2 The con-men of the production double-speak.

averaged $75. This would end up costing the producer over $56,000! No risk existed for the sound-editorial firm; the director was notorious for his changes and updates, so the expectation that each roll of fullcoat used would have at least one cut in it—and would therefore revert to purchase price—translated into money in the bank.

My advice to the producer was to purchase the desired-grade quality fullcoat directly from the stock manufacturer at $27 per roll. Since the production would use so much fullcoat, I suggested the producer strike a bulk-rate discount—which brought the price down to $20 per roll. This would give the producer a guaranteed line-item cost of $15,000, along with the peace of mind that any changes and updates could be made without collateral overages leaching from the budget's fine print regarding invasive use.

I then came across a paragraph describing library effects use. The contract stated that the first 250 sound effects of each reel would be free. A fee of $5 per effect would be added thereafter. First, most sound-editorial firms do not charge per effect. The use of the sound library as required is usually part of the sound-editorial contract. In the second place, no finite definition of what constituted a sound effect was given. If the same sound effect was used more than once in a reel, did that sound effect constitute one use, or was every performance of that same sound effect being counted separately each time? If the editor cut a sound effect into several parts, would each segment constitute a sound effect use? The contract did not stipulate. I might add that this picture went on to win an Academy Award for

Best Sound—but industry rumors placed the overages of the sound budget at well over one million dollars.

BUT YOU SAID IT WOULD BE CHEAPER!

While I was working on *Chain Reaction,* a studio executive asked to have lunch with me because he wanted to unload some frustrations and pick my brain about the rapid changes in post-production. For obvious reasons, he will remain anonymous, but he agonized over his Caesar salad about how he just didn't understand what had happened. "You guys said digital would be cheaper!"

"Wait a minute," I stopped him. "I never said that to you."

"I don't mean you. But everybody said it would cost less money, and we could work faster!"

"Name me one sound editor who told you that. You can't, because it wasn't one of us who sold you this program. It was the hardware pushers who sold it to you. You deluded yourselves that it would cost less and allow you to compress schedules. Now what have you got? Compressed schedules with skyrocketing budgets."

"So let's go back to film!"

I smiled. "No. Do I like working in nonlinear? Yes. Do I think that it is better? Not necessarily. Do I want to go back to using magnetic film again? No."

"Where'd we go wrong?" he asked.

"You expected to compare apples with apples—like with like. That's not how nonlinear works. With the computer and the almost weekly upgrades of software, we can do more and more tasks. Because we can do more, the director expects us to do more. You cannot expect us to have access to a creative tool and not use it.

"Are we working faster than before? Mach four times faster. Can we ignore using the extra bells and whistles and use the equipment as if it were an electronic Moviola? Absolutely NOT! The sooner you stop throwing darts at the calendar as you make up these artificial schedules and listen to your craftspeople's advice, the sooner you are going to start injecting sensibility into your out-of-control post-production budgets and start recapturing an art form that is quickly ebbing away. Otherwise, you had better take a deep breath and accept the fact that today's post-production costs are out of control, fueled by directors who find themselves in a studio playpen with amazing creative toys at their disposal. They are going to play with them!"

BUDGET FUNDAMENTALS

One of the most frequent agonies in the birthing process of a film is the realization that the budget for the sound-editorial and/or rerecording process was inadequately structured and allocated. Because these two processes are ranked among the most misunderstood phases, they are the two that often suffer the most.

The process is not alleviated by those who strive to help the new independent producers or unit production managers (UPMs) by trying to develop "plug-in" budget forms, whether printed or via computer software developed by those who know even less about the post-production process. More often than not, these forms are copied from budgets acquired from someone working on another show or even from someone trained during a different era. Not understanding the process, the software writer or print-shop entrepreneur copies only what is seen, thereby carrying only those line items and detail (especially the lack thereof) of whatever is on the acquired budget breakdown—including all the mistakes.

We often have been shocked to find that the producers or UPMs did not allow certain critical line items into their own budgets because they did not see an allowance for a line item in their budget form. Not understanding the sound-editorial and mixing process themselves, they did not add their own line items as needed. The ignorance and ensuing budget disaster is carried from project to project, like bad genes in a DNA strain, photocopying the blueprints for disappointment and failure onto the next unsuspecting project.

UNDERSTANDING THE BUDGET LINE ITEMS

Following are some important budget line items to consider. Remember, these costs directly impact the soundtrack. These line items do not include creative noise abatement allowances. Use common sense and draw upon experienced craftspersons to assist in planning a successful soundtrack.

Production Sound Budget

In addition to the time allocated for the production sound mixer, the smart producer budgets time for the mixer to come on a location field-trip—to see and hear the natural ambiance, to walk the practical location and hear the potential for echo, to note nearby factories and highways, to detect the presence of aircraft flight paths. In addition, the mixer takes a quick overview of where power generators might be parked and to note whether natural blinds exist to help block noise or if acoustic gear should be brought to knock down potential problems.

For a pristine dialog track, the boom operator is the key position. The production mixer is the head of the production sound crew, but even the mixer will tell you the boom operator is more important. If the microphone is not in the right position, what good is the subsequent recording? More often than not, the producer or UPM always underbudgets the boom operator slot. I have seen production mixers shave some of their own weekly rates so that those extra dollars can bolster the boom operator's salary.

Most smaller pictures cannot afford the cable man (the term "cable man" has stuck, regardless of the technician's gender). The cable man also handles the second microphone boom and other assistant chores. On one picture the producer had not allowed the hiring of a cable man, alleging that the budget could not support one. One night, the crew was shooting a rain sequence at a train station. The production mixer was experiencing many pops on the microphone because the rain was heavier than had been anticipated. Needing the rain bonnet, he asked the director for five minutes so that the boom operator could fetch one from the sound truck. The director said no—"We'll just loop his lines later in post-production." The following night, the actor was tragically killed in a stunt crash during filming. What do you think it cost to fix the rain-pelted production track, as opposed to the cost of the requested five-minute wait the night before?

ACCT		ACCOUNT TITLE		PREP	PROD	POST		RATE	TOTAL
3400		SOUND (Production)							
3401		SOUND MIXER		1 wk	6 wks	2 dys			
3402		BOOM OPERATOR		2 dys	6 wks	1 dy			
3403		CABLE MAN		1 dy	6 wks	1 dy			
3404		PROD. FX RECORDIST		2 dys	2 wks	2 dys			
3405		PLAYBACK OPERATOR							
3410		Equipment Package rental							
		analog/digital (for DIA)			6 wks				
3412		Equipment Package rental							
		analog/digital (for FX)			2 wks				
3415		Recording equip supplies							
3420		Purchases							
3425		Rentals							
3430		Walkie-Talkies / comm			6 wks				
3440		Repairs							
3460		Daily Transfer --Digital--							
3461		time code DAT rental			6 wks				
3462		digital transfer labor			6 wks				
3463		Audio File Back-Ups							
3470		Daily Transfer --Film--							
3471		film mag stripe							
3472		film transfer labor			6 wks				
[____]		[_____]							
[____]		[_____]							
[____]		[_____]							
[____]		[_____]							
3480		Fringes (___%)							
3481		Sales Tax (___%)							
					Prod SOUND ACCT TOTAL:				

Figure 4.3 Production sound budget.

On large productions, especially those with a great deal of specialized equipment, vehicles, or props that may be expensive or impossible to acquire later, increasingly more producers factor a production FX recordist into the budget. Usually these individuals have a reputation for knowing how to record for sound effect use and for effectively interfacing with the post-production crew to ensure needed recordings. They often work separately from the first unit, usually arranging to work with vehicles or props not being used at the time, taking them out and away to areas conducive to quality recordings.

For instance, a Trans-Am may be the hero vehicle for the picture. The director may want the Trans-Am recorded to match the production dialog, but recorded as a stunt-driven vehicle to give the "big sound" for post-production sound editorial. Recordings of this type are usually done in off-hours, not while the shooting unit is in need of any of the special props or locations in question.

Those occasions do arise, though, when the production FX recordist will record during actual shooting, such as recording cattle stampeding through a location set. It may be a financial hardship to field the cattle and wranglers after the actual shoot just to record cattle stampeding. Recordings like these are best orchestrated collaboratively with camera and crew.

Each situation requires a different problem-solving approach. Common sense will guide you to the most fruitful decision. However, production effects recording during principal photography demands attentive regard for suppressing inappropriate noises made by the production crew. Such events are incredibly challenging and seldom satisfying from the sound mixer's point of view.

The project may require that precise wild track recordings be made of an oil rig, say, or a drawbridge spanning a river. These types of sound recordings should be entrusted to a recordist who understands the different techniques of recording sound effects rather than production dialog (major differences are explained later in this book). The production FX recordist is not usually on for the entire shoot of the picture, but is brought on as needed, or for a brief period of time to cover the necessary recordings.

Production recording mixers can and prefer to use their own equipment. This is of great benefit to the producer for two reasons. First, the production mixer is familiar with his or her own gear and probably yields a better-quality sound recording. Second, in a negotiation pinch, the production mixer is more likely to cut the producer a better equipment-package rental rate than an equipment rental house. Remember too that the production mixer is usually responsible for and provides the radio walkie-talkies and/or Comtech gear for crew communications. Communication gear is not part of the recording equipment basic package, but is handled as a separate line item.

As you consider the kind of picture you are making, the style and preference of the production recording mixer, and the budget restraints you are under, you will decide whether to record in analog or digital—single-channel, two-channel, or multichannel. This decision outlines a daily procedure protocol from the microphone-to-picture editorial—how to accomplish it and what you must budget.

Without question, the vast majority of dailies today are delivered to picture editorial digitally. There are three ways of doing this. The first two choices involve having the production mixer's daily sound tapes (whether analog or digital) transferred to another medium for picture editorial assimilation.

1. You may choose to have the laboratory do it. This in-lab service may be more convenient for you, as they deliver you a video telecine transfer with your sound already synced up to the picture. The downside is that it is a factory-style operation on the laboratories' part. Very few lab services have master sound techs who think beyond the time code numbers and sound report's circled takes. The precision and attention to detail is often lost with the necessary factory-type get-it-out

schedule. A more important problem is that you introduce, at the very least, a generation loss by virtue of the videotape and, at worst, a lot of new noise and hums, depending on the quality of the telecine. I do not care what the laboratory tells you—all video transfers introduce degradation and system noise to some degree. I have inherited numerous projects in which producers had the laboratories handle sound transfer in this manner and I have been underwhelmed with their level of service and expertise.

2. You may choose to have your own assistant picture editor transfer (digitize) the sound straight into the AVID, locking to the digital picture internally. This certainly bypasses the video-transfer generation loss, but it places the burden of quality control and the personal project nuances on the picture editorial team's plate. This technique is mandatory if you hope to utilize the OMF procedure later in post-sound editorial. I never trust any material that was handled by a film laboratory, whether telecine transfer or even digitized audio files, if I ever hope to use OMF in the post-sound edit equation. (OMF, open media framework, is covered in greater detail in Chapter 14.) Your third choice is to have your production sound mixer do it—so to speak. By this I mean that the sound mixer would be recording sound to either the Deva II or to the new Nagra V—both of which record FAT16 WAV with BWF (Broadcast Wave Format) audio files. (Chapter 5 talks about the Deva, and Chapter 22 is devoted to the Nagra V). Time code and other scene/take reference data are included in the directory information of these files, making them instant "drag-and-drop" transfer items into non-linear picture and audio workstations. As you will read in more detail later, your sound mixer will simply pull the DVD-RAM back-up (if by Deva II) or the Orb drive (if by Nagra V) out of their recording set-up and ship it straight to picture editorial, ready to be data-transferred into the computer.

On the other hand, you may either have the budget for or the production philosophy for wanting to have your dailies transferred onto mag stripe film as well. There are two good reasons for this.

1. The obvious first reason is that the producer, director, and/or picture editor may want to cut traditionally on film using a Kem or a Steinbeck. This choice may be made for a whole host of reasons that we will not go into here.
2. You may wish to conform your 35mm workprint and 35mm mag stripe from your AVID EDLs (edit decision lists) so that you can conduct progress screenings more easily using interlock projection equipment in a traditional theatre—especially if test screenings are in "sneak" environments.

Music Budget

Once the producer settles on the music composer and they thoroughly discuss the conceptual scope of work to be done, the composer outlines a budget to encompass the financial requirements necessary. I am not going to pretend to be an authority about the budget requirements for music, just as I would not want a music composer to attempt to speak for sound-editorial budget requirements; therefore you should consult your music director and/or composer for their budgetary needs.

ACCT	ACCOUNT TITLE	POST	RATE	TOTAL
4600	MUSIC			
4601	COMPOSER(s)			
4602	LYRICIST(s)			
4603	CONDUCTOR			
4605	MUSICIANS [_____]			
4605	ARRANGER/ORCHESTRATOR			
4608	COPYIST			
4609	SINGERS/CHORUS [_____]			
4610	VOCAL INSTRUCTORS			
4611	Special Instrument Rentals			
4612	Labor/Transport-Instruments			
4613	Studio Rental			
4614	Studio Equipment --			
	rentals -&- set-up			
4615	MUSIC RECORDIST			
4616	RECORDIST ASST.			
4620	MUSIC EDITOR			
4621	Music Editor SET-UP			
4650	multi-track MIX-DOWN			
4651	STOCK:			
	Digital multi-track			
	Digital protection			
4652	Stock & Source Music			
	license fees			
4654	Music publishing			
	Copyright costs			
4655	Reuse Fee			
4660	Administrative expenses			
[_____]	[_____]			
[_____]	[_____]			
[_____]	[_____]			
[_____]	[_____]			
4680	Fringes (___%)			
		MUSIC ACCT TOTAL:		

Figure 4.4 Music budget.

Sound Editorial Budget

The "Labor" line items of the sound editorial detail illustrated in Figure 4.5 are geared toward a medium-sized feature film with a heavy action content. (I discuss the individual job slots and their contribution to the soundtrack later in this book.)

"Room Rentals" refers to the actual rooms where editorial equipment, whether Moviolas, benches and trim bins, or digital workstations with monitors and computers are set up and used by the editorial talent. This cost does not reflect the equipment, but many sound-editorial firms do include 9 to 12 gigabytes of external drive storage in the use of the room.

Each sound editor has a workstation system requirement. A sound designer has a lot more gear than a dialog editor. Assistant sound editors have different equipment requirements than do sound editors. The workstation system rentals obviously vary from one requirement to another.

Sound editors need more hard drives than the 9 to 12 gigabytes their room rental may allow. This need is dictated by how busy and demanding the sound editorial requirements are; again, every show is different.

The "custom FX recordist" may, at first glance, look like a redundancy slot from the sound (production) budget page. It is not. The production FX recordist covered the vehicles, locations, and props unique to the filming process. Later, usually weeks and even months later, the sound-editorial team is up against a whole new set of needs and requirements. It may need to capture specialized backgrounds that were not part of the original location, but are needed to blend and create the desired ambiance.

The stunt vehicle may have looked great on film, portrayed as a huge and powerful hydrogen jet car, but in actuality it had only a little four-cylinder gasoline engine that, from a sound point of view, is completely unsuitable. Now the supervising sound editor, in a calculated design to create the hydrogen jet car, must have the custom FX recordist record jets taking off, flying by, landing, and taxiing as a faraway military air base. The sound editor may need to have the recordist go to a local machine shop and record various power tools and metal movements. These recordings, as you can see, are completely different from those of the production FX recordist, who was busy recording a controlled audio series of the real props or vehicles as they actually sounded.

Referring to the "back-up media" line item, back-ups can never be stressed enough. Every few days, sound editors turn their hard drives over to the assistant sound editors, who mount them to a mass storage device, such as a DLT, using back-up management software such as Retrospect—or the DVD-RAM.

"Temp dub allowances" is a highly volatile and controversial line item. Directors have become fanatical about having temp dubs because they know their work is being received on a "first-impression" style viewing, and anything less than a final mix is painful. Studio executives want test screenings for audiences so they can get a pulse on how their film is doing—what changes to make, where to cut, and where to linger—all of which necessitate showing it with as polished a soundtrack as possible.

Extra costs may be needed to cover the preparation of the temp dubs separate from the sound preparation for final mix predubbing. The producer(s) and supervising sound editor(s) may want a separate editorial team to handle most of the temp dub preparation, because they do not want the main editorial team distracted and diluted by preparing temp dubs. (Temp dub philosophy is discussed later.)

ACCT	ACCOUNT TITLE	POST	RATE	TOTAL
4700	SOUND EDITORIAL			
4701	Labor:			
	SUPERVISING SOUND EDITOR	12 wks		
	CO-SUPERVISING SOUND EDITOR	12 wks		
	SOUND DESIGNER	7 wks		
	DIALOG SUPERVISOR	7 wks		
	DIALOG EDITOR #2	5 wks		
	A.D.R. SUPERVISOR	9 wks		
	A.D.R. EDITOR	4 wks		
	SOUND EFFECTS EDITOR #1	6 wks		
	SOUND EFFECTS EDITOR #2	6 wks		
	SOUND EFFECTS EDITOR #3	6 wks		
	FOLEY ARTIST #1	10 days		
	FOLEY ARTIST #2	10 days		
	FOLEY SUPERVISOR	6 wks		
	FOLEY EDITOR #2	4 wks		
	1st ASSISTANT EDITOR	12 wks		
	2nd ASSISTANT EDITOR	9 wks		
4702	Room Rentals			
4703	Workstation Set-ups (designer)			
4704	Workstation Set-ups (editors)			
4705	Workstation Set-ups (assistants)			
4706	Hard Drive Rentals			
4710	CUSTOM FX RECORDIST	2 wks		
4711	Equipment Package rental (FX record)	2 wks		
4715	back-up media (DLT / DVD-RAM)			
4716	Expendable Supplies			
4720	Courier / Shipping			
4730	Special Edit Equipment Rentals			
4735	Other Rentals			
4740	TEMP DUB allowances			
4750	Workstation Transfer Exports			
4760	CD-ROM / DVD services to client			
4765	Transfer STOCK and/or MEDIA			
4770	Payroll taxes			
4780	Fringes (___%)			
4781	Sales Tax (___%)			
[_____]	[_____]			
[_____]	[_____]			
		SOUND EDITORIAL ACCT TOTAL:		

Figure 4.5 Sound editorial budget.

"Workstation transfer exports" refers to the common practice of sound editorial to make "crash downs" (multichannel mixes) of certain segments of action from digital workstations and to export them as single audio files for picture editorial to load into the AVID and sync up to picture, thereby giving picture editorial little work-in-progress sections, such as action scenes, to assist the director and picture editor as work continues. Figure 4.6 illustrates the raw stock supply for the production recording mixer. Note the back-up DATs!

Transfers and Stock Purchase

Unless you are cutting your picture on film, the "Stripe for transfers" line item hardly affects you. This is where you would budget your 35 mm mag stripe and fullcoat costs if you were cutting on film.

Very few of today's post-production facilities are still recording ADR or looping sessions to analog 24-track 2-inch tape anymore, but you may run into one or two of them along the way, so you should understand the format. If you find that you need to use a service that still uses 2-inch stage, refer to the ADR "string-offs" line item. You need to consider the following—five 24-track rolls cover a 95- to 100-minute motion picture. Unless you have extremely complex and overlapping ADR, you should require only one set of 24-track rolls. You will require a second set of 24-track rolls if you are planning to record Group Walla, especially with today's stereophonic microphone set-ups. (ADR and looping technique and recording format options are discussed in Chapter 15.) If you are recording your Foley to 24-track 2" tape (refer to the "Foley string-offs" line item), the same considerations apply as before. Some films require more Foley tracks than others, so you would simply allow for a second set of 24-track rolls. Sometimes Foley requires only a few extra channels; if the Group Walla requirements are not too heavy, you can set aside the first few channels for the overflow Foley tracks and protect the remaining channels for the Group Walla.

In both the ADR and Foley stage-recording requirements, note that I have not mentioned recording straight to an editing workstation hard disk. We will talk more about this in Chapter 15 (for ADR/looping) and Chapter 16 (for Foley). The majority of your post-production sound services will be recording your ADR/looping sessions and/or your Foley sessions straight to a hard disk via a nonlinear workstations such as Pro Tools. Though this procedure will not require a transfer cost in the traditional sense of "transferring" one medium to another medium, you will need to back-up the session folder(s) from the facility's hard drive to whatever medium you require to take to your editorial service. This medium could be CD-ROM, DVD-RAM, Firewire drive, or some other intermediate transport protocol you have decided to use. If that is the case, you need to budget for it under "Hard drive media back-ups."

You will probably not require fullcoat for ADR or Foley recording (see "Fullcoat requirements"). I have not heard of any ADR or Foley stages using fullcoat now for several years. The four-channel film recorders have, for the most part, been replaced by 24-track 2" analog tape and direct-to-disk workstation recording (i.e., Pro Tools or Waveframe).

Depending on which studio you choose to handle the rerecording chores of your project, you will probably require 35 mm fullcoat for some or all of the predubbing and final mix processes. Although most mixing is done digitally using hard drive MMR8s or MMR16s and straight-to-disk platforms such as Pro Tools and Fairlight systems, the best-sounding film tracks are still mixed to film. Nothing sounds as good as 35 mm fullcoat—nothing!

ACCT	ACCOUNT TITLE	POST	RATE	TOTAL
5000	TRANSFERS-&-STOCK PURCHASE			
5001	Raw Stock for Production Recording			
	DAT-and/or-1/4" (orig)			
	DAT Back-Up -or- DVD-RAM			
5005	Stripe for transfers			
	Dailies	X		
	Sound Effects	X		
	Dialog Reprints	X		
	Foley String-offs	X		
	A.D.R. String-offs	X		
	Worktrack 1:1's	X		
	Backgrounds (mono)	X		
	Temp FX -- (for Pix Edit)	X		
5006	Fullcoat Requirements			
	Backgrounds (stereo)	X		
	Temp Dub Mix stock			
	Foley (4 trk) Stock	X		
	A.D.R. (4 trk) Stock	X		
	Music Transfers	X		
	Predubs (all)			
	Final Mix -- Masters			
	Final Mix -- Back-Up			
	Final Mix -- Stems			
	M.&E. "Foreign"			
	Television Version			
5007	Stage Protection Stock			
	DAT-or-1/4" protection -- Foley			
	DAT-or-1/4" protection -- A.D.R.			
5010	Stock for Customization			
	DAT-or-1/4" protection -- FX			
5020	Courier service			
[____]	[_____]			
[____]	[_____]			
[____]	[_____]			
5081	Sales Tax (___%)			
	TRANSFERS-&-STOCK PURCHASES ACCT TOTAL:			

IF you are cutting your picture on FILM rather than non-linear digital

Figure 4.6 Transfer budget.

You must allow for protection back-up stock when you have ADR or Foley sessions (see the 'Stage protection stock" line item). Some stages still use 1/4" tape, but the vast majority use digital DAT. The sound facility with which you contract your stage work may include this cost in its bid. You must check this—make sure to take an overview of how many protection 1/4" or DATs are allowed and the cost per item.

Some sound facilities charge the client a per-foot "head wear" cost for using customer-supplied stock. This is nothing but a penalty for not buying facility's stock, which has obviously been marked up considerably. Find out the kind of stock the facility uses, and then purchase the exact brand and type of stock from the supplier. Not only will you save a lot of money, but you also will pull the rug out from anyone trying to substitute "slightly" used reclaim stock for new and fresh stock. This is a common practice.

Post-Sound Facility

On the "Temp dubs" line item in Figure 4.7, note that we have reserved four days for temp dubbing. This can be used as four mixing days with one temp, as two two-temp mixing days, or as one four-day temp mix.

We have a fairly good production track for this budget example, but we have several segments in which we need to loop the main characters to clean out background noise, improve performance, or add additional lines. We budgeted five days on the ADR stage.

For this project, we have fairly large crowd scenes, and although we expect that sound editorial has all kinds of stereophonic crowds in its sound effects library, we want layers of specialized crowd Walla to lay on top of the cut crowd effects. We budgeted one day to cover the necessary scenes (see the "ADR stage & group walla" line item).

Note that you need to check your cast budget account and ensure that your budget has a line item for group Walla. Many budgets do not, and I have encountered more than one producer who has neglected to allow for this cost. In this case, we budgeted for twenty actors and actresses, who all double and triple their voice talents. With four stereo pairs of tracks, a group of twenty voices easily becomes a chanting mob scene or terrified refugees.

Here we budgeted ten days to perform the Foley (see "Foley stage"), giving us one day per reel. This is not a big budget under the circumstances—action films easily use more time—but we were watching our budget dollars and trying to use them as wisely as possible. In a preliminary meeting with the supervising sound editor, whom we had already set for the picture, we were assured that ten days were needed for those audio cues that must be performed on the Foley stage. Other cues that could have been done on a Foley stage, or that could have been recorded in other ways or acquired through the sound effects library, were not included in the Foley stage scheduling.

When budgeting for predubbing, always think in terms that more predubbing means a faster and smoother final mix; less predubbing means a slower and more agonizing final mix with a higher certainty of hot tempers and frustration. (You will read a great deal about mixing styles and techniques as well as dubbing stage etiquette and protocol later in this book.)

This budget allowed eight days of finals (see the "Finals" line item). The first day is always the hardest. Reel 1 always takes a full day. It is the settling-down and getting up to speed process when you find out that the new head titles are two cards longer than the slug that was in the sound videos, so the soundtrack is twelve and a half feet out of sync—stuff like that. This always brings the we-will-never-get-there anxiety threshold to a new high,

ACCT	ACCOUNT TITLE	POST	RATE	TOTAL
5900	POST-SOUND FACILITY			
	(stage & labor -- 8 hour days)			
5901	Temp Music Transfer			
	Digital and/or Analog			
5902	TEMP DUB(s)	4 days		
	screening copy transfer(s)			
5903	A.D.R. STAGE -- sync voices	5 days		
5904	A.D.R. STAGE -- Group Walla	1 day		
5905	FOLEY STAGE	10 days		
5906	Dialog Reprint Transfer			
	Digital and/or Analog			
5910	Workstation Set-up(s) (stage)	25 days		
	[ProTools / Waveframe]			
5920	PREDUBBING			
	Dialog Predubbing	3 days		
	Foley Predubbing	2 days		
	Background Predubbing	2 days		
	Hard FX Predubbing	3 days		
5921	FINALS			
	Final Rerecording	8 days		
	Run thru -&- Updates	2 days		
	test screening mag transfer	10,000'		
5930	POST-TEST SCREENING MIX			
	Stem Transfer for Recut			
	Stem Remixing Updates	2 days		
5940	2-track PRINT MASTER	1 day		
5950	Optical Sound Mix Transfer	10,000'		
5960	Dolby & Surround Channel License Fee			
5961	Digital system License Fee(s)			
5963	Digital MASTERING (SDDS/DTS/SRD)			
5970	M.&E. "FOREIGN" MIX	1 day		
5975	TELEVISION VERSION MIX	1 day		
[_____]	[_____]			
[_____]	[_____]			
[_____]	[_____]			
5981	Sales Tax (___%)			
	POST-SOUND FACILITY ACCT TOTAL:			

Figure 4.7 Post-sound budget.

causing the producer to become a clock-watcher. But as Reel 3 is reached, one witnesses rhythm and momentum building—eight days is all right for this picture after all.

When the primary mix is finished, one then interlocks the final stems with the changeover projectors and screens the picture in real-time continuity. Dubbing reel by reel and viewing the film in a single run are two different experiences. Everybody always has plenty of notes for updates and fixing, so we budgeted two days for this process.

Now we want to take the picture out with its brand-new, sparkling soundtrack and see what it does with a test audience. We do not take our original final mix rolls out—we have the head mixer make a screening copy transfer, which is run through the mixing console so it can be monitored for quality control. We take this screening copy mix and our silent answer print and run an interlock test screening.

It is a good idea to have a test run-through of the interlock screening copy materials before the actual test screening. I have seen too many instances where the client cut the schedules so tight that the last couple of reels of the screening copy were actually being transferred while the first reel was rolling in the test screening—not a good idea.

After the test screening, we have notes for further changes and updates. We need to allot monies to have the dialog, music, and effects stems as well as the predubs transferred into nonlinear editing hard drives for sound editorial to update and prepare for the stage.

To save money and any potential generation loss, we remix the updated stems and predubs (see the "Stem remixing updates" line item) straight from Pro Tools systems on the stage and interlocked to the machine room. We budgeted two days to remix the updated stems and predubs. We wisely have another test screening. Once we sign off on the both the film and its sound mix, we need to make the "2-track print master."

Even in our digital world, we still need the matrixed stereo optical soundtrack. To accomplish this, we need to make a 2-track print master. At this point, we bring in the Dolby or Ultra*Stereo engineer, who brings the matrix equipment and monitors the transfer process of folding down the multiple stereo channels into a 2-track matrix. The engineer watches the peak meters closely, ensuring that the maximum levels will make optical, and that the vibrancy and dynamics of the mix is translating properly.

Many independent sound facilities do not have their own optical transfer departments. They subcontract this work out to reliable and reputable specialists. We must budget for the optical track to be shot and processed.

Do not forget the license fees. Almost all distributors now cover all the audio bases in one print, putting the various digital formats (Dolby SR-D, SDDS, and DTS) and the traditional 2-track analog optical on the same print. No matter what format the theatre has been built for, the same print plays in all of them.

Depending on the complexity and the sound-editorial preparation for M&E (Music and Effects only, with the dialog track as a separate transfer so that foreign distributors can dub in their own language instead of using subtitles) considerations, the "M&E 'foreign' mix" can take as little as half a day to as long as two days. We budgeted one full day for the M&E mix for our film. The last thing we need is for a foreign territory to bounce our M&E track and stick us with thousands of dollars in fix-it costs. (I cover techniques of preparation and delivery requirements of the foreign M&E track later in this book.)

Sound editorial goes through the picture replacing alternate lines or looping television coverage on the ADR stage. We budgeted one day for mixing our "Television version mix."

THE LOST SOUND DIRECTOR

Years ago we had an individual who followed the sound from the initial budgeting and scheduling, through the final 2-track print master and M&E delivery inventory. This individual was known as the sound director, who was, in a word, the QC (quality control) gatekeeper to the film's audio experience.

We have lost this position, unfortunately. In an age of filmmaking in which mismatching technologies have mushroomed out of control—when coordinating an audio track has literally become a global challenge and responsibility—we need the return of the sound director. This is not the post-production coordinator, as some people think. This is a management overseer, richly trained in the audio arts and with experience hash-marks up both arms. Wise will be the producer who writes this position in as a budget line item.

For budgetary reasons, the producer might want to hire the sound director on a consultant basis rather than as a weekly payroll position, especially because a sound director oversees more than one project at a time. However the position is structured, the project reaps the obvious creative and financial benefits.

These are only a few highlights of the pitfalls in the journey you are preparing to take. How you prepare for it determines whether you bask in the joy of success or anguish in a battlefield strewn with could-have-beens and should-have-dones. The technology is at your disposal and fine craftspeople can be found throughout the world—it is up to you.

Chapter 5
The Challenging Battlefield
of Production

"I'm sorry, David, but the #$%*!ing director won't give me two minutes to slap a couple of wireless mikes on the actors, and there's no room in the #$%*ing office for my boom man—so I had to stick the mike on the floor under the desk—so don't blame me if it sounds like #$%*!"

Lee Howell, commenting on production DAT-14 while working as a production sound mixer

Without doubt, the most difficult and arduous recording process in the audio-track development of a film is the on-camera production dialog recording. Here the lack of preparation and tactical planning rears its ugly and expensive head in the coming months of post-production. Here the ignorance and apathy of other production-unit department heads, usually consumed by their own contracted concerns, becomes apparent; they do little to help the sound recording team in what should be a collaborative effort to achieve ideal production audio tracks during the shoot. Only seasoned directors and producers appreciate the loss of both real money—spent to ADR actors' lines—and of the magic of on-camera performance, rarely recaptured and seldom improved.

Some actors have it written into their contracts that they will do no post-production looping. In other words, if the sync production track is not usable, or if the director or producer decides that a line should be read differently or replaced for whatever reason, the actor will not be available to come onto an ADR stage and reperform it. These additional contractual complexities add even more pressure to capture the most pristine production recordings possible—pressure that seldom concerns other production heads, who so often have an immediate and dramatic impact on the ability of the production sound mixer and boom operator to achieve such recordings.

I remember watching the production crew filming a medium angle of Jamie Lee Curtis at MGM. I was amazed to see a crewman standing just off to the side of the camera's view, calmly eating an apple. The penetration of his teeth was clearly heard each time he bit into the apple's skin. An electrician stood beside him playing with the loose change in his pocket. Neither was making this "sound clutter" on purpose; both were clearly audio-ignorant. Nevertheless, I was stunned at the lack of respect and professionalism they paid to their audio craftspeople during the sequence filming. I knew that a few weeks hence, some sound editor would heave a sigh of disappointment and spend an unnecessary amount of time and extra production dollars to clean out the audible intrusions.

I talked to hundreds of various craftspeople while writing this book, and was constantly surprised and fascinated by the wide range of views and perceptions regarding sound. The vast majority agree that sound is one of the most important components of a film, and many actually rate sound as more important than the visual photography itself—yet most crafts-people not working in sound do not understand their own contributions to the success—or failure—of the production soundtrack.

THE PRODUCTION RECORDING TEAM

Sound Mixer

Responsible for the quality of the sound recordings on the set, the head of the recording team is the sound mixer. During preproduction the sound mixer consults with the producer and director on the best ways to tackle the recording challenges of the production sound. Each project is different—each dictates its particular needs. One project may have fairly straight-forward requirements, so it has been agreed to record the dialog on a digital time code DAT while rolling a 1/4" 2-track (stereo) Nagra as back-up. Another project may require multiple simultaneous recordings of different actors in constant motion on a complicated set, thereby requiring individual wireless microphones on each actor, two channels of overhead "air" mikes, and two foreground boomed mikes. This would require at least one 8-track recorder.

The sound mixer must choose the right recording format for the project, rent or supply the necessary equipment to accomplish the task required, and use that equipment to the best of his or her abilities during the filming process. The sound mixer supplies picture editorial not only with the best possible recorded material, but also with a volume of copious notes and sound reports that help guide the picture editor, and later the sound editors, through the maze of sync recordings, wild tracks, and room tones.

Boom Operator

The boom operator has an incredibly important position; if he or she does not get the microphone into the right position at the proper moment, the actor's voice is off-axis and sounds off-mike. The boom operator must be strong, agile, attentive, and observant. He or she must know the exact positions of invisible boundaries below which the microphone dips down into the view of the camera; the boom operator also must memorize light throws and angles to keep the shadow of the microphone from being seen on any surface of the area being photographed.

For those readers who think it cannot be any big deal dangling a microphone around over a couple of actors—tie an unopened can of dog food to the end of an 18-foot pole and hold it (fully extended) over your head for four minutes. Now think about having to do this while concentrating on rotating and pivoting the pole to flip the microphone into position, first one way, then suddenly another way—all the while watching for microphone shadows and keeping it above view of the camera lens. You must accomplish all this without making any noise or vibration that will be telegraphed into the microphone's diaphragm. Getting tired yet?

The boom operator must also know the delicate workings of radio microphones. He or she must know how to wire an actor quickly, yet know how to work diplomatically with performers' often unpredictable personalities and temperaments. The boom operator has a personal kit—a tool or tackle box that holds the tools, tapes, batteries, supplies, and implements that make it all work. In a matter of moments, the wireless microphone must be placed on the actor in exactly the right spot. The wire must be carefully hidden under the clothing and run to wherever the transmitter is being hidden on the actor's body. This is an art form in itself.

The boom operator must be constantly on the lookout for anything making unwanted noise. Good boom operators do not complain and report problems to the sound mixer or first assistant director—they assess the problem and offer solutions for dampening the offending sound down or completely eliminating the audio intrusions from polluting the recording.

Cable Man

The cable man used to be known as the "third man." He or she is also known as the sound utility, and, when a second microphone boom is needed, the cable man wields it. The cable man literally clears the microphone cables and keeps the boom operator from backing into things or banging props or the side of the set with the fish pole when cast and crew are in motion. When a boom operator must make a backward maneuver to clear the way and reposition to capture the actors cleanly, the cable man guides the boom operator back with a hand on the belt or back, clearing cable or even silently moving things out of the way.

If a microphone cable has gone bad or is suspect, the cable man grabs another cable and changes it—instantly! The cable man is the one who creates an impromptu rain hat, using short sections of doweling and wrapping it with a thin liner of plastic cover from a dry-cleaning bag and a section of air-conditioning "hog hair" filter. He or she anticipates problems before they arise and quietly solves them so the boom operator can concentrate on the job at hand.

THE SEQUENCE OF PRODUCTION RECORDING

The production mixer understands the rhythm of the production shoot. He or she can tell when the first AD (first assistant director) is about to announce that they are ready to roll film for a take, and sets the sound recorder into a stand-by, or "test" position. This allows the electronics to power up and be warmed and ready to operate on command.

The production mixer's sound recorder has been parked in the pause ("Test") mode, keeping the electronics live and ready to roll. The mixer activates the recorder in the RECORD mode. The tape turns at the designated speed, and the indicator shows a steady and dependable speed. The mixer presses the slate mike on the microphone mixing unit to verbally slate the shot, "Scene twenty-nine Baker take three." Verbally slating the audio tape prior to the camera rolling can save valuable film negative. Many mixers actually preslate the upcoming take prior to the first AD's announcement to roll sound. The mixer will preslate and then place the recorder in pause ("Test") mode again—waiting for the first AD to call, "Roll sound."

Sure enough, the first AD calls out, "Let's have the light and bell." The production mixer is also responsible for the warning light (the revolving red light) just outside the stage or on the perimeter of the location set. When the first AD calls out, "Let's have the light and bell," the mixer flips the warning light on, which also sounds the bell (one ring duration). Work activity stops and the crew holds their positions quietly for the shot.

Satisfied that activity has settled on the set, the first AD cries out, "Roll sound!" The production mixer turns the recording machine into RECORD mode. When he or she is satisfied that the machine is up to proper speed and that time code or pilot sync is true and steady the mixer calls out, "Speed."

The first AD cues the camera crew: "Roll camera." The camera operator turns the camera on and gives it a moment to gain sound speed; then answers, "Camera speed."

The slate assistant (who is usually the film loader) holds up the slate with the vital information for the show and scene number written on it. It reads 29 "B" TK-3. Most camera crews have the slate assistant verbally slate the scene, "Scene twenty-nine Baker, take three." Some crews forgo doing this as an excuse to save film. It is really up to the protocol desired and the concern of film stock that dictates this choice of procedure. The slate assistant snaps the slate for sync and steps quickly out of camera view.

The first AD calls, "Cue background," and the second AD cues the background extras so that they will be in motion. The director allows the action to take a few moments so that precious seconds of presence with background movement will be recorded (it will match any "inter-filling" that needs to be done later by a dialog editor). Then the director cues the actors: "Action."

The preceding is the proper and ideal protocol for preslating, rolling sound, on-screen slating by a slate assistant, and creating pre-action presence with the natural action of background extras as it will sound during the internal action of a scene. If you were to record presence tone without the background extras, the intercut presence would sound horribly out of place, cut in between actors' lines, for instance, to replace a director's cue or an unwanted sound. With audio-aware directors and assistant directors, you will achieve this level of protocol and consideration consistently, rendering the best possible audio results.

THE BASIC RECORDING KIT

The composition and extent of the tools at the mixer's disposal differ with every picture and every budget. Whether the project has no money to speak of or is a multimillion-dollar blockbuster, the basic recording kit does not change much. You need the following items:

- Sound cart
- Tape recorder(s)—analog and/or digital
- Portable mixer
- Microphones
- Microphone cables
- Wireless RF microphones

- Fish pole(s)
- Shock mount pistol grip with zeppelins
- Windscreen covers
- Miscellaneous adapters, phase inverters
- Smart slate
- Communication radios/comtechs
- Voltage meter for AC tie-ins
- Battery supply
- Cables
- Extra plugs, batteries, etc.
- Plastic and/or blanket for protection from flying objects or weather

ANALOG OR DIGITAL

Whether to record digitally or analog is a decision that requires factoring numerous technical and philosophical requirements and attitudes. Never think that a new technology or fad is automatically better or more desirable. For instance, it is nearly impossible to convince someone that analog recording can be not only equal to, but superior to digital, unless they have used both a digital DAT recorder and an analog Nagra under comparable recording conditions and compared the results.

I have my own opinions and reasons for recording production dialog in analog—just as I insist on recording action sound effects in analog. I was getting tired of listening to my colleagues argue back and forth that digital was better than analog, and vice versa. So I decided that we would go out and record analog and digital formats side-by-side simultaneously, using identical microphones that were arrayed together (for precisely the same recording aspect) and identical cables. The difference would be the tape recording device—analog or digital, and the format. To help you appreciate the recording differences, review cue #22 of the audio CD provided with this book for "comparative medium recordings."

Many production mixers currently use the DAT format as their primary recorder; however, most are also rolling a 1/4" Nagra as back-up. Other production mixers take the opposite posture. Their 1/4" Nagra is their primary recording machine, and they use the DAT unit as a back-up of their analog recording work.

Contrary to the hype and advertising regarding the digitally recorded signal, serious audio craftspeople still prefer that the original recordings be made in the analog environment, whether they be production dialog, customized sound effects, ADR and Foley sessions, or the music-scoring stage. The hundreds of interviews I have held with various mixers, editors, composers, and engineers have reinforced my own preference. Very few of us disagree, however, that once the material has been recorded in analog, it should immediately be transferred into the digital environment for the post-production process.

The question of analog versus digital recording, then, seems to fall to the issues of the production challenges themselves, budget considerations and, of course, who handles the recording chores as mixer. I have worked with a handful of mixers who are extraordinary at recording digitally. Lee Howell (Los Angeles) is one; Paul Jyrälä (Helsinki) is another. Peter Meiselmann is, by nature a hardcore analog specialist, but was pressed into recording the production track for first-time producers digitally because they felt they needed that technology for some reason. It was Peter's first time using the DAT technology—but his years of disciplined analog technique served him well in adapting to the digital medium. In fact, I was stunned by the results, as I happened to handle this project. The usual flaws and recording mistakes that plague the digital world were not there. In fact, numerous sequences that had a screaming monkey, shotgun blasts, and other harsh concussive audio cues were not only recorded beautifully, but they were devoid of distortion and overload edginess—all of which were overcome because of Peter's analog experience and discipline.

Don't be lulled into thinking that the final outcome of a film's soundtrack is reflective of the production mixer's work. It can be, but not necessarily. I have handled films where every second of production recording was ultimately stripped out of the track and every syllable of the movie was revoiced.

BACK-UP TAPES

As discussed in Chapter 4, having back-up tapes may seem like an inconvenience and a waste of money—but when you first experience the shipping carrier losing the shipment on the way to the lab and sound facility, or the first time your primary DAT machine "eats" the tape at program number 88, you will wish that back-up tapes had been part of the budget.

The mixer should always hold on to the back-up tape, as the back-up tape obviously would be useless if shipped with the primary tape and the both of them were lost! The mixer also has the back-up to play for the director and producer should a critical question arise of "bad sound" or problems with actual roots in sound transfer. Many a sound mixer could have avoided being the scapegoat in a finger-pointing row between the producer and sound transfer over the poor quality of a daily soundtrack if they had had back-up tapes available. I know of several situations in which the sound mixer was vindicated because a back-up tape played the sound cues in question for the director and producer. On one particular picture, the studio was actually compelled to fire its own sound-transfer department as contractor and then contract the sound-transfer chores to a rival studio, because the mixer had kept a back-up tape in hand as insurance.

LINE-UP TONES

As described in greater detail in Chapter 6, it is critical that every tape, whether analog or digital, has a known line-up reference tone at the head of the tape. The sound mixer threads up the first tape of the day onto the Nagra, or inserts the first DAT cassette into the recorder. The first thing he or she does is record an announcement of what is what and where they are and what kind of line-up tone is about to be heard: "Good morning, we're out here today at Glacier Point for Silver Tip Entertainment's production of *Five Rings of Michael.* The date is Tuesday, June twenty-sixth, 2003. This is roll seventeen. We're recording on a Nagra IV-S in a flat-EQ mode at a tape speed of 15ips. Stand by for the reference tone which is minus eight equals zero VU." In this short and to-the-point pell-mell of information, you have given the most important hit points:

1. Where you are
2. Name of the production company
3. Name of the project

4. Date—name of the day, month, day, and year
5. What 1/4" (or DAT) roll number it is
6. What kind of machine you are recording on
7. What kind of equalization setting you are using
8. What tape speed (or sampling rate if digital) you are recording at
9. A clear definition of your line-up tone

One must approach recording the information header of a fresh roll of recording tape as if the tape itself will be the only thing that survives the shoot. The box will be lost, the data card will be lost, and the sound report will be lost. I once had a big box handed to me that was just a huge wad 1/4" tape from a shoot in the Philippines. No box, no reports, no reels—just thousands of feet of 1/4" tape. Anything and everything I was going to know about the material on it (once I unwound the scrunched up ball of magnetic ribbon) was going to be what I gleaned from the mixer's header information and verbal shot slates. With that kind of nightmare looming around you, keep in mind how vital clear and precise vocal slates and information headers are to everyone who will work with your material.

Location of recording: Though it is not vital to know, almost all sound mixers mention where the shoot is in the information header.

Name of Production Company: This identifies these recordings as the property of the company or individual that hired the recording mixer to do the assigned work.

Name of Project: Always list the name of the project. In the case of episodic material, always name the project along with the production number.

Date of Recording: Name the date. There are numerous information data entries that will follow the shoot that use the date as a reference. Many times we will check the date of one or more shoots to satisfy what may supersede earlier versions—and sometimes it is vital information to be used for legal purposes.

Roll Number: This is one of the most important pieces of information, as the roll number is entered alongside the negative roll number (picture) in the code book and shows up on the EDL (edit decision list) of the final cut version of the film from the nonlinear platform. It becomes the quickest way to access original roll material for reprints, alternate takes, or to make an "A–B" comparison between an OMF (Open Media Framework) file from the nonlinear platform to determine if a complete retransfer from source material will be required because the original digitized transfers were substandard (a subject we will discuss later in the book).

Type/Model of Recorder: Always say what kind of recording device you are using—whether it is analog or digital. The transfer facility will want to know this so they will not inadvertently try to transfer the material on a playback unit with the wrong head configuration.

Equalization Setting: It is valuable for the transfer tech or assistant editor to know what kind of equalization setting was used, whether or not you rolled-off any high or low end, and so forth.

Speed or Sampling Rate: Tell us what tape speed (analog) or sampling rate (digital) you are recording at. Do not think that it is always obvious. You would be surprised how many times things get screwed up because someone assumed that something was obvious.

Line-Up Tone: The line-up tone quoted above is written on the sound report as: −8 dB = '0' VU. Because there are so many variations of '0' levels that equal a prescribed peak meter level and other variations of recording equipment that use different levels and/or kinds of level protocols, it is an excellent technique for the mixer to verbally tell us what kind of line-up tone he or she is about record onto the tape, and what it means.

Once the line-up tone is defined, the mixer will lay down at least 8 to 12 seconds of line-up tone. The reference tone level quoted on the tape is interpreted to be referenced to "0" on the VU (volume unit) analog meter or is referenced to what level "0" is interpreted as on a digital peak meter (i.e., −18 dB equals "0" VU). Without this reference tone, one cannot accurately set playback levels or make exact 1:1 copies at a later time.

SOUND REPORT

The sound report is the key to the mixer's hard work and efforts; it is the road map of what is on the recorded tape and where to find it. If properly filled out, the sound report also offers a wealth of information through notations made by the mixer as work progresses. Some mixers are more note-oriented than others, but if mixers realized the value of their notes, they would probably pay more attention to making them. As a supervising sound editor, I know the invaluable contribution of a mixer's notes, especially when it comes to comments about airplane noise or undesirable talking (listed as VOX) that may have marred the recording.

The most valuable notes are those regarding wild tracks (listed as WT). When I begin a project, I immediately get a copy of the mixer's sound reports and quickly scroll through them, looking for any wild tracks or miscellaneous recordings that may determine what other recordings I may need to refer to or authorize to have done.

It is equally important to list a shot in which there is no sound. For one reason or another it may be decided to shoot a set-up in which the sound mixer is not rolling sound. He or she will list on the Sound Report the abbreviation MOS (which stands for "without sound"). The genesis of this abbreviation is as follows.

Back in the early 1930s, during the infancy of the motion picture sound process, a famous director was shooting a picture when he decided not to have the optical sound camera roll for some reason. He turned to his crew and in his heavy European accent he announced to them, "Awlright children, this vun vee do mit out sound." The continuity script girl did not ask what he meant by that, but listed the sound note of the shot as M.O.S. in the script notes, and to this day the abbreviation MOS has stuck.

Frankly, it is uncertain who actually coined the term. Every academic professor has his or her expert opinion, but I can guarantee you that none of them were there to witness it. I have heard of someone who claims to have been there, but when you scratch the surface of the claim it was actually hearsay. I have interviewed a number of my colleagues on this issue, several of whom date that far back, but none of them know the answer beyond a shadow of a doubt. Many think that it was the colorful, if not legendary Michael Curtiz who said it (*The Sea Hawk, Casablanca, The Egyptian, We're No Angels*). Curtiz certainly had an infamous reputation for mauling the English language. Others insist that it was Ernst Lubitsch (*The Shop Around the Corner, Heaven Can Wait, To Be or Not To Be, That Uncertain Feeling*) who said the immortal words. Hal Mohr, a cinematographer who had worked with Paul Fejos many years ago, attributes the quote to Fejos himself. Regardless of who said it, when the production sound mixer writes MOS on his or her sound report next to a scene/shot designation, every sound transfer facility in the world knows that the sound recorder was not rolling.

The real origin of the expression is almost certainly less romantic than this. Remember that back during the first two and a half decades of motion picture audio, production sound recordings were accomplished by "photographing" the microphone pick-up via the optical sound camera. When the director did not require sync sound for a particular shot, the recording mixer simply listed the abbreviation MOS on the sound reports to mean "Minus Optical Sound." Unlike hearsay stories, there are actual written sound report notes that explain this use of the abbreviation.

More and more mixers are adopting a full-page-width sound report, which gives considerably more room for notation. The slender version of the sound report that dominated the industry for decades was designed so that you could fold it over and simply lay it inside the box of a 5" or 7" reel of 1/4" tape. Unfortunately, this convenient width also inhibited mixers from writing sufficient notations, and, believe me, we in the post-production process will read as many notes, ideas, and warnings as the mixer will write.

As you study a typical sound report (Figure 5.1), note the types of vital information displayed there. Believe it or not, even the title of the picture is important. Too many times the transfer department is hung up by trying to find a scene and take of a print only to discover that it picked up a similar-looking box assumed to belong to the same show because no markings indicated the contrary; hence valuable time is lost as the transfer department searches for the right roll number from the wrong show title. Worse, when the "right" scene is found and the transfer department takes and prints it, it is sometimes discovered too late that it is from the wrong show.

Many times mixers do not fully complete the information header, which has often confused transfer departments. Sometimes unusual head tone levels are utilized; these must be carefully noted.

If the mixer is using a DAT machine, he or she enters the PNO (program number) that the DAT recorder automatically assigns each time it starts a new recording. The PNO locator system has been a wonderful thing for us in post-production. You simply enter the program number of the scene and the take you want and hit the "play" button. The DAT machine spins at 200 times speed in search of this number, automatically stops, and aligns at the head of the recording and plays it—what a great time-saver!

Next to the DAT PNO the mixer lists the scene and angle designation number of each recording. Generally, a mixer enters the scene number only once, then draws a line vertically alongside all the takes until the next angle (see Figure 5.2). For example, the mixer lists scene 105 "A" in the scene box, then take 1. He or she lists take 2 below that and take 3 below that, all the while drawing a vertical line from 105 "A" until that angle is a wrap. The next set-up is 105 "B." Each take has its own line. Do not list all the takes together on one line. It is not only more convenient for the mixer to write, but it is much faster for an assistant editor or transfer tech to find material as the writing will "eye-scan" much more easily and efficiently.

A mixer may use a single microphone but have it split on two channels. The first channel (left) is recording at standard level; the second channel (right) is recording the same information but at a lower level (often −10 dB) in case of sudden bursts of sounds, such as gunshots, crashes, screams, and so forth. The mixer makes this notation accordingly.

Sound Report

TITLE _____ ROLL # _____ SHEET # _____ - OF - _____

COMPANY _____ MACHINE _____ TAPESPEED _____

PROD. NO# _____ HEAD TONES _____

MIXER _____ SYNC _____ _____ dB = _____ VU

BOOM _____ **PRINT CIRCLED TAKES ONLY**

SCENE #	TAKE	PNO	LEFT CHANNEL	RIGHT CHANNEL	COMMENTS	TIME CODE
						: : :
						: : :
						: : :
						: : :
						: : :
						: : :
						: : :
						: : :
						: : :
						: : :
						: : :
						: : :
						: : :
						: : :
						: : :
						: : :
						: : :
						: : :
						: : :
						: : :
						: : :
						: : :
						: : :
						: : :
						: : :
						: : :
						: : :
						: : :

Figure 5.1 Sound report.

PNO	SCENE	ANGLE	TAKE	LEFT CHANNEL	RIGHT CHANNEL
1	—	—	—	LINE-UP TONE	LINE-UP TONE
2	8 7	"B"	1	overhead boom	split -10dB mono
3	{	{	2	{	{
4	{	{	3	{	{
5	8 7	"C"	1	actor #1 - Rita	acto #2 - Jeff
6	{	{	2	{	{
7	{	{	3	{	{
8	{	{	4	{	{

Figure 5.2 Listing scenes and takes in a sound report.

In the middle of the roll, a mixer may decide to use two microphones and keep them on dedicated channels. He or she notes that actor #1 is on channel number one (left), and that actor #2 is on channel number two (right).

In the comments column, the mixer makes any pertinent comments that he or she feels the post-production people may need. I love it when a mixer makes a comment such as "Great door slam," "Neat machinery ka-thumps," or "Watch out for airplane in track." During interviews for this book, mixers confessed that if they really thought their notations were being read and utilized by anyone after the day's shoot, they would certainly make a bigger effort to write them. Sadly, many mixers do not feel that, in today's compressed post-production schedules and budgets, anyone takes time to glean through their notes or ferret out wild tracks recorded for post-production applications.

Many transfer departments use sophisticated calibrated vari-speed controllers. Many times, a director wants a set-up photographed off-speed, such as over-cranking the camera at 30 fps or higher for a slightly slowed-down effect, or under-cranking at 18 or 20 fps, which ultimately speeds up the shot when projected at a normal 24 fps. If the director does not want the harmonic pitch and timbre of the voice to sound pitched in relationship with the over- or under-cranking, then the vari-speed unit correctly pitch-shifts the audio up or down; this way, when it is played back at 24 fps, the visual action is slow-motion or accelerated, but the pitch and timbre of the soundtrack sounds normal.

One particular underwater monster picture was entirely shot two frames per second slower than sound speed (22 fps), making the pace of the action faster. This not only allowed the producer to tell a 103-minute story in only 95 screen minutes (which also proved more desirable to the distribution company), but it also allowed a performance edginess and tension to be instilled because the cast was speaking and moving slightly faster. If such notations are made in the comments column, the transfer department can effect the transfer accordingly, making daily transfers to match the picture.

Note that the last column is formatted for time code notations. In today's world of smart slates and time code dailies, the far right-hand column, which used to be reserved for transfer notations, is now being utilized by the production mixer to list time code starts for each take.

MICROPHONES

Pick-Up Patterns

The primary tools in the arsenal of weapons at the mixer's disposal are the various kinds of microphones with their different pick-up patterns. Good mixers have carefully chosen kits of microphones they can mix and match, depending on the location and challenges of the sequence to record. Following is an explanation of the basic kinds of microphones used for production recording (see Figure 5.3).

Omnidirectional Microphone

This condenser microphone has an omnidirectional pick-up pattern, as illustrated in Figure 5.3. The good thing about the omnidirectional microphone is that it has a relatively even pattern that picks up everything around it. The bad thing is that it has a relatively even pattern that picks up everything around it, including but not limited to camera noise, feet shuffling, crew downrange who are whispering, aircraft high overhead, the eighteen-wheeler truck making the grade five miles away, and so forth. As with the use of any microphone, you must choose the right microphone for the right job. In some situations you could not be better served than by using a good solid omnidirectional microphone.

Cardioid: A Directional Microphone

Both dynamic and condenser microphones can be cardioid. As indicated in the diagram, the cardioid microphone has a directional pattern of some degree, or what is called a "heart-shaped' pick-up response. It picks up more signal directly in front of it than to the sides and very little signal behind it. It is not just a matter of sound level that is affected. It is a matter of axis. As the actor moves off-axis, or to the side of the microphone, the character and richness of the voice thins and the frontal presence falls away. This is referred to as being "off-mike."

Dynamic microphones do not require phantom power and are known for being rugged and able to handle a wide dynamic range of sound-recording situations. Vents run alongside the microphone shaft, allowing sound to enter from behind, striking the diaphragm and canceling out some of the same ambient signal that enters from the front, which gives the directional microphone its unique function of cancellation. Signal cancellation is crucial for clear dialog recording, especially when working in exterior situations. Sound of identical character that enters the rear of the microphone as well as the front and that strikes the diaphragm equally is canceled out, thereby cutting down the amount of ambient noise in relationship to the unique sound being recorded directly in front of the microphone, such as the actor's voice. The more sound allowed in from behind the diaphragm, the more directional the pattern.

As you can see, this kind of microphone is more suited for precision miking of actors on a location set already filled with an abundance of unwanted ambient noise. The challenge is to keep the center of the pattern right on the origin of the desired sound; otherwise you suffer "off-mike" recordings.

Hypercardioid: Highly Directional or "Mini-Shotgun" Microphone

Like its directional cousin (the cardioid), this type of microphone is more than just somewhat directional, hence its nickname the "mini-shotgun." The longer the microphone tube, the

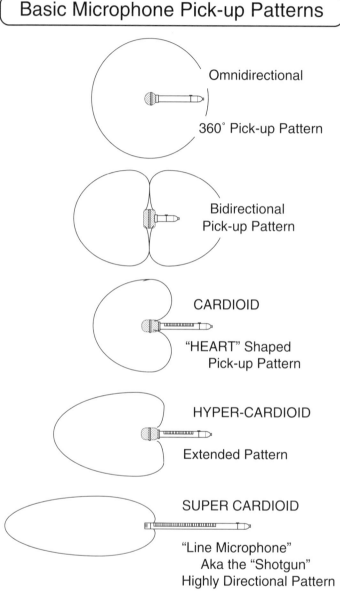

Figure 5.3 Basic microphone pick-up patterns.

greater the number of vents (to allow for rear-pattern cancellation and frequency compensation) required and the more directional the microphone.

Supercardioid: Ultra Directional "Shotgun" Microphone

Early supercardioids were called line microphones, or rifle microphones. The supercardioid is just that—highly directional, and equally more difficult to keep directly on the desired spot of origin for the most pristine of recordings. This microphone is not a good choice if your actor is doing much moving or if you have more than one actor on the set to cover; however, for single set-ups or two-shots where you cannot get in close with a fish pole and a traditional microphone, the supercardioid can really reach out and grab the signal.

The biggest mistake in using any microphone is forgetting that it does not have a brain. In other words, it cannot tell the difference between your voice and noise. Every application has a requirement; the right microphone exists for the right job. Your job is to know which to choose. For music applications, certain microphones can handle the sound-pressure levels that a kick drum might give out, or the brash brass of a trombone or saxophone. Other microphones cannot handle the percussiveness as well but have a much better reproduction of the top-end for use in recording violins and triangles.

Unfortunately, in our industry many craftspeople try to make one microphone do too many chores. The veteran mixer will have developed a taste and style of recording, either personally owning or insisting on the rental of a precise mixed assortment of quality microphones to fill his or her arsenal of recording tools.

The "Smart" Slate

Figure 5.4 shows the Denecke "smart" slate. This slate device is very handy, and is especially used in music video work and fast location shooting scenarios. A wireless transmitter hooks up to the time code "out" connector of your audio recorder—which, of course, needs to have a time code generator (either built-in or outboard hook-up). The time code that is being embedded into your recording sync signal is exactly what will be transmitted to the smart slate.

As you can see in the photograph, there is a small wireless receiver (usually fitted with a patch of velcro on the back). NOTE: when you plug the connector wire into the receiver from the smart slate, the receiver's little red indicator light will come on, thereby powering it up automatically. On the backside of the slate is a small toggle switch that is seated on a slim metal battery case. If you flip the toggle switch one way the time code numbers will illuminate on "low" intensity. If you flip the toggle switch "ON" the other direction, the time code numbers will illuminate on "HI" intensity. Obviously, high intensity will make the numbers easier to see in brightly lit situations—and of course, just as obviously, the "HI' intensity choice will wear out your "C" cell batteries a lot more quickly (the smart slate uses eight "C" cell batteries).

The slate assistant holds the smart slate up after he or she has hand-written the scene-angle-take information on the front, as with traditional slates. When the recording mixer rolls the audio deck, the time code will advance on the slate. When the slate assistant snaps the slate, the time code number will freeze on $00:00:00:00$ for a moment and then turn off. There are two small flush-mounted contact points near the end of the clapper arm; when the two touch at the snap point, it activates the time code to cut off.

Even though this is a seemingly convenient and visually easy thing to see for picture editorial, the fact of the matter is that many mixers find that sync is not precise. You may experience as much as plus or minus two frames accuracy. For those of us who come from the old school of precision, this is just not precise enough.

The Studio Microphone Boom

The studio microphone boom is a large-wheeled perambulator with a small platform on which the boom operator stands while operating the traverse wheels that not only lengthen

Figure 5.4 The smart slate.

or shorten the boom extensions but also rotate and pivot the actual microphone position at the end of the boom arm. When properly operated, the boom functions silently and smoothly.

Studio microphone booms are used less often on feature films today because of complex and realistic set construction and the widespread use of practical locations being filmed under accelerated shooting schedules that don't allow the sound crew time and space to use the traditional perambulator boom. These silent microphone arms still have an important use in television production, though, especially when taping live-audience situations.

The techniques are considerably different than those for booming with a hand-held "fish-pole" style boom. Not only does a studio boom operator need coordination and dexterity to operate the traverse wheels accurately and smoothly, but he or she also must learn how to turn a microphone and extend the boom arm quickly (so as not to allow air buffeting to affect the delicate microphone diaphragm), and then rotate the microphone back into position once the boom arm has been thrust out into position. It is a technique best learned from the veteran boom operators who have worked the boom arms for many years, a technique that cannot be mastered overnight.

The Shock Mount and Wind Screen

Two of the biggest enemies of good exterior recordings are vibration and wind buffet. All microphones are mounted onto something, whether a plastic friction clip or the cradle of a rubberband-mounted yoke. Budget restraints can motivate you to new levels of inventiveness. Through experimentation and test recordings, you will develop a wide range of techniques to insulate the microphone from the vibrations of, say, a car as you hard-mount your microphone on the rear bumper to favor tailpipe exhaust. You will learn how to stuff foam around your mike and cram it into a crevice or lodge it between solid substances. You will learn how to detect wind direction and swirl patterns and how to effectively block them. You will learn to grab an assistant and physically place him or her between the source of unwanted breeze buffets and the microphone diaphragm.

An effective way to control both vibration and wind buffet is a combination of the pistol-grip shock-mount fitted with a windscreen tube called a Zeppelin (see Figure 5.5). The microphone is fitted into the plastic ring clips, which hold it in place and protect it from undue vibration by the rubber-band trapeze.

Be careful to guide the microphone cable through the small, round cutout at the bottom of the plastic ring, then snap the rear cap of the Zeppelin into place. Do not pull the microphone cable too tight, as the microphone shock mount works best if a little play of cable remains inside for movement. Depending on the breeze factor, you can either slip the gray "sock" over the Zeppelin or, if the breeze is fairly stiff, you might slip on the Ryocote "Wind Jammer" (also referred to as a "Wooly," "dead cat," "furry dog," or the Sennheiser High Wind Cover) instead. These remarkable furry wonders have done much to knock down the kind of wind buffet that ruined many sound recordings in the past.

"Fish-Pole" Microphone Boom

As the name implies, the fish pole is a long pole with a microphone socket attachment to hold the microphone shock-mount. Most microphone fish poles are lightweight aluminum tubes that slide out and extend the length of the pole. Unlike with the studio microphone boom, do not extend the length of the fish pole during the recording process. You must lengthen or shorten the desired length of the fish pole by unscrewing the friction locks and extending the second or third extension tube, then screwing it tight again before rolling sound.

Good Microphone Boom Techniques

Most microphone boom work is done by placing the microphone over the actors' heads, higher than the line of sight of the camera lens, pointing downward toward the spoken word. Some mixers want the microphone to be pointing straight down, using an omnidirectional pattern diaphragm mike, because it picks up a uniform ambient background recording, regardless of which way the performance comes at it. The unfortunate reality of having an omnidirectional microphone in a full-down position is that it tends to pick up many footstep sounds. Foot shuffling and movements will seem to dominate. Again, it depends on the circumstances and the surface of the floor.

Some boom operators cradle the fish pole downward, pointing the microphone up at the actor's voice, keeping the mike low enough to be out of camera view. Again, this lends

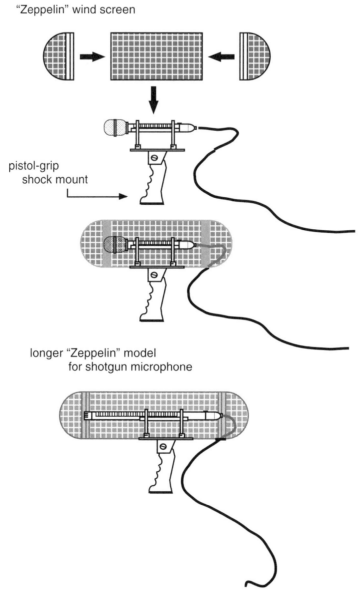

"Zeppelin" wind screen

pistol-grip
shock mount

longer "Zeppelin" model
for shotgun microphone

Figure 5.5 Shock mount and Zeppelin.

itself to a less-than-desirable characterization of recording and does not always serve the project well. This technique is most often used for documentary or news work, where one is not concerned about the precise timbre or quality of the vocal recording or whether the microphone is seen in the frame. Many consider it a lazy man's cradle.

Truthfully, the best sound recording can be obtained by holding the fish pole high above your head and pointing the microphone at a downward, but slightly tilted, angle, aiming right at the throat of the actor. Some boom operators will tell you that the ideal target to aim the directional pattern at is at the bridge of the nose. Others will tell you they aim at the upper chest, where the voice originates. They swear that the resonance of the chest is vital to the timbre of the recording. Still other boom operators aim right at the mouth, from where the voice issues.

These are all valid opinions that I have heard repeated many times. Each boom operator uses the technique that best serves the mixer and most successfully captures the desired vocal performance. Whatever technique you and/or your boom operator use, be consistent! Changing technique in the middle of recordings changes the timbre colorization from scene to scene.

Without a doubt, holding a fish pole above your head for takes is a grueling and punishing task (boom operators are perhaps the most physically fit craftspeople on the set). Because of this, it serves the recording team well for its members to look after each other. On one particular shoot, a boom operator held a big Sennheiser 815 supercardioid microphone on a fully extended fish-pole boom to cover an extremely slow dolly shot that moved in closer and closer on Lloyd Bridges, who gave a four-and-a-half minute performance at a pulpit. At the height of the sequence, the cable man could see that the boom operator was fatiguing badly. He carefully brought his own boom in, which was equipped with the same kind of microphone, and cautiously lowered it down next to the boom operator's. At a slight pause in Lloyd Bridges's delivery, the mixer faded from the first microphone to the cable man's mike and whispered into the boom operator's headset on his PL (communications term for "private line"). The boom operator raised his boom up and out of the way and stepped back silently. He lowered the fish pole and allowed himself a moment to rest, then raised his pole and reinserted his microphone alongside the cable man's. Again, as Lloyd Bridges paused to draw a breath, the mixer faded from the cable man's mike back to the boom operator's so that he could finish the take. Without that kind of teamwork, it just would not have been possible to sustain a fully extended, heavy mike recording for that length of time.

As a general rule, the master wide shot does not sound as good or pristine as the other close-up coverage angles. It is simple practicality: you have more set to cover, with more lights to watch out for and more potential noise to consider.

Boom Operator During Set-Up

One of the first things good boom operators do when starting on a show without a prior working relationship with other department heads, is to find out who serves as the "keys." They also must identify the gaffer and key grip and introduce themselves, as these people decide how to fulfill the DP's (director of photography) lighting wishes. They decide exactly where a light is set and how the light is controlled, using flags, cutters, and scrims.

The importance of establishing a good relationship with fellow crew personnel is illustrated by the following example. A grip may "cut" (light control) a lamp by putting a "C"-stand on one side of the light. At the same time, the boom operator may really need that spot for maneuvering and properly booming the actors' movements. The grip could just as easily place the "C"-stand on the other side and use an elbow joint to put the scrim in the original position, thereby leaving the floor space available for the boom operator. However, if the boom operator has not made introductions and explained what is needed to fulfill the microphone placement requirements, then he or she can blame no one else if the microphone cannot be placed in the necessary spot when the director is ready to roll camera and make a take.

The smart boom operator "baby-sits" the set. The boom operator gets the fish pole and stands by while the crew lights the set. The boom operator may wear headsets, slid down around the neck. This way everybody knows the boom operator is there, standing by to assist in the lighting collaboration; now he or she can follow the action without a boom shadow thrown somewhere on the set where the camera lens will pick it up. Boom shadows are the quickest way to fall into disfavor with the director and DP.

Being a good boom operator is also being a good gaffer or a good grip. One must know how to read the lights. One must know where to stand, where the camera will be, what size lens is used. Often a boom operator asks a simple question of the camera operator, such as, "What size lens are you using?" Sometimes a simple question like this causes the DP to be more attentive and to ensure that the crew cooperates more fully with the boom operator, allowing sound to get in and do its job effectively.

Director and cinematographer John LeBlanc has lensed and directed both feature films and commercials. "If the boom operator is not in there with us setting up the shot, I have no sympathy for the sound crew. I want good sound! I know that good sound will only help to make my work play better, but if the sound crew is not dedicated to getting in and showing us where the boom and microphones need to be while we're lighting the set, then it's their problem if they can't get in because they are suddenly making shadows."

As you can see, boom operators must know everyone's jobs in addition to their own to maximize the efficiency of the work. Unfortunately, although physical and technical demands on boom operators make theirs one of the most difficult jobs on the set, many production mixers will tell you they truly believe that boom operators are given the least respect—except, of course, from the production mixers themselves.

Checking with the Prop Department

The boom operator is responsible for talking to the prop department to discover pertinent information that will affect the sound recording, such as whether the firearms handler will use quarter-load, half-load, or full-load rounds in the guns to be fired on-screen. If full loads are used and a multitude of weapons are discharging, you will be deaf by the time you run through the sequence master and the various angles a few times. The microphones amplify the signal, and, with today's digital headsets for monitoring, the mixer and boom operator will have a bad time of it.

Many unfortunate situations occur when scenes using a practical weapon are rehearsed one way but actually performed differently. An example now gone to court is where an actor had rehearsed a scene during which he fires a pistol three or four times, then backs up and delivers his line. The mixer and boom operator compensated, covering the gunshots as rehearsed, then the actor lowered the pistol and began speaking. Right in the middle of his delivery, the actor whipped the pistol up and fired again. The Mixer and boom operator flung their headsets off as they grabbed their ears in pain. They had already altered their record levels for the actor's voice, not his pistol shot, and they had been exposed and vulnerable.

Using the Wireless Microphone

Obviously, many situations occur in which the boom operator cannot take the microphone boom where traditional microphones with microphone cables can or may go. The answer is to break out the RF (radio frequency) mikes. These wireless devices come in a multitude of models, but basically adhere to a simple and uniform configuration. A small microphone capsule can be either clipped or taped in a position somewhere on the upper part of the body, usually against the chest just above the heart. The capsule has a small wire that runs under the clothing to where the transmitter pack is attached. The transmitter pack is belted, taped, or otherwise affixed to the actor's body and has a short but critical transmission wire (antenna) taped in place to broadcast the signal to the mixer.

Batteries are consumed rapidly when using a radio microphone, so the boom operator should be prepared to change the batteries every couple of hours. It is not practical to turn the transmitter pack on and off between takes, so leave it turned on from the time you "mike" the actor to when you either wrap the actor or reach a point where the batteries, starting to show signal degradation, must be changed.

Before the boom operator approaches the actor, he or she goes to the wardrobe department to coordinate fabrics and textures as well as any special requirements, such as cutting holes inside the costume to allow wires of radio microphones to be connected to the transmitter worn somewhere on the talent's body.

Some fabrics, such as silk, wreak havoc with radio mikes, because they cause much noise. Another consideration may be whether an actress is wearing a brassiere. If so, the microphone wires can be hidden easily in the bra material, circling around the chest to the back. The wire can be taped as it descends down to the transmitter, which is often hidden in the small of the back. The absence of a bra necessitates carefully taping the wire to the body so that it does not move and show up as it pushes out against the fabric of the costume. Boom operators must approach the task of placing radio microphones on acting talent in an extremely professional manner, concentrating on the primary mission: hiding the microphone where it will not be seen by the camera, where it captures the best recording of the actor's voice, while anticipating and solving potential problems with wardrobe fabrics and design.

Radio microphones are a fact of the entertainment world, and their use is increasing. A good boom operator not only understands the delicacies of the job but also is very sensitive to the feelings of all actors. The boom operator articulates clearly and succinctly what he or she requires of the performing talent in placing a radio mike on them. Humor and innuendoes are completely inappropriate and do not contribute to the professional trust factor that must be instilled and maintained. Every situation is different, and every actor responds differently. The boom operator adjusts the style of communication and demeanor to each, taking cues in comments or attitude. Again, the boom operator must never do or say anything to break the essential trust developed with the acting talent.

Rusty Amodeo was handling the boom operator chores on an interview shoot with Barbara Walters and Jay Leno, and the mixer warned Rusty to get it right the first time. "Get the microphone in the right place where it can't be seen and can't be heard, because Barbara won't let you get back in and adjust it." As soon as Barbara entered the room, Rusty approached her to introduce himself. "Barbara, I'm Rusty Amodeo and I'm here to put a microphone on you."

"Well, give me the microphone and I'll put it on." she replied.

That's a tough situation for any boom operator. The microphone must go into an exact spot, and, more important, the place must be fabric-managed. The boom operator must run the wire so that the camera will not see it, and the transmitter must be situated properly with the transmission wire placed in a precise attitude for a clear signal.

"Fine, you want to put the mike on," Rusty answered as he held out the tiny microphone, pointing to a precise spot in the center of her chest, "then I need you to place the microphone right here, just under this flap of material, and then I need you to run the wire under and across to this side and tape it in place so that the connector will be—"

Barbara stopped him. "Well, maybe you should do it."

Rusty knew he had convinced her to allow him to do his job, but now he needed to win her confidence and trust. The two went upstairs, where her wardrobe department made the gown choice. Rusty opened his kit and removed the toupee tape (a clear durable tape sticky on both sides) to start affixing the microphone wire to her blouse.

"What are you doing?" she asked.

As Rusty continued to work he explained that he did not want to just put a mike on her. He wanted her to look her best, and using toupee tape would rigidly hold the microphone wire in place and prevent the button-down front from bulging open as she turned and flexed. It also would be in her best interest to protect the microphone from rubbing. In other words, Rusty was doing his job to make her look and sound as good as possible. Later, during the shoot, Barbara did not hesitate to allow Rusty to readjust, as now she was convinced that a truly dedicated professional was looking out for her and her image.

Because of wardrobe or camera coverage, boom operators constantly must consider new hiding places for the radio transmitter pack. Sometimes the small of the lower back is not an option, due to lack of clothing or a tightly fitting costume with the camera covering the back of the actor. Sometimes a boom operator hides the transmitter pack in the armpit. The toughest of all situations is when scanty clothing is worn, and all options above the waist are ruled out. More than once a boom operator has had to revert to hiding the transmitter high on the inside of the thigh.

Although it is most desirable to place the microphone in the upper center position of the chest, you are not always able to do this. For instance, it is difficult to hide the microphone there if the actor is not wearing any shirt. Such was the case on a Paul Mazursky picture, *Moon over Parador,* starring Richard Dreyfuss. Jim Webb (not to be confused with the songwriter of the same name), the production mixer, and his boom operator struggled to figure out where to put the microphone.

As Mazursky rehearsed the actors, the boom operator noticed how the character that played Dreyfuss's valet followed him around like a shadow. The boom operator pointed it out to Jim, and the two of them hit upon the idea of literally making the valet character a traveling microphone stand. They placed a wireless microphone very carefully on the forward edge of the scalp of the valet, hidden just inside his hairline. The valet, who spoke no lines of dialog during the scene, followed Dreyfuss back and forth in the bedroom of the manor, picking up Dreyfuss perfectly.

Getting Room Tones and Wild Tracks

The production mixer must anticipate the audio trials and tribulations that will come during the post-production sound-editorial phase. The mixer who works with the mindset that he or she is the one to make the material work is much more attentive to potential dialog lines or sequences, recommending recording pick-up wild lines with the actor after the camera has stopped rolling.

The mixer can either record such lines right then and there, while the crew holds still and the camera does not roll, or, what happens more often than not, the mixer can take the actor to a quiet area with a dead ambience and have the actor say the lines a number of times. These are usually short pieces of dialog spoken by a bit or minor character that were not clearly recorded during the actual on-camera shoot because of complex miking problems, practical equipment making noise that drowns out the line, or something like a door slam or a vehicle startup overpowering the dialog.

Aside from wild track pick-up lines, ambient room tones are also needed. Many mixers try to record room-tone ambience whenever possible, but it is very difficult to get a full-scale camera crew to freeze in place and truly be silent while capturing a good thirty seconds of ambience. So many times, we have gotten a room tone that has only a second or so of usable material. The mixer rolls tape, but the crew has not completely settled down, and there is still the sound of feet shuffling. By the time the crew has actually come to an ideal audio texture, the director, extremely antsy to move on to the next set-up, usually comments that that is enough, thinking the mixer has had a full sixty seconds, when in fact only three or four seconds of usable material can be salvaged.

People not sound aware often think that room tone is needed only for those little occasional holes or to patch over a director's voice cuing actors in the midst of a scene. They forget that we may be required to patch-quilt entire scenes in which one actor is looped but the other actors are not. Hence production dialog editors make a three-second ambient piece fill a sequence lasting several minutes on-screen, as it must underline all the ADR dialog of the second actor who was looped. We often are stuck using a very loopy sounding ambience because the production crew did not religiously and seriously record room-tone ambience.

More times than not, the assistant director is responsible for helping the sound mixer get the necessary presence recordings. I have heard too many reports from mixers and boom operators of uncooperative assistant directors who do not care about or understand the needs and requirements of anything but sync sound, which has inhibited presence recordings. The smart assistant director understands that by working with the sound mixer to record presence fill and wild track pick-up lines, or even to arrange prop series sessions, such as recording a rare or unobtainable prop aside from the shoot, he or she is saving the production company literally thousands of future dollars that otherwise would be spent to recreate or fix something that hadn't been solved right then and there.

One of the most banal excuses I hear from those in positions to make decisions having collateral sound-cost consequences is that they are visual people. I have news for them: so am I, and so are my fellow craftspeople in the sound industry. Someone claiming to be "visually oriented" really is admitting to being sensory-deprived. That person has immediately told me he or she knows very little about the storytelling process of making film. It is because we in sound are also visually empowered that we can design and create spectacular audio events to make the visuality rise to new heights of production value, the whole becoming a more thrilling spectacle than visual-only thinking can produce.

Splitting Off Source Sound

Very often, the production mixer has a scene to record that has a practical television in the shot. The television audio should not play back and be heard by the actors' mikes, so the mixer takes an audio feed from the video source feeding the television and records it onto a dedicated channel.

In many cases a mixer records on a 2-track Nagra or DAT. The mixer line-feeds the video source onto channel 2 as he or she records the actors' dialog onto channel 1. This eliminates all the conversion speed-rate issues; it also facilitates exact sync by having the live-feed material "transfer-recorded' in this fashion.

X–Y Microphone Configuration

The X–Y microphone configuration is important when you are recording a left–right stereo spread with two matching microphones. Recording stagnant ambiences with two matching microphones spread wide apart from one another is usually a problem, but whenever you have a situation in which there is a sound-emanating source (such as a car, airplane, or motorcycle) that is moving, ever changing the distance from itself and the two microphone diaphragms, you will experience phasing.

As depicted in Figure 5.6, a sound source such as a car passing across the median axis of a bilaterally symmetrical pattern of both microphones experiences a phase wink-out. As the car approaches, the sound of the engine takes slightly longer to reach the far mike than to reach the closer mike. As the car approaches, the time it takes to reach the far microphone decreases to the point that, as it hits the axis (center) point, the two microphones switch roles. Now it is taking increasingly longer for the sound to reach the far left mike. At this crossover point is a phase wink-out, or drop-out of signal.

The severity of the phase wink-out is proportionate to how far apart the two microphone diaphragms are from each other. The closer they are to each other, the less the phase wink-out. That is why stereo microphones have the two diaphragms in the same capsule, either side by side or one on top of the other.

If you are using two monaural microphones to record stereo material and you have the potential for audio sources such as cars, trains, or aircraft, then you may wish to place the

Crisscross the microphones, with the diaphragms as close to each other as possible, so as to reduce "phasing" as much as possible.

Figure 5.6 The X-Y pattern.

Note that the notch indicator shows the center axis of the microphone diaphragm—it can be adjusted by degrees of separation for the desired stereophonic effect.

Figure 5.7 Stereo capsule microphone.

two mikes in what is called an X–Y pattern. In this configuration the left microphone is facing to the right, covering the right hemisphere, and the microphone on the right is pointing to the left, covering the left hemisphere. This places the microphone diaphragms physically as close as possible to each other to greatly reduce the difference in the time the audio source signal takes to reach each microphone diaphragm.

Figure 5.7 depicts a typical dual-capsule stereo microphone. Note how the diaphragms sit as closely as possible to each other, one on top of the other. The top diaphragm capsule rotates to increase or decrease the degrees of separation as desired. Be careful to maintain the correct up-and-down attitude of the stereo microphone, to keep the left and right coverage in correct aspect. The advantage of using a stereo "dual-capsule" microphone is that the left and right diaphragms are much closer together than by placing two monaural microphones in an X–Y pattern. The chances of experiencing phase cancellation and "wink-outs" are minimized greatly.

The Illusion of Monitoring Field Recordings

Eric Karson has been on many a shoot, both domestic and abroad, learning well the difference between what you think you've got and what you really have.

"We're on location, in the heat of battle, making the picture, and we are given head-phones to monitor what we believe is actually being laid down on tape. Later when we wrap the shoot and settle into the picture editorial process, we discover that it does not really sound how we remembered it. Oh, it is what the actors had said, but the perceived quality value that we thought we had at the time was not really on tape. As a producer or director, you learn that lesson early on and sometimes in a very hard and brutal way."

In another case, John LeBlanc was asked to serve as director of photography on a low-budget western. The producer had made commercials successfully for several years but was inexperienced in the handling of feature projects. I received a call from John, asking if I would mind if he brought the producer, the director, the UPM, and the gentleman the producer had hired to handle the production mixing chores.

The following day, we met and discussed the various aspects of the show as they related to sound. Unknown to me, John had heard the production mixer talk about how he would handle recording on the set during previous preproduction meetings, and, knowing a few things about feature sound, several mental red flags had gone up. John segued the conver-sation into having the young man convey his intentions for me to hear for myself.

With a great amount of eagerness, he explained how he would record on a DA-88 so he could use up to eight channels at once, placing microphones all around the set. He wound up his dazzling litany with the warranty that the producer need not waste money on Foley, as his production soundtrack would make all that obsolete.

John turned to me. "Well, Dave, whad'ya think?"

I did not know whether to laugh or cry. "I think that you are hurtling toward an apoc-alyptic collision with post-production hell, that's what I think."

The young man was offended by my comment, but I felt the need to make my point. "Tell me, son. How many feature films have you mixed sound for?"

He tried to change the subject. He started to detail all the big-name features he had mixed. I grabbed the previous year's edition of the *Annual Index to Motion Picture Credits* pub-lished by the Motion Picture Academy as I calmly began pointing out that one should not try to equate working on a post-production rerecording stage in a totally controlled envi-ronment with the combat-zone style rigors of recording in the field.

The young man finally admitted that this was going to be his first time, but he had had more experience with digital sound than anyone else on the face of the earth. He actually extended his hand to me and said I could kiss his ring.

I returned to the *Annual Index.* "I don't see your name listed here under two of the titles you mentioned." He explained that he had not mixed on the actual soundtrack for those films but had handled mixing the sound for a making-of-a-film television program. John LeBlanc rose and shook my hand, as he knew nothing more was to be said.

Despite that afternoon's revelation, the producer decided to have the young man handle the production mixing job anyway, based on the digital sleight of hand that was offered—and I am sure a lot of it had to do with the temptation to save monies earmarked for the Foley process.

Several months later, John showed up with a video of the film. It was a work in progress, but clearly revealed the caliber of work of the mixer. John recounted how the production mixer had become progressively more bogged down during the shoot, totally underesti-mating the reality of the work. It had gotten to the point that the crew was even making fun of him. Not only did the producer have to go ahead with the original plans to have the Foley performed, but much more work in sound effect development became necessary, and potential ADR requirements also had grown. Instead of trying to reinvent the wheel, the producer would have been far better off using veteran experts and following their advice. With extremely few exceptions, we do things the way we do for good reason—because we have practiced our craft enough that we have developed it into an art form.

Multichannel Mixing

When we speak about production recording in a multichannel format we refer to two channels, either a 2-track Nagra or a 2-channel DAT. Nagra's 1/4″ digital deck allows 4-channel field recording, and a very few individuals may from time to time record to a DA-88 8-channel.

When you think of the grandfather of multichannel production sound recording, you must be thinking of the renowned Jim Webb, who handled the production recording chores for the legendary film director Robert Altman on such pictures as *California Split, Buffalo Bill, Three Women, A Wedding,* and *Nashville,* the first Dolby 2-track matrixed stereo mix (this picture earned Jim the British Academy Award for Best Sound).

On *A Wedding* Altman doubled the *Nashville* format. Jim Webb found himself recording on two 8-track machines simultaneously. Altman shot with two cameras amid fifty actors all interrelating with each other. Jim played musical microphones as he was mixing one group of actors holding a conversation, with camera set-ups moving from group to group. There was no real script, as Altman worked best with impromptu performances, so Jim had to be ready for anything.

For each set-up, his cable man went out and made a character ID strip of tape with numbered assignments on each of the radio mikes affixed to the actors. When he came back to the sound cart, the cable man laid the assignment tape right across the bottom of Jim's fader pots on the mixing console so that he would know who was on which microphone.

"It was nuts. I had an assistant keeping the log on who was on what track just so that the script supervisor could keep all the material straight, as there was no time for me to keep an accurate log!" he remembers.

On *California Split* Jim had the challenge of not only having to record 8-channel production dialog, but doing so while on a practical traveling location, a bus en route to Nevada. Keep in mind that, today, 8-channel mixing boards are commonplace, but in the 1970s Jim Webb's techniques were way ahead of mainstream production recording. The eight channels of signal had to be fed through two 4-channel audio mixers into the 1″ 8-channel tape-recorder located on the bottom shelf of the cart near the floor. A 1/4″ Nagra was fed a combined mix-down signal for protection back-up purposes. Jim Webb operated the first 4-channel mixer while his boom operator, Chris McLaughlin, operated the second 4-channel mixer.

Recording Practical Phone Conversations

For *All the President's Men,* director Alan Pakula told Jim Webb, "I don't want a throw-away soundtrack." (A throw-away soundtrack is basically a guide-track recorded so the actors can loop their lines later in an ADR session.) Jim could not have agreed more, so for every aspect of the production recording process Jim left no stone unturned.

Warner Brothers removed the wall between sound stages 4 and 11 to build the full-scale set of the *Washington Post* newsroom through the breadth of both stages.

"We had one shot that was a 180-foot dolly shot inside the four walls of the set. In order to eliminate what would have been a nightmare of ballast hum due to the entire ceiling being filled with rows of fluorescent lamps, the construction crew rigged a huge rack for the ballasts just outside the sound stage and bundled the wiring in groups that fed back into the stage to the fluorescent tubes themselves," Jim recalls. "As you know, it seems that half the picture was performed on telephones. Well, they didn't want the traditional style of actors having to act out a telephone conversation with no one on the other end of the phone to play off on, so it was decided early on with the help of the special-effects crew to build a practical telephone system into the set. We had five lines that you could switch back and forth on as Redford might put one call on hold while he answered another or place a second call while keeping one or two other lines on hold. Each off-camera actor was on the other end of the phone conversation and was set up in an isolated area of the stage."

Jim warns that simultaneously recording an on-screen actor clean while also recording the telephone feed must be handled carefully. "All the multiple phone calls are recorded in real time, which can be a problem if the on-screen actor's voice is in the phone feed. What you need to do is take the transmitter out of the handset of the on-camera actor's phone so that you don't experience 'double up' of the live mike with the phone-line tap. You set up the actors on the other end of the phone with headsets so that they are hearing the on-camera lines from the production mike (prior to the record head) so that you do not get that delay as heard from playback. The nice thing about this technique is that the off-camera phone feed has total isolation because the on-camera actor has the receiver right to his ear, listening to the off-camera voice so there is no acoustic leakage. Dialog overlaps are never a problem as you have both actors in complete isolation, recording each actor on a dedicated channel. This allows dialog interplay in real time."

It was the first time Robert Redford had ever used this kind of telephone technique while shooting a picture. After the director sounded "cut' on the first rehearsal, Redford looked up and exclaimed his excitement over being able to act and react to a live actor on the other end of the line. Jim could not have been happier with the results. "It really sets the actor free to act rather than try to play to nothingness, or to carefully avoid overlaps of lines being read off-camera by the script person."

Was all this extra effort worth it? *All the President's Men* was awarded the Academy Award for Best Sound that year.

Perils of Recording in Snow

In the winter of 1989, digital production recording was anything but mainstream. Long before inclement weather digital recording was being mastered, Paul Jyrälä had endured 105 days of production recording in freezing temperatures, handling the literal trench-warfare chores of mixing the war epic *Talvisota: The Winter War* in his homeland of Finland (see Figure 5.8).

Moisture, hot and cold temperature extremes, dirt, and grit—all the sensitivity issues that inhibit DAT machines from working to their optimum potential plagued Paul during the grueling shooting schedule. His boom operator and cable man worked hard to wrap the equipment with cellophane and pad them with thermal blankets to keep moisture and cold at bay.

"There were times we thought we should be awarded, I think you Americans call it the Purple Heart," chuckled Matti Kuortti, boom operator. "No matter how careful the

Figure 5.8 Production sound mixer Paul Jyrälä sits bundled against the freezing cold, his digital DAT and 1/4" Nagra protected by thermal blankets and battery-operated heating units. The boom operators wear machinist face shields and padded jackets to protect them from flying rocks and debris during explosion effects while recording spoken dialog. (Photo by Ulla-Maija Parikka)

special-effect crew was, there is always the possibility of something going wrong. During one scene where we filmed birch trees being blown apart, a rather large sliver of wood flew past the camera and pierced the director of photography in his shoulder. All of us had to be on guard, as there was danger everywhere."

Paul used four Sennheiser 416 microphones, backed up by two Vega and two Micron wireless microphones. The team used Ryocote 'Woolies" to combat wind gusts and air concussion from explosion pots. Unlike American production recording techniques, Paul encoded the production recording on *Talvisota* with DBX II onto the original 1/4". After the crew wrapped shooting for the day, Paul returned to the location barracks and carefully transferred the day's work himself. He decoded the DBX II signal and then re-encoded a noise reduction called Telecom (a European version of the Dolby noise-reduction system) as he transferred the dialog dailies onto 2-channel 17-1/2 mm fullcoat film. The first channel was a "flat" transfer, with no Telecom encoding, making it convenient for the picture editor. The second channel was the Telecom-encoded version Paul would work with later during the post-production process.

Because of the meticulous attention to detail that Paul Jyrälä brought to the production mixing chores, the picture only had 5% of its dialog looped later in an ADR session—an astoundingly small percentage given the difficult recording circumstances of snow, mud, flying dirt, and debris. Paul earned his fifth Jussi (the Finnish version of the Academy Award) for Best Sound, and *Talvisota* was one of the seven finalists that made the American "sound effect bake-off' for consideration for an Academy Award nomination.

Figure 5.9 Don't judge the Deva by its size. This little package carries a tremendous amount of direct-to-disk recording firepower. Using a keyboard, (out of view) the screen unit on the shelf above allows the mixer to enter all kinds of important data into the audio file directory. (Photo by David Yewdall)

Recording Straight to Hard Disk

With the advent of the Zaxcom Deva II, a direct-to-disk digital audio recorder, the production sound mixer brings a highly durable unit into any recording scenario without the sensitivity factor of traditional computer disk recording systems. The Deva II can record up to four dedicated channels of 48 kHz information (see Figure 5.9).

The high-quality 24-bit analog-to-digital converters on both the microphone and line inputs ensure a wide dynamic range. The AES interface can make transparent transfers of 24-bit material from other digital sources. The Deva can record a Sound Designer II audio file or either mono- or polyphonic Broadcast Wave audio files. By utilizing a small keyboard, shown in Figure 5.10, the production mixer enters pertinent data into the audio file directory.

The Deva uses a 40-gigabyte removable internal hard drive. Zaxcom claims these hermetically sealed drives can withstand as much as 100 "G"s—certainly twenty times more

Figure 5.10 The Deva with Cameo mixer.

than I intend ever to endure—but it does bring a lot of recording time for the mixer on the set. A separate DVD-RAM unit is easily hooked up so that the mixer can lay back protection copies to a recordable DVD, using the hard drive as a working medium only to record and manage files. Once the DVD is made and the material is safe in the hands of the post-production transfer facility, the mixer can wipe the drive clean and use it again, or put it in the archive for safe keeping as a back-up protection for all the dailies.

The mixer may choose to put the Deva into an "Intermittent" mode, which allows the unit to automatically make back-up recordings to the DVD when the Deva is not in "Record" mode. As soon as the "Record' mode is off, the Deva automatically continues recording back-up audio files to the DVD-RAM over the SCSI connector. "Turbo" mode allows recording to the Deva hard drive and to the DVD simultaneously.

The unit always maintains a ten-second "pre-roll" in the RAM buffer, so if the mixer presses the "Record' button, the previous ten seconds are automatically laid down to the hard drive, thereby doing away with waiting for the pre-roll. This feature is extremely helpful on a busy shoot, where the mixer must review previous recordings or where the director either does not understand pre-roll protocol or has not thought to warn sound that he or she is about to go for a "take" and roll cameras.

Rather than being caught right in the middle of playing back a previous cue and finding yourself totally incapable of spinning down to virgin tape to start recording again, simply hit the "Record" button, which automatically starts recording to the hard disk. You will not damage or record over the material you are reviewing, as it is impossible to accidentally record over a section of the hard disk that has already been used. Remember, computers do not work in a linear fashion. You can change from single-channel recording to multiple channels for the next recording set-up by simply touching the proper buttons to tell the Deva how you want to record. In addition to industry standard XLR connectors, the Deva has a break-out cable with a multipin connector for line inputs.

Note that the flat screen display for the Zaxcom Cameo mixer clearly shows the four audio channels, running line-up tones in Figure 5.11. Using a keyboard (not shown), the recording mixer quickly enters the scene, angle, and take data, which show up in the "slate" icon in the upper right hand corner. This entry along with the time code is embedded in the directory of the audio file itself, thereby streamlining and removing possible errors by the assistant picture editor later in assimilating the material into the nonlinear editing system being used.

Several other companies are actively engaged in perfecting direct-to-hard-drive recording systems for the field. The ability to mirror duplicate back-up drives quickly to cost-effective media and to build in data files to the directory of each audio file as they are created greatly enhances not only speed issues but also defeats the chances of error in data assignments later at the laboratory or at picture editorial.

THE ULTIMATE GOAL AND CHALLENGE

The challenges of production sound recording make it a difficult and arduous job. Production mixers and their teams face the daunting and often disheartening struggle with the ignorance factor of the producer(s) and director and their lack of personal empowerment by not knowing what is possible and what preparations and techniques can most efficiently accomplish the mission. If they do not understand what is possible (and they will not understand

Figure 5.11 The Zaxcom Cameo mixer.

that unless you have at least certain tools and procedural protocols), and if they do not understand the importance of what "quiet on the set" really means, then how can they hope to deliver what is truly possible? How can they dream to deliver the magic opportunities of production sound?

Nearly every director I have worked with in post-production jumps up and down insisting on how much he or she wants the magic of production, but in reality so many of them do not do their part to assist the production mixers and their teams to bring that magic of performance to its fullest possible potential. So many times the opportunities are lost in the logistical heat of battle, in the sheer struggle of shooting the film, getting the shot before they lose the light. If ever a phase of the creation of the motion picture cried out for the discipline and regimentation of a military operation, it is the challenging battlefield of production.

Chapter 6
From the Set to
the Laboratory

"That's a wrap for today!" shouts the assistant director. The camera crew breaks down the camera gear and carefully packs the cases into the camera truck. The second assistant camera person (known as the clapper loader in England) is responsible for the exposed negative. He or she sees to it that each roll of negative is carefully placed back in its opaque black plastic bag and secured inside the aluminum film can. The can is then taped so that it will not spill open accidentally. With a black Sharpie or a permanent felt marker, the second assistant labels each can, making sure the identification roll number matches what is on the camera report. The laboratory copy of the camera report is taped to the top of each can. When all the cans have been securely packed, taped, labeled, and have their corresponding sound reports taped on properly, each film can is then packed in a moisture-proof bag. The second assistant camera person places all the film cans in a thermal box for delivery to the laboratory and gives the script supervisor a copy of each camera report to include with the paperwork. Another copy of each camera report is sent to picture editorial, and a third copy is sent to the production office.

The sound crew breaks down the mixer's sound cart, carefully packing the gear into the sound truck. The production mixer packs up the master DAT and/or 1/4" rolls, or the DVD-RAM or Orb cartridge to be shipped back to sound transfer or directly to picture editorial. The original copy of each sound report is folded up and placed into its corresponding box of 1/4" tape, or wrapped around each DAT. Just like in the camera department, the sound mixer gives the script supervisor a copy of each sound report to include with the daily paperwork. A copy of each sound report is also sent to picture editorial and to the production office.

Before the film and sound rolls leave the set, the script supervisor reviews and confirms all circled takes with the picture and sound departments. If the location is within driving distance of the film laboratory and sound transfer, then a PA (production assistant)

shot on Film -- cut on Film

Exposed Picture Negative

Analog 1/4" -or- Digital DAT Production Recordings

1-light picture 35mm workprint

35mm monaural mag-stripe

Dailies are synced together and go to telecine for a video tape transfer.

The picture and sound rolls go to picture editorial after daily screening.

Picture Editor cuts both picture and sound film on Moviola or on a flat bed such as this KEM.

VHS video is sent to the set for purposes of continuity review.

35mm dailies (picture and sound) are screened before returning to Picture Editorial Dept. for coding and cutting.

Figure 6.1 Transfer protocol (film only).

drives the rolls of film negative and sound rolls to their respective processing facilities each night.

DELIVERY FORMAT

The negative has been developed, but what does the laboratory deliver to the client? Will the project be cut on film or cut digitally? This choice determines the protocol the production company follows to successfully carry the show through the various phases of post-production to completion. Before the cameras even begin to roll, the director, producer(s), director of photography, and picture editor discuss the various ways to handle the picture editing process (described in more detail in Chapter 7). Once the picture editing process is determined, the technical parameters and spec sheet for delivery virtually dictate themselves.

Cutting on Film

If it is decided to cut on film, then the laboratory must print 1-light daily workprints of all the circled takes advertised on the camera report. Sound transfer must transfer a monaural 35 mm mag-stripe of all circled takes on the sound report. On rare occasions, a project such as music events requires multichannel dailies. In such a case, the production company may require that 2-, 4-, or even 6-channel 35 mm fullcoat transfers be made.

Early each morning, the picture editorial runner drives to the laboratory and picks up the 1-light workprints, then drives to sound transfer and gets the rolls of single-stripe audio track. Once the picture assistant and apprentice sync all the dailies (discussed further in Chapter 7), they run the reels late in the afternoon or early evening when the director, producer, and picture editor convene to review the material. The first picture assistant must scrutinize the audio sync carefully during the projection of the dailies, as anything that may play back out of sync must be corrected before the reels of picture and their corresponding reels of mag-stripe are edge-coded.

Once the dailies are screened, the first picture assistant and apprentice return the reels to their cutting rooms to make any last-minute adjustments to fix sync issues that may have been noticed during the screening. Once these adjustments are complete, the reels of picture and track either are sent out to an edge-code service or the picture editorial crew may have rented their own edge-code machine, such as the Acmade, so they can do the work themselves. It is absolutely imperative that this edge-code process be done precisely with a focused attention to perforation accuracy and keeping the code number assignments straight. The edge-code number is printed onto both the picture and the mag-stripe film. Note that the numbers must line up exactly parallel to each other (see Figure 6.2).

On the 1-light workprint are two sets of numbers. The first set is the key edge numbers. These numbers are latent images that have been photographically printed into the original negative by the manufacturer at the time of its creation. The colloquial term is "picture keys," or often just "keys." These numbers are printed identically into the 1-light workprint, if the laboratory's optical printer exposes the edges of the film at the same time as the picture image.

These numbers serve basically two functions. First, a piece of film can be picked out of the bottom of the trim bin or off the cutting-room floor, and, by reading the key edge number,

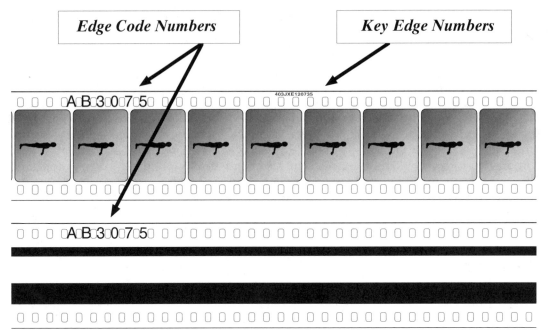

Figure 6.2 The two code numbers on the film workprint that are vital to your success.

you can look up the designation number in the code book (see Chapter 7). From there, you determine exactly what scene, angle, and take number it is, as well as from what camera roll of negative it was printed.

Second, the negative cutter uses these numbers not only to find what negative roll to access but to visually match the exact frame to make the cut. I can vouch for the ease and necessity of this system, as I have had to match far too much footage by visual image alone.

The edge code numbers are printed onto both the picture workprint and the mag-stripe film in exact sync to each other. If they are not in exact parallel sync, then having the edge number is obviously useless.

More than one numbering technique can be utilized in edge code. Some like to lock the start mark at the head of the roll and then reset the prefix code and footage counter, thus yielding the traditional letter and footage as follows: AA 1000. Some picture assistants like to set the number codes according to the day of the shoot; in this case, the first day of the shoot is AA, the second day is AB, the third AC, and so forth. Since a single day's shoot very rarely yields over 9,000 feet of dailies, it follows that no need would exist to move on to prefix AB until the second day's dailies.

Many first picture assistants who use the Acmade edge coding machine to print their own edge code numbers onto the workprint like to print the edge code numbers in a sequence that lists the scene, angle, and take as the number prefix, followed by the footage count, such as: 37A1000. This means that this is scene 37, set-up A, take 1. Custom-coding each "angle" and "take" in this manner obviously takes much more time than simply setting the start mark at the beginning of the roll and letting the entire roll of film run from top to bottom. However, the organization and speed gained later by the incredible ease of being able to pick up a trim of picture and/or production audio track and instantaneously know the scene and take, is of inestimable value.

Cutting on Nonlinear Systems

If the film is to be cut electronically, using a digital system such as the Avid or the very popular Final Cut Pro, a series of refined decisions must be made to structure a procedural protocol to deliver the picture and production sound into the digital nonlinear environment. These decisions must be made in preproduction, as they affect the entire post-production process to come (see Figure 6.3).

The decision may be made that the laboratory will develop the negative and make a reverse (positive image from the negative) video transfer to a high-resolution videotape such as the Beta-SP. Circled takes are not necessary for the laboratory process with this style of delivery. All the footage is transferred to tape, thus giving picture editorial access to all the footage, rather than just the circled takes. This tape would come to picture editorial without sound, leaving the process of syncing the production audio track to the assistant picture editor and the apprentice.

Many laboratories offer services for handling the daily sound rolls as well, including syncing the slates. The producer decides whether to pay out of pocket to an assembly-line style of delivery, or have the film's own crew personally do the work, adding the care and passion that a project's own picture editorial team is bound to bring to the effort.

Digital Food for Thought

Careful thought should be given to the choice of which nonlinear editing system to use. All systems are not created equal. All too often, I have seen a production company make a decision based on the belief that a particular system was much cheaper to use and therefore should be more cost-effective, only to find out that the collateral ramifications of going cheap on the nonlinear system inflicted numerous extra costs on the post-production budget later when the sound editorial process commenced.

Another mistake is in unquestioningly believing the laboratories and sound facilities when they tell you they are equipped and qualified to do specific services you may require. I knew one laboratory that told the producer that the film was being developed right there on site, but in actuality it was being flown counter-to-counter to Los Angeles for processing by another laboratory subcontracting the work. The first laboratory did not want to take time away from the services and handling they did do. The problem then, and still is, that the more you subcontract and fragment the services, eliminating those craftspeople who could truly be handling the QC (quality control) of your lab work, the more mistakes, lost footage, misunderstandings in specifications, and general lack of personal involvement and commitment to excellence you will find.

Before you settle on a laboratory or sound facility, do yourself and your production budget a big favor and check out various possibilities. Talk to other producers and especially to post-production supervisors who deal with numerous laboratories and sound facilities. Talk to those draftspersons who have had actual working experience with the laboratories or sound facilities you are considering. First-hand trench-warfare experience by those who work with these facilities is invaluable in guiding you through your production minefield.

shot on Film -- cut Non-Linear

Exposed Picture Negative

Analog 1/4" -or- Digital DAT Production Recordings

1-light picture 35mm workprint

Production Dialog is carefully transferred digitally, then backed up for protection before sending to Picture Editorial for syncing.

Telecine transfer of "picture only" dailies to Beta SP video for input into Avid.

Assistant Picture Editor enters dailies for exact syncing.

Picture Editor commences cutting sequences.

VHS video output of either dailies with sound or cut sequences for the Director to review on location.

Daily footage transferred to VHS from reversed negative for daily review of footage on location.

Figure 6.3 Transfer protocol (nonlinear).

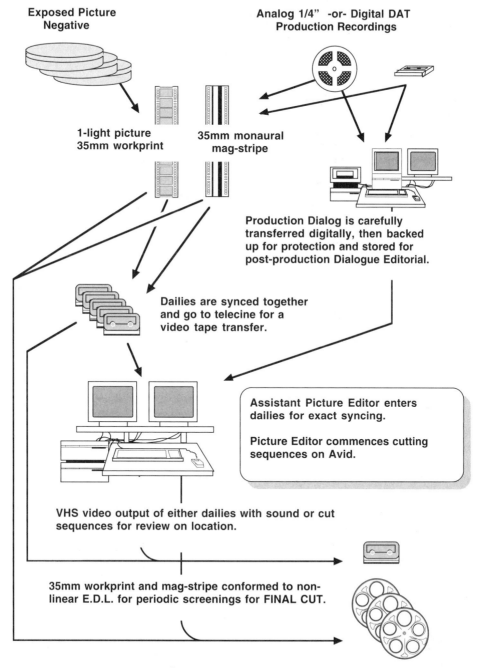

shot on Film -- cut Non-Linear
with Film to conform for screenings

Exposed Picture
Negative

Analog 1/4" -or- Digital DAT
Production Recordings

1-light picture
35mm workprint

35mm monaural
mag-stripe

Production Dialog is carefully
transferred digitally, then backed
up for protection and stored for
post-production Dialogue Editorial.

Dailies are synced together
and go to telecine for a
video tape transfer.

Assistant Picture Editor enters
dailies for exact syncing.

Picture Editor commences cutting
sequences on Avid.

VHS video output of either dailies with sound or cut
sequences for review on location.

35mm workprint and mag-stripe conformed to non-
linear E.D.L. for periodic screenings for FINAL CUT.

Figure 6.4 Cut and conform.

DATA IS GOLDEN

Regardless of whether you decide to edit on film or digitally, regardless of what editing platform or protocol is chosen, the underlining constant to all procedures is that at this stage in the negative-development through syncing of dailies, the precise and correct entry of data is crucial. Whether the key and edge code numbers are manually entered into the code book or into the information buffer of audio and picture files in the digital domain via the computer keyboard, this information is incredibly difficult to correct once entered incorrectly. Untold time and energy will be wasted trying to find a negative or sound roll because the code book data has either not been entered or the entries are sloppy and/or incorrect.

Unfortunately, this critical moment in the organizational structure of a project suffers the worst from fatigue and dyslexia. Many of us in post-production have discovered that more draftspersons suffer from some form of dyslexia than one might think. Be careful to recognize such tendencies in yourself and either delegate certain critical responsibilities for data entry to someone else or be extremely cautious and thorough, double-checking numbers before you proceed. Incorrect data entry completely invalidates the ability to successfully utilize OMF functions later. In today's highly pressured schedules, losing the ability to use either the OMF or Post Conform function severely slows down dialog editorial, potentially costing thousands of extra dollars to have dialog takes retransferred from source, or having to endure the slow and painstaking process of phase matching (discussed in Chapter 14).

35MM MAGNETIC STOCKS

Figure 6.5 illustrates the four kinds of 35 mm media used today, explained in detail in the following sections.

35mm Picture

The 35 mm film stock on the far left of Figure 6.5 is photographic stock. Numerous types of photographic stock exist, most of which are used to capture the visual action of a motion picture. Another reason for using photographic stock may be, for instance, to transfer the 2-track matrix stereo sound mix into the optical image that is combined photographically with the visual picture on the final release prints. The example shown has the classic four perforations per frame. Regardless of the incredible advancements in 24P and high-definition digital projection, 35 mm film stock is still the most popular, and, to date, it renders the most cost-effective image resolution, which will carry the industry well into the next century. 35 mm film is also a global standard. Whether you take your film to Europe, Australia, China, the far reaches of Africa, or upper Siberia, the technical specifications of 35 mm are worldwide.

35mm Mag-Stripe

This 35 mm stock is used for monaural audio sound applications. The wide magnetic stripe on the right side of the film is for the sound. The thinner stripe on the left is called a "balance" stripe

35 mm Film and its magnetic stock variants

Figure 6.5 35mm magnetic stock variants.

(also known as the "guide" stripe) so that the film does not undulate as it tracks along in the Moviola, on the KEM, or especially on the rerecording stage playback machines. The balance stripe allows the film to roll up onto itself with an even thickness due to the emulsion layer.

35mm Magnetic Three-Stripe

This 35mm stock is also used for audio sound applications. A nearly obsolete variant of stripe formats, three-stripe has been recently revived at several major studio sound departments. It is far easier to work with because it uses an acetate base that tears, unlike fullcoat, which uses a polyester base that does not break. It is also far more economical than fullcoat for the preparation of stereo and multichannel sound work.

35mm Magnetic Fullcoat

This 35mm stock is also used for audio sound applications. Fullcoat is the most popular and dynamically the best-sounding audio format for motion picture and television production. Because of the high rate of speed (90 feet per minute) with which the film passes over the head-stack array, and because of the breadth of the sound heads, the user can load up and saturate the magnetic properties of the film much more heavily than with other analog media, such as 24-track audiotape.

Figure 6.6 The transfer facilities at Weddington Productions never rest. In the foreground, Bruce Balestier is transferring dialog loads from the original production source for a dialog editor. In the background, Rusty Amodeo prepares to thread up a 2-inch roll of 24-track audiotape for a session layback. (Photo by David Yewdall)

Most "digital" motion picture releases today are first mixed to 35 mm fullcoat in a 6-track configuration to take advantage of the full and rich dynamic range. Because fullcoat has a solid magnetic surface, the user can utilize one of a variety of configurations.

Line-Up Tones

The disciplined use of line-up tones is the only basis for creating and later duplicating a precise and matched level of audio reproduction. Without it, we can only take our best blind guess, which even at its best never reproduces an exact duplication of the original. For this reason, the vast majority of audio draftspersons and sound facilities throughout the world have adopted and conformed their specifications and recording levels to uniformity by using SRTs (standard reference tapes). Equipment manufacturers design and build their products to operate to these standards. Facilities use SRTs to adjust their playback machines to properly reproduce the standard. This guarantees that a tape recorded halfway around the world will reproduce virtually identically in the studio environment so that 1:1 prints (the first one is identical to the copy made from it) can be transferred from the tape source as exact copies of the original.

In theory, if everyone used the identical reference tape and adjusted their machines correctly, recording a sample of the tones on the head end of recordings would be unnecessary. However, since a variety of reference levels can be used, not all machines record perfectly, and not all operators set up their machines correctly, the recorded tones at the head of a tape ensure that the recording is reproduced correctly.

Line-up tones are usually sine (for sinusoidal) wave or pure tones, not square waves. Line-up tones are laid down on the magnetic stock prior to the start mark. If the audio transfer is analog, as with 35 mm magnetic film or analog magnetic tapes such as 2-inch 24-track

Figure 6.7 VU and digital meters.

analog tape, the line-up tones are recorded at "0" level on the VU (volume unit) meter, unless specifically specified differently on the tape's content label.

A 1 kHz (referred to as a "thousand cycle tone") sine wave is the standard tone. If the transfer department is interested in very precise line-ups being made later, they follow the 1 kHz with a 10 kHz tone to adjust the high end, and a 125 Hz for adjusting the low end. Many who have been around awhile prefer to have a 40 Hz tone for the low end, but few sound facilities use it today.

If you are working with digital transfers, you do not have a VU meter, but a peak meter. In the digital world, "0" dB represents full scale or the absolute maximum recording level possible. Standard level then becomes some number of dB below full scale. Because digital and analog devices work together to accomplish recordings and rerecording jobs, an agreed-on correspondence must exist between standard digital level and standard analog level. I have already discussed the standard analog level, but, in the absence of a precise digital standard, everyone has a different opinion on what the "0" VU is for them and their own recordings. The generally accepted standard digital level has been changing during the last few years.

When gray-market DAT machines were first available in the late 1980s, some sound facilities adopted a –12 dB as "0" VU. Those of us who worked with high-concept high-velocity sound effects projects discovered very quickly that –12 dB would not give us the headroom required for the thousands of vibrant and robust sound effects we were developing and delivering to the rerecording stages. Those who used –12 dB as "0" VU discovered clipping and a plethora of digital spiking. The hardest lesson to teach the creative user was that the digital world has only so many ones and zeroes.

Let us pause for a moment to clarify something that probably puzzles many creative audio users who do not hail from an engineering background. In digital audio, the number of bits assigned to each sample (not the sampling rate) limits the dynamic range. If you are working in a 16-bit system, you have 65,636 possible volume levels to work with in each sample of the recording. If you try to drive the signal to 65,637, you will experience clipping and distortion because no more ones and zeroes are left to use.

Of course, the volume-level saturation geometrically increases as you work at a higher bit rate. If you were working in a 20-bit system, you would have 1,048,576 choices, and working in 24-bit would give you 16,777,216 for each sample!

It did not take long to find out that all the hard work of analog sound effect recording of the past couple of decades was being squashed and spiked, especially when the mixer had recorded the material very hot, saturating the tape. Recordists and sound facilities alike quickly discovered that the dynamic characteristics of many of their recordings were just too powerful to be properly translated into the digital realm.

In 1990, through a series of collaborations between manufacturers, sound mixers, and engineers, the theatrical and television industries settled on –18 dB as the digital peak meter equivalent to "0" VU, even though many of the DAT developers were designing their equipment for –16 dB. For several years, –18 dB seemed to be settling in fairly well.

Obviously, the best way to control overloading (clipping) the maximum level of your digital recordings is to bring the volume of the sound down by adopting a lower decibel level as a "0" VU equivalent. Several of the high-concept sound editorial firms have moved even lower to –20 dB, and a couple have gone so far as to adopt an extreme – 22 dB or –24 dB as "0" VU. Their audio engineers tell me they have come to the point that they need those extra decibels of headroom. I personally do not agree with this extreme choice.

PINK NOISE

Pink noise is an electronic signal that has equal energy levels at all frequencies across the range from 20 Hz to 20 kHz. Pink noise is often used to make measurements of electronic systems and acoustic spaces. It has an advantage over simple tones in that all frequencies are present simultaneously, allowing the user to make frequency response measurements quickly. Using an audio spectrum analyzer, a "flat" system or acoustic space is represented as a flat, easily interpreted line on the display. Users of pink noise must be careful to utilize analyzers that offer signal averaging over time due to the rapidly changing characteristics of pink noise. They must also be certain that the measurement microphone has a flat response.

LINE-UP TONES FOR YOUR OWN USE

Sound cues 2 through 8 of the audio CD provided with this book were carefully mastered so that you can use these line-up tones to check the performance, speaker assignment, and balance of your own system.

Audio CD cue #2 is a 1 kHz sine-wave line-up tone that was mastered to read –18 dB on the digital peak meter ("0" VU). Audio CD cue #3 is a 1 kHz sine-wave line-up tone only

Figure 6.8 1 kHz sine wave and square wave.

heard through channel one—the left speaker of your system. Audio CD cue #4 is a 1 kHz sine-wave line-up tone only heard through channel two—the right speaker of your system. Audio CD cue #5 is a 10 kHz sine-wave line-up tone that was mastered to read –18 dB on the digital peak meter ("0" VU). A 10 kHz tone is used to calibrate equipment to properly record and reproduce high-end frequencies.

Audio CD cue #6 is a 40 Hz sine-wave line-up tone that was mastered to read –18 dB on the digital peak meter ("0" VU). The 40 Hz tone is used to calibrate audio equipment to properly record and reproduce low-end frequencies, though many sound facilities use a 100 and/or 120 Hz tone instead. Audio CD cue #7 is pink noise that was mastered to read –18 dB on the digital peak meter ("0" VU). You can place a spectrum analyzer in the ideal listening "apex" of the room and study your speaker reproduction characteristics. (Many consumer-level electronics stores offer excellent spectrum analyzer and audio pressure meters for amateur and professional use.) Audio CD cue #8 is a 1 kHz square-wave line-up tone that was mastered to read –18 dB on the digital peak meter ("0" VU).

TIME CODE: THE OBNOXIOUS ELECTRONIC CRICKET

What is time code? How is it used? Should we worry about more than one? Some of the most frightening post-production war stories revolve around misunderstanding and misusing time code. I have seen craftspeople fall back against the wall and slump to a heap on the floor, holding their heads and crying with mental fatigue because of mismatching time codes or because thousands of dollars of video and layback transfers were rendered useless after time code parameters were entered incorrectly. Time code is one of the most confusing and frustrating subjects to deal with in the post-production process. It is important to get a good grasp on time code, what it does and how to use it as a valuable tool. Let us take a moment and appreciate its relationship to time and space.

In the beginning, before color television (and time code), there was black-and-white television, which operated at 30 fps (frames per second). Color television was introduced in 1953, and, to make color television compatible with the large number of black-and-white receivers, the engineers made a small adjustment to the television signal. They changed the frame rate from 30 fps, to 29.97, which slowed it down by one-tenth of one percent.

No one noticed and no one cared—until time code came along. The first time code was used in videotape editing and counted 30 fps. If this time code was operated at exactly 30 fps, the time code generator and a normal clock agreed. After viewing an hour of program material, the time code and clock agreed that exactly 60 minutes and zero seconds had passed.

However, because the television system operates slightly slower than 30 fps, the time code and the real-time clock do not agree. Imagine that you have two clocks, one with a slightly dead battery and one with a fresh battery. The clock with the slightly dead battery might run slower than the clock with the good battery. Because they are not both running at precisely the same rate, they do not stay in synchronization. Each counts hours, minutes, seconds, but their rates do not match.

When a television program assistant starts a stopwatch at the beginning of the program and then stops it at the end, time code and stopwatch will not agree. To make the slower-running time code address match the real time of day, the counting sequence was altered. It is important to remember that the time code rate was not changed; it still runs at 29.97, but the counting sequence was changed. The 0.1% speed change resulted in a difference of 108 frames per hour.

As we have discussed, American National Television System Committee (NTSC) systems run at 29.97 fps. Exceptions where video is run at 30 fps occur when special video-tape machines are utilized during principal photography using motion picture cameras to film a television monitor screen. The television video feed is set to run at 30 fps to eliminate the black roll bar that would be visible on the television screen.

Keeping Film in Exact Sync

The most precise standard to maintain synchronization with film is the synchronizer, also known as a sync-block. When working with film, one can interlock the 16 mm or 35 mm picture and one or more 16 mm or 35 mm mag-stripe rolls of sound together, side by side on sprocketed wheels (known as gangs) which are coupled to each other with a solid metal rod. When one wheel turns, the others turn at exactly the same rate, because they are physically coupled.

The synchronizer does two things. First, it keeps track of the position of the film by footage and frame number. Every frame has a unique identity. Second, it keeps the strands of film in exact synchronization. No matter how quickly or slowly the wheels are turned, the strands remain in perfect synchronization. This works because the film has sprocket holes (also known as perforation holes) that lace perfectly over the ever-revolving teeth of the synchronizer wheel. The film is kept on the sprocket teeth by a locking arm that is lowered and clicked into place. Each locking arm has two rollers with groove glides that allow the sprocket wheel teeth to pass through; yet the roller holds the film in place against the wheel, so the film does not slip and slide out of sync with the picture or other mag-stripe strands.

Figure 6.9 The editor's equivalency of "going postal" when the E.D.L.s do not match.

Each rotation of the wheel equals one foot of film. Numbers 0 to 15, in the case of 35 mm film, on the front of the wheel identify each frame around the circumference. An analog or digital numerical footage counter keeps track of how many times the synchronizer wheel has been rotated. If the wheel is turned 152 times, that means 152 feet of picture and tracks have passed through together in exact sync.

Invisible Sprocket Holes

Think of time code as an electronic multi-gang film synchronizer. Time code provides the same two functions for nonsprocketed media such as audio and videotape. In the case of videotape, every frame of picture has a unique identity, and, although sound can be subdivided into units smaller than one frame, we also refer to it in terms of frames. Time code uses hours, minutes, seconds, and frames instead of films' feet and frames.

We call the time code identity the time code address. Time code also enables synchronization among two or more elements (equipment) by providing a means to measure and control the speed, or rate, of the material. If a videotape and an audiotape each have matching time code, then we can use a computer to keep the two in sync by making sure that the time code address and speed (rate) match. It is important to think of these two different functions: address and rate. As long as the addresses and rate match, it does not matter at which absolute speed the material is played. The rates, however, must match exactly for the two elements to remain in sync.

The "Pull-Down" Effect

Film cameras are operated in the United States at 24 fps. If the film is never converted to television, it will always run at 24 fps from the camera to the theatre projector. When film is converted to a television format for broadcast, a change is required.

If NTSC television ran at 30 fps, the conversion from 24-frame film to 30-frame television would be fairly straightforward. As the telecine transfer is made, it pauses the film every fourth frame and duplicates the fourth frame again; then it rolls four more frames and duplicates the eighth frame again; then it rolls four more frames and duplicates the twelfth frame again, and so on. By doing this six times every second, the extra six frames needed for 24 fps film to fit a 30 fps format are achieved. You can see this for yourself by sticking a videocassette of a movie into your machine at home, then taking the remote control and pausing the action. Now push the single-frame advance button. The action advances a single frame. Push the button a few more times with a slow and rhythmic pace, so that you can study the single-frame movements. You will see that every fourth frame has been duplicated. Aren't your eyes quick enough to see those duplications in real time? No, neither are mine.

This does not fully solve the problem of film-rate conversion to television, however. NTSC television operates at 29.97 fps, or 0.001% slower, so when film is transferred to television it is necessary to slow, or pull-down, the film rate by the same 0.001% to 23.976 fps. When sound editors use a system that has a 29.97 fps video source, they must make sure that the production recordings, which are made with 30 fps time code, are slowed down by the same amount as the picture was slowed down when it was converted to television.

Addresses and Rates

There are four time code address types and four time code rates. The addressing serves only to uniquely identify each frame, but the rate is essential to maintaining synchronization. As you review the following time codes, remember that computers count from 0 and not from 1.

Addressing Modes

24-frame	Each frame is numbered from "0" to "23"
25-frame	Each frame is numbered from "0" to "24"
30-frame nondrop	Each frame is numbered from "0" to "29"
30-frame drop-frame	Each frame is numbered from "0" to "29" (but there is a unique counting sequence)

Frame Rates

24 fps	American film systems run at this rate
25 fps	European film and television systems run at this rate
29.97 fps	American (NTSC) television systems run at this rate
30 fps	American standard for non-television-based materials run at this rate

There are six normally encountered time code formats. The valid combinations of addressing modes and rates are as follows:

24-frame addresses and 24-frame rate
25-frame addresses and 25-frame rate
30-frame nondrop frame addresses and 30-frame rate
30-frame nondrop frame addresses and 29.97-frame rate
30-frame drop-frame addresses and 30-frame rate
30-frame drop-frame addresses and 29.97-frame rate

These combinations cover 99% of the normally encountered addresses and rates.

Audio Time Code Signal

Time code is recorded onto video and audiotapes as a special audible signal. It sounds very raucous, much like a constipated electronic insect with a bad temper, but time code-reader electronics can interpret this sound and convert it into computer-readable addresses. The computer listens to the time code and notes when transitions occur in the recorded signal. A transition occurs when the recorded signal changes from a positive-going waveform to a negative-going waveform, and vice versa.

The transition is important to the time code reader. The easiest transition to detect is a rapidly changing one. A very gradual transition is difficult for the computer to detect. Square waves have rapid transitions. As the time code signal is copied from one tape to another, it is possible for the shape of this square wave to become distorted, and the transitions become more difficult to detect. When the time code signal is rolled off, it means that the transitions are not rapid, and the time code reader is having difficulty detecting them.

Time code Specifications for Video Transfers

When ordering video transfers of either cut film or from nonlinear picture editing platforms, you want the videotape to be transferred with certain information windows and a precise designation of time code rate. Remember to be very specific about which time code format you want.

1. Transfer at 29.97 nondrop frame
2. Monaural production audio on Channel 1 (left)
3. Audio time code on Channel 2 (right) with visual time code address burned into the upper left of screen
4. Film footage and frame numbers visual burned into the upper right of screen
5. VITC (vertical interval time code, explained later in the chapter) on lines 17 and 19
6. Academy picture starts at exactly 000 feet and 00 frames, and time code corresponds to exactly 00 minutes, 00 seconds, and 00 frames
7. Time code "hour" designation matches the film reel number. For example, Reel 3 shows up as 03:00:00:00
8. 30 seconds of time code preroll before the Academy picture start
9. If VHS videocassette tapes are being created, time code and production audio are recorded on the normal analog channels

Drop-Frame Time Code

Drop-frame Time Code is so named because the counting sequence skips, or drops two frames, every minute except at the tens of minutes. The time code address increases from 59 seconds, 29 frames (00:59:29)—stepping past, or dropping, the 1 minute, 0 seconds, and 0 frames (01:00:00)—to 1 minute, 0 seconds, and 0 frames (01:01:00.02). The same number of frames per second is still there—each frame is still uniquely identified—they are just labeled differently.

Check for Drop/Nondrop

You have picked up a videotape that does not have a properly completed transfer label: it does not designate whether the video transfer was made drop or nondrop. Simply insert the videotape into a playback machine and spin the image down to the nearest one-minute address. By putting the controller into a flip-frame job mode and carefully flipping from frame 00:59:29 to the next frame, you will know instantly if the tape was transferred drop or nondrop. If there is no 01:00:00 frame, and the next frame is 01:00:02, then the tape was transferred drop-frame.

VITC

VITC (pronounced "vit-see") stands for vertical interval time code. VITC is time code recorded in the television picture. It is not normally seen by viewers and is similar to the frame line that exists between frames of film. When projected, the film frame lines are not visible, and if one were to write numbers in the masked area between frames, these would not be seen during normal presentation. However, if the editor subsequently handles the film, the numbers are easily read. VITC operates in the same way. VITC is written into the television vertical interval. When the video machine is stopped, computers can read this time code very accurately.

Mixing Drop-Frame and Nondrop-Frame Sessions

Most picture editors prefer to use nondrop frame time code even though they are cutting on systems that are in fact running at 29.97 NTSC rate. The reasons vary, but perhaps they are related to the facts that some early editorial systems could not handle drop-frame time code and that the calculations involved in adding nondrop time codes were much easier than those for adding drop-frame time codes. Since the picture editors then were probably using nondrop, it made things easier when the sound and picture used the same addressing scheme.

With today's faster computers and much more sophisticated software utilities, however, it does not make much difference whether you use drop frame or nondrop frame—as long as you are consistent and all of your people are using the same format. Even if they are not, the synchronization computers are capable of doing the math so that nondrop- and drop-frame addresses can be easily synchronized.

USING OUTBOARD A TO D ENCODERS

If you are interested in having the best-quality digital sound transfers made from analog tapes or from 35 mm film, insist on having the material encoded and decoded through high-quality D-A/A-D (digital-to-analog/analog-to-digital) converters, such as the Apogee converters. Most people do not know that to make digital technologies such as the 8-track DA-88 recorders cost-effective and attractive, the manufacturers sacrificed high-end quality at the analog-to-digital and digital-to-analog conversion. Remember, there is no such thing as a free lunch. A "really good deal" often looks that way because something, somewhere, was eliminated, sacrificed, or degraded to offset the expense.

Digital DA-88 recorders are fading away in favor of higher-quality encoding platforms (such as the 888 24-bit Digidesign interface and their new HD platform)—not only because of the better-sounding reproduction qualities, but also because of the limitation of only eight channels per tape and the fact that digitizing eight channels of a Foley session, for instance, requires a transfer process. Interlocking to time code meant "stem" type transfers, which yield eight audio files that eat up a solid amount of disk space at the rate of eight times five megabytes per minute (or 700–800 megabytes for a twenty-minute reel). The net "performance" passages were usually 15 to 20% of that—or 80 to 85% disk waste).

This is why MR8 and MR16 technologies, which can record a Pro Tools session straight to a removable hard drive, quickly gained favor. Straight-to-hard-drive recording in the ADR and Foley stage, rerecording predubing, and final mixing is becoming the standard, no longer the exception.

Just as DA-88 technology served as a "bridging" medium, so too look for DAT technology to fade in popularity. With direct-to-disk recorders, such as the Deva and the new Nagra V both utilizing high-quality straight-to-disk recording, the DAT will soon find fewer and fewer users in the production and post-production sound facility world. Keep this in mind as you plan the technical protocols for your project.

Chapter 7
Picture Editorial and Use of the Sound Medium

THE BASTION OF ABSOLUTES

From the moment daily film and mag transfers arrive from the laboratory and sound transfer, to the moment when the edge code number is applied to both picture and track after running the dailies with the director and picture editor is the most critical time for the regimentation and precision of a film. It is during the daily chore of syncing up the previous day's workprint and corresponding soundtrack that the assistant picture editor and picture apprentice must practice their skills with the strictest regard to accuracy and correct data entry.

When the film arrives, the picture assistant and apprentice swing into action, racing to sync up all daily footage in time for that evening's screening. Errors made at this point in lining up the picture and soundtrack in exact sync are extremely difficult to correct later. Seldom have I seen sync errors corrected once they have passed through the edge coding machine.

The technique and discipline of syncing film dailies is not as straightforward as it may sound. For some reason, film schools allow students to learn to line up and sync their film dailies on flatbed editing machines. I do not care what any film school instructor tells you— a flatbed editing machine is not a precise machine. Veteran editors and prized professional picture assistants also will tell you that flatbed editing machines are inaccurate by as much as plus-or-minus two frames! (Most moviegoers notice when dialog is out at two frames.)

This is not an opinion or one man's theory. This is a fact, without question. The only way to sync film and mag track precisely is to use a multi-gang synchronizer. Because so much hinges on having picture and mag track placed in exact sync to one another, it never ceases to amaze me when someone knowingly uses anything but the most accurate film device to maintain rigid and precise sync.

Before you can actually sync the dailies, you must first break down all the footage. As you wind through the rolls of workprint, you develop a rhythm for winding through the film very quickly. You watch the images blur by, and every so often you notice several frames that "flash-out." These are overexposed frames for which the aperture of the camera was left open between takes, washing out the image. These flash-out frames are at the heads of each take. Pause when you come across these flash-out frames, pull slowly ahead and, with the help of a magnifying loop, determine precisely at which frame the slate sticks meet as they are snapped together. That is where the clap is heard on the mag track.

Use a white grease pencil in marking the picture once you have identified the exact frame in which the slate marker has impacted. Mark an "X" on that frame of film where the sticks meet, then write the scene number, angle, and take number (readable from the slate) across the frames just prior to the "X" frame. Find the scene and slate number on the lab report form included with the roll of workprint, and mark a check next to it. Roll the workprint quickly down to the next group of flash-out frames, where you pause and repeat the process. After you have marked the slates on the entire roll of workprint, take a flange (a hub with a stiff side to it—or, if you like, a reel with only one side) and roll the workprint up. Watch for the flash-out frames, where you cut the workprint clean with a straight-edge Rivas butt splicer. Place these rolls of picture on the back rack of the film bench, taking time to organize the rolls in numerical order. You should probably practice winding film onto a flange without using a core. This is not as simple as you might think it is, but you will quickly master the technique.

After you have broken down all the picture, take a synchronizer with a magnetic head and commence breaking down the sound transfer. The sound transfer always comes tails out. Take the flange and start rolling the mag track up until you come to the ID tag. This is an adhesive label, usually 3/4" wide by a couple of inches long. The transfer engineer places these ID tags on the mag film just before rolling the scene and take the ID tag identifies. Break off the mag, keeping the ID tag. Then place the mag track into the synchronizer gang and lock it down; lower the mag head down to read the mag stripe. Roll the track forward. You hear the production mixer slate the scene and take, then you hear a pause, followed by off-mike words from the director. Within a few moments, you hear a slate clap. Continue to roll the mag track through until you hear the director call "Action."

It is at this point that most sync errors are made, because not all head slates go down smoothly. During the course of the picture a host of audio misfires occur. Sometimes you hear a voice call to slate it again; sometimes you hear the assistant director pause the sound roll and then roll again. Also, you can mistake a slate clap for a hand slap or other similar audio distraction. If you are shooting multiple cameras, be careful which slate you mark for which workprint angle, unless all cameras are using a common marker, which is rare. Sometimes the slate clap is hardly audible; a loud, crisp crack often irritates the actors and takes them out of character.

When you are satisfied that you have correctly identified the slate clap, use a black Sharpie marker to make a clean identification line across the frame exactly where the sound of the clap starts. Do not use a grease pencil in marking the slate impacts on the mag track. Once a grease mark has been placed on a magnetic track, it can never be completely rubbed off. The grease cakes up on the sound head and mars the soundtrack. The ink from a Sharpie does not harm or alter the sound on the mag track.

Remember that 35mm film has four perforations to the frame, which means that you can be 1/96th of a second accurate in matching sync. The more dailies you sync up, the more you will study the visual slate arm as it blurs down to impact. You will get a sense of which perforation in the frame is the best choice. You are now changing the mechanical technique of syncing dailies into an art form of precision.

Using the black Sharpie, write the scene, angle, and take number just in front of the slate clap mark on the mag track in plain sight. Roll up the head end of the mag track back to the ID tag and place the roll of mag track on the back rack of the film bench alongside the corresponding roll of picture.

Once you have finished, you will have a back rack filled with rolls of picture and track. You will have rolls of W.T. (wild track) with no picture. You will have rolls of picture with no track. Check the labels on the rolls of picture that do not have any corresponding rolls of soundtrack. They should all have a designation of MOS on the label.

Check the lab reports and sound reports. Every item on the material inventory should have your check marks next to it. If not, call either the laboratory or the sound transfer facility to order the missing workprints or mag tracks.

You are now ready to start building your daily rolls. Professional picture editorial departments always build the daily rolls starting with the smallest scene number and building out to the largest. By doing this, the director and picture editor view an entire scene and its coverage starting with the master angle; then they review the Apple ("A") angle takes, then the Baker ("B") angle takes, then the Charley ("C") angle takes, and so on. You also review scenes in order; for instance, you would not screen 46 before you would screen 29. This helps to begin the process of continuity in the minds of the director and picture editor.

Once you have built a full reel of picture and track, put head and tail leaders on these rolls. It is traditional to use a black Sharpie marker for the picture label and a red Sharpie for the sound label. With this kind of color coding, you can identify a picture or sound roll from clear across the room. Head and tail leaders should look like the labels shown in Figure 7.1

To the far right of the label, "HEADS" is listed first, then "PIX" (for workprint, often abbreviated from "picture") or "SND" (for mag track, often abbreviated from "sound"). The next piece of information to add to the head label is the format in which the picture is to be viewed. This is rather helpful information for your projectionist, as he or she must know what lens and aperture matte to use. After all, it's not as easy as saying, "Oh, we shot the film in 35." Okay, 35 what? The picture could have been shot in 1 :33, 1:85, 1:66; it could have been shot "Scope" or "Super-35" or any number of unusual configurations.

Do not write the format configuration on the sound roll, but list what head configuration the projectionist must have on the interlock mag machine. The vast majority of film projects have monaural single-stripe daily transfers, so list "MONO," for monaural. However, some projects have unusual multichannel configurations, such as those discussed in Chapter 5. When using fullcoat as a sound stock medium, picture editorial can use up to six channels on a piece of film.

The next label notation to make is the roll number. Each editorial team has its own style or method. Some list the roll number starting with the initials of the project, making roll "54" of the feature *Dante's Peak* list as "DP-54" or "DPK-54." Some do not list the initials of the show, just the roll number. Some editorial teams add a small notation on the label, showing which of that day's daily rolls that particular roll is. "DPK-54" could have been the third of five rolls of dailies shot that day, so it would be shown as "3-of-5."

Figure 7.1 Head and tail leaders for film. This is standard labeling for daily rolls.

Most editorial teams also list the date. Last, but not least, list the title of the film. The tail leaders should have the same information, but written in the reverse order.

I always make my head leaders first on 3/4″ white paper tape, then I apply the labels onto color-coded 35 mm painted leader. Different picture assistants use their own combinations of color-coded painted leader, but the most common combinations are yellow-painted leader for picture, and red-painted leader for sound. I run five or six feet of the painted leader, then I splice into picture fill, because picture fill is considerably cheaper per foot than painted leader.

Roll the picture fill down about twenty feet on both picture and sound rolls. At this point, cut an Academy leader "header" into the picture roll. The Academy leader roll frames are well marked as to where to cut and splice.

The frame just prior to the first frame of the "8" second rotation is called "Picture Start," and it means just that—PICTURE START. At this point, apply a 6″ strip of 3/4″ white paper tape, covering five or six frames of the Academy leader with the "Picture Start" frame right in the middle. With a black Sharpie, draw a line across the film from edge to edge, on the top and bottom frame line of the "Picture Start" frame. Place another strip of 3/4″ white paper tape, covering five or six frames of the picture fill leader of the sound roll. Again, with a black Sharpie draw a line across the film from edge to edge somewhere in the middle of the tape, as if you are creating a frame line on the tape. Count four perforations (equaling one frame) and draw another line across the film from edge to edge. Draw an "X" from the corners of the lines you have drawn across the tape, so that this box has a thick "X" mark. With a hand paper-punch carefully punch a hole right in the center of this "X" on both rolls.

Figure 7.2 The start mark. Exact synchronization between the picture and sound tracks are critical.

(The punched hole is for light to easily pass through, making it much easier for the projectionist to seat the frame accurately into the projector gate—which is traditionally a rather dimly lit area.)

Figure 7.2 illustrates the start marks. Snap open the synchronizer gangs and place the picture leader into the first gang (the one closest to you) so that the "X" that covers the "Picture Start" frame covers the sprocket teeth that encompass the "0" frame of the synchronizer. Close the gang until it locks shut. Place the sound leader into the second gang, the one with the magnetic sound head on top. Align it over the "0" frame in the same fashion as the picture roll. Close the gang on the sound roll until it locks shut.

From here on, these two pieces of film run in exact sync to one another. Anything you do to this film, you do to the left of the synchronizer. Do nothing to the right of the synchronizer; to do so would change sync between the two rolls of film and cancel out the whole idea of using a synchronizer (sync block) in the first place.

The biggest mistake beginners make when they start syncing dailies is that they pop open the gangs for some reason. They think they must open them to roll down and find sync on the next shot. Not only is this not necessary, but it is a phenomenal screw-up to do so. Remember, once you have closed the synchronizer gangs when you have applied and aligned your start marks, never ever open them—even when you finish syncing the last shot of the roll.

After the last shot, attach an Academy leader "tail" on the end of the picture roll and fill leader on the end of the sound roll. When the Academy leader tail runs out, attach a length of fill leader and run the two rolls an additional fifteen or twenty feet. Roll them through the synchronizer and break or cut the film off evenly on both rolls; then apply your tail leader identification tapes accordingly. You have just finished syncing dailies for the first roll of the day—great! Move on to the next roll. Time is running out, and you still have nearly three thousand feet of film to go.

I am sure many of you think that all this information on the process of syncing dailies is a waste of time. Film is dead—nonlinear is where it is at, right? I would counsel caution for those who love to sound the death knell of film. Years ago, when videotape came out, I read articles that predicted the demise of film—yet film is still with us. A few years later, David Wolper was shooting a miniseries of Abraham Lincoln in Super 16mm. I remember reading various professional publications of the time sounded the death knell for 35mm film. Again, 35mm film is still with us, and healthier than ever, even with the advent of high-definition and 24-P technologies offered today.

When studios all shot their films on location, I read articles about the death of traditional sound stages. Not only do we still have sound stages, but within the studios and independent arenas there is a resurgence of building sound stages throughout the world. Stages that had been converted for mass storage suddenly booted their storage clients out and reconverted back to being sound stages.

Not too long ago, I also read of the supposedly impending death of old-fashioned special-effects techniques, such as glass paintings and matte shots. These types of effects, it was claimed, were no longer necessary with the advent of computer-generated technologies. Not only have we experienced a rebirth of glass paintings and matte shots, but a renaissance is also underway of the older "tape-and-bailing-wire" techniques.

Every so often I am still approached by various clients seeking shoot-on-film/cut-on-film options to produce their new projects. Having worked on nonlinear productions, they have decided it is preferable to return to film protocols. I would not sound the death knell for film-driven post-production just yet.

"BUT WE ARE NONLINEAR!"

Do not slip into a factory-style mentality when it comes to the quality and technical disciplines that your dailies deserve. Just because a laboratory offers you a sweet deal for "all-in" processing, syncing, and telecine transfers does not guarantee technical excellence. More than one producer has ended up paying considerable extra costs to have work done over again because it wasn't done correctly to start with.

Precise attention to detail is crucial in syncing the dailies and creating the code book. It is shocking to witness the weeks of wasted work and the untold thousands of squandered dollars that result when the picture assistant and apprentice do not pay attention to detail and create a proper code book. I cannot overemphasize the importance of this moment in the process. The code book becomes the bible for the balance of the post-production process. Any experienced supervising sound editor or dialog editor will confirm this. Once you have performed a sloppy and inaccurate job of syncing the dailies, it is nearly impossible to correct. With today's nonlinear technologies and the promise of faster assemblies from such advanced software applications as OMF and PostConform, these tasks become nearly automatic. If you sync sloppily or enter misinformation in the directory buffer, you nullify the ability of OMF or PostConform to work correctly. Remember, a computer knows only what you tell it. If you tell it the wrong number, it only knows the wrong number. It's the cliche we always banter about—"Junk in, junk out." You can either be the hero, or you can be the junk man.

THE CODE BOOK ENTRY

For some reason, many inexperienced picture assistants and apprentices think that once they get the sound onto the mag film transfer for the KEM or into the computer for the picture editor, that is the end of it. What further need would anyone have to know about sound rolls and all that? It's in the computer now, right? Wrong. On more than one picture where the inventory was turned over to me for sound editorial, I was shocked to find that either no code book whatsoever existed or that the code book was only filled out regarding negative. After all, the crew did understand, at some point, that a negative cutter would be needed to assemble the original negative together for an answer print. However, when I looked to the sound rolls and all information regarding sound, nothing was filled in. The excuses for this ran the gamut, all of which were just that, excuses. In our industry, things work the way they do for a reason. Entry spaces are under certain headings for a reason: someone needs that information. Fill in all the entry spaces. Fill in all of the codes for negative, sound roll number as well as edge code numbers. If in doubt, ask. It is best to check with sound editorial to confirm what they need from picture editorial so that sound editorial will have a complete code book at turnover. After picture editorial has finished the director's cut and is locking the picture for sound editorial turnover, a team of sound craftspersons and negative cutters depends on your thorough and accurate code book log entries.

Figure 7.3 depicts a typical page from a code book generated by the picture-editorial team. Note that the title of the film and the number of day of shooting, followed by calendar date of the shoot, are listed at the top of the page. Note that the edge code series number is listed at the bottom of the page. When you three-hole-punch the page and start building up a thick binder, it is much easier to simply flip through the edges of the pages to search for the edge code number than if it were at the top.

The scene and take number is the first item listed on the far left. A description entry is for the assistant editor to make important notes, such as "tail slate," "2nd stix" (for "Sticks"), and, if the audio transfer comes from a different source on the "B" camera than from the "A" camera, "B cam sound." Notes make information quick and efficient to find.

The "C.R.#" is where the camera roll number is listed. Note that the picture assistant precedes the roll number with which camera was used. This greatly aids in such tasks as syncing dailies, where the assistants verbally call out their assigned camera slates:

"Camera 'A' marker" (followed by a slate clap)
"Camera 'B' marker" (followed by a slate clap)
"Camera 'C' marker" (followed by a slate clap)

How are you, the picture assistant, going to know which slate clap on the mag roll syncs up with which workprint picture shot simultaneously from three cameras? Of course, you could pick one, sync it, and lace it up on a Moviola to see if the actor's lips flap in sync. But what if the action is far enough away that a 3×4–inch Moviola screen is not big enough for you to see sync clearly enough? What if the much larger KEM screen is not big enough either?

You would probably eventually figure it out, but it is good to know how—for those oddball shots that missed seeing the slate clap, or for when there is not a slate at all. I promise that you eventually will cut sound in late because the assistant director did not give the sound mixer enough time to warm up or to follow production protocol in waiting until the mixer

"Dante's Peak"			Day 7 shot: Tuesday 8-20-'96		
scene / take	Description	C.R. #	acmade code	key number	S.R. #
64 "D"-1 (B)		B 44	054-1023-1269	K 125-7734-4474 -4711	8
-2 (B)	2nd stix		1270-1442	K 125-7734-4721 -4893	
64 "E"-2 (A)	A cam snd	A 57	1443-1515	K 139-8549-2222 -2294	
-3 (A)	Tail slate		1516-1573	K 139-8549-2305 -2362	
-4 (A)			1574-1667	K 139-8549-2376 -2469	
-2 (B)	B cam snd	B 45	1668-1745	K 125-8122-1126 -1193	
-3 (B)	Tail slate		1746-1810	K 125-8122-1203 -1267	
-4 (B)			1811-1892	K 125-8122-1278 -1359	
				054-1000	

Figure 7.3 The code book. This is the bible of data by which all production picture and sound tracks can be found.

calls "speed" before the action proceeds. You will have several seconds of silence before sound comes up, but the entire visual action has been shot. And, of course, who can forget those occasions when they tell you they will "tail slate" the shot, and then, during the take, the negative runs out in the camera before the slate can be made?

You must find some bit of sound. Do not look for anything soft. Look for sudden, instant sounds that make a precise point. An actor claps his hands with glee in the middle of the sequence, and there is your sync point. I have often used the closing of a car door, even the passing footsteps of a woman walking in high heels (of course, figuring out which heel footfall to pick was interesting). Knowing how to sync when production protocol goes afoul is important—but you do not want to spend your time doing it unnecessarily. You must develop a fully thought-through methodology of how to handle dailies given any number of combinations, including weather, number of cameras, mixed camera formats, mixed audio formats, use of audio playback, splitting off of practical audio source, and so forth.

The next entry is for the edge code number, listed in Figure 7.3 as the "acmade code" (the numbers discussed in Chapter 6 that are applied to both the picture and sound precisely after your daily screening). In this case, the editorial team chose to code its picture by the camera roll method rather than individual scene-and-take method. This method is commonly referred to as "Kem rolls."

For exhibition purposes, note that the first number always is 054 on this page, as this daily roll is #54. The second number is the last four digits that appear at the head of each shot, followed by a dash; the third set of numbers is the last four digits that appear at the end of each shot. Scene 64 "D," take 1 starts at 054-1023 and ends at 054-1269, plus or minus a foot for extra frames. You can instantly tell that this shot is 246 feet in length, which means that it is 2 minutes, 45-1/2 seconds long.

The next entry is the "key number," the latent image number burned into the negative by the manufacturer. This is the number your negative cutter looks for to image-match the workprint and negative, or, if you cut nonlinear, from your EDL. Its from-and-to numbering entry is in the same format as the edge code number entry, but only the last four numbers that appear at the end of the shot are entered.

The last entry is the sound roll number ("S.R. #"). Unless you want to have your sound editorial crew burning you in effigy or throwing rocks at your cutting room, you are well advised not to forget to fill in this blank.

One of the biggest and most serious problems in code book assimilation occurs when the picture assistant and apprentice do not make their entries clear and legible. I often have trouble telling the difference between "1" and "7" and distinguishing letters used for angle identifications.

With today's computerized field units such as the Deva, much more data entry is done right on the set, as the camera is rolling. In many respects, this is very good. Information is fresh in the minds of the production mixer and boom operator. The loss of precious code numbers is less likely, especially when the production is using timecode smart slates. Conversely, all this can lull the editorial team into a false sense that they do not have to pay strict attention to data entry and the code book. Again, a computer is only as good as what you tell it. If misinformation is put into it, unwinding it and getting it straight again is incredibly difficult and time consuming, often adding extra costs to the production. If for some reason the fancy timecode and software "wink out" or crash, you are dead in the water. When it works, a computer can be wonderful, but nothing replaces a trained professional's eyes and ears in knowing what must be done and doing it correctly and efficiently. The better your code book, the smoother the post-production process that relies on it. It is just that simple.

THE DANGER OF ROMANTIC MYTHOLOGY

I have been both amazed and dismayed to hear film students talk about "cutting-in-the-camera" and other techniques and regarding cinematic history and mythology as if they were doctrine to adopt for themselves. These romantic remembrances really belong in the fireside chats of back-when stories; they are only interesting tales of famous (and sometimes infamous) filmmakers whose techniques and at times irresponsible daring have no place in today's filmmaking industry. Sure, it's fun to tell the story of John Ford on location in Monument Valley: when told that he was seven pages behind schedule, he simply took the script, counted off seven pages, and ripped them out as he told the messenger to inform the executives back at the studio that he was now back on schedule. Do you think, though, that John Ford would dump seven pages of carefully written text that was a blueprint for his own movie? Some actually tell these mystical antidotes as if they had constructive qualities to contribute to young, impressionable film students, who often mistake these fond fables for methods they should adopt themselves.

THE POWER OF COVERAGE

The most important thing a director can do during the battlefield of production is to get plenty of coverage. William Wyler, legendary director of some of Hollywood's greatest pictures (*Big Country, Ben-Hur, Gentleman's Agreement, Mrs. Miniver*) was known for his fastidious style of directing. It was not uncommon for him to shoot twenty or thirty takes, each time just telling the crew, "Let's do it again." The actors struggled take after take to dig deeper for that something extra, as Wyler usually would not give specific instructions, just the same nod of the head and, "Let's do it again."

Cast members tried to glean something from their director that might finally allow them to achieve whatever bit of nuance or detail Wyler had envisioned in the first place. As usual, though, precious little would be said except, "Let's do it again."

Not to diminish the fabulous pictures he made or his accomplishments as a director, but the truth of the matter is William Wyler shot so many takes because he was insecure on the set. He did not always know if he had the performance he was looking for when it unfolded. What he did know and understand was the post-production editing process. He knew that if he shot enough coverage, his picture editor could take any particular scene and cut it a dozen different ways. Wyler knew that the editing room was his sanctuary where he could massage the film and create the picture as he had really envisioned. After closer examination, it is easy to understand why the job of picture editor is so coveted and sought after. After the director, the picture editor is considered the most powerful position on a motion picture project. Some even argue that, in the case of a first-time director or a director possessing even the perception of having a tarnished or outdated resumé, the picture editor is at least equal to if not more powerful than the director.

I have been in strategy meetings where a heated argument arose among studio executives over who would handle the picture editorial chores. The picture editor does more than just assemble the hundreds of shots from over 100,000 feet of seemingly disorganized footage. For example, a sequence taking one minute of screen time and portraying action and dialog between two characters usually appears to occur in one location cinematically. In actuality, the sequence would have been broken down into individual angles and shot over the course of days, even months, due to appropriate location sites, availability of actors, and other considerations. Sometimes what seems to be one location in the movie is actually a composite of several location sites that are blocks, miles, or even continents apart. Some actors who appear to be in the same scene at the same time performing against one another actually may never have performed their roles in the presence of the other, even though the final edited sequence appears otherwise.

LEANDER SALES

With one foot planted firmly in a General Patton–like editing-on-film philosophical style, Leander Sales takes no prisoners. Veteran of numerous Spike Lee films, Leander's technique

Figure 7.4 Leander Sales, film editor and editing faculty instructor at the North Carolina School of the Arts, School of Filmmaking. (Photo by David Yewdall)

and creative dogma is infectious. Yet with his other foot firmly set in the digital nonlinear reality of today's post-production world, Leander stays anchored in the discipline and ultimate realities of film.

"I grew up here in Winston-Salem, North Carolina. I graduated from East Forsyth High and was very active in the drama department. As an editor, you are deciphering performance, and having this training as an actor just helps me that much more when I am looking at those various takes of film and deciding which performance feels better.

"It is all about the performance. To me, I think that it is what editing is about. Of course, there is a technical aspect to it, but it is about a gut-level response to what I see on screen when I analyze the dailies."

"So that's where it started, in drama. But that experience just led me into editing, and I love it. Because in editing you get a chance to work with everything—you get a chance to work with the work of the screenwriter, because often times you are cutting things out and adding things in—looping and ADR. You're working with the cinematographer's work, you're cutting things out and putting them back in. You're working with the production sound recordist's work—everything.

"A lot of times it gives you a chance to show the director things that he or she didn't see. Being an editor allows you to be objective. When the director is on set, often times he doesn't see certain things because he is so worried about other things. But as an editor, who is not on set, it allows me that objectivity."

"Those are the moments that you look for. Those are the moments that actors look for, those true moments. You just feel it, and you can't repeat it—it just comes. That's the reason why Woody Allen says he never loops, or Martin Scorsese says he won't loop a certain scene because he says you can't recreate that emotion, because you don't have the other actor to bounce off of. It makes a huge difference."

"Another important thing for a film editor, I feel, is just to live—life. You have to understand emotions, behavior—because basically that is what you are looking at when you are studying those performances. You are looking for the emotional context that you are trying to distill a truth and honesty. The more you live, the more it helps you to get to that truth. I lived in Italy for a while, and I have traveled in Africa. Over there just helped me to understand life, and it opened so many doors for me as far as interest and just experimenting with things and trying to, I guess, see where I fit into the big picture of the world. That's important—how you fit into the big picture. That goes back to editing, you see; you cut this little scene, but how does it fit into the big picture.

"Editors are the only people who really get a chance to see the film from the first scene in dailies through to the release prints. I love that process. It's seeing the baby born, and then you put it out into the world."

MARK GOLDBLATT, A.C.E.

"Inappropriate editing can destroy a film," declares Mark Goldblatt, A.C.E. Like so many of today's top filmmaking talents, Goldblatt learned his craft while working for Roger Corman on B-films *Piranha* and *Humanoids from the Deep*, learning how to creatively cut more into a film than the material itself supplied. Goldblatt went on to cut *Commando* and *The Howling*, then vaulted into mega-action spectacles such as *The Terminator, Terminator 2: Judgment Day, Rambo II, True Lies, Armageddon*, and the space epic *Starship Troopers*.

"The picture editor must be sensitive to the material as well as the director's vision. On the other hand, the editor cannot be a 'yes man' either. We should be able to look at the dailies with a fresh eye, without preconception, allowing ourselves to interface with the director, challenging him or her to stretch—to be open to trying new ideas. Sometimes you have to work with a director who has an insecure ego, who can't handle trying something new, but the good ones understand the need for a robust and stimulating collaboration."

When the picture editorial process is completed properly, the audience should be unaware of cuts and transitions. It should be drawn into the story by design, the action unfolding in a precise, deliberate way.

Figure 7.5 Mark Goldblatt, A.C.E.: picture editor.

"Consistency is vital," comments Mark Goldblatt. "The actor performs all of his scenes out of order over a period of weeks, sometimes months. It's very difficult to match and reduplicate something they shot six weeks apart that is then cut together and played on the screen in tandem. Sometimes you have to carve a consistent characterization out of the film, especially if the material isn't there to start with. You have to help build sympathy for the protagonist. If we don't care for or feel compassion for the protagonist, the film will always fail. If the audience doesn't care what happens to our hero, then all the special effects and action stuntwork money can buy will be rendered meaningless."

COST SAVINGS AND COSTLY BLUNDERS

Knowledgeable production companies bring in the picture editor well before the cameras start to roll. The picture editor's work starts with the screenplay itself, working with director, writer, producer, and cinematographer to determine final rewrite and decide how to capture the vision of the project onto film. At this time, the decision of film editing protocol is chosen: whether to shoot on film and cut on film (using a Moviola or KEM) or whether to shoot on film and digitize to cut on a nonlinear platform such as Final Cut Pro or an Avid.

Close attention must be paid to the expectations for screening the film, either as a work-in-progress or as test screenings. Needs also are addressed for screening the film in various venues outside of the immediate cutting environment. Is the project a character-driven film without many visual effects, or is it filled with visual special effects that require constant maintenance and attention?

These considerations should and do have a major effect on the protocol decision. The choice of whether to cut on film or nonlinear (and if nonlinear, on which platform) should not be left up to the whim or personal preference of the picture editor. The decision should serve the exact needs and purposes of the film project. Not too long ago, I was involved in a feature film that wasted well over $50,000 because the project had left the choice of the nonlinear platform to the picture editor. The collateral costs required for the platform's unique way of handling picture and audio files cost the production company thousands of dollars that would not have been spent if the appropriate nonlinear platform had been chosen for the project requirements.

Vast amounts of money also have been saved by not filming sequences that have been pre-edited from the screenplay itself, sequences deemed as unnecessary. Conversely, the opposite also is true. A number of years ago, I supervised the sound for a feature film that had a second-generation picture editor (his father had been a studio executive) and a first-time director. The film bristled with all kinds of high-tech gadgetry and had fun action sequences that cried out for a big stereo soundtrack. Halfway through principal photography, the director and picture editor deemed that a particular scene in the script was no longer relevant to the project, and, by cutting it, they would have the necessary money to secure a big, rich stereo track.

The producer was caught off-guard—especially as he had not been factored into the decision-making process—and threw a classic tantrum, demanding that the scene be shot because he was the producer and his word was absolute law. The director was forced to shoot a scene everybody knew would never make it into the picture. The amount of money it took to shoot this scene was just over $100,000! Consequently the picture could not afford the stereo soundtrack the director and picture editor both had hoped it would have.

All who wondered why this film was mixed monaurally have now been given the answer. All who do not know to what film I am refering, just remember this horror story for a rainy day—it could happen to you. By authorizing the extra bit of stop-motion animation you really want or an instrumental group twice as big as your blown budget can now afford, you or those in decision-making capacities can wipe out what is best for the picture as a whole by thoughtless, politically motivated, or egotistical nonsense.

SHOOT THE MASTER ANGLE AT A FASTER PACE

Millie Moore, A.C.E once said, "I love master shots, and I love to stay with them as long as possible, holding back the coverage for the more poignant moments of the scene. However, to be able to do that, the master must be well staged, and the dialog must be well paced. If the dialog is too slowly paced, you are limited to using the master only for establishing the geography of the actors and action. The editor is forced to go into the coverage sooner simply to speed up the action, rather than saving the closer coverage to capture more dramatic or emotional moments. At one time or another, every picture editor has been challenged to take poor acting material and try to cut a performance out of it that will work. A good picture editor can take an actor's good performance and cut it into a great performance."

"My work should appear seamless," remarks Millie Moore, picture editor of such projects as *Go Tell the Spartans, Those Lips—Those Eyes, Geronimo, Ironclads,* and Dalton Trumbo's *Johnny Got His Gun*. "If I make any cuts that reveal a jump in continuity or draw attention to the editing process, then I have failed in my job. An editor should never distract the audience by the editorial process—it yanks them right out of the movie and breaks the illusion."

Figure 7.6 Millie Moore: picture editor.

Planning and executing a successful shoot is handled like a military operation, with many of the same disciplines. The producer(s) are the joint chiefs-of-staff back at production company headquarters. The director is the general, the field commander, articulating his or her subjective interpretation of the script and ideas to manifest the director's vision on-screen. His or her lieutenant commanders—first assistant director, unit production manager, and production coordinator—hold productive and comprehensive staff meetings with the department heads (i.e., casting director, production designer, costume designer, art director, director of photography, sound mixer, picture editorial, grip and electrical, stunt coordinator, safety, transportation, craft services).

From the first read-through to the completion of storyboards with shot-by-shot renderings for complex and potentially dangerous action sequences, literally thousands of forms, graphs, maps, breakdowns, and call sheets are planned and organized, along with alternative scenes that can be shot if inclement weather prohibits shooting the primary sequences. Like a great military campaign, it takes the coordinated and carefully designed production plan of hundreds of highly experienced craftspersons to help bring the director's vision to reality.

Whether the film is a theatrical motion picture, television show, commercial, music video, documentary, or industrial training film, the basic principles don't change. Coverage should still be shot in masters, mediums, and close-ups with total regard for "crossing the line" and direction of action. Tracking (dolly) shots and crane shots must be carefully pre-planned and used when appropriate. Many of today's movies suffer from the belief that the camera must be constantly moving (what I call the MTV mentality). More often than not, this overuse of the camera-in-motion without regard to storytelling becomes weary and distracts the audience from the purpose of a film—to tell the story.

The editing style is dictated by the kind of film being made and the actual material the editor has. The picture editor knows which style is most appropriate after he or she has reviewed each day's footage and assimilated the director's concept and vision.

"You can take the same material and cut it any number of styles, changing dramatically how you want the audience to respond. You can build suspense—or dissipate it, setting the audience up for a shock or keep them on the edge of their seat. It's all in how you cut it," explains Mark Goldblatt. "I can get the audience on the edge of their seat, realizing danger is about to befall the hero, because the audience sees the danger, and all that they can do is grip their seats and encourage the hero to get the hell outta there—or I can lull them into thinking everything is fine, then shock them with the unexpected. It's the same footage—it's just the way I cut it.

"The picture editor's job is to determine which style is appropriate to that particular scene in that particular film. The picture editor may cut it completely differently for some other kind of film. The experienced picture editor will study the raw material and, after due consideration, allow it to tell him or her how it should be cut; then the editor just does it."

THE NONLINEAR ISSUE

"There's a mythology to electronic editing," sighs Goldblatt. "Don't misunderstand me, digital technology is here to stay—there's no going back—but there is a common misperception of the advantages. The technology makes it much easier to try more things. Let's face it, when you can do more things, you try more things. This way the editor can have his cut, the director can have his cut version, the producer can have their cut version, the studio can have their cut version(s) (often more than one), and, of course, they want the audience test screenings the very next day!

"The problem is that working in digital doesn't give you as much time to think about what you're doing. When we used to cut with film on Moviolas and splice the film together with tape, we had more time to think through the sequence—you know, problem solving. In digital, we can work much faster, so we sometimes don't get the chance to think the process through as thoroughly. Nowadays, you see a number of movies that obviously look as if they had not been given the opportunity to completely explore the potentials and possibilities of the material, often without respect of post-production schedules being totally out of control."

Many editors regard this problem as "digital thinking"—conceptualization driven by the executive perception that digital is cheaper. Unfortunately, most studio executives who currently make these kinds of creative decisions are not trained in the very craft they affect.

"I think that the editorial process is given short shrift since the coming of electronic editing," comments Millie Moore. "Because it is faster to cut electronically, less time is being scheduled for the editorial process. That could be fine if all else stayed the same; however, such is not the case. While post-production schedules are shrinking, many directors are shooting considerably more footage per scene—the more the footage, the more time it takes the editor to view and select.

"Also, because it is so fast to cut electronically, the editor is being asked to cut many more versions of each scene, which is also time-consuming. Compressing post-production schedules while increasing the workload defeats the advantage of electronic editing. Although it may be faster, it does not create the 'art form' of editing that takes know-how and time. The more you compress the time schedule, the more you crush the creative process.

"There is no doubt that digital is here to stay. However, there needs to be a greater awareness of what we have lost in the transition. Only when the time-tested values of film editing are honored will digital technology fulfill its potential. This starts at the grassroots level—film students who understand that digital manipulation is not the art form. It is a tool, just like the Moviola—it just works differently.

"Years ago sound editors didn't have magnetic stripe to cut sound; they cut optical track, having to paint their splices with an opaque fluid to remove pops and ticks that would otherwise be read by the exciter lamp in the sound head," Millie remembers. "When magnetic-stripe technology came along in the early fifties, it didn't change technique and principals of creative sound editing or sound design. It was a new tool to make the job easier. Now digital has come along to accelerate the process of cutting picture as well as sound. The technique and principals of how you cut a scene or design sound have not changed—we're just using a new kind of tool to do the job."

SOUND AND THE PICTURE EDITOR

Millie Moore, A.C.E. at one time contemplated her career. "Prior to pursuing a career in the picture editing arena, I was a post-production supervisor and an associate producer making documentary films for Jack Douglas. We were the first people to use portable 1/4" tape. Ryder Sound had always handled our sound facility transfer and mixing requirements. Loren Ryder had brought in the Perfectone, which was the forerunner of the Nagra, which was manufactured in Switzerland. Ryder Sound used to come up to Jack Douglas's office where we would shoot the introductions to the show."

Millie was head of all post-production for Jack, turning out fifty-two shows a year and a pilot. Eventually, Millie was sent down to Ryder Sound to learn how to use the Perfectone herself so that Jack did not have to always hire a Ryder Sound team for every need. For some time, Millie was the only woman sound recordist in Hollywood, using this new 1/4" technology from Europe.

On more than one occasion when Millie went to Ryder Sound to pick up recording equipment, Loren asked her what kind of situation she was heading to shoot that day. "He would often suggest taking along a new microphone that they had just acquired or some other pieces of equipment that they thought might be of value. In short order, I became experienced in various kinds of microphones and amplifiers—of course, I spent half my time on the telephone, asking questions of the guys back at Ryder.

"I ended up teaching other people to use the equipment for Jack, especially when we went global in our shooting venues. Jack wanted me to move up to a full-fledged producer, but I turned him down. Frankly, I didn't want to live out of a suitcase.

"It was then I decided that I wanted to move over to picture editing. It became very satisfying. I was working on several projects at once, either hands-on or as a supervising consultant for Jack. If there was anything really special that needed care, he and I would go into a cutting room and close the door and go over the material together.

"It was very challenging for us, as we shot on both 16mm and 35mm film. On-location material was shot in 16mm, and interviews were shot in 35mm, so we had to combine these two formats. For a long time, I was the person who had to do the optical counts."

It was time to move on. Millie wanted to move into features, but in those days it was extremely hard for women to get lead position jobs, especially under union jurisdictions.

The independently produced *Johnny Got His Gun* was Millie's first feature film. The producer, who had worked at Jack Douglas's, wanted Millie to handle the Dalton Trumbo picture, an extremely powerful antiwar film.

"Every director with whom I worked was a new learning experience. However, I feel that I learned the most from working with Michael Pressman. He and I were still young when we first paired up on *The Great Texas Dynamite Chase*. Although it was not my first feature film as an editor, it was his first film as a director. Since then, we have collaborated on various projects, which have given me the opportunity to watch him develop his craft and grow. I have learned a great deal about the editing process from him. Aside from directing films, he has wisely spent a great deal of time directing theatre productions. I feel that his work in the theatre has allowed him to gain a greater understanding of staging and blocking, as well as an expertise in working with actors. His background in theatre has broadened him, enabling him to get more textured and full performances as well as more interesting visual shots. When I look at dailies, I can frequently tell when the director has had theatrical training. Whenever I talk to young people getting started, I always encourage them to get involved in local theatre so that they can gain skill in staging and blocking, as well as working with actors."

Millie is very discerning with her craft. "The best editing is invisible. You should walk away from seeing a picture without being aware of the cuts that were made, unless they were made for a specific effect."

"For the most part, I do not believe in using multiple editors. It's a very rare case that you don't feel the difference of each editor's sense of timing. I mean, what is editing, but an inner sense of timing—setting the pace of a film? In fact, one of the most important jobs of the picture editor is to control the tempo and the pace of the story. Through the cutting art of the picture editor, sequences can be sped up or slowed down, performances can be vastly improved, intent and inflections of dialog radically redesigned, giving an entirely new slant on a scene and how it plays out. When you keep switching from one editor to another through the course of the film, it lacks synchronic integrity. Even if you don't see it, you will feel a difference. It takes a rare director to hand over a project that utilizes multiple picture editors and end up with a fluid and seamless effort."

"Whenever I had to have a second picture editor on the team, I always tried to have the choice of that editor. Very simply, I wanted that editor to have a pace and timing as close to my own as possible—so the picture would not suffer. Most often, I turned my own picture assistants, whom I had trained to have a taste and feel for the cutting to be similar to my own, into the second picture editor."

Millie has cut several projects on an Avid, but she does not allow the technology to dominate her. "Nonlinear editing is just another tool, but God bless it when cutting battle scenes, action sequences, or scenes with visual special effects. For me, this is where the non-linear technology makes a substantial contribution."

Millie has altogether different feelings if she is working on a project that does not require special visual effects. "I don't need all the electronic bells and whistles if I am working on a character-driven film. It is much more satisfying, and frankly, you will be surprised to learn, a lot cheaper. Once all of the collateral costs are shaken out of the money tree, working on film with either a Moviola or a KEM is more cost-effective. Additionally, you will discover that you are not as restrained by screening venues as when you are working in digital.

And for those of you who discount the Moviola because it is looked upon as old or even "museum" technology, maybe you need to check out the end credits on Steven Spielberg's 2002 feature film *Catch Me If You Can*—cut on a Moviola. If you do not know the various tools of your trade, you may find yourself losing out on opportunities because you are deceived by the perception that technology is the driving force, and not the art form of your craft.

"I miss the Moviola. Cutting on an Avid is much easier physically, but it is much quicker to become brain-dead. Working on the Moviola is a kinesthetic experience—the brain and body working together, preventing dullness and brain fatigue. I could work many more hours on the Moviola than I can on an Avid, and stay in better physical shape as well. Working on a digital machine, there is too much interference between you and the film—it fractures and dissipates your concentration. The wonderful thing about the Moviola is that there is absolutely nothing between you and film. You touch it, you handle it, you place the film into the picture head gate and snap it shut, and you are off and running.

"To me, editing is as much a visceral as it is a mental act. Consequently, I love being able to touch film and have it running through my fingers as it goes through the Moviola. Even though working directly on film has a number of drawbacks, such as the noise of a Moviola, broken sprocket holes, splices, and much more, working on a keyboard gives one very little of the tactile experience of film. The young people today who are becoming editors have been deprived of this experience, and I think that it is very sad.

"Young editors today are not learning to develop a visual memory. When you cut on film, you sit and you look and you look and you look. You memorize the film. You figure out in your head where you are going, because you do not want to go back and tear those first splices apart and do them over. On film, you know why you put the pieces of film together the way that you did. You've spent time thinking about it. While you were doing other chores or running down a KEM roll to review and out-take, your subconscious was massaging your visual memory through the process—problem solving. On a computer, you can start hacking away at anything that you want to throw together. If it doesn't look good, so what—you hit another button and start over. There is no motivation to develop visual memory."

The use of visual memory is critical, for both picture editor and sound editor. "There is as much to do in sound as in picture editing. At a running, someone might say 'Oh, Millie, that shot is too long,' and I would answer 'No, wait. Sound is going to fill that in.' Love scenes that seem to drag on forever in a progress screening, play totally differently when the music is added. When I cut the sequence, I can hear music in my head, so I cut the rhythm and the pace of the love scene against that."

Young editors are not developing this ability because it is too easy to put in an audio CD and transfer temp music cues into the computer to cut against. This works when they have CDs on hand, but what about if they need to cut a sequence without them? Ask them to cut film on a KEM or a Moviola in the change room of a dubbing stage, and watch the panic set in! The training is just not there. Some new editors panic if they don't have a time-code reference to which they can pin their work."

Master picture editors will tell you that if you want to learn how to construct a film, watch it without sound. Sound tricks you—it carries you and points you, unawares, in many directions. By the same token, for many films if you only listen to the soundtrack you do not have the director's entire vision. The visual image and the audio track are organically and chemically bound together.

Sound effects and music are as important a "voice" in films as the spoken dialog; the audience uses them to define the characters' physical being and action. Sound effects go right in at the audience; they bypass the dialog track in that they are proverbial—like music, they hit you right where you live. They also are extremely powerful in the storytelling process. In the performance of a single note, music sets the tone for what you are about to see and probably how you are about to feel. Good picture editors know this, and, as they sculpt and shape the pace and tempo of the film, they keep the power of the coming soundtrack well in mind.

HOWARD SMITH, A.C.E

Howard Smith, A.C.E., veteran picture editor of both big-action and character-driven pictures (*The Abyss, Near Dark, Dante's Peak, Twilight Zone: The Motion Picture*), made the transition from cutting picture on film with a Moviola and a KEM to cutting nonlinear via the Avid.

"As the picture editor, my primary task is to work with the director to try to shape the material so that it is the most expressive of what the film is intended to be. You try to tell a story, and tell that story as effectively as it can be told."

"It has been said that the editing process is essentially the last scripting of the movie. It's been scripted by a writer, the project goes into production, where it is written as images, and then it goes into the editing process—we do the final shaping. Obviously, we are trying to achieve the intent of the original written piece. Things will and do happen—in produc-

Figure 7.7 Howard Smith, A.C.E.: picture editor.

tion through performance, through art direction, through camera—that happen through stylistic elements that can nudge the storytelling a little that way, or this way. One has to be very responsive and sensitive to the material—I think that is the first line that an editor works at.

"They look at the dailies, preferably with the director so the director can convey any input as to his intentions of the material. There may be variations in performance, and without the input from the director it will be more difficult to know his or her intentions versus happenstance, in terms of the choice of performance.

"Early takes of a scene may be very straight and dramatic. As the filming continues, it may loosen up—variations could bring countless approaches to how you may cut the sequence. Which way does the editor take it? The material will give all kinds of paths that the editor can follow.

"Years ago, there was a movement for editors to go on location, to be near the director and crew during production. This can often be a good thing, as a good editor can lend guidance and assistance in continuity and coverage to the shoot.

"As we have moved into electronic editing and the ability to send footage and video transfers overnight via air couriers or even interlocking digital telephonic feeds, the pressure for editors to be on location with the director has lessened. Personally, I do not think that this is necessarily better. At the very least, we lose something when we do not have that daily interaction as the director and editor do when they share the process of reviewing the dailies together.

"During production, the editor is cutting together the picture based on the intention of the script, and the intention as expressed by the director. By the time the production has wrapped, within a week or two the editor has put together the first cut of the movie.

"The director has traditionally gotten some rest and recuperation during those first couple of weeks before he returns to the editing process. For approximately ten weeks, as per the DGA contract, the director and editor work together to put the film together in its best light for the director's cut.

"What editing will do is focus—moment to moment, the most telling aspects of the scene. When you do this shaping, it is such an exciting experience, the mixing of creative chemistry. Most directors find that the most exciting and often satisfying process of the film-making experience is the film editing process. It is during these critical weeks that everything really comes to life. Sure, it is alive on the page of the script, it is alive on the set during principal photography, but when you are cutting the picture together, the film takes an elevated step that transcends all the processes up until that point—it really becomes a movie.

"Obviously the addition of sound effects and music, which will come later after we have locked the picture, will greatly elevate the creative impact of the film, taking it to new heights—but that is only to take the film to a higher level from a known quantity that we have achieved through picture editorial. Great sound will make the movie seem to look better and be more visually exciting; a great music score will sweep the audience into the emotional directions that the director hopes to achieve—but the greatest soundtrack in the world is not going to save or camouflage bad picture cuts.

"With the advent of nonlinear technology we are now able to add in temp music and sound effects in a far more complex way than we ever could with a Moviola or KEM; we are able to work with sound and music even as we are cutting the picture—as we go along. We now see editors spending more time, themselves, dealing with those elements. I don't know if that is a bad thing—especially if you have the time to do it.

"I remember when I was working on *The Abyss*. We were not working digitally yet. There were many, many action sequences. Jim Cameron [the director] expressed to me that you can't really know if the cut is working until the sound effects are in. I thought that was very interesting. It was the first time that that way of thinking had ever been put to me—and you know Jim and sound!

"On a visual level, if you are working on a big special-effects picture with a lot of visual effects, and they are not finished, what have we always done? We used to put in a partially finished version along with one or more slugs of SCENE MISSING to show that there is a missing shot, or we shoot the storyboard panels that represent the shots.

"When I cut an action piece, I always cut it anticipating what I know the sound designers could do with the action. I have a car chase sequence, and the vehicles are roaring by the camera. I will hold a beat after the last car has passed by, giving sound effects time to pan a big 'whoosh' off-screen and into the surround speakers. If I do not give that beat, the editor is not going to have the moment to play out the whoosh-by sound effect, and the rerecording mixer is not going to be able to pan the whoosh off-screen and into the surround speakers.

"That was part of my editing construct, based on my editing experience previously. It would leave a little bit of air for the composer, knowing that music would have to make a comment, and music needs a few seconds to do that, and then sound effects would take over.

"I remember Jerry Goldsmith [film composer] saying, 'They always want me to write music for the car chase, and I know that you are not going to be able to hear it—but I write it anyway.' We know that even if the sound effects are very loud, if you did not have the music there, you would feel its absence. The emotional drive is gone. Through experience, these are things that you learn over a period of years.

"Because of the Avid and the Final Cut Pro, I am now cutting sound effects into the sequences almost as soon as I make my visual cuts. I layer in visual type sounds, temp music, etc. Now, when I am playing the newly cut sequence for the director for the first time, I have a rich tapestry of picture and audio for him to evaluate, rather than the way we did it before nonlinear days, when we would watch the cut sequence with only a production track and mentally factor in sounds to come, sounds that definitely have an effect and influence on the pace—the rhythm and the voice of the scene. This tells the director if the film is working on an emotional level. It adds this emotional component immediately, so you can feel the effectiveness of the sequence, in terms of the storytelling overall.

"These sounds are not cut in to be used as final pieces. Do not misunderstand. I am not doing the sound editor's job, nor do I pretend to be able to, nor do I want to. I know full well that when we turn the picture over to sound editorial, my sound effects and temp music are going to be used only as a guide for intent, then they will be stripped out and replaced by better material.

"Working with Cameron was a real concept for me. He would bark, 'Let's get some sound effects in here right now! Let's see if this scene is kicking butt—right now!' So we would."

This puts the supervising sound editor and his or her sound designer to work, problem solving these questions and needs far earlier than in the traditional thinking that most budgets allow. Traditional scheduling and budgeting not only fail dismally to fulfill the Camerons of the filmmaking industry (who already understand this audio equation to picture editing) and an ever-growing number of filmmakers inspired and empowered by understanding what is possible—yet trying to function with outdated philosophies to budget means and old-thinking time schedules are doomed to make future cinematic achievements even more rare.

JULIAN SEMILIAN: NOT AFRAID TO TRY NEW THINGS

"There is an off-beat way of editing, as though the editor went and did all the things most editors would say they would never do. And because everything is so frenetic, it works very well—but it is clearly, purposely done that way, and it doesn't have a staccato rhythm. This was not like having nice little rhythms—and I think there is a connection between jazz music and editing. There are very interesting rhythms that exist in jazz, in the way a saxophone plays something or the vibes, that can give you a clue of how to observe what goes on in a scene, and how to cut in an interesting way—and still not feel that the rhythm is off or that it is not right."

Julian is certainly not a big fan of the "MTV"-style of picture editing that has overwhelmed the perception of commercial editing. However, he does not dismiss it completely. "One good thing about what MTV did, is that it allowed more editors to be daring in transitions. But, on the other hand, that frenetic fast cutting can certainly get on your nerves. If you look at the work of good editors back even sixty or seventy years ago, you can see some of these styles used at the right moment, you can see these styles used for the right kind of things for the right reasons for a few cuts. So MTV is not all that new.

"It is just like taking a delicate textured food and sticking it in the microwave for fifty times longer than the package recommends—it just wears you out and draws the audience's attention from the film and says, 'Look ma, I'm editing a movie!'"

Figure 7.8 Julian Semilian, film editor and editing faculty instructor at the North Carolina School of the Arts, School of Filmmaking. (Photo by David Yewdall)

Julian does not edit by whims, fads, or shocks. "If it is appropriate, I use it. Otherwise I do not want to break that thread of connection between the audience and the image on the screen by distracting or pulling them out of the film."

Julian learned his art form the old-ashioned way; he studied film, making it yield its secrets of why some films work and others do not. It is the craftsmanship of editing that most often makes the difference.

"I immigrated to the United States when I was seventeen years old. I worked in Minnesota as a photographer, which evolved into making scientific film studies of various animal behaviors. I became very interested in how these pieces of film were put together to tell a story. In those days we didn't have videotape. I went to the movie theatre and watched the films over and over again from the matinee until the last showing. I started taking notes on how scenes were edited, watching them on the screen and one time writing the sequence and the next time trying to catch how much time they would hold on a shot. So I was constantly making movies in my head. Then when I started to make my own movies, it came very naturally. I love to watch movies and get new ideas and discover new things."

Julian is one of the most popular faculty instructors at the North Carolina School of the Arts School of Filmmaking, and especially inspiring to his students in the editing discipline. "Even though it has been said that you cannot teach creativity, I want to give my students an opening in learning how to *see*. One of the ways I do this is by looking at films and analyzing what good editors have done. And even though you may not be able to tell everything because you don't know what material they had to work with, I have enough experience to conjecture, and get a sense of what might have happened. I want them to open up to the validity of their own imaginations. I think that is the most important thing, for them to become confident with their imagination. The other thing I want them to do is to become diligent in pursuing that.

"For instance, a lot of times they perceive that something is not working well, but they do not allow that perception to take effect—to work on that piece—how to change it, how to carve it, how to enhance it. And they know very well it doesn't work, because if you show them, they say 'Oh, yeah, it doesn't work.'

"And I'll say, 'Okay, but have you done anything about it?'

"They know there is something they could do, but they avoid that perception in the back of their minds. I want to push them as much as I can into becoming aware, becoming sensitized to how they really feel.

"You assume that most of them, if they are here, have it in them to do it—they have gotten this far just to qualify to attend film school. But some of them are too mentally blocked for me not to get through. Maybe it will happen in the future—you know, the light bulb goes off because you plant a seed in them—and maybe not. But at least I know that I am doing my job by going as far as I can with them."

In addition to the plethora of hands-on editing assignments for students to cut picture using Avids and Final Cut Pro nonlinear workstations, Julian helps empower his students to think like editors, by studying classic films and how they were cut. "Say you are doing a dramatic picture, and you have a number of problems. One problem is that you have an actor who is not working out. Then how do you carve out, how do you whittle a performance—how do you get to recognize the so called 'good bits,' and how do you recognize a context where those bits can work very well?

"If you have good actors, how do you use editing to enhance either a moment or a performance? There is a wonderful bit, for instance, that I show students from *One Flew Over the Cuckoo's Nest*. Jack Nicholson is being interviewed at the beginning by Doctor Spivey (played by Dean Brooks). I show this two-person scene to the students and then ask them, 'Is this good editing?' And they'll shrug and say, 'Well, it's regular editing.'

"Then I'll ask them, 'What do you think the editor did?'

"Then there is this kind of silence. 'Well, uh . . . he kinda . . . cut the scene . . . mmm,' being very vague.

"So I show them certain segments in the scene and help them recognize what problems the editor might have had at each moment. To give you one little example; Nicholson takes out his cigarette pack and asks if he can light a cigarette, and the doctor says 'Fine.'

"He takes the cigarette out and puts it in his mouth, and the shot clearly continues with him lighting the cigarette. As he puts the cigarette in his mouth he looks over at the doctor, and the doctor is doing something, I don't remember what it is, and then you cut to Nicholson lighting the cigarette. So a wonderful little moment was created simply by understanding what made an interesting moment. By cutting Nicholson's performance into two shots, with the doctor in between, you give the scene a new kind of dynamism.

"For instance, in the same scene, the doctor reads Nicholson's file. Instead of staying on the doctor reading the file, you stay on Nicholson. And the shot of Nicholson—it's at the very beginning of the film when we know nothing about Nicholson's character as the doctor reads Nicholson's file. He's done this, he's gotten in fights, he's done this and this—but the shot stays on Nicholson and not on the doctor reading the file. It's wonderful—you have the person and you know who he is. The editorial choice is simple, but a lot of people would never have thought to do it like that. Then the moment when you cut back to the doctor—who says, 'You lazy . . .' and the way he moves his head as he says his last line. Then the doctor looks at the file. Then you cut back to Nicholson, who looks up at him in that Nicholson 'upward-way' and he says, 'Chewing gum in class?'

"And the doctor glances up at that moment at Nicholson, and then the shot cuts back to Nicholson who kind of does this cool face expression—and then back to the doctor taking it all in. And it is such a perfection of looks, moves, and reactions. The timing and dance of this is so perfect and there is meaning that is created through that kind of editing."

TOUCH IT, LIVE IT

Leander Sales also helms the picture editorial discipline at the North Carolina School of the Arts School of Filmmaking with Julian. Even though he has similar thoughts as to style and the art form, he approaches it differently. If Julian teaches the way a psychiatrist works, then Leander is the boot camp drill sergeant. It is the two styles of instruction that is turning out such powerful, empowered, and qualified picture editors from the North Carolina School of the Arts School of Filmmaking.

Leander knows the vital importance of the synchronizer and flatbed editing machines. "If you are going to be in film school, then *touch* film. Get to know film and the whole process. If you can get a chance to cut on a Steenbeck you will get a true sense of history. If the kids would just work with the film on the flatbed, I think they would understand the history of film a lot better, because they are living it. Of course, that's where I came from; I learned cutting on film, but now everybody is cutting on the Avid or the Final Cut Pro—including me. I appreciate those formats as well. But I used to work on film and it is amazing how you can manipulate it, how you can look at every frame, just hold it up to the light and you can look at every frame. We are living in a digital world and will never go back to cutting on film, but I still think people should understand that history.

"I remember working with an editor by the name of Sam Pollard. He would just hold the film up and look at where he made his marks and how he made his cuts and, wow—you look at it and it is like life is just frozen in that frame. Now you run them all together through the machine, at twenty-four frames a second, and you create something new.

"I remember the first scene I was cutting. Sam Pollard gave me an opportunity to cut a scene in *Clockers*. He gave me the footage and he said, 'Here it is, go cut it.' That was it— go cut it. I remember it was the scene of the guys crushing up the car—pretty much two-camera coverage with all these jump cuts in it. And I was like, wow, this is my first scene. It was so exciting to put it together and at the end of the day, have Sam come up and look at it and say, 'Okay.' Then another scene came and another scene came. So, I was very happy to finally get a credit as an editor.

"What's interesting is that Sam doesn't like assistants who are working with him but do not want to cut because the next growth step should be to cut. As an assistant you should want to move up to be an editor. I feel the same way. When I hire somebody as an apprentice, your desire should be to move up to be an assistant, and then an editor. And if your heart isn't there, I'm thinking that I could have hired somebody whose heart would be there—who would really have a strong hunger to edit—not someone who just wants to hang out in the editing room, but someone who wants to do it. It's really important to have that hunger, because once you have that hunger, nothing else can stop you, nothing! And with the accessibility of editing equipment right now with Final Cut Pro, there is absolutely no excuse. Go and get a little mini-DV camera and shoot. There is no reason why you shouldn't be making a film—especially if you want to do it.

FINDING AN EDITING JOB

Going to a film school is one thing, but how do you go out and actually secure your first job to start building a resume of experience and learn your craft by the tried and true method of on-the-job training? When I ran my post-production companies in Los Angeles, we had adopted the Roger Corman approach to training and bringing new blood into the industry's workforce. Personal introductions were vital to us. Flashing a diploma from USC or UCLA did not mean squat. In fact, we had one graduate from USC whom we first had to wean from the misinformation he had learned there and retrain him in the real world. Today he is a very successful sound editor who is supervising his own product, and we are extremely proud of him and the other thirty four apprentices we brought in and trained.

I would give apprentices one month to figure out if they were in love with the *idea* of working in post-production or if they were in love with *working* in post-production. Therein lies the first major hurdle. If they worked hard and showed initiative and responsibility, they were advanced to become second sound assistants within a few months. Before too long, they would start cutting practice sessions (Foley was always a great starting place to learn the art of synchronization and using the equipment) or cutting background effects. If they showed the right growth in technique and creative philosophical style, they would be entrusted with a real cutting assignment as they evolved into an editor's role. When the time came we would write letters to accompany their paycheck stubs to verify days of employment if and when they wished to join the union.

These kinds of opportunities are not as available as one might think, and even when they are there is great competition for the precious few apprentice starting positions open. How then do you "break in?" Some get that first break through creative fiction, along with a lot of self-confidence and the ability to be a quick study. This is exactly how Julian Semilian bluffed his way into his first job.

"While I was still in Minnesota I had a job syncing dailies, so I at least knew how that part of the job was supposed to be done," remembers Julian. "So I came out to Hollywood. The second day I was there I walked over to A.F.I. (American Film Institute), and there was a notice posted that they needed an editor. I walked in and thickened up my Rumanian accent to talk to the director and said, 'Hi, I'm Julian Semilian and I'm an editor. I'm just new in town, and I'd like to do your film.'

"They weren't paying anything, but I just needed to get the experience. He asked me if I had a resume, and I told him that I didn't have it with me, but that I would bring it by the next day. So I went home and pulled out my typewriter and invented this whole little career on paper. I took it back to the director the next day and he said 'Okay, good, you've got the job.'

"I had never even used a Moviola before. Fortunately, they hadn't shot the film yet, so I was in good shape. There was a guy cutting a film next door to the room where we were going to cut. I walked in and again I thickened up my accent and introduced myself, 'I'm very new from Rumania. I was an editor there, but we never used this kind of equipment.'

"He was very helpful in showing me how to use a Moviola. After a while he showed me what he did. I already knew how to use the splicer and the rewinds, but I needed to master the technique of using the Moviola as a tool. So by the time the film crew actually started shooting I think I was pretty much up to speed with the equipment."

For Leander Sales it started with an introduction from his uncle, who was and is a successful character actor. "After I spent two years in Italy it was my uncle, Ron Dortch, who said that he knew a guy who was a sound editor—go and talk with him. So I went to see Rudolph Gaskins, who was working out of a sound facility by the name of Sound One in New York at that time. I sat with Rudy and said that I was looking for a job and that I would really like to get into editing. He said, 'Well, I don't know of anything that is happening right now.'

"So I told him that if he found anything to let me know—and that I would do it for free! During the day I was selling sofa beds and at night I could do whatever this editorial job would be. 'You don't have to pay me.' I told him. 'I just want to learn what happens in the editing room.'

"He said, 'Alright, I'll keep that in mind. No one has ever offered to work for free.'

"Two weeks later he called back. 'There's this guy coming back from Atlanta and he's going to start sound editing and he is looking for an apprentice sound editor for a film entitled *School Daze*. The director is Spike Lee.'

"Oh, wow! Spike Lee!' He gave me his number and told me to give him a call. I gave him a call. Spike came to the phone and said, 'Yeah, this is Spike.'

"I said, 'This is Leander Sales and I would like to apply for that job as apprentice sound editor.'

"He said, 'Talk with Maurice Schell, the supervising sound editor.'

"I went to interview with Maurice and he said, "This is only a four-month job.'

"I replied, 'Yo, man, please, please, I really want this' job.' Maurice asked if I had ever worked on a film before. No, I hadn't. He asked if I had ever gone to film school—no. He asked if I had a resume—no, nothing. I just have a desire to do this.'

"He said, 'Well, we'll think about it.' That was his reaction—we'll think about it.

"He called me up on a Monday and he said that I would start working on Wednesday. And I said, 'I'm there!!'

"I had four months to learn what I could—four months! That's how I saw it. They would say, 'Go and get this or go and get that.' And I would run to get it! And I would run back, because I didn't want to miss anything. Syncing dailies, marking up track, threading up the Moviola—all of that. So I would run to get their breakfast or coffee and run back—and they kept saying 'Boy, that guy is fast!' "

Leander also helped a few new talents along the way. "Determination and desire is where it is at. I remember there was this guy who wanted to get into editing. He was with craft services for one of Spike's films where he would set up the food for dailies. You know, people would come and have dinner while they watched dailies. And then one day he said to me, 'Man, I'm really interested in editing. Do you think I could hang out in the editing room after I finish craft services to watch you guys put these dailies back together to get ready for the next day?'

"I said, 'Sure, come on.'

"And every day he would break down the craft services very quickly after dailies. It was my turn to say 'Wow! That guy is fast!' He would come back to the editing room with us to watch and learn, and now he's editing, he is a sound editor."

People with handicaps are handicapped only if they allow it to become a stumbling block. Steve Rice, whom you will read about in Chapter 14, was missing his left foot due to a Viet Cong rocket during his service in the Vietnam War. Nobody wanted to hire him at first, until I offered him his first job as a combination grip/gaffer for a documentary I shot on the Navajo reservation. To my surprise, he overcompensated (as many people with perceived handicaps do) and worked as hard as three men.

A few months after that I asked if he wanted to learn post-production editorial, so I asked him to show up at the studio two hours before the boss arrived—and in two hours I taught him how to sync dailies and log them in properly. With just that two-hour instruction and his desire and passion to do the work, the head of the studio hired him on the spot. Steve went on to become one of the most amazing dialog editors I have ever known.

Conscious or subconscious prejudices and negative perceptions are probably the single most inhibiting obstacle anyone with a handicap will have to overcome—and not just physical handicaps.

Leander had a similar opportunity to give a handicapped person a chance. "We had a guy come in who had a condition with his leg, so he was hobbling along with a cane. He could not walk without this cane, but he said, 'I want to be the apprentice.'

"I looked at him and said, 'I don't know, because you've got to run to the city and get these heavy dailies, these sound rolls and film from the lab. Do you think you can do this, are you up for this?'

"He said, 'I really want to do this, man, I really want this.'

"I asked, 'What about your leg?'

"He told me that he was in physical therapy but he knew he could do it if he was just given the opportunity to try. So I told him that I would try him for a week. Oh man, he worked so hard. He went and did his physical therapy on the weekends. He would hobble, but he always got those dailies to us."

MORE CRAFTSMEN AND WOMEN OF COLOR

"I think I was fortunate—no, I was lucky to have worked with Spike Lee. Spike is one of the most prolific filmmakers in our time. Here is a filmmaker who said he wanted to make a certain number of films, and he is doing just that. I worked on nine of his films, back-to-back—starting out as an apprentice and working my way up to editor, with *one* filmmaker. Oh, I worked on other films in between and after that, but I have been so fortunate to have that opportunity to work with someone who works year after year, and not just as a filmmaker, but just trying to get more people of color into the unions. Because it is lily white out there. For example, you go to a set with an all-white crew and all-white cast, and most people think, okay, that's just normal, that's the way it is. But as soon as you get a black crew, or a mostly black or half-black crew, people start thinking 'What's wrong with this picture?'

"What's wrong with this picture is that many white people think people of color should never be in positions of power."

Now may be a good time to review Chapter 4 before you start shooting your film; this way, as you press on into the post-production phases described in Chapters 8 through 19, you will develop a conscious determination to plan for success.

Chapter 8
Temp Dubs and Test Screenings: A Critical Objective View

"We've just had a test screening, and the upshot is that we are throwing out the first reel and starting the picture with reel two."

John Carpenter, director, after a last-minute test screening during the predubbing of Escape from New York

Okay, so you think you have a sure-fire hit—the most important picture of the year. Of course, every other producer and director believes that his or her film is the one, but that's only to be expected. You lived with the project for months, perhaps even years. You know every word, every moment, every cut. Actually, all this places you at a tremendous disadvantage. You have lost your objectivity, especially if you were in the throws of the love–hate evolution that so often grips intensively involved craftspeople who are completely immersed in their project.

TEST SCREENING

The time comes to arrange a test screening. Don't screen the picture for your friends and colleagues—they are not the audience that buys the millions of tickets you hope to sell. You made the film with a particular audience in mind, one that buys the tickets for the genre you are carefully nurturing. You kept a keen eye on your audience during the writing of the script; you kept your audience in mind as you set up the shots; you kept your audience in mind as you started cutting the sequences together—or maybe you didn't.

If you took the popular and myth-ridden stance that you make a film to suit your own taste—a movie you would like to see—without considering the ticket-buying audience, then you really must have a test audience screening, and quick! Of course you made a movie you would like to see, but that does not mean you throw away the collaborative and advisory powers of a carefully planned test audience screening.

Keep in mind the words "carefully planned" in preparing a test screening. The last thing you want is to have a test screening for just your friends. They often do not give an accurate and critically objective judgment of how your film will be received. Oddly enough, this is one area many filmmakers fail to handle correctly, often getting distorted results.

Several years ago, my team and I handled the sound design and editorial chores for a first-time director's feature film. The producer contracted a firm to recruit a test audience to attend a quiet test screening on a studio lot. We sat in the back row with the producer and the nervous director as the opening scenes rolled. Within ten minutes, audience members got up and walked out. In the middle of the third reel, the action on the screen portrayed roving vampires as they entered a quiet country bar and had just begun feeding on the patrons. Bill Paxton rose up from sucking the blood from a victim's neck with great delight and said, "Finger lickin' good!"

Test audience viewers suddenly rose in groups and left the theatre en masse. From an audience of just over 300, we counted 152 people who had walked out by the middle of the film. The director, Katherine Bigelow (later to direct *K-19: The Widowmaker*) was hiding in the back row, tears rolling down her cheeks.

Many producers would have been sharpening the razor and drawing the warm bathwater by this time, but the veteran producer of this picture had been here before. He knew what had happened. The test screening firm had recruited the wrong audience by telling them that the picture was a country-western version of *Raiders of the Lost Ark*, an action-adventure film. The audience expected a PG-rated, fun-filled action picture, but got an R-rated blood-and-guts story with a very dark and graphic edge. Instead of panicking, the producer knew to schedule another test screening, this time making sure the right kind of target market audience was recruited.

Jim Troutman, supervising sound editor for such films as *Duel, Sugarland Express, Jaws, Charlie Varrick,* and *Midway,* recalls how a test audience screening saved a very important and legendary moment in *Jaws.* "We thought the picture was ready to try out on a midwestern audience, so we took it to Dallas, Texas, for a test screening preview. Verna Fields [vice-president of production at Universal] and I sat in the middle of the theatre with an audiocassette recorder. We recorded the audience's vocal reactions against the film's audio track as it played on the screen. It was the scene where Roy Scheider is chumming off the back of the boat, trying to attract the great white shark. He turns to look back at the cabin— the shark lunges up full-screen behind him. It's an enormous shock scare. The audience went nuts! We thought we had allowed plenty of time for the audience to settle down as Roy backed up into the cabin where he delivers his line to Robert Shaw, 'You're gonna need a bigger boat.'"

"Well, when we played back the cassette tape to listen to the audience reactions, we discovered that the pop-scare was so big that it took far longer than we had anticipated for the audience screams and chatter to settle down—they never heard Roy's punchline. So we went back to the cutting room, found the trim boxes of that scene, and pulled the 'out' trims of the sequence. We reconstructed an additional thirty-five feet of action showing Roy's shocked reaction and a more deliberate pace in backing up into the cabin. This gave enough time for the audience to settle down and hear Roy's delivery, giving the audience a much needed moment of comic relief."

All through the post-editorial process of *Escape from New York,* Debra Hill and John Carpenter had not test screened the picture for an objective test audience. We were deep into the sound mixing process, so deep in fact that we were nearly finished with the predubbing process on Stage "D" at Goldwyn Studios and about to commence with the final mix. Just as we were wrapping a predub pass, John Carpenter and his picture editor, Todd Ramsay, came onto the stage, looking a little pale and unable to hide the fact that their confidence was shaken. They informed us that they had just had a test screening, and much to their surprise a number of comments motivated them to rethink the final cut. They were going into an emergency tactical meeting with producers Debra Hill and Larry Franco.

When the dust settled, it was decided to scrap the entire first reel of the picture. In essence, the film would now start with Reel 2. So the heist scene at Denver's Federal Reserve was cut, the subterranean subway flight from Denver to Barstow was cut, as was the subsequent ambush by a federal police SWAT team and the take-down of Snake Plisken. Was it the right decision? According to preview cards of the test screening, it was.

With the advent of the Internet, producers and studio execs are having a difficult time having test screenings without finding their film posted all over the Internet within hours of the test—even though they are weeks or months away from actually finishing the film. This is making it extremely hard to trust a film to an intimate "test" group and feel confident about keeping the warts and unfinished misperceptions out of instant global chat rooms. Many producers are reacting by saying that they will dispense with the practice of test screenings—but we all know that is not a realistic option either. Somehow you have to get the ultrasound image of the mother's womb to see if you are going to have a healthy bouncing baby or if you are about to hatch a fungus-amungus. Somehow you have to deal with test screenings!

USE OF TEMP DUBS

As the cost of making motion pictures has increased, so too has the use of test screenings. Directors and producers are reticent to show their work-in-progress films to studio executives, potential distributors, and test audiences with only the raw production track. The barroom brawl looks laughable with the actors flying wildly from Sunday haymakers with no chin-punch impacts and body falls. What will the audience think of this long dolly shot that moves at a snail's pace and does not seem to progress the action? Arnold Schwarzenegger jumps the fence, swings his powerful 45-caliber pistol up, and shoots—the production track sounds like a kid's cap gun! The new computer-generated image of the tyrannosaurus rex rises over the actors and spreads its jaws in a menacing roar, but no sound emanates because the beast is nothing but a CGI (computer-generated image) composited against live actors filmed months earlier against a blue or green screen.

Enter the temp dub. The producer calls in the supervising sound editor and reviews the list of needs. We require punches, body falls, furniture breaking, and vocal "args" and efforts for the barroom brawl. The director chooses music from a CD of a previously released movie for temp music during the long, slow dolly shot to manipulate the audience's emotions and make them appreciate the moment's grandeur and magnificence. We must have high-velocity, bigger-than-life, Hollywood-type pistol shots with bullet zip-bys for Arnold's pistol. We need a sound designer to immediately develop some T-Rex vocals—something no one has ever heard before. The producer wants the hair on the back of the audience's necks to stand on end with anticipation and terror. And—we need this all for a temp dub tomorrow afternoon!

Do not laugh. This kind of unreasonable request happens all the time. For some reason, directors and producers think that sound editorial can throw any kind of sound at any sort of visual problem instantaneously—after all, isn't that why the motion picture industry turned digital?

Granted, a sound editorial team can make many things happen very quickly. Standard fare such as fistfight sound effects and weaponry are easy enough to whistle up. Most of us keep a large array of animals, both real and fantastic from previous projects, at our beck and call via CD-ROM storage. These can be transferred into a nonlinear digital workstation quickly and efficiently enough. However, new conceptual sound effects, such as noises no one has ever heard before, take a little preparation.

Unexpected temp dubs are the worst. A producer is very wise to decide on and set the supervising sound editor and sound editorial team early on; the smart producer also has empowered the sound editorial unit to begin developing conceptual sounds.

I like to have access to review special-effects work as early as models are being made or even when concept drawings are approved. On John Carpenter's *The Thing,* key members of my crew and I attended not only daily screenings of the first unit from Alaska, but also dailies from the visual effects studio. John wanted us to have every moment of creative thinking and experimentation at our disposal so we could make no excuses like "If we only had enough time, we could have. . . ."

When a temp dub is set on the schedule, the supervising sound editor sits down with the producer, director, and picture editor to finitely outline what sound effects and dialog work must be covered. (For example, "Do we need to bring in one or more actors for temp ADR or additional wild lines that do not exist in the production track?") Defining the scope of work that must be done for the temp dub is extremely important; without that, the work wildly and scatteredly goes on, focusing on very little and spinning everybody's wheels to no avail. What sound effects, dialog, and music are needed to tell the story?

Many low-budget pictures do not have the financial luxury of bringing in cast members for temp ADR; they often must resort to using members of the immediate production company as temporary voices for star actors. Later, during the final sound editorial preparations, the star actor is brought in to replace the temporary ADR with his or her own voice.

Swimming in the swift waters of theatrical post-production and not colliding with the temp dub syndrome is very difficult. By wanting conceptual material too quickly, too soon, producer and director are exposed to truly temp sound effects—material that we have only stuck in for test screening purposes, and do not intend to use in the final mix.

Temp dubs are a good news, bad news thing. The good news is that we get to try out different concepts ahead of time to see how the material works—the bad news is that the director and producer listen to the stuff back and forth all day long in the editing room for weeks and it gets etched in their brains like a tattoo. Temp dubs often close down their thinking to new concepts. Even when we make the real sound effects the way we intend for the final mix, the client has become so used to the temp effects that it is very difficult to break through and germinate new concepts.

Temp dubs can suck the creative lifeblood right out of a crew. On Andrew Davis's *Chain Reaction,* co-supervising sound editors John Larson and David Stone were faced with a daunting series of temp dubs and test screenings that marched week by week right down the schedule to the week prior to commencing the predubbing process for the final mix itself.

I was brought onto *Chain Reaction* with a very focused mission—design and cut all the major action sequences throughout the picture, passing any sound editorial chores that I did not want to be bothered with off to the two sound editors on either side of my room. However, I was not to concern myself with or be distracted by any of the temp dubs. If I had any material that was cut and ready that could be added to the temp dub process, that was great. But I was not to divert design and cutting energies from the final mix. If it happened to help the temp dub process along the way, that was great, but my focus was on the only sound track that really counts—the final mix!

It is exactly this kind of supervisorial philosophy that separates a great soundtrack from one hardly more than a compilation and revision of one temp dub after another. I have heard many a sound editorial crew agonize over the fact that there was never a chance to design and cut the final mix. The post-production schedules and test screenings were so compressed and intensive that they could barely make the first temp dub. From then on, it was not an issue of being able to design and cut new material, it was only about updating the picture changes between test screenings quickly enough to make the next temp dub update and subsequent studio or test screening.

In the "old days" (early and mid-1980s), a temp dub was a couple of units of temp music transferred from CDs and two or three units of sound effects. The dialog track was usually a 1:1 of the editor's cut production track that the dialog editor had run through, flipping out various unwanted sounds and adding some temporary additional lines. Today, temp dubs are gargantuan preparation events, even requiring predubbing. Commonly, motion pictures have four- to seven-day temp dub schedules. After two or three of these temp dubs, your post-production budget is shot. A temp dub used to be a monaural 35 mm single-stripe mix, suitable for interlock just about anywhere in southern California for test screenings. Today, many temp dubs are elaborate stereo mixes, complete with Surround® channel. This means 35 mm fullcoat mixes with 4- to 6-track head configurations, greatly reducing the number of possible test screening venues.

I do not dispute the actual need of producing a temp dub and of having test screenings. Producer and director, though, must embrace the counsel and advice of the supervising sound editor and structure a schedule and battle plan to achieve the mission, rather than just throw mud at the wall and see what sticks.

Chapter 9
Spotting the Picture for Sound and Music

"The studio jet is waiting for me, so we're gonna have to run through the picture changes as we spot the music, the dialog, and sound effects all at once—okay?"

Steven Spielberg announcing his combined spotting-session intentions as he sat down behind the flatbed machine to run his segment of Twilight Zone: The Motion Picture

Spotting sessions are extremely important in the ongoing quest to produce the desired final soundtrack. They present an opportunity for the director to mind-meld with the music composer and the supervising sound editor(s) on the desired style and scope of work in a precise sequence-by-sequence, often cue-by-cue, discussion. The various functions (music, sound effects, and dialog/ADR) have their own separate spotting sessions with the director, allowing concentration on each process without thinking of or dealing with all other processes at the same time.

During this time, the music composer and supervising sound editor(s) run through reels in a leisurely and thoughtful manner, discussing each music cue, each sound effect concept, each line of dialog and ADR possibility. This is when the director clearly articulates his or her vision and desires—at least theoretically. Very often, the vision and desires are very different from the style and scope-of-work concepts—these often are completely different from each other from the start and probably will be so even at the final outcome, for practical or political reasons.

The spotting process also is an opportunity for the music composer and supervising sound editor(s) to share thoughts and ideas collaboratively—so their separate contributions to the soundtrack blend together as one, keeping conflict and acoustic disharmony to a minimum. Sadly, the truth is that often very little meaningful collaboration occurs between the music and sound editorial departments. This lack of communication is due to a number of unreasonable excuses, not the least of which is the continuing practice of compressing post-production schedules to a point that music and sound editorial do not have time to share ideas and collaborate even if they want to. (I briefly discuss the swift political waters of competition between sound effects and music in Chapter 18.)

SIZING UP THE PRODUCTION TRACK

Before the spotting session, the condition of the production dialog track must be determined. To make any warranties on the work's scope and budgetary ramifications, the supervising sound editor must first screen the picture—even if it is only a rough assemblage of sequences. This way, the supervisor obtains a better feel for both audio content and picture editorial style, which will definitely affect how much and what type of labor the dialog editors need to devote to recutting and smoothing the dialog tracks. Reading the script does not provide this kind of assessment. The audio mine field is not revealed in written pages; only by listening to the raw and naked production track itself through the theatrical speaker system will the supervisor be able to identify potential problems and areas of concern.

One vital thought on production track assessment is as follows: Clients almost always want you to hear a "temp-mixed" track, especially with today's nonlinear technologies. Picture editors and directors do not even give it a passing thought. They use multitrack layering as part of their creative presentation for both producers and studio—but it does not do a lick of good to try to assess the true nature of the production dialog tracks by listening to a composite "temp mix." Clients usually do not understand this. They often want to show you their "work of art" as they intend it, not as you need to listen to it. This often leads to unhappy producers who complain when you return their VHS work-in-progress tape, with nothing retransferred but the raw production dialog—which means that they have just wasted money and time having the videotape transferred for you in the first place. Avoid this by supplying them with a "spec sheet" (precise specifications) telling them exactly what kind of videotape transfer you require. To assess properly the quality of raw production track, listen to it in a venue that best replicates the way it will sound on the rerecording stage. This dispels any unwanted surprises when you get on the rerecording dub stage and hear things you never heard before.

Never try to assess track quality on a Moviola, on a flatbed editing machine (such as a KEM or Steinbeck), or even on a nonlinear picture editorial system such as an Avid or Final Cut Pro. All picture editorial systems are built for picture editors to play tracks as a guide for audio content. I have never found a picture editorial system that faithfully replicates the soundtrack. Many times picture editors must use equipment on which the speaker has been abused by overloading to the point that the speaker cone is warped or damaged. Few picture editors set the volume and equalization settings properly, so track analysis is very difficult.

For these reasons, I always insist on listening to the cut production track on a rerecording stage, and, if the sound facility has been selected by this time, I want to run the picture on the very rerecording stage with the head mixer who will be handling the mixing chores. This is the best way to reveal all warts and shortcomings of the production track. You will then know what you are dealing with, what your head mixer can do with the material, and how it can be most effectively prepared for the rerecording process (see Chapters 12 and 13). The screening also gives the director, producer(s), and picture editor(s) an opportunity to hear the actual, and often crude, condition of their production track—transparent to the ears through the theatrical speaker system without the benefit of audio camouflage that temp music and temp sound effects often render. I guarantee you will hear sounds you have never heard before—usually unpleasant ones.

TEMP MUSIC AND TEMP SOUND EFFECTS FIRST

The picture editorial department must understand the necessity of going back through its cut soundtrack and removing any "mixed" track (where the dialog track has been temp mixed with either music or sound effects) and replacing it with the original raw sync dialog track; hearing the dialog with mixed music or sound effects negates any ability to properly evaluate it.

The smart picture editor who cuts on a nonlinear platform will wisely keep any temp sound effects, temp crash-downs, temp music, or any other nonpure production sound cues on separate audio channels. The first two or three audio channels should be devoted to production dialog only. Any revoicing, added wild lines, even WT (production wild track) must be kept in the next group of channels. In this way the picture editor will have a very easy time of muting anything and everything that is not production sound. I have had to sit and wait for over an hour while a rookie picture editor, faced with the fact that we are not there to listen to the total cut vision, has had to find and mute each cue, one at a time, because he or she has them all mixed together without separate track assignments.

The dialog mixer is the one who mixes it, the one who fixes it, to create the seamless track you desire; this is your opportunity to get the mixer's thoughts and comments on what he or she can and cannot fix. The mixer runs the work track through the console that ultimately will be used to accomplish the dialog predubbing. During this run, the mixer determines what he or she can accomplish, often pausing and making equalization or filtering tests on problematic areas, thereby making an instant decision on what dialog lines most likely will be saved or manipulated. What dialog cannot be saved obviously must be fixed, using alternate takes or cueing material for ADR. If temp music and temp sound effects are still left in the cut production track (as a mixed combine), your head mixer cannot discern what is production and what is an additive.

AFTER THE "RUNNING"

You had your interlock running with your head mixer on the rerecording stage—and had to call the paramedics to revive the clients after they discovered their production track was not in the clean and pristine shape they had always thought. The preliminary comments stating that the production track was in such good shape and that only a handful of ADR lines were anticipated fell apart in the reality run-through, which yielded a plethora of notes for ADR. Suddenly, you cue this line and that line for reasons ranging from airplane noise to microphone diaphragm popping, from distortion or off-miked perspectives to off-screen crew voices. The next step is for everybody to go home, take two Alka-Seltzers, and reconvene in the morning to address the issues afresh.

The supervising sound editor is wise to split up the upcoming spotting session. Clients often try to make one spotting session cover all needs. Unfortunately, as one facet of the sound requirements is being discussed, other audio problems and considerations tend to be shut out.

It is much smarter to set up a spotting session in which the supervising sound editor(s) and both the dialog editor and the ADR supervisor sit with the director, producer(s), and picture editor to do nothing but focus on and address the dialog, ADR, and group walla needs. The supervising sound editor(s), along with the sound designer, then schedule a spotting session specifically to talk about and spot the picture for sound effects and backgrounds. The supervising sound editor(s) may have one or more of the sound effect editors sit in on these spotting sessions as well, for nothing is better or clearer than hearing the director personally articulate his or her vision and expectations as you scroll through the picture.

CRITICAL NEED FOR PRECISE NOTES: A LEGAL PAPER TRAIL

During a spotting session, both the supervising sound editor(s) and the attending department heads take copious notes. If the sound editorial team does not understand something, they must pause and thoroughly discuss it. It is very dangerous just to gloss over concepts, assuming you know what the director wants or intends. If you assume incorrectly, you waste many valuable hours of development and preparation that yield worthless efforts. In addition, you lose irretrievably precious time, which certainly erodes the confidence level of the clients.

The failure to take and keep proper spotting notes can cause calamitous collisions later. On many occasions, a producer has relied on either my own notes or the notes of one of my department heads to rectify an argument or misconception that simmered and suddenly boiled over. Consequently, your spotting notes also act as a paper trail and can protect you in court should the rare occasion of legal action arise. Remember, sound creation is not an exact industry. It is an art form, not a manufacturing assembly line. Boundaries of interpretation can run very wide, leading you into potentially dangerous and libelous territory if you have not kept accurate and precise spotting notes. The purpose is to accurately map and follow the wishes of the director and producer, and to achieve the same outcome and creative desires. Some supervising sound editor(s) go so far as to place an audiocassette recorder in plain view to record the spotting proceedings; the tape then can be reviewed to ascertain the precise words of the director and producer when they articulated their creative desires and asked for specifics.

THE SUPERVISOR'S BIBLE

Because spotting sessions often move at a rate considerably faster than most people can push a pencil, most of us resort to a series of shorthand-like abbreviations or hieroglyphics to jog our memories later. Therefore, you must take time soon after the spotting session to go back through your notes and type a much more formal narrative with appropriate footnotes and directions for others going through the sound editorial adventure with you. Using a personal computer notebook in a spotting session is not a good idea. You cannot write or manipulate the information on the document quickly enough. Write your notes by hand during the spotting session, and transcribe them to your computer later.

The supervising sound editor dedicates a binder (sometimes more than one) to amass the steady flow of notes, logs, EDLs, schedules and all revisions, and copies of faxes and memos from the producer's office—from the director as well as from picture editorial. In short, this binder contains all the pertinent data and paper trail backups that guide the development of the soundtrack to successful fruition and protects you from future misunderstanding.

As a result of all the care taken, you will develop an awareness and observational focus that is extremely important in the spotting session process. You will notice things the picture editor and director have not seen, and they have lived with their film for months, in some cases even a year or more before you are called in to spot the picture with them. One such case occurred during a sequence where the actor came to his car, opened the door, got in, and closed the door. I put my hand up for a question. The editor stopped the film. I asked on which side of the cut they wanted the door-close. The editor and director looked at me like I had just passed wind at the lunch table. "When the door closes, you match the door close. What could be easier?" asked the picture editor.

I pointed out that as the actor got into the car, the door closed on the outside cut, and, when they cut inside the car with the actor, the door closed again.

"The hell you say," replied the editor.

I asked them to run the sequence again, very slowly, so we could study the cut. Sure enough, actor David Carradine got into the car and the door closed; as the angle cut to the inside, you clearly could see the door close again. The editor, who had been working on the picture for just over a solid year, sighed and grabbed his grease pencil to make a change mark. All this time he had never seen the double door-close.

SPOTTING SESSION PROTOCOL

The spotting session can be one of the most volatile atmospheres with regard to client insecurity and creative sensitivity. One must learn the art of using diplomatic language when discussing various problems—especially when the filmmakers have delivered an atrocious mess for you to fix. On one of my earlier pictures, I spotted the picture with a picture editor I had known for a number of years, dating back to Corman days. I had not worked with the director before. We finished running through a particular scene where actor Donald Pleasance was discussing a crime scene with a woman. I commented to the picture editor that the actress could not act her way out of a paper bag. The picture editor's brow furrowed as he gave me a disapproving glance. At the end of the reel, the director, noticeably fatigued, left the room for a smoke break. The picture editor grabbed the next reel off the rack, leaned over, and informed me that the actress was the director's wife. After that colossal faux pas, I learned to research diligently who was whom in the production team and in front of the camera.

Other sensitive situations can arise when you have a tendency to count things and are spotting the film with a picture editor who thinks his or her work is beyond reproach. Such was the case when we held our spotting session on the sci-fi horror film, *The Thing*. I brought my core team with me, as was my custom. I had already handled two pictures for the director, so I was not concerned about unfamiliar ground. I knew he was very comfortable and secure with himself.

The problem arose because I tend to count things, almost subconsciously. I developed this habit while supervising soundtracks and having to think on my feet during spotting sessions. In the case in question, a scene in the film depicted the hero checking out a helicopter outside when he heard a gunshot from within a nearby laboratory building. He jumped off the chopper and ran into the building and down the hallway, hearing more pistol shots. He reached the lab, where a crazed scientist was warning the rest of the staff to stay away. In a matter of moments, the team outmaneuvered and subdued the scientist after he emptied the last two bullets from his pistol.

I raised my hand with a question. The picture editor paused the film. I glanced around to my team members and then to the director. "Do you really want us to cut eight gunshots?"

I was taken aback by the picture editor's response. "You can't count! There are only six gunshots!"

I was willing to let it go. I knew full well that the editor had meant to have only six, so I would just drop two from the guide track. But the director loved to have fun. He grinned like a Cheshire cat at the opportunity. "Let's go back and count 'em."

The picture editor spun the reel back to the exterior with the helicopter. He rolled the film. The first off-stage gunshot sounded, and everyone counted. "One."

The hero jumped off the chopper skid and dashed into the building, past boxes of supplies as another shot rang out. "Two."

The hero reached the doorway to the lab. He was warned that the crazed scientist had a gun. The scientist turned from swinging his axe at the communication equipment and fired a warning shot at the hero. We all counted, "Three."

The hero told the guy next to him to maneuver around to the doorway of the map room. As the other actor reached the doorway, the crazed scientist fired another warning shot at him. "Four."

The actor ducked back as the bullet ricocheted off the doorframe. The scientist stepped into the center of the room as he fired two more on-screen shots. The image cut to the doorframe, where we saw three bullets hit and ricochet away. Everyone counted, "Six and. . . ." Nobody dared continue.

The picture editor stopped the film and growled at me. "So you'll cut two of them out." As it turned out, we could only drop the one as the hero was running down the hallway because it was off-stage. The way the picture editor had cut the sequence as the scientist emptied his pistol could not be trimmed without the picture editor first making a fix in the picture, which he was unwilling to do.

WHAT REVELATIONS MAY COME

Other, more costly ramifications, constructive or not, certainly can come out of a spotting session. I was spotting the sound requirements on a superhero-type action picture when the director and I reached the point in the film of a climactic hand-to-hand battle between the hero and the mobster villain. At the very point where the villain literally had the upper hand and was about to vanquish his nemesis, a door at the back of the room opened. The mobster villain's young son entered to see his father in mortal combat—at the same time the villain turned to see his son. Taking full advantage of the distraction, the hero plunged his huge knife into the villain's back.

The director noticed my reaction and stopped the film, asking me what the matter was. I politely asked, "I guess I missed something somewhere in the picture—but who was the hero?" The director was shocked at my apparent lack of attentiveness. If I had been paying attention I would have known that the whole picture revolved around this guy on the floor, our superhero, and how he was taking revenge against the forces of the underworld for the loss of his family.

Yes, I did notice that. I also pointed out that in the blink of an eye the director had changed the hero from a sympathetic hero to a moralistically despicable villain. Not only had he stabbed the mobster villain in the back, but he performed this cowardly act in front of the villain's son.

A steel curtain of realization dropped on the director. This elementary storytelling had just blown its tires while hurtling down the highway of filmmaking. The director told me to commence work only on the first nine reels of the picture, as he was going to meet with studio executives to decide what to do about the ending.

A few weeks later, the set, which had been torn down in Australia, was being rebuilt in Culver City, California (where they shot *Gone With the Wind*) precisely as it had been. Frames from the master angle of the film were used to meticulously re-place broken shards of glass that lay on the floor so that the two filmed segments would match. Actors were recalled from all over the world. Lou Gossett, who played the police lieutenant and had crossed through the carnage at the end of the action sequence when it was first shot in Australia, was not available—so the director had to employ the industry's top rotoscope artist to painstakingly rotoscope a moving dolly shot to carefully mask out the tell-tale knife protruding from the mobster's back from the original Australia shoot that had Lou Gossett crossing through.

Other audio challenges resulted from the reshoot when we discovered that the boy portraying the mobster's son had grown since the original shoot, and his voice was changing. This meant pitch-shifting the boy's dialog tracks upward by degrees until we could accurately match the pitch and timbre of the original material shot months before in Australia.

The observant problem-solving approach to spotting sessions is invaluable. Learn to glance at a building, then turn away. Now ask yourself how many floors the building has. How many windows are in a row on each floor? Are they tinted or clear? Develop your observation skills to accurately recall and describe what you see, and it will serve you extremely well.

Also learn to listen to what people say. People often repeat what they thought someone said, or their own perception of what they said instead of what was actually said. These kinds of skills are invaluable in dialog editing and transcribing muffled or garbled words from a guide-track to cue for ADR. You do not transcribe the gist of what they said, or an interpretation—you must write down PRECISELY what they said. Even if you intend to change the line later in ADR, you first must know exactly where you are, before you can continue forward.

Chapter 10
Custom Recording Sound Effects: The Real Fun and Adventure

"Why do you have to go clear out to Oklahoma to custom record the Steerman? Save the money—use our crop-duster sound effects from *North by Northwest.* Nobody will ever know the difference!"

MGM/UA executive, dissuading the producer from custom recording sound effects for The Aviator

I laid behind the low wall of rocks hastily piled together as an impromptu bullet-resistant shield to protect myself from the spray of lead I knew would be flying toward me at any moment. Having just signed a release of responsibility should I be accidentally wounded or killed, my partner, Ken Sweet, and my first assistant, Peter Cole, still tried vigorously to talk me out of placing myself in such a dangerous position. "Why can't you just leave the tape recorder and microphones there and clear out of the line of fire?" Ken asked.

I gazed up at my concerned partner as I slipped on my headsets. "Have you ever recorded bullet zing-bys before—let alone stereophonically?"

Ken sighed. "No."

"Well, neither have I." I powered up the Nagra recorder. "I don't have the slightest idea what to expect, so I wouldn't have a ghost of a chance of making a qualified preset. The only way I know how to do this is to stay here and monitor the tape as we are recording, then make quick adjustments between volley fire."

"It's a bad idea," growled Ken.

"We're wasting time. Get back to the firing line and keep accurate notes," I insisted.

Ken and Peter gave up and went back the 400 yards to the firing line, where the two contractors and clip loaders were finishing preparations. Over the past three days, we had recorded twenty-seven different machine guns. We had recorded in a variety of acoustically different locations west of Las Vegas, chewing up over 9,000 rounds of ammunition.

I rolled over to check the equipment again. The microphones were live; the batteries were strong. In a few minutes the shooting team would be ready. I tried to relax. How had I ever gotten myself into this position in the first place?

I had been on Stage "D" at Goldwyn Studios in the midst of a temp dub on *Twilight Zone: The Motion Picture* when Don Rogers, head of the sound department, asked if I could step outside a second.

Out in the hallway, Don told me that they had an awkward situation. A Chuck Norris picture was temp dubbing over on Stage "C" and the director was throwing quite a tantrum. It seemed that the sound editing crew had cut inappropriate weapon sounds, and, to make matters worse, the supervisor was calling every firearm on the screen an Uzi. Don wondered if I would mind coming back to Stage "C" to try to inject some damage control.

As soon as I walked on stage, I was introduced to Steve Carver, the director of the film, *Lone Wolf McQuade.* He ordered the reel to be run. As the work print flickered on the screen, Steve would point and demand, "What kind of gun is that?!"

I felt like I was being flashed silhouette identification cards in a precombat briefing. "That's a Mac-10."

On screen another stuntman jumped into view, brandishing another kind of weapon. Carver pointed again. "And that?!"

"That's an M-16."

Another stuntman kicked in the door of the cabin. Carver grinned as he pointed once more. "What about that one?"

I smiled as I recognized the weapon. "Oh my, I've never seen a Ruger Tri-Automatic before."

Carver signaled the mixer to halt the projection as he turned to me with a curious expression. "Then how do you know it is one?"

"I meant I've never seen one in action—just in last month's issue of *Guns and Ammo.*"

Steve smiled. "Then you have the sounds of these weapons in your library."

"Not yet, but I will soon."

That was how I came to lay there, waiting for the first machine-gun burst. The radio crackled, and my assistant asked if I was ready. I turned on the Nagra and radioed back that I had speed.

I heard a faint distant burst, and a beat later I could barely hear the bullets flying high overhead just prior to impacting the far cliff wall. I lifted the radio. "No, no guys. You're way too high. You have to bring it down lower."

A few moments passed, and then another burst was heard, followed by a flight of projectiles passing somewhat lower, but still not low enough. I lifted the radio. "Still too high. You have to come lower still."

A short time passed before I felt a series of impacts and disorienting debris. I had been struck in the back of the head, and, since I knew being struck by a bullet probably would not feel like what you think, I experienced a moment of disbelief and shock. Instantaneously, another 9 mm slug somehow flew between the crevice of two rocks, came under my head, and struck the ground two inches from my left eye. It then flew forward, striking a river rock and flipping back in front of my face on the ground as a mangled lead lump.

I moved my hand cautiously behind my head and gingerly felt my scalp for blood or an open wound. Fortunately, I had been struck by a rock and not by a bullet. I suddenly felt immense relief that I was not mortally wounded, more than happy to endure a nasty lump rather than a hole in the head. My eyes focused on the still-hot lump of lead in front of my face. I was intensely aware that this piece of metal had flown under my head. I picked it up and set it in the palm of my hand to look at it.

I suppose several awkward moments had passed and the firing line crew had not heard from me. The radio crackled. It was Peter calling. "David . . . David?"

Snapping back into reality, I picked up the radio. Unfortunately, however, I did not pay strict attention to my exact choice of words. "I'm okay Peter; I have a bullet in my hand."

Peter's voice wailed away, "Oh, my gawd!! We've shot David!!"

Listen to cue #23 of the audio CD provided with this book for the actual recording of "Auto Bullet Bys" recorded that day. Note that each succeeding flight of bullets gets closer and closer.

I am the first to encourage you not to record weapons like this. I was lucky—but stupid and irresponsible. Although we captured some of the most remarkable bullet flights in a you-are-there perspective, far better ways are available today to record such effects without putting yourself in harm's way. If that bullet had grazed one of the rocks as it passed through the stone barrier, it could easily have changed course and struck me in the head, instead of passing just underneath my eye. It is better to plan the process with a safe and sane philosophical agenda. Problem solve how you could monitor your tape recorder and make adjustments in another way instead of placing yourself in a dangerous and compromising position. Be smart and survive. This does not diminish the excitement or thrill of recording live action sound effects. After all, you will be able to enjoy practicing your art form for a much longer period of time.

Most sound editors do not know one weapon from another. Because we were serving a director who was fanatical about the audio signature of weapons used in the film, we had to find some way to help the sound editor identify and use the correct sound effects with on-screen gunfire. We took a page from classic World War II aircraft identification posters, the ones with a series of aircraft silhouettes. If you see this silhouette, then it is this kind of airplane—so you use these sound cues to be authentic. I cut out photographs from numerous periodicals and books that showed the weapon profiles and carefully listed the applicable recordings.

I called it "see-a-gun/cut-a-gun." If you see an actor using a weapon that visually matches one seen in any of these sound effect catalog pages, then one or more sound effect cues listed under each picture are the appropriate ones to cut.

THE ADVENTURE OF CUSTOM RECORDING

Custom recording sound effects is probably my favorite phase of the soundtrack creation process. Maybe it is because of my memories of venturing out to capture the exact kinds of sounds needed to successfully mount a project. Maybe it was the freedom I felt as I packed my car with recording gear and any special props I might need and simply got out of town. You cannot help but feel a bit like Indiana Jones as you set out to capture new sounds.

A wonderful side benefit from custom recording is the incredible learning experience that goes with it. If you truly are dedicated to the sound job, you cannot help but immerse yourself totally in the subject, learning the mechanics of how things work by studying sounds that emanate from whatever you are recording.

Figure 10.1 "See-a-gun/cut-a-gun." We incorporated photographs of the exact weapons we recorded, then grouped sound cues that pertained to each weapon together. The sound editor could flip through the pages of the catalog until he or she recognizes the weapon being used in the film—a different spin on the police "mug-shot" book idea. (Photo by David Yewdall)

Sometimes the adventures were short and poignant; sometimes they became multiteam military-style operations involving thousands of dollars and careful planning. No matter how small or large the custom recording undertaking, my commitment to new recordings had a great deal to do with my growing reputation as a supervising sound editor and my marketability in the industry in the early 1980s.

SUPERVISING SOUND EDITOR

Ideally, the supervising sound editor is set for the project early enough so that he or she can screen dailies, or at least view significant event sequences long before picture editorial is ready to lock picture and turn it over for sound editorial work. Early on, you will discover that the screenplay, the scripted roadmap of how the movie is intended to be made, is not the last word in the actual outcome of the visual adventure ultimately turned over to sound editorial. The smart supervising sound editor uses this only as a guide of expectations and challenging promises. Once he or she actually sees footage, then the precise audio needs make themselves crystal clear.

After an overview of the sound effect material either in the sound library or in any wild track recordings the production mixer may have gotten on the set during principal photography, the supervising sound editor starts to list needs for custom sound effect recording. The supervising sound editor usually has one or more favorite locations that have been successful sites to record exterior sound effects. From prior experience, he or she knows air traffic patterns and temperature inversions that affect wind currents. In addition, the supervising sound editor has probably developed a relationship with local authorities or with individuals who occasionally enjoy developing sound effects and are willing to lend a hand.

More often than not, the supervising sound editor personally goes out and custom records the sound or teams up with other sound effect recordists in larger sessions that require multiple microphones and a team effort.

Increasingly more custom sound effect recording is done by specialists who devote much of their career to custom sound recording. These men and women all have various reputations for specialties. A supervising sound editor may hire one individual because he or she is known for quadraphonic background recordings. A different sound effect recordist may have a reputation for eerie organic sounds, and another is known for being good with vehicles. The supervising sound editor considers who is best suited for each job, and then checks for schedule availability. Once the recordist has been set, the supervising sound editor usually runs sequences of action with the sound effect recordist, reviewing certain details of action and the concept of the performances. For instance, it is vital to articulate precisely how an engine should sound. Should it be cherried up? Should they unbolt the muffler and shift it back a little? Should it have a couple of spark plug wires removed? Should they even physically remove a spark plug? How heavy-handed does the sound recordist get? By the time the supervising sound editor completes the briefing, the scope of work is well defined, and the sound recordist has a clear picture of the mission to accomplish.

Steven Spielberg's *Jaws* required a great deal of attention and creative forethought. Contrary to what one might think in light of its history, *Jaws* was not intended to be a big picture. In fact, it was the little horror picture for Universal that year, a small project to add to the package of big films that the studio was offering. Box office history has shown that the year's other big pictures were comparative failures, and that *Jaws* saved the financial future of the studio.

No one could have made that kind of prediction during the principal photography phase of the picture. The post-production budget was not only unremarkable, but low-budget and bare-boned in design. Jim Troutman, the picture's supervising sound editor, had to make do with what little he had, and do it quickly. One of the better decisions was allowing him to custom record the *Orca*, the sharking boat used to search for the dreaded great white.

"The *Orca* played throughout a good third of the picture. We had to record it doing all kinds of things to match the action in the movie," Troutman remembers. "They had been very smart and had brought the *Orca* out to Los Angeles along with the Swedish captain who maintained and operated the boat for the studio." Jim and his recording team set up early in the morning. The captain took the small boat beyond the breakwaters of the L.A. harbor, out where Jim could get good, clean recordings.

"We recorded the flapper on the exhaust bouncing and spitting; we recorded the engine cruising along, under strain, with trap door open, with trap door closed—and then I happened to glance over the gunnels of the boat, and I began to pay closer attention to what was going on."

Jim stepped over to the captain. "Excuse me for asking, but this is a very interesting optical illusion. We seem to be riding lower in the water than we were a couple of hours ago."

The captain calmly replied in his heavily accented English, "Ja, we are sinking." Jim's eyebrows shot up as he immediately announced that he had recorded enough material of

Figure 10.2 Sound effects specialist Eric Potter and Charles Maynes record a passenger train as it speeds southbound at 80 mph. (Photo by David Yewdall)

the *Orca* heading west, and now he thought they should record the more important "flank speed" "flank speed" segment as they headed back to port!

One of the more interesting underwater recordings made earlier in the day utilized an underwater hydrophone. Jim and his team had tried to make underwater point-of-view recordings of the Orca, with mixed results. At one particular point, the mixer had Jim listen to a very strange emanation through his headsets. After a moment, Jim asked the captain if he knew what was making the peculiar sound. After listening to it, the captain nodded that he indeed had some experience with this back in Scandinavian waters—they were listening to the sound of shrimp eating. This is the strange and almost alien sound you hear as the movie begins. The Universal logo has just faded to black, and before the underwater title shot fades up, all we hear is Jim's recording of shrimp eating. From before the first frame of visual picture, Jim had set a weird and unearthly mood for things to come. *Jaws* won an Academy Award for Best Sound that year.

WHY A CUSTOM RECORDING SPECIALIST?

Why have special custom sound effect recordists record sound effects when you have the production mixer and all his or her gear out on location anyway? I have met very few production mixers who understand how to record sound effects. A production mixer's prime directive is to capture the spoken word on the set. When the actors speak, the production mixer does everything to record the actors' performances as cleanly and vibrantly as possible. As discussed in Chapter 5, the production mixer must overcome incredible ambience adversities to do this. He or she knows where the microphone must be placed to capture the best timbre of the human voice.

Good mixers know the necessity of doing everything to keep extraneous noises out of the production track. Audio intrusions such as generators, airplanes overhead, footsteps, cloth rustlings, and close proximity camera noise are some of their daily nemesis. The valuable experience of the seasoned production mixer is a precious commodity indeed. Despite all this, I would not hire a production mixer to record custom sound effects, especially vehicle series. They just do not understand the dynamics and intricacies of required performance cues and, more important, where to put the microphones.

When I was working on a period picture (circa 1919) entitled *Moonbeam Riders*, the authentic motorcycle engines of this action-adventure racing story challenged us. I was told the production mixer had exactly custom recorded what I would need for the Aero Indian motorcycle in the final reel of the film. Of course, I was more naive back in 1978. Our reels were due to start predubbing first thing in the morning, and, as often happened, we found ourselves cutting late into the night to finish the work on time.

By 3 A.M. I had finally completed the old Harley and turned my attention to the Aero Indian. I pulled the 400-foot roll of 35 mm wild track from the back rack of my table, laced the film over the sound head of the Moviola, and started to audition it. With every foot that passed over the sound head, I became more and more dismayed. If the sound recording was not suffering from vibration distortions, then it was the mixer talking during the performance or drastic changes in level as the bike performed. As the roll grew smaller in my hand, my blood pressure rose correspondingly higher. The recording was worthless! I knew the material needed was not there.

This was only one of many instances in which a production company has had a perfect opportunity to custom record historically rare or one-of-a-kind props—only to squander the opportunity. In 1998 I was asked to cut sound effects on a major action picture being filmed in Europe. The supervising sound editor had me view a videotape of the editor's assembly for the first 50 minutes, revealing some of the hottest car chase sequences I had ever seen. I knew that the car sound effect series required by the picture's vehicles would not be found around town; even if they could have been, the breadth of action and the demand of high-performance engines and screaming gear boxes would require extensive custom recording. To add to the requirements, most of the action was filmed on cobblestone streets. Understandably, the director would be very demanding, with all the publicity and care taken to shut down whole sections of a city to film these incredible sequences.

I sat down with the supervising sound editor and shared my concerns about the car sound effects and the need for an expert sound effect recordist to handle the custom recording of each vehicle and the cobblestone street segments. While the sound effect recordist was there, he could also capture a number of stereophonic European backgrounds for us to lend greater spice to the track.

The supervising sound editor shook his head. We would not need all that. He knew the production mixer, an old buddy of his. They could do the job perfectly well—right? Privately, I sighed, knowing what would come of this. I knew the picture would bog down in this area because the supervising sound editor was not taking my advice. Of course it did not help that I knew one of the producers on the picture—second-generation Hollywood who thought was expert enough in these matters that he neglected to allocate money for custom sound recordings into the budget of the production.

We would receive an abundance of sound recordings from the production mixer recorded after he had completed an intensive and exhausting production schedule. The last thing this weary man would be able to do would be rev up enthusiasm to tackle the daunting chores of custom recording these vehicles in steeplechase action for our sound requirements. In the past, the work had been dumped onto me to fix. This picture was more important than that. It should not just be fixed—it should be done right. When a movie costs $65,000,000 and the sound editorial firm is set to do the picture as early as principal photography, the scope of work should be structured and tactically designed by the supervising sound editor to deliver the best material possible to augment the creativity and excitement of the action.

I decided to decline working on the project, as I knew that it would be a hellish headache without custom recording, and I did not want to reward a producer who should know better—or perhaps did know better and wanted to be cheap. I just did not need the headache, especially after such extensive involvement on *Starship Troopers* the previous year. Ironically, a couple of months later, the supervising sound editor asked to see me. He wanted to know if I could give him the name of the sound effect recordist who I had recommended that we would have sent over to Europe to do the work in the first place. I knew then that his production mixer buddy in fact had not come up with the audio goods to make the car action sequences work. I heard later that they had gone to great expense to get what they needed—over four times the cost that we had quoted to do it the right way at the outset. In the end they had to rent a racetrack for the high-speed chase sequence recordings and have at least two of the vehicles shipped over from Europe, as they were not even on the market yet. I am sure finding enough cobblestone in California to duplicate the tire-thumping requirements proved very challenging.

It is one of the most important lessons to learn as a producer or director—rather than dictating what you think will be the quickest and most cost-effective method of producing a great soundtrack, listen to your supervising sound editor's advice—he or she has a hundred times more experience than you do. Learn from their experience. In the end, they will save you precious thousands of dollars and get the job done correctly the first time. Do not find yourself a victim of the old post-production adage, "They can't find enough money or time to do it right, but somehow they find more money and extra time to do it over!"

FEAR OF BEING STEREOTYPED

By the end of the 1960s, legendary director Robert Wise was afraid of being typecast as a director of period costume pictures. While looking for a project that would completely change his image, he got a call from an associate at Universal who talked up a wacky science-fiction thriller written by a young kid named Michael Crichton (*The Andromeda Strain*). Wise jumped at the opportunity. What a change from *Helen of Troy*! It had the potential to rival his other science-fiction classic, *The Day the Earth Stood Still*.

Joe Sikorski studied the *Andromeda* script and reviewed the sound effect material on hand at the studio. Very little lived up to the level of both story hardware and visual art direction that Wise was capturing on film. Sikorski met with Wise to discuss the concerns of having the new and modern sounds the picture needed. Although Joe Sikorski and fellow sound editor Bob Bratton had tackled a similar style high-tech computer film the year before

(*Colossus: The Forbin Project*), *The Andromeda Strain* went way beyond anything they had done in *Colossus*.

Sikorski proposed custom recording all types of stuff to make the underground bio-tech lab come to life. But where could they do it? Wise told Sikorski he would get back to him. Three days later, Wise called Sikorski to let him know that he had secured the cooperation of the Jet Propulsion Laboratory in Pasadena.

For two full days Sikorski had a sound mixer, boom operator, cable man, and access to all the high-tech "toys" he would want to record. Nitrogen fill tanks, a vacuum pump on an electron microscope, centrifuges, laboratory ambiance backgrounds, clean room doors, hydraulics, air compressions, transformers, switches, air vents, mechanical hand movements, sterilization processes, cutting-edge telecommunication gear—Sikorski not only had access to the real sounds, but also to the best technical advisors to guide him in their use.

At the time, Robert Wise did not consider *The Andromeda Strain* a big sound job, as we think of big soundtracks in today's acoustical barrages—but it was. Each moment of the picture had a precise and focused audio event that underlined and supported the visuality. It did not blast you out of your seat with a wall of sound—instead, it reached out with a special singularity in the storytelling process. The unique custom recorded sound effects added a fresh spin that really captured your attention.

SOUND EDITORS RECORD THEIR OWN MATERIAL

Some of the best sound effect recordists have come from the ranks of sound editors. They are driven to record out of frustration because they need specific characterization in their sound effects to make their edit sessions really come alive. Others record because they love the challenge and freedom of using the world as their sound stage. Either way, sound editors bring editorial experience with them that dramatically affects how the material is performed and consequently recorded. Some of the best sound effects I have ever heard have been recorded by sound editors who learned how to record their own material.

Before I draw up battle plans to custom record a whole series of sound effects, I always sift through the production sound reports first, noting the wild track recordings and listening to them before I make commitments on what to record. Needless to say, the more sound editors become frustrated by lack of material in the studio's sound library and improperly recorded wild tracks from production, the more they venture out to custom record their own sounds.

In the old days, by strict union definition of job functions, sound editors were not permitted to record their own sound effects. I knew of several editors who got slapped with $500 fines by the union for doing the work of a Local mixer. Like a shark that has tasted the blood in the water, though, once we had recorded sounds for our precise and unique applications and had cut them into sync to the picture, we had to have more. We liked the results and refused to turn back. Many of us decided to have dual union membership.

If we were 38 miles from the intersection of Hollywood Boulevard and Vine Street in Hollywood, we were legally outside union jurisdiction. This is the main reason I started returning to my hometown of Coalinga to custom record my sound needs in the late 1970s. A secondary reason for recording away from the Los Angeles area should be painfully obvious. In terms of controlling ambient sound, a city is one of the worst places to record—

unless, of course, you need busy streets and noisy neighborhoods with police helicopters patroling overhead.

At the beginning of my sound editing career, I did some limited custom recording for one picture or another, especially while contracting Roger Corman films (*Humanoids from the Deep, Battle Beyond the Stars*). *Escape from New York* was the film that swept me into serious field recording and made me understand the unique styles, challenges, and disciplines of stereo. Suddenly, I was no longer thinking monophonically. Now I thought in three dimensions—left-to-right, right-to-left, and in the surround channels. At first, though, trying to problem-solve the stereo requirements for the many audio challenges of a motion picture can be mind-boggling.

CUSTOM RECORDING VEHICLES

For *Escape from New York* we staged our first serious sterephonic car-recording expedition. The Coalinga morning air was cold and still; a light fog lingered through the early afternoon. I soon learned that such conditions are perfect for sound effects. The best recording trips have been during the late fall and winter. Sound carries very well through cold air, and crickets and other pesky insects are frozen and silent.

I have developed a special background for recording vehicles—born out of the frustration of trying to make an old library car effect series work on a sequence without the proper components of recorded material to make the action come alive. I had recorded many vehicle series over the previous five years with mixed results, but it was John Carpenter's *Christine* that focused and galvanized the style and standards by which I would record vehicles in the future.

For *Christine* we had a vehicle that had to sound sad and beat-up during some sequences, but needed to sound tough and beefy in other sequences. This would require a mechanic and whatever assistance he or she would need for the car to sound a variety of ways.

When recording vehicles, you must be very sensitive to the local authorities. Not all roads fall under local jurisdiction. If you are not careful, you can find yourself in deep trouble if you record car stunts on the wrong stretch of highway. I have yet to find one highway patrolman or county sheriff who does not like to assist and be involved in recording hot cars for the movies—but you must involve them in your early planning and listen carefully to their recommendations.

For *Christine*, the highway patrol suggested that it would be much easier, with much less "maintenance observation" required on their part, if we hired a security officer to be with us as we worked. This benefited both parties. A uniformed officer with experience in traffic management and radio communication with the local authorities gave us instant access should a troublesome situation arise. He also lent a visual symbol of authority and legitimacy to people driving through the recording zone.

We quickly discovered, however, that we could not use the road we first had in mind because it fell under state jurisdiction, making necessary a mountain of complex paperwork and approvals from the state capital to use a state highway. Local authorities noted several alternative roads that fell under county jurisdiction, making it vastly easier to receive permission and clearances to perform various stunt driving for the express purpose of recording sound effects.

We did not choose a location at which to record simply by fingering the map and picking a place at random. We drove out (at the same time of day the recording was planned) and stopped on each road, got out and walked the length, listening to the ambience—considering potential audio problems posed from a nearby factory, airport, field pumps, and so forth, not the least of which was daily wind shift patterns. On some locations, we discovered that if we had not gotten our recordings by noon we were doomed to winds that kicked up for the remainder of the day.

I secured the assistance of Tim Jordan, a school friend who owned his own automotive shop in my hometown. Tim served as head mechanic and vehicle liaison officer, knowing who in town owned what kind of car. I briefed him on the sound effect requirements and the range of automotive changes and challenges he would make on the performing vehicles while we were out in the field. In a matter of moments Tim and his assistant could remove spark plug wires, in some cases removing a spark plug completely for a really raspy clatter. The two men would detach the muffler and move it back slightly, causing a gap, or they would change the timing. All of these alterations had to be done quickly, and often with the result that the desired effect still was not realized. In a matter of minutes, though, the car was ready to make awful (but necessary) noises.

Christine was the first picture on which I used two recording teams. The first recording unit, or "close-up" perspective team, would always set up on the road itself, close to the car. The second recording unit was the "semi-background" perspective team, set off the road twenty or thirty yards to get a softer performance. Approach recording a car series with the material needs of the sound editor in mind. You seldom record a single performance with all the elements of that recording working together in their proper balanced volumes. The undercarriage may overwhelm tire hum; engine dynamics disappear under tire skids. A perfectly balanced mixture of elements in one recording almost never happens. Therefore, do not approach recording cars with the idea that each recording is an end unto itself. Every recording is but one piece of the puzzle of sound effects that must be cut and blended together to make a slick car sequence work. With this understanding deeply rooted, the intelligent custom sound recordist breaks the action into traditional parts. Smart supervising sound editors always record cars in the same groupings, from which a sound editor can create any movement.

The following list is a typical vehicle performance series as broken down into single cues. Of course, your own needs for vehicle recordings vary, but this is a good guide.

Vehicle Mechanicals
Trunk open and close
Hood up and down
Hood and/or trunk release mechanism
Driver door open and close
Passenger door open and close
Into car movement/out of car movement
Seat belts movt. and buckling up
Window cranked (or motor) up and down
Emergency brake set and release
Shifter movt. into-gear, reverse movt
Glove compartment open and close
Cigarette lighter movt.

Radio switch on and off
Cassette player movt.; cassette in and out (or CD player)
Rummage through glove compartment
Gas flap release (on newer vehicles)
Gas cap key and off and on movts.
   (especially older vehicles)
Various dashboard clicks, knobs, and lever settings
Keys into ignition movt.
   (be careful not to use a keychain)
Turn-signal relay clicking
Windshield wipers—recorded dry (various speeds)
Windshield wipers—recorded wet (various speeds)
Brake squeaks (with squeaky brakes, roll car down
   Slope with engine off, brake to stop—various)
Roll car over light gritty asphalt
Roll car off asphalt onto shoulder of road
Pry off and put on hubcaps
Overhead light
Convertible roof open/close mechanism (if applicable)
Moon/sun roof mechanicals
Pedal movt.
Mirrors (if motorized)

Now you must record the performance of the car engine itself. Contrary to those who would assume they know how car sound effects are recorded, let me assure you that the best series are recorded in a very methodical, often boring manner. Note that the perspective of the recording from the tailpipe area sounds completely different from the recording made before the front bumper. Likewise, a recording made from the side of the car sounds different than that from either front or back. These positions become extremely handy and critical later in sound editorial when the actual demands of the visual picture may require the car to start, have a short idle, then pull past the camera and away. Another shot may require a rear perspective view, where a front-end microphone does not sound appropriate. It all boils down to common sense.

Following is a list of idles and revs required in a static position. Note that "jump" revs are recorded in a static position; the car does not actually leave the ground and fly by. (Review cue #17 of the audio CD provided with this book for examples of "idle" and "rev" cue sounds.)

Start, idle, and off (close front perspective)
Start, idle, and off (close tailpipe perspective)
Start, idle, and off (mid-side perspective)
Start, light revs, and off (close front perspective)
Start, light revs, and off (close tailpipe perspective)
Start, light revs, and off (mid-side perspective)
Start, medium revs, and off (close front perspective)
Start, medium revs, and off (close tailpipe perspective)
Start, medium revs, and off (mid-side perspective)

Recording CAR START and IDLES -- CAR REVS
(from two perspectives simultaneously)

Figuer 10.3 Recording a car—START and IDLE.

Start, big angry revs, and off (close front perspective)
Start, big angry revs, and off (close tailpipe perspective)
Start, big angry revs, and off (mid-side perspective)
Start, "jump" revs, and off (close front perspective)
Start, "jump" revs, and off (close tailpipe perspective)
Start, "jump" revs, and off (mid-side perspective)

I have met few car owners who take kindly to having their vehicles "jumped." Actually, vehicles seldom make such a sound when they leave the ground. It has become one of those Hollywood audio clichés, a metaphor we expect or even feel satisfaction from because we believe the way it fits the action on screen. To add to the sensation of flight, move the microphones away from the engine as the engine peaks in its "freewheeling" rev, duplicating the sensation that the vehicle is passing by in flight.

Start, short idle, and away—various speeds (close front and by perspective)
Start, short idle, and away—various speeds (close tailpipe away perspective)
Start, short idle, and away—various speeds (mid-side away perspective)

In addition to the three basic perspectives, you also need the driver to perform each take with a different emphasis. One start-and-away should be slow and lethargic. Another should be at normal speed, with yet another a little faster, building to a fast and hard away, throttling downrange.

Using the same philosophy as the start-and-aways, now you must deal with variations of where the car actually stops. One of the most overlooked approach-and-stop cues is having the vehicle approach and pull up into a driveway. This cue sounds so much different from simply pulling up to a stop on the street. (Review cue #19 of the provided audio for examples "in-to-stop" cue sounds.) Refer to the following list.

close -to- away perspective recording team

pass-by perspective recording team

**Recording CAR START and AWAY
(FLAT perspective & IN-and-BY to STOP)**

Figure 10.4 Recording a car—START-and-AWAYs. Following is a list of variations on the start-and-aways. (Review cue #18 of the audio CD provided with this book for examples of "start, idle, and away" cue sounds.)

close in-to-stop perspective recording team

pass-by to-stop perspective recording team

**Recording CAR IN-to-STOPs
(FLAT perspective & IN-and-BY to STOP)**

Figure 10.5 Recording a car—IN TO STOP.

Long in approach and stop, engine off—various speeds (stop close front perspective)
Long in approach and stop, engine off—various speeds (close by and stop tailpipe perspective)
Long in approach and stop, engine off—various speeds (mid-side away perspective)

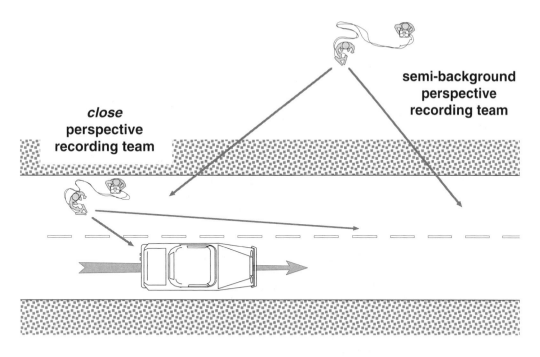

**Recording a CAR BY
from two perspectives simultaneously**

Figure 10.6 Recording car—BYs.

The car should not always stop directly in front of or to the side of the microphones. Performances that have the car pass to a stop a bit past the microphones are not only a good idea but vital for perspective placement. You might also have the driver approach, slow as he or she nears, then pass by 8-to-15 yards from the microphone and U-turn back in to stop. These types of in-to-stops are excellent for estate driveways.

I have never encountered a sound effects library that has too many approach-and-bys for any given vehicle series. Remember, don't record for only the film you are working on, but for any future uses. (Review cue #20 of the provided audio CD for examples of "approach"- and-"BY" cue sounds.) Refer to the following list for guidelines.

Approach, by, and away—various speeds (stop close front perspective)
Approach, by, and away—various speeds (close by and stop tailpipe perspective)
Approach, by, and away—various speeds (mid-side away perspective)

You should not only record numerous variations such as sneak by, slow by, normal by, medium by, fast by, and race by; you also must think about accelerating or decelerating on the by—upshifting or downshifting just prior to or just after the by itself. You should also not record all your approach-and-bys from the same location. If a seam or a tiny piece of debris is in the road, you will discover later that you got a rhythmic click or thump in the same spot in the performance, quickly making the vehicle BYs predictable and uninteresting.

semi-background
perspective
recording team

close
perspective
recording team

Recording a car series
CAR "maneuvers"
(from two perspectives simultaneously)

Figure 10.7 Recording car MANEUVERS.

Start-and-aways, in-and-stops, approach-and-bys are all very obvious. They are the "getting there" cues, but vehicles do not drive only like that—they need transitions and dipsy-doodles to tie the "getting there" cues together into a single ribbon of reality.

Maneuvers are one of the most vital, yet frequently overlooked, performances for a vehicle. As a sound editor, I can cut bits and pieces of vehicle maneuvers and weave them into the transitional moments of screen action in a way that not only bridges one "getting there" effect to another, but also injects a variety of interesting moments that bring the vehicle to life and create a character—a performing actor made of metal and rubber.

You should most certainly record several sets of maneuvers, moving from one location to another, because the surface on which the tires bear down is revealed to the microphone more dramatically than any of the other "getting there" cues. Remember that the sound of a tire on asphalt is totally different from the sound of a tire on cement or a tire on a dirt road. (Review cue #21 of the provided audio CD for examples of maneuver cue sounds.) Refer to the following list for the ranges of maneuvers.

In and maneuver about—slow and deliberate (perspective #1)
In and maneuver about—slow and deliberate (perspective #2)

In and maneuver about—normal (perspective #1)
In and maneuver about—normal (perspective #2)
In and maneuver about—fast and aggressive (perspective #1)
In and maneuver about—fast and aggressive (perspective #2)

Last but not least, record a variety of onboard constants. I usually set a pair of microphones on the back bumper, pointing downward toward the road and being influenced by the tailpipe. The second pair of microphones is inside the vehicle in a wide separation with the windows up. Later, in sound editorial, I cut the tailpipe constant alongside the interior constant to develop the right blend.

One of the most important points about onboard recordings is the illusion of speed. Many vehicle onboard recordings I have heard from other sound libraries are flat and lifeless, a dead giveaway they had been recorded literally. When you record onboards, find a road with a very long, gradual grade so that the performing vehicle engine always "works" and does not freewheel. Very often we must drive at slower speeds in lower gears to simulate higher speeds, an audio illusion to learn early. Recording reality is not always the most desirable.

To add to the recording challenge, *Christine* had been filmed during both rainy and dry weather. I did not want to cheat the wet tire sound effects under a dry car recording any more than I had to, so we decided to record the vehicles both dry and wet. This required hiring a water truck and driver. It was a hot August day when we custom recorded the wet car series. The water truck operator surely thought we were out of our minds when he arrived. He glanced about for a dirt road or construction site to wet down as he asked me where I wanted the water. I gestured down the hot broiling asphalt of the highway. "Are you nuts? The water will evaporate in a matter of minutes!" he snapped.

I assured him I understood that, but the work order did specify a mile-and-a-half stretch of county road. He asked me if I knew how much this load of water cost. Again I assured him I did, especially since I was paying for it. I asked him if he was getting paid for doing the job, and, if so, why should he care where and how the water was being utilized?He shrugged. "Whad'ya want me to do when I finish dumpin' it?"

Smiling, I stated, "I guess you had better go back and get another load. At the rate of evaporation, you're gonna be busy all day." For the next six hours, the water truck shuttled back and forth, laying down a fresh surface of water on the stretch of road. *Christine* had another unique problem. After the car was beat up and hurt, "she" limped back to the garage to heal. The rerecording mixer was capable of adding echo to the sound effects as the car rolled into the garage, but I wanted to customize a really unique audio event into the recording when *Christine* gets back to the her "nest" in the garage. A somewhat surprising location presented itself. Regrettably, my California hometown had been decimated in the 1983 earthquake, destroying 360 buildings and eleven square blocks of downtown. The powerful quake had also rendered the Sunset School buildings unusable for several years. Originally, the school had been designed with a unique open hallway and concrete corridors between buildings that had a roof but no walls between the wing groupings of classrooms. I knew recording a vehicle in a real garage with enclosed walls would add so much reverb to an engine recording it would be unacceptable. Here at Sunset School, the semi-open corridor provided a taste of enclosed reverb, but still allowed the major echo build-up usually accompanying interior recordings to escape into the open grassy breezeways. It was perfect. We just had to maneuver the performing vehicles up concrete steps into the hallway corridors.

Once we experienced the subdued reverberation, I knew we must customize several exact shots, as I just loved the sound of Christine's puffing engine, achieved by having four spark-plug wires removed and the exhaust pipe unbolted. This procedure worked well for the sequence in the movie where Christine blows up the gas station and returns to the garage. She enters the shelter with her entire chassis sizzling from the fire, turning past Robert Prosky as he watches her in disbelief. We had recorded very slow pass-bys in the corridor, allowing the performing car to basically idle as she passed. The Doppler effect of the tailpipe was perfect, and the entire effect built toward the crowning moment when she backed into her stall and switched off.

A signature effect of Christine in the movie was a complete gift of chance. While out on the county road recording start-and-idles, we discovered that the hydraulic system of the car wheezed and whined as it relaxed. At first, Tim Jordan was apologetic about it, jumping out of the car to cure the unwanted sound. I asked him to leave it alone for a moment, as we should specifically record the comical little wheeze with the pathetic metallic edge. Later during sound editorial, we decided to factor the sound into the sequence where Christine backs into her stall and turns off. The wheeze/whine became her pitiful exhalation. When John Carpenter (director) heard it on the rerecording stage, he asked if we could also use it in the last shot of the movie when the camera moves in close on the compressed block remains of Christine in the wrecking yard, and a little piece of her grill flexes.

Do not record vehicles in the same way you record production dialog. For recording dialog you put your microphone out on a fish pole and hold it up in the air just above the actors as the ideal placement to record their voices. Dialog recording mixers follow the same philosophy for recording sound effects—but that does not yield the most vibrant and exciting performance for sound effects. Oddly enough, I have my microphones very low to the ground, especially when recording the tailpipe perspectives. Also pay very close attention to what comes out of the tailpipe, should you choose to take up position there, as I discovered with *Christine* on the "angry revs." You need to try various placements until you find what pleases you the most.

Rule of thumb—"If it sounds good, it is correct." The placement of the microphone is an illusion of the reality you are creating for the screen.

Because sound travels better in colder air and fewer people and vehicles are out at night, so, too, less ambient gray noise clutters the atmosphere. Some of my best vehicle recordings were done during the late fall through early spring season, around or after midnight. The only allusion we have to nighttime is the sound of crickets, but crickets are also heard during the day, even though they are not as lively.

RECORDING MULTIPLE POINTS-OF-VIEW SIMULTANEOUSLY

With the advent of digital nonlinear editing technology, it has been much easier to record and develop complex multichannel "points-of-view" performance recordings. During an action chase sequence, such as in the movie, *Road Warrior,* the audience's point-of-view is all over the big tractor-trailer rig. One moment you are up in the cab with Mel Gibson; the next moment you are back on the rear of the tanker with the rear gunner; and the next moment you are on the front bumper of the tractor with Vernon Wells. Each one of these angles is going to sound, and should sound totally different. With the decelerations and the accelerations as the big rig maneuvers about, the powerful engine is going to be the foundation character. The RPM rate, whether it is rising or falling, and what gear the tractor is in cannot and should not suddenly be different from shot to shot. The ever-changing dynamics of the truck should have continuity, linking the series of shots together in a binding motion.

To cut a vehicle series together from individual cues that were recorded separately has always been a very challenging and arduous task. With today's technology we can easily record and re-master multiple points-of-view in synchronous stereo pairs so that if we cut from one angle to the other the dynamics of the engine will always be exactly at the correct RPM, whether decelerating or accelerating, making the sound editorial task vastly easier.

For a similar assignment, Eric Potter and his team had gone out to custom record the big Kaiser 5-ton Army Truck with the turbo charger for an action chase sequence. After studying the sequence in the picture with the supervising sound editor, the two had worked out the various actions that needed to be covered. In addition to a standard series of recordings, a list of specialized moves and road surfaces were noted.

Eric had decided that the best way to tackle the problem was to hire several other recording colleagues to join the team, bringing not only their own expertise but also their own equipment to use. In all, Eric had a twelve-man recording crew. Some of the recorders were digital DAT machines; some were 1/4" stereo Nagras. After evaluating the microphones in their arsenal, the recording teams agreed on what type of microphones and recording formats would work best in the various positions chosen.

Each recording team had a 5-watt communication radio. Three recording teams were positioned in a huge triangle configuration out on the desert salt flats. The stunt driver would perform the vehicle in its "chase" sequence action by driving around in a huge one mile circle, allowing each of the three "ground" recordists to have a close drive-by point-of-view followed by a long away and a long approach.

The fourth and fifth recorders were in the cab of the truck, recording action as miked from the front bumper and from inside the cab angled toward the driver's feet. The sixth recording team had their microphones positioned between the tractor and the box, able to get bright and "ballsy" exhaust raps. The seventh recording team was positioned on the rear of the truck, with microphones attached on shock mounts to the rear underside, favoring suspension and rattles.

Eric used a toy clicker as a sync slate, which he held up to his 5-watt communication radio when he clicked it. Each recordist had his own radio receiver held near his own slate mikes of their field mixer so that each recording would have a very short click point to be used later by the sound librarian to edit and align the material for mastering (as described in Chapter 11).

As with recording car series, it is very important not to allow tire skids or screeches into the performance. The primary task is to record a wide and full range of engine revs, accelerations, and decelerations that can be cut clean. If tire skidding is heard in the recording, it is very difficult to cut out later, denying the sound editor the use of clean engine sounds where the tire skid has been heard. A sound editor will invariably not want the skids that are in the recording for the sequence he or she is cutting, but would rather add separate tracks of skids so that they can be properly controlled and balanced later in the mix.

RECORDING ANIMALS

Recording animals can be extremely challenging. Many movements or vocals that must be recorded are so subtle that you must record the animals under very strict audio controllable conditions. Many choose to record animals on a Foley stage, which can work for various kinds of animal recordings, but some animals do not respond naturally in an alien environment. The biggest problem in recording real animal vocals and movement performances is that the vast majority of animal trainers who contract with entertainment industries train their animals to react to vocal or signal commands. This makes it impossible to get a clean recording when working with a trainer who is constantly blowing his or her whistle or snapping a clicker or shouting vocal cues, most of the time either on top of or intruding into the desired part of the animal's vocal.

One animal trainer who does not rely on making unwanted noises or speaking to his performing animal during sound recordings is Karl Lewis Miller of Animal Action. Karl trains his dogs to perform on cue or make desired reactions or vocals by use of visual signals. Only once or twice during the recordings of his dogs did he actually have to speak. Daddy, the big Saint Bernard that played the title character in *Cujo*, ambled up to the stone Karl had set on the ground as Daddy's "marks." I had advised my boom operator, Chuck Smith, to extend the microphone pole to give some distance between himself and the big dog. Chuck waved me off, thinking Daddy was about the most docile canine he had ever come across, and therefore stood far too close to the mark. I rolled the Nagra and announced "speed." Karl silently got Daddy's attention, then stuck his finger out, pointing at Daddy's nose, then made a wide sudden gesture. The dog lunged forward, stopping within inches of the microphone, his giant jowls snapping, reminding us how he had made *Cujo* so terrifying. He growled, barked, and lunge-snapped. After a full minute of canine viciousness, the trainer made another motion. The massive dog stopped his performance, backed up on the stone mark, and returned to his docile and friendly self as if nothing happened. Chuck had turned pale with fear. Perspiration streamed down his forehead as he immediately began to loosen the microphone pole tube locks and extend the pole to its maximum 18-foot reach.

An interesting trick the trainer used to keep his dogs from barking, while still allowing the animal to perform vicious growls and vocal gutturals when desired, was to insert a tennis ball into the dog's mouth. The ball was a toy, so the dog was having fun, but it inhibited the animal from barking.

As animal trainers strive to be in demand, more and more are learning to train their animals to perform to visual, rather than audio cues. Such noise cues end up on production tracks over the dialog when the animals perform on screen, spoiling many a soundtrack and making preparations in sound editorial much more difficult.

RECORDING AIRPLANES

Recording airplanes is similar to recording vehicles. After all, you still want to record engine start, idle, and offs. You still want to record engine start, rev ups and downs. You still want to record engine start, taxi, and aways as well as taxi in toward mike, stop rev, and offs. The major difference is in where you position the microphones for maximum yield, and, especially with propeller craft, not to be subject to massive wind buffeting.

Several unique positions are necessary to get the power of the propeller aircraft engine on tape. I took up position just in front of a single-engine Steerman biplane while my assistants held onto the tail section of the plane and the pilot revved up the engine to a very high RPM. The amazing harmonic rise and fall from these recordings became vital for power dives, in-flight maneuvers, strained pull-outs, and so forth. We also had the aircraft perform a figure-8 around us doing variations: some with engine revving up, some with engine decelerating.

While recording the 1920s-era biplane aircraft for *The Aviator,* we were challenged not only to find the precise and authentic aircraft with the correct engine, but to find them in a part of the country remote enough to safely record without jet aircraft interference or distant traffic noise. After calling Oshkosh, Wisconsin, the home of aviation, we were quickly referred to Hurley Boehler, an aviation expert and liaison out of Tulsa, Oklahoma. Hurley was able to put together not only the exact engine combinations called for by the producer, but was able to locate an excellent area in which to record the aircraft where we would be unfettered by unwanted audio intrusion.

We had two recording teams, each recording with a Nagra IV-S at 15 ips (inches per second) for maximum saturation. Our two-week recording expedition took in three biplanes and six period automobiles from the second-largest private car collection in the world, out of Muskogee, Oklahoma. Each day, we wrapped the recording session between two and three o'clock in the afternoon, then shipped all the 1/4" tapes back to my studio in North Hollywood, where they were edited and logged by the sound librarian. That recording adventure taught us some very important lessons. First, always tell the recordist who will be inside the aircraft recording onboard perspectives that you have asked the pilot to simulate engine failure as the plane is diving and swooping. As the Steerman went roaring past us, the pilot flipped the magneto off and on to simulate major engine trouble. All we could see was our recordist, his eyes big as saucers, fingers embedded in the fabric of the cockpit lining with an abiding certainty that he was about to meet his maker. You can review cue #24 of the audio CD provided with this book to hear the 1927 Steerman biplane as it approaches with simulated engine trouble and passes overhead.

Second, try to find a high position to record the aircraft fly-bys and especially the long lazy turns that work well for exterior in-flight constants. If you record these cues too close to the ground, you run the risk of picking up ground reflection as well as bird chirps and creature noises.

The ultimate recording is made from a unique "third-position" aerial platform. Such platforms do not exist naturally—unless you have a very tall tower in a recording environment with no wind. Try to find that! The serious aviation recordist will have a special all-welded metal hot-air balloon "basket" rig made to eliminate every conceivable noise-generating source for which conventional hot-air balloon baskets are notorious. This multi-tier platform is made of light-weight aircraft metal and has two levels. The top position is the pilot/safety officer platform, whose job it is to turn the burner off during the actual time of recording and back on when the recorders are turned off. As the safety officer, this person also maintains radio communication with all recording mixers and boom operators—just below the aircraft, on the ground, or in the performing aircraft—as well as the performing pilot. The safety officer is, therefore, responsible for the overall control of action and subsequent safety precautions.

The recording mixer sits with the boom operator in side-by-side seats with body harnesses on the lower level of the metallic rig. The multitrack recorders are strapped into a foam-insulated roll-bar type welded rack in front of and alongside the recording mixer. The boom operator is strapped into the seat next to the recording mixer. The boom operator has control of the "hot-head" type pillow block pylon that runs through the center of the dual level basket. This absolutely silent pillow-block mechanism allows the boom operator to rotate the lower deck from side to side or completely around in a 360-degree movement as required to keep the fixed angle multimicrophone set-ups in perfect spatial positioning as desired.

With this unique recording position, the usual audio clutter associated with point-of-view microphones that are confined to the ground are eliminated. The hot-air balloon drifts with the prevailing wind—so breeze buffet, which often plagues recordings (especially after 11:00 A.M.) is cut down tremendously. The trick is for the performing pilot to understand that the hot-air balloon is the center of performance—the bys and maneuvers must be large, circular arcs around the hot-air balloon in addition to hard BYs. Just think of it as recording a car for "estate" driving and the creative possibilities will all become clear to you.

This is also where multirecorder points-of-view style philosophy pays off. Careful breakdown and mastering of these audio cues back in the studio by the librarian will be crucial. (This is explained in detail in Chapter 11.)

RECORDING EXPLOSIONS

As a precaution, I made arrangements for the Westside Fire Department to stand by one Sunday morning at the Federal Pit as we detonated a custommade explosive device for the helicopter explosion in John Carpenter's *The Thing*. The nine firemen watched with interest as a one-foot hole was dug in the ground. I then poured five pounds of black powder into a steel pipe. On either side of the pipe, we strapped two small one-inch pipes filled with black powder. I placed the bottom end of the pipe bundle into the hole, then placed an upside-down trash can on top, knocking out a hole through which the top of the pipe would fit. My assistant then shoveled gravel into the trash can in and around the pipes. We set a second trash can, right-side up, on top of the base can and filled it with high-octane gasoline. The two smaller pipes would actually make the "bang"; the main pipe was to launch a short steel sleeve up through the bottom of the second trash can, igniting the fuel and blasting it up and out.

To simulate helicopter debris for the explosion, my assistant, Peter Cole, had absconded with all kinds of metal siding and scrap found alongside the road, including some old signs still being used by the county. (Fortunately, the fire captain had a good sense of humor about the roadside markers.) We ran the detonator wires back about 200 feet, where Peter had the battery and ignition switch. I had taken up a position about 50 feet back from the device with my microphones spread wide left and right, where I hoped to catch an acoustical concussionary slap off the far wall of the pit.

The fire crews and their trucks pulled back 200 yards to safety. All were instructed not to verbally react or say anything until well after the event. I told Peter I would yell "rolling" and he should silently count to three, then hit the switch. After being satisfied that the tape recorder was rolling properly, I yelled "rolling" and waited for the detonation. Almost ten seconds passed without an event. I peered out of my foxhole to see Peter struggling with the battery. It was not strong enough to set off the detonator through that much wire. I quickly called out for him to stop trying.

I jumped up and ran over to check the device. Gasoline was starting to leach from the upper can. We had to do something quickly, before fuel drenched the pipes below. I yelled to the top of the pit for someone to drive my car down. Within moments someone delivered my Dodge Diplomat down into the Federal Pit to Peter's position. I lifted the hood and pulled the detonation wire over to the car battery. Grabbing a hold of Peter to get his undivided attention, I yelled, "Whatever you do, when you touch these two wires, do not hesitate or wait for the explosion. Touch the second wire and instantly drop to the ground, as fast as you can. Do you understand?"

Peter nervously nodded. As he took the detonation wire, his hands were shaking. I repeated my previous instructions. "I will say 'rolling,' then you count silently to three and touch it off. Got it?"

I ran back to my foxhole and turned on the tape recorder. "Rolling!" Three silent moments passed, and then the air was split by the explosion. Peter was actually starting to drop for the ground when the second wire touched the car battery terminal. The main pipe split open and flattened out, flying over Peter's head like a Frisbee, landing 200 yards away, only three feet from a fireman.

The fireball mushroomed out like a miniature atomic explosion, blowing over my foxhole, then rising skyward. Metal debris flew everywhere. Most of the Federal Pit was ablaze when the fire trucks headed down to douse the flames. Satisfied that I had captured the audio event, I stood up from listening to the playback of the recording to find the fire captain standing next to me, watching his men mop up the aftermath. He turned to me and winked. "Well son, that was about as good as sex." Then he continued on down the hill. I was not quite sure what to say to a comment like that; I doubt that Roger Ebert ever gave a thumbs-up rating with a quote like that.

As it turned out, I learned some very valuable lessons about recording explosions. First, always work with a professional explosives contractor who knows what he or she is doing.

Second, unlike the bullet flights discussed at the beginning of this chapter, explosions are definitely recordable without your having to be with the equipment. The most important part of the explosion is the first fraction of a second after the initial blast ignition. If you are not set to properly record that, then the rest of the recording is meaningless. I usually use the horn of a big car at semi-close proximity, such as a Cadillac, to act as a pseudo on-site recording-level test. It is only a guess, but it gets you close to a safe recording level. As with recording gunfire, your first few shots are either overmodulated or underrecorded, until you find the ideal record setting. Do not depend on one explosion.

That is one of the primary reasons we like to record these kind of high-maintenance high-cost-per-performance events with multiple tape recorders. On the first explosion, if one recorder overmodulated, there is a good chance that one of the others did not. After the first explosion, each recorder should be carefully rewound and reviewed for you to hear the playback of the blast. The sound effect recordist should pay strict attention to the VU meter, as a quality speaker monitoring system cannot be on-site to audibly analyze the recording. Headsets should only be used as confirmation that the recording was successfully made; they should not be depended on to render a quality analysis of the frequency breadth of the recording.

Third, do not rely on record limiters to keep from overmodulating. If your first explosion is overmodulated, then make a new level adjustment. By using record limiters, you invite unwanted signal compression that ruins the desired effect.

Fourth, record gunfire and explosions at the fastest tape speed you can. At the very minimum, record with an analog tape recorder at 15 ips. If can get your hands on an analog tape recorder capable of field recording at speeds of 30 ips, you truly will be ecstatic with the results! (Review cue#22 of the provided audio CD for a comparison of how the same rifle-shot sounds recorded by an audio cassette at 1-5/8 ips, an analog Nagra recording at

Figure 10.8 When using explosives, it is always safety first!

7-1/2 ips, an analog Nagra recording at 15 ips, a digital DAT, and a direct-to-disk digital recording on the Deva. Each recorder is using Electro-Voice RE-16 microphones in an X–Y configuration. Absolutely no equalization or signal manipulation occurs prior to the audio CD mastering. Each rifle shot cue is presented absolutely raw for better quality comparison.)

Fifth, and most important, do not try to integrate debris into the recording of the explosion. As explained in Chapter 12, debris such as the metal signs and junk should not be used in a staged explosion. Debris should be recorded as separate audio cues and cut together with the explosion blasts later during the editorial process.

To achieve a unique explosion sound, try taking several recordings of the same explosion, recorded on different tape recorders using different microphone configurations, and then blend them together. Often, one set of microphones delivers a more "crackly" character to the explosion, with little low-end. Another stereo pair has a rich bottom-end boom, with little high-end. A third stereo pair may have more mid-range with a near overtone tail to it. Putting all three stereo pairs together during the sound editorial process delivers a combination that none of the stereo pairs alone could capture.

SMALLER IS OFTEN BIGGER

Just as you record vehicles in slower low gears to create the illusion of speed, you must look to other, smaller props to sell the illusion of size. Glass and metal chains illustrate this point. Big chains do not make big chain noise—they make very disappointing clunky sounds. Accurately judging how chains will sound is extremely difficult when you go to the hardware store to pick the correct size and grade of chain for your recording. I take along my tape recorder and listen to the chains through the microphone I intend to use. How does the microphone hear the chain metal? Small links of brass or brass alloy metal work best, but you must test them by listening to their movement and clanks through the recorder's microphone, as not all chain links are created equal.

Imagine you have a sequence in which a huge storefront window is smashed. Do not buy thick sheets of storefront glass. They only sound dull and "thunky." Single-thickness glass sheets make the biggest sounds. We discovered that holding the glass sheet horizontally in the air, then swinging a solid steel bar upward from underneath just as you let go of the glass, produces the best results with longer air-flight time for glass shard ring off.

Remember, you must wear eye goggles. It is also advisable to wear thick motorcycle gauntlets and wrap your body in packing blankets for protection. However, be aware of unwanted cloth and leather glove movements with all this protective armor. One of the best glass breaking sequences I recorded was performed outdoors. My father and I went to an old concrete bridge that crossed a dry streambed. I placed one set of microphones near the glass sheets, and the other set down near the bottom. My father then dropped one sheet of glass at a time, making sure it clipped the edge of the bridge railing. The glass burst into shards, cascading a wonderful shower of glass down to the concrete slope below, where I got a very nice impact and shard slide.

An amazing glass recording I made fifteen years ago still is being used around town today: the exploding light bulb smash for *The Philadelphia Experiment*. We took an 8-foot 2 × 12 and drilled 5 rows of 20 holes the exact width to screw in a light bulb. Into these 100 holes we screwed 100 6-inch fish-tank bulbs. Taking the prop to the Foley stage, I had an assistant hold the bottom of the board so it would stand upright. The assistant wore heavy gloves and eye goggles; several thick packing blankets were also draped over him. Slipping on my eye goggles, I took an iron bar to the light bulbs in one smooth swing. The result was an astounding explosion of glass.

The largest wood rips and tears are not recorded with huge logs or thick lumber, but with thin plywood sheets exposed to the weather. The lamination on the plywood comes apart after being soaked in water and baked in the sun for several years. Stand back a couple of feet from the microphone and pry the layers apart with various intensities. These recordings produce amazing results when combined with the wrenching whine a tree makes as it begins to fall from being chopped through. Veneer and plywood "separation" rips truly sell the desired moment.

IMPORTANCE OF SCRIPT BREAKDOWN

Every producer, director, unit production manager, production coordinator, director of photography, and anyone aspiring to these jobs should read this section very carefully. The described incident is not unique to the film discussed herein, but is one of many. Setting your supervising sound editor before you commence principal photography is an excellent and advisable idea. After reading the script, the supervising sound editor apprises you on a number of sound editorial requirements that lay ahead. Don't just listen to the sound editor's advice—follow it! It will save you tens of thousands, if not hundreds of thousands, of dollars.

Producer Ross Hunter was looking for a full, exciting sound job for his 1970 smash hit, *Airport*. Hunter sent a copy of the screenplay to Joe Sikorski at Universal Studios. Joe carefully read through the script, making numerous notes and underlining areas of concern. A few days later he sat down with Hunter and reviewed his notes. He had made a precise list of approximately 120 sound events that concerned him deeply. The producer must guarantee that these recordings would be made during the principal photography process, because all the equipment and manpower necessary to create these sounds would be available at that time.

The production company secured the St. Paul Airport in Minnesota, with exterior runway and tarmac filming to occur when the airport was shut down in the evenings. Months passed. The production company had wrapped the shoot and returned to Los Angeles. Several weeks later, Hunter called Sikorski about doing a temp dub for the sequence where George Kennedy tries to get a stuck Boeing 707 out of the soft ground between two runways. The congo line of snow plows and scrapers lines up, awaiting Burt Lancaster's order to move forward and plow the distressed airliner off the airfield, making room to open up runway Two-Niner for the inbound bomb-damaged Trans Global airliner to land. Hunter wanted to have a temp sound effect job underline the visual excitement of the sequence to show it to a test audience and see how it played. Sikorski said they would be happy to oblige. "You need to send over the sound effect recordings that we asked you to make while you were up there filming."

After an awkward pause, Hunter replied, "We forgot. We didn't get any."

Sikorski explained that the studio's sound library did not have the sounds the sequence required, which was why he had given the painstakingly precise sound-event notes to the producer in the first place. Hunter understood, then asked Sikorski to work up a budget of what it would take to custom record the sounds he needed. Several days later, Sikorski received a call from Hunter, who had just reviewed the custom recording budget. "Are you out of your mind? This is half the budget of the picture! Couldn't we just go down to LAX [L.A. International Airport] and record this stuff?"

Sikorski explained to the producer that, even if they could get permission and cooperation from the FAA to record at Los Angeles International, his team certainly would not be able to get the clean, isolated recordings that sound editors need. He suggested they might try putting together some odds and ends, mixing them together to get through the temp. This ray of hope delighted Hunter. "Anything, try anything!"

In addition to a multitude of other sound effect requirements for the temp dub, Sikorski pulled numerous sounds of jets, motor whines, turbine start-ups, and other noises and cut them into elements to remix as new sound effect masters for the jet revs. A couple of weeks later, Sikorski was on the dubbing stage, supervising the temp mix with Hunter. An exciting sequence grew to a climax. Burt Lancaster orders the line of snow plows forward. The flight assistant glances at George Kennedy in the pilot's seat, while the aircraft shudders from the engines, straining to pull itself out. "Petroni, she won't take much more!"

The furrows on Kennedy's brow deepen with determination as he chomps on his cigar. "Well, she's gonna get it!"

Kennedy shoves the engine controls forward with a resolution to either get her out of the mud or tear themselves apart in the effort. Sikorski's newly created jet revs scream out, adding to Alfred Newman's exciting musical score. The angle cuts to a close-up on the landing gear as the tires mash down on wood plankings. Sounds of wood moaning and twisting tell of the incredible weight bearing down. Suddenly the 707 wallows up from the soft ground and lunges out onto the taxiway; the engine revs peak and settle down into a reverse to slow. To be sure, it was an exciting audio moment and a memorable sequence in theatrical film history.

Joe Sikorski soon found himself manufacturing various sound events from other sounds to make do. It was not what he wanted. Customized sound recording undoubtedly would have brought the picture to an even higher level of achievement. It is, however, a tribute to what a creative sound editorial team can do when faced with having to make do with what's at hand.

Sound editors often must work with what they have even when the producer went to the trouble of recording wild tracks. I was working on a helicopter action movie that involved several very stylish-looking choppers. To add delight to the project, the cinematography was fairly good, especially the aerial action footage. The picture editor had thought through the material and had cut it with an eye for action stereophonic sound. I had been informed that the production mixer went to great lengths to record all kinds of helicopter action sounds. Eagerly gleaning the 1/4" production tapes, I tried to find the golden recordings that would jump to the forefront and make the show come to life. To my dismay, only a handful of cues were usable; during the recordings, crew members were constantly talking.

Later, on the rerecording stage, we were mixing the sound effect predubs when one of the producers (also an owner of one of the helicopters) got up. "That's not a Hughes 500! Why didn't you use the wild tracks of the helicopters we recorded?"

I had had it!! I spun around on him with fed-up looks to kill. "I would have loved to have used your wild track recordings! But your crew couldn't keep their mouths shut. If they had kept quiet while your mixer was trying to record your helicopters, then I could have used your wild track recordings! Maybe next time you'll teach your crew how to keep their #$%*ing mouths shut when your production mixer is trying to get a priceless recording!"

Suffice to say, I didn't hear another word out of him during the rest of the mix. It is infuriating to spend hours poring over what should have been fabulous production recordings only to find them filled with voices and other noises.

PREPARING FOR SUCCESSFUL RECORDINGS

Put together a kit of supplies and tools to take along on location recording sessions. The one thing you can count on is that unforeseen problems and "whoopsies" are parts of your recording adventure. The larger the crew and the more complex the scope of work, the more Murphy's Law ("Whatever can go wrong, will") rises up to try and frustrate you.

Probably the most common shortcoming in field recording is lack of an adequate and dependable power supply. You do not find an abundance of AC wall outlets built into the rocks in the field. Therefore, pay attention to the inventory of batteries necessary to sustain your equipment during your session. Not all batteries are created equal, especially battery packs unique to certain recording devices and custom designed for use only with those units. This is where the analog Nagra 1/4"machines show themselves as such great workhorses. The internal battery cavity holds twelve "D"-cell batteries, which, when the recorder is properly used, easily sustain the machine all day long, and longer. Have a full set of back-up batteries securely packed and sealed in case your battery meter test suddenly plunges.

The other great thing about "D"-cell power is that if you do break down in the middle of nowhere with battery shortcomings, just go to the nearest convenience store and you are back in business. I shy away from using any tape recorder, whether analog or digital, that has custom designed batteries unique to that unit. Where do I find emergency battery supplies if I am up in the high Sierras? I doubt the local trading post has any custom batteries in the stockroom, let alone the JMV-3871/X88 rectangular power cells required by a particular portable digital machine.

Towels are extremely useful for covering and insulating equipment, drying things that got wet, or even in helping isolate wind buffets in emergencies. I usually keep a couple of bath towels and several hand towels in the trunk of the car for such use. In addition to traditional towels, packets with premoistened wipes are extremely handy. Keep several plastic clothes bags from the dry cleaner in a separate paper bag. Plastic clothes bags make excellent microphone and equipment wraps when recording in damp, drizzle, or even a full-fledged downpour. Use 3/4″ paper tape to wrap the plastic clothes bag tightly around the recorder or microphone(s) so that loose plastic does not flap about, making unwanted noise.

Adhesive tape is very handy. You should use a wide but gentle paper tape if you need to tape microphone cable firmly against the side of a vehicle to keep cable vibration from spoiling the recording. You do not want to pull the tape up and have the paint job come with it. I like to have a roll of 1/2″ Scotch Magic Tape for paperwork or lightweight applications, and a roll of gaffer's tape or at least duct tape for heavy-duty needs. I also keep several colors of 3/4″ paper tape for color-code labeling. You will also need several Sharpie markers of different colors.

Always keep a tool kit, including both a full-sized Phillips screwdriver and a flat-head screwdriver (in addition to a fine-instrument size of each). You should have a claw hammer, a 1-inch paint brush never used for painting, a pair of needle-nosed pliers, and a standard set of pliers. Include large and small sets of Allen wrenches.

Stock a separate head cleaner kit, with a can of compressed air to blow dust and debris out of the equipment, along with head cleaner and head cleaning swabs secured in heavy duty zipper-lock freezer bags.

Include a steno or small notepad so that you or your assistant can jot down recording information to assist in the sound library work that soon follows.

Pack a set of flares in the car for both emergency use and traffic control. Also pack a fire extinguisher, just in case.

Purchase at least two heavy-duty flashlights for your kit. Many recording sessions are done in the night. You can also use flashlights as microphone reference points for the shooter to see. As your recording experience increases, you will develop a system of signaling with flashlights rather than risking audio intrusion on a recording by speaking. Always have a personal safety kit. This should include a standard first-aid kit with the basic bandages, gauzes, iodine, medical tape, and snake bite kit. Fortify the first-aid kit with good eye wash, petroleum jelly, calamine lotion, strong sunblock, and insect repellent.

Include several pairs of ear plugs to protect the eardrums from the sound of close proximity gunfire. The personal safety kit should also include several pairs of eye-goggles and heavy construction gloves. You should have a little accessories bag to keep in the personal safety kit that has safety pins, a good pair of scissors, and a box of industrial single-edged razor blades, and/or an Exacto knife.

When recording sound effects outdoors, especially in desert regions, dehydration and sunstroke are real dangers. Many technicians get deeply involved and forget that the sun is beating down on the tops of their uncovered heads, or they forget to use SPF 35 sunscreen

Figure 10.9 Looking for the ideal recording venue.

on their faces and arms. Three hours later, they wonder why they feel funny and their skin feels tight and crispy.

You should also include a water spray-bottle. Being able to spray water onto the body or onto a prop you are recording is also very useful.

Take along a change of comfy and warm clothes, especially socks and shoes. I have lost count of recording trips where, for one reason or another, I either fell into or found it necessary to get into water, such as a mountain stream, pounding surf, flooded fields, swimming pools, or other liquid masses that will spoil your attire. I especially remember what the sloppy mud and clay of Oklahoma can do, not only to your clothing but also to your equipment and vehicle mats.

When you know you must put yourself into the wet and muck to properly achieve an audio performance, do what is necessary, no matter what you are wearing. Hence, you should record in junk clothes, taking a change of clothing with you. Wear cotton clothing rather than nylon or plastic, because synthetic fibers make "shushy" noises when you move, obviously spoiling your recording.

Proper planning and preparation of equipment and supplies goes a long way toward helping you achieve supremely recorded sound effects. The rest is limited only by your own imagination.

Chapter 11
The Sound Librarian:
Curator of an Audio Empire

"I know you need a body fall—but is that a body fall on cement, on wood, grass, on soft dirt, hard dirt, into shifting sand, into dried brush, garbage, a wood pile, metal dumpster, starship decking, onto the hood of a car—is it fleshy or lots of clothing—do we hear an argh or no vocal at all?! You gotta be more specific here, Steve!"

Mollie Gordon, librarian of Creative Café, responding to an exasperated editor on Twister

Just recording sound is not enough. If you ever hope to efficiently work with the recordings you spent so much time making, adopt a sound library system that not only assimilates the data but offers swift and easy access to it. A dedicated sound librarian developing and maintaining the sound library helps, but because few of us can afford such a luxury, we must do it ourselves. I am too protective of my material not to do it myself. This is not necessarily bad. Being your own librarian gives you an incredible edge because you have an intimate knowledge of not only each cue's labels, but you also know exactly how you entered and "cleaned" the material.

THE EVOLUTION OF FINDING IT

Supervising sound editors know they must work quickly and be extremely flexible in custom recording and gathering precise sound cues from the sound effects library to mount their film or audio project. Before the advent of digital sound technology, the most common media in which to store sound effects were 35 mm magnetic film (both monaural stripe and fullcoat for multichannel stereo), 1/4" inch tape, and audio cassette tape. A few unique libraries transferred sounds to 4-channel 1/2" tape or 24-track 2" tape (using time code as a reference), but they were not really part of the mainstream theatrical sound editorial community.

Figure 11.1 At Weddington Productions, thousands of 1/4″ tapes are kept in a temperature- and humidity-controlled environment, even after they have been digitally transferred to DAT cassettes. These tapes await retransfer as soon as technology significantly improves analog-to-digital converters or geometrically higher sampling rates and bit depth. At that point, it is worthwhile to return to the original 1/4″ tapes to take advantage of the analog source. (Photo by David Yewdall)

For sound effects, nothing sounds better than 1/4″ analog tape recorded at a speed of 15 ips. Most of us have custom recorded our sound effects on 1/4″ tape, then have had sound librarians carefully edit and "leader-out" the individual sound cues by splicing in white 1/4″ leader. They physically wrote the cue number on each white section of white tape. This allowed the transfer operator to easily count the white leaders that would spin across the sound head at high speed. Some librarians used a red Sharpie to edge every tenth sound cue leader, making it even easier for a transfer operator to identify and spin down to cue 46, for instance. He or she simply counted as four red-edged leaders flew by and then paid closer attention to counting the last six white leaders.

OPTICAL SOUND TO MAGNETIC FILM

Thousands of priceless sound effects have filtered down to us from previous years on magnetic 35 mm film—many were carefully remastered from 35 mm optical track. These first sound effects were originally recorded in a device known as a sound camera. The equipment was so bulky it had to be mounted inside a vehicle called the sound truck to move it quickly

Figure 11.2 35 mm film optical track.

from one location to another. The sound mixer recorded directly into the sound camera, which "photographed" an image of the sound onto the area just inside the perforation holes of 35 mm film.

This continually undulating area of "photographed" sound is known as an optical track. Optical track technology still is used today in theatrical presentations of features presented in theatres with no digital technology and in the audio presentation of 16 mm prints. The sound is created through an exciter lamp in the sound camera that creates one of many kinds of optical track formats. The film is then sent to the laboratory and developed. The optical soundtrack can then be played on a synchronizer, Moviola, or projector also equipped with a playback exciter lamp optical head. Light passes through the optical soundtrack image of the film and strikes a photoelectric cell, causing current fluctuations that accurately reproduce the analog audio signal for playback.

During the first three decades of motion picture sound, sound editors had to work with their tracks very carefully. An editor would take much greater care in ordering the needed sound effects, especially the number of repetitions. If cutting a gun battle, you ordered enough repetitions of a particular gun to cut the sequence. If you suddenly came up short, or ruined the material with which you were working, the remedy was not as easy as it is today with digital technology. Now we simply highlight the needed sound and duplicate it with a computer keystroke. An editor back then, though, would have to order the desired sound cue from the sound librarian, who would build the master effect into a roll with other 35 mm optical masters, which would then be shipped with a work order to be loaded onto an optical camera and shot over and over again onto a fresh roll of 35 mm film. The magazine of film would then be shipped to the laboratory to be developed. Depending on how busy the sound department and laboratory were, a day or two could easily pass before a sound editor would receive reprints of the necessary gunshot effect to complete the work.

Not only did the sound editor need to be careful about the amount of material ordered, but also with handling the film. Most sound editors wore at least one white cotton glove so that fingerprints or skin oils would not be left inadvertently on the track. The emulsion of the track could easily be scratched, causing pops and crackles. The sound editor laced up the

Figure 11.3 This Moviola is equipped to read both magnetic and optical sound. The editor has flipped up the magnetic sound head (single track) out of position to check the optical soundtrack from a section of release print. Note the thick cylindrical unit protruding from the film. An exciter lamp inside shines a narrow beam of light through the optical track. The light is read and translated into modulations. (Photo by David Yewdall)

optical track on the sound head of the Moviola. After adjusting the sync point of the sound effect, the sound editor carefully noted on the film the exact foot and frame point for the sound assistant to build the cue into individual reels of sound called "sound units." These units held numerous individual sound cues, spaced precisely apart by "fill leader" (35 mm film that was usually recycled newsreel or release prints).

The sound editor assembled sound cues with the fill leader with Mercer clips. This roll was then sent to assembly, where the assistant hot-spliced the sections of film together; and, using "blooping ink," the assistant made sure the splice points did not have any exposed

Figure 11.4 Projector optical reader head. (Photo by David Yewdall)

scraped emulsion areas that would cause loud pops and snaps due to a bright burst of light leaking into the optical reader.

With the advent of magnetic film in the early 1950s, the cut-and-assembly technique changed dramatically. Although the sound librarian still had to send assembled masters of sound effects to the transfer department for quantities of reprints to be made for sound editors, 35 mm magnetic film was not developed at a lab. Once it had been removed from the 35 mm magnetic film recorder, it was instantly ready to be broken down and used by the sound editor.

The sound editor still threaded the 35 mm magnetic film under the sound head of the Moviola or synchronizer, and still made precise sync notations—but instead of preassembling the sound cues with sections of filler using Mercer clips for hot-splicing, the sound editor merely hung the cut sections of magnetic sound effects on a series of hooks in a trim bin.

After the sound editor completed cutting the reel, the trim bin was rolled into the assistant's room, where an apprentice assembled the individual sound cues into the sound units. As before, the empty distance between sound cues was spaced out with fill leader—but instead of hot-splicing the cuts and painting the splices with blooping ink, the apprentice used a Rivas tape splicer and taped the backside of the film.

Whether the sound editor cuts with optical sound, magnetic film, or with modern digital technologies, the basic techniques and demands on the sound librarian have changed very little. As this book has repeated over and over—only the tools change; technical disciplines, artistic techniques, strategies, and philosophy of sound always have remained the same—and always will.

ORGANIZING A SYSTEM TO FIND STUFF

At the heart of the sound editorial world is the sound library—a vast wealth of sounds, both historical and designed. The sound library must be a highly organized and protected shelter, safe from the ravages of heat and moisture, safe from destruction or loss—yet available at a moment's notice as demands may require. The sound librarian is the gatekeeper, shepherd of the flock, and audio accountant, charged with the responsibility of organizing and protecting the limitless frontier of sound bites.

The sound library is never complete, but is ever growing and expanding. Challenges to the sound librarian include not only the management and care of hundreds of thousands of sounds, but also keeping track of the continually evolving technology by which the library is archived, cataloged, accessed, and protected.

I find sound library work both relaxing and enriching. I have learned much about our world through listening to and working with my own sound library. Some of the most enjoyable times in my audio work have been dealing with historical sound effects, especially recordings of that which does not exist today, or of museum pieces no longer utilized. When was the last time you heard a Daimler-Benz engine of a Messerschmitt 109 approach and rip by at emergency war speed? What distinguished the sound of a P-38 Lightning with its turbocharged engines from all other aircraft? One can almost catch the acrid smell of burned oil in the nostrils after a long day of processing and remastering these fabulous historic recordings. It can be very stimulating, and your work goes toward preserving and archiving these vanishing wonders.

Assigning Sound Cues Part Numbers

No industry standard exists by which to build and maintain a sound library. The first and foremost starting point for precise identification and accessibility of an audio cue is carefully assigning a "part number" to each sound cue entered in the library. Regardless of whether a computer database is utilized, nothing is more accurate than a dedicated part number.

"Topic-Roll-Cue" System

Some sound libraries are set up with initials to designate the topic, prior to the actual part number—such as CR6-87. "CR" stands for crashes, "6" stands for sound roll number, and "87" stands for cue #87. The transfer operator reads the sound effect numbers from the transfer order form, seeing the need to print CR6-87 for a sound effects editor. From the tape rolls stored on the library shelf, the transfer operator withdraws tape CR6, loads it into the playback machine (usually an analog 1/4" or 1/2" tape, but sometimes a digital DAT), and spins down to cue #87. If the material is archived on 1/4" tape, the transfer operator listens to the 40-cycle tone voice slates, which at high speed "beep" as they fly by the playback head. If the material is archived on 1/2" tape, the transfer operator enters the time code reference, which spins the tape down to the precise point on the tape. The transfer operator decides on which of the three available channels the desired sound cue can be found.

If the material is archived on digital DAT, the transfer operator simply enters the PNO (program number) on the keypad of the machine or remote on the unit's keypad and then presses the "play "button. The machine spins at 200 times speed to find the precise PNO requested.

As library part numbering systems go, the "Topic-Roll-Cue" system at least allows for an ongoing growth of the sound library, in a linear fashion, while keeping common topic sound effects together. Instead of sound rolls numbering from 1 and progressing numerically, sound rolls have initials for topic designations and any number of rolls in that category. This is not a common system.

"Linear Numbering" System

Many sound libraries use a linear style of numbering rolls and sound effects, making for an easy and universally understood way to cross-verify material. This system works especially well when mastering sound cues to consecutive digital DATs. This system can be applied whether you are sending a transfer order to have analog transfers made (i.e., 35 mm fullcoat or 35 mm single stripe) or you are sending an order to have the sound cues downloaded into a nonlinear computer editing system such as Pro Tools. If the transfer order notes that DAT 0120-73 must be transferred stereophonically, the transfer operator knows it is the 120th DAT in the sound library, puts the DAT into the machine, and punches in 73 as the PNO.

DAT Mastering System

Even in today's computer audio file environment, having your sound library mastered to digital DAT as a foundation system is a very wise and economically sound insurance policy. Most of us have crossed over from the days when we cut the sound for our projects on 35 mm fullcoat and 35 mm single stripe. Many of us adapted to the changing technology and growing success of our businesses and scope of work. Extremely few of us working today remember recording sound effects from a sound truck with the optical camera (no, I am not one of them). Most of us remember venturing out from our editing rooms to record with Sony TCD-5 audio cassette recorders, then graduating to Nagra 1/4" and higher-quality microphones, as budgets allowed. With early experimentations in digital recordings, many of us tried the clumsy and cumbersome Sony F-1, while others ventured into the incredibly expensive digital tape decks that were only teases of things to come. Then, in the late 1980s, the first gray-market digital DAT decks were adopted by those who wanted digital technology in the field. This evolving technology gave us a sound effect library compilation filled with a frightening intermixture of technologies and formats.

As a sound library tool, digital DAT is the answer to many technological and organizational problems, not the least of which is the ability to defeat print-through of overmodulated sound effects such as gunshots, explosions, crashes, metal, and so forth. Sound librarians jumped with joy as they were able to record a digitized program code number with each sound effect recorded on the DAT. During search-and-seize time to make transfers of these sound effects, nothing is faster in the tape format world.

DAT technology presented a great opportunity to retransfer our multiformat sound libraries into digital-based realms—realms that would solve a host of problems that had plagued sound artists for decades. By 1987 the race was on to convert to a DAT master system. Naturally, a new set of problems and disagreements arose, not the least of which was understanding the differences between the standard VU meter, which sound craftspeople had been using for decades, and digital peak meters the digital DAT machines used. This misunderstanding caused thousands of overmodulated transfers to DAT. This costly mistake

Figure 11.5 As the sound librarian at Weddington Productions, Steve Lee carefully edits original 1/4″ tapes before having them digitally transferred to DAT master tapes. Eventually these DATs will be retransferred to CD-ROMs and DVDs as carefully prepared Sound Designer II audio files. (Photo by David Yewdall)

is still felt today, as many libraries had to return to their 35 mm mag and 1/4″ originals vaulted away in cold storage and remaster them all over again!

Even the manufacturers of the digital DAT machines disagreed on what "0" VU equaled on their DAT meters. Many claimed it was at –12 dB on the peak meter; most thought it was –16 dB. Still others who did not understand the calibration differences at all simply thought that, like Nagra machines, they should set their "0" dB reference tone at –8 dB on the digital peak meter. All these choices resulted in overmodulation.

After several years of disagreement and trial and error, most of us now generally accept and understand that the "0" VU level equals –18 dB on the digital DAT peak meter. Since many action sound effects, such as gunshots, explosions, crashes, and impacts, were recorded in the "saturation" style (see Chapter 10), that extra headroom certainly would be needed to properly remaster the analog recording. A few sound editorial facilities, especially those with a reputation for high-concept sound effects, are even starting to use –20 dB as "0" on the VU meter.

Mastering to CD-ROM

The CD-ROM is still the most cost-effective per megabyte for drag-and-drop storage medium. With a maximum capacity of 700 megabytes, the cost hovers at around a penny per 15 megabytes of storage. As the cost of DVD-RAM recorders and cartridges continues to

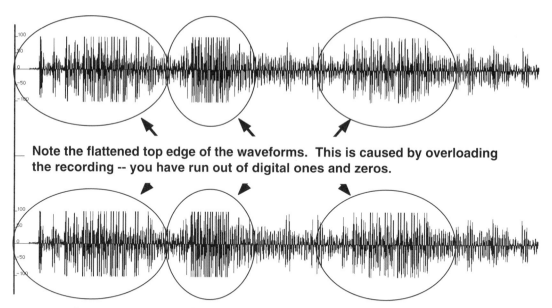

Note the flattened top edge of the waveforms. This is caused by overloading the recording -- you have run out of digital ones and zeros.

Figure 11.6 Sound Designer II audio file with flattened overloaded top edge.

drop, the cost per megabyte for storage will fall below even that of the CD-ROM. The advantage, at present, is that one DVD-RAM equals eight to nine CD-ROMs in terms of storage capacity. Depending on the depth of mastering on the DVD, the medium will offer anywhere from twelve to twenty times the disk storage capacity of a single of CD-ROM. Even so, the CD-ROM is assured considerable life as a high-capacity, affordable way to record to a medium that, if properly stored and maintained, has the ability to sustain a very long shelf-life.

Unlike a digital DAT or other analog media, CD-ROMs and DVDs can be scanned by computer archival software, and in a very short time you can build at least a rudimentary database in which to find the material you need.

Following are three important things you must be aware of in handling CD-ROMs.

1. Do not touch the data surface of a CD-ROM. Do not set a CD-ROM on a table top, and never slide the disk's data surface across anything. Doing so is liable to cause scratches or damage that does not allow the CD-ROM player's laser to properly read bytes of data, causing error and possible permanent loss of audio files.
2. Do not store CD-ROMs in an environment that is too hot, or atop equipment that radiates heat. If the disk warps, you cannot get it to read correctly in a CD-ROM player, resulting in the loss of material on it.
3. Do not store CD-ROMs in bright light for any length of time. Whenever I transport my CD-ROMs from one facility to another, I either pack them in black leather carrying cases with zip flaps, or, if I am moving full racks of CD-ROMs, I spread heavy towels over them to avoid exposure to direct sunlight in transit.

Several of us in the sound community ran fade tests on various brands of CD-ROMs, placing them in direct sunlight as it shone through an open window for various lengths of

Figure 11.7 CD-ROM file for burning. Once you have put together your folder of audio files, you must run Norton Utilities software on it, as well as computer virus and worm checks so that you do not include dangerous anomalies onto your CD-ROM and DVD masters. Once satisfied with the folder content and precautions, make a disk image before you "burn" your CD-ROM files.

time to test the stability of the disks after bright light. We discovered that not all CD-ROM brands are created equal. Two of the brands tested faded, resulting in a permanent loss of data after only fifteen minutes of direct exposure to sunlight. Others lasted for several hours, and some took two weeks of day-in and day-out exposure to show fade damage. Regardless of the rate of fade damage, such a test should motivate you always to keep your CD-ROMs stored in a dimly lit and temperature-stable environment.

To prepare audio files for CD-ROM mastering, the sound librarian first "cleans up" (explained later in this chapter) each audio sound file until he or she is satisfied it should be committed to a CD-ROM.

The sound librarian creates a folder and names it—in the case of my own sound library, and the example being shown, the disk name is YEWD 1561. YEWD 1561 is the CD-ROM "disk address." If you want a custom icon on your CD-ROM you must highlight a file icon that has the desired image on it. I always leave an empty file folder with my library icon image on the desktop of the computer. Then you will Apple keystroke/ "i" to open the information window. The icon image will be shown in the upper left corner of the information window. Move the cursor over and highlight the icon image, then copy the icon by using

Apple keystroke/ "C." Move the cursor to the upper left-hand corner and tap on the little gray box to put the window away. Next, you will highlight the new CD-ROM file folder that you just created and open its information window. Highlight the file icon in the information window and paste the custom icon (Apple keystroke/ "V") that you have just copied from your master icon image.

With the assistance of color-coding and the infinite variations of custom icons available, your CD-ROMs are easily recognized as a workstation copy from a vault master or a work-in-progress back-up from a finished CD-ROM master. I use unique icons to distinguish Foley backup CD-ROMs or dialog back-up CD-ROMs from anything else I am using.

You create additional topic folders that reside inside the CD-ROM master folder. You place audio files to be mastered inside these topic folders.

After the CD-ROM master folder is filled (not to exceed 690 megabytes—thus allowing a 10-megabyte buffer from the disk maximum designation of 700 megabytes), you should run Norton Utilities' Disk Doctor and at least one anti-virus software to ensure that the data directories and resource forks are not damaged or missing. It does not do any good to master an audio file and not be able to use it later because it is damaged or does not open and function. The sound librarian then defragments the drive using Norton Utilities Speed Disk.

Close the CD-ROM master folder and click on it twice. The folder menu will pop up, displaying the inner topic folders. Now is the time for you to reposition the folder window on the computer monitor screen exactly the way you want it to appear whenever the disk is used later, for this is exactly the position and configuration with which the CD-ROM will permanently format it—the way it will always open.

Once these processes are complete, boot up the CD-ROM recording software, such as Adaptec's "Toast." Select the DATA option on the software window to burn a CD-ROM. Drag-and-drop the folder, in this case "YEWD 1561," of the master file to be burned onto the "Toast" window. The software scans it and shows it to you in its own menu window. The drawer of the recorder opens as a software prompt asks for a blank CD-ROM to be loaded. Place a fresh CD-ROM in the CD-ROM recorder drawer and close it—commencing the recording of data, called "burning." A menu will appear, asking at what speed you wish to burn the CD disk. Even though today's ultra-high-speed CD-ROM burners that can burn at 16x and faster, I still burn my master CD-ROMS at 4x speed maximum. I find I suffer fewer errors and artifacts by burning at the slower speed.

Note the open folder to the left in Figure 11.7. This is only to show you how the folders inside the computer disk drive look. Note that the software window shows YEWD 1561 as a disk icon (the custom icon is shown as the first item as a document). The audio files inside the first folder show exactly as they did in the original drive.

Burning a master back-up copy always is wise, as it can be stored in a dark, temperate place so that, if necessary, it can generate additional copies in the future. A work copy is also made for day-to-day use in the workstation environment.

BASIC "CLEANING-UP" OF AUDIO FILES

The sound cue rarely comes directly from the microphone into the recording device in a pristine configuration. Though many of us learned and taught our colleagues and recording assistants to speak as little as possible when recording sounds in the field, unwanted vocals always need to be removed. In addition, the audio action does not always start on cue or play out as planned.

We always try to record everything during a session. Even if it goes wrong, the sound event that follows has value and a use sometime, somewhere. While recording sound effects for *Christine,* I had briefed the dual recording team not to speak or react, even if disaster struck. If an accident occurred, I wanted the sound of it to be clean. As it turned out, the stunt driver lost control of the car during a power reverse on a section of highway just wet down by the water truck. He spun off the road and slid right for my brand new Cadillac El Dorado. In my heart, I knew he could not avoid a collision, yet I held the stereo microphones steady as I watched. Fortunately, the stunt driver narrowly missed my car, after slamming the transmission into first gear and gunning the engine so hard that it threw a rooster tail of mud and dust across not only my own car but two others. One unplanned bonus from this near catastrophe was that we got a great clean recording of a high whine gear box with tires spinning in mud, swerving up onto the pavement and a great wet spin-out skid as the car throttled down the road. And not one person on my team let out a vocal reaction—not even a heavy breath—UNTIL I yelled "and CUT!!" Then, of course, everybody came unglued.

The point was that I was prepared and disciplined to keep my mouth and the mouths of my team SHUT. My recording crews did the same. However, many recording crews often talk and react, making all kinds of unnecessary movements and extraneous noise such as eating, gum chewing, or jingling coins in their pockets while recording. I do not like editing out these voices every time I need to use the audio cue. If a sound editor is pressed for time and has to cut the sound cue for an edit session hurriedly, he or she is more likely to overlook vocals and extraneous noises and movement, which only show up on the rerecording stage later. Therefore, make sure that all nonperformance vocals are edited out of the master, and that you have carefully gone through the sound cue to ferret out other problems, which must otherwise be edited out and fixed repeatedly during sound editorial sessions. Cutting and cleaning the sound cue once prior to CD-ROM or DVD mastering prevents all this unnecessary work.

Listen for digital ticks, zits, or glitches, and be prepared to remove them. Using the digital pencil, you can "draw" out a digital tick simply by zooming in very close, so that you can clearly and easily connect the waveform from the exact point at which it suddenly shoots straight up to the point (usually only a few samples in length) to where the tick returns to the normal waveform (see Figure 11.8). By drawing across it in this manner, the digital tick itself disappears, and you probably will not hear any residual after-effect. (Listen to cue #14 of the accompanying audio CD to better understand the sounds of digital ticks, zits, and glitches.)

Drawing out the digital tick is not always possible, especially when working with a very active sound that has a busy frequency field. Sometimes with harmonic sounds it is impossible to completely purge the audio file without hearing a bump. Another option for removing ticks is to cut them out, being careful to select cut points where the audio wave is at a curve point that matches smoothly and does not cause yet another tick or snap. When all else fails, import the audio file into a Pro Tools edit session, cut out the offending problem using the "shuttle" option, then build in cross fades until you are happy with the resulting playback.

Sometimes neither one of these options solves the problem. In such cases, it is necessary to create a Pro Tools edit session, import the audio file into the session, find the

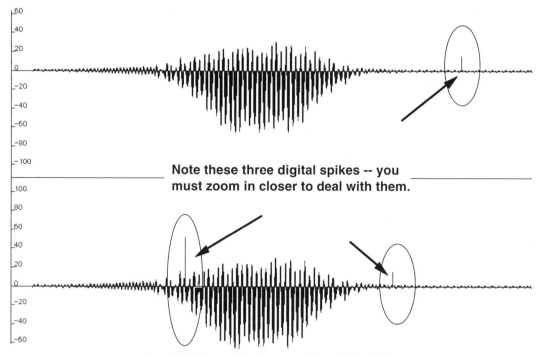

Figure 11.8 Sound Designer II: three digital ticks.

offending problem(s), and then cut and cross fade to blend away the bump that a direct cut cannot solve. Once I have cut, cross faded, and reviewed the audio file, I then create a new copy by using the Bounce-to-Disk option. (The mechanics of digital editing and manipulation are discussed in Chapter 17.) Once the new audio file has been rerecorded using Bounce-to-Disk, I then throw the original file into the computer trash can and flush it away. The new bounced file becomes the audio file to master the CD-ROM or DVD—free of those bedeviling ticks and snaps.

COMPLEX SOUND EFFECT MASTERING

When I transfer my sound effects into the digital realm of my workstation, I utilize the strengths of both digital and analog technologies in what I refer to as a grass roots, common sense approach. I do not like to over-process the sound cue or cut raw material. My goal is to deliver to the rerecording console a cut session of sounds that do not require the mixer to signal process and noise gate to the degree it does when material comes completely raw.

Depending on the rawness and dirtiness of the original recording, the effort devoted by the mixer to each cue can take a staggering amount of stage time. As the hourly rate ticks by, the mixer can be stuck with the time-consuming task of trimming equalization on each cue or feeding some cues through noise gates.

On the other hand, prepolished sound mastering is not a task for beginners. The most common mistake made by sound editors who start working with signal processing is that

Figure 11.9 A simple but extremely effective signal path for entering sound into the digital domain. The DAT sends the analog signal from the Sony deck, up to the 30-band Klark-Teknik equalizer, down to the Night Technologies EQ3, down to the Eventide Harmonizer, then into the Pro Tools interface.

they lay on excessive amounts, using the various DSP functions with the finesse of a rhinoceros suffering from diarrhea. They try to make the sound effect as pristine as if it were a final mix. You can over-process the sound effect to a point that the mixer cannot unwind or use it for the project. The beginner does not understand that the dynamics and character of sound change when cues are layered together. What may sound good when played by itself may be completely lost and overwhelmed when layered in against other sound cues. If you remove or manipulate the audio file's frequency and dynamic qualities too much before mastering, you may limit its potential use later during sound editorial.

If I am transferring sound effect cues into the computer, I use a Night Technologies EQ3 equalizer in tandem with the Klark-Teknik DN 30/30, a 30-band graphic equalizer (see Figure 11.9). The signal path of the sound goes from the DAT machine (analog outs), through the two equalizers, then into the Pro Tools interface, where it is digitized into the computer. The Night Technologies EQ3 equalizer allows tremendous flexibility in a virtual non–phase shift environment to manipulate the range of frequencies to emphasize, especially in the high-end, referred to as the "air" bands. I experience tremendous success with all kinds of sounds that need extra help with high-end clarity. Adding such high-end emphasis with any other equalizer always brings a rush of bias hiss or unwanted "shushy"-type anomalies.

Although nonlinear editing is wonderful and convenient, DSP (digital signal processing) functions, especially equalization options, are still a bit "edgy" for my ears—lending an undesirable sterility and a noticeable footprint of signal processing to the sound. There are those who can make magic with these plug-ins—but not very many. It is kind of like the adage that anybody can pick up a bow and draw it across the stings of a violin—but not many really make music.

I digitize my sound into the computer in two ways. In the first method, I transfer an entire sound effect DAT or 1/4" tape into a Pro Tools session. Then I break the transfer audio file down into the desired individual cues. As I make each cut I will tap twice on the cue (which will pop up the NAME AS option) and rename the segment as I wish the new audio cues to be named. If the audio files are stereo, I name the left channel (always ending the name with .L). Then I highlight the name and copy the name (Apple + "C" key) so that every letter and space will be exact. I then tap twice on the right channel of the cut clip. The NAME AS option window appears. I highlight the name that is there and paste in the copied name from the left channel (pressing Apple + "V"). I then back up two spaces (to erase .L) and type in .R. I move on to the next cut audio cue and rename it.

After I have cut up and renamed all of the cue clips I want and eliminated the unwanted audio material, I highlight all of the cut audio segments—then I go up to the upper right-hand side of the Pro Tools session window to the AUDIO bar and open that menu, come

Figure 11.10 Digitizing (recording) audio data into a Pro Tools session.

Figure 11.11 The Output Options window for "Exporting Selected as Files."

three-fourths of the way down the list of options to "Export Selected As Files," and release. Up comes the OUTPUT OPTIONS menu (see Figure 11.11). You must make a series of choices to ensure that your final audio files are exactly as you want them and exactly where you want them.

Under FILE FORMAT: You may choose to output your new audio files in either Sound Designer II (SDII), AIFF, .WAV, snd Resource, Quicktime, or Realsound formats.

Under RESOLUTION: You can output your new audio files in either 8, 16, or 24 bit.

Under CHANNELS: You can output your audio files in either Mono (1), or Stereo from .L/.R(2). If you have stereo audio files and intend to work with them in nonlinear environments, you will want your stereo .L and .R files to be output as Mono (1). The stereo output option is for when you are making audio files that you wish to burn later as audio CD disks—which means that they will be at a sampling rate of 44.1 kHz and interleaved as stereo from your .L/.R source.

Under SAMPLE RATE: You can output your files at the following sample rates—48000 (DAT); 44100 (CD); 22254 (Old Mac); 22050 (Power PC/IBM PC); 11127 (Old Mac); 11025 (Power PC/IBM PC); or CUSTOM setting.

Under CONVERSION QUALITY: You can choose how good the quality of the output will be. Like most things, higher quality means less speed. You can output at Low (fastest), Good, Better, Best, or Tweak Head (slowest). I never opt for anything but the "Tweak Head" speed. With today's gigaflop speed CPUs there is no reason to opt for anything of less quality.

Under DESTINATION DIRECTORY: Push "CHOOSE" and a window will come up for you to select the path for the computer to place your new audio file outputs into a particular target folder.

Under RESOLVE DUPLICATE FILENAMES BY: Choose how you wish the computer to deal with any accidental duplicates. This will not become an issue if you are targeting a file folder simply to hold your new files for later disbursement.

I also record and prepare my audio files in Digidesign's Sound Designer II software as a stand-alone function. I am so insistent about this that I have the Audiomedia 3 card installed into my computer to support the Sound Designer II software because Pro Tools-24 does not support Sound Designer II as a stand-alone option. Even though I know that the software language is dated and old, I still have not found a better program that can offer the tools and precision I am used to. Digidesign offers DSP functions in an Audio Suite menu function in the Pro Tools session for those who prefer to work the plug-ins that way. The Audiomedia 3 is no longer available from Digidesign—their new high-definition "M-Box" replaces the Audiomedia 3. However, with the M-Box you will find that you have to do all of your audio work on the Pro Tools session window, using the Audio Suite menu—or you can use third-party software to work as the stand-alone Sound Designer II does. Chapter 17 discusses other options for working with your audio files.

Because we must work within the boundaries of hard-drive storage space, the actual utilization of each byte is vital to a sound editor. A typical sound editorial workstation uses a quad array of high-speed 40- to 100-gigabyte removable drives. When loading a drive with audio files or cutting sessions, do not fill the storage capacity of the drive beyond the recommended 10% margin. On a 100-gigabyte drive, this leaves you with a relatively safe working storage volume of 90 gigs. That may be a lot of computer memory to some, but those of us who cut theatrical-style sound know we need much more drive space, as disk memory gets chewed up in a hurry. This is primarily why I spend seemingly immense, yet appropriate, preparation time before cutting. Recognize the need to prepare and polish sound effects before you cut them, a concept often overlooked in the heat of battle when cutting complex sequences.

My primary thought in prepping audio sound files is to distill them down to a reasonable and workable size, cutting out unnecessary and wasteful parts that gobble up valuable disk storage space. Once the sound is trimmed to a realistic size, I decide whether I should spend the time and effort to polish it even further, such as building in fade-ins and fade-outs. Be very careful in making fade decisions in the audio file master, because they cannot be removed from the editorial session later. Conversely, as you become proficient in the art of complex audio cleaning and preprep, you will discover that sounds with logical permanent fade-ins or fade-outs built into them save time for the editor later.

Listen to sound cue #15 on the audio CD included with this book. This depicts a before-and-after comparison of identical sounds. The "before" version is the raw recording as played back from the DAT master. The "polished" version is the same sound, but after I muted the

DAT Machine

EQ³ Equalizer

N.T.I. EQ 3

Graphic Equalizer

Audio Outputs

ProTool Interface

Computer C.P.U.

External Hard Drives

Audio Mixer

Speaker Amplifier

to Left Speaker

to Right Speaker

Figure 11.12 A typical workstation signal path.

space between performances, being very careful not to clip the overtones on the end too tightly, and then added short but effective fade-ins and fade-outs.

I prefer to have front-end sync sound effects, such as door-opens and closes, gunshots, impacts, face punches, telemetry beeps, and other precise cues prepared whenever possible for drag-and-drop or spot-mode sync cutting. These benefit the sound editor who is frame flipping across countless visual special effect computer graphic scans for the purpose of cutting precise, frame-accurate bursts and trills. When the clock is ticking and you are cutting a complex gun battle with multiple shooters wielding various weapons, nothing speeds the ability to assemble a full and dynamic fire fight more than having the weapons mastered with spot-mode preparation. Thorough preparation of audio file masters to better achieve this editing style is time-consuming, but the untold hours of future schedule time it saves is well worth the investment.

Now is an appropriate moment to comment on the monitoring system used when you are working on complex mastering of your audio files. Do not attempt this by only listening to your material through headphones. In 1988 the Hollywood sound editing community got a fabulous boost by the advent of Sony's MDR-series dynamic stereo headphones. Editors stood aghast as they heard sounds in their own material that had been inaudible through conventional headphones. Many editors adopted these headsets as the new standard. At my own shop, we insisted everyone use them, as we did not want disparity between what editors heard. Regardless of the new technological breakthrough in these headphones, we discovered the hard way that a sound editor does not hear the full and complete frequency range needed when determining cut points during editing. We got the material to the rerecording stage only to discover that editors were clipping off the long low-frequency overtones of metal rubs, explosions, and gunshots because they could not hear the low-end frequencies in their headsets.

To properly monitor the full frequency and dynamic value of audio, pay close attention to your speakers. Be very picky about choosing a good close-proximity speaker. It should perform with a transparency that allows you to properly evaluate the material and not worry that the speaker is adding any color. Nothing is worse for a sound editor than to hear the session play as desired at the workstation, only to take the material onto the rerecording stage and discover that the realities of the material do not translate.

This is why I do not fill my room with artificial amounts of subwoofer toys. I have listened to numerous editors having a great time playing with sounds in their rooms, cutting massive helicopter chases or moving the framework of the walls with concussive explosion effects—but the truth is that they are only fooling themselves. The material never sounds like it did in their editing suite on the rerecording stage. The client will not understand.

Audio file preparation is not simply a case of distilling the effect to a workable size to make more disk storage space for other sound effects. This is not about just cutting out unnecessary audio within the effect (i.e., recordist voices, unnecessary bumps, and movements as the recordist repositions or prepares for another performance). This is about internal signal integrity and gleaning the maximum richness each sound effect cue can yield. For lack of a better term, I call it *dynamic expansion.*

Listen to sound cue #16 on the audio CD included with this book. The recording is of two men pushing a grand piano on a hollow wood floor. The first task was to distill the 2-1/2 minutes of raw sound recording down to a workable 30 seconds. Another task was remedying the fact that the maximum volume peaks of the wheels striking either grit or hardwood floor seams were suppressing the wonderful low-end richness of the piano's wood frame, which was reverberating from the vibration of its internal strings. Using the DSP "normalize" function (in Digidesign's Sound Designer II) as a global parameter would not achieve any further richness. Sure, I could have used a dynamic envelope algorithm that would act like a noise gate and a gain brain expander, but such tools are only good for quick bandage-type work—often yielding disappointingly flat and sterile results. (I use the zoom in function to get extremely close so I can study each waveform, often enlarging the waveform image to single samples, ferreting out digital ticks and zits. I study and remove distortion patterns and often redraw the waveform itself to repair and salvage, rather than cut and remove, the offending material.) It took me four hours to bring the rolling piano effect to a full richness, bringing out the resounding piano chords and the rumble and weight of the instrument.

Most sound designers and sound editors choose to use one or more software functions to accomplish DSP. Of course, I use DSP parameters as well, but not as an end-all and

This distortion crash must be drawn out with a digital pencil or cut out and smoothed.

Figure 11.13 Sound Designer II: Signal "crash" breakup.

certainly not as a defining formula to accomplish a desired result. I listen to each sound, not just what it sounds like, but what it tells my instincts about how to maximize its potential. At this level, I audition and understand the dynamic possibilities that lie within the overall performance. I then highlight precise regions, even within a fluid action, and lay on DSP functions ranging from normalization to pitch shift to parametric equalization. This kind of decision making can only come from years of experience supervising pictures, cutting and combining millions of sound effects, and working on the rerecording stage with the mixer to learn what one should and shouldn't do to an audio file prior to the rerecording mixer for the predubbing process. Listen to cue #43 of the audio CD provided with this book to listen to two examples of using the normalization DSP function and simple equalization.

AUDIO FILE PROTOCOL

It is very frustrating to find audio files that have been mastered onto a CD or DVD with incorrect stereo designations. This is a direct result of ignorance on the part of inexperienced librarians importing audio files from 1/4", DAT, or any other outside audio source into the Pro Tools nonlinear workstation via a Pro Tools session rather than into Sound Designer II software using the recording menu—where Sound Designer II import automatically assigns the .L and .R stereo designations correctly.

Pro Tools works with stereo files in single split "left" and "right" monaural files, which, when laced precisely together, make a stereophonic image. The file designations contain an "L" for left channel, and an "R" for right channel. When entry recordists import audio directly into a Pro Tools session as the recording platform, Pro Tools automatically names the incoming file according to the channel into which it was imported, and it assigns a sequence designation. If you import a stereo pair into a Pro Tools sessions on the first two audio channels, the resulting designation assigned to the recording by the Pro Tools software is as follows:

Audio 1-01
Audio 2-01

Rename Audio 1-01 by double-clicking on the file waveform of Audio 1-01. A "name" window will appear. It will ask you to name the region. As an example, you may rename it "Peckerwood Canyon 0078/02." To designate the stereo left/right position, you must add a period (.) immediately followed by an "L". You want the option "name region and disk file" highlighted so that the file name is altered. Before you choose "okay," you should highlight the window with the new designation and copy it with the Command/C keystroke.

Audio 1-01 now reads "Peckerwood Canyon 0078/02.L." Now double-click on Audio 2-01. The "name" window will appear. Paste in the copied name so that the exact duplication of the name and use of characters and spacing is assured. Back up one space to erase the "L" and replace it with "R". It now appears as follows:

Peckerwood Canyon 0078/02.L
Peckerwood Canyon 0078/02.R

This gives you a proper stereo pair. If your workstation is configured to support Sound Designer II as stand-alone software, you can double-click on the audio file icon; it will boot itself and its stereophonic mate with it. The point to this whole left/right designation issue is that only one way exists to properly prepare a Sound Designer II audio file so that it boots correctly into a Sound Designer II stand-alone format. The period (.) and "L" or "R" must appear as outlined here, or it will not boot up correctly, if at all.

Figure 11.14 shows several examples of files seen at other sound facilities where inexperienced craftspeople did not understand audio file protocol. These designations are noted incorrectly, and Sound Designer II software does not allow them to boot up into its stand-alone platform.

The left/right designation does not come before the description; it does not have the period (.) after the "L" or "R"; it does not appear in parenthesis or brackets. The stereo left/right designation only works at the end of the file name and only with the period (.)

Incorrect designation	Should be:
44 Pistol (L) ext shot	44 Pistol ext shot.L
44 Pistol (R) ext shot	44 Pistol ext shot.R
0366-47 Big Death Laser L	0366-47 Big Death Laser.L
0366-47 Big Death Laser R	0366-47 Big Death Laser.R
Rooftop Traffic TR-412 L.	Rooftop Traffic TR-412.L
Rooftop Traffic TR-412 R.	Rooftop Traffic TR-412.R
L Mustang start/out CR/478	Mustang start/out CR/478.L
R Mustang start/out CR/478	Mustang start/out CR/478.R

Figure 11.14 Left/right audio file designations.

immediately preceding it. I have wasted countless hours retransferring and relabeling sound files from other sound libraries. The lack of disciplined library procedure throughout the industry is staggering. Editing talent gets bogged down with file management work that should have been done correctly in the first place. The cost of wasted CD-ROMs and DVDs with improperly labeled audio files is compounded by the additional time and expense of downloading the material to a work drive, readdressing the mastering and labeling chores, and then remastering to CD-ROM or DVD.

Contrary to the opinion of some librarians, it is not necessary to put a period (.) and an "M" at the end of a monaural sound file. If there is no designation, it is de facto a monaural sound file without a mate. Many librarians put this on the end of a monaural file so that it will not be confused with an interleaved stereo file that has no dot (.) designation at the end of the audio name.

I like to use the computer's color codes under "Label" in the menu bar to color-code my audio files for quick recognition. Pink designates monaural sound files, and dark blue indicates stereo pairs. I use orange to designate audio files that are raw entries and/or files I have not had time to open to edit and clean. Once I change the color code as a sign to indicate completed work on either a monaural or stereo file, I must make a change, however slight, in that audio file's name designation so that the computer does not confuse it with an original version of the same file. When using a source material designation such as "Peckerwood Canyon 0078-02," I enter the sound file and then 0078-02. Later, after I have opened the sound file in Sound Designer II and have cut, cleaned, and processed the effect the way I want to remaster it, I then change 0078-02 to 0078/02. This subtle but effective change keeps any other copies of "Peckerwood Canyon" without edits and processing from causing conflict and preventing sessions from opening.

MULTICHANNEL MASTERING TECHNIQUES

You can record only single or stereo pair channels into Sound Designer II software. With a limitation of two inputs, you must record wider formats directly into a Pro Tools session, where you are limited by the number of inputs of the I/O interface. For instance, if you are recording into a Digidesign 888 I/O, eight (8) discrete channels can be recorded simultaneously. Be careful to make sure that you have your XLR inputs plugged correctly. XLR #1 goes into input channel one, XLR #2 goes into input channel two, and so forth. Before opening the Pro Tools recording session, check your inputs to ensure proper calibration. (You can learn how to check your equipment and recalibrate your system interface under the heading "Line-Up Tones and Calibration" in Chapter 6.)

Once satisfied that your inputs are calibrated correctly, you can either open or create a Pro Tools session to record multiple channels. If you are recording eight channels simultaneously, you need to create eight audio tracks using "File" in the menu bar.

Open the mix window under "Display" in the menu bar and verify that the inputs are coming in accordingly. Make sure that each audio track has its own voice and will not be in conflict with another track, either because of voice assignment or duplicated input channel assignments.

Turn off the record safeties on each audio track, which illuminate white with red lettering. Hit the return bar on the computer keyboard, returning the digital sound head to the 000+00. Open the transport window under "Display" in the menu bar. Press the round "Record" button on the far right in the transport window control bar. Roll your source tape and press the "Forward" button on the transport window (the single triangular button just to the right of the black, square "Stop" button). If you have followed these steps correctly, all eight channels will start laying down a red band path, in which you will see waveforms drawn shortly after you hear sound.

When you reach the end of the material you wish to record, press the black, square "Stop" button in the transport window control bar. The recorded red bands will suddenly turn white, showing their automated name designations.

Say that this is a live concert multitrack recording. The production mixer would have completed a track assignment sheet (review Chapter 5 on multitrack recording). Rename the audio files so they are easier to work with later in an edit session. After studying the production mixer's track assignment sheet, you may rename the audio files as described earlier and as shown in Figure 11.15.

Figure 11.15 Eight-channel music transfer.

After I have recorded in a number of synchronous eight-channel cues and renamed them, my preference is to color-code the groups of eight with alternating color designations. I color code the first set red, the second set pale blue, the third set red, the fourth set pale blue, and so forth. This checker boarding effect makes the hundreds of audio files easily stand out in their groups of eight as they are listed in the drive partition window.

MIXED MEDIUM SYNCHRONOUS MASTERING

An interesting technique in today's action-oriented sound effect world is using multiple recorders during custom recording sessions to record the same action from various points of view (see Chapter 10). Any time multiple points of view are desired, especially when the dynamics and action are constantly changing, this technique of recording and subsequent mastering is of supreme value.

A sound librarian received seven sets of raw recorded audio rolls from Eric Potter, who had been contracted to put together and cover the recording session of a 5-ton Kaiser truck. These rolls had not been recorded in interlock or time code. The stereo Nagras had their crystal sync modules in during recording, so the material was resolved to sync during transfer by the sound librarian. Recording with a digital DAT using absolute time is extremely accurate, causing no concern about speed drift. The material had been recorded with different types of tape recorders in different formats, yet each recording was of the same audio performance event recorded at the same time by different recordists in different points of view.

The sound librarian first loaded each version of the recordings into the computer. Following the sound reports very carefully, the sound librarian was careful to account for each matching set of cues for each of the seven recorders. After entering the hundreds of cues, the sound librarian created a Pro Tools edit session just to align, trim, and remaster each recorded event in its seven discrete angles. He then dragged in the first seven stereo pairs. Finding the "clicker" sound at the head of each cue, the librarian zoomed in extremely close to align the click sync point of each stereo pair exactly together.

That was the easy and obvious part. From then on, the librarian had to watch out for and correct the drift of the recordings, finding occasional points easily aligned and matched, such as a gear box clunk, sudden burst revs from the exhausts, and so forth. (An experienced sound editor who understands this type of waveform matching and editing usually performs this task.) At each cut and/or move, the librarian used an appropriate cross-fade to heal the cut, avoiding the potential for digital ticks due to mismatching waveforms at the cut point or a difference in the rise and fall of the engine's performance.

A series of recordings like this is incalculably valuable for the sound editor throughout the sound editorial process. The editor can choose one angle over another according to the visual on the screen, or can use one or more angles played together to further dramatize the action, knowing that the rise and fall of the engine and the dynamics of the performance will always match.

After the raw recordings had been aligned and cut to match each other, the sound librarian opened the mix window under "Display" in the menu bar. He checked that each stereo pair was set for output channels one and two. Then the librarian performed a Bounce-to-Disk of each stereo pair by highlighting the entire sound cut, making sure that all the cuts

Figure 11.16 Multi-angle recording of a Kaiser truck maneuver.

and fades had been included. Bounce-to-Disk is found under "File" in the Pro Tools menu bar. A "Bounce" window will appear.

Under "Bounce Type," the librarian chose the "split stereo" (two mono files, best for Pro Tools) option. Then the librarian chose "Bounce," which brought up a window for naming the new files and designating where to store the new material. Some librarians like to store a shorthand of information that helps the sound editor know what kind of recording medium was used (in some cases, the initials of the recordist), which helps track style patterns throughout the entire recorded series. Using this technique, the performance cue may be retitled as shown in Figure 11.17.

These fourteen audio cues (seven stereo pairs) represent the simultaneous recording of a single audio event. You can see how easy it would be for a sound editor to recognize the desired files. "5-TON" denotes the vehicle. The take (or cue) of the audio file is listed as "t01." The take number is placed in this precise order in the name, as the take number automatically lines the groupings of recordings together in their stereophonic pairs. If the take number was placed at the end of the audio file name, the computer would look at the alphabetically first word used in the description. In this case it would be an "S."

A very short description of action is listed next. A complete description can be entered into each audio file by opening the information window and leaving the entire text there.

The recording medium is listed next, noted as "DAT" or "Nag," for Nagra. The recordist's initials are listed after the recording medium, followed by the appropriate stereophonic designation period (.) "L" or period (.) "R."

Figure 11.17 Five-ton truck rename files.

THE SOUND EFFECT INVENTORY DATABASE

As you amass an audio empire, it becomes very difficult to recall material. The thousands of audio files become a blur as you struggle to remember where you put the "inverted numb-knuckle lock screw metal squeak." The best weapon in the arsenal of organization for the sound librarian is a good computer database. You can acquire database software that has been specifically designed and written for sound library work, such as Leonardo or Metropolis, or you can use one of the numerous off-the-shelf programs, such as FileMaker Pro or ClarisWorks, and structure your own. Regardless of whether you purchase sound librarian software or tailor your own from preexisting software, you must have a structured regimen whereby the entered data can be retrieved in various ways.

DiskTracker

If you have a very tight budget—and the vast majority of us do—you will get a lot of service and firepower from DiskTracker. (You can find DiskTracker on the Web at DiskTracker.com.) The fee is amazingly reasonable ($30), especially in light of what you can do with it.

Once you have installed your DiskTracker software, you will want to find the application icon program in the DiskTracker folder and highlight it. Open the information window (Apple/keystroke "i") and increase the memory allowance. Because of the size of the scanned data I keep I have had to increase the memory allocation to ten times the original size.

Boot up the software and make a new library file. Scan a few disks and then quit. Go back into the DiskTracker folder to find the document you just made. Highlight it and make an alias (Apple/keystroke "M"). Drag this alias out onto the desktop of your computer—I place my library alias in the lower center of my screen. From now on, if you need to access DiskTracker to search for audio files or scan in new CD-ROM disks—all you have to do is tap twice on the alias icon on the desktop.

Once you have burned a sound effect library CD-ROM, put it back in the CD-ROM tray and boot up your software from the desktop file icon. When your CD-ROM appears on the desktop, open the "Scan Mounted Volume" option under the "Scan" window in the menu bar. The window will open and show all the data volumes that your computer is seeing. Your internal and external drives will show up as drive icons. Your CD-ROM will show up as a CD disk icon with its assigned name next to it. Highlight the CD-ROM icon and press the "Scan" button on the lower right of the window. The DiskTracker software will scan the disk. Once the scan is complete, put the CD-ROM in the trash can to eject it.

It is a good idea to save after each disk scan. The software has a tendency to crash if you scan too many disks without saving, and you can save yourself the work of having to face doing it all over again by simply getting into the rhythm of this habit.

Notice in Figure 11.18 that the CD icons match your original files exactly. You can open the folders and physically look through the ranks of audio file data. By going up to the menu bar to "View" and selecting "List Views . . .", you may select exactly what kind of data you wish to be shown by Name, Size, Kind, Type, Creator, Created Date, Modified Date, Free Space, Scanned Date, Items, Serial Number, etc.

I keep my viewing data extremely simple—Name, Size, and Kind. I can always change it later, but I really do not need to wade through a lot of visual text on a day-to-day basis.

Print-Outs

You may print a hard copy of disk data. I do not use the DiskTracker printing option because I find the material too difficult to read. I simply open the disk icons and folders in the DiskTracker software window that I wish to reveal, then I go up to "View," open the "List Views . . ." option, and turn off all but the "Name" option.

Figure 11.18 DiskTracker scanned data file.

I then highlight the entire data scan by pressing Apple keystroke/ "A"—or, if I want to print data on only one or a just few CD disks, I simply highlight with the cursor only those disks I wish to capture. I then move over to the word processing software (such as Apple-Works or Word) and paste (Apple keystroke/ "V") the selected data in.

Now I can quickly tidy up the data document by highlighting and changing font selections for disk titles so that they will stand separate from audio files. I also keep an "icon art" palette in my word processing folder from which I can highlight CD disk icons or folder icons. By quickly scrolling down the page and pasting (Apple keystroke/ "V") in disk icons or folder icons I can make a very easy document for the eye to scan. For permanent hard copy outputs I even go back and color-code all of the audio file names just as they appear in the original data field.

Duplicate Files

At one time duplicate files were a huge problem, especially if you were your own librarian and also handled the chores of supervising projects and cutting reels for the stage—when would you have time to physically research the duplicate audio file issues? DiskTracker can do that for you. When you are between projects and want to do some library maintenance, open up the software and go up to the menu bar to "Search," and highlight the "Duplicate Item Criteria" option. The menu will offer you a number of choices. You can create a filtering combination by cross-referencing files by duplicate Name, Size, Kind, Label, Creation Date, Modification Date, Depth, Item Note, Finder Comment or file Type, Creator or Version.

I simply choose Name. I then press the "OK" button and go back up to the "Search" menu and select "Find Duplicate Items." When that window comes up, make sure that the upper box is checked— "Check Only Items Which Match the Filter."

You will need to select the kind of folders, applications, or icon files that you wish to ignore or wish to see. Then select that you want to look at your entire scanned list, and engage. The software will scan through its data and present you with a detailed list of any and all things that have duplicate names (or whatever filter you opted to utilize). You can print this out to a hard copy if you wish, or—if your audio files reside on drives within your server—you can actually sit and carefully weed out your duplicates by highlighting a name in the scan and eliminating it (Apple keystroke/ "X"). The software will not only remove the audio file data from the software but will remove the audio file itself from the hard drive if the hard drives are connected to the CPU you are using. Be careful when eliminating data from the scan file.

As you learn to use this option with skill you will be able to use it like a surgeon's scalpel—but until you master the technique I highly suggest you use caution. I have found myself going back to cold storage CD-ROM back-ups to restore several files that I had accidentally eliminated from the data scan, only to find that it had also eliminated them from the computer hard drive I was using.

Looking for Audio Files

Now you have an up-to-date data scan of your sound-effect CD-ROM library. You are given a cutting task and find that you need to pull dozens of sound effects, many of which you cannot locate. Boot up your alias icon and go up to the "Search" option in the menu bar. Select "Find . . ." and a window will appear (see Figure 11.19).

Figure 11.19 "Search" menu to find audio files by matching name data in DiskTracker.

The first rule of the DiskTracker search technique is, do not attempt to enter the exact name of what you are looking for. Chances are you will not get it right and you will just be frustrated. Remember that a computer only knows what you tell it. It only knows what has been entered and it does not read your mind. This is a major reason why I do not like unrelated nicknames given to sound files. An audio file that has been named "Joe's Magic Whirly" has nothing in the name that you can grab onto in a "subject-style" search. The effect may be a powerful wind-up and constant motor that you recorded at a local car wash and used in sound project for a prop or scene that was a magical machine wind-up that belonged to Joe. Or maybe the recordist's name was Joe. Years later, when you are trying to find this sound that you know is perfect for your needs, but you cannot remember the exact name and you cannot even use something like "machine" or "car whoosh" to search for it, you will be sorry you named it "Joe's Magic Whirly."

That lecture over, let us move on to searching for things that do have something in the name that we can find easily. Think in terms of topic names or a piece of a name that you would probably have used. There is a favorite New York traffic recording that I love to use, but I can never remember where I put it. All I can remember is that a good friend of mine

Icon	Name	Size	Kind	Created	Modified
	(39) bodyfalls	420 K	Snd Designer II™ 2.8.3 document	3/11/99	3/11/99
	-035/07 bodyfall (subtle dirt)	3.1 MB	Snd Designer II™ 2.8.3 document	2/17/01	2/17/01
	-230/04 wood bodyfalls	564 K	Snd Designer II™ 2.8.3 document	2/13/01	2/18/01
	0359-18 bodyfall.L	7.0 MB	Snd Designer II™ 2.8.3 document	1/28/97	1/28/97
	0359-18 bodyfall.R	7.0 MB	Snd Designer II™ 2.8.3 document	1/28/97	1/28/97
	1118-1 AdultDinoBodyFall.L	3.9 MB	Snd Designer II™ 2.8.3 document	7/26/97	7/26/97
	1118-1 AdultDinoBodyFall.R	3.9 MB	Snd Designer II™ 2.8.3 document	7/26/97	7/26/97
	180/06 bodyfalls (softer) L	5.8 MB	Snd Designer II™ 2.8.3 document	7/6/00	7/6/00
	180/06 bodyfalls (softer) R	5.8 MB	Snd Designer II™ 2.8.3 document	7/6/00	7/6/00
	64/105 Bodyfall dirt/silt L	744 K	Snd Designer II™ 2.8.3 document	7/9/00	7/9/00
	64/105 Bodyfall dirt/silt R	744 K	Snd Designer II™ 2.8.3 document	7/9/00	7/9/00
	64/105 Bodyfall dirt/silt.L	744 K	Snd Designer II™ 2.8.3 document	7/9/00	7/9/00
	64/105 Bodyfall dirt/silt.R	744 K	Snd Designer II™ 2.8.3 document	7/9/00	7/9/00
	64/110 BODYFALLS (Talvi) L	5.1 MB	Snd Designer II™ 2.8.3 document	7/9/00	7/9/00
	64/110 BODYFALLS (Talvi) R	5.1 MB	Snd Designer II™ 2.8.3 document	7/9/00	7/9/00
	BodyFall METAL #1/70 .L	1.2 MB	Snd Designer II™ 2.8.3 document	8/30/96	9/14/97
	BodyFall METAL #1/70 .R	1.2 MB	Snd Designer II™ 2.8.3 document	8/30/96	9/14/97
	BodyFall wood floor #34 .L	1.1 MB	Snd Designer II™ 2.8.3 document	8/30/96	11/18/96
	BodyFall wood floor #34 .L	1.1 MB	Snd Designer II™ 2.8.3 document	8/30/96	11/18/96

Figure 11.20 The results of searching for "Bodyfall."

from New York gave it to me, and that she had used "Bronx" in the title—so, whenever I want it I simply enter "Bronx" and up it comes.

But what if you can't remember any part of the title? What if it isn't just one audio file, but a series or genre of sound? That is when "topic" works best. When I want to pull some bulkhead wrenching sounds for a deep pressure dive on a submarine, I don't look under "Submarine." That sound is made by metal, and I know that I would have put it in with the metal sounds. Entering "metal" in the "Find" window may retrieve several hundred audio files (and folders) that have the word "metal" in them, but it takes much less time to scroll through several hundred audio names than it does to search through a quarter of a million audio files in the entire data scan. Besides, once you begin scanning the list of genre or type of sounds, looking for the one you remembered, you will come across dozens that will trigger your imagination and give you ideas that you had not previously thought of. That is another reason why I like to take a little time and just "wade" through the files.

As you use the system, you will develop short-cuts to get to your desired destination. Perhaps you need a variety of bodyfalls. Instead of listing "Bodyfalls" as a plural in the "Find" window, list it as "Bodyfall," which will return both files with "Bodyfall" and "Body-falls" in the title (see Figures 11.19 and 11.20).

After you enter the name to search for, hit the Return key and the software will scroll out a "Search Results" window, as shown in Figure 11.20. Notice the bidirectional arrow near the upper right-hand side, just to the right of "Modified." If you touch the bidirectional arrow with your cursor, the "Size / Kind / Created / Modified" data field will change to "Path." This field will show you exactly where your desired audio file can be found. It will list the CD-ROM designation name and then the folder name in which the audio file resides.

THE TRADITIONAL CATALOG DATABASE

The data itself, and how it is entered into the computer will determine the ease with which you find specific material and the amount of customized filtration you need to search for information. By entering data with a slant toward accessibility, you will quickly discover that adding terms or abbreviations increases the ease of finding material later. As you build a sound library, regardless of whether the root master is on digital DAT or analog tape, you need to compile a linear log.

Figure 11.21 is an example of a root master log. This is 1/4" tape AFS 1909 from the Weddington Sound Effects Library. When Steve Flick and Richard Anderson worked on

---

<<<<<< AFS1909 >>>>>>

THE FINAL COUNTDOWN

SPEED: 7.5 ips	**FORMAT:** 1/4-inch Fulltrack Mono
TONE: 1kHz	**FLUX:** '0' VU = 120 nWb/m
NR: None	**DATE:** 07/31/'79
NOTES: Formerly MX-11	

Jets on USS Nimitz

Cue	Description	Fmt	Time
01	F-8 JET LAUNCH: on aircraft carrier. With burners	M	00:40 MX11-1 DAT 1266-35
02	16 JETS PASS BY: aircraft carrier. PA vox over beginning. You can't really count the number, but it sounds pretty good. Good trail off	M	01:09 MX11-2 DAT 1266-36
03	JETS IDLING: on aircraft carrier	M	01:25 MX11-3 DAT 1266-37
04	F-8 JET IDLE: ECU on aircraft carrier. RLA's note sez "good for constant." still sound like white noise	M	00:42 MX11-4 DAT 1266-38
05	A-6 JET IDLE: ECU on aircraft carrier.	M	00:25 MX11-5 DAT 1266-39
06	F-14 JET WARM UP/IDLE: on aircraft carrier. White noisey. A-6 in B.G.	M	01:30 MX11-6 DAT 1266-40

Figure 11.21 Catalog: jets on USS *Nimitz*.

The Final Countdown, they had a sound recording team on the aircraft carrier USS *Nimitz* recording anything and everything they could, from interior ambiences of the Combat Information Center (CIC) to the explosive shriek of steam catapults hurtling F-14 Tomcats into flight.

Every audio file mastered into a sound library comes from another source, whether recorded on a Foley stage, a scoring stage, on location during production, or from a custom sound effect recordist. These sources have different formats and are on different original mediums. Part of the data entered into a library should be a notation of its source.

In the case of the example shown, note in the header data of the catalog under "Notes" that AFS 1909 used to be known as MX-11. The librarian has also noted at what recording speed the analog tape had been recorded, that the format of tape was 1/4", and that it was recorded on a fulltrack monaural head stack. Listed as well is the date on which the material was recorded. Most logs today also note the recordist's name. The header relates to the project for which the sound was specifically recorded, in this case for *The Final Countdown.* The tone is 1 kHz (one thousand cycles), and the flux notation signifies the strength of the recording, the amount of magnetic influence.

Each cue is listed in numerical order. The sound librarian enters the "Description" information in a way that makes cross-referencing easy. In the case of the first cue, a sound editor can ask the computer to find all the jets; if the sound editor is interested in a strong engine/afterburner sound, "launch" or "launching" can be requested. Maybe the editor is interested in aircraft carrier material. The filter parameters the editor sets in the search request narrow the material displayed for review. If the sound librarian does not enter a detailed enough description into the catalog entries, the computer cannot accurately search and retrieve the material that is being sought. Hence it is unwise to list only cute nicknames that add no meaningful information to the content.

The sound librarian will want to keep track of the monaural or stereo format (Fmt). The length, or time duration, of the sound cue is helpful. In the case of this catalog data entry, the original 1/4" roll and cue number is listed, as well as the subsequent digital DAT master roll number and program number (PNO). In this case, AFS 1909 was digitized to DAT 1266. Most of us have digitized our 1/4" and 35 mm mag masters to digital DAT masters. Do not discard the 1/4" originals! There are advantages in being able to return to the original 1/4" source and redigitize after better technologies and techniques have been developed. The analog-to-digital encoders on many early digital systems were not as good as they could have been, and, for the sake of our libraries' integrity, many of us have decided to use outboard analog-to-digital encoders as augmentations to the mastering system.

If you decide to try 24-bit audio technology, you have no choice but to go back to original 1/4" and 35 mm mag source to capture the deeper bit rate and geometric breadth of the audio. To simply convert 16-bit audio files to 24-bit files is a waste of time because that conversion will not provide any additional signal fullness. To achieve a broader richness, you must go back to the root source. Those of us who started building our sound libraries back in the days of 35 mm mag and recording 1/4" analog (many still prefer high-speed analog recordings to digital) never throw original analog recordings away. We put them into cold storage, waiting patiently for the next upgrade of technology, when we pull them out of the vault and redigitize them with new digital possibilities.

With data carefully and thoroughly entered, the sound librarian can ask the computer to print out catalog pages to provide a linear compilation of the library's root masters, in sequential order. If an editor is interested in jets and enters "jet" into the search parameter,

Cue	Description	Fmt	Time
1266-31	F-14 JET TAXI: on aircraft carrier.	M	00:20
1266-34	F-14 JET LAUNCH: on aircraft carrier. Very good. "Double cat shot." Very flamey, phasey sound. Launched w/double catapult.	M	01:15
1266-40	F-14 JET WARM UP/IDLE: on aircraft carrier. White-noisey. A-6 in B.G.	M	01:30
1266-52	F-14 JET TOUCH & GO: two of them	M	01:00
1266-54	F-14 JET TAKE-OFF: burners very long. Good!	M	01:10
1266-59	F-14 JET PASS BY: low and slow. Good, clean recording	M	01:10
1266-60	F-14 JET PASS BY: low and slow. Same as 1266-59 but better. Then F-4 PASS BY, around which time the tape gets mysteriously hissy. I dunno	M	02:15
1266-62	F-14 JET PASS BY: low and slow.	M	00:40
1266-63	F-14 JET PASS BY: low and slow.	M	00:50
1266-33	F-8 JET TAXI: on aircraft carrier.	M	00:20
1266-35	F-8 JET LAUNCH: on aircraft carrier. With burners	M	00:40
1266-46	F-8 JET TAKE-OFF: w/burners, Very long and good Crisp, w/some overmod, though quite useable	M	01:35
1266-78	F-8 JET TOUCH & GO: nice whistle on approach, wheels touch and engines throttle up and out	M	00:55

Figure 11.22 Index: jets.

he or she can scroll through all the sound entries that have "jet" listed. Note that each of the F-14s is listed together in a group because the sound librarian had listed the make of jet first. If it hadn't been done that way, the computer would have looked at the first word of the description and listed all sound cues of "jets" in alphabetical order based on the first letter of the first word, making it much harder to group the types together. Input by a specific jet type, such as F-14 or 737 makes locating the effects you desire easier to retrieve.

Note that the "Cue" numbers are not sequential. In this case, the computer is alphabetically lining up to "F" first, then the number. Although an F-8 is a lower designation than an F-14, the computer is looking at the first number after the "F". The number 1 is lower than 8, therefore the F-14 comes up on the computer before the F-8. To perform good data entry as a sound librarian, think of sound with the cold logic of a computer. Only then will you produce a database with the greatest flexibility and information access.

Chapter 12
Sound Design Myths
and Realities

As my partner Ken Sweet and I seriously immersed ourselves into sound effect development chores for John Carpenter's *The Thing,* we decided to try using a sound designer for the first time. The term had hardly been born, and few pictures presented the sound crew with the time and budget to allow experimentation. We called some colleagues to get recommendations for sound design talent.

The first place we contracted used a 24-track machine, something we did not use much in feature film sound work. The concept of layering sounds over themselves for design purposes appeared promising. The film-based Moviola assembly at sound editorial facilities like ours could not layer and combine prior to the predub rerecording phase. Ken and I sat patiently for half the day as the multitrack operator ran the machine back and forth, repeatedly layering up the same cicada shimmer wave. The owner of the facility and the operator kept telling us how "cool" it would sound, but when they played their compilation back for us, we knew the emperor had no clothes on, at least at this facility.

We called around again, and next were recommended to a hot young talent who had something called a Fairlight. We arranged for a design session and arrived with our 1/4″ source material. We told the eager young man exactly what kinds of sounds we needed to develop. Ken and I could hear the concepts in our heads, but we did not know how to run the fancy gear to expose the sounds within us. We explained the shots we wanted, along with the specially designed cues of sound desired at those particular moments. The young man turned to his computer and keyboard in a room stacked with various equipment rented for the session and dozens of wire feeds spread all over the floor.

Once again, Ken and I sat patiently. An hour passed as the young man dabbled at this and fiddled with that. A second hour passed. By the end of the third hour, I had not heard one thing anywhere near the concepts we had articulated. Finally, I asked the sound designer if he had an inkling of how to make the particular sound we had defined so clearly.

He said that he actually did not know how to make it, that he just played around and adjusted things until he made something that sounded kind of cool, and then he laid down the sound on tape. His previous clients would just pick whatever cues they wanted to use from his "creations."

Deciding it was going to be a long day, I turned to our assistant and asked him to run to the nearest convenience store and pick up some snacks and soft drinks. While I was digging in my pocket for some money, a quarter slipped out, falling onto the Vocorder unit. Suddenly, a magnificent metal shring-shimmer ripped through the speakers. Ken and I looked up with a renewed hope. "Wow!! Now that would be great for the opening title ripping effect! What did you do?"

The young man lifted his hands from the keyboard. "I didn't do anything."

I glanced down at the Vocorder, seeing the quarter. I dropped another quarter, and again an eerie metal ripping shring resounded. "That's it! Lace up some tape; we're going to record this."

Ken and I began dropping coins as the helpless sound designer sat rolling tape. Ken started banging on the Vocorder, delivering whole new variants of shimmer rips. "Don't do that!" barked the young man. "You'll break it!"

"The studio will buy you a new one. At least we're finally designing some sound!"

Ken and I realized that to successfully extract the sounds we could hear within our own heads, we would have to learn and master the use of the new signal-processing equipment. It was one of the most important lessons we learned.

I always have had a love–hate relationship with the term "sound designer." Although it suggests someone with a serious mindset for the development of a soundtrack, it also rubs me the wrong way because so many misunderstand and misuse what sound design truly is, cheapening what it has been, what it should be, and what it could be. This abuse and ignorance led the Academy of Motion Picture Arts and Sciences to decide that the job title "sound designer" would not be eligible for any Academy Award nominations or subsequent awards.

I have worked on mega-million-dollar features in which a sound designer was contractually listed in the credits, but whose work was not used. One project was captured by a sound editorial company only because it promised to contract the services of a particular sound designer, yet during the critical period of developing the concept sound effects for the crucial sequences, the contracted sound designer was on a beach in Tahiti. (Contrary to what you might think, he was not neglecting his work. Actually, he had made an agreement with the supervising sound editor, who knew he had been burned out from the previous picture. They both knew that, to the client, sound design was a perceived concept – a concept nonetheless that would make the difference between contracting the sound job or losing the picture to another sound editorial firm.)

By the time the sound designer returned from vacation, the crucial temp dub had just been mixed, with the critical sound design already completed. Remember, they were not sound designing for a final mix. They were designing for the temp dub, which in this case was more important politically than the final mix, because it instilled confidence and comfort for the director and studio. Because of the politics, the temp dub would indelibly set the design concept, with little room for change.

The contracted sound designer in this case is one of the best in the business. At that moment in the time and schedule, the supervising sound editor only needed to use his name and title to secure the show; he knew that several of us on his editorial staff were more than capable of accomplishing the sound design chores for the picture.

THE "BIG SOUND"

In July 1989 two men from Finland came to my studio: Antti Hytti was a music composer, and Paul Jyrälä, a sound supervisor/mixer. They were interested in a tour of my facility and transfer bay, in particular. I proudly showed them through the sound editorial rooms as I brought them to the heart of our studio. I thought it odd that Paul simply glanced over the Magna-Techs and Stellavox, only giving a passing acknowledgment to the rack of processing gear. He turned his attention to studying the room's wraparound shelves of tapes and odds-and-ends.

Paul spoke only broken English, so I turned to the composer with curiosity. "Antti, what is he looking for?"

Antti shrugged, then asked Paul. After a short interchange, Antti turned back to me. "He says that he is looking for the device that makes the Big Sound."

I was amused. "There is no device that makes the Big Sound. It's a philosophy, an art—an understanding of what sounds good together to make a bigger sound."

Antti interpreted to Paul, who in turn nodded with understanding as he approached me. "You must come to Finland so we make this Big Sound."

I resisted the desire to chuckle, as I was up to my hips in three motion pictures simultaneously. I shook their hands as I wished the two men well, assuming I would not see them again. Several weeks later, I received a work-in-progress video of the picture on which Paul had asked me to take part. Still in the throws of picture editorial, it was falling further and further behind schedule. My wife and I watched the NTSC (National Television System Committee) transfer of the PAL (phase alternating line) video as we sat down to dinner. I became transfixed as I watched images of thousands of troops in this 1930s-era epic, with T-26 Russian armor charging across snow-covered battlefields.

The production recordings were extremely good, but like most production tracks, focused on spoken dialog. In a picture filled with men, tanks, airplanes, steam trains, and weaponry, much sound effect work still had to be done. The potential sound design grew within my head—my imagination started filling the gaps and action sequences. If any picture cried out for the Big Sound, this was the one. *Talvisota: The Winter War* was the true story of the war between Finland and the Soviet Union in 1939. It proved one of the most important audio involvements of my professional career. It was not a question of money. It was an issue of passion—the heart and soul of a nation beckoned from the rough work-in-progress video.

I made arrangements to go to Helsinki and work with Paul Jyrälä to co-supervise this awesome challenge. I put together a bag filled with sound effect DAT tapes and a catalog print-out to add to the sound design lexicon that Paul and I would have to use.

This project was especially challenging, as this was before nonlinear workstations. The film was shot on 35mm with a 1:66 aspect. They did not use 35mm stripe or fullcoat for sound editing, but they did use 17.5mm fullcoat, and had one of the best 2-track stereo transfer bays I had the privilege to work in. To add to the challenge, we only had nine 17.5mm Perfectone playback machines on the rerecording stage—which meant that we had to be extremely frugal about how wide our "A," "B," "C" predub groups could be built out. We had no Moviolas, no synchronizers, no Acmade coding machines, no cutting tables with rewinds and no Rivas splicers. We did have two flatbed Steinbeck, a lot of veteran know-how, and a sauna.

AMERICAN SOUND DESIGN

Properly designed sound has a timbre all its own. Timbre is the violin—the vibration resonating emotionally with the audience. Timbre sets good sound apart from a pedestrian soundtrack.

Sound as we have seen it grow in the United States has distinguished American pictures on a worldwide market. Style, content, slickness of production, rapidity of storytelling—all make movies produced in the United States generally better, but the sound on American pictures is far superior to that of a vast majority of pictures made anywhere else in the world. Most foreign crews consider sound only a background behind the actors. They have not developed the Big Sound concept.

For those clients understanding that they need a theatrical soundtrack for their pictures, the first hurdle is not understanding what a theatrical soundtrack sounds like—but how to achieve it. When you say "soundtrack," the vast majority of people think of the music score. The general audience believes that almost all nonmusical sounds are actually recorded on the set when the film is shot. It does not occur to them that at least as much time and effort was put into the nonmusical audio experience of the storytelling as was put into composing and orchestrating the music score.

Some producers and filmmakers fail to realize that theatrical sound is not a format—it is not a commitment to spend giga-dollars or hire a crew the size of a combat battalion. It is a philosophy, an art form that only years of experience can help you understand.

The key to a great soundtrack is its dynamics and variation—with occasional introductions of subtle, unexpected things: the hint of hot gasses on a close-up of a recently fired gun barrel, or an unusual spatial inversion, such as a delicate sucking-up sound juxtaposed against a well-oiled metallic movement for a shot of a high-tech device being snapped open.

THE SOUND DESIGN LEGACY

When you ask a film enthusiast about sound design, the tendency is to recall legendary pictures with memorable sound, such as *Apocalypse Now* and the *Star Wars* series. I could not agree more. Many of us were greatly influenced by the work of Walter Murch and Ben Burtt (who worked on the above films, respectively). They not only had great product opportunities to practice their art form, but they also had producer-directors who provided the latitude and financial means to achieve exceptional accomplishments.

Without taking any praise away from Walter or Ben, let us remember that sound design did not begin in the 1970s. Did you ever study the soundtracks to George Pal's *War of the Worlds* or *The Naked Jungle*? Have you considered the low-budget constrictions that director Robert Wise faced while making *The Day the Earth Stood Still*, or the challenges confronting his sound editorial team in creating both the flying saucer and alien ray weapons? Who dreamed up using soda fizz as the base sound effect for the Maribunta, the army ants that terrorized Charlton Heston's South American plantation in *The Naked Jungle*? Speaking of ants, imagine thinking up the brilliant idea of looping a squeaky, pickup truck fan belt for the shrieks of giant ants in *Them*. Kids in the theatre wanted to hide when that incredible sound came off the screen.

When these fine craftspeople labored to make such memorable sound events for your entertainment pleasure, they made them without the help of today's high-tech digital tools—without Harmonizers or Vocorders, without a Synclavier or a Fairlight. They designed these sounds with their own brains, understanding what sounds to put together to create new sound events—how to play them backward, slow them down, cut, clip, and scrape them with a razor blade (when magnetic soundtrack became available in 1953), or paint them with blooping ink (when they still cut sound effects on optical track).

DO YOU DO SPECIAL EFFECTS TOO?

In the late summer of 1980 I had completed Roger Corman's *Battle Beyond the Stars*. I was enthusiastic about the picture, mainly because I had survived the film's frugal sound editorial budget and all the daily changes due to the myriad of special effect shots that came in extremely late in the process.

I had to come up with seven different-sounding spacecrafts with unique results, such as the Nestar ship which we created from human voices—it is the Community Choir from my hometown college of Coalinga. Choral Director Bernice Isham conducted her sopranos, altos, tenors, and basses through a whole maze of interesting vocal gymnastics, which were later processed to turn forty voices into million-pound thrust engines for the Nestar ship, manned by clone humanoids. Cue #33 of the audio CD provided with this book has several examples of sound effects developed from choral voices. We developed Robert Vaughn's ship from the root recordings of a dragster car, then processed it heavily to give it a menacing and powerful "magnetic-flux" force—just the kind of quick-draw space chariot a space-opera gunslinger would drive.

The day after the cast and crew screening, I showed up at Roger's office to discuss another project. As was the custom, I was met by his personal secretary. I could not help but beam with pride regarding my work on *Battle*, so I asked her if she had attended the screening—and if so, what did she think of the sound effects?

She had gone to the screening, but she struggled to remember the soundtrack. "The sound effects were okay, for what few you had."

"The few I had?"

The secretary shrugged. "Well, you know, there were so many special effects in the picture."

"Special effects! Where do you think the sound for all of those special effects came from?" I snapped back.

She brightened up. "Oh, do you do that too?"

"Do that TOO?" I was dumbfounded. "Who do you think makes those little plastic models with the twinky-lights sound like powerful juggernauts? Sound editors do, not model builders!"

It became obvious to me that the viewing audience can either not separate visual special effects from sound effects or has a hard time understanding where one ends and the other begins.

A good friend of mine got into hot water once with the Special Effects Committee when, in a heated argument, he had the temerity to suggest that to have a truly fair appraisal of their work in award evaluation competition they should turn the soundtrack off. After all, the work of the sound designer and the sound editors were vastly affecting the perception of visual special effects. The committee did not appreciate, nor heed my friend's suggestion, even though my friend had over thirty years and four hundred feature credits of experience behind his statement.

I have had visual special effects artists drop by to hear what I was doing with their work-in-progress "animatic" special effect shots, only to be inspired by something that we were doing that they had not thought of. They would go back to continue work on these shots, factoring in new thinking that had been born out of our informal get together.

SOUND DESIGN MISINFORMATION

A couple of years ago I read an article in a popular audio periodical in which a new, "flavor-of-the-month" sound designer had been interviewed. He proudly boasted something no one else supposedly had done: he had synthesized Clint Eastwood's famous .44 magnum gunshot from *Dirty Harry* into a laser shot. I sighed. We had done the same thing nearly twenty years before for the Roger Corman space opera, *Battle Beyond the Stars*. For nearly two decades Robert Vaughn's futuristic hand weapon had boldly fired the sharpest, most penetrating laser shot imaginable—which we developed from none other than Clint Eastwood's famous pistol.

During the mid-1980s I had hired a young enthusiastic graduate from a prestigious southern California university film school. He told me he felt very honored to start his film career at my facility, as one of his professors had lectured about my sound design techniques for Carpenter's *The Thing*. I felt a rush of pride, which was swiftly displaced by curious suspicion. I asked the young man what his professor had said. He joyously recounted his professor's explanation about how I had deliberately and painstakingly designed the heartbeat throughout the blood test sequence in reel ten, which subconsciously got into a rhythmic pulse, bringing the audience to a moment of terror.

I stood staring at my new employee with bewilderment. What heartbeat? My partner, Ken Sweet, and I had discussed the sound design for the project very thoroughly, and one sound we absolutely had stayed away from because it had screamed of cliché was any kind of heartbeat.

"Heartbeat?! Horse hockey!! The studio was too cheap to buy fresh fullcoat stock for the stereo sound effect transfers! They used reclaim, which had been sitting on a steel film rack that sat in the hallway across from the entrance to Dubbing 3. Nobody knew it at the time, but the steel rack was magnetized, which caused a spike throughout the stock. A magnetized spike can't be removed by bulk degaussing. Every time the roll of magnetic stock turns 360 degrees there is a very low frequency 'whomp.' You can't hear it on a Moviola. We didn't discover it until we were on the dubbing stage—by then it was too late!!"

The young man shrugged. "It still sounded pretty neat." Pretty neat? I guess I'm not as upset about the perceived sound design where none was intended as I am about the fact that the professor had not researched the subject on which he lectured. He certainly never had called to ask about the truth, let alone to inquire about anything of consequence that would have empowered his classroom teachings. He just made up a fiction, harming the impressionable minds of students with misinformation.

In that same sequence of *The Thing* I can point out real sound design. As John Carpenter headed north to Alaska to shoot the Antarctica base-camp sequences, he announced that we could not go too far in designing the voice of *The Thing*. To that end, I tried several ideas, with mixed results. Then one morning I was taking a shower when I ran my fingers over the soap-encrusted fiberglass wall. It made the strangest unearthly sound. I was inspired. Turning off the shower, I grabbed my tape recorder and dangled microphones from a broomstick taped in place from wall to wall at the top of the shower enclosure.

I carefully performed various "vocalities" with my fingertips on the fiberglass—moans, cries, attack shrieks, painful yelps, and other creature movements. When John Carpenter returned from Alaska, I could hardly wait to play the new concept for him. I set the tape recorder on the desk in front of him and depressed the "Play" button.

I learned a valuable lesson that day. What a client requests is not necessarily what he or she really wants, or particularly what he or she means. Rather than developing a vocal characterization for a creature never truly heard before, both director and studio executives actually meant "We want the same old thing everyone expects to hear and what has worked in the past—only give it a little different spin, you know." The only place I could sneak a hint of my original concept for the Thing's vocal chords was in the blood test scene where Kurt Russell stuck the hot wire into the petri dish and the blood leaped out in agony onto the floor. At the point where the blood turned and scurried away was where I cut those sound cues of my fingertips on the shower wall, called "Tentacles tk-2." I wonder what eerie and horrifying moments we could have conjured up instead of the traditional cliché lion growls and bear roars we were compelled to use in the final confrontation between Kurt Russell and the mutant Thing.

DAS BOOT: MIKE LE-MARE

I believe "legendary" is the only word properly describing the audio storytelling achievement that Mike Le-Mare (*Blow-Up, Ronin, Andersonville, She's So Lovely, Neverending Story*) and Karola Storr, along with their British-German team, accomplished in 1981 with *Das Boot*, a film directed by Wolfgang Peterson. Never before had anyone been nominated twice for an Academy Award in the sound arts on the same picture. Mike Le-Mare was nominated for Best Sound and for Best Sound Effect Editing.

Many attribute the successful experience of *Das Boot* to the careful and thoughtful sounds Mike gave to the film. The sound effects, by design and intent, were profoundly responsible for the psychological, claustrophobic terror during such sequences as the depth charge attack, which left the audience with sweaty palms, gripping the armrests. Who could not be affected by stress creaks of the metal hull of the U-boat enduring the pressures of the North Atlantic? Mike's broad palette of audio textures—unsettling air expulsions, pit-of-the-stomach ronks, and low-end growls—seized the audience, making real to them the vulnerability and mortality of the submarine crew in a way that transcended the visual picture.

Such a track did not magically happen because Mike Le-Mare could hear the potential sound design in his head. Nor did it happen because he willed it. Granted, such beginnings are vital, and the will to strive for excellence is essential. But without rolling up his sleeves

Figure 12.1 Mike Le-Mare and Karola Storr in their Los Angeles sound editorial facility Tape Effects.

and attending to the countless details and processes, without challenging himself and his crew to take the extra effort to achieve more, such sound experiences are not possible.

Le-Mare had been brought onto the project early enough to be able to do a significant amount of custom recording. The production company had access to a World War II–era German U-boat. To record the authentic diesel (for surface) and electric (for underwater maneuvering) engines, Le-Mare was allowed access to a permanently moored U-boat at Wasserburg where he made carefully controlled recordings of the submarine engines. Many variations were required for the various sequences. Precise notes were kept, with strict attention paid to microphone aspect, engine gears, and revolutions per minute (RPM) written down (such as "U-Boat: CLOSE—diesel engine startup and CONSTANT—nice tappets, then engine shuts down [in 2nd gear at 202 rpm]"). Recordings were made of the engine in all gears, under strain, cruising, at flank speed, reversing—recorded close up, medium perspective, down the companionway, or as heard from the conning tower.

Le-Mare made most of his recordings with a 1/4" Uher 4200 Report Monitor and Nagra III tape machines, using both Sennheiser and Neumann microphones. He obtained some authentic German hydrophone recordings that had extremely detailed notations, such as "HYDROPHONE: destroyer approaches and passes overhead, 250 rpm slows to 160 rpm (2 shaft—4 blade) then slows to stop TK-1."

From his own extensive sound effect library back in London, Le-Mare pulled a variety of ship horns, bilge water slops, tanks flooding with sea water, tanks blowing with air, vents, safety pressure valves, ASDIC pings, and all the metal and metal-related groans and rubs he could put together.

To help focus and define the authenticity of his sound design, Le-Mare brought in numerous German naval veterans who had served on U-boats during the war. He would tell them the use of each sound cue grouping, and then he would play it. "No, it did not sound like that," the submariner would say. "It sounds more like the bulkheads cry out in agony."

Sometimes Le-Mare would get emotional reactions from the men as the sounds evoked still-present realities from their memories. "There were times that I would have conflicting opinions," Le-Mare explained. "I resorted to acquiring World War II–era recordings, unsuitable for theatrical use, but I would listen to the texture and timbre of them and do an A–B comparison to see that our audio recreations were on the right track. This and the U-boat servicemen really helped me out a lot."

Unlike most submarine movie crews that build the practical set open on the side so that the cameras can get the shots easier, U-96 was built in two sections—front and rear. To this day, the two halves (now joined together) are still on display at Bavaria Studios in Munich.

"After wrapping principal photography, they took the two sections out to mount together for the tourist display. We were fortunate to get twelve of the actors to come back later to custom record them running through the companionway from back to front and back. This kind of action would be just about impossible to duplicate correctly on a Foley stage," recalled Le-Mare. "We laid down a series of Neumann microphones alongside the floor's metal plates so that we could properly hear the texture of the footsteps and body movement as the men ran forward. They would grab grip bars above the hatchways as they frantically swung through and continued on. This kind of sound lent an incredible realism for the audience and really helped to draw the viewer in as part of the crew, rather than just watching the film at arm's length."

Le-Mare brought onto the Foley stage all kinds of electric motors for the sounds of the echo range finder, compass, depth gauge, generator, and other equipment for controlled isolated recordings. He brought in switches and various mechanisms for periscope handle movements and fine adjustments, ballast tank operations, rudder controls, hydroplane wheel turns, and so forth. Each item was carefully recorded, making numerous variations for the future sound editorial process.

Le-Mare had Moviolas and Acmade's Pic-Sync Competitors shipped in from London to supply his British sound editorial crew with the equipment it felt most comfortable and confident using, while the German crew used flatbed Steinbecks. German rerecording stages were challenged by the amount of tracks it took to mount the required sound for *Das Boot*. With a limited number of soundtracks generally used in film production, picture editors usually ran the mixing sessions, but not with *Das Boot*. Aside from Klaus Doldinger's haunting music score, Mike Le-Mare came onto the dubbing stage with as many as 110 hard effect tracks and an average of twenty Foley tracks in addition to the dialog, ADR, and backgrounds. In fact, Le-Mare was asked to get behind the console and help in the mixing at some busy moments, since he was the only one who had a grasp of the material and how it all would work together. For all this, Le-Mare was nominated not only for Best Sound Effects Editing as the supervising sound editor, but also for Best Sound as one of the rerecording mixers.

It was one of the most complex soundtracks ever to be mixed on Stage "A" at Bavaria Studios. So thorough was the feature's preparation and the attention to detail given it, a month after Le-Mare and his sound crew had finished the two-and-a-half-hour feature version, the director and producers decided that Le-Mare and his team should prepare the television version. They went back to the drawing board to prepare the new five-and-a-half-hour version. Of course, the conventional method would have been to cut down the feature version, but, in this case, new scenes were actually added and existing materials were extended to generate a longer picture.

More producers should consider hiring quality theatrical editors to handle foreign language conversions, but it comes down to money. Remember this—you get what you pay for. So many foreign language remixes seem comical and often slipshod. The producers must be willing to pay for fine craftsmanship to achieve a high quality standard.

Mike Le-Mare's career as a supervising sound editor dates back further than he may be willing to admit. Certain young and ambitious studio executives sneer at a resume that dates back very far (known as the "gray list"); they believe veterans are not hip and up-to-date enough for modern feature work. Those who believe this nonsense should see John Frankenheimer's 1998 action thriller, *Ronin*. Mike Le-Mare and his team tackled the ultimate car chase sequence put to film yet.

"Recreating the unique European car exhaust systems for the picture was very challenging; it became a virtual orchestration of the variety of engines and mechanicals. The final result was very satisfying indeed."

The major chase sequences were filmed MOS. Mike Le-Mare eventually hired Eric Potter as his post-production sound effect recordist to custom record the myriad car sound effects, whining gear boxes, all kinds of tire skids and slides (don't forget the challenge of cobblestone streets), and mechanical demands. The climactic chase through Paris is a rare treat. Except for occasional dialog exclamations, the sequence is almost entirely done with sound effects and Foley alone. The audio detailing is delightful, giving the action sequences a whole new dimension. With years of experience and know-how, Le-Mare did not waste time figuring out what worked and what did not. Because of his experience, he knew exactly what had to be done: focusing on the audio events to be brought to life and spending his energies and team resources to accomplish a very difficult and challenging job.

THE DIFFERENCE BETWEEN DESIGN AND MUD

Supervising sound editor David Stone, winner of the Academy Award for Best Sound Effects Editing in 1993's *Bram Stoker's Drakula*, is a quiet and reserved audio artist. As sound design field commanders go, he is not flamboyant, nor does he use showmanship as a crutch. What he does is quietly and systematically deliver the magic of his craft—his firm grasp of storytelling through sound. Though he loves to work on animated films, having helmed projects such as *Beauty and the Beast*, *A Goofy Movie*, *Cat's Don't Dance*, *Pooh's Grand Adventure: The Search for Christopher Robin*, and *The Lion King II*, one should never try to typecast him. Stone has time and again shown his various creative facets and the ability to mix his pallet of sounds in different ways to suit the projects at hand. He leaves the slick illusionary double-talk to others. For himself, he stands back and studies the situation for a while. He makes no pretense that he is not an expert in all the fancy audio software, or that he was up half the night trying to learn how to perform a new DSP function.

"Being a computer vidiot is not what creates good sound design—understanding what sounds go together and when to use them does," Stone reminds us. "Otherwise we run the danger of making a pile of mud. Many times I have watched young sound editors simply try to put together two or more sound effects to achieve a larger audio event, often without satisfaction. A common mistake is to simply lay one pistol shot on top of another. They do not necessarily get a bigger pistol shot; in fact, they often only diminish the clarity and character of the weapon because they are putting together two sounds that have too many common frequency dynamics to complement one another—instead the result is what we call mud."

A good example of this is the Oliver Stone film *On Any Sunday*. As I listened to the presentation at the Academy theatre (it was not a substandard speaker system for the performance venue) I was completely taken out of the film itself by the badly designed football effects. The lack of clarity and "roundness" of the sound was, instead, replaced by overdriven effects with an emphasis in the upper mid-range that cannot be described as anything other than distortion.

A newly initiated audio jockey may naively refer to such sound as befitting the type of film—the "war" of sports needing a "war" of sound. Frankly, such an answer is horse-dung. Listen to the sound design of *Road to Perdition, We Were Soldiers,* and especially *The Pianist* and *Saving Private Ryan.* These are also sounds of violence and war in the extreme—and yet they are designed with full "roundness" and clarity. Each audio event has a very tactile linkage with its visual counterpart.

I have harped on this throughout this book and will continue to do so, because it is the keystone of the sound design philosophy—if you take the audience out of the film because of bad sound design—then you have failed as a sound designer. It's just that simple.

Steve Flick (two-time Academy Award winner for Best Sound Effects Editing for *Robocop* and *Speed*) asked if I would come to Weddington to help cut sound effects on *Predator 2*. Several days later, John Dunn, another sound effects editor, asked if I could bring some of my weapon effects to the opening shootout in reel one. I brought a compilation DAT the following day with several gun effects I thought would contribute toward the effort.

Just after lunch, Flick burst into my room (as is his habit, garnishing him the affectionate nickname of "Tsunami") and demanded to know, "How come your guns are bigger than mine?!"

"I never said my guns are bigger than yours, Steve."

Steve shrugged. "I mean, I know I have big guns, but yours are—dangerous!"

With that, he whirled and disappeared down the hall just as suddenly as he had appeared. I sat in stunned aftermath, pondering his description of "dangerous." After due consideration, I agreed. The style by which I set my microphones up when I record weapon fire, and the combinations of elements I use to editorially manufacture weapon fire to create audio events that are supposed to scare and frighten, have a "bite" to them.

Gunfire is an in-your-face crack! Big guns are not made by pouring tons of low-end frequency into the audio event. Low-end does not have any punch or bite. Low-end is fun, when used appropriately, but the upper mid-range and high-end bite with a low-end underbed will bring the weapon to life. Dangerous sounds are not heard at arm's length where it is safe, but IN YOUR FACE. They are almost close enough to reach out and touch you. Distance—what we call "proximity" triggers your subconscious emotional responses to determine the danger.

I compare blending multiple sound cues together in a new design to being a choir director. Designing a sound event is exactly like mixing and moving the various voices of the choir to create a new vocal event with richness and body. I think of each sound as being soprano, alto, tenor, or bass. Putting basses together will not deliver a cutting punch and a gutsy depth of low end. All I will get is muddy low-end with no cutting punch.

The Pro Tools session shown in Figure 12.1 is a rifle combination I put together for a recent action-adventure period picture, circa 1925. We had several thousand rifle shots in the

Figure 12.2 The "Mauser rifle" Pro Tools session.

battle scenes—for each, I painstakingly cut four stereo pairs of sounds that made up the basic signature of a single 7.62 Mauser rifle shot. The reason is simple. Recording a gunshot with all the spectrum characteristics envisioned in a single recording by the supervising sound editor is impossible. Choice of microphone, placement of microphone, selection of recording medium—all these factors determine the voice of the rifle report. Listen to cue #30 of the audio CD provided with this book to listen to 7.62 Mauser rifle shot design.

As an experienced sound designer, I review recordings at my disposal and choose those cues that comprise the soprano, alto, tenor, and bass of the performance. I may slow down or speed up one or more of the cues. I may pitch-shift or alter the equalization as I deem necessary. I then put them together, very carefully lining up the leading edge of each discharge as accurately as I can (well within one one-hundredth of a second accurate). Then I play them together as one new voice. I may need to lower the tenor and/or raise the alto—or I may discover that the soprano is not working and that I must choose a new soprano element.

If possible, I will not commit the mixing of these elements at the sound editorial stage. After consulting with the head rerecording mixer and considering the predubbing schedule, I will decide whether we can afford cutting the elements abreast and leaving the actual mixing to the sound effect mixer during predubbing. If the budget for post-production sound work is too small and the sound effect predubbing too short (or nonexistent), I will mix the elements together prior to the sound editorial phase, thereby throwing the dye of commitment to how the individual elements are balanced together in a new single stereo pair.

The same goes for rifle bolt actions. I may have the exact recordings of the weapon used in the action sequence in the movie. When I cut them to sync, I play them against the rest of the tracks. The bolt actions played by themselves sound great, but now they are mixed with the multitude of other sounds present. They just do not have the same punch or characterization as when they stood alone. As a sound designer, I must pull other material, creating the illusion and perception of historical audio accuracy—but I must do it by factoring in the involvement of the other sounds of the battle. Their own character and frequency signatures will have a profound influence on the sound I am trying to create.

This issue was demonstrated on *Escape from New York*. During sound effect predubs, the picture editor nearly dumped the helicopter skid impacts I had made for the Hueys upon descent and landing in the streets of New York. Played by themselves, they sounded extremely loud and sharp. The experienced, veteran sound effect mixer, Gregg Landaker, advised the picture editor that it was not necessary or wise to dump the effects at that time, because they were in a separate set of channels and could be easily dumped later if not wanted.

Later, as we rehearsed the sequence for the final mix, it became apparent that Gregg's advice not to make a hasty decision paid off. Now that the heavy pounding of the Huey helicopter blades filled the theatre along with the haunting siren-like score, what had sounded like huge and ungainly metal impacts in the individual predub now became a gentle, even subtle, helicopter skid touchdown on asphalt.

WHAT MAKES EXPLOSIONS BIG

For years following *Christine* people constantly asked about the magic I used to bring such huge explosions to the screen. Remember, *Christine* was mixed before digital technology, when we still worked to an 85 dB maximum. The simple answer should broaden your design thinking into areas aside from just explosions. I see sound editors laying on all kinds of low-end or adding shotgun blasts into the explosion combination, and certainly a nice low-end wallop is cool and necessary—but it isn't dangerous. All it does is muddy it up. What makes an explosion big and dangerous is not the boom—but the DEBRIS that is thrown around.

I first realized this while watching footage of military C4 explosives igniting. Smokeless and seemingly nothing as a visual entity unto themselves, they wreak havoc, tearing apart trees, vehicles, masonry—the debris makes C4 so visually awesome. The same is true with sound. Go back and listen to the sequence in Reel 7 of *Christine* again, the sequence where the gas station blows up. Listen to the glass debris flying out the window, the variations of metal, oil cans, crowbars, tires, tools that come flying out the service bay. Listen to the metal sidings of the gas pumps flying up and hitting the light overhang atop the fueling areas. Debris is the key to danger. Prepare tracks so that the rerecording mixer can pan debris cues into the surround channels, bringing the audience into the action, rather than allowing it to watch the scene at a safe distance.

THE SATISFACTION OF SUBTLETY

Sound design often calls to mind the big, high-profile audio events that serve as landmarks in a film. For every stand-out moment—however, dozens of other equally important moments designate sound design as part of the figurative chorus line. These moments are not solo events, but supportive and transparent performances that enhance the storytelling continuity of the film.

Undoubtedly, my reputation is one of action sound effects. I freely admit that I enjoy designing the hardware and firepower and wrath of nature. Yet some of my most satisfying creations have been the little things that hardly are noticed: the special gust of wind through the hair of the hero in the night desert, the special seat compression with a taste of spring action as a passenger swings into a car seat and settles in, the delicacy of a slow door latch as a child timidly enters the master bedroom—little golden touches that fortify and sweetly satisfy the idea of design.

REALITY VERSUS ENTERTAINMENT

One of the first requirements for the successful achievement of a soundtrack is becoming audio educated with the world. I know that advice sounds naive and obvious, but it is not. Listen and observe life around you. Listen to the components of sound and come to understand how things work. Learn the difference between the Rolls Royce Merlin engine of a P-51 and the Pratt-Whitney of an AT-6, the difference between a hammer being cocked on a .38 service revolver and a hammer being cocked on a .357 Smith & Wesson. What precise audio movements separate the actions of a hundred-ton metal press? What is the audio difference between a grass fire and an oil fire, between pine burning and oak? What is the difference between a rope swish and a wire or dowel swish? How can one distinguish blade impacts of a fencing foil from a cutlass or a saber; what kind of metallic ring-off would go with each?

A supervising sound editor I knew was thrown off a picture because he did not know what a Ford Cobra was, and insisted that his effect editors cut sound cues from an English sports car series. It is not necessary to be a walking encyclopedia who can regurgitate information about the South American Kerrington mating call or the rate of fire of a BAR (if you even know what a BAR is). What is important is that you diligently do research so that you can walk onto the rerecording stage with the proper material.

I remember predubbing a helicopter warming up on stage. Suddenly the engine wind-up bumped hard with a burst from the turbine. The sound effects mixer quickly tried to duck it out, as he thought it was a bad sound cut on my part. The director immediately corrected him, saying that it was absolutely the right sound at exactly the right spot. The mixer asked how I knew where to cut the turbine burst. I told him that, in studying the shot frame by frame, I had noticed two frames of the exhaust that were a shade lighter than the rest. It seemed to me that that was where the turbo had kicked in.

Reality, however, is not necessarily the focus of sound design. There is reality, and there is the perception of reality. We were rehearsing for the final mix of Reel 3 of *Escape from New York,* where the Huey helicopters descend and land in an attempt to find the president. I had been working very long hours and was exhausted. After I dozed off and fell out of my chair several nights before, Don Rogers had supplied a roll-around couch for me to sleep on during the mixing process. The picture editor paced behind the mixers as they rehearsed the reel. He raised his hand for them to stop and announced that he was missing a "descending" sound.

Gregg Landaker and Bill Varney tried to determine to what element of sound the picture editor was referring. The exact components of the helicopters were all there. From an authenticity point of view, nothing was missing.

I rolled over and raised my hand. "Roll back to 80 feet, take Effects 14 off the line. Take the feed and the take-up reels off the machine and switch them; then put on a three-track head stack. Leaving Effects 14 off the line, roll back to this shot, then place Effects 14 on the line. I think you will get the desired effect."

Everybody turned to look at me with disbelief, certain I was simply talking in my sleep. Bill Varney pressed the talk-back button on the mixing console so that the recordist in the machine room could hear. "Would you please repeat that, Mr. Yewdall?"

I repeated the instructions. The picture editor had heard enough. "What is that supposed to accomplish?"

I explained. "At 80 feet is where Lee Van Cleef announces he is 'going in.' The next shot is the fleet of Hueys warming up and taking off. If you check the cue sheets, I think that you will see that Effects 14 has a wind-up from a cold start. Played forward, it is a jet whine ascending with no blade rotation. If we play that track over the third channel position of a three-channel head stack, which means the track is really playing backward while we are rolling forward, I think we will achieve a jet whine descending." Listen to cue #31 of the audio CD provided with this book to listen to "Huey helicopter descending."

From then on, more movies used helicopter jet whine warm-ups (prior to blade rotation) both forward and reversed to sell the action of helicopters rising or descending, as the visual action dictated. It is not reality, but it is the entertaining perception of reality.

In today's post-production evolution, the tasks of equalization and signal processing, once considered sacred ground for the rerecording mixers, increasingly have become the working domain of sound designers and supervising sound editors. Accepting those chores, however, also brings about certain responsibilities and ramifications should your work be inappropriate and cost the client additional budget dollars to unravel what you have done.

If you twist those signal-processing knobs, then know the accompanying burden of responsibility. Experienced supervising sound editors have years of "combat" on the rerecording mix stage to know what they and their team members should do, and what should be left for rerecording mixers. I liken my work to getting the rough diamond into shape. If I over-polish the material, I risk trapping the mixer with an audio cue that he or she may not be able to manipulate and appropriately use. Do not polish sound to a point that a mixer has no maneuvering room. You will thwart a collaborative relationship with the mixer.

The best sound design is done with a sable brush—not with a ten-pound sledge hammer. If your sound design distracts the audience from the story, you have failed. If your sound design works in concert with and elevates the action to a new level, you have succeeded. It is just that simple.

Sound design does not mean that you have to have a workstation stuffed full of fancy gear and complex software. One of the best signal process devices I like to use is the simple Klark-Teknik DN 30/30—a 30-band graphic equalizer (see Figures 12.3 and 12.4). Taking a common, but carefully chosen steady wood flame, I used the equalizer in real time, undulating the individual sliders wildly in waves to cause the "mushrooming" fireball sensation.

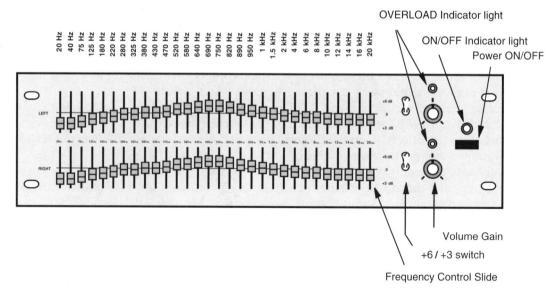

Figure 12.3 The Klark-Teknik DN 30/30 graphic equalizer. If you turn up the volume gain full to the right (which equals +6 dB level) and flip the +6/+3 dB switch up into the +6 position, this will give you a total of +12 dB or −12 dB "gain" or "cut."

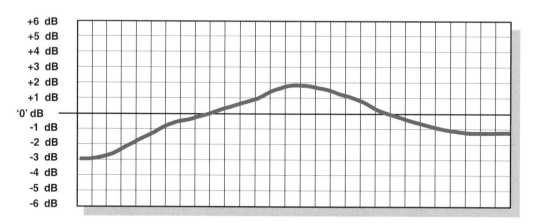

Figure 12.4 The frequency response of the graphic curve setting seen in Figure 12.3 on the 30-band equalizer.

Listen to cue #32 of the audio CD provided with this book to listen to the development of "Mushrooming flames."

WISE ADVICE TO CONSIDER

I learned more than one valuable lesson on *Escape from New York*. Never tell the client how you made the magic. *Escape from New York*'s budget was strained to the limit, and the job was not done yet. The special effect shots had not been completed, and the budget could not bear the costs of a traditional feature special effect shop. They decided to contract the work to Roger Corman's company, because he had acquired the original computer-tracking special effect camera rig that George Lucas had used on *Star Wars*. Corman was making a slew of special effect movies to amortize the cost of acquiring the equipment and offering special effect work to outside production companies, *Escape from New York* being one.

The first shots were delivered. John Carpenter (director), Debra Hill (producer), Todd Ramsay (picture editor), Dean Cundey (director of photography), Bob Kizer (special effects supervisor), and several members of the visual special effects team sat down in Projection "A" at Goldwyn to view the footage. It has been suggested that the quality expectation from the production team was not very high. After all, this was only Corman stuff—how good could it be?

The first shot flickered onto the screen—the point of view of Air Force One streaking over New York harbor at night, heading into the city just prior to impact. Carpenter, Hill, and Cundey were amazed by the high quality of the shot. After the lights came up, John asked the visual special effects team how it was done. The team members, proud and happy that Carpenter liked their work, blurted out, "Well, first we dumped black paint on the concrete floor, then we let it dry halfway. Then we took paint rollers and roughed it up, to give it the 'wave' effect of water at night. Then we made dozens of cardboard cut-outs of the buildings and cut out windows . . ."

Carpenter's brow furrowed as he halted their explanation. He pressed the talk-back button to projection. "Roll it again, please."

Now they viewed the footage again—only with the discerning eye of foreknowledge of the illusion's creation. Now they could see the imperfections, could see how it was done. The reel ran out, and the lights came up.

Carpenter thought a moment, then turned to the visual special effects team. "No—I am going with what I saw the first time. You fooled me. If I ever ask you how you did something again, don't tell me."

The lesson of that afternoon was burned indelibly into my brain and I have referred to it time and time again in dealing with clients who want to know how something was made. Do not destroy the illusion and magic of your creations by revealing the secrets of how you did them—especially to your clients. Here endeth the lesson.

Chapter 13
Sound Editorial:
Sync-Sync, Chop-Chop

"Address the bench and prepare your tracks in such a way that any mixer can get in and mix them!"

Ken Sweet

All through a film's evolution, sound endures uneven recordings, mismatching formats, missed opportunities, temp voices, temp music, and temp sound effects. It suffers clipped lines, radio interference, line static, digital zits, dramatic level shifts, noisy backgrounds, fluorescent ballast, power hums, and just about every other insult and shortcoming a sound engineer can imagine—in addition to ignorance, carelessness, and mindlessness. The project experiences noncommunication, miscommunication, misinformation, improperly entered data in the code book, improperly transferred material, lack of notations in the production sound report, and physical misplacement or total loss of materials. Just because the negative and original sound rolls are vaulted at the laboratories and sound transfer facilities does not mean something unexpected cannot happen to them. Murphy's Law is ever present and devilish in thwarting creative and idealistic expectations. All during this time, one person or another inevitably will say, "Oh, don't worry about it; we'll fix it later in post."

Guess what. Post is here! The production sound and locked picture will be turned over to sound editorial. You can have no "fix-it-later" attitude here. Sound editorial must gather the various broken pieces of the production sound process and put them back together again, in addition to creating the sound effects and ambiances that creatively bind the entire sound-track together.

The head of the sound editorial team is the supervising sound editor; in the case of a big, complex feature project, two editors team up as co-supervising sound editors. Like a field commander carefully deploying forces, the supervising sound editor divides the work, assigning a specialist to each aspect of the sound tasks. The supervisor organizes and coordinates each editor's efforts, focusing the creative work so that when various components of the sound elements are brought together in the rerecording process, the result is a seamless audio experience performing with a transparency of reality.

WHO IS WHO IN SOUND EDITORIAL

Figure 13.2 illustrates the sound editorial structure of a typical medium-budget action picture. (This same sample crew was outlined in the budget breakdown in Chapter 4.)

Supervising Sound Editor

The supervising sound editor is the creative authority of the sound preparation process, working hand-in-hand with the director, picture editor, and producer(s) in realizing the audio potential of the film. The supervisor's shoulders bear far more than the limelight of the title. His or her taste in sound and choice in sound crew—sound editors, sound designer(s), Foley artists, transfer department crew, ADR and Foley stage mixers, and the choice of the final rerecording stage and mixing team—are pivotal factors that focus the combined efforts of all toward an artistically successful soundtrack. Such expert guidance vastly increases the production value of the film. Conversely, inappropriate taste in sound or choices of team members can lead headlong to disaster, plunging the project into a budgetary hemorrhage and irreparably destroying the chances of a quality sound experience. Directors and producers are well aware of this.

The supervising sound editor enters into a series of meetings with the director, picture editor, and producer(s), covering a wide range of audio concepts and concerns. As discussed in Chapter 4, unwise clients decide what mixing facility to use without including the input and professional experience of the supervising sound editor.

As today's post-production schedules become increasingly complicated and more outrageous, the supervising sound editor literally is becoming a tactical field commander whose talent assignment and schedule problem-solving skills are often considered more important than the ability to sound design or cut sound. After all, these chores can be assigned to specialists hired as needed. In simplistic terms, the supervising sound editor's job is to hold the hands of the director and producers through an often arduous and anxiety-filled post-production process.

The supervising sound editor holds the promise of a wonderful and inspiring soundtrack to come, all while scrambling to deliver these promises without budget overruns. On top of all of this, the supervising sound editor must deliver these promised audio ingredients to the rerecording stage on time, while enduring the inevitable hail of changes, both in the film and the director's heart and mind.

The supervising sound editor receives a script from the production company considering him or her to head the project. The supervisor reads it carefully—breaking out all the audio events and potential challenges to be addressed. Budgeting and bidding on a project based solely on reading the script is extremely difficult, however.

As soon as the supervising sound editor is asked to consider a show, research must begin. The supervisor first should determine who the director and producer(s) are, and then look them up in the *Annual Index to Motion Picture Credits*, published by the Academy of Motion Picture Arts and Sciences, gleaning any information about screen credits and earlier

The Basic Phases of Sound Editorial

1/4" TAPE   DIGITAL DAT

PROD. DIALOG is reprinted for DIALOG EDITING

from sound transfer dept.

downloaded into sound edit system by Assistant

work drive

"LOCKED" PICTURE" is transferred to picture dupe or to video tape

35mm color film "dupe"

1/2" VHS -or- 3/4" video tape w/time code

ADR ("Looping") Replacing Actors Lines as well as Group Walla.

FOLEY Foley Artists perform footsteps and minor props in sync to the projected picture.

SOUND EFFECTS Custom recorded sound effects -- "sound designed" made effects through electronic manipulation as well as sound effects pulled from the sound effect library.

Orb 2GB

Figure 13.1 Sound editorial crew flow chart: basic phases of edit.

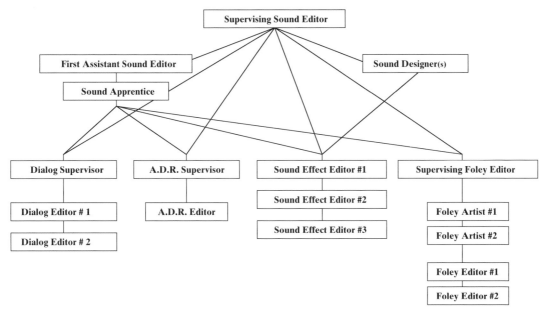

Figure 13.2 This sound crew tree is a typical crew for a medium-budget feature project with an average schedule and temp dub requirements.

work. Sometimes the supervisor charts the projects, especially for someone unknown, showing the evolution of a first-time director who rose through the ranks of cinematographer, picture editor, or producer. This kind of information lends a feel for a director's expectations, in regards to sound. If the director has previous projects listed, the supervisor takes time to review them on various video media to determine the style of sound exhibited in other work. The supervisor does the same in regard to the producers, especially noting if and on what project(s) the director and producer(s) have worked together before.

The supervising sound editor may want to trace the present project back to either commencement of principal photography or announcement in the trades (*Hollywood Reporter* and *Variety*), where back issues can yield any publicity information on creative and political footnotes. The Internet has also become a valuable resource, providing nearly instantaneous information. All of this provides the necessary information for developing a philosophy and tactical strategy that helps the supervisor better serve the project at hand.

Next, the supervisor insists on personally listening to raw daily recordings in a playback environment that accurately reveals any problems affecting the scope of work to be done. Experience has taught me that a picture editor's opinion on the quality of the dialog track is not always an accurate determination, though it can be a weather vane of expectations. The supervisor immediately gets a feel for not only how difficult the dialog preparation is liable to be, but how much ADR is needed, how much Group Walla is necessary, how broad and detailed the sound effect editing will be, and how much Foley should be scheduled. The supervisor then makes up an asset plot chart, mapping out in a timeline what labor should be hired at which point and for how long (see Figure 13.3). In a relatively short period

Sound Editorial Crew Flow Chart	week #1	week #2	week #3	week #4	week #5	week #6	week #7	week #8	week #9	week #10	week #11	week #12	week #13	week #14	week #15	week #16	total weeks
												Rerecording MIX schedule					
Supervising Sound Editor	X	X	X	X	X	X	X	X	X	X	X	X	X	X	X	X	16
First Asst. Sound Editor	X	X	X	X	X	X	X	X	X	X	X	X	X	X	X	X	16
Sound Apprentice	X	X	X	X	X	X	X	X	X	X	X	X	X	X	X	X	16
Dialog Supervisor		X	X	X	X	X	X	X	X	X	X	X	X	X			13
Dialog Editor # 1			X	X	X	X	X	X	X	X	X	X					10
Dialog Editor # 2				X	X	X	X	X	X	X	X	X					9
A.D.R. Supervisor		X	X	X	X	X	X	X	X	X	X	X	X	X	X	X	15
A.D.R. Editor						X	X	X	X	X	X	X	X				8
Sound FX Recordist			X	X													2
Sound Designer		X	X	X	X	X	X	X	X	X	X	X	X				12
Sound Effects Editor #1			X	X	X	X	X	X	X	X	X	X	X				11
Sound Effects Editor #2			X	X	X	X	X	X	X	X	X	X					10
Sound Effects Editor #3				X	X	X	X	X	X	X	X	X					9
Supervising Foley Editor		X	X	X	X	X	X	X	X	X	X	X					11
Foley Artist #1							X	X	X								3
Foley Artist #2							X	X	X								3
Foley Editor #1								X	X	X	X						4
Foley Editor #2								X	X	X	X						4

Figure 13.3 The supervising sound editor carefully charts out the labor requirements for the most efficient use of budget dollars.

of time, with much experience from previous projects to help assess the new project, the supervisor arrives at a cost-to-complete.

After the supervisor is chosen by the client for the project, he or she must carry out the tasks of developing, cutting, and overseeing the mixing of the project soundtrack, while staying within the boundaries of the contracted budget and schedule. Schedules and budgets, as well as changes and renegotiations, are an entire science unto themselves, and this book is not designed to address those issues.

First Assistant Sound Editor

The first assistant sound editor is the supervising sound editor's secret weapon in the war of organization and technical discipline. The first assistant is the direct conduit from the picture editorial department. Picture dupes, videotapes, change notes, code books, sound reports, EDLs (edit decision lists), and all transferred materials pass through the first assistant's domain and control before the editors receive them. If they do not, the first assistant cannot vouch for the material being current, correct, and viable. The first assistant is the organizational foundation on which the entire sound editorial project rests.

Figure 13.4 First sound assistant Peter Cole rewinds a thousand-foot transfer onto a projection reel for the Foley editor. The first assistant is the first to be hired by the supervising sound editor, and the last to be laid off. His or her work literally makes or breaks the ability of the sound editorial team to successfully mount and complete a project and to keep editorial costs from rising unnecessarily.

Sound Apprentice

Shortly after the first assistant sound editor commences work, the sound apprentice is hired. This position is not to be confused with the second sound assistant. The term "sound apprentice" is being used less in the industry, replaced by the term "intern," as more editorial facilities try to sidestep a potential union position. In past years the apprentice was the break-in position, but as union domination slowly ebbed, so has the structured ways of entering the industry's workforce.

Regardless of this position's name, the apprentice is an assistant to the assistant, and, working at the job, he or she will begin to learn and understand the process—why we perform tasks a certain way. The reasons behind procedures are among the most important factors in building a strong base of technical and procedural discipline. Unless you understand why, you will never appreciate the procedures to successfully achieve the desired result.

Sound Designer

Depending on the post-production schedule restrictions and the complexity of the project, the supervising sound editor may want to contract a sound designer to create sound effects, ensuring the continuity and efficiency that will satisfy the director's taste and vision. This is especially true for high-concept projects. This work used to be done by the supervising sound editor, but since the late 1980s the supervising sound editor has shifted the ever-growing sound development needs to sound designing talent on a full-time basis. (Review Chapter 12 for more detailed information on the role of the sound designer.)

Dialog Supervisor

The dialog supervisor is called the co-supervising sound editor on some projects, and the ADR supervisor on others. Regardless of the title, the task is of primary importance. Music and sound effects may be used or discarded in the mix, but dialog almost never is discarded. When the actors' lips flap, vocal utterances must be heard. Hence strict attention must be given to the preparation of dialog tracks; whether original production recordings or ADR "looped" lines, they must be seamlessly edited so that the audience is unaware of the editing process. (See Chapter 14 for an in-depth review of the importance and editorial philosophy of the dialog editor.)

ADR Supervisor

For weeks prior to "turn-over," the picture editor, director, and producer(s) become increasingly aware of the quality shortcomings of their production track. On some pictures, the ADR supervisor is hired separately from the supervising sound editor and sound editorial crew. Often the ADR supervisor is the political trade-off to secure a project. The ADR supervisor, more than any other post-production craftsperson, interfaces and works with the acting talent. When temperamental or difficult talent is involved, the producer's first concern is who handles the ADR politics and responsibilities.

A special talent exists for cutting ADR lines. Most of the time, an ADR line never just falls from the actor's mouth. The actor or director has signed off on the line because of the performance, more than anything—so it falls to the ADR editor to massage (cut) the actor's words in such a way as to lend a seamless and natural delivery, yet still fit the lip movements. This is not so easy a task! (Review Chapter 15 for more detailed information on the role of ADR supervisor/editor.)

Sound Effects Editors

The experienced supervising sound editor will know the editing style and talent of the sound effects editors with which he or she works. Almost all sound effects editors tend to lean toward their own favorite tasks or specialties. Some are more talented in cutting animal

Figure 13.5 Wendy Hedin, a New York–based supervising sound editor working at her nonlinear workstation. Note the various digital tape deck formats, including two DA-88 machines, time code DAT recorder, audio CD player along with both 3/4" Umatic and 1/2" VHS video decks. Using both analog and digital DSP plug-ins, Wendy has all of the tools she needs to design and cut project assignments.

vocals; others are better versed in cutting vehicles and mechanical devices. Few sound editors can truly say they are proficient at cutting all sounds. Understanding how to sync up sound and make it work is one thing; it is far and away another to know how to massage the material and make a special audio event from a handful of common audio cues.

With today's digital nonlinear systems, a supervisor can assign a particular type of sound to a single sound effects editor to cut throughout an entire picture. Some supervisors call this "horizontal editing." This lends a greater precision in continuity to a picture. The sound effects editor who cuts the windshield wipers on the car in Reel 2 is the same editor who cuts the windshield wipers in Reel 9, thereby guaranteeing a matched style and rhythm.

In the track chase sequence in *Raiders of the Lost Ark*, the driver turned on the windshield wipers as the truck barreled through the water duct. The sound effects editor interpreted the material one way and cut the windshield wipers "swish-thunk, swish-thunk, swish-thunk." The chase crossed over into the next reel, and the sound effects editor who cut his portion of the chase checked with the other sound effects editor to make sure he was using the same windshield wiper sound effect—but he had neglected to ask the interpretation. He cut it "thunk-swish, thunk-swish, thunk-swish." This certainly was not the end of the audio world, but is a little humorous "oops" recounted as a valid example of the detailed techniques and thinking that must be addressed.

Foley Supervisor

Some pictures do not have a Foley supervisor. Each sound effects editor (or sometimes the supervising sound editor) marks up the Foley cue sheets, noting the precise cues to be performed in each reel. The advantage of having a dedicated Foley supervisor, especially on a picture in which thorough and complete coverage is expected, is that the style and design of the layout are consistent from reel to reel.

The best intentions of the supervising sound editor to mark up the Foley sheets and oversee the Foley walking are often side-tracked by other demands, such as future client meetings, having to sit on another stage for the previous project's M&E or airplane version, or unscheduled emergencies.

Some Foley supervisors not only mark up the Foley cues, but also serve as lead Foley artists on the stage. This is an added bonus, as they lay out the cue assignments in the most logical ways, develop a working relationship with their Foley mixers, knowing how the two of them like to work, and help make the flow of work most efficient.

Foley Artists

The term "Foley artist" has become the preferred designation for the Foley walker, who was even earlier was known simply as the "stepper." These people perform the footsteps, cloth movement, and prop work as requested on the Foley cue sheets. Foley artists work on a Foley stage, performing footsteps and props while they watch the action in real time as projected on a screen or television monitor in front of them. (See Chapter 16 for a thorough overview of Foley.)

Foley artists are often hired for their strengths and specialties. If the supervising sound editor is working on an important feature project, he or she may hire a Foley artist known more for the ability to give texture and characterization to the footsteps, rather than just providing common footfalls. The trade-off, however, is usually that the footsteps are not walked precisely in sync. If the footsteps are performed to frame-accurate sync, then texture and character are sacrificed, and vice versa. A good supervisor always opts for texture and character, knowing full well the sync issue can be fixed by good, disciplined Foley editing. The last thing the supervisor wants is common, "clunky" Foley.

I do not endorse the "hang-and-pray" technique. I have heard many producers say they would prefer to have their Foley walked to sync and hung in the mix. They really are saying that they do not want to incur the costs involved in transfer and precision sync editorial. When you get on the mixing stage, all the practical trade-offs are quickly forgotten when they grumble that the sync is rubbery and the performance does not seem to be what it should—a performance always helped out by the Foley editor.

Other Foley artists are known more for creative prop work, and not so much for good footsteps, just as others are not skilled at prop work but specialize in footsteps. Of course, one should have a relationship with a number of Foley artists, with a thorough knowledge of their strengths and weaknesses, so that appropriate Foley artists for a project can be contracted.

STRATEGY BREWS

The director engages the supervising sound editor in sweeping concepts for the soundtrack rolling around in his or her brain for months, now bursting at the seams to manifest itself into dramatic and bold audio events. The producer meets with the supervising sound editor in private and bemoans the fact that the picture is over budget, over schedule, and teeters on the edge of disaster. Of course, they are counting on sound to save it.

Large calendar pages are taped to the wall in monthly progression, with dozens of yellow sticky notes showing the turn-over date of "latched reels," various progress screenings, spotting sessions, ADR and Foley stage bookings, temp dub(s), test audience screenings, commencement of predubs, and when finals start. This is the battle map upon which the supervising sound editor will deploy forces. Start talent too soon, and no money will remain to maintain the crew through to the predubs; hold back too long, and the supervisor risks delivering to the stage late or compressing necessary creative time for properly producing the work.

The biggest danger is from the director and producer themselves. In their zeal to develop a temp soundtrack to commence test screenings, they all too often deplete and exhaust precious time and financial assets. Although one or more temp dubs are scheduled and budgeted, invariably the project is sapped by the little "nickel-and-dime" needs that irreparably detract from the final product. The experience of veteran supervising sound editors pays off here, for they have been in this situation numerous times, dealing with the same old requests that weaken the sound editorial assets inch by inch.

To cut corners and save costs, both client and inexperienced post-production supervisor will hire cheaper labor. Experienced, veteran talent does not work for a union rate card minimum. For good work, you must hire good talent with experience, which costs more than the skills of the aspiring apprentice. Producers and production accountants with "bean-counter" mentalities look at the higher paid, experienced craftsperson as just a more expensive craftsperson. However, those who have been around the block a few times understand how the industry works and realize that the extra cost for the veteran actually saves money because of their ability to do the job better and faster than the apprentice.

This is not to say that apprentices should never be used. On the contrary, as an industry, we have a responsibility to train and build a workforce to fortify the veteran ranks. The best way for new talent to learn their craft is from veteran craftspeople.

THE TURN-OVER

When picture editorial begins to turn over material to sound editorial, it turns over a fairly standard set of materials, which is received by the first assistant sound editor. Nothing should be picked up and used by the supervising sound editor or other department sound editors until the first assistant has logged it in and prepared it for use.

A binder should be kept to record materials received. Not only the day should be recorded, but also the exact time at which it was received. You will be surprised how many times you need to prove what time something was received to avert misunderstandings, untrue warranties by third parties, and even court action. Keep a binder also tracking materials that leave sound editorial. The listing should show what materials were removed from the premises and who ordered the removal of said materials. This person usually is responsible for the materials while they are off-site, but if not, the person who is responsible for the materials also should be listed. The log should also show what date and time said materials left the premises and where the materials were destined. As with the receipt binder, this tracking binder also proves invaluable in keeping the sound editorial firm legally safe.

Dupe Picture and Video Dupes

In the old days we received 35 mm black-and-white "dupes" of the editor's color workprint. By the late 1980s, 35 mm color "dupes" were becoming more affordable. With today's nonlinear technology, almost all post-production sound work is now done on videotape with time codes for sprocket holes.

The supervising sound editor almost always asks for two formats of videotape transfers. Most sound editors are working on 1/2" VHS tape (make a distinction between traditional VHS and Super VHS format), and some sound facilities (where ADR and Foley stage work is done) prefer to use 3/4" tape.

Because picture editorial almost always makes video transfers directly from a nonlinear system (the cost is much lower), you must never allow picture editorial to deliver final hard sync cutting copies that have been transferred directly from a nonlinear system. These are very inaccurate in sync. Think of them as a pool of constantly undulating tide. They lose and gain time, drifting along on the average. Nonlinear systems do not sync to time code, contrary to general perception. They are run by time stamp, a completely different discipline. The only accurate way to make videotape copies from the nonlinear editor's cut is to take the system drives to a video telecine equipped to read these drives and precisely resolve the time stamp to the time code equivalent.

From the outset, establish a very clear understanding with picture editorial that you will accept video transfers made directly from a nonlinear system for spotting and temp effect development only. When hard sync cutting is being done for final work, however, let picture editorial know you will only accept video transfers done by a legitimate telecine facility that will resolve their drives.

Traditional cutting reels are approximately 900 feet long. We refer to them as "thousand footers." When we say Reel 1, Reel 2, Reel 3, we are referring to the traditional configuration. These reels are mixed in their thousand-foot configurations; then the supervising sound editor and assistant sound editor join them to make the 2,000-foot "AB" configurations that are ultimately sent to movie houses around the world for theatrical presentation.

With nonlinear technology, most work is turned over to sound editorial in prebuilt theatrical presentation. These are known as Reel 1AB, Reel 2AB, Reel 3AB, and so on. Traditional thousand-foot Reels 1 and 2 are combined to make a 2,000-foot projection reel known as Reel 1AB. This means that the cut reels combine as follows: Reel 1 and Reel 2 become Reel 1AB; Reel 3 and Reel 4 become Reel 2AB; Reel 5 and Reel 6 become Reel 3AB; Reel 7 and Reel 8 become Reel 4AB; Reel 9 and Reel 10 become Reel 5AB. You can always tell the difference between theatrical film and television post-production craftspeople. Television editors rarely refer to the cut reels as "reels." Instead, they refer to them as "acts."

Never have more than one reel transferred onto a single videotape cassette. Because of the logistics of sound editor specialists who need access to different reels simultaneously and because changes are made to some reels and not others, it is wise to have each reel of the film transferred to its own dedicated videotape. In addition, ask for more than one copy of each tape. The number of copies you request depends on budget and needs, but it always seems that never enough copies are around.

Today, many of your sound editorial houses are using digital picture to cut to, whether digitized in-house from the clients video tape ouput, or using digital output via OMF means. In either case, the disciplined attention to accuracy remains the same.

Production Audio Source

You must take possession of the original production sound tapes, whether they be DATs, 1/4", or audio files generated by the digital Deva or a Nagra V field recorder on the set. Prepare the dialog by utilizing the OMF option (see Chapter 14). Regardless of whether you can successfully use OMF, you still need to access the original audio source at some point.

Make certain that the client has a precise inventory accounting when the material is delivered to you. This information is listed into the receipt binder. Rarely does a film have every roll accounted for when the material is delivered to you. If you sign for the material blind to any shortcomings, you are the responsible party.

If you utilize the OMF option, make special arrangements with picture editorial to develop a precise EDL along with copies of the audio files to build the dialog editor's Pro Tools session. (This process and protocol is discussed in detail in Chapter 14.)

Code Book

As discussed in Chapter 7, the bible of where to find this information is the code book. Picture editorial will supply a photocopy of the code book, which spends most of its time in the dialog editing department. Sometimes an extra copy of the code book is made, so that the first assistant sound editor has a dedicated copy in the assistant's room.

Lined Script

Photocopies of the lined script, including opposing pages of notes, are supplied by picture editorial. The ADR supervisor needs a copy for reviewing and cuing the picture for loop lines. The dialog editor needs one at the workstation, and the first assistant sound editor needs a dedicated copy in the assistant's room.

Cast List

The production office supplies you with a cast list, identifying who is playing which character. This list is vital to the ADR supervisor.

Continuity

Picture editorial supplies a *continuity*, an outline form breakdown of each reel with the scene numbers included, along with a very short description of action. Each member of the sound editorial team receives a copy of the continuity, which makes it much easier to find their way around the picture, knowing the sequences included in each reel.

LFOP Chart

The LFOP (last frame of picture) chart, also known as the LFOA (last frame of action) chart, is supplied by picture editorial to rectify and compare notes with the first assistant sound editor. First assistant sound editors double-check and verify the validity of these charts, and usually make their own for accuracy.

As discussed in Chapter 7, in sound we must count "Picture Start" on the Academy leader as "000" feet and "00" frames, not frame "1." Most LFOP charts start out wrong because picture editorial often ignores the practical disciplines of post-production and insists on counting "Picture Start" as frame "1"; this can cause delays of time and wasted money because of sound editorial's delay in redoing these charts.

Another strange phenomenon is getting picture dupes or video transfers with either no tail pops at all, or tail pops that are not precisely 3 feet, zero frames from the last frame of picture. I am constantly puzzled that some picture editorial teams simply put one wherever they want one, arbitrarily.

In 35 mm film, the head pop is precisely 9 feet, "00" frames from the Academy leader "Picture Start" frame. That is represented by a single frame of "2" on the picture. Precisely 3 feet, "00" frames from the head pop is the first frame of picture. The same is true for the tail pop, only in reverse—precisely 3 feet, "00" frames from the last frame of picture. Experienced picture assistants often punch a hole through this frame with a hole punch so that it visually "blips" when you hear the one frame of "pop" and shows up clearly in the video transfer. Some picture assistants use a black Sharpie to draw a frame line around this tail pop frame and then draw an "X" from corner to corner, or they write "tail pop" in the frame itself.

Those who do not know what to use for audio "pop" for both head and tail pops should take a single frame from a 1,000-cycle tone (1 kHz). All kinds of line-up tone can be cannibalized on the head end of your 35 mm mag stripe dailies. If you are working entirely in the digital nonlinear domain, simply ask a sound editorial service to supply you with a "tone" folder of audio files. Any reputable sound service will be more than happy to supply you with the correct material, or you can access the line-up tones off the audio CD inside the back cover of this book. (I discuss how to digitally access this material from the CD-ROM drive of your computer in Chapter 17.) Also remember that an important difference exists between "video pop" and "film pop." If you are working on television material that has been shot at 30 frames and no "drop frame" is used, you use a "video pop." Editors who work in time code reference rather than feet and frames in their nonlinear software forget this fact. For them, one frame is 1/30th of a second. Therefore, when the sound is mixed together and transferred to film, the sound assistant rolls down the mixed fullcoat master on a synchronizer to find the head pop, only to discover that its duration does not quite reach the next frame line. Hence, it is important when working on a nonlinear editing system to develop your "pop" frame while working in the foot-and-frame mode, and not in time code.

A quick way to check the "pop" audio file in your tone folder is to simply drag it in and spot it precisely to a frame line, making sure that your session is in foot-and-frame mode. Zoom in extremely close so that you can see the end of the "pop" very clearly. If it does not precisely reach the next frame line, then it is not a "film pop."

DEVELOPING THE CUT LIST

The show is turned over for sound editorial work. The supervising sound editor delegates the production dialog editing chores to the dialog supervisor (as described in detail in Chapter 14). The ADR chores are turned over to the ADR supervisor (as described in Chapter 15). The Foley tasks are turned over to the Foley supervisor, or the supervising sound editor may opt to do them (as described in detail in Chapter 16).

Most supervising sound editors develop their own cut lists, rather than leaving the sound effect creative decisions up to the individual sound effects editors. Much of the time, they do this because they have a more thorough knowledge of the sound effects library; occasionally, they may be exercising fanatical control over each and every sound tidbit cut. Mostly, the cut list is meant as a creative guide. It helps the sound effects editor cutting sound for a particular reel or sequence establish continuity with the supervisor's vision for the sound as well as with other sound effects editors who may be cutting the same kind of action in other reels.

In the old days of cutting sound on magnetic film, supervisors assigned entire reels to a sound effects editor. With today's nonlinear technology, we are moving into more horizontal editing. One sound effects editor, known for a mechanical hardware style of sound editing, may be asked to handle the robotic sounds throughout the entire film—and nothing else. Another sound effects editor may be asked to handle just animal vocals throughout the film—and nothing else. Predub these "horizontal" layers separately, then play them back together to make the full soundtrack.

The supervising sound editor uses one or more computers to audition sound effects as he or she writes a cut list on a second computer. Because we are experiencing almost daily changes, we seldom list the foot and frame of the sound cue to which we are referring. We use the continuity, which was supplied by picture editorial, to list the scene number with a one-line description. Below that, we list the various sound event moments that need attention. Under these subheadings, we list the sound effect number and file name. For those sound editorial firms that have their libraries completely computerized, the description data, even if it does not apply to the picture at hand, is also printed.

We depend on the hired sound effects editors to know what we talk about within the context of a scene. If they are puzzled and do not understand, then we depend on them to ask specific questions. Most supervising sound editors allow their sound effects editors to be creative and add material into the mix as well, but first they must cut and fulfill the cut list.

WHICH PREPARATION TECHNIQUE?

No absolute exists as to how to approach the cutting and predub breakdown of any given film. Every project dictates its own spin, demands its own style, and challenges you to overcome the various hurdles of budget shortcomings and unrealistic schedule demands. Two basic kinds of approaches can be adopted: "all in and mix" and "A-B-C."

"All in and Mix" Approach

The "all in and mix" approach is used when the budget is small and the dubbing schedule is short, loosely referred to as the movie-of-the-week schedule, an anachronism for "put it up and just mix it without the frills." This style of preparation is contingent on the film not being a heavy sound effects design show without events such as big car chases, gun battles, flying space ships, or medieval warfare. If the show consists of simple vehicle work, such as door opens and closes, or phones ringing with pick-ups and hang-ups, it can be done as an "all in and mix."

```
Date : 01/08/97              Editor's Cut List         Page 10
                  THE 5TH ELEMENT

MOTOR -- LOWER FRIDGE

        CWK0003-91    AIRCRAFT: Flaps, electric, Cessna 172, buzzy.
        SPT

        CWK0003-92    INDUSTRIAL: Forklift, electric

HUM -- GUN IDLE
        DAX0034-03    CREDIT CARD SCANNER: touch phone beeps followed
                      by electronic information beeps.  RESTRICTED!!

        DAZ0034-14    MOTOR: small CU pool motor, steady constant
                      idle -- no on or off.  Watch perspective.

ELEVATOR DOORS OPEN

        DAT1126-28    LEONOV POD DOOR:  sweetener for R-7.
        MPT

        DAT1473-020   SPACE SHIP DOORS:  "Star Trek" like space
        MPT           doors, hissey hi-end slide w/small click
                      impact.  GREM2 NOTE:  Clamp elevator doors

PANEL SLIDE
        CWK0005-29    TRIPOD LEGS, SMALL: Smooth, metallic sliding
        SPT

        CWK0005-32    TRIPOD: Slide telescoping leg in.
        SPT

        CWK0005-36    TRIPOD: Slide telescoping legs, single stage
        SPT

        CWK0005-42    COPY MACHINE:  Slide table tray
        SPT

        DAT1365-001   PNEUMATICS/SERVOS:  a variety of wheezy
                      metallic slides -- much like hatch closures.
```

Figure 13.6 A single page of the "cut list" from R-2 of *The Fifth Element*.

Cut your most important sound cues in the first few soundtracks, moving out toward the last few reserved for backgrounds. The total number of soundtracks you are able to cut, to mix all at once, is contingent on how many inputs the dubbing console can handle and how many channels can be exported from the machine room. The other factor that must be dealt with is the number of channels required by production dialog, ADR, and Foley—as they must come along at the same time to achieve the concept of "all in and mix."

It will behoove you to make a field trip to the dubbing stage contracted to mix the film, even if you have worked there in the past, as the sound facility may have upgraded the stage since last you mixed there.

A drawback to the "all in and mix" approach is that little margin exists for adding sound effects, especially ones that must be designed and cannot be thrown easily into the mix on a Pro Tools unit hooked into the console. Your delivered tracks must be as polished and final as you can make them.

The advantage to "all in and mix" is that nothing sits by itself, naked to the client during predubbing. Rather than predubbing only the backgrounds and having the client fuss and nit-pick little flaws or choices, all the tracks are running at once, helping each other camouflage the inevitable imperfections each may have on its own.

STARSHIP TROOPERS   editor: **Yewdall**   **R-5**   v.14 -- **Final turnover**

A-FX	B-FX	C-FX	D-FX
Spaceship Engine: DRONE Spaceship Engine: back-out of space dock Spaceship Engine: Rev up and warp drive	Servos & Motors Hydraulics	Bulkhead door Impacts "POD" Rotation Pier Coupler Release Metal Ronks & Movt. -- moving out --	System "whine" Telemetry Beeps "Collision" Alarm Warp Drive Targeting
Laser Rifle "Power-Ups" Laser Rifle "SHOTS" (Blue rifles)	Laser Rifle "SHOTS" (Red rifles) Laser Rifle "MOTOR" (recharges)	Laser METAL impacts Laser "FLIGHTS" Laser "BODY IMPACTS"	Laser "SIZZLES" Laser "ELECTRICAL"

Figure 13.7 Predub group strategy assignments for A-FX, B-FX, C-FX, etc. for R-5 of *Starship Troopers*.

"A-B-C" Approach

Soundtracks that are taken seriously are almost always mixed in the "A-B-C" approach. Essentially, all the basic elements are predubbed by themselves, then polished and refined exactly as intended. This approach also gives much more control over the basic elements when you reach the final mix.

"A-B-C" refers to "A-FX," "B-FX," "C-FX." The supervising sound editor tells the sound effects editor which approach to take for preparation. If the "A-B-C" approach is chosen, then the sound effects editor knows to break out the basic sound effect groups. On complex sound effect shows, the supervising sound editor often does this. He or she makes a chart and lists "A-FX," "B-FX," "C-FX," and so forth.

Beneath each heading, the supervisor lists what kinds of sound groups are desired in each designation. Often the supervisor uses a color-coded felt marker, giving each group a color code and then marking the cut list print outs of each color code by each sound effect listed, to avoid any error.

For example, take the sequence of Reel 7 in John Carpenter's *Christine* where Christine slams into and destroys the gas station. I cut the car engine sound effects on "A-FX." Nothing else was in this predub pass except the car engine. I could cut other sounds in this "A-FX" group only if they occurred before or after the car engine, but never during the car engine material, which had to be completely by itself. In the "B-FX" pass, I cut the tire skids and the wet-road effects. I could cut other sound effects in this pass prior to or after the gas station scene, but never during tire skids or wet road cues. In "C-FX" I cut metal-oriented sounds: suspension movement, collision impacts, bumper tears, gas pump metal impacts and falls, debris for explosions, and so forth. In "D-FX" I cut the various layers of the explosions.

Predub these by themselves, and when you play them back together you have much better control over the individual concepts. If the director asks to favor the skids more, you have not married them to the engines, or vice versa. This technique is simple in principal, but oddly enough falls apart in the heat of battle for beginners. Only after enduring the dubbing stage and gaining the logical and methodical style of a rerecording mixer, does a sound editor truly learn how to break down sound effect sequences to maximum effect.

This is another problem that nonlinear technology has brought to the learning process. In the old days of working on mag film, all of my editors came to the dubbing stage. We would call back to the shop at a certain point in the dubbing process of a reel so that everyone could come watch the playback. The sound editors definitely were on stage for their reels.

With nonlinear technology allowing horizontal editing, as many as eight or ten editors may have worked on a single reel of sound on big action pictures. Having eight or ten sound editors sitting on the stage while part of the reel while their own work is being mixed just is not practical or economical. Therefore, we are losing whole groups of new sound editing talent who have not experienced the intimate techniques, styles, and tricks of interaction with rerecording mixers.

MARKING SYNC ON FILM

To mark sync on film, as we have discussed, you use a Moviola and a synchronizer. After you have cut the sound cue in the desired fashion, mark the closest even foot inside the sound cue.

In Figure 13.8, the footage marked is "723." Using a black Sharpie, box either side of the frame, then write the footage in the frame itself. The ink of the Sharpie does not harm the soundtrack. Behind it, mark an abbreviation for the show—especially when you have more than one show in the shop at a time. In this case "MH" is the abbreviation for *Moscow on the Hudson*, which was in the shop with two other projects. Mark the "A-B-C" pass designation and then the FX channel number. Anyone picking up a piece of film lying on the floor knows exactly where it belongs because of these abbreviations.

The sound assistant rolls fill leader through the synchronizer and marks the frame (723) where the four cues land. The assistant backs out the fill leader strands, to the left of the synchronizer. Each sound cue then is taken off its respective trim bin hooks, one by one. The assistant carefully lays the boxed footage mark over the marks on the fill leader, then carefully guides the front end of the sound cue to the leading edge. At this point, the assistant turns both fill leader and mag film over and splices white 35 mm splicing tape on the backside to bind them. In the course of a single motion picture, it is not unusual to chew up half a million feet of fill leader, nearly a million feet of 35 mm mag stripe, and a hundred thousand feet of 35 mm fullcoat.

Each roll of built sound cues is known as a *unit*. If you have cut sixty tracks of sound for "B-FX," then you have sixty thousand-foot rolls of sound units built and delivered to the stage for predubbing. These racks of film units hold as many sound units as I cut for Reel 9 of *Leviathan*, which had over 450 tracks at the height of the destructive climax. By the time the sea floor laboratory was destroyed by the monster, Mike Le-Mare and I had broken the sound action into "A-through-W" predubs. Imagine the sheer weight of film stock that had

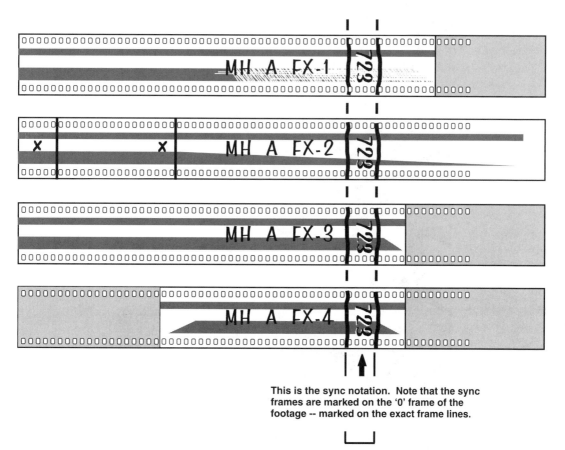

This is the sync notation. Note that the sync
frames are marked on the '0' frame of the
footage -- marked on the exact frame lines.

Figure 13.8 Cut sound cues showing several types of scraping and/or "wiping" techniques used on 35 mm mag stripe. Note the "thatching" technique in the upper track.

to be carried around by the editorial team. I always felt sorry for the assistant sound editor and apprentice when they delivered units to a dubbing stage that had a machine room upstairs, with no elevator or dumbwaiter to raise the tons of film. Hauling around a motion picture keeps you in better physical shape than working nonlinear.

SEPARATION OF SOUND CUES

Now the wisdom of custom recording sound effect cues in single cue actions becomes crystal clear. It is nearly impossible, and only a fluke of luck when it does occur, that you can record a single piece of action that covers everything. First, aside from being impossible, you would not have control over the levels of individual components. That is why you do not want your tire action sounds to be married to the engine. While you are recording, it is fun and thrilling. Now, however, at your workstation, you are cursing yourself for being foolish and allowing the stunt driver to do spin-outs and skidding noises over the precious engine maneuvers. Yes, you want the tire skids and road texture, but you want to control them—putting them where you want, not where your recording dictates.

Figure 13.9 Pictured is a four-gang synchronizer. The cut picture is in the first gang, closest to the front. Sound cues are built into fill leader, with sync footage notations bracketed around the even foot frame.

LEADING EDGES

Study the chart of the four tracks of sound cues from *Moscow on the Hudson* in Figure 13.10. Note that no leading edge of mag track actually touches the leading edge of the splice. Scrape the mag track away from the leading edge, just prior to the actual sound cue itself. This inhibits any "ticks" that may occur from a magnetic signal striking the sound head as the splice passes over it. The most common technique is to scrape across two perforations (half a frame) at a 45-degree angle.

magnetic 35mm "cut-&-scrape" preparation

Figure 13.10 Marking sync on film with a black Sharpie.

Other techniques can also be used, such as a gentle fade-in (as in FX-2). This kind of fade was especially useful in the fade-out configuration, instead of enduring sudden cut-offs of overtones or unwanted ambiance presences.

The "thatched" fade-in technique as depicted in FX-1 is the only kind of track manipulation that nonlinear digital has not mastered yet, contrary to what any digital software writer tells you (they probably do not understand what it is). We frequently used this technique to break up and thin out vocal tracks, such as vocals over a radio that were coming and going in clarity as the operator rotated the frequency dial. We also used it in the fine thatched form depicted in top track (FX-1) of Figure 13.8. This thins out the volume of something that "banged" in too hard. Digital software writers state that this technique could be achieved by using the volume control—but it is not the same.

Whenever I need the thatched track effect for vocal break-up, I transfer the sound to a 35 mm mag track, break out the single-edged razor blade, and go at it. Then I transfer it back to a DAT and transfer that into the computer as a Sound Designer II file for the Pro Tools edit session.

Another technique that demonstrates what degaussed single-edge razor blades are good for is crescent notches. I have tried to duplicate the effect with counter digital cross fades to varying degrees of success, but it is never as precise as what mag stock and a razor blade could do.

These comparisons are not meant to negate nonlinear. On the contrary, as a sound editor who worked nearly twenty years on mag and made a fruitful transition to nonlinear digital, I love it. I write about it to challenge and explain to digital software writers that the

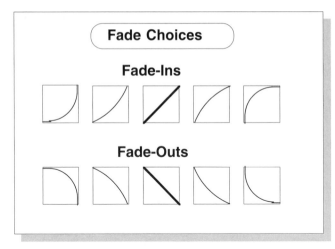

Figure 13.11 The five fade-in and five fade-out choices available in a nonlinear Digidesign Pro Tools session.

editorial tasks to emulate are not completely mastered yet. Thatching would be a fabulous ability to have in digital mode. Crescent notching would be another. To master these techniques, however, you must sit down with the film veterans who used them in order to understand why they are used and why they are still needed. Then you will be able to write the software equivalents.

Fade techniques are obviously not reserved for magnetic film editing alone. The same technique is used in digital nonlinear preparation. The experienced editor knows to add a fade-in or fade-out to a cue, however short or long, as shown in Figure 13.11.

For veteran sound editors who cut on 35 mm mag film, the greatest joy about working with nonlinear digital is not having to scrape fade-ins and fade-outs as in the past, wearing out a 100-count box of single-edged razor blades. Many used the foul-smelling and finger-staining Track Wipe for years, which became known as a carcinogen, thought to have been responsible for more than one death among the sound editor workforce. (Track Wipe was a mixture of 50% acetone and 50% film cleaner. The percentages differed depending on the strength and cutting desire of the editor using it.)

The real advantage of working with nonlinear digital is the ease with which undesirable fade-ins and fade-outs can be erased. In addition, unlike with magnetic film cutting, cross-fading between tracks is possible. This is a great boon to cutting and compositing sounds.

CUTTING BACKGROUNDS

I absolutely love backgrounds. When I started *Escape from New York*, I knew that rich stereo backgrounds were not only nice to have, but vital. The stereo background predub is the stereophonic canvas upon which the entire motion picture soundtrack sits. Music will not play all the time. Hard effects do not play all of the time. Foley, dialog, and ADR are monaural in nature. Group walla can, and ought to be recorded and cut stereophonic whenever appropriate and possible, but crowd scenes do not occur all the time. What does play all the time are the backgrounds, always present—so don't slough them off.

Unfortunately, most pictures do not have stereo backgrounds prepared thoroughly. A common tendency is to hold them down during predubbing, rather than letting their full potential thrive, adding yet another dimension to the film. How does the client know what wonderful textures are available if they are not heard during predubbing? If you choose to hold down the backgrounds during the final mix, fine, but do not squash them during predub. In more than one final mix I have had to stop the dub to have the machine room recall a background unit because a client was requesting something that had been held down and out during predubbing.

Another problematic area is the mastering process of the material itself. Not all sound effects libraries are created equal, as discussed in Chapter 11. Not all sound librarians see to it that the material is carefully cleaned and gleaned before the audio file is mastered to a permanent storage medium such as CD-ROM or DVD. Many effects, even at big sound editing facilities, have scads of sound cues with distortion, glitches, digital zits, drop-outs, and other blemishes. Unfortunately, many forget that sound editing means playing through and editing the material.

Having premastered material that has been carefully cleaned and polished is fabulous, and, as you become familiar with the material, you will gain confidence in each sound cue, remembering where its peculiar peccadilloes are located. However, if you expect the rerecording mixer to use your background material with trust, not only must you listen to it carefully and make sure it is smooth and polished, you also must "dramatically" listen to it against the action on the screen. Although it sounds extremely basic, you would be surprised how often this is not done. Most sound editors think of backgrounds as generic, nonsync audio texturing. I cut backgrounds to help tell the story of the action, often finding little bits of action that I can sync up to something in the background to give it a sense of belonging.

The real magic of backgrounds does not happen when you cut one stereo pair. It happens when you lace up two or more stereo pairs. Two sounds played together are not $1 + 1 = 2$. They become $1 + 1 = 3$ or 4. They become a whole new sound. Listen to the background carefully as it plays against the production dialog track. If it distracts instead of adding, then change it.

Sometimes the most wonderful thing about a background is its magnificent power (e.g., the omnipresence of spaceship engines throughout entire scenes within a battle cruiser), and sometimes it is its delicacy and intimate subtlety (e.g., the quiet and musty basement of an old house prior to dawn). Backgrounds set a mood—like choral inversion airs or tonal presences. Two of the most requested backgrounds I have used in films are "Pipe Test" and "Peckerwood Canyon."

"Pipe Test" was developed from only two frames of a 1" metal deck rustic grind, sampled and processed, then manipulated over a two-and-a-half minute long evolving growth—an unearthly presence that often fit the producer's request for "something we have never heard before."

My wife Lisa and I recorded "Peckerwood Canyon" just south of Yosemite Valley in the Sierra Nevada Mountains. It is the slow movement of air through the pine trees, with no bird calls, no movement, no insects—about every minute and a half is the most wonderful echo of a woodpecker as heard from about a hundred yards away. Producers and directors

Figure 13.12 Note the outgoing audio tracks and incoming audio tracks overlap one full frame during the Fade-in/Fade-out cross-over.

want audio cassette transfers made of this background to play in their cars while they commute. (Listen to sound cue #25 of the audio CD provided with this book for a series of examples on layering stereo backgrounds to create an environmental envelope for the audience. Each background example will add one additional layer to itself every four seconds, giving you the opportunity to study and evaluate the effect of layering.)

To keep the rerecording mixer from taking the backgrounds casually, I often work on rather important sound cues, which can be justified to be in the background pass. By doing this, the mixer must listen to them and address their valuable addition, as they cannot be ignored.

Note the extreme close-up of the backgrounds in the Pro Tools session graph pictured in Figure 13.12. At a scene change or a perspective split, I overlap the material by one full frame. This same technique is used, whether cutting on mag film or cutting nonlinear. This overlap, with a one-frame fade-in on the incoming background tracks and a one-frame fade-out on the outgoing background tracks, lends a smooth transition. By not using this technique, you risk a digital tick at the scene change, or at the very least you will experience a strange "edginess" to the cut, something not quite settled.

When stuck for a stereo background and all you have is a monaural recording, make a "pseudo stereo" background version by following this simple procedure. After importing your monaural background into the Pro Tools session, drag it over into channel #1. Now highlight the background with the "hand," hold down the "Control" and "Option" keys and drag down a duplicate copy of the background into channel #2. Now cut the background right in the center. If the background is 100 feet long, cut it at the 50-foot mark. Now drag the second half of the background forward in front of the first half, allowing them to overlap about 6 to 8 feet. Now blend the two ends with at least a 5-foot cross-fade. Move both sections of the cut background so that the cross-fade is in the middle of the background on channel #1. Now, using the "Cut/Reveal" tool, open both ends of the cut background so that the lengths of the backgrounds of channel #1 and channel #2 are identical. Highlight and play the background. Most monaural backgrounds can be given a startling stereophonic illusion by using this process. The trick is, you must cut out any obvious impacts or sounds that show up a bit later in the other channel, thus giving away what you have done. (Listen to sound cue #26 on the audio CD provided with this book for a series of examples on developing "pseudo stereo" backgrounds from monaural material without using electronic delay techniques. Each example will play the original material monaurally for four seconds, then it will suddenly open up into its "pseudo-stereo" potential.)

LAYERING TECHNIQUES

Figure 13.13 shows a moment in an artillery barrage of a French Foreign Legion fortress in North Africa in the feature film *Legionnaire*. By now it is probably apparent that layering sounds is how sound editors develop these rich and vibrant audio events that are so enjoyed.

Figure 13.13 Pro Tools session—Cannon barrage predub from *Legionnaire*

(Listen to sound cue #27 on the audio CD provided to hear the component cues and final combustion.)

The layering technique made the artillery field piece feel truly dangerous. From studying the C-FX session shown in Figure 13.13, you can see that I made the field piece by layering four stereo pairs of effects. These effects are only for the actual firing of the cannon, not for shell impact or any collateral debris effect.

The first effect is a rich black-powderish low-end whomp explosion called "Nitroglycerine Blast." The second layer gives the cannon a dangerous "bite," achieved by using a Civil War cannon shot, which surprisingly does not have much low-end fullness, but does have a wonderful cutting edge that will cut through almost anything. I made several vari-speed versions of this effect, adding a speed recognition addendum to the audio file name—(0.0) meaning normal speed, (2.0) meaning half-speed, (4.0) meaning quarter-speed, and so on. The third layer is the shell flight of an M-4 Sherman tank's 75 mm cannon firing downrange. This gives the overall sound a historic "period" feel. I cut off the actual shot of the 75 mm cannon, using a quick fade-in of the projectile "whirring" away toward the target.

Although the final designed cannon shot sounds as if it had been recorded today with modern digital technology, it also sounds exactly correct for the period of the picture, which is 1925. I had exactly the concussionary "shot" I wanted with "Nitroglycerine Blast" and the Civil War (0.0) recoil. I wanted the effective shell whir as the 75 mm projectile flew downrange. Adding the discharge shot of the Sherman tank to both Nitroglycerine Blast and Civil War (0.0) recoil would only muddy the combination of sounds and detract from the fullness already achieved. The fourth layer is a short high-end shell flight of an incoming mortar shell. This shrill high-end sweetener works much like the Civil War cannon "bite," giving danger and menace to the flying shell projectile.

Refer to the three cannon shots shown in Figure 13.13 The second one shows the shell flight happening a little later than the first or third. This goes back to picture editorial issues discussed in Chapter 7. The picture editor did not make a thorough study of the material. Physics tells us that if the target is in the same place, and the cannons have not moved from their primary location, then the shell should take the same number of frames to travel from cannon discharge to shell impact. The biggest challenge I had in the cannon fire was to make each shell flight sound natural and believable; some flew for a long time, and others were instantly at target.

WHIP PAN TECHNIQUES

The example shown in Figure 13.14 is a moment in the B-FX predub of *Starship Troopers* when infantry trainees are working out with "tag" laser rifles. This session is eighteen channels wide. It contains three groups of three stereo pairs of sounds. (Listen to sound cue #28 on the audio CD to hear this cue.)

Three stereo pairs work together to create the laser fire from one rifle. I did something here that I very rarely do and almost never recommend. If you look closely (you may need a magnifying glass), you will note that the fade-in and fade-out configurations on each stereo pair do not match! The reason for this is actually quite simple: no mixer on earth could have panned these laser shots quickly or accurately enough from left-to-right and right-to-left—so I decided to prepare the material with prepanned laser fire by virtue of radical inverted

Figure 13.14 Pro Tools session of laser tag fire fight elements from R-5 of *Starship Troopers*. Note the carefully sculpted fade-outs for fast left-to-right and right-to-left flight-bys.

fade combinations. This must be undertaken very carefully; if prepared improperly, the mixer mostly likely will not be able to unwind it, requiring rework.

I started using this technique of prebuilding pans into the material by using fade-ins and fade-outs for the Wesley Snipes picture *Boiling Point*. The rerecording mixing schedule was woefully inadequate, especially considering that the sound effects mixer would have to devote several days to pan-potting all the car-bys needed for street traffic. By using this technique, though, the sound effects mixer needed to make only minor adjustments in balance and volume, leaving him free to pay closer attention to far more important sound effects. The fade panned car-bys simply performed as designed, crossing left-to-right or right-to-left as planned.

This places much responsibility on the sound editor and especially on the supervising sound editor should these prebuilds not perform as anticipated. What sounds like a piece of heaven at your workstation in the cutting rooms can easily degenerate into an ugly finger-pointing disaster when a producer watches the stage clock ticking off hundred-dollar bills because your "designed" pan-bys are not working correctly. However, situations such as the two described above frankly point to this technique as a time and money saver. The best way to rally support from your mixing colleagues for using this method is to consult with them first, well in advance of predubbing. No rerecording mixer will be your ally and support you if it blows up in your face because it does not perform as you expected if you had not consulted him or her ahead of time. Mixers most likely will bounce the reel to save their own skin, sending you back to the editing room with egg on your face as you recut it.

USING AN OFF-THE-SHELF AUDIO CD SOUND LIBRARY

An advantage to buying ready-made sound effects from commercial CD sound libraries is the ability to amass thousands of sound effects in your audio arsenal very quickly. By the mid 1990s, audio CDs were finally starting to offer theatrical-style sound effects, which gained a wider acceptance among those accustomed to custom recording their own material.

Not all sound CD offerings are created equally. Many have that flat documentary-type sound, of little value to theatrical sound editors. Others are developed through synthesized means, which also offer little. Some sound libraries offer a few good sound effects on a CD, with the rest of the material pure junk. Before spending money, try to listen to the product first.

One sound publication firm that has truly excelled in serving the feature film market is Sound Ideas, based in Toronto. Starting with their 6000 General series, Sound Ideas began to develop a rich theatrical feel for its product. Their subsequent library series have been as good, if not better.

Regardless of what audio CD series you use, the most disappointing flaw is the lack of sufficient variations. For instance, when cutting an action car sequence, you require numerous variations in the car-bys or maneuvers so you are not using the same cue over and over. When it comes to complete vehicle series, whether aircraft, boats, cars, trucks, motorcycles, what have you, you will be extremely hard pressed to find any audio CD that gives you all the nuts and bolts you require. Here comes that same speed of car-by with that same road texture and that same little bump in the pavement "thump" at the same place. When you think through your road texture and performance variations, you are looking at twenty-five to forty variations—not the three or four usually offered on CD libraries.

Having good sound effect CDs in your library for secondary and miscellaneous sounds is absolutely necessary, but for key action vehicles, consider custom recording. Review Chapter 10 for further details on custom recording a complete vehicle series.

TECHNIQUES IN CUTTING VEHICLES

Almost everybody thinks cutting cars is easy, until they get in and try cutting anything but the standard in-and-stops and start-and-aways—let alone complex maneuvers and car chases. Before getting into and understanding complicated cutting, let me start by saying that the usual first mistake of a learning-to-cut sound editor involves how a car starts and stops. In many a film sequence, the sound editor does not take the time to observe the physics and mechanics of how a car actually works. The sound editor cuts the sound of the engine so that the RPM rises as the car visually moves forward, and I have watched many a scene where the engine sounds completely out of touch with the car coming to a stop. Observe the real thing before you try to duplicate it on film. Note that a car engine starts to accelerate before you see the vehicle move. Obviously, you must play with it. If you allow the acceleration to begin too soon, it sounds odd—if you accelerate with the visual,

Figure 13.15 Pro Tools session for a car predub from R-6 of *Jackie Brown*, including into car movt, door, keys, Cadillac start, back-up, and away with tire grit and swerves.

it feels equally odd. Move the acceleration against the picture and play it against action until it feels connected.

Other things almost magically fall into place. Little bits of noises and nuances you heard before but did not make any sense of suddenly fall where they should, such as the engagement of a transmission, little clunks that, when massaged for sync, bring the action to life. (Listen to sound cue #29 on the audio CD to hear the car sequence cue and its components.) For demonstration purposes, I have not cut this in an A-FX, B-FX, C-FX style, but in an "all in and mix" style, so that you can hear all the separate elements as well as how they work together.

The sequence cut in Figure 13.15 (sound cue #29) is for Robert Forster getting into a late model Cadillac, starting it up, and driving away (from R-6 of *Jackie Brown*). Listening to the single combine, you may think it unremarkable, until you realize that the movements in the sequence are a careful weave of single audio events. Stop thinking of finding one sound cue that does it all, and start thinking of the component parts from the palette of sounds at your disposal, so that you may paint your own reality.

I audition my file of various keys into door locks, looking for the more solid metal sedan key, not the CJ-5, which has a more hollow metal lock over-ring, and not the Honda, which sounds too small. I lengthen the unlocking movement as the man on film fiddles with the door longer than my sound effect lingers, and I shorten the part of the key extraction to speed up the urgency the actor displays.

I always cut two stereo pairs of car door opens and closes. Move in tight and match the latch movements on both effects exactly, or they do not sound as one door. No two are ever identical, nor should they be. If you do not match the latch movements, the two door effects only sound like one door cut on top of another, with no relationship to each other. Once you match the latch movements, the two doors sound as one door—one plus one equals a new one! You can create an unlimited variety of doors and textures by mixing and matching doors. Experience and technique helps develop your own favorite combinations.

Car warning alerts, such as door open "dinging" or seat belt "jingles," are optional. I usually do not cut them in unless the client specifically asks for them, and when I custom record vehicles I always try to defeat the warning alerts on the car prior to recording. On the screen, they are often distracting.

I cut an "into-car" movement track. When I custom recorded the cars for *Christine*, I captured what has become one of the most used into-car seat movements in the business— better than Foley and with an interesting character of seat springs and cushion movement. Just sync up the seat spring point where the actor's weight has bottomed out (excuse the pun), then shorten or extend the ins and outs.

I usually cut two different key movements into the key ignition, depending on key ring and desirability of jingle. It is important to pay attention to the make of the car series you are using to cut. Many discerning ears, whether of the rerecording mixer, the producer, or the general viewer, are quick to point out when the cut sound effects are of a Dodge instead of the Ford depicted on-screen. The two vehicles sound different, so pay attention. That is not to say you do not use creative license, but certain signature elements, such as the throat of the engine that can take a viewer out of the story, are so wrong that they are distracting.

I have the entire car series residing in a file folder on an external drive, where I can access it. I cut an engine start-up, and probably have to shorten the duration of the engine settling down into an idle. I cross to another track for the acceleration of the engine as the car backs up. I sweeten a little brake squeal on another track if it fits the character of the car. I cut in a little transmission clunk movement as the driver changes from reverse to drive. In this particular case, the driver is anxious and pulls out quickly, turning hard left, then accelerates down the street. On a separate track I cut in a little tire sweetener to sell the tire turn as it grinds down on the pavement with the strong acceleration away.

SPLITTING OFF TRACKS

Pay attention to preparing the sounds so that it is as easy as possible for the rerecording mixer to work with your material. This is especially true for fast action sequences, where perspective shifts change quickly. Sure, a rerecording mixer can make the perspective shifts on the console; sometimes it is necessary, for technical reasons, such as harmonic sounds that must not be split. However, most sounds can be split for perspective. If you do not prepare the material so that all the mixer does is set perspective volume levels and/or equalization shifts on one set of channels over another, you quickly will find your mixing counterpart becoming more perturbed with you, eventually bouncing reels back to the cutting room for more thorough preparation.

Say I am using five channels of sounds playing together to make the flying reality of an Apache helicopter. I cut the cues into FX-1, 2, 3, 4, and 5. Those five channels will be my "close-up" group. The action is working fine, and then I come to a cut where we favor the enemy tank as it barrels along on the ground with the Apache maneuvering in the background. I split off the material from FX-1, 2, 3, 4, and 5 and move the cues over to FX-6, 7, 8, 9, and 10 as a background group. As with the one-frame overlap technique shown in the cutting of backgrounds, I extend the leading edges of this perspective split, fade-out the out-going channels, and fade-in the incoming channels.

The action holds on the enemy tank for a few moments, then cuts back to the close angle of the helicopter. Again, I split the five channels of sound back to FX-1, 2, 3, 4, and 5. This process goes on throughout the entire sequence of action. Analyze each shot, deciding where the perspective splits should be placed. Often I need an additional five channels for more complex coverage, as I may need a medium-angle group. In that case, I reserve fifteen channels in a row to handle the perspective preparations for five channels of sound, split into three basic angle perspectives.

The next time you watch a car chase, such as the chase through Paris in John Franken-heimer's *Ronin*, note how many layers of material must have gone into the preparation for the two key vehicles. Engines, gear-box whines, tires on cobblestone and asphalt, suspen-sion, skids—all need perspective splits made to control the two cars as they race through city streets.

The best way to understand the concept of when to split, how to split, and where to place the split-off material is to put yourself in the shoes of the rerecording mixer. If you had to mix this insane tidal wave of sound coming at you in real time, when would you want the material split-off, how would you like it split, and where would you want the material? Study the action—the film tells you where it wants to be split.

The danger is that you can over-split the material, called the "ping-pong" effect. As you develop experience, you will learn when you are running the danger of over-splitting. The best advice I can give you is this: first, if your mixer is hindered, you are not splitting it well. Remember, part of your job is to make that task as easy as possible so that time is not wasted in track management, but is spent creatively mixing the material to a higher level of enter-tainment. Second, if the audience is distracted from the story, you have failed. Anything that draws attention away from the stream of storytelling toward the fact that you are making a movie is wrong.

BUILDING IN VOLUME GRAPHING AND EQUALIZATION

With nonlinear workstations, it is easy to build in volume graphing, equalization, and other signal-processing additives. Today's editors exchange and talk about their "plug-ins" like kids trading baseball cards on the playground. Play all you want—be as creative as you want—pump your signal-processing gear until you are blue in the face. Just remember this: When you have had your fun and think you're only decibels from an Academy Award nom-ination, walk onto the dubbing stage, turn your cue sheets over to the rerecording mixer, and face the responsibility for what you have done.

Very few sound craftspeople working today can signal process successfully prior to the dub stage. Many do it—many think their work goes to the stage and is mixed just fine. Many do not know their work is dumped and others are brought in to recut and reprepare the material because their processed work is unmixable. With every signal-processing adjust-ment made, you are inching out on the limb a little further. After a while, the breeze starts to kick up a bit; the branch becomes a bit more unstable. Decide how far out on that limb you are willing to go. Your next job may depend on the reputation of how much time and trouble you caused by having to have material reprepared or remixed because you went too far.

Volume graphing is not nearly so crucial an issue—in fact, many mixers do not mind a little volume graphing to help them understand the intent of the sound editor and facilitate the mix. It is not a good idea, however, to be finite about your levels, especially when you attempt to lower them too far.

CUING THE PICTURE

The vast majority of post-production sound editorial work today is done in the nonlinear realm with videotape transfers of either the cut workprint or the Avid or Final Cut Pro edit sessions. However, many would prefer to mix, or at the very least, check our predubs or final mix in a playback mode against the final 35 mm picture. Most picture editorial teams strive to either conform the 35 mm workprint against the locked EDL or have the silent first trial print on the dubbing stage for the rerecording mixers to use during the mixing process.

When the 35 mm workprint or first trial (often called the "black track" because there is a black mask where the optical soundtrack eventually goes when the final mix is complete) is made available, the first sound assistant cues the picture. The sound assistant calls the dubbing stage and asks the head mixer what kind of picture cues are wanted and how.

"Ten-Ten" Cues

Some mixers prefer what are called "ten-tens." The sound assistant has a template, usually a strip of tape on the bench between the two rewinds. A line has been drawn on the left end of the tape. Ten frames of 35 mm film from that line cross from left to right. There is a bold cross drawn on the 11th, 12th, and 13th frames. The frame count continues to the right. Three more bold crosses are drawn on the 24th, 25th, and 26th frames. As the sound assistant winds the picture slowly from the left rewind to the take-up rewind on the right, he or she watches for the changes in shots. By this time, the assistant has the film virtually memorized. Where perspective and/or scene change cues need to be made, the assistant brings the film down to the tape template, placing the frame line at the line on the left side of the template. He or she takes a grease pencil (some mixers even dictate what color grease pencil—so ask) and boldly marks the two sets of three crosses where the template crosses are set.

As the film runs through the projector at 90 feet a minute, these crosses appear as a mere "one," "two" beat prior to the perspective split or scene change. Where the third set of crosses would have occurred is where the change takes place.

"Wipe" Cues

Other mixers prefer the "wipe" cue, which is often not quite as precise in nature. The wipe cue is accomplished by drawing a diagonal straight-edged line with a grease pencil from left to right across the film—usually one foot prior to the perspective split or scene change. At the frame line of the wipe, the assistant uses the grease pencil to draw a thick line across the film, emphasizing the frame line itself. As the film runs through the projector, the wipe suddenly travels across the screen, ending in a "blip"-type frame line.

Presentation

A most vital concept to keep in mind is presentation. Dozens of sound effects must work together to make a reality. Very often, however, either confidence or doubt is set with the very first effect played by the effects mixer as the track is auditioned in a "solo" mode to determine what is truly there.

If you do not lead off with your strongest cue, you are inviting doubt, from the effects mixer back to producer and director. Make a good first impression. You do not want to give a perception of weak material, so why put your sweetener or support material in the first tracks the mixer auditions? Nobody cares if your support effects are not as strong, just as long as they are not your foundation sound pieces.

Cue Sheets: Hand-Made or Computer-Generated?

Cue sheets are not only the blueprint of the soundtrack you have spent weeks and months preparing. They are also the first key to the philosophy of presentation. I have seen many fine sound editors who could cut up a storm, who knew how to make magic of sound, but who also neglected the presentation of their cue sheets. Their cue sheets were sloppy, often with words misspelled. Before the first sound cues hit the screen, the producer and director had glanced at them and cringed, wondering what kind of soundtrack they were getting. Even if the work itself was superb, already the atmosphere of doubt was set.

Some editors still prefer to hand-make cue sheets, citing the personal touch and their last authorship of the design. It gives them the opportunity to make side notes and draw flow lines or add color-coded underlines. Most, however, use a computer program that extrapolates an exact map of what was cut. The smart sound editor takes the time to ripple through the computerized columns to erase unnecessary number information, or to rename files from the sound master file according to the action on-screen.

The information header should have specific information naming the show, who cut it, what kind of session it is, and what version date the cut represents.

Think about the comfort and the visual flow of the cue sheet so that the mixer is not wasting effort and time trying to figure out the cue sheet, taking away time from turning the dials and equalizing the material.

Show Title: I have seen rerecording mixers trying to figure out a reel with cue sheets that belonged to the same reel of an entirely different project. (No wonder nothing was in sync!!)

Editor: The editor's name should always be on the cue sheet. Not only is this an indictment of the guilty party to throw rocks at if everything blows up, but more important,

show: **"Starship Troopers"**	editor: **David Yewdall**	reel #: **5**	group: **"D"-FX**	version: **v.18**

Figure 13.16 The top of your cue sheet should have clear, neat and pertinent information so the rerecording mixer knows the name of the show, what reel it is, who cut it, the predub group, and the version.

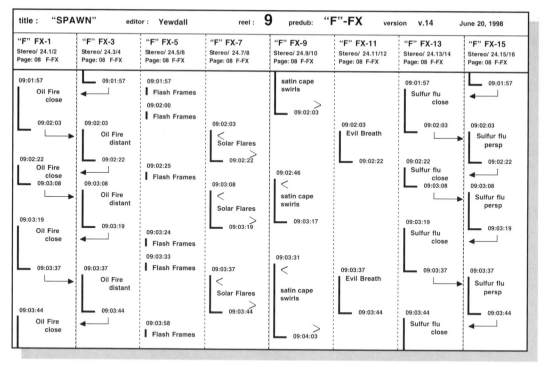

Figure 13.17 A typical computer generated "dubbing" cue sheet. Note the regimented line-up of time counts and the "cleaned-up" audio file names for ease of use on the rerecording stage.

it tells anybody working on the mixing console who should know the content of the reel most intimately, should questions arise that need swift and accurate answers.

Reel #: The rerecording mixer should be able to see in large, clear print what reel he or she is working with.

Predub Group: The cue sheet needs to clearly show what predub group the cue sheets represent. Remember, the cue sheets are a blueprint—a road map to most efficiently guide the rerecording mixer through the contents to be dealt with.

Version : Do not forget the version number. If the sound effects are not working in sync, the first thing the rerecording mixer is going to do is check the version number on the cue sheets and the version number on the picture (or videotape). If they do not match—well, get it off the stage until sound and/or picture editorial can bring the most current versions that have both a matching picture and cut audio elements. Some crews use the date rather than a version number. Both techniques work fine, but it is not a good idea to interchange these techniques.

Study the cue sheet pictured in Figure 13.17. This is a computer-generated cue sheet that has been "cleaned-up" for the dubbing stage. What that means is that any computer cue sheet program is going to display the data of the audio cut with all of the precise computeresque exactitudes. By that, I mean that the actual cue "Oil Fire" is actually listed in my library as "097/42 Oil Fire w/low+6." When the computer software displays it in the "cut region" the data may shot up as 097/42 Oil Fire w/low+6-18.R.

The computer is showing you the entire name—then the 18th cut in that session—then the right channel is displayed to you. I really do not want all that in each data window—it is just too much data clutter. So I eliminate everything except what I want the mixer to see—and in this case I will add a perspective description—"close" or "distant." I will then highlight this new name and copy the text "Oil Fire close," then scroll down and paste it into each "cut-region" in which the entire name shows up, thereby giving me a name "Oil Fire close." I will repeat this technique in each displayed channel and change any "cut-region" field data that I wish to simplify.

If you look up at the channel data window, you will see that you can combine left and right channels into a single track. The reason that ".R" will show up at the end of the clip name is because I have combined all the stereo channels into one track, so the computer shows only the one track name that represents both the left and right sides. The data window tells you this by showing you this information expressed as "Stereo/24.1/2."

This means that this single represented channel of sound is actually two channels of sound, because it takes a left and a right channel. The "24" means that the medium has been transferred onto a 24-track tape to go to the dubbing stage. The "1/2" means that the stereo left and right channels have been transferred to channels "one" and "two" of the 24-track tape. As you can see, this will save a lot of cue sheet paper by condensing stereo cues, and save on the wear and tear of dubbing mixers' eyes. An additional help to the mixer is not to read the entire audio cue as "097/42 Oil Fire w/low+6-18.R"; therefore, I will go into the computer program and "clean-up" the cues, removing unnecessary data that will mean nothing to the rerecording mixer.

In addition, computer programs do not make "split-arrows" suach as you see in "FX-1," "FX-3," "FX-13" and "FX-15." I make an arrow template and put these in manually—because when an audio track is split for perspective and/or volume shift issues, a rerecording mixer is really thankful to see where the event is going.

You might want to check out computer cue sheet programs before you buy them. I stay away from one program in particular because it makes you change the names of your audio files so that it will read them a certain way in the cue sheet. This is like the tail wagging the body of the dog—it is engineered backwards. Other computer cue sheet programs are designed to be much more friendly to editors—who are usually having to make their cue sheets in the middle of the night or minutes before the actual mix commences and do not have time to put up with a lot of backward computer program engineering.

The sideways "V's" in "FX-7 and "FX-9" tell the mixer that the effect has built-in fade-ins or fade-outs. These symbols are built into the computer program and will show up automatically. If you are a precise editor who builds in one-frame fade-ins and fade-outs to guard against digital ticks, the computer will not show this any differently from a thirty foot fade-in or fade-out. So here again, I remove any fade-in or fade-out symbols that do not truly represent an important fade that the mixer may be interested in knowing about.

PACKED AND READY TO GO

The sound assistant has gone over the flow chart of the material advertised from the various departments. He or she has seen to it that the editors have cut to the proper versions. The assistant has seen to it that the sessions have been backed up and protected. Finally, he or she has seen to it that the cue sheets have been properly made and that the various editors are speaking with one style and voice, as far as presentation is concerned.

Since 1978, I have taken an organizational chart template to an economy copy center and have special 10 × 13-inch white envelopes printed up. Each envelope holds a reel of dialog cue sheets (including ADR and group walla), Foley cue sheets, hard effects cue sheets, or stereo background cue sheets. As each group of cue sheets is completed, the sound assistant check marks the appropriate box on the front of the envelope, along with the show title, editor's name, type of cue sheet groups, completion of predubbing on the material, and so on. On the bottom is a large box in which the supervising sound editor can write notes while on the dubbing stage with the mixers. He or she can pencil in update notes to be made before the final mix.

This is not only a good way to keep the flood of paper work straight and easily accessible, but it is also good presentation to your client. They see how you work with clean and neat envelopes with precise notes that are easy to find. It instills confidence in you and your ability to handle the complex job of developing their soundtrack, and they are more willing to listen to your advice when the chips are down because they have seen your neatness and orderly procedure.

Chapter 14
Dialog Editors:
Hollywood's Unsung Heroes

How many times have you sat in the theatre, enjoying the movie and sighed with admiration for the dialog editor's skill and handiwork? "Wow, that was great cross-filled presence. It's so transparent, you can't even tell the difference between those two angles."

Of course you haven't. If you did notice what kind of job the dialog editor did, it would be because he or she did a poor one. Dialog editing is an invisible art form. If the work is good, the audience never notices it. An expert dialog editor takes a dialog track that is a patchwork of hundreds of cuts and pieces of presence and prepares it so that the bits of production audio fit together seamlessly. Only editorial colleagues know the work's excellence, and only they know the contribution of dialog editing to a motion picture.

How big of a contribution is it really? Sound effect design may be used or discarded, backgrounds may be used or discarded, music cues may be used or discarded—but the dialog track always plays—always! The dialog track is the most important audio element in the film, yet, as discussed in Chapter 5, it is one of the more neglected aspects of the production shoot.

QUALITY CONTROL BEFORE POST-PRODUCTION

On a Jesse James picture in which I was involved, the production team had been working on a flatbed KEM and had never listened to the raw production track in a quality-controlled environment. To make a precise assessment of the ADR requirements, I insisted on running the picture with the contracted rerecording mixer, Bob Glass, Jr., on his stage. We barely got into the second reel when I called over to the editing room and told the producer we would wait until they came over to hear it for themselves. Unbeknownst to them during the production shoot, the production mixer had been experiencing condensation popping on the microphone diaphragm. The cold morning air warmed up, and, as the sun rose toward noon, condensation was affecting the track with periodic popping noises. The producer and director listened in disbelief. Surely it must be something in the sound transfer. Could it have been introduced on the KEM? It couldn't have been that way on the set!

My first assistant pulled 1/4" tapes arbitrarily from the boxes that had arrived from the lab. We laced them up one at a time and spun down and stopped randomly to listen. The popping noises were in the original 1/4" recordings. Vast sections of scenes filmed outdoors were affected. Glass and I advised the producer and director that as much as 80 percent of the picture had to be looped to fix the problem. Panic seized the studio executives. Nobody had budgeted for the tens of thousands of dollars in ADR costs that would be required to fix a problem that should have been discovered, flagged, and problem-solved during the production shoot.

As it turned out, we saved the studio vast sums of money by spending just a few thousand dollars in a cleverly prepared series of dialog tracks that were then carefully "scrubbed" and processed with an audio software known as Sonic Solutions.

The key was not processing raw dailies. Dwayne Avery, the dialog editor, prepared the flawed dialog tracks in edited form, then downloaded the separate "cut" dialog tracks into the Sonic Solutions system to be fixed. This process is known as "declicking." While we were at it, we had the Sonic Solutions subcontractor do selective surgical processing on several problematic dialog angles that would have been virtually impossible for our rerecording mixer, Bob Glass, Jr., to accomplish with a traditional analog mixing console.

DIALOG EDITING STRATEGY

The supervising sound editor hires a key dialog editor, often referred to as the dialog supervisor. Depending on the size of the project, the length of the schedule, and other monetary factors, the dialog supervisor may decide that one or more other dialog editors are needed to assist in the work to be done.

During the course of sound editorial work, the supervising sound editor may go over the work expectations from the client, including one or more temp dubs, as well as the calendar time frame within which the work must be accomplished. The two also discuss what degree of polish and how much preparation are needed for the temp dub. The lead dialog editor should always be part of the "spotting session(s)" described in Chapter 9. She or he is there during those critical discussions with the director, picture editor, and producer that evolve into a finite battle plan to accomplish any temp-dub wishes and to define the final expectations for a polished dialog track.

In turn, these discussions also focus the budget demands accordingly. If the director and producer expect a more polished dialog edit for the temp dub, more dialog editors are hired to get the work done quicker so as to better serve the temp-dub needs. Conversely, if the director and producer are using their "editor's cut track" (also known as the "editor's work track") as the dialog portion of the temp dub, with perhaps a few fixes for clarification or correction of a particularly bad passage of production sound, then that requires a much lighter dialog team on the temp dub and allows the dialog editor to properly cut the dialog over the sound-edit schedule.

footage	Edge Code #	Scene/Angle & Take #	Sound Roll	Notes:	# of Reprints
9		"POP"			
12	023-1033	36 - 3	21	master	x 1
27	024-1216	36 "C"- 2	22	close of Woods	x 1
42	023-1896	36 "B"-2	21	close of Savage	x 2
56	024-1475	36 "C"- 4	22	close of Woods	x 1
59	023-1660	36 "A"- 2	21	medium two shot	x 2
78	023-1033	36 - 2	21	master	x 1

title: "SALVADOR" Editor: Steve Rice Reel: 4 page: 1-of-14

Figure 14.1 Dialog sequence sheet.

DIALOG SEQUENCE SHEETS OR EDL

When the turnover materials discussed in Chapter 13 arrive at the first sound assistant's bench, he or she immediately starts preparing material for the dialog editor. Before any cut editor's tracks are handled by anyone in sound editorial, they are first sent to sound transfer, where 1:1 copies (exact duplicates) are made, not only for protection, but because other departments (ADR, Foley, sound effects) need a copy—not the original—of the editor's cut track. The dialog editor must have the original.

If the dialog edit is to be done on film, then the turnover includes 35 mm picture dupes and the original cut editor track. If the dialog edit is to be done on a nonlinear platform such as Pro Tools, then the assistant will be responsible for providing a 1:1 copy of the cut production track (found on the left channel of the video output).

The need and technique of using a guide track in editing is the same whether cutting on film or digitally with a nonlinear system. After preparing at least one picture dupe, the sound assistant gives a picture dupe and its corresponding cut editor track to the sound apprentice to make a "dialog sequence sheet" (Figure 14.1).

The sound apprentice laces up the picture dupe and the editor's cut track into a synchronizer, placing the start marks on the "0" and zeroing out the footage counter. She or he lowers the sound head of the synchronizer onto the mag track and plugs headsets into the workbench mixer, then rolls through the track, carefully watching for splices in the soundtrack. When one arises, the apprentice pays close attention to the edge code numbers, described in Chapter 6. In my shop, our technique was not to list every splice cut, as some do. Instead we listed the cuts only when the edge code number changed, since this represented a change in the sound roll. If splices occurred within a sequence where the edge code numbers did not change in sequential order, or changed very little, we knew that the picture editor had simply tried a cut, did not like it, and put it back together, or had made an internal cut, which we knew our own dialog editor would be able to sequentially match. We did not want to clog the dialog sequence sheet with hundreds of repetitious notations that we knew full well the dialog editor does not need. The dialog editor needs to know which rolls of reprints are necessary to commence cutting chores.

The apprentice enters the first even-foot number that lands within the dialog cue to be listed, then lists the first edge code number that appears on the edge of the film. He or she keeps rolling down, entering new edge code numbers as the scene/take/angle changes. After finishing that task, the apprentice looks up each edge code number listed in the code book and writes the scene, angle, and take next to the edge code number entry. In the "Sound Roll" column the original source tape number is entered. The apprentice makes a photocopy of the sheets completed, three-hole punches them, and places them in the supervisor's "bible." Once this is done, the first sound assistant turns over a picture dupe, the editor's cut track, and the dialog sequence sheets to the dialog editor.

The dialog editor laces up the picture dupe and editor's cut track in the Moviola and runs the reel, pausing every so often to enter any notations in the "Notes" column. After the dialog editor has run through the entire reel, he or she decides how many dialog reprints are required from the original 1/4", or DAT, source. The dialog editor photocopies the completed dialog sequence sheets and gives a copy to the first assistant, who will put together a transfer order so that sound transfer can complete the reprint work as quickly as possible.

If the film and subsequent sound editorial work is being done electronically, the first assistant receives an EDL (edit decision list) (Figure 14.2). The EDL is cleaned up and easy to read. It takes hours to do this, as the picture department originally sends over a tidal wave

Project: FOOLS GOLD				Pull List for REEL 2AB (Picture 2) -- page 2 of 48			
Bin: REEL 2AB				Tue. July 14, 1998 5:25 PM			
Sequence: REEL 2AB							

REEL 2AB: Pull List — 284 entries, handles = 0, 1 dupe, 30 opticals

	Footage	Duration	First/Last Key	Lab Roll	Cam Roll	Sc/Tk	Clip Name
21.	156+15 163+04	6+06	KC 11 8267-5060+08 5066+13	062	123	14/2	14/2.omf
22.	163+05 172+11	9+06	KC 27 8267-5060+08 5069+14	063	124	17C/1	17C/1.omf
23.	172+12 174+01	1+05	KC 45 5140-3218+12 3220+01	054	103	21H/3	21H/3.omf
24.	174+02 189+07	15+05	KC 45 5140-3377+06 3393+11	054	103	21H/4	21H/4.omf
25.	189+08 212+02	22+10	KC 45 5140-3752+01 3772+11	054	103	21J/6	21J/6.omf
26.	212+03 219+14	7+11	KC 45 5140-4137+14 4145+09	054	103	21K/2	21K/2.omf
27.	219+15 226+05	6+06	KI 01 8078-1790+02 1796+08	056	105	21M/1	21M/1.omf

Figure 14.2 Edit Decision List (EDL) EDL list.

of numerical data. For some reason, most picture departments become confused about what data should be requested when they generate an EDL.

Most of the time, sound editorial receives an EDL perfect for negative assembly, but that does not do sound editorial much good unless you request the scene/take as well as the sound-roll entry. The lab roll is the sound roll. Most of the time the picture EDL is sent to us, which is significantly different from the sound EDL. All picture editors will overlap sound-tracks, steal alternate readings, put in a bit of off-screen dialog that was not there before. A picture EDL will not reflect these cuts, but picture assistants forget to think about that when they choose the EDL menu options. Picture editorial must call sound editorial prior to making the EDLs to double-check the necessary items.

The EDL handles much the same chores as the dialog sequence sheet. It shows at what footage (or time code, if you prefer) each cut takes place. It shows the duration of the clip until the next cut, and it shows the first and last of the key edge numbers. Remember, we do not have edge code numbers in the digital realm; only if we sync our dailies on film and edge-code them prior to telecine and digitization do we have edge code numbers. The picture digital workstation does not have those edge code numbers, but it does have the negative key edge numbers. Sometimes these numbers are helpful to the dialog editor trying to find something in the code book.

The EDL also lists scene/take and clip name. The computer is extremely literal. If you make a cut, it acknowledges it. We often get fifty to sixty pages of an EDL for a single reel, with the computer listing every single cut, even if it is the same scene and take over and over. The smart supervising sound editor makes a copy of the EDL and then cleans it up, so as to make the mass of data much easier to read by the dialog editor. Choose a clear, easy-to-read font and a large font size. Sound editors usually work in dimly lit rooms. Small font sizes or fonts with characters squashed together are extremely hard to read, causing eye fatigue and editor burnout in a short time.

Suppose the supervisor sees that Scene 21J-3 is listed five times in a row, which is unnecessary. If an internal cut has been made, the dialog editor can figure that out in two seconds. The supervisor erases four of the repetitive listings, thus saving the dialog editor from scanning unnecessary lines. The next line reflects the next true change in a scene, angle, and take that the dialog editor must know.

Once the supervisor has finished cleaning up the reel, a copy is made and collapsed even further. All but the scene, angle, takes, and sound-roll (or lab roll) notations may be eliminated. Finally, all redundancies are eliminated. Only one of any scene, angle, and take, remains. The supervisor then rearranges the data according to sound-roll numbers. The result is printed and forwarded to the first assistant to make up a transfer order so that sound transfer can complete the dialog reprint work as quickly as possible. You may find that what would have been sixty pages of massive number printouts have been reduced to twelve to twenty pages.

AUTO ASSEMBLY: OMF OR PHASE-MATCHING SYNC

Most EDLs denote the clip name showing ".omf" after the scene/take designation. It is important to transfer the dialog from the original source to use OMF software to extrapolate a Pro Tools session of exact cuts from the editor's work track. Unfortunately, many projects have to be completely reprinted from the original production tapes because the original digitization by the picture assistant was poorly done. Sometimes there is a tremendous loss in clarity, and noise may have been introduced into the dialog recordings either because of poor line connections prior to use of the workstation's digital interface, or because cheap digital-to-analog encoding equipment was used.

OMF (Open Media Framework)

When OMF (open media framework) works, it is wonderful. It saves the extra step and cost of retransferring the source dialog material into the digital domain for dialog editing. It saves precious time in preparing for temp dubs as well as for finals. The key is in how well the picture department did its job when first entering the dailies into the digital picture workstation such as Avid or Final Cut Pro.

Here is demonstrated the classic example of the adage, "Garbage in, garbage out." If the material is not put in clean, with attention to exact signal-path disciplines, the result is a tainted and dirty dialog track from the OMF file that is not as good as one from the original source. If you do not pay attention to the exact disciplines of syncing dailies, the OMF audio file will never line up in precise sync. Your only hope for gaining true sync rests on how good the eyes and ears are and how many years of battle-line experience you have.

Consider the following example: I was finishing a temp dub on a film when the picture editor starting ranting and raving about our out-of-sync cutting. I quietly slipped behind the stage Pro Tools unit, booted up the dialog session, and zoomed in extremely close on the very passage in question. The reprint was laid precisely in sync to his work track, and when he realized that, he stepped back and said, "I don't get it. How is that possible?"

Everybody on stage knew how it was possible. His department was anything but the poster child for procedure and discipline. I allowed him to save face by telling him that this was just a temp dub and that we had not had the time to prepare the material fully, but that it would be in sync by the final mix—which it was. My dialog editors spent agonizing wasted days visually resyncing material that they should have been able to match-sync to a picture editor's 1:1 guide track.

To Trust or Not to Trust OMF Media Files

The first question a supervising sound editor must answer is whether the audio integrity of OMF media files is good enough to use for final sound editorial. My first assistant makes a Pro Tools edit session by using the OMF software to extrapolate a reel of dialog. The transfer engineer then pulls several tapes advertised on the EDL and makes half a dozen cues from various parts of the reel, choosing one for intimate dialog, another for exterior ambiance, and so forth. I drag the new dialog transfers into the Pro Tools edit session, phase-matching them against the OMF audio file that already exists in the session. I then pull the drive and take it onto the dubbing stage, where we can listen to and assess the quality of the material through the stage speaker system where the film is dubbed.

We boot up the session on the stage Pro Tools unit and make an "A-B" comparison, first listening to the OMF file, then flipping back to the new transfer from the original tape source. If we do not hear a difference in the two, we feel confident enough to use the OMF media files for dialog editing and final rerecording. If we do hear a difference, we know that picture editorial did not enter the original audio into the workstation properly.

We have resorted to reprinting more often than being able to use the OMF media files as supplied by picture editorial. If you must transfer the material over again, you will spend several thousand dollars unnecessarily because picture editorial did not do its job correctly the first time. This is part of what I mean by collateral costs.

Hence the experienced producer or post-production supervisor will always ask who is handling transfer chores. Clients make a deal with a sound facility for handling the dailies and having a guaranteed individual handling the work because they know that that particular transfer engineer doesn't just roll the stock and push the "Record" button. They know that that particular individual handles the job like an artist, maintaining the "magic" of a good production track.

It is extremely rare to get this kind of service at the major laboratories or factory-style sound facilities. This is a specialty service usually found only at the independent boutique sound houses that specialize in theatrical craftsmanship. Entire feature projects have been pulled away from facilities when the client discovers that the specific individual promised or contracted to do the work is not actually doing it.

One very important sound house was trying to cut costs on a project because it had other financial issues in the facility. One of the projects it was handling were the dailies of a rather important picture. It had gotten the contract to do the job on the understanding that a particular transfer man was going to handle the work. The picture editor knew, from a previous picture, that this transfer man handled the daily chores of transfer to 35 mm stripe with a simultaneous mastering to a Pro Tools session so that the digital dialog audio files were already mastered. The picture editor knew this person's work—he knew the kind of sound transfer notes this person made, including a separate list of interesting WT (wild track) and important audio notes to pay attention to. This kind of work is not done by 99 percent of transfer personnel.

The sound house needed to save money, so it replaced this transfer man with a less costly person. Within twenty-four hours the picture editor called up screaming—followed by the producer, who also called up screaming. Because the sound house was caught trying to shortchange the project, the daily transfer job was pulled from the facility. The collateral damage was that the word spread around to other producers. This sound house suddenly lost transfer work right and left and was eventually dropped from being considered to handle any post-production editorial chores. Sounds like an isolated case, huh? You would be shocked to know how much this goes on all the time. Just know that this kind of game playing goes on, and remember this one important fact—*studios do not make motion pictures— PEOPLE make motion pictures.*

Reprinting Dialog Cues from Original Source on Film

The transfer engineer opens the 1/4" tape box and pulls out the sound report (if the original sound is on digital DAT, it is usually folded and wrapped around the DAT cassette like a hot dog bun). (Flip back to Chapter 5 to refresh your memory on the sound report and to study the information at the top of the form. The information listed is key to how the transfer engineer is able to make a perfect duplicate of the original source.)

The 1/4" tape usually syncs to a Pilotone or to sixty cycles, which resolves via a crystal controller, known as "crystal sync." The 35 mm film recorder has a precision stepping motor that has been engineered to resolve to sixty cycles at precisely 24 or 25 frames per second (fps) depending on whether the transfer engineer chooses the American 24 fps or the European 25 fps, by the simple press of a button.

The transfer engineer threads up the 1/4″ tape (stored tails out) or the DAT cassette, which should always be stored rewound back to heads when not in use. The engineer spins the 1/4″ tape at high speed. The tape should not be dragged over the sound head, but should glide just off the head. Even though it is not touching the playback head, the engineer can count the takes as they spin by. "Clicks" are heard, which at normal speed are the tail tones the production mixer enters. These clicks make it much easier to locate a precise cue quickly. When one is found, the engineer stops the tape machine, then plays the verbal slate that the production mixer recorded prior to rolling action to verify that the correct take is identified. The tape is rewound to just before the slate and stopped.

The transfer engineer writes a scene/angle/take designation on a label that was placed prior to the actual material being transferred. She or he rolls the 35 mm film recorder and when it obtains "speed," pushes the "Record" button. The engineer then rolls the 1/4″ or DAT machine. The production mixer is heard slating the desired take. Slate sticks are heard, and the scene plays out. These transfers are broken down by the first assistant or apprentice and forwarded to the dialog editor.

Nonlinear Reprinting

There are two ways to transfer production dialog into the computer for editing purposes. The first technique is very basic and grassroots in nature. When the scene is originally shot, a "Smart Slate" with a time code generator is not used. It is basically running on a tape recorder using crystal sync. The scene is slated, making a sync mark, either by using a clapper slate or by an actor verbally slating the take and clapping hands in plain view of the camera. Experienced dialog editors know how to drag this kind of transfer into an edit session and phase-match the sync against the editor's work track.

Some picture budgets are so low that they cannot afford to rent the more expensive sound equipment to have the basic necessity of time code transfers or crystal sync resolution. We actually transferred the 1/4″ tapes and/or the DAT cassettes into the computer without the benefit of a sync resolver. The transfers inevitably would drift slowly out of sync—but my dialog editors were of the "old school" of editing disciplines, and as long as they knew what they had, they could sync anything! Fortunately for us, our equipment would drift longer rather than shorter, thereby making it easier for the dialog editor to simply pull the material up, back into sync, rather than having to lengthen it, which makes the entire process much more difficult.

The second technique is taking advantage of the time code signal and using Post Conform to accurately extrapolate a Pro Tools session with all the cuts in place, ready for the dialog editor to separate and massage. The transfer engineer carefully transfers the material into the computer using a Lynx to precisely guarantee sync resolution. Once the transfer is recorded into the Pro Tools session, the engineer double-clicks on the audio file waveform, which allows renaming the file with the exact scene/angle/take designation. The engineer then pulls down the menu option to time-stamp the transfer, placing a precise time code address in the audio file's directory. This procedure is critical to linking and extrapolating a Pro Tools edit session with all the cut and edit decisions the picture editor made in exact sync.

PostConform gives you the benefit of using the power of the computer to extrapolate an editing session where the exact cuts have already been brought into sync to the editor's work track, saving the time of the phase-matching that is traditionally part of the dialog editor's job. Consequently, the dialog editor can spend more time on massaging the material to make it cleaner, working out the presence-fill problems, splitting out the production effects, and so forth.

The advantage of PostConform over OMF is that transfers are made from the original audio source, whereas OMF gives the audio file that the picture assistant or apprentice entered into the picture workstation. With OMF you are at the mercy of the technique and discipline of the picture department, or lack thereof.

FIRST ASSISTANT BECOMES A TRANSFER ENGINEER

In today's ever evolving industry the task of sound transfer into the digital domain has changed dramatically. Sound transfer used to be the sacred task of sound transfer departments, and, for many kinds of transfer requirements it still is. However, a great amount of audio transfer is now being handled by sound editors themselves as well as assistant sound editors and even apprentices. This book does not address the union jurisdiction and philosophical arguments involved because whether these tasks are handled in the traditional way through the sound transfer department or by other personnel, the audio disciplines detailed here still apply.

Today first assistants take the responsibility of transferring back ADR from recording sessions as part of the editorial preparation. They enter the material from DATs, from 1/4" tape, from DA-88s and download audio files from both studio and field direct-to-disk hard drive systems. Assistants must learn the signal-path disciplines as well as how to time-stamp audio files correctly.

LAYING OUT THE DIALOG TRACK STRATEGY

Dialog editors must be predictable. They must always prepare their sessions in the same methodical manner, always laying out the tracks the same way. Such consistency makes the job of the dialog mixer much easier when predubbing commences. Mixers do not like to reinvent how they mix material from one reel to the next. They want each reel to match in style and technique, which not only allows them to get into and maintain a rhythm and a flow, but adds continuity to the track.

Whether dialog editors cut on a Moviola and build sync on a sync block (synchronizer) or whether they cut nonlinearly in a Pro Tools session, the technique and approach are the same.

The first track is a copy of the editor's work track. I slave-transfer my work track directly off the videotape supplied to me, thereby guaranteeing that I am matching exactly what was on the videotape, which has the editor's work track. Most videotape-machine audio outputs are 10 dB lower than "0" level. Hence most dialog editors have a difficult time matching waveforms; the editor's work track transferred in from the videotape is 10 dB lower than the levels of their dialog reprints.

After I transfer the editor's work track, I save and quit the Pro Tools session. Then I find the editor's work track in the audio file folder of the session and boot it up in Sound Designer II. I select the entire file and draw down the menu to "Change Gain," then I raise

Figure 14.3 Typical dialog edit session.

the level +10 dB. This gives a waveform far more accurate for phase- matching than would be the case if I had left the −10 dB level the way it was.

Another way to raise the level is to have a "4–10" box, which converts the −10 dB signal upward as needed. This box allows the entering of material into the Pro Tools recording as already elevated where desired. Panasonic DAT machines such as the 3500 and 3700 formerly had a "4–10" switch on the back panel of their rack-mounted machines, but more recent models have done away with them.

Once the dialog editor has the editor's work track in, he or she checks that the head pop is precisely on the 9+00 foot and frame. The dialog editor adds several more audio tracks to the Pro Tools session. Most dialog editors who work nonlinearly keep the number of dialog tracks to eight. The editor clicks on the audio track designation twice so that it can be renamed. The tracks are retitled– DIA-A, DIA-B, DIA-C, DIA-D, and as many DIA channels as the editor thinks are needed for the actual recut dialog. Then several other audio tracks are added, and they are renamed X-DIA and P-FX. Some dialog editors have more than one X-DIA and often more than one P-FX track. Figure 14.3 shows a typical dialog edit session.

The X-DIA track holds any bits of sound used by the picture editor that the dialog editor is not using in the primary A, B, C tracks. These are the bits not meant to be used in the dialog predub; however, never throw away any production track a picture editor has cut—never! There will come a time, and rather often it seems, when the picture editor is pacing behind the rerecording mixers wondering what happened to her or his track and must be able to account for it. In the X-DIA, track(s) are usually lines that cannot be used for the final soundtrack and must be looped, or they can be bits of noise and junk you do not want in the predub.

The P-FX is where valuable sound effects that occurred during the production recording are split off, sounds you absolutely want to protect for the M&E version (foreign soundtrack). Often these little tidbits of sound are mastered up into a sound editorial library as magic tracks for future shows.

Different dialog editors approach the posturing of sync dialog cues on the A, B, C tracks differently. Some dialog editors working on character-driven projects that often have intimate controlled dialog recordings find it preferable to favor a particular character to be on DIA-A and another character to be on DIA-B. This can be done on films shot in controlled-ambiance environments such as a sound stage.

Films shot in a mixed bag of locations—inside cars in traffic, on city streets or practical interiors, even office locales—prohibit the character-per-track approach. Instead, the dialog editor keeps the same recorded material in the same dialog track. Take, for instance, a scene shot on the loading dock of a shipyard. The scene is covered in a master angle, a medium shot, two over-the-shoulder opposing shots, and two close-ups. Unavoidably, each angle has a slightly different colorization in the ambiance of the background. Every time that microphone changes position, the background ambiance is going to sound differently—that's pure acoustical physics. The dialog rerecording mixer reaches up on the console and twists the parametric equalizers to adjust and match each angle to another to make them sound as flawlessly the same as possible. The mixer may even send the signal out of the console to an outboard rack to the right, where the favorite signal-processing equipment is kept, such as a universal dip filter. The mixer may pause and play the angle back and forth several times until satisfied with the equalization and/or compression and/or noise reduction that the track must be run through to achieve what is necessary.

The scene cuts to the opposing angle, and the dialog editor puts that cut on the next dialog track down—DIA-B. The mixer goes through a similar procedure to balance that angle. At the next picture cut, or even several picture cuts into the scene, the picture editor returns to the same scene, angle, and take as the earlier cut where the dialog rerecording mixer had run through the signal-processing gear—but the editor did not remember to put it in DIA-A!

This kind of mistake is one of many reasons why dialog editors must think carefully about their cuts. In these instances, the dialog sequence sheet or the EDL aids the dialog editor in thinking through the placement of the cuts. If scene 36A-2 was cut into DIA-A, and several cuts downrange in the sequence the picture editor used 36A-2 again to continue the action, then make sure all cuts of 36A-2 always show up in DIA-A. This makes it much easier for the dialog mixer to predub, as he or she does not need to stop and repatch the signal path to chase 36A-2 to a different channel.

The dialog editor's success depends on always laying out the dialog tracks in the same style and technique, keeping identical material in the same dialog tracks, splitting out throw away material to the X-DIA, and separating all production sound effects to be kept for the M&E version (foreign) of the P-FX track(s).

LIP SMACKS, TISKS, AND OTHER UNWANTED NOISES

Most people who do not work with raw production sound recordings are amused when they hear, for the first time, a favorite actor smacking his lips, "tisking," or clacking his or her dentures! Many distracting and odd sounds emanate from the human face.

One job of the dialog editor is to decide what "lip" business is really acting, and what is nervousness, loose dentures, or a "ham-in-the-rye," which is what most big lip smacks are.

Dialog editor craftspersons who cut on 35mm film often have a special "diamond" punch for quickly eliminating "smacks" and "tisks." This stainless steel punch has a sharp diamond pattern that is placed, pointing end-to-end, on the mag track. The playback head does not detect a dropout, not at 90 feet a minute, and the procedure is faster than physically cutting in a frame of fill track or taking a degaussed razor blade to it.

The dialog editor must be careful, however. Some lip smacks are part of the performance and must be left intact. When we start a new show, we often discuss the philosophy of lip smacks and tisks with the director, picture editor, and producer during the spotting session. Include the client in the decision-making process whenever possible; this way the sound editorial team does not go out on a limb, making an erroneous decision.

Fixing denture "clacks" is not as easy. These either must be carefully scrapped down with a razor blade or surgically filled. This is where the ability to cross-fade material in the digital domain of Pro Tools really pays off, for you cannot do this with 35mm mag film.

P-FX PREPARATION

Not all production sound effects must be split out and protected for the foreign M&E. You may want the Foley to reduplicate the production sounds, so splitting them out for protection is not necessary. Sound effects may be developed that are better than what was recorded on the set. However, you may want to keep many little production-recorded jewels. Make sure these sounds do not have any dialog over them, as that defeats the whole purpose of saving them for the M&E.

Sometimes I like a particular prop that makes a specific sound, but the sync dialog take has an actor speaking while that prop makes its peculiar noise. If I am very interested in salvaging it, I listen to the alternate readings of the scene to see if the prop performs its unique sound between actors' lines—and then I steal that sound cue, just for the prop noise.

On many occasions I review the reel with my dialog editor, pointing out particular production sounds I do not want left in the dialog tracks. Sounds that would "muddy up" and diffuse the precision of a sound effect specifically developed for that moment must be dropped and "filled." In such cases, the dialog editor extracts the production sound effect, moves it down to the X-DIA, and then fills the hole in the dialog track with matching ambiance to prevent a dropout.

I remember cutting dialog on the opening reels of *The Punisher* starring Dolph Lundgren. I was the supervising sound editor and knew exactly what kind of sound effects I was going to lay into the various sequences. In reel 3, Lou Gossett, Jr., drives to a blown-up mansion in his unmarked police car. He greets his partner, opens the car door, gets out, and closes the door as he carries on a conversation. I did not like the "edgy" sounding production car or its distorted door sounds, so I cautiously extracted them, making sure not to encroach on Gossett's lines or those of his partner. I took another reprint of the same angle and take to pull pieces of production presence, pieces that did not have either car noise or dialog but did have the production movement of the disaster team digging out the rubble, as this movement was the underlying presence of the shot.

After I cut in the pieces of ambiance "fill" and feathered the splice with a degaussed single-edged razor blade, no one could tell I had ever touched it; of course, you heard Gossett and his partner talking, and the background activity—you just did not hear the car come in-to-stop or the car door open and close.

When we predubbed the reel on Dubbing 3 at Warner Brothers, the head mixer, Wayne Artman, noticed the delicately cut stealth vehicle with absolutely no anomalies to the dialog being spoken. He glanced over at me and smiled, knowing we would have a really good mix, realizing he would not need to grapple with having to control unnecessary production effects, which often get in the way of a well-designed sound effect track.

It is not always easy for dialog editors to make precise decisions on extracting production effects. Most dialog editors are not involved in the sound design process and must review the reel with the supervising sound editor for specific instructions on what to move into the X-DIA and what to move to the P-FX. A thin line exists between a supervisory judgment call and a dialog editor's responsible preparation.

MAGIC AND TRANSPARENCY OF GREAT DIALOG EDITING

There are dialog editors—and then there are dialog editors. Cutting dialog is not just the mechanical procedure of phase-matching reprints, filling holes, or extracting lip smacks and unwanted noise—it is the massaging and evolutionary improvement of an actor's performance. Master dialog editors take the time to review alternate takes, looking for a better reading, a clearer articulation, whatever brings the polish of a diamond to the spoken word. Remember, the dialog track always plays; it is truly the star of the soundtrack, so it is appropriate that a tremendous amount of attention be paid to making it as clear and pristine as possible.

On *Twilight Zone: The Motion Picture*, my partner, Ken Sweet, handled the dialog editorial chores throughout the entire picture. One challenging sequence occurred in the first episode when Vic Morrow is dragged to the train in the rain.

Morrow tragically was killed during the filming, so we did not have access to him for ADR. The train sequence had been filmed the night before the accident. The artificial rain deluge was extremely heavy, thwarting any attempt by the boom operator to keep water from popping the microphone diaphragm without a rain bonnet. The director dismissed the need, saying they would ADR the scene later in post. We were not allowed to use a "soundalike" for looping the few lines obliterated by rain pelting, so Ken Sweet rolled up his sleeves and scrounged the production track in a way I have never seen a dialog editor do before.

He spent days cutting bits and pieces, sometimes as wide as one-fourth of a frame (a single perforation), from alternate takes to reconstruct a fluid piece of dialog that worked, without hearing the giant impacts to the microphone from the rain machine. Remember,

Twilight Zone: The Motion Picture was cut years before digital nonlinear editing. Ken did not have the luxury of cross-blending two pieces of audio files with a digital cross-fade. Everything he cut was on 35 mm film mag stripe.

Another challenging sequence occurred in the Spielberg episode when Scatman Crothers offers the elder members of a retirement home a second chance at youth. Scatman was eighty-one years old when he filmed this magical segment, and understandably had trouble with precision in diction and enunciation. Ken Sweet tackled the dialog editing as a labor of love because of his admiration for Scatman and went the extra distance to pore over alternate takes—stealing Ds, Ts, and Rs from outtakes where the actor had properly enunciated the consonant or vowel. Often Ken would steal such pieces from words or phrases entirely different from the word or phrase on which he was working. He would lift wherever he found a matching piece that could work, for he could not run the risk of making a single noticeable cut. Not one insert could be made that would give away the fact that Ken was resculpting the delivery of Scatman's speech. This was truly a work of editorial art.

Steve Rice faced a similar dilemma on *The Aviator*. When we spotted the picture with director George Miller, we were informed that Christopher Reeve was halfway around the world on another shoot and unavailable for any looping whatsoever. Somehow Steve would have to save all the production lines that dealt with the actor's voice. This was no small task, as Christopher Reeve wore a thick aviator's leather jacket throughout the majority of the picture. Naturally, the wireless microphone was positioned in such a way that the jacket was constantly rubbing the microphone any time Reeve moved.

I glanced over at Steve and we grimaced together, as we knew full well what challenges lay ahead. However, Steve Rice had been trained in the art of dialog editing by Ken Sweet just a few years before, and he had learned his art well. As far as tenacious work habits, I have never seen better. Steve never came to me with a problem; he came to me with a solution to a problem. He had launched his dialog editing career with me on *Battle Beyond the Stars* and *Escape from New York*, and with Ken Sweet's tutelage, he became a master dialog artist.

CREATING THAT WHICH IS NOT THERE

When we started *Moscow on the Hudson*, we were faced with a potentially costly situation that Paul Mazursky has already conceded would be necessary. In the sequence where Robin Williams is standing in a long, cold line at night, waiting to buy shoes, he pauses to talk to Leonid, an old friend (Alexander Narodetzky), also waiting in line. When the scene was shot, Robin's close-up angle was fine, but, on Alexander's angle, the sound of the wind machine that gently blew a snowfall dominated the audio track, making his close-up sync dialog completely unusable.

Les Fresholtz, the head dialog mixer on Warner Brothers Dubbing Stage 5, had earlier advised Mazursky to loop the actor. The picture editor, Richard Halsey, agreed with the director that it was a definite redo. To ADR this actor would require flight costs as well as daily expenses for at least the director and picture editor to fly to Munich to loop the actor's lines. Including the cost of an ADR stage, the funds needed to bring the actor back, and other stock expenses, Mazursky was facing at least a $10,000 black eye to the budget.

I suggested to Paul that he hold off on making that kind of commitment until my dialog editor dug through alternate readings in an attempt to rebuild the original performance. Halsey scoffed at the idea, saying that Fresholtz had written it off as unsalvageable. I asked Paul if waiting another week would make that much of a difference on the schedule—after all, it was ten thousand dollars. Paul shrugged and gave us permission to at least try it. I told Steve Rice to work on that sequence first to see what could be done.

Late the following week, Mazursky asked me what the verdict was on the Alexander Narodetzky dialog. I turned to Steve, who gave me the "high" sign that it worked just fine. I told Paul that the $10,000 did not need to be spent. Halsey was doubtful of the quality of the recut and asked Fresholtz to listen to it on the big screen in Dubbing 5. We assembled behind the sprawling console in Dubbing 5 the next day to run the sequence. Where the harsh and intrusive wind machine had marred the dialog track Steve had masterfully recut it from alternate angles where the wind machine had been. The trick had not been just using alternate takes—this is done all the time. The trick had been in finding usable alternate takes and making them fit in the full face-front close-up angles ruined by the wind machine, making the mouth movement precise, and especially in not changing or altering the inflection of the actor's performance.

This last point is the key to the entire art form of dialog editing. It is not enough just to understand and master the ability to sync lip-flapping movements with words. You carefully must guard and protect the performance and inflections so vital and cherished by the client.

Richard Halsey was so stricken by the flawless, seamless work of Steve Rice that his knees literally gave out and he collapsed in front of the credenza.

WHEN TO EQUALIZE AND SET VOLUME GRAPHING

A basic rule is to never use signal processing on any cut dialog. You want interesting-sounding vocals for monsters and ghouls? Prepare the material "flat"—signal processing is done by the rerecording dialog mixer on the stage. You do not have the proper acoustical environment to make such a decision in the editing room on a nonlinear workstation. The result would be something that cannot be unwound and reprocessed at the mixing stage; a smart dialog editor does not pre-equalize or preprocess the cut material in any way.

Prepare the elements of the material so that no matter how you wish to use it in processing the "vocal," it is easier work for the mixer. For example, cut the voice on channel 1 and cut any additives, such as animal growls or inorganic pieces, on channel 2 in exact parallel to the cut dialog. In this way, the rerecording mixer can assign the two tracks into a Vocorder or Harmonizer and play with it while the director and producer attend. Thus, it is their taste and creative desires you ultimately serve, not your own.

Many dialog editors are using volume graphing more and more, building in volume shifts. A few years ago this practice was seen as an absolute editorial sin, but today it is done to a greater degree than ever before, with better results as dialog editors learn how to use the software.

As the evolution of nonlinear workstations and rerecording mix stages causes the two to meld more and more into one and the same, there will be a greater need for dialog editors to work in rooms that truly do emulate the acoustical representation of a dubbing stage, as they will be asked to not only cut and prepare but to be responsible for the signal-processing function—even to the point of mixing and delivering a dialog predub stem to the stage for a final mix.

Eventually, of course, more and more product will be prepared and mixed completely on "mini" stages rather than on full-scale dubbing theatres. Indeed, more of this work is being done today than you might think, which is why we are seeing a lot of disparity between the soundtracks of important feature films versus other soundtracks.

Chapter 15
ADR and Looping: Getting the Lips to Flap in Sync

I believe in the magic of the original recorded production track. Most producers and directors believe in the magic of their original production track and they usually get dragged screaming and kicking onto the ADR (automatic dialog recording) stage with a multitude of more lines to replace than they had hoped to have to endure. They complain that ADR is so often sterile and stilted—that it stands out from the original performance.

To that I have no argument whatsoever. There are two ways to keep the sterile and stilted performances out. One, the directors and producers need to pay more attention to getting better production dialog recordings, both by budgeting better for it and by listening to the advice of their production mixers in the first place.

The second way is explained in this chapter and describes how to go about recapturing the magic of the actors' performance through not only the technique of ADR, but the utilization of an older and little used method called "looping"—a very liberating technique which gives actors a clearer and less confusing opportunity to focus on their acting art.

Before we proceed with the subject of ADR, we need to clarify the difference between it and looping. Today we often use the term "looping" when we talk about an ADR session. We say, "We need to loop these lines," or, "She does not loop well," when we are really referring to the process of vocal replacement and not the technique itself.

The technique of looping goes back to the beginnings of motion picture sound. In order to reperform dialog over an existing visual performance, a "looping editor" would have to roll both picture and optical track through a synchronizer, listening for the lines using the optical head mounted over the second gang of the sync block. Once the editor found the line to be looped, he or she would cut both picture and track out, precisely in sync—making a mark with a grease pencil on the matching frame lines. The editor would add a little extra on either side of the line so that the actor would have a lead-in. Both picture and sound were then spliced head-to-tail, making a film loop, with the start frame clearly marked and punched in the center.

The loop editor would then take a grease pencil and make a angular one-foot-long cue on the picture. This was a visual reference for the actor to see when the first frame of modulation of the line to be reperformed actually started.

The punched hole in the film was to assist the projectionist when she or he would slide the looped picture into the gate of the projector. It was often extremely difficult in the dim light of the projection booth to see the grease-pencil marks once the film was inside the gate area, but there was no mistaking the bright illumination coming through the punched hole, even when the douser of the projector was closed.

Once the picture film loop was loaded into the projector and the audio film loop was loaded into an optical playback dummy (the term used for a play-only machine that slaves to other machines), the projector and playback dummy were "put on the line" (interlocked together by a distributor drive unit) so that when the projector ran forward, the playback dummy would run forward exactly in sync.

The looping mixer was given a green light, and the mixer would tell the looping editor and actor on the stage that the next cue was ready. Then the mixer would "roll" the projector, which of course rolled the playback dummy. The cue to be reperformed would be seen on the screen, along with the grease-pencil cue that would cross the screen (usually from left to right), ending with the beginning of modulation of the line to be replaced. The original recording was also being heard as the actor would spend a few moments rehearsing it.

When the actor was ready, the loop editor would tell the mixer, and the mixer would have the recordist put the optical film recorder "on the line" with the projector and playback dummy. Once the mixer rolled the projector and got up to speed, the actor would perform the line. The loop would continue to go around and around, allowing the actor to re-perform the line several times—sometimes giving variations and different reflections to the performance.

Once the actor and looping editor were satisfied, the mixer would stop the projector, and the crew would take down the picture and audio loops and put up the next cue loops. This is the way it was done for many years, although in the early 1950s optical sound recording was replaced by 35 mm magnetic film recording.

Understand that there was no way to stop and back up and listen to these recordings. The projector, reproducer dummies, and recorder were incapable of operating in reverse. What became known as "rock-and-roll" technology, which allowed projector and playback equipment to stop and reverse in sync did not come into existence until the mid 1970s. As late as 1978 I worked on a picture that was mixing at the Warner Brothers sound department where we still could not stop and back up.

A variation of this style of looping was done at a few studios that specialized in a heavy amount of looping, especially as they were handling vast amounts of television shows. These looping rooms used the same technique of using physical film loops, but with an important difference: at the end of each day's shoot two copies of the circled takes were transferred to 35 mm mag-stripe by the sound department. These copies were made on two interlocked mag-stripe recorders simultaneously. The picture editorial apprentice would pick up one set and the loop editor would pick up the other set. The loop editor would break down all of the lines that each actor said, carefully making notes of scene/angle/take. Each actor's lines were then made into a loop—but a slightly different kind of loop. The loop editor would not bother with picture film; it was too costly and took too much time for the process to run the cycle through the laboratory and back to sound editorial. Instead, the loop editor would make each loop the length of the performance and again as long with two extra beats of fill. This would allow room for the actor to comfortably repeat the line during the blank period of the loop after he or she had just heard the original portion of the track played back in the headsets.

These loops were carefully marked with show code number, actor name, scene, angle, and take. Then each actor's loops were placed in 2000-foot film cans and stored on a rack. The following day, after the actor had completed that day's shoot, she or he would report to a "looping room" where all of the lines performed the day before would be relooped. This procedure gave incredible latitude to picture editorial, and subsequently to sound editorial after picture lock, greatly speeding up the post-production phase as they rarely had to call actors back in except to change performances with different dialog than originally written.

These so-called looping rooms did not project picture. The machine room loader threaded the loop onto a sprocketed 35 mm playback machine. As the loop played, it traveled around and around over the playback head, first playing the actor's original performance, then falling silent as the blank 35 mm fill passed over. This process allowed the actor in the booth to repeat the line he or she had just heard. As the loop continued around, the actor would hear the loop again and then, during the blank spot, and would repeat the line, altering the performance and giving a different inflection or emphasis. The process continued until the actor had delivered ten or fifteen variations, from which the loop editor and director could choose the best.

Once the cue was finished, the machine room loader removed the first loop and loaded the next, continuing the same process through the listed cues. The recordist placed a hand-written note of the next loop's code number on a piece of tape and placed the tape on the 35 mm mag-stripe (*after* the record head) to help the loop editor assistant break down the recordings later on. Once the tape was ready, the green light would come in, notifying the room that the loop was mounted and ready to roll. The looping mixer would roll the loop for the actor to listen to and get comfortable with. Once the actor signaled that he or she was ready, the recordist would place the 35 mm mag-stripe film recorder "on the line," inter-locking it to the reproducer dummy.

The actor simply stood next to a music stand that held the looping editor's notes and printouts of the actor's lines. This procedure gave actors a tremendous advantage. They could close their eyes and concentrate on listening to the performance and then reperforming it, either as an exact match or with variations. Actors thus had the freedom to *act*, rather than being overwhelmed with having to watch picture, take notice of cue stripes or hear beeps in the headset, or try to match lip flapping to the visual. All such nonacting demands would distract and pull actors out of the realm of delivering an audio performance.

We will address the subject of how to recapture this almost lost art form in the last part of this chapter under "Looping Today in the Digital Realm."

This technique will also serve you well when actors are unavailable for an ADR stage or looping room, for example, when they are shooting a film in the jungles of Africa or the Antarctica—definitely nowhere near an ADR stage—long after your post-production schedule and the two-track print master has already been delivered to the laboratory. I will discuss the mechanics of this location looping technique later in this chapter under "Remote Location Looping."

ADR—THE POPULAR AUTOMATIC SYSTEM

In the mid 1970s, with the advent of the "rock-and-roll" system in which projectors, repro-ducers, and recorders could stop, reverse, and roll forward again in absolute sync, the system of ADR came into being.

Contrary to some beliefs, ADR does not stand for "All Dialog is Ruined," although some directors would certainly argue the point. Indeed, the initials ADR are often quoted two ways: "automatic dialog recording" and "automatic dialog replacement." Of course, ADR does not replace anything—it takes an ADR editor to do that.

What the term ADR really refers to is the ability to program into the stage automation equipment the precise foot and frame that the mixer wishes the three pre-roll beeps to be heard—the film recorder to enter record mode and when the recorder should come out of record mode.

Based on these numbers that were physically entered into the automation using analog pushbutton switches, the equipment would react to preset parameters to roll at high speed (in those days six-times speed was high speed) down to the desired line, sense the proxi-mity of the foot and frame, and automatically slow down and park itself so many feet prior to the line. As computer programs started to drive the automation equipment, programming became even more complex and more detailed—ushering in a digital reality. As video trans-fers of the cut work picture became popular, time code began to be used (as we discussed in Chapter 6), so ADR stages had automated setups that allowed the mixer to choose whether to work and enter in-and-out cues in either feet and frames or time code.

The mixer would roll back and forth through the line for the actor to get a sense of the performance. Precisely three feet prior to the foot and frame entered by the mixer, the automation would trigger the ADR beeps, so that the actor would hear three very short rhyth-mic tones just prior to the actual line to be looped. These are known as the "beeps" (or "pips" to many English editors), spaced every sixteen 35 mm frames apart, equal to one beep every foot. Where the fourth beep would have landed is silent (known as the fourth silent beep), and this is the exact frame where the actor must begin to speak the line being replaced, otherwise referred to as "first frame of modulation."

The idea was that the actors could also watch their physical performance projected up on the screen. Thus there was no need for laborious grease-pencil cues to be marked on the film, as the three beeps prior to action provided the actors with an accurate rhythmic cuing. Since the actors had a chance to watch themselves, they became quite aware of "things" about them in the movie realm that they might want to react to and that might influence their new performance.

This was a great toy. The studio where I was working in mid 1977 was putting their new ADR stage, and I became very involved in this new process. We quickly discovered that some actors are perfect for ADR-style reperforming and others are totally intimidated by it—some to the point that they would devise all kinds of strange personal techniques in order to face the microphone.

Many who supervise performing talent on an ADR stage have noticed how some actors are intimidated by the beeps that precede the dialog cue to be reperformed, not being used to hearing the beeps and especially not used to the rhythmic timing. The rehearsal exercise in Figure 15.1 is for those who would like to be better prepared before stepping onto an ADR stage costing dollars by the minute. Follow it as you listen to and emulate the three cues—#36, #37, and #38—on the audio CD provided with this book.

CUE #	Character	
301	SAMANTHA	"I don't know how to get to him -- you tell me!"
START:	242+07	
TO:	244+00	

CUE #	Character	
302	MARCUS	"This ain't what I pay you for, Sam -- so don't give me no excuses, awright?!"
START:	244+08	
TO:	247+00	

CUE #	Character	
303	SAMANTHA	"I don't give excuses -- I just give headaches to knumb skulls like you."
START:	244+08	
TO:	247+00	

Figure 15.1 ADR practice exercise to help you get used to the timing of the "beeps."

THE PRACTICE OF ADR LINES

Just as you will experience on a professional ADR stage, you will hear three rhythmic beeps on the CD, then a piece of production dialog, which is the line intended to be revoiced. The beeps and dialog cues are repeated six times, to assist you in getting used to the rhythm of the beep cues and the silent fourth count that is the cue to lip-sync your voice against the production dialog.

To further the practical realism of line replacement, the practice cues have noisy ambiences, making it difficult to hear the original dialog at times. As you listen to the CD cue with the beeps and production cue repeated six times, try to repeat the line in perfect sync. As you master the ability to match sync, change the inflection and performance, while still keeping the temp and rhythm in perfect sync. This practice session is designed to help actors overcome the fear of working with the beeps and better understand what is expected as they work on today's ADR/looping stage.

ADR SUPERVISOR

The ADR supervisor, more than any other post-production craftsperson, interfaces and works with performing actors. When temperamental actors are involved, the producer's and director's first concern is who will handle the ADR responsibilities—and the politics.

Some actors love to ADR. They see it as a chance to get back on stage and improve their own performance, to massage it, fine-tuning it in a way not possible on location. On the other hand, many other actors dislike ADR immensely. They are intimidated or inhibited by the ADR stage process. To them, the on-screen sync track was the magic performance they provided while filming the scene on location. Many actors do not listen to the production track with a discerning ear. They hear only their own performance and, once satisfied with that, often refuse to loop a requested cue. Many are not audio aware. These actors do not always notice the intrusive airplane flying overhead marring the recording; neither do they hear the distorted brittleness in the track where they shouted or suddenly burst forth in a dynamic shift, catching the production mixer off guard and causing the voice to be overmodulated.

This is where strong and politically smart ADR supervisors really earn their salaries. If a supervisor gains an actor's confidence in his or her sincere interest in improving and magnifying the performance, the actor almost always defers to the supervisor's recommendations.

An ADR supervisor does not always have to be the best ADR editor in the world (one can always hire ADR editors with reputations for cutting good sync), but the ADR supervisor does have to appear on stage neatly dressed, with a professional bearing of calm self-confidence. The supervisor also must be extremely well organized, able to locate the right paperwork at any moment. If the supervisor does not have the answers literally at the fingertips, he or she must know where and how to get it in a timely manner without fuss.

The ADR supervisor must articulate clearly, to both the actor and the director and producer(s) as needed, why certain cues are added and how they will improve the outcome of the final soundtrack. The ADR supervisor should not give the perception of being just the bearer of bad news or a presenter of problems, but rather of a professional presenting solutions.

An ADR supervisor works hard at surgically gleaning out problematic dialog lines (for both performance and technical issues). He or she compiles a complete list of lines to be looped and devises tactical solutions for gaining access to remote actors not available for formal looping sessions.

Nothing is worse than being on an ADR stage or, even worse, on the rerecording stage and having a director or producer notice that lines were missed. It is bad enough when a director or producer decides on additional dialog needs after the fact; it is altogether a most undesirable situation to overlook lines that either clearly were requested in the initial spotting session(s) or were not gleaned out by common sense by the ADR supervisor while cuing the ADR lines at the workstation.

LISTEN CAREFULLY TO THE PRODUCTION TRACK

One pitfall that the director, picture editor, and producer(s) constantly encounter is losing touch with their production track. Remember, they have lived with the picture and their production track for weeks, often months, and on occasion even years. They know every word, every production sound effect, every dropout, every flaw. They have grown so close to it that they have lost the ability to hear it anew, as heard by an audience for the first time. It is often very difficult to convince directors and producers that a dialog line must be looped when the repetitious playback of that line is indelibly etched in their minds.

In a spotting session, I hear a problematic line. The director, picture editor, and producer are not flagging it. I hold up my hand. "What did they say?" Invariably, the director or picture editor will *tell* me what the actor said instead of realizing that my not understanding the line was related to its lack of clarity.

The best ally a supervising sound editor and ADR supervisor can have is the dialog mixer who helms the ultimate rerecording of the project. Many times a director or producer will disagree with or try to badger the ADR supervisor, claiming nothing is wrong with a particular line. "You can make that work." However, when the dialog mixer says to loop it, nobody questions it. After all, the dialog mixer is the ultimate authority through whom all dialog tracks must flow. He or she has the power to bounce the reel off the stage and refuse to mix it if the material cannot be made to work because of the way it has been prepared. It is for this reason that, as supervising sound editor, I always insist on having the sound facility set in place and the mixing crew contracted at the outset of commencing the post-production sound editorial chores. The first thing I want is an interlock running of the picture with the dialog mixer, who usually helms the stage. Naturally, I have my dialog editor (responsible for cutting original production tracks) as well as my ADR supervisor on stage for the running. More important, I want the director, picture editor, and producer(s) in attendance to hear exactly what the dialog mixer says about one cue or another.

The dialog mixer runs the production track through the very mixing console used during the predubbing process. Often this is when the picture editor, director, and producer(s) hear the track truly for the first time, through quality theatrical speakers that are extremely transparent—that is, they do not color or hide the flaws of the recordings. *All* is revealed.

Many dialog mixers explain that they have a three-count rating system as the team discusses the various dialog lines. If they rate it a "one," that means they have no problems with the technical characteristics of the line and can make it work; however, if they want to loop it for performance reasons, that is the call of the director and/or producer(s). If they rate it a "two," that means they do not like what they hear. Either there is a "fringy" edge (usually the threshold of distortion) or some kind of hum or noise, such as overhead aircraft, offstage traffic, or other intrusive sounds. The dialog mixer feels that he or she can work with the line if necessary, but would rather have it looped. If they rate the line a "three," that means there is no choice but to loop the line, as the dialog mixer cannot equalize it or work with it to make it sound right. Do not even argue with the dialog mixer about his "three" count—even actors who have died can and do have line replacement done by "sound alikes."

From time to time the dialog mixer pauses and lays on a few equalization moves or runs the sound through a universal dip filter to make sure that some offending noise can be notched out without encroaching on the characteristics of the voice. By the time the running is over, there is usually no question as to the scope of work to be done. The mental alignment of the sound editorial team and picture editor, director, and producer(s) becomes fairly well set. With a short conversation regarding tactics of dialog preparation and perhaps other options to save certain critical lines, such as using Sonic Solutions or renting specialized signal-processing gear for the dialog predub process, everyone leaves the running focused on the job ahead.

Having an interlock running with the dialog mixer at the beginning also relieves the mixer of responsibility with you. It is one thing to show up on the rerecording stage for dialog predubs and have the dialog mixer zinging the sound editors because something was not done, but when the dialog mixer is part of the decision-making process from the beginning, she or he is bound to the sound editorial team as well as the director and producer(s) by what was counseled before work began.

APPROPRIATE USE OF LANGUAGE

Language is a very delicate and extremely important part of the soundtrack. Few producers, directors, or writers truly understand the ramifications of using excessive or inappropriate profanity in the dialog track. This is not about what previously was known as the television network standards and practices board. This is a question of common sense and a calculated decision on the part of the producer of defining the audience for the film.

In an industry immersed in an assault on the senses, where we are exposed to extremes of cinematic content, most of the new generation of filmmakers unfortunately is desensitized and perhaps suffers from ignorance of this controversial and delicate subject. Seriously ponder for what audience you have been making the picture, then rethink the use of profanity or slang used in the script. I have witnessed several projects that could have done much better commercially but were banished to a harsher MPAA rating because of the careless use of blasphemy and profane dialog.

Not an issue of Victorian prudishness, this is the experience of being associated with over one hundred theatrical motion pictures, watching their creative evolutions through to box-office success or failure, and witnessing elements that made them successful and those that weakened them, turning off audiences. The topic is broached here because it is during the looping process that you may wish to rethink your dialog track through one more time with a critical eye toward this cause-and-effect issue; you still have a chance at this point to make changes that will improve the film's commercial worth.

Aside from primary content consideration, you must address television coverage. After you finish the M&E (foreign) mix, you will need to prepare a television version. You will not find an official "no-no word list" anywhere. Probably out of fear of violating the First Amendment, nobody wants to dictate and formally publish such a no-no list—nor will I. However, many sound editorial firms, especially those dealing with network television, have lists compiled from meetings and verbal edit strategies. Of course, the list is constantly changing. At one time, certain words could not be said on television or even in movies—that are now heard on a regular, desensitizing basis. Each network and cable channel has its own threshold of acceptance.

Determining what is profane or what will trigger a harsher MPAA rating is not as obvious as you might think. The word "hell" is a good example—an extremely common and virtually everyday word that has lost much of its impact. If an actor says, "Oh, what the hell," this is not a problem. But if an actor turns to another actor and says, "You go to hell!" this is a problem, for now it is used in a spiritually damning way against another human being. Therein lies the difference.

The most powerful and surefire trigger to not only doom your film to a harsher MPAA rating but also to turn off a huge cross section of the audience is the use of blasphemy. Should an actor place the word "God" in front of the word "damn," the most profane word has been uttered—yes, it is even worse than the "F" word.

It is just amazing to me how badly warped the cable censorship community has become. American Movie Classics and other popular so-called family channels will bleep out the defecation "S" word, yet they will leave in the harshest of all obscenities, the blasphemous "G-D" words. This is not an indictment based only on Christian ethics. "God" is a global term that applies to the specific spiritual names that define the pinnacle deity of almost all religions. Therefore, using it in a blasphemous way once is worse than using the "F" word as many times as Al Pacino did in *Scarface*. If you do not understand what I am talking about, then I suggest you check out the Ten Commandments that Moses brought down from the mountaintop to the Israelites—it is the only verbal utterance that is forbidden by God.

The "body count, bullets and blood" mentality that desensitizes the audience will erode (and is eroding) the viewing tolerance. I should know. I have worked on many films that I would not, by choice, go to see. I have been bombarded by images and language that for long periods of time have desensitized me. Hollywood argues that their studies tell them the kind of movies that the public wants to see. Statistical studies, however, yield different information depending on exactly how you present the question. We did not believe Hollywood's box-office studies of the public taste and demand, so we made our own study, including moviegoers and patrons of local video rental shops. It revealed that middle-age and older moviegoers were going to the theatre less and less often, not because of a lack of desire to go see a movie in a theatre, but because of the content of today's movies, especially the language.

Language was the number-one reason why a significant number of potential patrons either stopped going to the movie theatrs entirely or became far more picky about which films they wanted to see. Many comments surprised us, especially in regard to the specificity of objectionable words. For instance, many viewers reacted very badly to the word "crap" or "crappy" in film dialog, saying they actually would prefer to have heard that other overused defecation "S" word.

While it is true that some of these comments came from areas many refer to as the Midwest or the "Bible Belt" audience, filmmakers forget that that audience accounts for a giant share of income and can certainly wield powerful critical acclaim or disapproval. Many filmmakers have failed to consider the collateral loss of dollars that they did not know about, because they did not know what was possible to begin with.

The movie *The Rookie*, starring Dennis Quaid, is an excellent example of a picture that has heart, passion, emotion, action, interesting photography, good sound and music score, and yet does not have one curse word. By the way, it was rated G, disproving the Hollywood hype about G-rated films being poison at the box office.

This is not just a question of ethics or morals, but of good business practice based on *possibilities*. It is wise to remember the audience a film is targeted for, and analyze the visual images and dialog track with that audience in mind.

Furthermore, since, as we have discussed in this book, foreign sales stream income now dominates the domestic market, filmmakers should likewise consider the tastes and tolerances of foreign markets. Each overseas audience market has its own reactions to film language. Sometimes offensive words may be translated out, but certain words are universally recognized. This is not to say that you cannot or should not make R-rated films. They definitely have their market. This is about recognizing what market your film is really speaking to and making sure that the content matches that market.

A few years ago I was supervising the sound on what should have been a cute little PG-rated robotic film. We had just sat down to commence the spotting session when the lead actor turned and used the "G-D" word—not once, but several times. I raised my hand for the editor to stop. I turned with a puzzled expression to the producer and said, "So you're making an R-rated film?"

He recoiled at my comment. "What gives you the idea that we're making an R-rated film? This will be rated PG!"

I shrugged. "That's what I thought your market was going to be. But you sure have an R-rated film now."

The producer asked how I came to assume that. I explained that after working on more than a hundred theatrical motion pictures, including many in which I was privy to the interactions of the producer and the MPAA, I have come to know what will trigger certain ratings—and using the "G-D" word will get you an R rating.

The producer scoffed at me. What did I know? I was just a sound editor! Several months later, when we commenced the final rerecording process, the producer burst onto the dubbing stage with a deluge of profanity. How could the MPAA have given them an R rating? I glanced knowingly at the head mixer, who smiled with an unspoken "I-told-you-so" acknowledgement.

Rather than take the time to go back in and loop the offending lines and resubmit the film for a new MPAA rating, the producer did not understand that it was this simple language issue that had garnered the R rating, so those lines were never replaced. Consequently, the picture was released as an R-rated film and never reached the audience for which it was designed. The film failed miserably, all because of a dozen "G-D" outbursts in the dialog track.

Another point for filmmakers to remember is that television standards forbid certain words, so if they don't want their film playing on a well-known cable channel with muted dropouts in the soundtrack, they should accept the advice from the ADR supervisor regarding getting dialog for a television version while actors are on stage for the primary ADR session.

CUING ADR LINES

After a thorough run-through and discussion with the director and producer on actor performances and availabilities, the ADR supervisor goes through the film to cue the dialog, noting both replacement and added lines to be recorded.

The ADR cue sheet (Figure 15.2) is always typed. Never take handwritten ADR cue sheets to the stage. Never give an actor a handwritten ADR cue sheet, unless you are adding or collaborating on new dialog on stage *with* the actor. The neatness and precise look of the ADR cue sheet is your ambassador of professionalism and trust. Watch for misspelled words or crossed-out lines with handwritten corrections. Many actors are intimidated by the ADR stage already. If you give the actor handwritten cue sheets, you do not instill confidence and inspire the actor, and you may find yourself soon replaced. That decision may not be up to your supervising sound editor but commanded by the director or producer(s).

Note that each ADR line in Figure 15.2 has a cue number. Almost all ADR supervisors use the reel number as the first designation, so all cues in Reel 4 are the 400 series; 401, 402, and so on. In addition, many supervisors leave a blank box in between each cue, allowing space to add lines on the spur of the moment, but also making it much more comfortable for the actor to find and read the lines in the dim light of the ADR stage. The actor must concentrate on the image projected on the screen to match sync, and not waste time looking for the written cue on the page.

List each part by the character name, not the actor's real name. Every ADR supervisor has a specific technique and preference as to how to prepare ADR sheets. Many supervisors list ADR cues just as the ADR form is displayed in Figure 15.2. In other words, ADR cues are listed in a linear order, in sequence of performance, listing each character. Other ADR supervisors choose instead to put all the lines for each character on a separate page. Their contention is that this is not as confusing to the actor on the ADR stage. I simply take a yellow highlighter to all Richard's lines, and on another copy I highlight all Jeanie's lines, thereby making it immensely easier for the actors to focus on their own dialog requirements.

EDITOR: Boguski REEL : **4**

MIXER / RECORDIST Schwartz / Porter TAKE PREFS NOTES:

CUE	Character			
401	Jeanie START: 01:10:02 TO: 01:15:00	"You tell me where all the animals have gone!"		
CUE	Character START: TO:			
402	Jeanie START: 01:15:10 TO: 01:21:00	"Two weeks ago this entire archipelago was crawling with exotic creatures."		
CUE	Character START: TO:			
403	Richard START: 01:22:07 TO: 01:32:00	"Maybe they're just timid -- wrong time of day to come or something."		
CUE	Character START: TO:			
404	Jeanie START: 01:31:20 TO: 01:38:00	"I hardly think so, besides the air itself -- it lacks that certain aroma."		
CUE	Character START: TO:			
405	Richard START: 01:40:12 TO: 01:48:00	"Aroma? -- Aroma of what? (beat) "You mean their stink?"		
CUE	Character START: TO:			
406	Captain START: 01:48:15 TO: 01:57:00	"She's right, my boy. The air was full of life."		

Figure 15.2 ADR cue sheet.

As supervising sound editor, I prefer ADR sheets in linear order. With today's computer software, it is easy to extract "per-character" variants from the master cue list and print them for the actor on stage, but I do not want to fumble through a dozen separate sheets looking and accounting for lines of dialog.

Each line has a "start" and "to" designation. This designation either is listed in feet and frames or in time code. Many veteran theatrical editors still like to work in feet and frames, but video outputs from the cut picture are offering fewer and fewer opportunities to use feet and frames. Moreover, a few ADR stages cannot even display feet and frames anymore, so time code is the only choice in those instances. (Always check with the stage before starting this task.)

When cuing the line to be ADR'ed, list the exact frame in which the first audible modulation can be heard—exactly! At the end of the line, add one foot extra for overtones to die off. Not all ADR mixers like their "start" cues the same way. Some want it two frames prior; others want it as much as eight frames prior; and still others want it right on the frame of modulation. You will probably use more than one ADR stage to complete all ADR work for the picture. Each stage may want the "start" cues slightly different. Either tell the mixer that all your cues are right on the frame so that specific preferences can be utilized, or print out new sheets with the preferred frame specifications already listed for each recording venue.

The ADR supervisor soon has a list of the stages, both local and around the world, that will be dealt with to accomplish the looping chores of the picture. The ADR supervisor discusses preparation preferences as well as media requirements from the ADR mixer and/or audio engineer of each facility. It often is necessary to prepare separate ADR sheets for individual ADR facilities, customizing the data to best accommodate that facility's own capabilities or limitations.

Some ADR supervisors have an added line of notations for each cue. They list a reason why the line is to be reperformed—that is, noise, distortion, performance, television coverage, and so on. This practice has developed as a result of some frustrating experiences of ADR supervisors, supervising sound editors, producers, directors, and rerecording mixers, who, in the final analysis, have to make it all work. Initially, the producer or director may perceive that the dialog for the film is basically in good shape and does not require much looping. Then the ADR supervisor and supervising sound editor run the reels with the rerecording mixer on a dubbing stage to analyze the true quality and nature of the production sound. It never fails to shock the producer and director—who have never truly heard their production track in this theatrical environment—to discover just how bad and brittle their soundtrack is.

Now come the lines added because of unwanted vocal overlaps that were unnoticed before, for instance, airplane noise not detected on the little speakers of a picture editorial workstation. The rhythmic ticking was not noticed because of early morning condensation affecting the microphone diaphragm. If you loop the passenger character in the front seat of the car talking, you either must loop the driver or cross-fill all the noise from the driver's dialog under the passenger character to avoid a series of checkerboard dropouts—which ultimately accomplishes nothing if you were intent on getting all that noisy background out from behind the passenger character's lines in the first place!

Now the ADR lines start adding up. At an average of ten minutes per line to successfully record, the producer and director get nervous. Their "good shape" dialog track is now escalating into several hundred, even a thousand-plus ADR cues. Then suppose you have to send an ADR kit to, say, South Africa to an actor on location but with access to an ADR stage in Johannesburg for an afternoon. The budget cannot afford for the ADR supervisor to fly down there to oversee the session. What comes back is a marked-up ADR sheet with only a fraction of the ADR lines done. The actor often does not understand or does not care about the technical problems of the scenes. The actor usually considers his or her performance fine.

I received a 1/4" backup master from an ADR stage in Florida, where a name actor had performed his ADR session unsupervised. Without due consideration of why the ADR cues had been written up, and without calling the editor in Los Angeles to ask why he was expected to loop certain lines, he arbitrarily decided not to loop certain lines but would go ahead and loop others. As I ran the 1/4" backup master, I could hear the actor scoff as the film rolled. He demanded to know what idiot had cued the lines. He crossed out a line and wrote "omit." Of course, he did not pay attention to the background noise, which the ADR supervisor knew would give the dialog rerecording mixer absolute grief later. Guess who caught the criticism from the rerecording mixer when he heaved a sigh and said, "I can't make this work! Why didn't you loop this line?"

By making notes as to why the particular ADR line has been cued, the ADR supervisor not only informs and educates the actor to gain cooperation but also makes a paper-trail that may be necessary to prevent later blame and to show the producer and studio executives that the ADR supervisor had prepared the job correctly in the first place.

Note in Figure 15.2 the six squares to the right of the ADR line. The ADR supervisor keeps a close record of which takes are most desired. This is kind of like the "circled" takes on a production sound report. Before direct-to-disk digital recording systems, such as Pro Tools, Waveframe or Fairlight, ADR was recorded to multichannel magnetic stock. At first it was three-channel 35 mm fullcoat, and as the 35 mm four-channel head stack came out in the late 1970s, we were thrilled to have one extra channel. Then stages started adapting 24-track 2" magnetic tape, especially when Dolby Laboratories made the Dolby "A" 24-channel noise-reduction encoder/decoders. This practice became even more popular with the Dolby "SR" (Spectral Recording) encoder/decoder. Cue sheets during these years had twenty-four square boxes for the ADR editor to keep notes in, especially notes on what take was on which channel.

With today's direct-to-disk recording systems, the question of "what channel" is irrelevant. It becomes a matter of "what take," as everything all resides on the hard drive unless thrown away by the user. It really falls to the ADR mixer assistant to help the mixer keep the take numbers straight, as after recording a line, the mixer needed to tap twice on the recorded audio track to rename it. That renaming would become critical for future reference. It becomes very easy to record numerous takes before the director chooses one or more to "print" which is an old term that meant that the sound transfer department should make a 35 mm mag-stripe copy for the ADR editor to cut. With today's digital technology we do not "print" anymore, though the term still sticks; today it just means that the ADR editor will want to pay strict attention to the director's choices. The ADR supervisor also makes notes as to how to cut the line. The director may ask for the first part of the line from Take 3 with the second part from Take 9.

ADR STAGE: THE CREW

ADR Mixer

The ADR mixer not only must be highly experienced in the use and placement of various microphones, but also must know how to listen to the production track and match the colorization and timbre of the ADR stage microphone so that the actor's voice blends into the production track as seamlessly as possible. In addition, the ADR mixer must be a politician, knowing when to guide and hand-hold and when to remain quiet and step back.

The ADR stage is known for everything from making magic to provoking bouts of fisticuffs. Tempers flare, and feelings get trampled. The ADR mixer de facto becomes both host and problem-solver, but the mixer almost always has the last word. Most of the ADR mixers I have met are slightly reserved, politically smart individuals who know how to focus on the good of the show and how to guide the temperaments of all concerned toward a constructive end.

The great ADR mixers are extremely comfortable and smooth with their equipment. With what seems like effortless magic, the mixer rolls the tape, presses the inline mike, and slates the multitrack and DAT backup recorder: "Cue four-oh-three take five, channel six."

A beat later the three rhythmic ADR beeps sound, and, on the silent "fourth," the actor performs the line. Without being asked, the mixer quickly rewinds the tape and hits the talk-back button so all on the stage can hear. "Playback."

The tape rolls, and everybody hears the production track. At exactly the right moment, the mixer mutes the production dialog as Take 5/Channel 6 plays back the new performance. The mixer smoothly slips out the production track exactly at the end of the cue so those on stage can get a sense of how the new line sounds.

We wait for a response from the director. Is it a circled take, and we go on to the next cue, or do we try another take of this cue? It is a circled take, and yes, the director wants to try another one. The mixer calmly switches off Channel 6. "Save Channel 6, moving on to Channel 7." The recordist makes the appropriate note on the ADR protection report, and they roll the videotape to try it again. The instant feedback may help the actor relax and, in general, facilitate success.

ADR Recordist

The ADR recordist supports the ADR mixer. The recordist is responsible for receiving either the film dupes or the videotapes of the picture prior to the ADR session. If the session is being synced to videotape, the recordist spins down to the one-minute time code designation and checks if the tape really is "drop" or "nondrop" time code as advertised on the label. Many times people just assume the label is filled out correctly, and even more frequently the video transfer facility fails to list the technical specifications at all.

If the videotape is "drop" frame, the visual time code numbers (note the semicolon for the frame count) jump from 01:00:59; 29 to 01:01:00; 02, skipping over two frames. Obviously, if the tape is "nondrop," the visual time code numbers (note that it is a colon and not a semicolon for the frame count) simply flip from 01:00:59:29 to 01:01:00:00.

Once the time code rate has been determined and verified, the recordist makes sure that the proper number of multitrack audiotapes (such as 2" 24-track analog or 1" 48-track digital) have been properly degaussed and time code striped for the upcoming work. The recordist prepares all labels for both the multitrack masters as well as the 1/4" or digital DAT backups.

The recordist also lays down line-up tones on all tapes, making sure that all channels are recording properly and that the stock is stable and reproducing properly. The recordist further confirms that the signal path from the mixer's console is patched through the noise-reduction encoders and that the right console fader assignments indeed go to the correct input channel on the recorder.

The recordist also does a shakedown run of the videotapes supplied by the ADR supervisor, making sure that the time code is reading correctly and that the production track on Channel 1 is playing clearly. Videotapes are not all transferred with equal attention to quality or time code. The last thing you want is to run an ADR session and discover that your videotape has dropouts in the time code. If you do not have a good backup tape at your disposal, the entire session can come to a screeching halt, or at least to a short-tempered delay.

At the start of the ADR session, the recordist takes the ADR sheets from the ADR supervisor and sets them up so that the mixer is only concerned with the business at hand. The recordist keeps all paperwork and organizational chores out of the mixer's way so that the mixer can focus on balancing the microphones and capturing the actors' performances clearly without distortion or unwanted noise.

As the ADR session progresses, the recordist methodically and carefully maintains the backup digital DAT, checking that each cue has its own program number (PNO) and determining which takes are requested by the director as "circled" takes. The recordist monitors the playback head of the multichannel, vigilantly listening for any breakup, distortion, or other anomalies that would inhibit a successful audio conclusion.

Up to this point, all of the excuses made down the line all the way from production recording through picture editorial is "we'll fix it later"—but not anymore. There is nobody after us to "fix it." Post production sound is the end of the line. The buck stops here. You either get the recording clean or you fail. At the first sign of clicks, pops, distortion, or other unwanted noise, including squeaks from the actor pivoting around on a stool too much, the recordist flags the mixer (who may not be hearing it from the prerecord head position), who then asks for a retake or diplomatically informs the actor that she or he is making unwanted noise.

The recordist ultimately is responsible for seeing that the master multitrack is either delivered to the client, goes to the transfer department to transfer the circled takes to whatever medium the editor dictates, or downloaded into a digital workstation format such as Pro Tools or Waveframe.

MICROPHONE CHOICE AND PLACEMENT

A most important factor in good ADR recording is the choice of microphone. As discussed earlier, not all microphones have the same colorization or character. The ADR mixer needs to know exactly what microphones the production mixer used on the set, so that the same model of microphone can be used to record the ADR. Figure 15.3 shows an example of matching microphones.

Often I pick up a production roll and find no mention of the microphones on the sound report; not even the model or head-stack configuration of the sound recorder itself is listed. Although many production mixers do recite an audio checklist at the head of each production roll before they roll their line-up tone, it must be assumed, as often is the case, that the production roll is not in easy access to the ADR mixer; if the production mixer had

Figure 15.3 Pictured are two Sennheiser 416 microphones used on an ADR stage. Although there is no need to use windscreens indoors, the mixer leaves on the windscreens because they were used on the microphone during exterior filming. The mixer tries to recreate the exact colorization of the microphones so that the ADR lines better match the production performance.

listed the recorder and microphone information on the sound report, it would be instantly available.

At any rate, the ADR mixer needs to know the model of microphone used in order to duplicate the audio texture and colorization, so that the new ADR lines flow as seamlessly as possible with the original production material against which they are cut. Otherwise, the audience will be mentally yanked out of the performance of the scene because the ADR lines glaringly stand out from production.

Most ADR stages have two matching microphones set up for the session. The first microphone is approximately two feet from the actor, slightly higher than the forehead and angled downward toward the mouth. At this distance, a "depopper" screen in not needed, but some actors have a well-trained stage voice that requires protection from their powerful "P"s, or, as Christopher Lee apologized to me once, "Ah yes, I have vented many a theatre."

The second microphone is placed farther back from the first, between four to six feet, depending on the perspective required. This microphone is also slightly higher than the closer mike. With this configuration, the ADR mixer can switch from one microphone to the next to achieve a more desirable perspective in matching the original production track. Without the two-microphone setup, the ADR mixer constantly must get up, go out into the stage, and readjust the microphone position from cue to cue, wasting precious time and accelerating the fatigue and irritability factors. The only time to move the close-up microphone any nearer the actor is on those rare occasions when recording intimate whispering and

ADR -or- Looping
The ADR editor cues actors lines to be
replaced. Actors and/or replacement voice
talent are brought in on an ADR stage to
reperform their lines against their original
performance.

Figure 15.4 Mike placement to actor.

extremely subtle vocals that require the microphone to be ultra-close. Be very careful about the popping "P"s and hard consonants with this in-your-face proximity. Figure 15.4 shows an example of mike placement.

ADR PROTECTION REPORT

The ADR supervisor sits on the ADR stage near the acting talent, interacting with them and the director. The recordist maintains the multitrack recorder and digital backup DAT. The recordist keeps track of the ADR cue number, listing each take and its channel. If the backup is made to 1/4" tape, the recordist notes the time code start. If the backup is made to a digital DAT, the recordist notes the PNO (program number) that the DAT machine assigns to the tape each time it rolls. Figure 15.5 shows an ADR protection report.

The recordist also circles those takes the director and/or ADR supervisor want to keep. These takes are protected on the multitrack recorder. The mixer does not record over those channels if additional attempts at the performance of that cue are requested.

Note that the protection report also lists microphones used, tape speed, whether noise reduction was used and what kind, and so forth. Always prepare these forms as if someone with absolutely no knowledge of your procedures and protocol is working with the material and cannot converse with you on the phone if he or she has questions. Additionally, a copy of the ADR protection report is kept in the multitrack tape box. A copy is also given to the ADR supervisor. It is especially valuable because of the DAT PNOs.

Several years ago a mixer shipped out a good amount of material in great haste, without filling out the necessary information. He simply told the messenger that the transfer man should call with any questions the next day. Sad but true, the mixer had a fatal heart attack that evening. Also sadly, the transfer man was left with many unanswered questions.

A.D.R. PROTECTION REPORT

TITLE: ———————————— ROLL #: ——— DATE: ————— STAGE: ————

PROD. CO.: ————————

☐ 7.5 IPS ☐ NAB ☐ DOLBY A ☐ DOLBY SR

MIXER: ————————

☐ 15 IPS ☐ CCIR ☐ NON-DOLBY

RECORDIST: ——————

☐ FULLTRACK ☐ OTHER SYNC on channel ———

☐ TWO TRACK ☐ COPY

HEAD TONES: —————

☐ 59.97 ☐ 60 Hz ☐ TIME CODE ———

MICROPHONES : —————

CUE #	TAKES	CH	1/4" TIME CODE	DAT PNO	NOTES

Figure 15.5 ADR protection report.

ISDN TELECOMMUNICATIONS INTERLOCK

Sometimes it is not possible, for economic or scheduling reasons, that directors and actors can be in the same place at the same time. Increasingly, telecommunication ADR sessions are necessary. Suppose three actors in a film live in New York. The director must oversee their ADR session but also must remain in Los Angeles for another post-production task. Fortunately, many ADR stages now offer digital interlockable sessions. You can therefore book an ADR stage in New York and schedule the three actors to show up for their lines. At the same time, you can book a small ADR or viewing stage in Los Angeles. Both stages hook up and interlock using an ISDN line.

Logically, these kinds of sessions are simply referred to as "ISDN session." One line handles the time code feed, while a second line handles the digital audio feed of the actors' performance as heard through the mixer's console. A third line handles the communication feed for the director and/or ADR supervisor to communicate with the actors just as if they were on stage with them.

The New York and Los Angeles stages in our example would both have identical prints (or videotapes) of the film with production track. The third line, with time code, interlocks the Los Angeles videotape machine and slaves it to the mechanism of the New York machine. The digital audio feed is decoded through a quality digital-to-analog decoder on the Los Angeles stage and played through a good speaker system. The ADR lines are recorded on equipment in New York and subsequently shipped overnight to Los Angeles for editorial. The price of the hours of phone lines is a fraction of the cost of flying the actors to Los Angeles, paying per diem and expenses, or for the director and/or ADR supervisor to fly back to New York.

RETURN OF THE "LOOPING" TECHNIQUE

As frustration mounts over the issue that the director cannot get his actor to recapture the magic of the production track, one starts to look for alternatives. Naturally, if the production track just did not have that jet noise over the dialog, or if the actor had not been so far "off-mike"—the "what if's" mount up like dead insects in a bug-zapper.

Forget the "what-if's." You will just have to place more emphasis on giving the production mixer what he or she needs to record better production tracks for your next project. You have to overcome the frustration of the here and now. When you have acting talent that is not classically trained, you are almost always going to have to replace more dialog during the post-production phase.

Almost all first-time actors are inhibited and intimidated by the beeps in the ears and concentrating on a poorly projected image of themselves on a screen or on a monitor as they try to match the lips in sync. As they have to pay attention to doing all of this, they cannot possibly concentrate on "acting"—the performance. Yet, isn't that what all of this is about?

Consider this scenario: the actress just could not make it happen. The stage clock was clicking off the hourly rate, the director was frustrated that he wasn't getting the performance, and the actress could not walk and chew gum as the producer's thermometer was rising, foreshadowing an oncoming stroke.

I turned to the ADR mixer and signaled him to shut it down. He was recording straight to a Pro Tools session. I asked him to cut away the production track on either side of the actress's line, highlight the line as much after it and a couple of seconds more. "Go up to 'options' and select 'Record Loop.'" I told him.

I went onto the stage where the actress was about to pull her hair out. The director was literally pacing. I gestured to my ears for her. I told her that she would hear her line in her headsets, then there would be a silent space and then she would hear her line again. Forget looking at the screen, forget trying to sync your lips to what you see, I advised her. "Close your eyes and listen to your line—and then during the silence that follows, perform your line. All I want you to do is focus on being an actress and bring forth your character. You will hear it again, and you will perform it again, with a different inflection maybe. Forget the technical bull%#!* and just act."

The director looked at me suspiciously as I turned. I winked at him and gave the ADR mixer the signal to roll. The actress held her headsets close to her ear and closed her eyes. After a couple of times just listening to her line, she started to repeat it, reperforming it—and the difference was night and day. Suddenly we were getting a performance; the character that was on the screen started to come to life.

Sounds just like the technique we talked about at the top of the chapter, about the studio that had all the actors "loop" all of their lines every day, no matter what. Well it works. And using the "Record Loop" option in the Pro Tools menu makes it easy.

It is also amazing how much material you can do in an hour using this method. Rather than six to eight lines an hour using the ADR method, we were easily doing ten to fifteen! You sacrifice the "toy" playback machine for the director to roll back and forth after each take and review the ADR line in sync—which is not in sync most of the time anyway. What you gain is an actor who can become an actor again. Which method you choose to employ is up to you.

Recording Dialog Using the "Looping" Technique

The technique is the same, no matter what nonlinear system you use. Figure 15.6 shows a Pro Tools session with a line of dialog that has been isolated and highlighted so that the line will play back for the actor, and then the same amount plus a couple of extra seconds during the silent phase so the actor can reperform the line that he or she just heard. Once the recording head (the line that crosses from left to right) reaches the end of the highlighted area it will immediately "loop" back and repeat again.

The key is to get set up properly. First of all, whether you were going to hold an ADR session or a "loop" session, you would have transferred the "cut worktrack" from the locked picture into your work session. Refer to Chapter 17, "Importing the Editor's Cut Track."

Prior to the "looping" session, the ADR editor (who has now, technically, become a "loop editor") would have built a session for each reel of film. In this case the actress's character name is Sara. The loop editor would break out and isolate each character's lines to be looped and place them in their own channels. Rename each audio channel with the actor's character name. Refer to Chapter 17, "Renaming Audio Channels."

This makes it much easier and more efficient during the actual looping session to jump to the next line to be done, thereby not wasting the actor's time by making her or him wait for the looping mixer to scroll down and find each line and prepare it during the looping stage time.

Move the track that has the character lines that you are going to be looping to the top of the session. Name the second audio channel "RECORD." This is the channel

Figure 15.6 Recording dialog using the "looping" technique with the "Record Loop" function.

where you will actually record the new "looped" lines that the actor on the stage will reperform.

Activate the "Solo" buttons on the character channel (in this case, Sara) that you wish to hear as well as the "RECORD" channel that you are going to record to. This will mute all other channels in your session.

Open the "Show Mix Window" under "DISPLAY" in the menu bar. You need to assign all of your character channels—those channels that have the cut-up production track and are meant for the actor to listen to—to Output One (1). Refer to Chapter 17, "Show Mix Window."

Some actors wish to be able to hear their own voice as they are reperforming the line during the silent space. Others would rather not hear it as it may be distracting. If the actor wants to hear his voice, then you need to also assign the Output of the "RECORD" channel to Output One (1). If not, simply assign it to Output Two (2) so that only the looping mixer can hear it in the booth and the director and loop editor can hear it through their own headsets.

This means that you need to have a headset signal path that can bifurcate the playback signal from the actor and the director and loop editor. The loop editor will control who will be able to hear what from his outboard mixing console.

While you are in the "Show Mix Window" mode, make sure that your Input channel assignment for the "RECORD" channel is the same channel that the "line input" feed that carries the signal from the stage microphone(s) are plugged into. Refer to Chapter 17, "The Interface I/O."

Make sure you engage the "Rec" button on the "RECORD" channel. This is an "arming safety." You will not record anything if this button is not on.

Now select "Show Transport Window" under "DISPLAY" in the menu bar. The Transport Window will appear. This is your "tape recorder"—complete with all the controls to interlock, record, play, stop, etc.

Using the "LINE" tool, highlight from the front edge of the cue to be looped and continue on again as long, and a couple of seconds longer. This allows a comfortable amount of time for the actor to reperform the cue in between the playback phases. If the actor is a little slow in responding to reperform, you may have to open the distance up a little wider. With a cue or two you will immediately sense how much extra time you should allow for each actor's style and ability.

Take the cursor and press the button on the far right-hand side of the Transport Window. This is the Record ARMING switch. Once you have armed the Transport Window you are ready to roll. When you press the "Play" button, (the button with the triangle button that points to the right) the record head (line) will start scrolling across the the highlighted area. You will hear the dialog line from the channel above, and then during the following blank area, the actor will reperform the line, which will be recorded in the "RECORD" channel.

Once the actor has reperformed the line (as many times as the actor and/or loop editor and director may want), then press the black square button in the center of the Transport Window. This is the "Stop" button. A bold filename will appear in the region list. It will read "RECORD 01" (refer to Chapter 17, "the Region List"). You can tap twice on this filename of the cue you just recorded. A window will pop up for you to rename this cue. Simply enter the "character" name and "cue number" that is advertised on the loop editor's ADR sheet.

NOTE: Remember that if you end a filename with a number, it is a good idea to put a slash after it. Take the cue above as an example. The time code hour tells us that this is Reel 1. The loop editor's cue sheet shows this line as Cue 107. You tapped twice on the file and named it "SARA 107/." This will avert disk-management confusion when the cue is cut. Pro Tools automatically renames a cut clip with a dash and sequential number assignment (i.e. -01, -02, -03). If you named the audio cue "SARA 107," a cut clip name may read "SARA 107-07." A visual scan may become confusing to the human eye. If, on the other hand, you named it "SARA 107/,"a clip name will read "SARA 107/-07"—a much easier number to visually scan.

This procedure will also prevent you from relying on Pro Tools to automatically name your audio clips, a practice that presented us with a disaster when we inherited a show that had been started by another sound editorial facility. Their protocols were not anywhere near professional and experienced, and they had allowed Pro Tools to autoname based on the name of the audio channel. During the course of the ADR sessions, they had a particular actress come in over seven sessions. Each session started with a new session. When we got the show we discovered that we had seven identical names for seven different performances. "JANICE-09" was being seen by the computer seven different times, and, of course, the computer did not know which "JANICE-09" was the correct one to select to boot up the Pro Tools cut session. In such a case it defaults to the first one it sees—which most of the time is the wrong one.

So you can see that there is more than one reason to be particular about your audio cue name protocol!

Remember what we talked about in Chapter 11—this is the "part number" for this series of performances for this line.

Once you have completed recording the loops for this reel, simply "Save" and "Close" this reel session and open up the next reel session and continue the process.

Once you have with one actor, simply move the track that holds the original lines (in this case SARA) down from the top position, somewhere below the "RECORD" channel, and then move the next character channel up to the top to more easily work with the next actor. You will find that you can move along very swiftly and the difference in the performance material will amaze you.

If the director wishes to see a line in sync with the picture, you can easily pull the line in from the region list, align the waveform against the original line, place the session in interlock by "apple" keystroke "J" and playing the videotape back.

The director should not be encouraged to do this too often as this will slow the session down to a snail's pace. The director should get used to reviewing the scene prior to looping the sequence and then listening to the actor reperform. Remember what we said about the loss of "developing a visual memory" in Chapter 7? The same is true for directors.

REMOTE LOCATION LOOPING

By now the ADR supervisor has all but two of the film's actors accounted for; those two are on other projects. One is on location in Lapland in the northern part of Finland, and the other is shooting in Kenya—both remote locations with no ADR facilities nearby. The ADR supervisor has talked to the production companies of both projects, and both are willing to collaborate in getting the dialog looped. Great! But how do we actually do it?

Using a variation of looping, you take a page from that technique manual and give it a little bit different spin. The ADR supervisor scrolls through the picture editor's cut track (also known as a DIA 1:1, PIX DIA track) on the digital workstation, ferreting out all the lines the two actors must reperform. The ADR supervisor (or assistant) digitally copies each line and groups them together, one after the other. Put a digital DAT into your workstation's DAT machine and feed in 30 seconds of −18 dB line-up tone. Then highlight the first line, and again as much blank with an extra couple of beats as blank space. Go up the "Options" menu and drag down and choose "Loop Playback." Now roll your DAT tape and play the line and subsequent blank space. It will play, then loop and play again, loop and play, loop and play again. Let it record at least twelve to fifteen repetitions. Then stop the playback. Do not stop the DAT machine immediately. If you press the "Rec Mute" button, the DAT machine will record five seconds of silence before it stops and parks itself in a "record stand-by" pause mode. This also allows the actor on location to know you are moving on to the next cue.

Highlight the next dialog cue the same way you did the first one; then repeat the recording process. Take clear and accurate notes of which dialog cues are at which DAT PNO. Put each of the two actors on his or her own separate DAT tapes, as they are heading off to two different parts of the globe.

When the digital DAT and a copy of your ADR notes arrives in Lapland, the actor and production mixer get together after their day's shoot or on their day off. The production mixer in Finland should know where to find a good acoustically "flat" sounding environment to record. It is helpful if the ADR supervisor adds any interior or exterior notes. Such indications guide the production mixer in deciding the kind of environmental deadening necessary. She or he may string up a couple of packing blankets or angled cardboard sheets to trap and flatten reflection or slap.

The production mixer sets up a DAT machine to play back the source DAT you sent. The mixer then plugs in a set of headphones for the actor so that the actor can hear the dialog lines as they repeat themselves "loop" style.

The production mixer sets up a second DAT machine or a 1/4" deck. The note that the ADR supervisor sent along also specifies the kind of microphones used on the original shoot. If the production mixer does not use the exact kind of microphone, one is chosen from the mixer's own set that comes as close as possible to the texture and colorization.

The production mixer lays down line-up tones, then rolls the playback DAT machine as the recorder is rolled. In the headsets, the actor hears the line to be looped, then repeats the line during the silent part of the recording, just as in the traditional looping procedures. This technique works extremely well when you have no method of getting your acting talent to a real ADR stage.

INHUMAN VOCALITIES

On many occasions you may want to use a human voice mimic to perform character grunts, whines, growls and barks of dogs, monkeys, cats, pigs, horses, rhinos—all kinds of creatures. Vocal specialists can emulate huge nostril snorts of bulls, for example; other specialists create unearthly creatures that defy description. As you can imagine, these talented individuals cost more for a day's work than a standard Group Walla vocalist. If you think their price too high, try going out in the pasture with your DAT machine and recording an angry bull snorting. Some cinematic creatures need an entire team of vocal specialists just to create the wide range of vocals, breaths, snorts, and gutturals–no one person can do it all.

GROUP WALLA

The director is filming two actors sitting in a lounge, talking over drinks in the intimate setting of a booth. A couple can be seen sitting in a booth behind the main characters. Occasionally someone walking by or a waitress delivering drinks can be seen. The rest of the bar is brought to life by cutting sound effects of, say, a bartender making drinks off-camera, maybe an occasional cigarette machine movement. Depending on the kind of bar scene, the editor might cut in occasional billiard sounds. The sound effects editor pulls some cocktail-lounge Crowd Walla, everything from intimate conversational murmur to three guys chuckling at the bar to occasional chatter from the back billiard room. This is a classic situation for Group Walla. The sound effects editor lays some library Walla tracks, but the unique specificity of the scene is developed and borne out of the recording of custom Group Walla.

Organized groups specialize in hiring out Walla groups as needed. The supervising sound editor and/or ADR supervisor will choose a group, then have the group leader look at a videotape of the film, along with some initial conceptual thoughts of their goals. After the group leader looks at the videotape, he or she meets with the supervising sound editor and ADR supervisor to go over the notes that were made. Working within the confines of budget restraints, they work together to structure how many voices the budget can afford and how much time will be allocated on an ADR stage. They discuss the need for specialized ethnic or dialect requirements. There may be a need for a session where vocal talent is auditioned for inclusion in the Group Walla session.

The more languages and/or different vocal inflections a vocal talent can bring to a session, the more apt that individual is to work consistently. Sounding different on demand throughout a film is very cost-effective. In big crowd sequences, every vocal performer in the group should field numerous voices, as the ADR mixer records the group several times in the same scene, layering each recording until the Walla Group of twelve to fifteen men and women sounds like hundreds.

There is an important footnote to atmospheric foreign-language Group Walla. Unless you personally speak the language, either ask the actors what they are saying or brief them with a strict set of performance parameters regarding slang. On one such picture, we were surprised to hear Vietnamese theatre goers laughing hysterically during a serious sequence where the hero is hiding in the reeds of a Vietnamese jungle while a North Vietnamese ambush patrol passes by. It turned out that the Walla Group performers had made up a bit of impromptu dialog in which the on-screen North Vietnamese are talking about their command officer, grousing that he was probably lost and did not know where the hell they were. Another performer commented that they were sure that they were going to be ambushed by a roving American patrol. The idea was not really bad–the humor was nice—except the vocalists peppered the dialog with Vietnamese profanity.

A good supervising sound editor works with both the director and ADR supervisor to write specific off-stage vocal dialog, scripting a more accurate and refined finish to a period picture or a film with much technical hardware. Research a period film, studying news events of the day as well as indigenous nomenclature and slang. Well-thought-out Group Walla scripting and texturing for specific sequences adds an immeasurable spin to the atmospheric hubbub.

For *Moscow on the Hudson,* I secured the services of a group of recently immigrated Russians, who would bring with them the latest and freshest of street terms and translation variations that would best fit the picture. I also used them to check over the dialog editing sessions before they went to the rerecording stage to make certain that there were no mistakes, as my English-only dialog editor did not speak a word of Russian. However, as I pointed out to Paul Mazursky, sound is sound; the phasing of dialog tracks (as we discussed in Chapter 14) would make it unimportant that my dialog editor could not speak Russian. He would be able to check alternate takes by audio relationships, and I would have a Russian translator, Anastasia, check his work to verify—that everything was just right. And it all was.

Recording Group Walla

In the past most Group Walla sessions were recorded monophonically. The new trend is recording stereophonically, especially for big crowd scenes. The Group Walla actors are placed strategically around the ADR stage, for a feeling of depth and separation. The ADR mixer records the entire scene with the Group Walla actors standing in a particular position on Channels 1 and 2; then the mixer rewinds to the top of the sequence as the actors move to change the spacial placement of their voices. They not only change their physical position in the room but utilize a different colorization and texture to their voices for the next recording pass.

The ADR mixer safeties the first two channels (so they cannot be accidentally recorded over) and then records the next stereophonic pass on Channels 3 and 4. The actors move again. The mixer records on the next stereo pair, and so on and so forth until they build up a layered crowd that captures the size and energy required.

All these recordings must be recorded flat. No echo or equalization beyond the removal of line or system hums is built into these recordings. It is vital to deliver this material to the mixing stage during predubbing as flat recordings in order for the rerecording mixer to echo and manipulate as desired. To add echo or other graphic or parametric equalization, especially noise gates or expansion dynamics, prior to the dialog predubbing only traps the dialog mixer into signal processing that cannot be undone if inappropriate.

TECHNIQUES OF CUTTING ADR

Cutting ADR is not like phase-matching production dialog. Although the words are the same (most of the time), the precise rhythm and timing is almost always a little different. Some actors are so good at ADR that the editor just imports the ADR line into the edit session and lines it up against the waveform of the production dialog track. When the editor plays it back against the video picture, it lays in precisely.

Sometimes it seems that no matter how the editor syncs it up, too much vowel or word squirts out in the middle or at the end. The editor must learn how to study the human mouth when people talk and see how the lips move when they form consonants and vowels. In doing so, the editor will learn all too quickly that when the human mouth closes, extra modulations cannot spill over.

Start by finding a hard consonant in the word you are trying to sync. Good consonant choices are "D"s, "B"s, or "T"s, as they are executed in one frame. Vowels are drawn out over several frames and, as a result, are not good choices to sync to. "S"s and "R"s are equally poor choices, as they begin modulation without a dramatic and precise movement of sync.

Some ADR editors use computer software that assists in sculpting the loop line in to sync to match the waveform from the production track. Like all technological tools, the software is only as good as those using it, and like most digital processing devices must be used like a fine sable brush rather like than a paint roller. The ADR editor probably will have more satisfying results by learning how to "edit" rather than by relying on algorithmic shortcuts. With a little practice, the ADR editor can learn to sync the hard consonants that dictate precision of visual sync, and then to adjust the vowels and blend them with various combinations and lengths of cross-fades.

With more practice and confidence, the ADR editor can also learn how to steal consonants and vowels from other readings and words and to massage them into the problematic loop line. This kind of work is advisable only for the master craftsman, the ADR editor who knows the actor's voice and inflections as well as his own. To misuse this technology and have the reel bounce on the rerecording mix stage can have disastrous effects and lose you the confidence of the director and producer.

The other side of the coin is pure magic. There is an art form of being able to take the actor's voice and, through the skilled hands of the ADR editor, bring forth a better performance than the actor originally gave.

During the ADR session, the director or producer might request that the ADR supervisor cut alternate readings, as they wish to see which performances work best. Tactically, it is not wise to go to the dubbing stage with numerous alternate readings. The rerecording stage costs anywhere from $400 to $800 per hour and is not to be used as a very expensive audition session.

The smart ADR supervisor has the director and/or producer come to the sound editorial room where the loop lines are prepared. The director and/or producer must listen to the cut material and make selective choices. If it turns out that the director simply cannot decide on a few lines until heard on the dubbing stage, the ADR editor prepares those lines as stage alternates, but this way at least dozens of other alternate preparations are decided on in advance of the dialog predubbing in a much less expensive environment.

Chapter 16
Foley: The Art of
Footsteps, Props, and
Cloth Movement

"They had to blame the failure of the picture on something. So they blamed it on Foley."

Gary Larsen, in a Far Side *cartoon*

In the early days of sound, when the silver screen first developed a set of lungs, relatively few sound effects were cut to picture. With rare exceptions, and only on major motion pictures, sound effects were cut when nothing was in the production dialog track. With each picture the studios turned out, fresh ideas of sound methods pushed steadily forward. Both audience enthusiasm and studio competition fueled the furnace of innovative approaches in sound recording and editorial, along with new inventions in theatrical presentation.

Artisans such as William Hitchcock, Sr. (*All Quiet on the Western Front*), Robert Wise (a director who started as a sound editor before he rose to become a picture editor for Orson Welles on *Citizen Kane* and *The Magnificent Amerbersons*), Ronald Pierce, Jack Bolger, Gordon Sawyer (Sam Goldwyn's legendary sound director), Roger Heman, and Clem Portman overcame more than just new creative challenges—they also overcame the problems presented by the new technology of sound, dealing with constant changes in new equipment variations and the difficulties resulting from nonstandardization.

JACK FOLEY

Even though Warner Brothers had been producing several synchronized sound films and shorts as experimentations with Vitaphone's sound-on-disk system, it was John Barrymore's *Don Juan*, which premiered October 26, 1926, at Grauman's Egyptian Theatre, that thrilled the audience and positively pointed the way for audience acceptance and appeal of sound. These early films synchronized musical scores and some sound effects as much as they could, but the following year it was Warner Brothers' production of *The Jazz Singer* that sent other studios scrambling to license, adapt, or develop systems of their own. Starting out as a stunt double in the Silent Era of the mid 1920s at Universal, Jack Foley soon found himself working as assistant director on several pictures filmed on location in the Owens Valley, then shooting inserts and shorts back at the Universal lot. When *The Jazz Singer* opened at the Warner's Theatre on October 6, 1927, with synchronized singing, segments of lip sync dialog, and a story narrative, it was evident that tremendous opportunities to overcome the new challenges would present themselves.

Universal had finished making *Show Boat* as a silent picture just prior to the premiere of *The Jazz Singer* when the studio realized its picture instantly was rendered obsolete. Universal would have to find a way to retrofit it with sound before they released it.

Like so many breakthroughs in technology or procedure, the mother of invention is usually forced into a dedicated ingenuity by individuals with little choice but to do something never done before, not because they want to, but because they have to. Such was the case with people like Jack Foley. Engineers set up a rented Fox-Case sound unit interlocking the recording equipment to the projector so that the picture would be thrown onto a large screen on Stage 10. A forty-piece orchestra, under the direction of Joe Cherniavsky, would perform the music visually to the picture. In an isolated area to the side, Jack Foley and the rest of the sound effects performers also watched the projected picture as they made various sound effects, even performing crowd vocals such as laughing and cheering, as well as clapping while the orchestra performed—a technique that became known as "direct-to-picture." The retrofitted sound track worked remarkably well, and soon other silent pictures that needed sound were brought to Universal to utilize Stage 10 for similar treatment.

During the first few years of the "talkies," sound effects almost always were recorded on the set along with the actors' voices. Many scenes were not filmed using sound equipment and thus required "direct-to-picture" effects to augment them.

Soon the advent of optical sound allowed editors to cut an ever-increasing amount of sound effects, including footsteps in precise sync to the picture. Such cutting was considered a "sweetening" process, adding something that did not already exist in the production sound track. As the quality of the extra sound effects grew, however, it became clear that cutting in new sound effects would make a much more dramatic and pristine final sound mix than most of the production-recorded sounds. A new labor force emerged, editors dedicated only to cutting sound.

The only footsteps heard in these first sound pictures were the actual footsteps recorded on the set. By the mid 1930s, editors were cutting in footstep sound effects (also known as "footfalls") from the growing new sound libraries to various sequences on an as-needed basis. The technique of cutting in new sound effects grew to the point that most sound editors commonly cut footsteps to all characters throughout the entire picture, all pulled from the studio's sound library. It became more and more difficult to find just the right kind of sounds in the sound library to meet the growing demand to cover subtle movements and props.

Jack spent most of his time "walking" the actor's performances over again, using the "direct-to-picture" technique. By now, Jack and his crew had slowly transformed a small sound stage into a full-time "direct-to-picture" facility (dedicated to sound effects only), with music being recorded on its own dedicated scoring stage. The film projector was synchronized to an optical film recorder (a specially built 35 mm camera adapted for photographing sound via light impulses) in the machine room. As Jack stood in the middle of the sound stage floor, he would watch the projected image on the screen and then custom perform the footsteps and cloth movement to whatever action the selected actor made. He would perform each actor one at a time, thereby layering the various footsteps and movements into a fabric of audio reality.

The recording mixer was seated behind what was referred to as a "control desk" (known today as a mixing console), where he or she carefully raised or lowered the volume level, sending the signal back into the machine room to the optical film recorder, watched by the recordist, who monitored the sound quality that came to it.

Of course, it was not possible to roll back the recording and listen to the performance for approval. Remember, these still were the days of optical sound. The sound image that had just been recorded went to the film laboratory and was developed before it could be heard. Even if it could be listened to, it could not be backed up and played. "Rock-and-roll" transport technology was still years in the future.

Sound craftspersons at Universal referred to the "direct-to-sound" stage simply as "Foley's Room," and when Desilu Studios built its own "direct-to-sound" stage facility, they officially honored Jack by naming their stage the *Foley stage*. The term stuck, and today it is used all over the world.

In those early years many sound editors performed their own custom effect needs, but, as it became possible for films to have customized footsteps from beginning to end, a special performer was needed to walk the entire picture, thereby guaranteeing continuity to footstep characterization and style. A few sound editors spent more time "walking" Foley cues for other editors, slowly evolving into full-time Foley artists.

During Jack Foley's forty-year career at Universal (Figure 16.1), he became the footstep performer of choice for movie stars on a regular basis, each of which had individual characteristics. Jack referred to Rock Hudson's footsteps as "deliberate," James Cagney's were "clipped," Audie Murphy's were "springy," Marlon Brando's were "soft," and John Saxon's were "nervous."

Sometimes the amount of sound work to perform would be so heavy that Jack would get his prop man involved, pressing him into "walking" with him or performing a piece of movement while he concentrated on the primary sound. When Walter Brennan was not busy working on his own picture as an actor, he often spent time walking cues with Jack over at Universal. It was Jack who suggested Brennan put a rock in his shoe, thereby giving Brennan his famous limp.

"You can't just walk the footsteps," recalls Joe Sikorski, a veteran sound editor of nearly 400 pictures, and colleague of Jack Foley during the 1950s. "When Jack performed a scene he got into the actor's head, becoming the character. You have to act the part, getting into the spirit of the story. It makes a big difference."

For the epic battle sequence in *Spartacus*, Jack was faced with a unique and exciting challenge in the scene where 10,000 battle-hardened Roman troops pressed forward in a deliberate rhythm as they approached the ridge where Kirk Douglas and the slave army stood. After consultation with director Stanley Kubrick, and knowing that trumpet brass and heavy drums would be used in the music score, Foley hit upon the idea of putting together hundreds of metal curtain rings and keys strung out on looped cords. He and his assistants stood together on the Foley stage and rhythmically shook the rings in sync to the soldier's

Figure 16.1 Jack Foley had a love and passion for life, which was exactly the way he approached his work. A robust man with an extremely talented mind, Jack always strove to support the story-telling of the film through his "sync-to-picture" customized approach, which the world now refers to as "Foley." (Photo courtesy of the Foley Estate)

feet, creating the extremely effective and frightening effect, uniquely underlining the military might of Rome.

MODERN FOLEY

Alas, the last of the old studio Foley stages has been torn down and rebuilt to service the demands of modern film. Today's Foley stages have evolved into efficient and precisely engineered environments, capable of recording either in analog or digital to a myriad of formats—but most of them lack that really "lived-in" world that made great audio character.

Figure 16.2 Director Robert Wise made a clean-room bio-suit and stainless steel security pylon available for Joe Sikorski to perform the custom sound effect "Foley cues" for the 1970 techno-thriller *The Andromeda Strain*. (Photo courtesy of Joe Sikorski)

A talented workforce of specialists known as Foley artists (a.k.a. "Foley walkers" or "steppers," although-those terms are now considered demeaning by many Foley practition-ers) spend a huge portion of their lives living in these acoustical cavelike stages amid an apparent eclectic junkyard. Figure 16.2 shows an example of a custom sound effect made for *The Andromeda Strain*.

These remarkable sound effects warriors immerse themselves in an amazing type of consciousness, consumed by attentive study of how people walk and move and realistic recreation of sounds that replicate a real-life auditory experience for the audience. Foley artists must create sounds with various available props on hand in order to make sounds like those of other props that are either not on hand or don't exist. The most dramatic body-fall impacts are also created on the Foley stage. Very few recordings in the field can equal the replication of a Foley artist. Years ago, David Carman, a humor illustrator, and his wife

"...Concrete bodyfall, take 2.."

Figure 16.3 Bodyfall.

visited our sound facility in North Hollywood. I gave them an audio demonstration, playing the various sound effects that make the dramatic magic used to acoustically sell the action. One such effect was cue 1030—02, "Groundfalls" (sound cue #39 of the provided audio CD). As I played the series of vicious body falls, David asked how we could make such wicked-sounding impacts.

Teasing, I replied deadpan, "My Foley artist, Johnny Post, lines up all the assistants in a row, and for each take he picks them up one by one and slams them to the concrete. Kind of tough on the body—that's why we go through so many." A couple of months later I received the following illustration that is Figure 16.3. Copies hang in many Foley stage recording booths in Los Angeles.

John Post is considered a grand old gentleman of the Foley art form. I have lost count of how many aspiring young Foley apprentices John has taken under his wing and trained. What he can do with a bowl of vegetables is truly disgusting, not to mention what he can do with an old broken camera, a leaf rake, or an old rotary-phone mechanism, all to create some new high-tech prop gadget on screen.

"Johnny Post is one of the most creative and resourceful sound men I have ever had the pleasure to work with," declares lead Foley artist Vanessa Ament. "He could pick up ordinary 'nothing' things from around the room and perform sounds that you would never imagine could be made with them. He inspired us all how to creatively think—to achieve the sounds we needed with everyday things that lay around us."

Many Foley artists are former dancers, giving them the added advantage of having a natural or trained discipline for rhythm and tempo. Some Foley artists, especially in the early days, came from the ranks of sound editors, already possessing an inbred understanding of what action on the screen is needed to be covered. This background is especially valuable for those hired to "walk" lower-budget films, where full coverage is not possible. Both the supervising sound editor and the Foley artist must understand and agree on what action to cover, and what action to sacrifice when there just isn't sufficient time to physically perform everything.

It is not enough to know that Foley artists perform their craft in specially engineered recording studios outfitted with "pits" and surfaces. Whether one is a supervising sound editor, Foley supervisor, or a freelance Foley artist, traveling to the various Foley stage facilities and researching them carefully is a valuable experience. I have taken many walk-through tours with facility executives anxious to show their studio services to potential clients. Most of these tours were extremely shallow, since most of those who tour a Foley stage really do not understand the true art form in the first place. They usually consisted of walking into a studio with the executive giving a cursory gesture while using the latest technological buzz words and reciting the productions that had just used their stages. When I got back to my shop, I always felt as if I had heard a great deal of publicity but had come away with little more knowledge than I had hadbefore I arrived.

Taking a "tour" is an extremely important beginning, though, especially for understanding the capabilities of the sound facility and for building a political and/or business relationship with executive management. Ask for a "facility credit list," handy during meetings with your client (producer). Discuss the pictures or projects each stage has done. Find out what Foley artists have used the facility recently. Talk to these artists about their experience on the stage in which you are interested, and, if possible, hear a playback of their work. This gives a good idea of the kind of results you can expect.

Look the credit list over thoroughly. Serious facilities are very careful to split out credits into the various services they offer, taking great care not to take undue credit for certain services on pictures that are not theirs. For instance, I noticed that one facility credit listed a picture in such a way as to give the impression that they had handled the Foley, ADR, and the rerecording mixing. I knew for a fact that another studio actually performed the final rerecording mixing, so I inquired about that accreditation. The facility executive was caught off guard, quickly explaining that they had only contracted the Foley stage work. I nodded with understanding as I commented that he might redo the credit list and split the work out accordingly in the future. It may seem superficial and unimportant to the reader, but a precise and verifiable credit list is an important first impression for those deciding which sound facility to contract. If one item on the credit list of your career resume can be called into correction when a potential client checks you out, it can cast doubt over your entire résumé.

Once you have had the facility tour and collected all the available printed information from the facility (including their latest "rate card"), politely ask if it would be all right to visit the stage on your own, both when a Foley session in progress and when the stage is "dark" (meaning, not working). This way, at your own leisure, you can walk around the Foley pits, study the acoustics, and visit the prop room.

IT'S REALLY THE "PITS"

You always can tell if a Foley stage was designed by an architect or by a Foley artist. Most architects do not have adequate experience or understanding in what Foley artists want or need, and, more often than not, they only research the cursory needs of the recording engineers and acoustical engineering. Granted, these are vital needs. Not addressing them properly is facility suicide, but many Foley artists are distressed that so few facilities have consulted them prior to construction, since the stage is their workplace.

Figure 16.4 The "pits" of a typical small Foley stage. The Foley artist stands in these variously sur-faced pits, performing footsteps in sync with the actors while they watch them on screen. Most Foley stages are equipped with both film and video projection. (Photo by David Yewdall)

Most of the Foley stages I have worked with over the years had to undergo one or more retrofittings after discovering their original design did not accommodate the Foley artists' natural work flow or was not isolated enough from noise for modern sensitive digital tech-nologies. They rebuilt the pits, changed the order of surface assignments, and grounded the concrete to solid earth (Figure 16.4). This last issue is of extreme importance, as it dictates whether your concrete surface actually sounds like solid concrete. Oddly enough, most Foley stages suffer from a hollow-sounding concrete surface because they are not solidly connected to the ground.

When I contract for a new job, I run the picture with the producer, director, and picture editor with at least a cursory overview. I have learned to notice how much concrete surface work I must deal with in Foley. If the picture is a western, it doesn't matter. If the picture is a science-fiction space opera, it doesn't matter. However, if the picture is a police drama or gangster film, concrete surfaces abound. Mentally I strike from consideration the Foley stages that I know have hollow-sounding concrete surfaces, because it will never sound right when we mix the final soundtrack.

Back in the mid 1980s I did a Christmas movie-of-the-week for a major studio. Part of the agreement was to use the studio's sound facilities. Since it was my first sound job using its stages, the sound director decided to visit me on the Foley stage to see how things were going. He asked me how I liked it. I told him, "Not very much." He recoiled in shock and asked why. I pointed out through the recording booth windows that the concrete sounded hollow. He charged through the soundproof access door and walked out onto the concrete surface, pacing back and forth. What was the matter with it? It sounded fine to him. I told the sound director that it did not do any good to try to assess the quality of the concrete surface out there; he had to stand back with us in the recording booth and listen through the monitor speakers as the Foley artist performed the footsteps. The sound director stood out on the floor defiantly and asked what good that would do. I explained it made all the difference in the world: what you hear with your ears is not necessarily what the microphone "hears."

The sound director came back to the recording booth, and I asked my Foley artist, Joan Rowe, to walk around on the concrete surface. The sound director stood there in shock as he heard how hollow and unnatural it sounded. He turned to his mixer and demanded why he had not been told about this problem before. The mixer replied that they had complained on numerous occasions, but that perhaps it took an off-the-lot client to get the front office to pay attention and do something about it. A couple of months later I was told that a construction team was over at the studio, jackhammering the floor out and extending the foundation deep into the earth itself.

When you return to revisit the Foley stage facility you are considering, walk around on it by yourself, and take the time to write detailed notes. Draw a layout map of the pits. It is crucial to know which pits are adjacent to each other, as it makes a difference in how you program your show for Foley cues. If you are doing a western and the hollow wood "boardwalk" pit is not next to the dirt pit, there will be no continuous cue for the character as he steps out of the saloon doors, crosses to the edge of the boardwalk, and steps off into the street to mount his horse. To cue such action in one fluid move, the Foley artist must be able to step directly from the hollow wood surface pit into the dirt pit. Now you begin to see the need for a well-thought-out Foley-pit layout.

Note the surface of each pit. Sketch the hard-surface floors that surround the pits and make a note of each one's type. You should have bare concrete (connected to solid earth), a hardwood floor, linoleum and/or tile, hard carpet, and marble at the very least. The better Foley stages have even more variations, including flagstone patio surface, brick, variations of carpet, marble, hardwood, and others.

One of the first surfaces I always look for is a strip of asphalt—real asphalt! A good Foley stage floor has a long strip, at least ten to twelve feet long and approximately two feet wide, of solidly embedded concrete, with a same-size strip of asphalt alongside it. It is annoying when concrete is made to sound like asphalt because no asphalt strip is available for on stage use. These kinds of subtle substitutes really make a Foley track jump off the screen and say, "Hey, this does not connect!"

If viewers are distracted enough to realize that certain sounds are obviously Foley, then the Foley crew has failed. Foley, like any other sound process in the final rerecording mix, should be a transparent art form.

The other important builtin feature is the water pit. No two stages have the same facilities when it comes to water. Before the advent of decent water pits, water almost always was cut in hard effects from the studio's sound effects library. On shows that needed more customized detailing, Foley artists brought in various tubs and children's blow-up vinyl pools. The problem with these techniques, of course, is that the Foley artist and recording mixer constantly must listen for vinyl rubs or unnatural water slap that do not match the picture. Not only does this dramatically slow down the work, but not enough sensation of depth and mass of water can be obtained to simulate anything more than splashing or shallows.

Only big pictures with substantial sound budgets could afford to pay for a major four-foot-deep portable pool to be set up on the Foley stage, as was done on Goldwyn's Foley stage for the film *Golden Seal*. Naturally, a major commitment was made to the Foley budget while the stage was tied up with this pool in place (at least a fifteen-foot-diameter commitment to floor space was necessary for weeks). A professional construction team set it up with extra attention to heavy-duty bracing to avoid a catastrophic accident should the pool break and flood the sound facility floors.

Today almost all major Foley stages have variations of a water pit. Ryder Sound was one of the first when it built Stage 4, their Foley stage, which also doubled for ADR sessions. Unlike many Foley stages, Ryder's water pit is flush to the floor and extends down into the earth three and a half feet. The audio engineer told me that the concrete foundation went several feet deeper, ensuring a solid grounding with the earth for all the pits and floor surfaces.

Invariably, almost all Foley stages with permanently built water pits suffer from the same problem: precise attention was not paid to the slope and surface of the edges of the water pit. Although these pits are deep and can hold enough water to adequately duplicate mass and heft of water for almost any Foley cue, they still suffer the "slap" effect at the top edges. I have yet to see a water pit with a sloped, textured edge.

If your project has hollow-wood-floor needs, check the hollow-wood-floor "boardwalk" pit. I do not know why, but several Foley stages use 2 × 4 wood planks. This size is far too thick to get a desired hollow resonance. Make sure that the boardwalk pit uses 1 × 4 non-hardwood planks, such as common pinewood. Walk on it slowly, listen to each plank, and test each edge. Foley artists often get a hammer and adjust these planks so that one or more of them has loose nails, allowing the artist to deliberately work loose-nail creaks into the performance if appropriate. This technique works well when a character is poking around an old abandoned house or going up rickety stairs. It is vital to be able to control just how much nail creak you work into the track—a little goes a long way.

Many stages have at least one metal deck, and, by laying other materials on top of it or placing the microphone lower to the floor or underneath it, you add a wide variety of textures. Roger Corman's *Battle Beyond the Stars* was an action-adventure space opera with various spaceships and futuristic sets. The entire picture had been filmed in Venice, California, in his renowned "lumberyard" facility, and the spaceship interiors were cross-breeds of plywood, cardboard, styrofoam, and milk crates—none of which sounded like metal at all. We knew we would walk the Foley at Ryder Sound's Stage 4, which had a smooth metal deck set flush to the concrete floor as well as a very nice roll-around metal ladder.

I knew, however, we would need much more than that. Contacting Bob Kizer, the picture editor, I advised him of the problem. "Could you ask Roger to cough up an additional fifty dollars so I could have something made to order?" The next day, cash in hand, I

Figure 16.5 For *Battle Beyond the Stars,* I had a steel diamond deck prepared with six-inch steel pipe legs. Recording microphones could be used under as well as above the deck for an entirely different sound. For this cue, a chain-link fence gate was laid atop the diamond deck to make the "mushy" metal surfaces to Camen's ship. (Photo by David Yewdall)

dropped by the nearest welding shop and sketched out a three-foot-long by two-foot-wide metal diamond deck contraption with angle iron underneath to support human weight (Figure 16.5). The deck was to sit on four six-inch-high steel tube legs and solidly welded in place so the microphone could be positioned under the diamond deck for an entirely different kind of metal sound as desired. Listen to cue #43 on the audio CD provided with this book to hear two examples of metal sounds.

By positioning this deck platform onto the concrete floor or onto the existing smooth metal deck of the stage, we could achieve numerous characterizations to the metal footsteps. We pulled a three-foot section of chain-link fence out of the prop room and laid it over the diamond deck for an even stranger type of spaceship deck quality. For years that metal diamond deck has been floating around town from one Foley stage to another. Every time I need it, an "all points bulletin" must be sent out, as I never have any idea who has it at any given time. Listen to sound cue #40 on the audio CD for several footstep cues performed on the various types of described surfaces. Refer to Chapter 17 regarding the making of a digital-to-digital transfer from an audio CD using Toast Audio Extractor (found in your "goodie" folder inside the Toast software folder) allowing you to make various audio format files for use in nonlinear digital workstations. You can reproduce pristine copies of these effects for your own cutting needs without any fear of signal degradation.

PROP ROOM

Another important place to search when checking out a Foley stage is the prop room. You can always tell the amount of professionalism and forethought given the building of a Foley stage by whether a real prop room was designed into the facility. If a stage has a prop room that is just a closet down the hall, work progress slows down, costing hundreds of dollars in additional hours taken by the Foley artist repeatedly leaving the stage to access the prop room and storage areas.

The prop room should be directly accessible to the stage itself, and large enough to amass a full and continuous collection of props (basically useless junk that makes neat sounds). This "junk" needs to be organized and deparmentalized to easily accommodate easy acquisition. Everyone greatly underestimates what an adequately sized room is. Only a Foley artist can properly advise an architect how to design a proper prop room, complete with appropriate shelving, small prop drawers, and bins for storage. Smart sound facilities will not only have a convenient and adequately sized prop room, but will actively collect various props for it. You never complete this task. Every project will have its own requirements and challenges.

One major studio had employed a sound man by the name of Jimmy MacDonald, who over the course of thirty-five years had custom-made several thousand devices and props for the studio's Foley stage. He was literally the backbone for the studio's reputation for unique sounds as custom-performed for their famous cartoons and animated features. Over the decades Jimmy's masterful craftsmanship continued to make these ingenious and valuable tools of the sound-creation trade. Studio carpenters built a wall with hundreds of various sized drawers with identification tags so efficient and detailed that each prop or group of similar devices could be carefully stored and protected for years of service, allowing quick access by a Foley artist without spending valuable time hunting through the entire prop department looking for what was needed.

In the mid 1980s, when the studio was wavering about whether or not to shut down its aging sound facility or spend millions to redevelop it, it brought in a young man to head the sound department and infuse new blood and new thinking. With hardly any practical experience in the disciplines and art form of sound, the new department head walked through the studio's aging Foley stage to recommend changes. All he saw was a huge room filled with junk. He ordered the place cleaned up, which meant throwing out nearly a thousand of Jimmy MacDonald's valuable sound props. Some were salvaged by quick-thinking Foley artists and mixers who knew their value, some were sent to Florida for an exhibit, but many were lost due to this new person's ignorance. The great sadness is that, with that unfortunate action, a large part of a man's life and contribution to the motion picture industry was swept away. It is difficult to say for how many more decades Jimmy's devices would have still been creating magic. If the young department head only had called a meeting of respected professional Foley artists and recording mixers for advice on assessment, reconstruction, and policy, the entire industry would still have Jimmy's full collection of sound effect devices.

Numerous excellent props have been painstakingly collected over the years from old radio studios by several Foley facilities specially built for making custom sound effects in the days of live broadcasts. One of my favorite sounds that is very hard to record in the atmospheric bedlam of the real world is the classic rusty spring of a screen door. Austin Beck, owner of Audio Effects and veteran of the days of live radio, acquired numerous props from an NBC radio studio, including half-scale doors, sliding wood windows, and thick metal hatches mounted on roll-around platforms. The metal spring in the screen door had been allowed to properly rust and age for years and was used to customize the most unbelievable sounds.

In the final shoot-out scene in Carol Franklin's film, *One False Move*, Michael Beach (Pluto), is mortally wounded by Bill Paxton in an exchange of gunfire, staggers out the back screen door and collapses to the ground in a slow, dramatic death scene. All the country insects and birds had quieted, reacting to the sudden outburst of gunfire. Music did not intrude; no one spoke; the moment was still, electrified with the energy and shock of the moment. The screen door slowly swung back and gently bumped closed. No one would ever suspect that it was anything but production track, but it was not. It was Austin Beck's NBC half-pint screen-door prop.

Foley artists appreciate a well-equipped prop room; although they are known to cart around boxes and suitcases of their own shoes and favorite props, they always want to know that they are working in a facility able to supplement their own props with a collection of prop odds and ends on stage. A Foley artist's boxes of props are the arsenal of tools that achieve countless sound effects. With so many modern films using pistols and automatic firearms, a Foley artist needs a variety of empty shell casings at the ready. Some artists keep a container filled with a dozen or so .45 or 9mm brass shell casings, a dozen or so magnum .44 shell casings, and a dozen or so 30–06 or .308 shell casings. With these basic variants, a Foley artist can handle shell-casing drops as well as single shots or automatic ejection clatters for any type of gunfight thrown their way.

Every Foley artist looks like a shoe salesman from skid row. The shoes in their boxes do not look nice and new. Most look as if the Foley artist had plucked them off street urchins themselves. These shoes are usually taped over to lessen squeaky soles; they have been squashed and folded over, and any semblance of polish has been gone for years. If Foley artists do not have at least ten pairs of shoes in their bags of goodies, they are not serious enough about their work. They should be able to take one look at a character and, regardless of the shoes worn, reach into their boxes to pluck out just the right pair for the job.

We attached sponges to the bottom of John Post's shoes so he would sound like squishy-footed mutants in *Deathsport*. The steel plates wrapped with medical tape on the bottoms of the motorcycle boots worn by Joan Rowe added a certain lethality to Dolph Lundgren in *The Punisher*. Foley artist Vanessa Ament has handled such challenging projects as *Predator*, *Robocop 2*, *Batman Returns*, and *Die Hard*, to name just a few. Outspoken and opinionated, Vanessa is passionate about what she does. "If I don't have the zeal for the work I do, then the creation suffers. There is no life to the performance without passion."

Vanessa submerses herself into the needs of the storytelling process. "That's what we do—we assist the director in telling his story in ways that he and the actors cannot. Try distilling the in-the-pit-of-your-stomach terror of an unseen spirit that is flexing the bedroom door of your bedroom through a spoken narrative. What's the actor going to do, sit up in bed and say 'Gee, I'm terrified?' He or she is so scared they can't talk; are you kidding? We make the audience experience the terror along with the frightened actor through created sound inventions—that's what we do."

Lead Foley artist Dan O'Connell (Figure 16.6) understands the world of audio illusion. From conceptual detailing for feature projects such as *Mouse Hunt*, *Total Recall*, *Star Trek II*, *III*, and *IV*, and *Dune*, to heavy-duty action pictures such as *The Rock*, *Cliffhanger*, *Con-Air*, and

Figure 16.6 Lead Foley artist Dan O'Connell works with his favorite bolt-action prop rifle, specially loosened and taped up to maximize the desired weapon movement jiggles. Dan also carries a belt of empty 50-caliber brass shell casings and nylon straps to recreate gear movement. (Photo by David Yewdall)

Armageddon, to historical pieces such as *Glory, Last of the Mohicans,* and *Dances with Wolves,* Dan O'Connell has developed a powerful and respected résumé for handling comedy, to fantasy, to heavy drama. In his studio in North Hollywood (One Step Up, Inc.), Dan and his associates revel in developing that sound that directors and producers always ask for—something that the viewing audience has never heard before.

"You have to have a passion about your work. Without passion you are just making so much noise to fill the soundtrack, instead of developing the story point with just the right nuance."

SUPERVISING FOLEY EDITOR

If the project is big enough and a supervising sound editor has the budget, a supervising Foley editor may be hired to oversee all Foley requirements. One of the industry's more colorful and successful Foley supervisors is Solange Schwalbe, often referred to as the Queen of Foley. With such challenging pictures as *The Color Purple, Jacob's Ladder, The Fugitive, Lethal Weapon 4,* and *Patch Adams* on her résumé, one can quickly see why Solange's in-the-trenches experience and hands-on style of work makes her a sought after commodity.

Figure 16.7 Foley supervisor Solange Schwalbe is very hands-on when it comes to her Foley. "I won't leave the stage until I know that the mixer and I are of one mind. Why do the cues over again when we can do them correctly the first time?" A mixer with an extremely good reputation, Jackson Schwartz (foreground) works ADR as well as Foley sessions. (Photo by David Yewdall)

In Figure 16.7, Solange runs a sequence with Jackson Schwartz, the Foley mixer, to discuss particular challenges for both surface texture and footstep characterization that may not be apparent by simply viewing the footage.

"When I am set as the Foley supervisor of a picture, I sit and spot with the supervising sound editor, then program the entire show for both footsteps and props. I will go to the stage to work with the Foley artists and mixer to establish the surfaces and props for that particular movie, but I do not sit around and watch every single cue being done. I would rather let the professional Foley artists work as a team with their mixer to expedite the work and not slow down the process with excessive presence. If the movie has special sound effect challenges that require a cue-by-cue decision and finesse, of course, I will stay and work with them to help develop and perform the right sounds. I do go to the Foley stage when they call and tell me that they are ready to play the reel for me. I'll review the work in a playback with them and point out the changes that I want.

"I am very particular about surface texture. If I don't like how the character of the surface is playing, I'll have them redo it. Most of the time, I have already had a thorough briefing with the Foley mixer and Foley artists, so we have already gone over those kind of issues. My lead Foley artist will demonstrate his or her intent for the various characters and surface textures that I have listed in the cue sheets, so before I return to the cutting room we all know exactly what is going to work and what doesn't. If I need to sit on the stage and oversee my Foley artists perform each and every cue then we hired the wrong crew."

I agree with Solange's tactics, for I, too, do not stay and oversee each and every cue my Foley artists perform. However, kicking off the first Foley session became a must-do practice after *Christine*. It was a very busy season that year, and Goldwyn Studios, known as Warner Hollywood today, was booked up. The only way we could squeeze in Foley sessions was to schedule them at night. I asked my lead Foley artist, John Post, if night sessions would be acceptable. He said yes.

The evening of the first session, I was still tied up with other matters back at the cutting room and could not shake free. John had helmed most of my important projects before, so I felt very comfortable with him starting on his own, even though he had never screened any of the film prior to the Foley session. Why should I worry? After all, I had Charlene Richards, one of the best Foley mixers in the business, handling the console. Several hours later, I called to see how things were going. Charlene informed me everything was fine, aside from the fact that the cue sheets did not match anything, but not to worry, as they were rewriting them as they went. I was not immediately suspicious about that disclaimer, but asked if I could speak to John Post. Charlene patched me straight onto the stage to speak to John, who welcomed a break to catch his breath.

John told me not to worry, everything was going fine, but, wow, there certainly was a lot of action in this movie. John asked if I had all those fancy helicopters in my sound library. My thought process skipped a groove. Helicopters? I asked him what he saw on the screen. John said he had never seen helicopters fly between and around buildings like that. I did not waste a moment. "Put me through to the projectionist."

When the projectionist answered the phone, I told him to look at the film rack and tell me what he saw. A loud, unpleasant exclamation burst forth. The daytime Foley sessions had been working on *Blue Thunder*. The projectionist had picked up and mounted Reel 1 of the wrong film, and John Post had been busy creating worthless Foley cues for three hours!

Back then we did not have any head or tail titles for a film until well into the final rerecording phase of the mix. The only way to tell one show from another was by paying strict attention to the handwritten labels on the ends of the film leaders themselves, which obviously that projectionist had failed to do.

EMPHASIS ON FOLEY CREATION

Charles L. "Chuck" Campbell received his first theatrical screen credit on a 1971 motion picture docu-feature entitled *The Hellstrom Chronicles*. "It was an amazing project to work on. Much of the picture was shot with macro-lenses, so we, the audience, are watching the insect-vs-mankind sequences on their level. We had to come up with all sorts of sounds that did not exist or would be virtually impossible to record, like insect leg movements, time-lapse photography of plants growing, opening in daylight, closing at night. I spent hours on the Foley stage to oversee and help make the kinds of sounds that we knew we would need."

Campbell supervised the sound editing on two of Robert Zemeckis's early films, *I Wanna Hold Your Hand* and *Used Cars*, which attracted the attention of Steven Spielberg. Spielberg was impressed with the detailing that Chuck brought to those films and, in turn, asked him to supervise the sound editorial chores on *E.T. the Extra Terrestrial*.

"Needless to say, it was a huge break for me. As is my style, I put major emphasis on creating much of the sound effect design on the Foley stage. I personally oversee it so that I can have immediate input and help the Foley artists focus on achieving the necessary sound cues."

Campbell's attention to detail and almost fanatical use of the Foley stage and its artists helped redefine for many of his peers the importance of Foley. Many rerecording mixers were using Foley as simply a filler (many still consider it such); if the production track or the cut hard effects were not making the action work, only then would they reach for the Foley pots.

Rather than using Foley as a last resort, Campbell shoved his Foley work into a dominant position. "I approach the creation of each sound effect from a storyteller's point of view. What is the meaning, the important piece of action that is going on? The sound must support the action, or it is inappropriate. That is one of the big reasons that I create the sound cues that I want in Foley. If I have them in Foley, why would I waste time and valuable editorial resources recutting them from a sound effect library? I just customized them exactly as I want them for that piece of action for that film."

This philosophy and technique served him and his partner, Lou Edemann, well. Campbell won the Academy Award for Best Sound Effects Editing three times (*E.T. the Extra Terrestrial, Back to the Future, Who Framed Roger Rabbit?*), as well as the British Academy Award for Best Sound Editing for *Empire of the Sun.*

SELECTION OF LEAD FOLEY ARTIST

It usually falls to the supervising sound editor to hire Foley artists. If the supervising sound editor has a dedicated Foley supervisor on board, then it would be wise to include the supervising Foley editor in the decision-making process of hiring the lead Foley artist.

If you are responsible for selecting the lead Foley artist, two issues will guide you into the proper selection. The first one is simple: first know your scheduled Foley dates (actual days booked at a particular facility for recording the Foley performances to picture). This narrows the selection of Foley artists at your disposal because many of them already may have booked Foley commitments. The second issue is the strengths and weaknesses of the various Foley artists available for your sessions. Some Foley artists are extremely good with footsteps. They may have a real talent for characterization and texture, having less difficulty with nonrhythmic syncopated footsteps such as steeplechase sequences, jumping, dodging, or stutter-steps. If you are forced to do a walk-and-hang (often referred sarcastically as "hang-and-pray") Foley job, hire a Foley artist with a strong reputation for being able to walk footsteps in precise sync. (I discuss the pros and cons of the walk-and-hang technique later.)

Some Foley artists are known for their creative abilities with props, especially in making surrogate sounds for objects either too big and awkward to get into a Foley stage or not at the immediate disposal of the Foley artist. Rarely do you find a Foley artist skilled at both props and footsteps, and those who are skilled in both are seldom available because of such high demand.

TELEVISION BREAKS THE SOUND BARRIER

Until a few years ago television sound was not taken very seriously. Most rerecording stages that mixed television series or movies-of-the-week kept a stereo pair of small speakers on the overbridge of the mixing console so they could do a "simulated" TV playback of the soundtrack. This way, they would be confident that the audio material would play through the little "tin" speakers of the home set.

Sound editors and Foley artists were looked upon in a feature-vs-television caste system—and often were deemed incapable of handling feature standard work if they worked on too much TV. I was one of those employers who glanced over résumés and made snap judgments based on seeing too much episodic television. Shame on me–and shame on those who still practice this artistic bigotry.

Since the early 1980s home televisions have evolved into home entertainment centers as consumers have become very discerning and more audio aware. Major home "theater-style" setups, once erected only by the audiovisual enthusiasts with expert knowledge of how to build their own home systems, are now within instant reach of anyone with enough cash for a ready-made system. Major electronics stores have hit teams that sell you the "kitchen sink" system, and another team moves it to your residence and sets it up. Consumer awareness and desire to have such prowess in the home is added to the fact that we are now able to produce sound tracks with as great, and in some cases greater, dynamics and vitality than those produced for your local cinema.

Donald Flick, the sound editor who cut the launch sequence of *Apollo 13*, believed that the film sounded bigger and better played from a DVD through my customized system at my home than he remembered it sounding in the theater. What does this mean to today's television producers or directors? The television show or direct-to-video movie has just grown a pair of lungs and insists that you think theatrical in audio standards. Never again should the flippant excuse be used, "It's good enough for television."

Along with this new attitude has cropped up an entire new cadre of television sound artisans, not only regarding program content, but also regarding working in, and continually excelling in, television's challenging mediums format. One such Foley artist who has done sensationally well in television is Casey Crabtree (Figure 16.8). Casey has specialized in creating Foley for television, both episodic such as *ER*, *Brimstone*, and *Third Rock from the Sun*, as well as movies-of-the-week and miniseries such as *Amelia Earhart*, *Peter the Great*, *It*, *Ellis Island*, *Keys to Tulsa*, *Police Academy*, and *Bad Lieutenant*, to name a few.

"With today's compressed schedules, editors rely on Foley more and more. I create absolutely anything. I have created car crashes, sword fights, lumbering tanks crushing through the battlefield—I even created an entire ten-story building collapsing—on the Foley stage," recalls Casey. "I am particularly proud of my horses. I create horse hooves and movements that are so real the editors want me to do all of it on the Foley stage because it sounds better than any effects that they could cut by hand."

I must admit I took the "horse" statement as being a little too self-assured, since I have been cutting horse hooves longer than I would like to recount. Casey grinned as she detected my skepticism. She proudly had her crew pull a Foley session reel from an episode of Bruce Campbell's *The Adventures of Brisco County, Jr.* I was impressed. Her horses sounded so natural and real—their hooves, the sound of their hooves on the texture of the ground, the sound of saddle movement, bridle jingles-it was as good as anything I would want for a feature film, and this was episodic television.

"For *ER* I do absolutely everything. I have my own prop 'Crash Cart' with all the devices and good-sounding junk that I use to recreate virtually everything from squirting blood vessels to syringes to rebreathers to blood pressure wraps. I even do the pocket pager beeps."

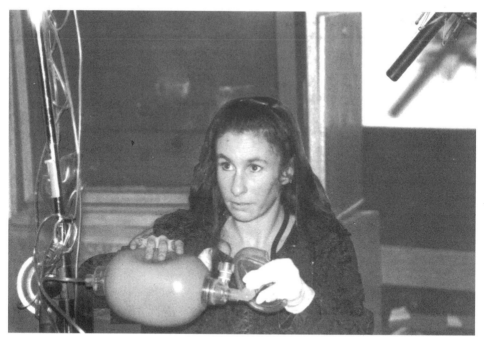

Figure 16.8 Casey Crabtree performs an "ambu" bag as an on-screen medical technician struggles to maintain life support of a patient for the hit television series *ER*. (Photo by David Yewdall)

Although Casey performs her craft on any Foley stage the producer requests, she is quick to point out that every stage has its own voice. "You can do the same kind of action on four different Foley stages, and you will get four different audio characterizations and colorations. Of course, I have my favorite Foley stages as well as my favorite Foley mixers—and I will discuss the options with the client accordingly. Ultimately, it is their decision where their facility deal is going to be, and I will abide by that.

"I had done several episodes of one particular television show over at Film Leaders, and then the producer switched to another Foley stage for one reason or another. They got the material to the stage and did not like how it sounded—not my performance, but the characterization and color of how my performance was reproduced through the microphones of the Foley stage. There is an acoustical imprint or influence that a stage itself has. You have to factor that knowledge into the equation as well."

OBSERVING THE FOLEY STAGE IN ACTION

Visit the Foley stage when it is working. Unless the stage is closed because of a film's sensitivity, most Foley stages do not mind visitation from qualified professionals (or serious "students of sound") for observation purposes. You learn virtually everything you want to know about the stage by quietly watching the recording mixer and artists at work. Watch how the mixture pay attention to the recording levels and the critical placement of the microphones. Although today's Foley artists adjust the microphone positioning themselves (except on special occasions), the recording mixer should be very attentive to how each cue sounds. If the mixer is not willing to jump up and run in to readjust the microphone stand, then that should be a red flag to you about his or her lack of commitment to quality.

Observe how mixer and Foley artist work together. Are they working as a team or as separate individuals just making their way through the session? The respect and professional dedication a mixer has for the Foley artist is of paramount importance. The Foley artist could be working as hard as possible, trying to add all kinds of character to the cue, but if the mixer is not applying at least an equal dedication to what the Foley artist is doing, the cue will sound bland and flat.

Watch the mixer carefully and observe the routine. Is the mixer taking notes on the Foley cue sheet supplied by the Foley supervising editor? Is the mixer exercising common sense and flexibility as changes arise or if the Foley artist requests them?

Do not be afraid to ask the mixer questions about particular preferences. Most mixers have different priorities regarding your cue sheets and notes that make their jobs more efficient. Listen to what the mixer says; if you do decide to use this particular Foley stage, and if this mixer will be on your show, take her or his advice and factor it into your preparation.

The worst thing you can do is not work with and/or collaborate with a mixer. If a mixer feels that he or she is being forced to effect a particular style or procedure without good reason, the Foley stage experience can be very painful. To get the collaboration of the mixer, explain the shortcomings and budgetary realities and constraints you are facing, and you will get a sympathetic ear. Encourage the mixer and lead Foley artist to suggest where you might cut corners. They are sources of good advice and pointers on joining forces to accomplish your job within constraints.

Pay attention to the quality of the sound recording. Does it sound harsh and edgy, or full and lush? Ask for explanations if you are unsure. Embrace the professionals you have hired and pull from their mental knowledge to enhance each cue and each track to augment the audio that you want. It will help you better understand what you need to ask to get you what you want. A big problem that the smaller Foley stages may have is inadequate acoustical engineering. Many times a recording mixer needs to go to the thermostat and turn off the air conditioner because the microphones are picking up too much low-end rumble. This is a sure sign of poorly designed bass trapping (special acoustical engineering to isolate and vastly diminish the low-end rumble) in the air ducts that feed the stage itself. Other low-end problems arise from insufficient isolation from nearby street traffic or overhead aircraft. The Foley crew and I have had to wait on many occasions for a passing jet or a heavy tractor-trailer because the stage walls or ground foundation were not properly isolated during construction.

A few years ago this was not such a problem. The standard microphone was a directional Sennheisser, and the recording levels were meant to be recorded as close to final intended level requirements as possible. In 1980, +6dB recording was adopted for the Foley sessions on *The Thing*. By recording the Foley at a higher level (+6dB) and then lowering it later in the final mix, the combined bias hiss of all the Foley channels being played back together was remarkably reduced, making for a much cleaner-sounding final rerecording mix. With the success of this elevated recording technique on *The Thing*, it instantly became an industry standard.

Digital technologies have accelerated the performance demands of today's Foley stages. Many have stages abandoned the traditional Sennheisers for more sensitive and fuller-sounding microphones, such as Neumann, AKG, and Schoepps. These sensitive and ultra-clean microphones uncover hosts of flaws in acoustical engineering and construction short-comings no matter whether the stages were built for the express use of Foley/ADR recording or not. If not positioned correctly, they literally pick up the heartbeat of a Foley artist. While doing the sound for *Once Upon a Forest,* an animal handler brought in several birds of prey so we could record wild tracks of wing flaps and bird vocals. The handler held the feet of a turkey buzzard and lifted the bird gently upward, fooling it into thinking it needed to fly. The giant six-foot wingspan spread and gave wonderful single flaps. After doing this routine several times, both bird and handler were tired and paused a moment to rest. The micro-phone picked up fast heartbeats as heard down the throat of the bird itself!

Make sure you step back into the machine room and take careful note of the various types of recording and signal-processing equipment. Most Foley stages can record to any medium that the supervising sound editor requests, such as 35 mm fullcoat or stripe, 24-track (2″) analog tape, or several variants of digital recorders such as the eight-channel DA-88.

Today we transfer Foley cues eight channels at a time into Pro Tools workstations. Many Foley editors prefer to use digitized picture, as it is much easier to scrub the image back and forth over the cue to determine exact sync. A great benefit of nonlinear digital editing is that now all Foley tracks can be heard playing against one another at the same time during play-back of cut sequences.

Many sound facilities not only offer the option of transferring the 24-track Foley session into a nonlinear environment, such as Pro Tools, but also of having their Foley stage record the Foley session directly to hard disk; in other words, they record directly into the Pro Tools session.

Solange Schwalbe vehemently dislikes direct-to-disk recording. "I am not a sound engi-neer. All I know is that I work with these [pointing to her ears], and I know what sounds good and what does not sound good. That is why every picture that I work on, I lobby as hard as I can to have the sessions recorded analog to 24-track, using Dolby-SR noise reduc-tion, because it sounds better!"

After the Foley editor cuts the Foley in the digital nonlinear environment, the edited session should be laid back (transferred) to an analog 24-track tape, having been re-encoded with Dolby-SR before being sent to the rerecording stage for predubbing.

Recording Foley cues directly into a direct-to-disk hard drive using digital editing soft-ware such as Pro Tools yields mixed results depending on what quality of D-to-A encoders have been used. Recording action type sound effects such as crashes, metal sounds, and impact sounds directly from the microphone straight into a digital direct-to-disk hard drive is a delicate job at best. Digital recorders do not successfully record hard impacts or concus-sive metallic sound effects that well. The warmth and lushness that analog can capture are often lost. Analog stock with a magnetic emulsion, such as 35 mm fullcoat or 24-track (2″) is far more flexible and forgiving than digital. However, digital transfers them just fine once they have been recorded onto analog via 1/4″ tape, 35 mm fullcoat, or 24-track tape. Our best results were accomplished by sending the signal from the microphone straight into a 24-track analog recorder, running at 15 ips (inches per second) to maximize the iron molecules exposed to the energy of the recording. As the tape passes from the "record" head to the "playback" head, the recorded signal is sent directly into the hard drive for the Pro Tools. This method combines the warmth and lushness of analog with the convenience of digital. With digital technology, you do not have to worry about signal print-through (phantom "echoes" of the high energy passages of a recording disturbing the magnetic properties on either side of the stock several seconds before and after the event), from the moment the tape wraps around on itself.

Most Foley stages have a recordist working with the recording mixer. The recordist works all day with high-quality headsets over both ears. While loading the recording machine, make labels, keep notes, and alert the recording mixer if any drop-outs, static, or distortion are heard from the playback head. In addition, the recordist also handles machine malfunctions, fields incoming phone calls, and alerts the mixer if the session is in jeopardy of running into meal penalties or overtime. The recordist's responsibility also includes proper setup and monitoring of the signal-processing equipment, such as Dolby-SR noise reduction cards.

The recordist also ensures that precise line-up tones (at least thirty seconds) are laid down at the head of each roll of stock. When a roll is completed, the recordist makes sure that it either goes to the transfer department with clear and precise notes on making the string-offs (continuous monaural 35 mm transfers of each channel) for the Foley editors to make precise sync adjustments, or it is set aside for pickup by sound editorial.

Some Foley stages have the recordist regenerating new cue sheets to reflect what is actually being recorded and onto which channel. This practice is based on sloppy Foley cuing done by inexperienced editors who do not understand Foley protocol and procedure. Unfortunately, this extra work diverts the energies and attentions of the recordist away from the primary job of monitoring quality control as outlined above.

CUING THE FOLEY

The best way to cue Foley is to pull out the trusty eight-channel cue sheets (Figure 16.9) and write it up by hand. Don't use cursive–print! And neatly. Remember, too, your recording mixer must be able to read this cue sheet in dim light, so do not use pencil.

The cue sheets is not meant to go to the dubbing stage later; it is simply a road map of intent and layout by which the recording mixer navigates. As the recording mixer executes each cue and the Foley artist is satisfied with the performance, the mixer makes a checkmark by the cue, thereby confirming that the cue was actually done.

As the Foley artist and recording mixer work their way through the reel, they may wish to make changes in your layout, usually to accommodate an item the Foley artist wishes to add; perhaps they feel the need to separate cues you had assumed would be done simultaneously. For instance, you may have made notes in a prop channel, such as Foley-7, that you need Jesse James to draw his pistol, snap open the cylinder, and reload six fresh cartridges. Because of intricate maneuvers with entirely different props to simulate the weapon, your Foley artist might tell the mixer that the "holster draw" and "bullet inserts" will be done in Channel 7 (Foley tracks are referred to as channels), but that he or she wants to redo the gun movt. (the subtle metallic rattle) and the cylinder "snap open movt." in Channel 8 to separate the two bits of action.

Plotting out Foley is extremely important. Cues of different character cannot be jumbled one after another without realistic separation. Be very predictable and consistent—think ahead to the eventual predubbing process on the rerecording stage and put yourself in the chair of the sound effects mixer. The standard rule is as follows: hero's footsteps in the first channel; second hero's (or first villain's, depending) in the second channel; secondary individual performances in the next channels; then background extras using one or more

editor: Tom Burke		cue sheet chart					pg. 1 of 18
FOLEY R-3		show: "Frank and Jesse"			FOLEY R-3		
Foley-1	Foley-2	Foley-3	Foley-4	Foley-5	Foley-6	Foley-7	Foley-8
0' Start	0' Start	0' Start	0' Start	0' Start	0' Start	0' Start	0' Start
9' "POP"	9' "POP"	9' "POP"	9' "POP"	9' "POP"	9' "POP"	9' "POP"	9' "POP"
12' Jesse's F.S.-boots on dirt	12' Frank's F.S.-boots on dirt	12' B.G. Footsteps "A"	12' B.G. Footsteps "B"	12' Frank's HORSE Milling	12' Leather SADDLE SQUEAKS	18' Hardware boardwalk prop movt.	12' CLOTH MOVT.
37'							
58' Jesse's	68'						
72'							

classic Foley cue organizational layout

Figure 16.9 Typical Foley cue sheet log with eight channel sheets.

channels; next, several channels of props—and remember to keep each performance isolated for the sound effects mixer.

Most of your work, unless the budgets are larger and the Foley schedule longer, fits effectively in the eight-channel format. This format fits most digital formats perfectly: eight channels fit into two rolls of four-channel 35 mm fullcoats perfectly. Thinking in groups of four and eight channels is the most logical way to proceed.

TECHNIQUES TO CONSIDER

Most of the Foley expertise you acquire is simply a matter of hands-on experience, getting in and doing it, trying different things, listening to how they sound in playback.

Self-Awareness Tips

You must learn from the start, when around these highly sensitive microphones, to breathe very lightly—not an easy task if you have just completed a rather strenuous cue. I often hold my breath or take very shallow breaths, holding my mouth open so as not to cause any wheezing sounds, for fear the microphone will pick it up.

After a recording mixer reports that a cue was ruined by some extraneous noise (which you probably caused) and it must be done over, you learn to cross the room noiselessly, pretending to be a feather, or you breathe with such a shallow intake as to redefine stealth.

I spent most of the time with my pants off while I was on the Foley stage. (Remember, Foley is performed on a dark stage.) I wore black, close-fitting cotton bikini shorts or a competition swimsuit. The reason was really quite simple: I could not risk unwanted cloth movement. As your ears become more discerning, you discover how intrusive various cloth materials are. If you wish to perform various props and/or non-cloth movement cues as cleanly as possible, you will do anything to achieve the desired level of sonic isolation necessary. Many female Foley artists wear leotards, aerobic exercise garments with little if any excess.

Grassy Surrogate

One of the best ways to simulate grass is to unwind a hundred feet or so of old 1/4″ recording tape. Place the small pile in the dirt pit. When bunched together or pulled apart for thinner textures, walking through grass, or leaf movement on bushes, is simulated amazingly well.

Snow

Probably the substance that most closely matches the sound of snow is cornstarch. Lay an old bedsheet down over the dirt pit or on a section of the concrete floor, then pour several boxes of cornstarch into the center of the sheet, making a bed approximately 1″ thick. With the microphone stand positioned close in and the microphone itself lowered fairly near to the floor, the result is an amazing snow-compaction crunch. Most Foley stages are equipped with two stands with identical microphones. As you experiment with placement and balance, you will find that having the second microphone placed back and a little higher affords the recording mixer an excellent opportunity either to audition and choose the better sounding angle or to mix the two microphone sources together for a unique blend.

The only drawback to tromping footsteps through the cornstarch, as you will experience when you spend a good part of the day performing in the dirt pit, is that you kick up a lot of dust and powder particles. It is unavoidable. The Foley stage should be equipped with powerful exhaust fans that can be turned on during breaks to filter the air or keep surgical filter masks available. Check the sensitivity of the smoke sensors on the stage, as they often get clogged and silently alert the local fire department to come unnecessarily.

Safety with Glass

You may need to wear a surgical mask if the film you are walking has a great deal of either snow or dirt effects to perform. A smart Foley artist keeps a pair of safety goggles in the box, especially for performing potentially hazardous cues such as broken glass or fire. For *The Philadelphia Experiment* (New World Pictures), we purchased one hundred 6′-long, 25-watt lightbulbs and mounted them in one hundred closely drilled holes on a 2′ × 12′ board. When we performed the sequence in the picture where the actor smashes vacuum-tube arrays with a fire ax, we had our biggest and strongest assistant kneel down to support the board in a vertical position. He wore heavy leather construction gloves and safety goggles. For added protection, we draped a section of carpet over him to shield him from the shower of glass shards. I also wore safety goggles, but I wore black dress gloves so as not to make undue noise.

Because we could not accurately estimate the dynamic strength of the recording, we brought in a backup 1/4" Nagra recorder. This gave us not only a direct recording to 35 mm stripe, but a protection 1/4" recorder in the machine room recording at a tape speed of 7.5 ips and a second 1/4" recorder on the stage itself recording at 15 ips! The 1/4" Nagra recording at 15 ips captured the most desirable effect as I swung a steel bar down through the one hundred lightbulbs, resulting in an incredible explosion of delicate glass and vacuum ruptures. I have been ribbed for years by Foley artists who claim that, every so often, they still find shards of those light bulbs.

Fire

Fire is another tricky and potentially dangerous medium to work with on a Foley stage. While performing some of his own Foley cues for *Raiders of the Lost Ark*, Richard Anderson used a can of Benzine to record the little fire raceways in the Nepal barroom sequence when Harrison Ford (Indiana Jones) is confronted by Ronald Lacey and his henchmen. After a few moments, the fire suddenly got out of control, and, as Richard quietly tried to suppress it, the flame nonetheless spread out quickly, engulfing his shoe as it raced up his leg.

In typical Richard Anderson fashion, he did not utter one word or exclamation, but pointed for his partner to grab the fire extinguisher. It had been moved before lunch, however, and was no longer in its place. Steve Flick dashed through the soundproof door to find one as Richard breathlessly jumped around trying to put out the growing threat. He saw the three-foot-deep water pit and jumped in–only it was not full of water, and in a seemingly magical single motion, he jumped instantly out again. He grabbed the drapes under the ledge of the screen and used them to smother the flames just as Steve Flick appeared through the doorway with another fire extinguisher at the ready.

Because of the increased hazard and potential injuries posed by performing various types of fire on a Foley stage, most sound facilities either discourage or forbid anything more than matches and a lighter. The days of burning flares and destroying blood bags with fire on stage (as I did for *The Thing*) are over. Except for instances of careful and exceptional planning with the sound facility and with the studio fire department in attendance, the supervising sound editor should plan for these sound cues to be performed and recorded in any venue other than the Foley stage. Even with the studio fire department supervising during custom recording of a blowtorch in *Jingle All the Way*, the glowing metal of a 55-gallon drum reached a certain dangerous hue, and the fire captain stepped in to say "enough."

Yuk and Guts

When it comes to slimy entrails and unspeakable dripping remnants, few have done it longer or better than John Post. Considered the inspirational sponsor and teacher of virtually half the Foley artist cadre of Hollywood, as stated earlier, John has trained more than his share of aspiring sound effects creators. As of the writing of this book, John is in his fifth decade of working the pits and creating the audio illusions that make his work legendary.

I always liked working with John. He brought a whole different performance to even the simple act of walking. Many Foley artists made footfalls on the right surface and in sync with the action on-screen, but Johnny took the creation to a whole new level. It was not just a footfall on the correct surface—the footstep had character, texture, and often gave an entire spin on the story. I remember being on the rerecording stage when the director stood up and

Figure 16.10 Foley artist John Post squishes paper towels dipped in a bowl of egg yokes to make "autopsy guts" for John Carpenter's *The Thing*. (Photo by David Yewdall)

paused the mixing process. He asked the mixers to back up and replay the footsteps of the actress crossing a room. After we played the cue again, the director turned to us with an amazed expression. He was fascinated with how John Post had completely changed the performance of the scene. Before Johnny performed the footsteps, the actress simply crossed the room. During the Foley session, however, Johnny built in a hesitation by the actress on the off-screen angle, then continued her footsteps with a light delicacy that bespoke insecurity. This not only completely changed the on-screen perception of the actress's thoughts and feelings, but also greatly improved the tension of the moment. Johnny's very act of craftsmanship separates the mechanical process from art. He always approaches his Foley responsibilities as part of the storytelling process. Many agree that John Post knew how to walk women's footsteps better than women. Sound cue #41 of the included audio CD actually is John Post performing the original autopsy sound effect cue for *The Thing*. This recording has been used in perhaps a hundred or more motion pictures and/or television shows since.

As a general rule, I do not reveal how an artist makes magic. Since this book is about sharing and inspiration, however, I will divulge to you how John Post made this famous sound. Johnny set up a large heavy bowl on the Foley stage (Figure 16.10). He then broke half a dozen eggs and mixed them thoroughly, just as if he were preparing a scrambled-egg breakfast. After the Foley mixer received a volume-level test and readjusted the microphone positioning, Johnny dipped several sheets of paper towels into the eggs until they were completely saturated. He then lifted the paper towels out of the brew and voice-slated what he was doing. Johnny proceeded to play with the paper towels, squeezing them, pulling them through his tightened fingers, manipulating the egg goo to replicate that to which our ears and imagination responded.

Hush Up!

You learn very early as you work on a Foley stage or out in the field recording sound effects to keep your mouth shut—even when the unexpected happens. If that crystal bowl slips out of your hands and smashes to the floor, you want a clean and pristine recording of a crystal-bowl smash, untouched by a vocal outburst of surprise or anger. After all, it may end up in the library as one of the proudest accidental sound effects. Every sound editor has a private collection of special sounds attributable to this useful advice.

Zip Drips

Another classic sound is the "zip drip" effect. This tasty little sweetener effect often is performed to add spice, such as the sizzling power line that extended over the downtown square in *Back to the Future* after Christopher Lloyd (Dr. Emmett Brown) made the fateful connection allowing lightning to energize the car that sent Michael J. Fox forward into the future. The Foley artist, John Roesch, burned a piece of plastic wrap from a clothing bag, causing the melted globule to fall past the microphone, making a "zip-drip" flight.

The same technique was used when I supervised *The Thing* four years earlier, only I burned the plastic fin of a throwing dart. As I studied the frame-by-frame action of Kurt Russell lighting a flare before descending into the ice cavern of the camp, I saw a small spark fly off the striker. I wanted to sweeten this little anomaly with something tasty, as there was a moment before the three men turned to go below. We recorded several "zip drips" for this, but as I played them against the action, I noticed that because of the Doppler effect caused by the globule approaching and passing the microphone so quickly, it made the "zip by" sound ascending instead of descending as you might expect. (If you listen closely to the above mentioned sequence in *Back to the Future,* you will notice that the globules falling from the power line sound ascending instead of descending.) Wanting the spark from the flare to have a descending feel, I simply took the recording of the "zip drip" and made a new transfer, playing the original recording backward. It may seem like a small, insignificant bother, but this kind of attention to detail adds up to a more pleasing overall performance, regardless of whether the audience is aware of the detail.

Solange Schwalbe agrees. "For years we have been brainwashed about how dumb the population out there is. I remember someone trying to tell us that the average education level of the viewing public was only fifth grade. What a bunch of hooey! The audience is not dumb. They are very intelligent and sophisticated, and they notice absolutely everything. I was very lucky when I started in Foley. Gregg Orloff, a Foley mixer, really changed my professional life and my awareness and attention to detail when he taught me the difference between a creak and a squeak. Think about it. What kind of a difference could that possibly make? Believe me, it makes all the difference in the world. Today, I take that very example that Gregg taught me and I pound it into those who I now train and inspire. Don't perform down to what Madison Avenue thinks the public is, set your sights higher and challenge the audience upward. It sure is a lot more fun."

EDITING FOLEY

In the days of magnetic film, we had transportation runners wheeling hand dollies into the editorial rooms stacked high with hundreds of pounds of 35 mm stripe—hundreds of 1,000-foot rolls. Each roll represented a single Foley channel of a single reel of a movie. These were called "string-offs" because they were transferred one channel at a time to one roll of film at a time. We threaded up each roll on the Moviola and interlocked the start mark with the Academy start frame of the Foley string-off. For hours we rolled back and forth, checking and correcting sync, cutting out frames to condense, adding frames of blank film to expand. Our Rivas splicers clacked and whacked every few seconds with another cut decision. It was not unusual to use up an entire roll of splicing tape on one channel roll of Foley. Back then, one roll of 35 mm white perforated splicing tape cost over $15. Each foot of 35 mm magnetic stripe film cost 2.5¢ (from the manufacturer) and as much as 7¢ a foot for the labor to transfer it. That means that every foot of stripe was costing approximately a dime. If we held the show to eight Foley tracks per reel, we burned off at least 80,000 feet of Foley stripe transfer. Some sound facilities were using an average of twenty-two to forty-four channels of Foley for action features.

The Foley cutter is just as much an artist as the person performing Foley on stage. An interesting axiom is that precisely cut Foley sometimes does not play as well as creatively cut Foley. While cutting Foley on *Predator 2,* during the sequence where Glover and Paxton chase the alien up to the rooftop, I cut each and every step in precise sync. The men burst out of the room and into the hallway, slamming up against the wall, turning and running down the hall, then turning and vaulting up steel stairs—steeplechase-style running and maneuvering. I cut it all in exact sync, using three rolls of splicing tape per Foley roll. Then I played it at real time. It felt funny. I knew it was cut in exact sync, but exact sync wasn't evoking the passion and rhythm of the sequence.

I pulled it apart and spent another day just cutting movements and turns to accent the sweep and moment of the action. I discovered that by changing the footsteps that had been performed, by moving the order around so that a more forceful footfall was replaced by a lighter one, and the heavier one placed in a more strategic spot to emphasize a particular change of body direction, I made the performance take on a whole different spin. Suddenly, power and energy backed up the visuals on the screen.

One of the harder techniques to master is cutting footsteps in precise sync when you cannot see the feet. Most beginners think this is easy stuff. After all, you cannot see the feet, so just let the footsteps roll. It doesn't play quite right, however. To cut footsteps when all you see are talking heads and torsos, watch the shoulders of the actors. Flip frames slowly. Each frame of walking has a natural blur to it except when the foot has just impacted the ground. That one frame has a perfect focus. To that frame you sync the footstep sound. If the footsteps still feel odd, try changing feet. Sometimes sliding down the left foot's impact sound and syncing it to the right footstep makes all the difference.

"For me, cutting sync is not a matter of exact precision. Because light travels faster than sound, I like to cut the footsteps one frame prior to focus frame [visual impact]," says Solange. "It gives a better appearance of sync when playing at normal speed as heard in the theater—it just feels better."

As opinionated as Solange is about having her Foley session recorded in the analog domain, she is equally stubborn about cutting in the digital domain. "I just love cutting digitally. I can do so many things in Pro Tools that I could never do in analog with film. One of the techniques I use is not be tempted to just dive into the session and start whacking and hacking. Before I cut, I must prep—you know, how your mother made you wash your hands before you sat down to dinner. I magnify the waveforms of the tracks so high that they become blocks of color. This way, I can see all of the most sensitive and subtle recordings without having to take the time to play it all. I will highlight and cut out all of the strips of silence in between the individual cues, then highlight and rename the regions. This way I can highlight and cut all the strips of silence between individual cues, then highlight and rename the regions. This way I can cut and fiddle around with individual cues all I want, but every cut won't just come up as Audio-01 and its subcut. It will always say, 'hero footsteps 13 or 14 or 15,' but it will always say 'hero footsteps,' or whatever that particular region has been named, whether it be footsteps or props. Otherwise, if I open up a session and just visually look over the cuts, I wouldn't know what Audio-01-23 was over Audio-01-48. They might be from the same sequence; they may very well be an entirely different cue within Audio-01. I have no way of knowing.

"I don't know why, but a lot of sound editors don't do this region prep, and then they have trouble with their audio files and cue sheets later. To me it's just common sense."

For many Foley artists who develop the rich footstep, movement, and prop creations prevalent in today's entertainment, the term "Foley" itself is no longer enough. Years ago, the process helped fill in the subtle, but important, footsteps and movement the production track lacked. Today, the Foley artist creates sounds that Foley walkers never dreamed about fifteen or twenty years ago. On *Extreme Measures*, Foley artists created the entire subway train, complete with the feel of massive tonnage, steel wheels shrieking on rails, cavernous echo—all of it! This is no longer Foley. This is custom sound effects creation at its most liberated.

PRO TOOLS—RECORDING TECHNIQUE USING DIGITAL DIRECT-TO-DISK

Recording straight to hard disk using a nonlinear system such as Pro Tools has become more and more popular, especially as the D-to-A converters have improved. The technique is easy (Figure 16.11), and with a little practice you will quickly develop your own preference for naming Foley cues and how to manage your track assignments.

Refer to Chapter 17 regarding setting up a new Pro Tools session. Once you have created your session, draw down from the "FILE" in the menu bar and select "New Track . . ." I usually start by creating eighteen tracks. The first track I rename "GUIDE," which is where I import the editor's cut worktrack—or 1-to-1. It is a good idea to have the editor's worktrack at the ready in case the Foley artist would like to listen to it, to get a sense of what he or she might need to do, such as evaluate a surface. I usually leave this track in the "MUTE" mode unless the Foley artist wants to review it.

Rename the second audio channel "RECORD." This is where you will record all of the incoming Foley performances. Think of this as a scratchpad—a place to record, dump it out if you do not like it, or keep it and rename it before you pull the cue down into the Foley channel where it will reside for subsequent editing and final predubbing.

Rename the rest of the audio channels "FOLEY-1," "FOLEY-2," "FOLEY-3," and so forth. This gives you sixteen Foley tracks. Remember what we talked about—thinking in groups of eight? Unless you are getting into complex action, sixteen channels of Foley should

Figure 16.11 A typical Pro Tools Foley session. Here a Foley artist is recording the sound of a character walking up a spiral staircase.

be plenty. If it turns out you need more, no big deal, you can add more as you need them. I always do.

Open the "Show Mix Window" under "DISPLAY" in the menu bar. Refer to Chapter 17, "Show Mix Window." Make sure that your Input channel assignment for the "RECORD" channel is the same channel that the "line input" feed that carries the signal that the stage microphone(s) are plugged into. Refer to Chapter 17, "The Interface I/O."

Make sure you engage the "Rec" button on the "RECORD" channel. This is an "arming safety." As we talked about in Chapter 15, you will not record anything if this button is not on.

Personally, I record in "GRID" mode. Note the highlighted rectangular box in the upper left-hand corner of the session window with the word "GRID." This means that I will record either exact second to exact second or exact frame to exact frame. I like to record in "GRID" mode with the "NUDGE/GRID" reference (shown on the upper right hand corner of the session window) in the "1 SECOND" option. This makes it extremely easy to accurately move cues up or down from one audio channel to another channel without loosing sync once I have recorded the cue into the session.

Now select "Show Transport Window" under "DISPLAY" in the menu bar. The Transport Window will appear. This is your "tape recorder," complete with all the controls to interlock, record, play, stop, etc.

Using the "LINE" tool, highlight from just in front of the spot you wish the Foley artist's performance to be recorded to a couple of seconds past the "out" cue advertised on the Foley Cue sheet. Pro Tools will automatically kick into "RECORD" mode when the timecode hits this highlighted area and will kick out when it reaches the end.

You do not have to highlight the cue area. If you would rather, you can simply place the record head "line" at the spot you wish to record, and later stop recording by hitting the "STOP" button on the Transport Window when you wish to stop.

Either way, you need to rewind the videotape approximately ten seconds prior to the start point you wish to record. This pre-roll is not only to allow the session to interlock with the timecode but it allows your Foley artist to get focused on the action that he or she is about to perform–especially necessary when it comes to rhythmic footsteps.

Once you have run the sequence for the Foley artist and she or he is ready to perform, take the cursor and press the button on the far right hand side of the Transport Window. This is the Record ARMING switch. Once you have armed the Transport Window you are ready to roll. Make sure that you are interlocked with the timecode signal, by pressing "Apple" keystroke "J." The little window at the bottom left hand corner of your session window will show "WAITING FOR SYNC." The little "clock" window on the far left hand side of the Transport Window will glow blue.

Roll the videotape. The timecode will be seen by the Pro Tools session and will interlock. The record/playback head (line) will start scrolling toward the top of your highlighted cue. When it hits the cue area the session will jump into "RECORD" mode.

Once you have finished the cue (Figure 16.12), the recording will either stop on its own (if you use the highlighted method) or you will hit the "STOP" button.

Figure 16.12 Once you have completed a cue, tap on the waveform twice and rename the cue.

Tap twice on the audio cue that you have just recorded. It will probably say "RECORD-01". Now enter what you want the cue to be called. I use a technique of entering a reference number in case I have to rebuild sync positions. If you will note, the cue started at the thirty-eighth second of the fourth minute. So, I enter "04/38/00" prior to a short action name. Should something happen to my original session, I can easily make a new session and throw the cues very quickly into "performed" sync locations by using the minute-second-frame designations. Pro Tools protocol will not allow you to use a colon in the name, as you would write out a timecode number, so I use a slash instead.

Once I have named my cue I will use the "HAND" tool and grab the cue and drag it down into the Foley channel where I intend for it to reside. On to the next cue.

IMPORTING FOLEY STEMS INTO PRO TOOLS FOR TRACK STRIPPING

Some Foley stages still use DA-88 tapes for recording Foley, or you may have a stage that is recording deluxe-sounding analog Foley to a 24-track with Dolby-SR noise reduction. Whatever the reason, you may receive material that will need to be imported into a Foley session as "STEMS." The "STEM" technique is extremely wasteful when it comes to disc space. It chews it up at 5 megabytes per minute, per channel. Which means that if you have a 24-channel Foley session of an A-B reel of film, you are looking at 2 to ½ gigabytes of memory per reel. Most of the timeline of the stems are empty blank space, with a few cues of Foley every so often. If you are blessed with unlimited memory resources, you do not have a problem, but many craftsmen do not have unlimited memory allocations. Even more important is the archival space that may be necessary to waste afterwards.

When I receive Foley sessions as "STEMS," the first thing I do is import them into a Foley session (Figure 16.13). If you are transferring from a source medium, slave the session

Figure 16.13 Foley "STEMS" are imported into a Foley session, ready to work with.

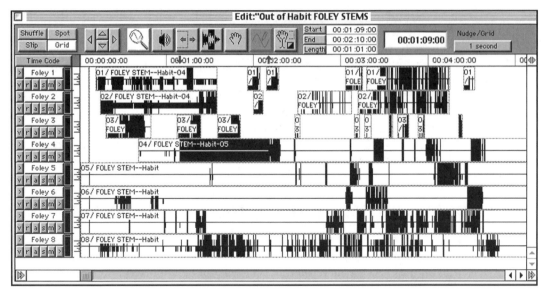

Figure 16.14 Increase the waveform signature to clearly see if there are any subtle Foley cues lurking about.

to the time code of the source medium (DA-88 or 24-track, etc.). The Foley stems will lay into your Foley session in sync. Once you have finished, go to the head and look at the first "six-second" position in the timecode. There should be a "pop" there. If not, you have no exact frame reference to start with. Your better Foley stages will always put a reference "pop" in their sessions.

To better look for any subtle recordings, increase the waveform signature by tapping on the "up" arrow (Figure 16.14). (Look at the four-arrow array in the upper left-hand corner of your session window, next to the magnifying glass). Tap on this several times until the track becomes thick black. Any subtle recordings will appear clearly now, and it makes it very easy for you to determine what wasted areas you wish to eliminate.

Software writers at Digidesign will scoff and ask me why I do not use their "STRIP SILENCE" option under "EDIT" in the menu bar. Well, I have used it—but even changing the presets to open the pre and post-roll and sensitivities, I have still experienced clipped overtones and giblet cut-up cues that are really inappropriate. I find it safer to just take a few moments and do the job manually. Like all good art form, good craftsmanship is done by human tactile interaction. And, like all "programmed parameters," computers only do things literally. They do not judge or evaluate, then make their own educated or creative decisions. Only human beings can do that.

Now I will quickly go through and decide which areas of silence I wish to eliminate. It is important to work in "GRID" mode with a "1 SECOND" "NUDGE/GRID" option for fast resyncing (Figure 16.15). Highlight the areas of silence you want to delete.

Once you have done that, tap twice on each cue and rename it (Figure 16.16). Once you have renamed the cues, highlight all the audio cues in the session. Then go up to the bar

Figure 16.15 Highlighting empty track areas in "GRID" mode with a one-second "NUDGE/GRID" setting, erasing the wasted silent sections.

above the region list with the "AUDIO" designation and open that menu. Come down to "Export Selected as Files." A menu will come up asking you what audio format you want, what sample rate, etc. Refer to Chapter 17, "Export Selected as Files." You need to choose a target folder to put these new audio cues. Once you have set the parameters of the export, initiate the transfer.

Figure 16.16 Refer to the Foley cue sheets for reference, then tap on each cue and rename the region.

The session will output each cut region as a new audio file, named with the new name that you gave the cut region in the session. Once the process is complete, (and it does not take very long, especially when using a Mac G4) go back up to the "AUDIO" bar and import these new files. They will line up as bold, black titles against the non-bold cut- region names. The bold, black titled audio cues are your new files. Now is when the "GRID" mode of "1 SECOND" really pays off. You can quickly grab and pull in and snap to sync each bold titled audio file against its cut-region counterpart very quickly.

Once you have done this, you can save and close your session. Open up your session folder where the original Foley STEMS reside and drag them into your computer's TRASH barrel and flush them away. Take a moment to be sure that all you are throwing away are the original STEMS and not your newly created audio files. You will probably discover that you have reduced your drive-space consumption for the Foley session by at least 60 percent and oftentimes as much as 80 percent.

Doing this makes your session far more efficient to work with, both for you and for those involved in shipping data and archival.

IT WILL ALL COME TOGETHER

If you have not worked on the creation of audio art, undoubtedly it is difficult to understand its techniques and philosophical issues, but, as you learn the process by which the sound track evolves, you eventually will come to understand everything better. Some of what has been described here will make sense to you as you read, but other parts will evolve into a sharp focus of understanding only as you practice one or more aspects of sound creation. Then, at the strangest moments, when you least expect it—and often to the amusement of those around you—you will swear you had an epiphany induced by extraterrestrial intervention. It was that way for me, like a bolt of lightning: suddenly two points of technicality collided to bring forth conceptual understanding, and then my mind became a sponge, soaking it up.

Just remember this: the best Foley, just like great dialog editing, is a transparent art form. If the audience is aware of what we do, we have pulled their attention away from the film reality we are creating, and therefore we have failed. So go out and make Jack Foley happy.

Chapter 17
Nonlinear: The
Digital Workstation

I slip into my ergonomic workstation seat with self-adjusting hydrolifts to support my back and correct my posture. I flip on the system. My liquid helium hard-drive cylinders glow to life. My system is not considered to be bulked up with memory, but I do like to have 3.4 terabytes of instant access, especially on the larger feature films. At times I can remember when we still struggled with 24-byte 48 kHz sampling-rate sound files. Drive management was so much more difficult then. That was when data was stuck on rigid surfaces that spun at high rates of speed. Now, with liquid helium, fragmentation never occurs because nothing moves, in the old sense of the word, and thus the concept of a computer crash has ceased to exist. I slip on the infrared wristband and boot up the newly installed Pro Tools 12.1 software. The blue laser of my optical computer drive flashes to life and stabilizes.

The Neurosine plug-in is becoming easier to work with. Its creative freedom has taught me to just lean back, relax my head into the neck pad of my ergo-lounger and simply think through the process. I do not have to manipulate a trackball or use a freehand pencil pad to articulate my DSP wishes, as we had to do a few years ago. Just a short time ago I used to have to watch each process unfold on my crystal monitor screen, but I have learned to trust my hearing more than my vision, so I simply close my eyes to begin my day's work.

The wristband interfaces with my nervous system straight into the audio software linkages, and the computer instantly extrapolates what I think. It took a while for the computer and me to bond. The personal filter files disregard the vast amount of "brain" noise, allowing only the focused solution-seeking elements of neurotransmission. In short, I am a creative person with a busy brain stem who also tends to be a little scatterbrained, but the Neurosine plug-in has really helped me with that.

I call up an old recording that Dr. Regusters of the Jet Propulsion Laboratory made in the Congo years ago. I go to work on separating the loud and hashy presence of the atmospheric insects from the distant cry of a Mokel Mobimbe. Within an instant, the holographic dynamic pattern hovers over the center of my workstation as well as in the center of my mind's eye. I study it carefully. Sound technology has changed so much with the advent of select timbre analysis. The traditional two-dimensional thinking had gone as far as it could. Now three-dimensional study and manipulation of sound has changed everything.

I see the insect noise in my head and wish for an overview of the exact components. Suddenly, color values are applied to all points in the timbre analysis, rendering what looks like a magnificent galaxy filled with trillions of multicolored stars. My brain rotates the overview so I can study the interwoven blends of colors. Like an onion being peeled, my thought pattern separates and assigns to the digital clipboard each color value that does not fit the desired outcome. Bit by bit the insect hash layers diminish.

I invert the audio envelope, like turning a positive into a negative, much as the old rerecording sound mixers used a universal dip filter to isolate and then revert to ferret out the precise scope of an offending noise.

The insect hash is totally gone. Now all I hear is the gentle sway of tall dried grass and the gentle lap of the lakeshore water—and every so often the mournful cry of the Mokele. My mind sweeps in closer on the image of its timbre. Now it is easy to isolate it from the grass and water lap. I do not want to lose the other sounds completely, so I mentally ask the computer to "Save As" and file it away under Africa, Grass, Regusters, and Water.

There, rotating in all its glory, is the undulating timbre wave of one of the most magnificent and lonely cries that natural history has probably ever heard. I wish for the enrichment plug-in to fill in the missing gaps the algorithm noted were lacking. Yes, please save. The revised audio file disappears into the vast molecular storage structure of cold liquid helium.

I feel a hand on my shoulder. I open my eyes to see my friend and dialog editor, Dwayne Avery. Oh, I must have been napping. I rub my eyes and wonder what happened to my wristband. I see that I was sitting in my stiff so-called "lumbar-support" chair—I swear, whoever does invent the ergonomic editing chair will make a fortune—and where did my Pro Tools 12.1 go? Oh yes, we are still some years away from that. But these very technologies are in development right now, some of them a lot closer to reality than you think.

PRACTICAL PHILOSOPHY

Each chapter of this book could easily be expanded into a complete book of its own; therefore, the focus is on the practical art form and technique that can empower you, whether you are writer, director, producer, picture editor, just beginning to venture into the hands-on applications of working with sound, or simply fascinated by the audio arts.

With that in mind, I present here an extremely basic overview of the nonlinear digital audio workstation and a few softwares that will launch you in the right direction. The tidal wave of hardware and software that exists can be daunting even to the experienced craftsperson. With very few exceptions, those individuals who truly understand digital applications and can use the softwares proficiently do not tend to be very great sound artists. Those who are great sound editors or can create audio works of art often struggle just to move around in the vastly complex world of software technologies. This is a phenomenon I have noted time and time again.

Some film school students who had a single course in Pro Tools and have been taught all kinds of tricks and shortcuts nevertheless lack an understanding ofbasic sound editing disciplines and techniques.

Yes, I use some simple "keystroke" shortcuts with the digital softwares, but I shun the "super-shortcut" tricks. Those who have the most trouble with edit sessions, and especially with exactitudes to synchronization, can trace the roots of their nemesis directly back to the use of "super-shortcuts." These techniques work only in ideal situations, where each preceding step is followed exactly and everyone does her or his job correctly. As has been demonstrated repeatedly, just the opposite usually prevails. The very art of editing is to problem-solve in addition to asserting one's own creative voice. How can one possibly hope to use "super-shortcuts" in a flawless manner amid the production and post-production tempest?

NONLINEAR EDITING PLATFORMS

With few cosmetic differences, most nonlinear sound editing platforms work pretty much the same way. Many have their own proprietary "somethings or others," and a few excel in exceptional signal-processing prowess over their competitors. But when it comes right down to it, if you understand the basic techniques of how to set up sessions, what drives sync for these sessions, how to route a signal path (both audio as well as time code) and the basic principles of audio signal processing, then you can move back and forth through the various manufacturers fairly easily.

Several audio workstation manufacturers can be found in the workplace today. Think of the nonlinear audio workstation as a digital Moviola, a digital synchronizer, a digital Rivas splicer, and a combination of all the other audio tools used by sound craftspersons through the decades since Alexander Graham Bell invented the telephone. For the sake of streamlining this chapter as we discuss the nonlinear world of sound editing, and because Pro Tools is arguably the dominant nonlinear audio workstation platform in the motion picture business, we will discuss the nonlinear issues in the context of the procedures and protocols of Pro Tools.

This book does not try to instruct in the full use of this software program—that subject would be a big fat volume of its own, and teaching Pro Tools is not the mission of this book. This chapter is meant to be a "get-start" primer to get you up and online and your wheels squarely on the track heading in the right direction. By the time you finish digesting this chapter you should be ready to tackle the owner's manual of your nonlinear system, and it will actually start to make sense.

Remember that virtually all audio software and hardware have been designed, and text manuals written, for music users. The vast majority of the consumer market for these products is not the sound editing market but music composers (and the thousands of "hope-to-be" music composers), music editors, and developers. Hence the user manuals talk in music terms; they are not written for sound design and sound editorial people directly.

One reason that user manuals are seemingly impossible to understand is that they are written with the supposition that you are a computer-techie who already knows how to use computers or basic softwares. Most of the problems I hear are, "I can't get it open" or "How do you get the software to see a file" or "How do I get from here to there?" and the proverbial, "Someone has erased part of my files." Therefore, I will include basic highlights that should problem-solve many of the get-start questions that I am constantly asked.

This book is not going to deal with the volatile and ever changing "keeping up with the digital Joneses" syndrome. We all know that Apple's OS-X operating system has caused major disruptions in the use of software developers and many favorite tools that editors have been using for well over a decade now. The fact that many of the favorite tools will not operate on OS-X and that some of the software developers who made those "favorites" are not even in business now does not help the situation.

The advent of high-definition systems does not alter the basic platform style and art form of editing—it simply adds more firepower to the processing refinements of sample rates and bit depths, with a greater accuracy for clarity and fullness.

As for this chapter, before you swim in the deep end, you first have to learn how to swim. Once again, let me remind you that a computer is only as smart as you are. When you call it stupid, you are really calling yourself stupid. You were the one who did not set the disk allocation logically. You were the one who did not set the session setup window correctly. You were the one who did not set the hardware settings before slaving sync to the videotape source. You get the idea.

NONLINEAR AUDIO SIGNAL PATH

As touched on briefly in Chapter 11, you must create a clean signal path from your audio file source, through your sound interface (such as the Pro Tools 888 I/O Interface), through the computer, back through the interface, out through your workstation mixer, out to your speaker amplifiers, and to the speakers. You must have a clean "input" path where you can digitize (record) both monaural and stereophonic analog sound into an audio file format that your workstation recognizes and uses. You also must have the ability to transfer material digitally (known as D-to-D) from DAT cassettes, such as a DAT recorder, using AES/EBU "Ins" and "Outs" or a coaxial digital processing cable. Many beginners do not understand that they must use a high-quality digital coaxial cable for D-to-D work, often mistakenly using common RCA connectors.

When it comes to your signal path, whether a digital or analog signal, it is wise to spend a few extra dollars to have the best quality connectors and speaker cable for your gear. Not only will they make the signal path cleaner and easier to listen to, but you can be assured that you are not adding noise and audio gunk to your recordings or downloads.

The Interface I/O

The Pro Tools 888 I/O Interface handles eight discrete channels of either analog or digital audio signal. Even though the 888 I/O allows sixteen "voices" (channels of material you can listen to simultaneously), you can input or output only eight discrete channels. If a bigger system is needed, add one or more 888 I/O. Each interface requires its own expansion slot in your computer's chassis, so always choose a computer designed with expansion-slot requirements in mind, such as the PowerMacs. Each interface gives eight more inputs and outputs as well as sixteen more voices. By the very virtue of how electronic hardware and software is developed, however, no sooner is this text written than it is already out of date.

I have a custom-designed workstation desk for my Pro Tools setup because I want my two Digidesign 888 I/O interfaces in front of me in an underbridge configuration. I use four 100-gig external hard drives in a pair of twin removable drive racks in my lower-right rack-mount cabinet.

Remember the outboard gear array shown in Chapter 11? That is where I have my touch "keypad"-activated DAT recorder, which makes calling up precise program number cues much easier than using a hand remote. The analog signal goes to the Klark-Teknik 30 band equalizer, then to the Night Technologies EQ3, then to the Eventide Ultra-Harmonizer—and then into the Pro Tools 888 I/O Interface. I also have a high-quality digital coaxial cable that allows D-to-D transfers directly from the DAT machine up to the 888 I/O.

You must have a cost-effective, but high-quality, workstation sound-mixing board. You bring the Pro Tools "outputs" up to your mixer. This unit is not for rerecording mixing, but for hearing the work you are doing in a controlled manner. Your mixer also has "inputs" and "sends" so that you can plug in your audio CD player and/or DAT machine for auditioning material separately from and prior to recording into the computer. Mackie makes excellent workstation mixers in a variety of sizes and capacities, with a transparent clarity exceptional for its price.

Your mixer has a 1/4" stereo headphone outlet with a dedicated volume control. A stereo pair "main outs" finally sends your audio signal either to your speaker amplifier or straight to your speakers, if they have built-in power amps.

Choose your speakers carefully. This is where so many sound designers and sound editors make a common mistake. You can beef up your workstation suite with powerful sub-woofers and all kinds of "tricked-out" gear. When you play your sessions, you are rocking and rolling, literally sending earthquake-like shudders through the studio's framework. You finish cutting your helicopter-chase sequence, absolutely convinced you have aced a sequence that will garnish an Academy Award nomination. Then you get to the rerecording stage and experience total shock when it does not play back anything like the sequence you remember cutting.

The reason is simple. You colorized your workstation environment to have acoustical fun, not to develop and cut serious sound for film and video applications. You must think in terms of being transparent. I say this to designer and editing colleagues alike. You want a workstation environment that reproduces your work as identically as possible to how it will sound when you get it to the rerecording stage. Keep all your ultra-subwoofer toys at home for personal use and fun, not at work when you are developing serious products. On the other hand, you do not want a speaker system lacking the rich low-ends your material must have.

SETTING UP A NEAT DESKTOP

I can always tell how organized a sound editor is by looking at how he or she sets up the desktop of the computer. The ones with troubles tend to have a cluttered desktop, with software and file icons mixed in with drive icons. Poor desktop layout slows down your work and frustrates you. I keep my desktop divided into three basic parts. The hard-drive icons always boot up on the right side of the screen; therefore, I use that side strictly for hard drives and nothing else.

I search out my various software tools, such as Sound Designer II, Final Cut Pro, Pro Tools, Sample Search, DiskTracker, Audio Extractor, etc. I make an alias of each software icon by highlighting it and using the "Apple" keystroke "M." I drag each icon to the desktop and line them up in a column on the left side of my desktop. These are my most used software tools, so I want ease of access to them.

I make a folder that I leave in the lower center quadrant of the desktop and name it "Sessions." Each evening, before shutting down for the day, I copy the sessions on which I have worked into this folder, giving each session a current date or code designation. The first time your external hard drive crashes with irreparable damage or melts down, you adopt this technique instantly. I make a couple of other work-in-progress-type folders, which hold word processing documents regarding work, sound design layout charts, spotting notes, EDL lists, and so forth. All the non-hard drive, non-software folders, and/or alias icons are kept in the lower center of my screen. The desktop is organized, easy to read—software icons to the left, work in the center, hard drives to the right. Keep as little "work" material on the desktop as possible, as it makes your computer work harder. Keep an organized desktop and drive-management routine (discussed next), and you will lose very little work and endure a lot less anguish.

DRIVE MANAGEMENT

The oft-repeated adage of "Garbage in, garbage out" also applies to the building and maintaining of your internal and external hard drives.

One of my hard drives on *Starship Troopers* was named "149 A." No matter what the project was, I always placed my Pro Tools edit sessions on the first drive of my SCSI chain. I placed some sound files on this drive, but basically kept the bulk of the sound library files on the following drives. I made individual folders that designated the reel of the project, using an abbreviation of the project, followed by the reel number. In the example displayed in the "149 A" chart in Figure 17.1, I have opened the folder for Reel 5 of *Starship Troopers*. In naming the file, I held down the "Option" key and pressed the "8" key to make a bullet prior to the name. Using bullets ensures that "bullet" folders group together when read under the View menu designation of "By Name." This gives the folder a name of "• STR R05" (Yewdall—all).

Since we had quite a team of sound editors on *Starship Troopers*, with many specialty assignments, I needed to make it clear that the materials in this folder were my sessions and not those of Warren Hamilton, Jr., Charles Maynes, or Greg Hedgepath.

One of the most important things you must consider when organizing work and designating files is working on the "heart attack" principle. Here you are, working on a motion picture with a production budget in excess of $150,000,000. After a grueling day's work, you have a heart attack, a stroke, an auto accident, and you are in the hospital in a coma or otherwise incapacitated. As cold and unfeeling as it may sound, someone must be able to boot up your computer with as little trouble as possible and carry on with your work with little lost time. Developing good disk-management techniques and disciplines go a long way toward helping others, should the need arise.

Inside the "• STR R05" (Yewdall—all) file is where I keep all my Pro Tools sessions involved with Reel 5. *Starship Troopers* was such a gargantuan project that I needed a

# 149 A			
339 items	83.1 GB in disk		17.9 GB available
	Name	Size	Kind
▷ ▦	TONES	826K	folde
▷ 🖿	YEWDALL FX tank	78.5 GB	folde
▷ 🗀	STR "TRAILER" DY-FX	64.3 MB	folde
▷ 🗀	● STR R- 1 (ship FX) Yewdall	191K	folde
▷ 🗀	● STR R- 3 "A"-FX	191K	folde
▷ 🗀	● STR R- 4 DY-FX	127K	folde
▽ 🖿	● STR R- 5 (Yewdall--all)	1.8 MB	folde
▽	🖿 STR R05 "A" FX + training #1	191K	folde
▷	🗀 Audio Files	zero K	folde
	🖸 STR R05 "A"-FX v.14	191K	Pro
▽	🖿 STR R05 "B" FX + training #2	254K	folde
▷	🗀 Audio Files	zero K	folde
	🖸 STR R05 "B"-FX v.14	254K	Pro
▽	🖿 STR R05 "C" FX + training #3	254K	folde
▷	🗀 Audio Files	zero K	folde
	🖸 STR R05 "C"-FX v.14	254K	Pro
▽	🖿 STR R05 "D" FX "pod"	318K	folde
▷	🗀 Audio Files	zero K	folde
	🖸 STR R05 "D"-FX v.14	318K	Pro
▽	🖿 STR R05 "E" FX v.14 (telem)	254K	folde
▷	🗀 Audio Files	zero K	folde
	🖸 STR R05 "E" FX v.14	254K	Pro
▽	🖿 STR R05 "F" FX v.14 (avio/ F S)	191K	folde
▷	🗀 Audio Files	zero K	folde
	🖸 STR R05 "F" FX v.14	191K	Pro
▽	🖿 STR R05 "G"-FX (hose)	64K	folde
▷	🗀 Audio Files	zero K	folde
	🖸 STR R05 "G"-FX (hose)	64K	Pro
▷	🗀 ● orig. audition sessions	381K	folde
▷ 🗀	● STR R- 6 (Yewdall--all)	103.1 MB	folde
▷ 🗀	● STR R- 7 Yewdall--all)	49.2 MB	folde
▷ 🗀	● STR R- 8 (Yewdall--all)	11 MB	folde
▷ 🗀	● STR R- 9 (explosions)	24.4 MB	folde
▷ 🗀	● STR R-10 (Yewdall--all)	22.3 MB	folde

Figure 17.1 Drive 149 A—fast and efficient work starts with good disk management. Neat, efficient layout makes it easy to find things and helps to prevent drive conflicts and corruption.

dedicated external hard drive just to keep the fade files from bloating up my session drive. This is not the case for most projects; usually you keep your fade-file folders in the Pro Tools session folder.

The second folder from the top was named "YEWDALL FX tank." This was the first of several folders, as well as external hard drives, where I kept sound effect audio files.

"TONES" FOLDER

Inside the "Tones" folder (Figure 17.2) are the basic audio files ensuring consistently clean head and tail pops, correct line-up tone, ADR blips, and a slug of "blank" files—audio files with no sound that sound editors often use for making notes to themselves, or other editors, on the Pro Tools session. These "notes" will show up on the computer-generated cue sheet and are perfect for making editor's notes to the rerecording mixer.

Carefully measure the "pop" audio file. As discussed earlier, many editors do not think that a video (30 fps) session shows frames shorter than film sessions (24 fps). Before you commence using someone else's "Tones" folder, take the time to drag the "pop" audio file into your session, set the "feet.frame" designation under the Display menu and actually check the precise length of the pop.

You should also drag the 1 kHz @-18 line-up tone out on the session, then digitally output the signal to your DAT recorder. It is important that you output the signal digitally to ensure that you can calibrate properly. You will not be able to assure yourself of a lack of signal-path impedance if you output the signal in analog.

If the line-up tone audio file is advertised at –18 dB, then it should read exactly –18 dB on the digital meter of your DAT recorder. If it does not, you should find out why. As discussed in Chapter 6, –18 dB is not necessarily an industry standard, but whatever the "house" standard is, the line-up tone audio files in the tones folder should reflect that.

Notice that there are two sets of "pops" as well as two sets of 1 kHz TONE. Each has been made in both 48 kHz as well as 44.1 kHz sampling rates so that you can work in either sample format. We place a 1 kHz tone in every channel of your session, usually at the end of

Name	Size	Kind
"POP"	272 K	Snd Designer II™
"POP" 44.1	272 K	Snd Designer II™
1KHZ @ - 18 44.1 1KHZ	1 MB	Snd Designer II™
1KHZ @ - 18 48 1KHZ	1 MB	Snd Designer II™
1Khz TONE -- 60 sec.	6.1 MB	Snd Designer II™
1Khz TONE -- 60 sec. (x2) .L	6.1 MB	Snd Designer II™
1Khz TONE -- 60 sec. (x2) .R	6.1 MB	Snd Designer II™
BLANK	544 K	Snd Designer II™
- 06DB (STEM TONE)	952 K	Snd Designer II™
1khz@-18db 48k Stagrd	272 K	Snd Designer II™
ADR BLIPS	408 K	Snd Designer II™

-Tones [full]

11 items, 18.5 GB available

Figure 17.2 The "Tones" folder holds your "pop" frames, line-up tones, and other everyday insert files in both 44.1 kHz and 48 kHz sample rates.

the session several seconds after the "tail pop." Many of us use the technique of staggering these tones two seconds apart, so that the machine-room engineer can scan the meter and watch each channel pop up to −18 on the peak meter and confirm that the signal path is playing at the correct level.

We also have a track of "ADR blips." I make my ADR blips by taking one frame of 1 kHz tone and then pulling it into a Sound Designer II software, where I make extremely short fade-ins and fade-outs. thus taking the digital harshness off the "blip." I then import the softened blip into a Pro Tools session in which I set the counter to "Feet" and "Frames" (not "Time Code"). I place three rhythmic blips in a row, each exactly one foot (twenty-four frames) apart. I then highlight from the leading edge of the first blip through the three blips and to the leading edge of four feet. This will yield three rhythmic blips with twenty-three frames of silence before the end of that audio file. I then "bounce to disk" (see "Bounce to Disk" later in this chapter) to make a new file (i.e., ADR BLIPS).

If you find yourself in a situation where you have to make an ADR session (and you do not have ADR software) you can easily make a very efficient and cost-effective session by using a Pro Tools session with your guide track in Channel 1 and placing copies of your ADR BLIPS audio file wherever you need to cue the actor. You slide the flip in using the Grid mode in a Frame setting (see headings on the modes of Shuffle, Spot, Slip, and Grid later in this chapter) and rear-syncing the first frame of modulation with the last frame of the ADR BLIPS audio file as you watch the "End" Counter in the upper toolbar.

BUILDING YOUR AUDIO FILE DRIVES

To make your audio files efficient and easy to access, you must plan to make them so. Some editors simply make a file folder they call "Load" that is supposed to hold all the audio files needed for the particular reel on which they are working. This method works fine if you are working on only one reel and if you have a precise cut list to work from with no deviations.

If you are working on more than one reel—if you have been given creative license—and if you think creatively rather than methodically—you will desire the alphabetical file system. I set my drives up in such a manner that the main library resides in an alphabetical format (Figure 17.3).

The most important way to facilitate smooth, efficient performance of your hard drives is to practice good drive-management techniques. For those confused by conflicting advice regarding the use of an optimization program, be aware that nonlinear picture editing platforms such as the AVID work more efficiently if the files *are* fragmented, which explains the contradictory advice from those who might tell you not to defragment your audio workstation hard drives. The contrary is true when it comes to Pro Tools and how it functions. I defragment my hard drives at least twice a week, and, when I am working on extremely complex sound effect pictures, I let my Norton Utilities "speed disk" function defragment my hard drives every time I wrap for the evening.

Sometimes defragmenting hard drives with Norton Utilities has led to damage or data loss in the audio file directories. A good maintenance software that protects audio file directories is DiskWarrior. Run this application before you defragment your drives, and you will notice dramatically less file corruption.

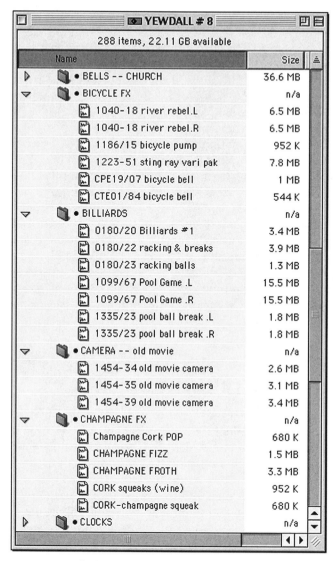

Figure 17.3. YEWDALL #8—a typical sound effect access drive. This is the alphabetical file system. Personally, I prefer to use a "bullet" and a space prior to the filename. This guarantees that all of these file folders will line up to the bottom of the list.

WORMS AND VIRUSES AND TROJAN HORSES—OH MY!

Before I tackle the creative sound editing challenges of the day, I run a worm scan and virus scans to check that the system is free of these nefarious demons. A sound editorial house at which I worked had downloaded a seemingly innocent software file from the Internet. Within twenty-four hours, nearly every workstation had been affected through the sharing of external hard drives routed through sound transfer. Once the virus had booted up into the transfer computer, it attached itself to every hard drive that came through there that night, affecting three major motion pictures. Worms tend to enter from D-to-D transfers of CD-ROM or audio CDs. Norton AntiVirus, Virex, and Worm Scan are valuable hard-disk protection tools to keep your software and hard work from contracting a fatal attraction.

TURNING THE COMPUTER "ON"

As silly as this may sound, the proper procedure for turning on the computer is the problem that I hear the most common frustrations about. Before you actually turn on the computer (CPU) itself, you need to make sure that the hardware devices that you are going to be using are already turned on and ready to be "seen" by your various softwares once you turn the computer on.

If you have external hard drives, check the SCSI connectors and make sure that they are fastened correctly and snugly fitted. Check to make sure that there is a terminator on the last drive of the chain and that the terminator is securely fitted on. We have seen many hard-drive towers melt down because terminators were not properly seated or not on at all.

Is the interface (sound I/O unit) turned on? In this case we are referring to the sound platform from the viewpoint of Pro Tools, using the Digidesign 888 interface. If you are locking up video picture to your session using time code, you are either using the Digidesign USD (Universal Slave Driver) or some other manufacturer's MIDI device that reads SMPTE time code. Make sure that this device is turned on. Your external drives have to be turned on and wound up to speed and stabilized before you start your computer.

It is always a good idea to reach over to your audio mixer and turn your monitor speakers down to zero before you press the start-up button, as very often a loud and nasty snap will burst forth from your speakers. Not only is that snap annoying to you and anyone else in the room to hear, but it will damage your speakers if it occurs often enough. Now go ahead and start your computer.

MAKING A "SESSION"

Click twice on the Pro Tools icon alias on the left side of the desktop. The software boots up, showing the Pro Tools icon in the upper right-hand corner of the menu bar. Over on the left-hand corner of the menu bar will be the word "File." Move your cursor up onto this word and press down on your mouse button. This will open the File menu (shown in Figure 17.4). Now simply drag your cursor down to the first option, "New Session . . ." and let go of your mouse button.

A menu appears; the upper window is for you to manipulate the path to direct the placement of your session on the desired drive. In the upper pull-down window of the menu, place your cursor on the bar and hold down the mouse button. In most cases, Pro Tools sessions work best when they reside on an external hard drive that is SCSI-connected to the Digidesign expansion card fitted into your computer. A narrow box in the middle next to "Name:" is where you would assign a name designation to your session (Figure 17.5). After you chose the drive and give your session a name, you need to choose what kind of "Audio File Type" you want to work in. Unless you change the file type, Pro Tools will default to SDII (Sound Designer II), at least for the present. It is very possible that this default may change in the not too distant future, as software development is constantly changing. You

File	Edit	AudioSuite	MIDI	Movie

New Session...   ⌘N
Open Session...   ⌘O
Close Session   ⇧⌘C
Save Session   ⌘S
Save Session As...
Save Session Copy In...
Revert to Saved...

Bounce to Disk...

New Track...   ⇧⌘N
Group Selected Tracks...   ⌘G
Duplicate Selected Tracks   ⇧⌥D
Split Selected Tracks Into Mono
Make Selected Tracks Inactive
Delete Selected Tracks

Import Audio to Track...
Import MIDI to Track...
Export MIDI...
Export Session As Text...
Import Tracks...

Get Info...

Quit   ⌘Q

Figure 17.4 The FILE menu in Pro Tools.

can choose to work in ".WAV" (Broadcast Wave) or in ".AIFF" (Audio Interchange File Format).

You need to make sure that the settings of the bit depth and your sample rate are what you want. If you do not change these settings they will default to 24-bit and 48 kHz.

Recall the differences in bit rates detailed in Chapters 6 and 11. Even as this book is being written, the use of 24-bit for anything other than music is being reconsidered throughout the industry. Back when we had only 4-gigabit and 9-gigabit hard drives to work with, the size of an audio file was significant. When you are an action specialist and you have thousands of audio files that need to be at the ready for access, you are concerned about file size if you have only so much space available.

But with today's increasingly larger drives and increasing speed, the size of audio files is not nearly the concern it once was. The problem is not so much whether we can work at 24-bit and 96 kHz for dialog and sound effect sessions as it is whether the audio files were originally digitized with the scope and clarity that fulfill the use of 24-bit and 96 kHz. What good is it to work at that kind of sampling rate if you rely on commercially prepared audio CD disks for your library and you strip a 16-bit 44.1 kHz sampled sound—which, by the way, has already been squashed and rolled off from its fullness?

In 1998 we tried using a Pro Tools edit session in 24-bit rate for retransferring 1/4″ source production dialog, and then using PostConform to extrapolate the editor's cut work track. We learned one major truth on this project. There is good news and bad news with regard to 24-bit production dialog. The good news is that you will hear so much more than you do in 16-bit. The bad news is that you will hear so much more than you do in 16-bit.

Figure 17.5 You need to name the session, assign it to a drive, set which audio file type you wish to work in, then choose the bit depth and sample rate.

The quality of the final result really depends on how good your production mixer is. It also begs the issue of recording analog production dialog at 71/2" per second or at 15 ips. And unless you have had the pleasure of preparing dialog from a project that was recorded at 15 ips, such as I had with *The Dead Zone*, you will have no idea what kind of audio opportunities you are missing—especially in regard to dynamic audio events that usually experience momentary distortion.

It also does not make much sense to work at a 24-bit rate when you have digital recorders that are not capable of recording at a 24-bit rate—for the same frustration of stripping 16-bit 44.1 kHz audio from audio CD disks. In order to work successfully in a 24-bit/ 96 kHz new world, you are going to have to structure the recording-to-editing-through-rerecording process from the top down. Producers and directors are going to have to work more closely with supervising sound editors to design a stem-to-stern protocol whereby the promises of 24-bit/96 kHz can be fully realized. Those who flippantly reply that this is really only for the music people are exposing their ignorance of what is possible for others.

Where this is going to really take off and be important is with the new family of field recorders, such as the DEVA II and the new Nagra 5 and other digital recorders that are recording at 24-bit as well as higher sampling rates. Therefore, if you have an average or below-average production mixer with common techniques you will notice a lot more junk and extraneous noise than you did before. If you have a superior production mixer such as Tommy Causey, Geoffrey Patterson, Ken Segal, Peter Meiselmann, or Paul Jyrälä, then you are going to experience an amazing improvement in quality. In the near future, 24-bit production dialog will likely become the standard and not the exception.

If you decide to use 24-bit instead of 16-bit, allocate an additional 50 percent of hard-drive space to accommodate the larger files. Fifty percent more space is a small price to pay for the exponential bit depth.

You cannot use 16-bit audio files in a 24-bit session. You can convert and import 16-bit files in batches. (Incidentally, you can easily distinguish a 16-bit session from a 24-bit session by the session icon "24" across the front.) I usually set up a session to convert and import hundreds of files at a time just before lunch break, as a fast computer easily converts up to 1 gig of sound files in an hour. Either that, or I can set up larger batches and let the computer crunch away when I wrap for the day to go home. When I come back I will highlight and color-code all of the new files to set them instantly apart from the 16-bit files.

Once you have set the New Session menu the way you want it, press the "Save" button. Your new session screen will open up with a toolbar at the top and a Region List on the right and no tracks whatsoever.

NEW AUDIO TRACKS

Drag down to "New Audio Tracks" to add more tracks to your edit session. A selection window will appear (as shown in Figure 17.6) offering you three decisions to make. First, how many tracks do you want to start with? The maximum number of tracks you can make in any one session will depend on your software and will change with each issued version of software. Consult the instruction manual specifying what the particular software version dictates. Usually I will automatically start with sixteen tracks and add more later as I need them.

Next, what kind of tracks do you want? Audio tracks, Auxiliary Input tracks, Master Fader tracks or MIDI tracks? For this session we are cutting a sound effect session, so we would leave the default of "Audio Track."

Once you have set this window, press the "Create" button. Bingo! Sixteen tracks will appear with a "track header" on the left-hand side of the screen. We will discuss the "track

Figure 17.6 New track.

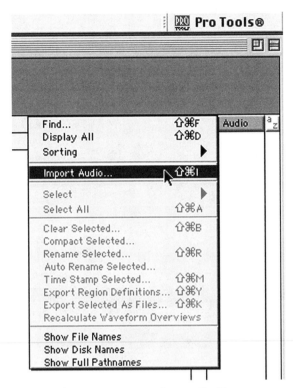

Figure 17.7 Importing audio files.

header" in more detail a little later. Each track header have a "name bar," and upon first creation, they will be named Audio-1, Audio-2, Audio-3, etc.

IMPORTING AUDIO FILES

When you are ready to import audio files (Figure 17.7) into your edit session to work on, you will move your cursor up to the upper right-hand side of your session window and place it on the "Audio" bar above the Region List window, which is the vertical column window that shows all of the audio materials that your session is working with. Hold your mouse button down and a small menu window will appear to the side. Draw your cursor down to "Import Audio" and let go of your mouse button. The Import Audio window will open (Figure 17.8).

This is your "fast-food drive-up window" to access, audition, and either choose or convert the audio files you wish to work with. Everything you need to know about each audio file that you highlight will instantly be displayed in the center of the window: what kind of audio file it is, how long it is, file size, bit depth, sample rate, and whether it is stereo or mono. Note the window to the right of the information window. In this case, it is telling me that the audio file I highlighted is a different sample rate. I can still bring it into the session and work with it if I wish, but it will not play at the file's original speed. This fact is extremely

Figure 17.8 The Import Audio preview window.

important when you are working with dialog and music, but not as vital when you are working with sound effect files.

At the bottom left you have an "audition audio" player. The audio file highlighted is shown in the window. There is a stop-and-play button, a two-channel peak meter. You can raise or lower the playback level with the adjustment slide to the right of the meter. The adjustment slide under the stop-and-play buttons can quickly advance you deeper into the audio file if you do not want to waste time listening to the file in real time. By either tapping twice on the desired audio file in the upper window or by highlighting the desired audio file and pressing the "ADD→" button in the lower center, you will add the audio files that you wish to "Import" into your session once you press the "Done" button at the lower right of the window.

If you wish to convert files due to audio type or sampling rate, you can highlight the desired files in the upper window and then press the "Convert→" button. Once you have chosen the file(s) you wish to convert, press the "Done" button and the computer will commence to crunch away at high speed, converting your files to Sound Designer II audio files in split .L-&-.R configurations at the sample rate and bit depth that your Pro Tools session has been set for.

These new converted files will be placed in your session's Audio File folder inside your Session folder.

THE EDIT WINDOW—YOUR AUDIO TRACK HEADER

Figure 17.9 shows the Edit window. Let's look at the actions you can perform here.

Renaming Audio Channels

The name for your audio track will default to Audio-1, Audio-2, Audio-3, and so forth, but you can retitle these tracks by placing the cursor over the name bar of the track and tapping twice. A "name" window will appear and you can rename your track. Be careful how long you make the name, as a name that is too long can cause complications later when you print out your computer-generated cue sheets.

Record (Rec)

Each track is equipped with a "Record" button. Think of this is a safety feature on a weapon. If the safety is on, the weapon cannot shoot. In this case, if the "Rec" button is not highlighted (white with red letters), it will not record an incoming signal. If you want to record audio material into this channel, you first must press this button. We will talk about recording into Pro Tools later (see Figure 17.18).

Read

The "Read" button is for using the automated volume graphing and other plug-in settings that you may be applying to your edited material as you cut and manipulate. If you place your cursor on this button and hold your mouse button down, a menu window will appear,

Figure 17.9 The Edit window—track header.

offering choices of Auto Off, Audio Read, Auto Touch, Auto Latch, Auto Write, and Trim. The default is Auto Read. These options work with outboard interface gear such as Digidesign's Pro Control.

Solo

Press the "Solo" button if you wish to listen only to this track or any selected tracks that you have "soloed" together. When you press "Solo" on this track, all other tracks not under the "Solo" designation will show a grayed-out "Mute" status and will not be heard.

Mute

The "Mute"s button makes the same kind of choice as "Solo," only in reverse. You press it to mute the track, so that it will not be heard, regardless of the the "Solo-Mute" option choice of other tracks.

Voice Auto

When you create new audio tracks, the software will automatically assign the new track a "voice" in numerical order of the tracks' creation. The number of voices that a system has dictates how many channels of sound that system can play for you simultaneously. If I have a thirty-two-voice system and I have forty-eight channels of audio playing at the same time, then only the first thirty-two voices will be heard. If an audio track in Audio 6 (which has Voice 6) is playing, and Audio 38 also has an audio track, then Audio 38 will not be heard, because they both share the same "voice."

If I have a thirty-two-voice system and I make four channels of sound, the software will assign Voices 1 through 32 to Audio Tracks 1 through 32 and then start over, assigning Voice 1 again to Audio Track 33, Voice 2 to Audio Track 34, and so on. Now if an audio cue that is playing in Audio 6 is complete and there is no audio cue in that track, then the software will kick in the audio playback of Audio Track 38 because that voice is now no longer being being used where it was first assigned. A little bit farther down the way, another cue comes into play on Audio 6; the audio cue in Audio 6 will supersede Audio Track 38, which will instantly cut off, allowing Audio 6 to play.

I often cut sessions with more tracks than I have voices if I know that I am shipping my cut sessions to a mixing facility that is going to be predubbing my sessions with Pro Tools stations that have sixty-four-voice systems. You need to always take into consideration the voice capacity of the site where the ultimate rerecording mix is going to take place.

Depending on the configuration of your computer's audio hardware/software, you will have either an eight-voice system (such as Pro Tools Free or LE) or you will have a sixteen-voice system or a thirty-two-voice system. Or if you have two 888 interface units and accompanying internal cards, you could double that to sixty-four voices. It all depends on the prowess of your hardware/software configuration.

Waveform

The "Waveform" option bar allows you to choose between viewing the audio file displays as simple blocks or with the waveform calculated and drawn out. An advantage of using

"Block" is that with older and slower computers, it does not take as much speed or crunch time to redraw and present the complex waveforms on the screen constantly. This was important back when we had primitive and slow CPUs, but with today's PowerMacs, especially the 9600s, G-3s, G-4s, and now the G-5s, this option is unnecessary.

You can also select "Volume," which will display the volume graph line across the entire audio line, allowing you to go touch the line with your cursor wherever you want to place "nodes" that will lock the volume position before you place another "node" and drag it either up (as much as +6 dB) in volume increase or drag it down to infinity attenuation.

You can also set the track to "Mute." With this setting, a line will appear that is much like the volume graph line except that it ist set all the way to the top. As with the volume graph line, you can use your cursor to place nodes on the line. When you place the node, a small box will appear next to the node saying "not muted." If you then grab the line between nodes and pull the line down, it will go to the bottom. These bottom-selected regions between muted nodes will play back whereas the rest of the audio track will not. When the audio track is played back, any audio file that has these muted nodes will suddenly cut in or out, depending on whether the node is an incoming point to come in or an outgoing pointing to "Mute" again.

Peak Meter

Each audio track has a small peak meter on the right side just before the "scale" ruler. If you are recording into this channel, you should never let the volume hit the top, which is red. When you are playing back audio files that you have imported into your session, the audio level of these files will also show up. If your audio file is hitting the upper red square, you will want to open up your volume-graphing option and attenuate the volume accordingly.

Track Sizing

If you place the cursor on what looks like a ruler scale on the right edge of the header block and hold your cursor there, an option window will appear, giving you a choice of what size you would like your tracks. They can range from as small as "mini" to as large as "extreme." It all depends on what you are doing and what you need to see while you are working. Personally, I find I can work with sixteen to-twenty-four channels quite comfortably by working in the "small" option. If I am recording material into the session, I like to work in at least "medium" or "large" so that I can watch and study the waveform as I listen.

THE SETUPS MENU

Before we start doing any work and before we start importing a bunch of audio files, we need to set some basic parameters to make sure that we will be functioning correctly.

Open the Setups window menu (Figure 17.10). Draw down to "Hardware." A Hardware Setup window will appear (Figure 17.11).

Hardware Setup is the foundation of getting off on the right foot. This is where we verify what audio card hardware is installed inside the computer. Sometimes the software

Figure 17.10 The Setups menu in Pro Tools.

will give you a warning telling you that you must open the Hardware Setup window and set the "Card" option.

Sampling Rate

You can work either in 48 kHz or 44.1 kHz sampling rate. In the theatrical feature film world, we are pretty much all working in 48 kHz today. Because the audio CD standard is 44.1 kHz, if you intend on making audio cues and material that is going to be for audio CDs, it might be easier to work in 44.1 kHz from the beginning. This is a decision you will have to make if you are about to build a library of sound effects for commercial/consumer sale. If you use commercially made audio CD disks for sound effects, you will most likely be using the Audio

Figure 17.11 The Hardware Setup window in Pro Tools.

Extractor software for high-speed stripping of audio files, and, of course, they will be in 44.1 kHz.

Sync Mode

If you are slaving to a time code videotape for picture lock, you need to make sure that the Sync Mode is set to "Internal." Use this mode in "digital" only if you are recording material in from another digital unit, such as a DAT machine, and you are importing the material D-to-D (that is, not decoding to an analog signal first). When you change back to an edit mode, you must change the Sync Mode back to "Internal" or you will have serious sync issues later.

Digital Format

You can record or play back digitally to an outboard deck (such as a DAT or other digital recorder) using either the SPDF or the AES/EBU mode. SPDF (which stands for Sony/Phillips digital format) are the RCA connectors for the ins and outs on the back of your DAT machine. AES/EBU (wich stands for Audio Engineering Society/European Broadcast Union) are the XLR connectors on the back of your DAT machines. Unlike analog, which requires a separate cable for each audio channel, the digital signal comes in through a single "In" or is sent through a single "Out" cable, both left and right audio channels sharing the same cable. Check to see which digital In and Out cables you are using, and then choose the appropriate option in the "Digital Format" box.

Ch 1–2 Input

The Ch 1–2 Input option serves what we just talked about. If you are recording material in from an outside source, do you want to record digitally or in analog? With digital you have no volume-altering capability. You are simply transferring ones and zeros data from an outboard machine into your computer. If you want to use any outboard signal-processing gear prior to entering your session as a recorded signal, then you need to enter your data as an analog recording.

It is a good idea to press the "Recalibrate Inputs" button prior to leaving the Hardware Setup window any time you have changed your settings, especially your Ch 1–2 Input mode. Once you are satisfied that your hardware setups are correct, press the "OK" button at the bottom and the window will disappear.

Open the Setups menu again and draw down to "Disk Allocation." The window shown in Figure 17.12 will appear. Check to verify that every track is pointed to the hard drive on which your session resides. This will ensure that all your fade files and any created audio files will be directed to this folder and not be sent to any other drives that you may have. I never choose the option of "Use round robin allocation for new tracks"—never.

If for some reason the drive name is not consistent on all of the audio tracks shown, simply hold the cursor down on the bar under "Root Media Folder" and select the drive to which you want it directed.

There are times that you might need to use the "Use round robin allocation." Let us say that you have to import sixteen channels of interlocked audio signal for a sustained period

Figure 17.12 Disk allocation.

of time. By using the "round robin" option you will be assigning the workload of importing this bulky amount of data over more drives, thereby cutting down on the risk of drive crash or system breakdown. This is especially true in the music industry, where twenty-four to forty-eight channels of audio imports are done every day.

Open the Setups menu again and draw down to "Peripherals . . ." The window shown in Figure 17.13 will appear. The first folder, "Synchronization," is what we are concerned about. Note under "Device" that "Universal Slave Driver" is shown. Next to it, under "Port," is "DigiSerial Port." This is correct for using a USD (Universal Slave Driver) with an 888 interface and its accompanying Digi card system that fits into the expansion slots of your CPU.

You may be using a VSD (Video Slave Driver) or a SSD (SMPTE Slave Driver). Under "Device" you will find both of these options as well as SSD + VSD.

You may decide to use a different manufacturer's unit to interlock your sessions for sync. Mark of the Unicorn makes several extremely reliable models. If you are working on a tight budget, you may like the Micro Express, which works very nicely. You would simply choose "Generic MTC Reader" under "Device," and then you will find that under "Port" the compatibility software that you installed when you set up your Micro Express will show "MicroExpress,Modm" as the proper option to choose.

Whatever device you decide to work with, you must make sure to make a clean, reliable signal path so that your editing platform software can read and lock up to the signal sent to it from your MIDI timepiece, USD, Slave Driver, or whatever.

Open the Windows menu at the top of your screen (Figure 17.14). There are a couple of things that we need to attend to here. The three main issues are your Mix window, your Session setup, and where you go to show your Transport deck.

Figure 17.13 The Peripheral menu.

Figure 17.14 The Windows menu.

THE SHOW MIX WINDOW

Open the Windows menu and draw down one set to "Show Mix." The Mix window shown in Figure 17.15 will appear. Each audio track has its own fade slide array, just like on a rerecording console. If you understand one, you understand them all. At the top is the "Input" designation. Note that "Audio 1" shows "#1/1|888." This means that the input signal path is routed through Channel 1 of Mix Card #1 input of the Pro Tools 888 interface. If you wish to change that input designation, you simply place the cursor arrow up on top of that button and hold it down; a little menu will appear to the side listing all of the input possibilities that you can choose from. Draw down to whichever input designation you wish and let go.

The next button is the "Output" assignment. In this case all of the audio channels are playing back through Channels 1 and 2. In the mode in which this Mix window is presently set up, each channel is playing equally through left and right speakers and therefore "phantoming" a signal in the center. Notice the little slide just below the "Solo" and "Mute" buttons. This little slide can be moved to hard left or hard right (or soft left and soft right, or whatever degree you wish) if you want to keep the output assignment as "#1/12|888."

Figure 17.15 The Mix "console" window.

Figure 17.16 The Session Setup window.

If I am cutting a stereo session, I may want each channel to be a "dedicated out" rather than setting the "pan" slides to hard left and hard right. If so, I will hold down the "Output" button and draw down to assign a single output channel; in this case it will read "#1/1|888," assigning Audio 1 to "Output 1" so that it will play only through the left speaker. The little "pan" slide will disappear, and the "Pan > 0 < " button just below the "Vol" button will also disappear, as they are no longer necessary.

The other buttons on each fader slide mirror the option buttons you have on the Audio Track header.

Note the little box with the letter "a" in it on both Audio 1 and Audio 2. This shows me that these two tracks are "grouped" together.

The fader slides below are automated and will rise up and down, following the volume graphing that you build into your edit session. We will talk about volume graphing later.

Open the Windows menu again and draw down to "Show Session Setup." The Session Setup window will appear as shown in Figure 17.16. Quickly scan the settings that you have set before. They should all be the same here, e.g., sample rate, bit depth, "internal" sync mode, etc. Now look at the small time code window in the upper right-hand corner marked "Session Start." Note that it reads one hour and zero minutes, zero seconds, and zero frames. With the exception of the hour designation, this is the correct minute, second, frame start for any session. The "hour" setting tells us what reel number we are on. If we are working on a feature film, we may have ten reels in a 95-minute film (if we use traditional reel sizes). If we are cutting in A-B configuration, we will have five reels in a 95-minute film.

In this manner we would name the hour of the session "01" if it is Reel 1, "02" if it is Reel 2, and so forth.

Note the black time code numbers just under the Session Start time code designated as "Current Time." This tells you exactly what time code your SMPTE timepiece (i.e., Universal Slave Driver) is reading from your video picture source. In the example shown in Figure 17.16, the videotape is standing by just prior to the session start of 01:00:00:00. This is good, as you always want to have your video source parked prior to where you want to interlock "in sync." This is known as a "preroll," the time code that precedes the "hour" designation start of your session. The edit software sees the time code and can lock up to the video source at the first frame of your session.

I do not agree with those who build a preroll into the session itself. First, it is unnecessary and leads to all kinds of complications when you are measuring, moving, transferring, or making some types of computer-generated documents. The preroll that counts is what is on the videotape prior to the first frame of the "start mark" (as discussed earlier in this book), the "start mark" being the one-hour designation of your time code followed by zero-zero minutes, zero-zero seconds and zero-zero frames.

You must set your "Frame Rate" correctly. It is vital that you know how your video source was transfered. Most professional video transfer services list this information on the video telecine label. When in doubt, call picture editorial and ask for the specifications that they gave the telecine transfer service. Or if they made the video transfer themselves, ask for the output specifications they used.

It used to be that a standard of 29.97 fps (which is non-drop frame) was the standard. But over the last few years various post-production editorial groups have been using different approaches. The most important issue is that whatever picture editorial used, you need to match it, or you will discover that your session will quickly drift out of sync when you get the rerecording stage.

You can review the frame rates and drop/non-drop issues as we discussed in Chapter 6 under "Time Code: The Obnoxious Electronic Cricket."

Because time code dropouts are a constant problem in making videotape copies for editors to work with, we build a buffer into the "Time Code Freewheel" option. You can set this window from 1 to 120 frames. That way, if the video time code feed has dropouts in it, the session will keep playing along, looking for a time code signal to lock on to. In the example shown in Figure 17.16, the "Time Code Freewheel" setting is forty-eight frames, giving the software two seconds to see and lock on to the time code signal again.

The last important item to set is the "Clock Reference" and "Postitional Reference" options at the bottom of the setup window. In this case we have both boxes set to "LTC" (Linear Time Code). Refer to Figure 17.16 again and note the menu boxes of various options. We are not going to take the time in this book to go into all of these options and their applications. Suffice it to say that "Linear Time code" is the most common approach to interlocking, so we are showing that display. Please refer to your owner's manual on your editing software to read about the other options.

Open the Display menu (Figure 17.17) and you will see an array of "show" options with arrows to the side. As you draw down to these various display options, a side menu will appear to the side of the arrows. A series of options will list what you want to have shown in your displays: big, small, narrow, wide, extra expansion windows to your transport deck, and so on. You can add I/O Views, Insert Views, and Send Views for your Mix or Edit windows, as well as other options. Personally, I do not like to junk up

Figure 17.17 The Display menu.

my screen. I like to keep it simple—easy to visually scan, easy to read, and right to the heart of the matter.

The "ruler" that crosses over the top of the editing field shows the timeline for editing precisely. You can have this ruler changed from "Bars:Beats" or "Minutes:Seconds" or Time code" or "Feet and Frames" or "Samples." If you want, you can have more than one ruler showing at a time. You can change the order in which you wish the rulers are displayed if you are using multiple rulers. By the way, "Feed and Frames" works in 35 mm terms.

If I am going to work in time code, then I do not want other rulers to complicate the view scan that a single ruler will provide.

THE TRANSPORT DECK

Open the Windows menu at the top of your screen and draw down to "Show Transport" (or use "Apple"-keystroke "1"). The basic transport deck as shown at the top of the Figure 17.18 will appear. If you want to add extensions and options to your transport, then open the Display menu and draw down to the "Transport Windows Shows." A side menu will appear with various options to expand the look and use of your transport deck. As with everything else that I do when I am editing or recording into Pro Tools, I like to keep the transport deck as sleek and simple as possible. The most important thing you need to know here is the way that the "tape recorder"–style control bar works.

Interlock Clock

In the far left window is the icon of a clock. When you interlock your edit session with the incoming time code signal sent from your video source, use the"Apple"-keystroke "J" keys and you will notice a small box at the bottom left-hand corner of your edit session will

Figure 17.18 The three basic Transport deck views.

suddenly say "Waiting for Sync." You will also note that the clock icon on your Transport window is flashing on and off (light blue).

When you roll your video picture, and the time code signal changes to a steady one and is read by your session, the lower left window will change to either "Play" if you are playing back audio in sync, or "Record" if you are recording in sync (such as ADR or Foley sync-to-picture sound effects). The blue icon will stop flashing and just stay solid light blue.

Back-to-Heads Arrow

The box just to the right of the icon clock is an arrow that points to the left with a line. If you press this, the playback head (also called an "I" bar or a "line") will go back to the top of the session.

Fast Reverse

The next box is a double arrow to the left. This is the "Fast Rewind" (or "Fast Reverse") button. If you are playing a cue and wish to back up quickly, you can press this and the playback head will reverse quickly until you release, and it will then continue to play.

Stop

The next box is a black square. This is the "Stop" button. You can either push this button or hit the space bar of your computer keyboard to stop a playback or a record mode.

Play

The next button to the right of the "Stop" button is the "Play" button. You can either push this button or hit the space bar of your computer keyboard to play or commence recording (if the transport is armed).

Fast Forward

The next button to the right of the "Play" button has two arrows pointing to the right. This is the "Fast Forward" button. As with the "Fast Reverse" button, you can press this button if you are in playback mode to skip ahead in the audio track. When you release it, the track will continue to play in real time.

Go to End of Session

The next button to the right of the "Fast Forward" button shows an arrow that points to the right with a line. This is the "Go to the End of Session" button. If you press this, the playback head will go to the end of the last audio cue in the session.

Record "Armed" Indicator

The last button on the right, next to the "Go to the End of Session" button is the "Record Armed" button. The center circle will flash bright red when the transport is armed and ready to record. When you roll, by either pressing the "Play" button on the Transport window or by pressing the space bar on your keyboard, the "Record" indicator will stop flashing and hold a steady bright red.

RECORDING INTO AN AUDIO TRACK

Importing the Editor's Cut Track

Okay, so you want to record what is referred to as a "guide" track or an "editor's cut track"—what the transfer department calls a 1-to-1 (1:1). Make sure than you have an audio cable from Channel 1 (left channel) "Audio Out" of your videotape machine. Patch it into one the "Analog Inputs" in the back of your audio I/O interface—in this case we are using the Digidesign 888 I/O. I usually leave a permanent signal-path hookup to my video deck to transfer guide tracks by using Input #4. That is strictly a personal choice.

Open the Mix window, as shown in Figure 17.15, and go up to the "Input" bar above the audio channel you wish to record to. Since I always place my guide tracks in the first channel, I will record the guide track into Audio 1. Reassign the Input designation to Channel 4—or in this case it will show "#1/4|888." Now I brought the signal path from the video deck, in through the audio I/O interface, and it will show up on the peak meter of Audio 1.

Press the "Rec" button on the Edit "header" window as described on page 352. This will arm the track, or, more precisely, it will allow any audio signal being seen by the input designation to that channel to be recorded. Also press the "Solo" button on the Audio 1 Edit header so that only that track will be heard (in case there are audio clips in other channels).

Without attempting to record, and not engaging time code interlock, I will simply roll the videotape to be assured that I am receiving audio signal from it. If I am receiving the audio signal, I rewind the videotape back about six to ten seconds prior to the session time code. If the time code setting of the session is 01:00:00:00, I will want to park the videotape back at 00:59:52:00, give or take a couple of seconds.

Now press the "Record Armed" button on your transport deck window. The red circle will flash as it waits to commence recording. Press "Apple"-keystroke "J" and the icon clock will start pulsing blue as it waits for time code. You are ready.

Remember: everything chases the clock. The clock is the time code fed from the video-tape. Roll the videotape deck. The time code on the videotape from Channel 2 (right channel) will be sent to the Universal Slave Driver, which in turns sends the correct signal to the computer software. Within a few seconds your audio session is seeing the time code, but it will not start recording until exactly 01:00:00:00. Suddenly it engages. The flashing clock icon and flashing "Record Armed" button stop flashing and hold solid. A wide, faint red band starts to march across the screen in Audio 1. Several seconds later you can make out a waveform being written behind the leading edge of the record head.

Unless your tape has a time code dropout that exceeds your freewheel setting, you will continue to record until either you stop the recording or the reel is finished and the video-tape cuts off the time code stream. Now you have a "guide" track. Highlight the track with the "hand" (described later in this chapter) and press "Apple"-keystroke "L". A little padlock icon will appear at the lower left-hand corner of the audio file. This audio track is now locked in place!

GROUPING TRACKS

The Group Tracks mode is a vital option when you are working with stereo or quadraphonic or any other eight-track, sixteen-track, or twenty-four-track audio files that must be locked together. It is also extremely useful if you are working with predub or final-mix stem updates. When cutting in stereo pairs, you will find Group Tracks very helpful. Click on an audio track that will be one of your stereo pairs. Hold down the "Shift" key and click on the other audio track you wish to lock together with the first as a pair. You can either drag down the File menu to "Group Tracks," or you can simply use "Apple"-keystroke "G" to group the highlighted tracks together. A menu window will appear, as shown in Figure 17.19. You can group the two tracks as "Edit" only or as "Mix" only, or you can use the default, which is locking both "Edit and Mix."

You will notice that each time you group two or more channels into a "Group" a "Group ID" letter will be assigned. This "Group ID" will also show up in your Mix Window, making it simple for you to see which tracks are grouped together. This is especially useful if you are grouping stems and multichannel signals (such as quadraphonic or eight-channel record-ings). Using "Group" keeps your left and right stereo sides from slipping out of phase with each other as you move them around and chop them up.

Group Tracks can also be extremely helpful when in conforming predubs or mixed stems, you want to group four, six, ten, or any number of audio tracks together (up to the maximum of your software version).

I often import two or three predubs into one Pro Tools session to update at once. Because you may cut and massage the material differently from one predub to another, do not want group them all together. Say you have a background predub and hard effects "A" and "B" together. Highlight all five audio tracks of backgrounds, group them together, then highlight all five audio tracks of "A"-FX and group them together. Now do the same to "B"-FX. The Pro Tools software assigns each five-channel group its own color code, making it even easier to see what you are doing as you cut and move sections around.

Figure 17.19 Grouping tracks.

MOVING TRACK MODES

The four small rectangular boxes at the upper left-hand side of the toolbar shown in Figure 17.20 are the four modes for moving and/or cutting audio regions.

Shuffle Mode

If you wish to cut material out of an audio cue and have the material behind it move forward to fill in the deleted gap, that is known as Shuffle mode. It can be a very handy way to quickly illuminate a lot of extraneous material from an audio cue and distill it down to what you really want. The downside is that as you "shuffle" the material from the right back to fill in

Figure 17.20 Left side of the toolbar.

the gap you just cut out, it is going to shuffle everything to the right—even audio cues down-range that you have already placed exactly where you want them and have now just knocked out of sync.

The way to avoid this catastrophe is to first go down to the cue to the right of the one you are cutting up in shuffle mode and "Lock" it down in place by highlighting it and using the "Apple"-keystroke "L" option. Once one cue is locked in the pathway, the shuffle mode will not affect anything behind it, therefore you need not worry about altering sync. Shuffle mode is also good for collapsing whole sections of audio files or stems that need changes or updates. Once an editor receives a change sheet from picture editorial, he or she can use the Group Tracks (Figure 17.19) and Grid to get exact measurements from the cut points indicated in the change sheet and then highlight the cut and change the mode to Shuffle, and thereby moving all the audio behind the cut to shuffle forward exactly into the new sync point.

Slip Mode

The rectangular box below "Shuffle" is "Slip." This mode is what you want to use when you are cutting creatively or phase-matching dialog reprints to the guide track. You can move your audio regions any amount—large or tiny, even down to one-sample moves if desired.

Grid Mode

The rectangular box to the right of "Slip" is "Grid." If you opt to use this mode, you need to go over to the right side of your toolbar (shown in Figure 17.21) and choose which grid size you wish to bump your audio regions by. You can move in one-"second" moves or one-"frame" moves (which are the two most common), or you can choose "quarter frame," "sub-frame," or "sample."

This mode gives you extreme accuracy in moving leading-edge audio cues into sync on frame lines or making absolute rhythmic audio events by using seconds and frames. The more you use it, the more you will find ways to utilize it.

Spot Mode

The rectangle box above "Grid" is "Spot." If you choose the Spot mode, then go over to the Region List column on the right side of your screen and choose an effect and drag it out on to the audio channel where you wish it to reside. A menu will appear asking where you want the leading edge. You can type in the time code, and the audio cue will go directly to that "spot."

Enlarge View-&-Waveform

The array of arrows and waveform icons to the right are for magnifying the waveform wave and moving in close. If you press this bar with the arrow that points to the left, the view of your edit session will progressively step backward, pulling farther away from close-up detail.

If you press the bar with the arrow that points to the right, the view will step in progressively closer, showing more detail.

If you press the little horizontal bar with the thick waveform, the size of the audio waveform in the audio track regions will increase. (NOTE: This does not change the volume of the sound, only the visual look.) If you want to decrease the size of the waveform, you press the little horizontal bar beneath it (with the thinner waveform icon). The 1 through 5 number blocks are zooms in percents. Press on the "3" box and you will move halfway in closer (approximately). Press on "1" box and you will move back out.

The Magnifying Glass

The really precise tool for working in close or moving out is the "Magnifying Glass." Touch and highlight this button. Now move your cursor (which has become a magnifying glass) down into the edit session area. Place the magnifying glass at the left side of the area you wish to zoom in on. Hold down your mouse button and drag the magnifying glass to the right until you have highlighted the area you wish to fill the screen.

The screen will instantly jump in closer. If you wish to go in farther in, repeat the same action. If you want to pull back to full view, simply tap on the magnifying glass twice and the screen will pull back to full view.

THE "THREE-TOOL PACK"

The three most used tools for cutting and manipulating are the "Razor Blade," the "I-beam" or "line," and the "hand." The long horizontal bar that straps these three tools can be highlighted so that you can use all three tools together, or you can highlight the individual icons and use them one at a time.

Razor Blade

The Razor Blade is a chop-delete tool. You can whack into tracks and dispose of the unwanted regions quickly. It is also a "reveal" tool. Suppose you realized you have cut too far or you change your mind about a cut. Place the Razor Blade cursor over your audio region. Note that there are two prongs pointing to the left. That means that you are to the left of the 50-percent mark or center of the audio cue. Anything that you chop off will come off from the left side of the tool—that is, the head end. Move the tool farther across your audio region until you pass the center 50-percent area. Note that the prongs suddenly flipped over and are now pointing to the right. That means that anything you cut will be lopped off the right side of the tool, or the tail section.

If you hold the tool over the audio region and hold your mouse button down, the tool will chop. But notice that if you do not release the mouse button and move the cursor to the left or the right, it will either shrink or reveal a part of the audio region that you had chopped off before. This is because Pro Tools is not a destructive audio software. When you make these "cuts" and "cross-fades" and other manipulations, you are not performing them on the actual audio file. Rather, you are building a set of directions—a "to-do" list for the software, telling it how to play what portion of what audio cue at what point, and while it is doing it, when to fade in or when to fade out. This set of instructions is known as an Edit Decision List. It is a convenient visual construct, for your benefit, of what you are telling the DAE to perform deep inside the computer.

Selector (or Line)

The icon in the center with the waveform and thick region-highlight line through it is called the "Selector" or the "I-beam" or the "line." You can highlight this icon box and then come down and place the playback head exactly where you want it. Simply move the cursor to the spot you want and tap the mouse button once. Now the Selector is exactly where you want it—or at least exactly where you placed it.

You use the Selector icon by placing it on the left edge of something you wish to affect, then holding the mouse button down and dragging the line to the right. This creates a highlighted region that can be used to play only from here-to-there. Highlight a region and hit the space bar of your keyboard. The tracks will all play from start to finish only in the region you highlighted.

You might want to place the Selector line just in front of an audio region, then tap down and drag into the audio region area to highlight many frames, or seconds and frames. Let go of the button and use the "Apple"-keystroke "F" option to create a fade. Go back to Chapter 13 and look at Figure 13.11. These are the "Fade" slope options. A menu window will appear showing you these Fade choices as well as any cross-fade combinations if you are cross-fading into another audio cue. After you choose the "Fade-in" slope you want, the fade-in will instantly be rendered, causing a fade-in region from the exact front leading edge of the audio cue in to the point where your highlight region ends.

If you do not like the result, simply highlight the fade-in region you made with the "hand" and hit the "Delete" key and make another fade-in region. The procedure is all non-destructive; you can work and rework it over and over.

Hand

If you want to physically grab tracks and move them forward or backward, or drag them up or down to another audio channel, go up to the toolbar and tap on the "hand" icon.

Your mouse cursor will become a hand. Move down into the edit field and grab whatever you wish to move by placing the hand onto the audio region and pressing down on the mouse button. You must hold the mouse button down to be able to move things. If your finger bobbles and deselects the audio file, it will drop off and perhaps sit in the middle of another audio file or across a bunch of fades that will be destroyed. You must instantly go up the Edit menu and draw down to the first option, "Undo." "Undo" will place the audio region back where it was without destroying any work that you might have wiped out with the mishap. Grab the hand and go back and move your audio region again, only this time be more careful.

Scrub Speaker

The icon next to the hand is a speaker with a vertical dotted line through it. This is a "Scrubber." Tap on this icon and move down into an audio channel. If you place the cursor, which

Figure 17.21 Right side of the toolbar.

is now a "scrub speaker" into Channel 5, for example, where you have an audio region, you can tap down your mouse and then drag to the right and back to the left. The speaker "head" will play either faster than or slower than real time. This tool is valuable to get in fairly close and scrub back and forth much more slowly than in real time to find the exact spot of a digital tick or other audio bobble that you are trying to ferret out.

Digital Pencil

The box next to the scrub speaker is the Digital Pencil. Most of the time you are not zoomed in close enough to allow the use of this tool. When you zoom in close enough to use it, the grayed-out image will appear solid as it shows in the toolbar.

The Digital Pencil works the same way that you use it in the Sound Designer II software, explained in detail later in this chapter. (NOTE: The Digital Pencil is a destructive application. When you use it, you are affecting the actual audio file, so you want to be very careful or make a copy of the audio file you wish to use it on first.)

Figure 17.21 shows the right side of your toolbar. These are your counters. If you were highlighting a region, the "Start" number would read where in the timeline the leading edge of your highlighted area begins. The "End" number would show where the trailing edge of your highlighted area ends. The "Length" would tell you exactly how long your highlighted area is.

You can open the downward arrow icons on the sides of the "Grid" and "Nudge" counters and change what increment of time you wish to move the tracks when you use the "–" or "+" keys on the calculator portion of keyboard to shuttle highlighted areas forward or backward.

You move in one-"second" intervals or one-"frame" intervals. These are arguably the most popular and most practical movements for editors to use. But you can also set the calibration of moves for "quarter frame," "sub-frame," or "sample" as well.

THE OPERATIONS MENU

Open the Operations menu (Figure 17.22) and notice the following important options.

Loop Record

We talked about the Loop Record option near the end of Chapter 15 (about recording dialog using the "looping" technique) with regard to actors reperforming their lines.

Operations	Setups	Display	Windows
Destructive Record			
Loop Record			⌥L
QuickPunch			⇧⌘P
Auto Input Monitor			⌥K
✓ **Input Only Monitor**			
Online			⌘J
Pre/Post-Roll Playback			⌘K
Loop Playback			⇧⌘L
Scroll Options			▶
✓ **Link Edit and Timeline Selection**			⇧/
Copy Edit Selection To Timeline			⇧⌥5
Copy Timeline Selection To Edit			⇧⌥6
Play Timeline Selection			⌥]
Play Edit Selection			⌥[
Mute Frees Assigned Voice			
Auto-Spot Regions			⌘P
✓ **Active In Background**			
✓ **Pre-Fader Metering**			
Calibration Mode			

Figure 17.22 The Operations menu.

Online

The Online option is what we have discussing regarding interlocking with the time code signal from your video source. To interlock your edit session, simply use the "Apple"-keystroke "J" option and your session will either be interlocked to your video time code source or unlocked.

Loop Playback

Loop Playback works just like Loop Record in that you highlight a region or highlight an entire audio file and press the space bar of your keyboard, and the playback head will play to the end and instantly start again.

This option can be very useful for a number of applications where it is easier to loop sections of track and output to another source rather than build out a timeline. The difference is that you cannot work any cross-fades in from the end of the cue to the beginning of the cue. So if the ambiance does not match at the end and beginning edges for some reason, the sound will bump.

Scroll Options

Scroll Options should be set before you commence work. This option determines whetherr your computer screen shifts with the playback head. You can set it so the screen will not scroll, but moves after you stop playback, or you can set it so it will not scroll at all. You can also set it so that it will "page" scroll, meaning that just prior to the playback line moving off screen right, the screen will shift over to the next "page" viewing area as the playback line enters from the left side of the screen. You can also set the Scroll Options so that the screen moves continually, as if it were a synchronizer wheel, always keeping the playback head in the center of the screen and the array of audio tracks moving across it. The choice is up to you.

THE EDIT MENU

Open the Edit menu (Figure 17.23). Here are highlights of some of the most commonly used and useful options in the Edit menu.

Undo/Redo

The Undo/Redo is one of my favorite options, especially when I want to correct something I have just messed up. It is especially helpful when you just slid across and crashed into a

Figure 17.23 The Edit menu.

pile of audio files because you were in Grid mode in "Second" steps rather than in "Frame" steps—or you just ripped a bunch of fade selections away that you did not mean to destroy and now you have to put them back the way they were.

A perhaps obvious but important tip for the beginning artisan is that if you must "undo" or "redo" the last move made, do not make another edit or move decision before taking advantage of the Undo option. If you cannot "undo" what you just did, this option shows up in light gray.

Cut

If you want to eliminate a highlighted section of the audio file, you can open the Edit menu and draw down to "Cut," or simply use "Apple"-keystroke "X." The software will quickly make a backup copy in case you wish to "Undo" the cut, then it will shuttle through and eliminate the material and redraw the waveform for display. Check your cut immediately. If you wish to "Undo" it, you must do so immediately; otherwise the cut will be permanent.

Copy

If you wish to copy a highlighted section of the audio file or even the entire audio file, open the Edit menu and draw down to "Copy," or simply use "Apple"-keystroke "C" to copy the desired material. You need to immediately move to wherever in the audio file you wish to paste, as it is held in RAM and if you pause to copy something else first, you will blow out the first thing you copied and will have to copy it again.

Paste

You can paste a copied section anywhere you want by tapping once on the Line window, going to where you want to insert the copied region, placing the line, and then opening the Edit menu, where you can draw down to "Paste," or simply use "Apple"-keystroke "V."

Clear

For clearing one or more audio regions, simply highlight the desired region(s) you wish to erase from the session, using either the "hand" or the "I-Beam" line tool, and then press the "Delete" key on your keyboard.

Duplicate

Highlight a cut region that you wish to duplicate, then simply use the "Apple"-keystroke "D," and a precise copy of what you have highlighted will appear at the end of the highlighted edge. If you highlighted the file as well as a certain amount of blank track behind it, "Duplicate" will make a copy of the region as well as the blank space precisely. This option is very useful for cutting rhythmic sound effects. Sometimes I will master the "tick" and the "tock" of a clock only once, then bring the audio file into Pro Tools, cut apart the "tick" from the "tock" and experiment with temp.

If I want a precise clock I will take the leading edge of modulation of the "tick" and place it at the leading edge of a second, then take the leading edge of the "tock" and place it at the leading edge of the next second. Next I will highlight the two tracks with the "Selector" tool and extend the highlighted region to the leading edge of the third second. Now, if I press "Apple"-keystroke "D" over and over again, I will quickly make a precisely ticking mantle clock.

Or I may experiment with making the "tock" two seconds from the "tick," then highlighting both cuts as well as the blank space down to the leading edge of the fourth second and start duplicating. Now I have made a grandfather-clock tempo.

Mute/Unmute

Occasionally, I am not sure whether I want to remove complex edited bits in a particular passageor keep them. In this case, I highlight the material I wish to mute and use the Mute option, or just use "Apple"-keystroke "M." The waveform of the file turns mid-gray, denoting that you will not hear it. In this manner, whatever was highlighted, the one piece or section within a group of other cues, can be muted instead of the entire audio track.

Lock/Unlock

After I make the cuts in the desired manner, I highlight across entire sections and use the "Apple"-keystroke "L" for "Lock," or press it again to "Unlock." As you gain confidence and wish to use the Shuttle mode before cutting material deeper in the session, remember to highlight the cut material and "Lock" it down. Otherwise, as you use the Shuttle mode, making any kind of move or deletion, all the material behind the cut in that audio track shuttles closer toward the head of the reel as well. A few moments of forgetfulness teaches you very quickly to remember to lock down material you do not want manipulated.

IMPORT AUDIO FROM OTHER MOVIE

One of the best applications for assisting in the swift and accurate conversion and importation of audio CD material into a nonlinear edit domain is "Import Audio from Other Movie" (Figure 17.24). All audio CDs have a sampling rate of 44.1. Using the "Import Audio . . ." option, you can go to the desktop and highlight the audio CD that you put in the CD-ROM player of your computer, then open it up and a menu of the audio cues that exist on that audio CD will display.

Inside you will see numerous cues simply named Track 1, Track 2, Track 3, etc. Select the sound cue to import and engage. It will automatically default to the Audio Files folder in the Pro Tools session that you are working in, so if you wish the imported files to reside somewhere else, you will have to target a different folder. Once you have imported the file(s) I suggest you save and quit your session, open the folder where the new audio files are, and rename them before you starting using them.

Figure 17.24 The Movie menu.

If your session sample rate is 48 kHz, this importation function will also convert the incoming 44.1 kHz CD file as a 48 kHz sample rate to match the session that is fetching it.

This option is nice, but I find using the Audio Extractor software that comes as one of the goodie-tools with Toast software a far more muscular software to use. With Audio Extractor you can choose more than one file to import at a time. In fact, you can strip the entire CD with one keystroke, asking the software to strip everything—go pour yourself some coffee while it does it—in excess of ten times the real-time speed.

Next, you can batch-import all of the 44.1 kHz audio files that Audio Extractor just made for you by using the "Import and Convert" option that we discussed earlier (shown in Figure 17.8).

THE MIDI MENU

Open the "MIDI" menu (Figure 17.25). Though MIDI is usually thought of as a tool for music applications, many sound editors use it as fire points preprepared leading-edge-type sound cues, such as gunshots or impacts—especially if they are going to be using a lot of them and they do not have much time or desire to massage variation into precise audio-event points.

Refer to the owner's manual if you want to know more about these options. There are entire books on the subject of MIDI applications.

THE AUDIOSUITE MENU

Open the "AudioSuite" menu (Figure 17.26). You can fill this menu with a host of power DSP plug-in tools. Just describing the length and breadth of their uses would make an entire book

Figure 17.25 The MIDI menu.

of its own. If you are going to do your own signal processing, whether it be in part or heavy-handed, you should first consult with the individual or team leader of the mixing crew who is going to rerecord your session. Also, remember that it is better to signal-process with a sable brush than a sledgehammer, and most first-time users seem to take the sledgehammer approach. Refer to your owner's manual and seek out other publications regarding specialized plug-in signal-processing tools.

"BOUNCE TO DISK"—SIMPLE INTERNAL MIXING

From time to time you may want to make either a monaural or a stereo combine of multiple cuts from one channel, or multiple cues over several channels. Before you "bounce" anything, you need to remember that a "bounce" will be made to either a single or a stereo (two-track) channel (Figure 17.27). If you are "mixing" together multiple stereo pairs, then you first need to open the "Mix" window and go up the Output bar, the second bar down from the top of each channel that is going to be contributing an audio signal. All these bars need to be set to 1 and 2, that is, left and right. If they are not set to 1 and 2, you may hear them in the playback as the tracks are bounced, but any audio signals assigned to any other outputs other than 1 and 2 will not be mixed together in the new "bounced" audio file itself.

After you are satisfied with the export channel assignments, close the Mix window. Use the "Selector" tool to highlight the exact section of sound cue(s) that you wish to record as a new audio file. Once you have highlighted the desired section, you are ready to make your new audio file via "Bounce to Disk."

Open the File menu and draw down to "Bounce to Disk . . ." The menu shown in Figure 17.28 will appear. You must select which "bounce" you want to make. If you are going to import the new "bounced" audio track back into a Pro Tools session, then you will want the

Figure 17.26 The AudioSuite menu.

stereo files to appear as two monaural files, to which the software will automatically assign .L (for left) and .R (for right). If you are making a stereo audio file that you wish to use to "burn" an audio CD, select the last choice, "stereo (interleaved)," which will appear as one audio file, but a stereophonic one. Remember, if you wish to burn the audio file to an audio CD disk, you must also convert it to a sample rate of 44.1 kHz.

After you have the selections set the way you want, press the "Bounce" button at the bottom right of the menu.

You need to target where you want the new audio file to reside after the "bounce" process is completed (Figure 17.29). Unless you decide to place it in some other library folder or some other disk, for whatever reason, the software will default to the Audio Files folder of the session that you are working in.

Figure 17.27 Bouncing to disk:first highlight the material you wish to combine into either a monaural or stereo-pair audio file.

Figure 17.28 Setting your "Bounce" protocol.

Figure 17.29 Finding the new audio file a home.

IMPORTING AUDIO TRACKS FROM ANOTHER SESSION

From time to time you may want to combine audio tracks from another session into the session you are working in, or to build a combination session from two or more specialty sessions (Figure 17.30). Open the File menu and draw down to "Import Tracks . . ."

Figure 17.30 Importing audio tracks from another session.

Figure 17.31 Point to the session from which you want to access the audio tracks.

You need to find the session that you wish to import the audio tracks from and high-light it (Figure 17.31). Once you have found the session icon that you wish to access, high-light it and press the "Open" button in the lower right. The "Import Tracks" data window will appear as shown in Figure 17.32.

It is vital that you take time to make sure that you carefully choose which audio tracks you wish to import into your session as well as the options shown to the right. You need to make sure that the time code settings of both sessions match, or you may have to import and then highlight everything in those new tracks and manually move them down into sync. (Remember what we talked about with regard to setting up sessions without preroll?)

Figure 17.32 The Import Tracks data window.

Figure 17.33 The Import Allocation window.

You always want to make a "Copy from source media" in transferring tracks. What if you only "Refer to source media" and it is on a different drive, and then at a later time that other drive may not be with you on the stage or that material has been deleted. You would find yourself up the proverbial river, wouldn't you?

Target the Audio Files folder of the receiving session that the tracks are being brought into as the place to store the new audio copies.

The "Disk Allocation" window (Figure 17.33) will appear. Check to make sure that the hard-drive disk of all the tracks match; otherwise, you will have copied material and fade files spread over additional drives.

You probably want your imported "copied" files to be placed in the Audio Files folder of the session that is receiving the imported audio tracks. Simply make sure that the Audio File folder is highlighted and that the correct name of your session is shown in the bar above, then press the "Choose" button (Figure 17.34).

New imported tracks will always show up at the bottom of your session. One of the little techniques I employ is to save and quit my session after the copying of files. I will than take the "Fade Folder" from both the session I "copied from" and the session that I have "copied to" and drag them into the trash and flush them away. Then I will boot up the session with the new copied files. Of course it is going to ask, "Where is Fade . . . ?" I will press the "Skip all Fades" button, which will cue the software to redraw all the fades all over again. This practice helps maintain a more pristine folder of fades and avoids possible corruption and confusion.

"SAVE SESSION"

You should practice saving your work often—say it with me: "OFTEN." You will probably learn this credo the hard way, but don't say I didn't warn you. Go up to the "File" menu and

Figure 17.34 Choose a target folder.

drag down to "Save" your session, or "Save Session As." This allows you to make a copy of the session and give it a new name or version, as you should do each evening when you wrap work. It is an invaluable habit tomakeg backup sessions at the end of each day and place a copy of them on a floppy disk, Zip drive, or some other hard drive where your work resides. I have heard blood-curdling screams of editors after discovering that their hard drive has just "melted" because someone using the system the night before had forgotten to hook it back up the way she or he found it, and then it was booted up without the terminator in place. All that hard work just melted down with it, there being no disciplined backup habits in place.

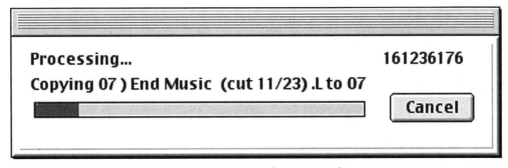

Figure 17.35 Processing new copies.

Figure 17.36 Import Tracks complete.

Occasionally, in the confusion of the heat of battle, a sound editor or an assistant blows material off a hard drive, thinking that a backup DLT or DVD-RAM was made when in fact one was not. On one occasion, we had one of the industry's top sound assistants, who has excellent work habits, enter the room and trip on a cord that had flopped onto the floor from a nearby desk. The assistant lost her balance and dropped a 9-gig drive. Upon its impact with the floor, all the work the dialog editor painfully had spent the weekend accomplishing was instantly wiped out. In this case, the dialog editor had been anxious to get home and had not made a backup session to a floppy for protection. Although the assistant could build another hard drive with all the dialog files backed up to a DLT when the PostConform session was originally made, none of the subsequent detailed editing work could be resurrected, because no backup session existed to rebuild it.

Get into a religious habit as part of your "wrapping work ritual" to make "Save Session As" copies of all work done throughout the day. If nothing else, make a folder on your computer desktop, drag the session icon over, and let it copy a backup into your desktop folder. The first time you lose a hard drive, you will be very thankful for the backups that mean instant resurrection of your lost work.

READY AND ARMED TO START CUTTING

Now that you have learned how to set up your session, how to sync to time code, how to make sure you are working in the desired bit rate and sampling rate, how to perform "bounce to disk," and how to import tracks from other sessions—now you can get started cutting and preparing your sessions. There is a lot more that you will need to know and learn in order to be truly proficient, much more than this book can cover. However, the information in his chapter can give you with a get-start understanding of how a direct-to-disk digital audio software program (in this case Pro Tools version 5.1.1) is meant to work and how you can utilize it. You have learned enough now to make the owner's manual a lot more understandable.

SOUND DESIGNER II AS STAND-ALONE PLATFORM

As you have no doubt come to realize by reading previous chapters in this book, I am passionate about working with my audio files in certain ways. One of those ways is to do mastering preparation in a stand-alone software program called Sound Designer II (SDII). This program is basically obsolete now. At least, it is obsolete to those who think you can accomplish the same things in AudioSuite in the Pro Tools platform. To a certain degree I agree with that opinion. But I do not like how AudioSuite makes new files, and I do not like the way I have to work with and manipulate the audio signal. I am a believer in embracing the best of the analog and the digital technologies together, and I like how Sound Designer II, as a stand-alone software platform, works. I can be far more accurate with the edits and far more discerning using Sound Designer II than using AudioSuite. Many in this field are looking for a high-quality equivalent to Sound Designer II. Of course, we need a software that can handle the higher sampling rates and larger bit depths that are now being recorded. I still maintain a workstation structured with an Audiomedia III card so that I can use Sound Designer II as a stand-alone platform. This card has also been discontinued by Digidesign, as I guess they found too many people were opting for it rather than their multi-thousand-dollar 888 interface with its need for expensive outboard hardware.

By the way, Pro Tools version 4.3 works very nicely on this Audiomedia III card, and it will sync to time code. I have cut numerous highly complex projects using just this simple little system, all for well under a thousand dollars (including the Mark of the Unicorn MicroExpress and the Mackie audio mixer).

First, you must understand that unlike Pro Tools (or other audio direct-to-disk editing platforms), Sound Designer II software is a destructive process. That is why I use it for mastering my audio effects and processing my various designs. I guess it served me pretty well

Figure 17.37 Booting up Sound Designer II.

on *Chain Reaction, Jingle All the Way, The Fifth Element, Dante's Peak, Starship Troopers, Jackie Brown, Lion King II,* and *Legionnaire* (to name just a few). It didn't seem to be a hindrance on those projects. It certainly made it vastly easier to maintain a controlled audio-management system in regard to naming files and cleaning out unnecessary audio junk to keep the system lean and mean.

You can record directly into Sound Designer II via the analog or the SPDF digital inputs in the Audiomedia III card, or you can bring in an existing file and boot it up into Sound Designer II (by simply dragging the file from the drive window and placing it onto the Sound Designer II icon alias that sits on the left side of your computer desktop screen.

In Figure 17.37, I have booted up the audio file entitled "MUSHROOMING FLAMES" (you can hear this sound effect if you wish to listen to cue #32 on the audio disk supplied with this book). The large part of the window shows the first two seconds of the left channel (on top) and the right channel (on the bottom) of this stereo file. The entire audio file (viewed as a single channel combine) is in the narrow strip above and just under the toolbar. We can see, at the far right of that waveform, that the file is 1.4 minutes in length. What can you use this software for? Why work in this platform rather than in the AudioSuite plug-in options of Pro Tools? Let's review what we can do with this software, and you can make up your own mind.

Like all File menus, the SDII File menu (Figure 17.38) is where you create a new SDII file (if you are going to be recording straight into the Sound Designer II software), or you can open other audio files to import all or highlighted portions.

Before I start work on "creating" a variation of or altering the audio file in any way, I first open the File menu and draw down to "Save a Copy . . ." I will make one change in the name—usually referring to my intentions, such as speed changes, pitch shifting, or, if I am simply cleaning and mastering, I will alter the designation as we talked about in Chapter 11.

Figure 17.38 The SDII File menu.

THE TOOLBAR FOR SDII

Following is a description of the basic array of tools to play, highlight, draw, record, and scrub your audio file.

Speaker

Highlight a region with the "Line" (the fifth box from the left) that you wish to listen to and then press the "Speaker" icon window (the second box from the left). You can also activate playback by simply hitting the space bar on your keyboard.

Box Zoom Window

Tap on the Box Zoom Window (the third box from the left) and then come down to enlarge the area desired. This window is explained in detail later on in this chapter.

Digital Pencil

The Digital Pencil is a very useful tool when you want to "draw out" mismatching wave-form curves that cause those nasty digital snaps and ticks. Note that the pencil is grayed out, which means that at this close proximity to the waveform, you cannot use it. You must zoom in close, where you can really see the individual rise and fall of the sine wave and effectively analyze and get your Digital Pencil in for precise work.

Figure 17.39 The SDII toolbar.

When you are close enough, the grayed-out appearance will change to a solid one like that of the other icons in the toolbar.

Remember that this is a destructive program, so when you draw the line, that is a permanent alteration. It is a good idea for you to do a lot of practice on a junk audio file so that you get the feel and manipulative prowess of this option. The Digital Pencil is described in greater detail later on.

Selector (Line)

The selector tool that I call the "line" is one that causes a vertical line to appear when you bring your cursor down and tap. But this point where the line appears is also exactly where the playback head will start playing from. It is also the leading edge of the region of the audio file that you might highlight. It is part of the defining parameters of the area that you may wish to alter through parametric or graphic equalization or pitch shifting. This is demonstrated for you later on in this chapter.

Enlarging Arrows

If you place your cursor over the arrow that is pointing to the left and tap, the waveform will step back—that is, you will see more of your audio waveform, just as if you had literally stepped back from the painting. If you tap on the arrow that points to the right, you will step in closer. As you tap more times on the same arrow, you will move in still closer, by steps, or you can back out by steps. Unlike the Box Zoom Window, where you physically draw a box parameter around the waveform segment you wish to fill the screen, here you simply press the arrow that points to the right to move in closer by steps, or the arrow that points to the left to move out by steps or the arrow that points upward to enlarge the waveform or the arrow that points down to reduce the waveform. If you place your cursor over the arrow that points upward and tap, the waveform will seem to grow in size, getting larger. Do not mistake this for volume shifting. This is simply a way to increase the dynamic look of your sine wave so that you can study it to manipulate it more easily. If you tap on the arrow that points down, you will obviously decrease the size of the waveform.

Markers and Inserts

I do not use the Markers and Inserts options, as I use Sound Designer II software only as an audio file manipulation and mastering tool. Editing options are accomplished in the Pro Tools editing platform.

Recording Deck

The Recording Deck is shown in Figure 17.40. When you press twice on this icon, the Recording Deck menu will appear. This window works just like a tape recorder. The transport controls work just like the Transport Windows described earlier in this chapter around Figure 17.8. You will note that you also have a two-channel peak meter as well as information on how much free disk space is left to use on your hard drive. The Recording Deck is what you

Figure 17.40 The SDII Recording Deck.

will use to record audio material, either analog or digital, into the nonlinear world of your computer.

Playback List

I do not use this option, as I do all my editing and mix work in the Pro Tools realm.

Playback Scrub

Playback Scrub is a very helpful tool when you want to "scrub," or listen to sound either faster or much slower than real time in order to help isolate precise points of pesky digital ticks or modulations of sound that are within a very active presence of other sounds that mask the waveform image.

USING THE RECORDING DECK

If you are going to record new material into your computer via the Sound Designer II software, you need to either boot up your SDII icon alias or, if the software is already open, go to the File menu and drag down to "New . . ." (or just use the "Apple"-keystroke "N"), and a menu will appear. The window will look identical to Figure 17.55, which will tell you that you are creating a new sound file and that you have options for what to call it, where to have it placed when it is made, and what bit depth and file format you want. In the lower left-hand box, you can choose to make special outputs for non-Mac PC computers or for other applications. You can make the following:

Sound Designer
Sound Designer II
Audio IFF (AIFF)
System 7 Sound
Compressed
.WAV (PC)
SDII Split Stereo

Once you have named your new audio file and made the appropriate choices, press the "New" button, and the Session window will open up.

Now go up to the toolbar and tap on the Recording Deck icon. The window shown in Figure 17.40 will appear. This is your tape recorder—a digital one. It is the portal from outside, working just the way you can record sound into your Pro Tools system. You have a two-channel peak meter that shows levels from –21 dB up to maximum. The name you chose is shown under "File Name." If you wish to change the sample rate, now is the time to do so. Close this window and open the Setup menu and draw down to "Hardware Setup . . ." A menu will appear that will tell you what kind of audio card you are using, your sample rate, bit rate, etc. You can choose from 48 kHz, 44.1 kHz, 22.05 kHz, or 11.025 kHz. You can also choose whether or not you wish to record your sound by importing it as an analog signal or whether you wish to record D-to-D (digitally).

Once you are satisfied with these choices, close this window and tap on your Recording Deck icon again. When you are ready to roll, simply press on the "Rec" button and you will be recording an audio file. The other buttons are obvious. "RTZ" is to return to top of the file. "Rew" is to rewind during playback. "Play" is for simply playing the audio file at normal speed. "FF"—is to fast-forward, or speed ahead, while you are in playback. "GTE" is to "Go to end," especially if you wish to add more recorded material to what you have.

If your recording is coming in too hot, you might want to open up the "Hardware Setup . . ." option in the Setup menu again. There is an option bar down near the lower left of the menu marked "More Options." Press on this and another menu will appear over the "Hardware Setup" window. This menu will allow you to set your input levels from zero down to –6 dB or up to as high as +15 dB, as well as select your digital input type (Tascam or S/PDIF). One assumes that the equipment that is used to playback audio to be imported into your software is working at a nominal, or "flat," level. Naturally, this is not always the case, so this volume option will be of great help to you.

Place your cursor over the Box Zoom Window (the third window from the left on your toolbar) and tap once. Now come down to your audio waveform and place the cursor above and to the left of the area you wish to enlarge. Tap down on your mouse and hold it down as you draw the window down and then to the right, creating the area parameter that you wish to enlarge. Let go of the mouse button and your audio waveform will instantly fill the screen according the parameters that you drew.

If you wish to pull instantly back to full view, place your cursor over the Box Zoom Window and just tap twice. The waveform image will enlarge to the default size. Remember, the main window is only a couple of seconds' view of your entire audio file. The long, narrow window just above shows your entire track.

When you first boot up your audio file, if it has not been worked on in Sound Designer II software before, or if you have just recorded a new audio sequence into the software, the

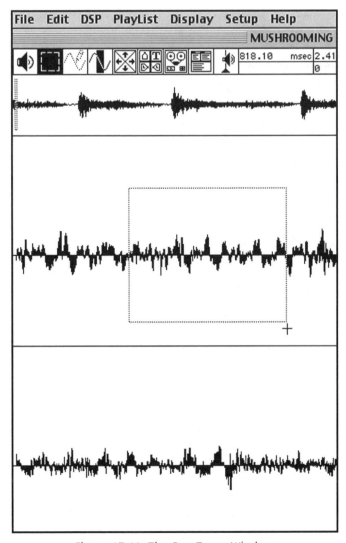

Figure 17.41 The Box Zoom Window.

long, narrow window will simply show measurement of time—either in seconds or in minutes with tenths of seconds designated at the end. In order to draw a waveform into that box to scan your entire audio form, move your cursor up into that long, narrow region and hold down the "Option" key. A little icon will appear whenever the cursor is in that long timeline region. Hold down your mouse button and a menu will appear. If your audio file is stereo, it will give you the choice of

Time Line
Left + Right
Channel 1
Channel 2

Figure 17.42 Medium enlargement of waveform.

If your audio file is monaural, the two choices will be "Time Line" and "Channel 1."

The waveform in Figure 17.42 is the same sound as shown in Figure 17.37, only now we have come in much closer—a medium distance.

The waveform in Figure 17.43 is the same sound as shown in Figure 17.42, only now we have moved in extremely close. Note that the Digital Pencil (Figure 17.44) is now solid, telling us that we can use it to draw on the waveform if we desire to do so.

Note how easy it is now to study the sine wave for imperfections, digital spikes, or other anomalies that you want to purge from your audio file before you send it into combat duty.

When you have enlarged your waveform close enough that the Digital Pencil appears solid, you are close enough to use it (Figure 17.44). This can be very helpful in eradicating the digital ticks and spikes or the mis-cuts when eliminating audio track that leaves a sine wave from up above the center line to a sudden drop below the center line, causing a tick or snap.

Remember that when you draw a new waveform, this is a destructive act. If you do not like the result, you need to go to "Undo" under the Edit menu immediately and change it; otherwise, you will be stuck with it or have to try to redraw it.

To highlight a region (Figure 17.45), go up to the toolbar and tap once on the Selector icon. Now your cursor is the playback head, or the tool to highlight a region of the audio file. If you place the Selector where you wish to start, press down on your mouse button and drag to the right until you encompass all that you wish to either play or affect through some editorial option or DSP signal processing.

Figure 17.43 Close enlargement of waveform.

THE EDIT MENU

Open the Edit menu, as shown in Figure 17.46, and take note of the following functions and options offered there.

Undo/Can't Undo

If you do not like what you just did, go up to the Edit menu and draw down to the first option, "Undo" (or simply use the "Apple"-keystroke "Z". If you are past the point that you can undo it, this option will say "Can't Undo."

Cut

If you want to eliminate a highlighted section of the audio file, open the Edit menu and draw down to "Cut" (or simply use "Apple"-keystroke "X"). The software will quickly make a

Figure 17.44 The Digital Pencil.

Figure 17.45 Highlighting a region.

backup copy in case you wish to "Undo" the cut, then it will shuttle through and eliminate the material and redraw the waveform for display. Check your cut immediately. If you wish to "Undo" it, you must do so immediately; otherwise, it will be permanent.

Copy

If you wish to copy a highlighted section of the audio file or even the entire audio file, open the Edit menu and draw down to "Copy" (or simply use "Apple"-keystroke "C") to copy the desired material. You need to immediately move to wherever in the audio file you wish to paste, as the material you are copying is being held in RAM, and if you pause and copy

| File | **Edit** | DSP | PlayList | Displa |

Can't Undo	⌘Z
Cut	**⌘X**
Copy	**⌘C**
Paste	⌘V
Clear	**⌘B**
Replace	⌘Y
Reverse	**⌘]**
Silence	**⌘E**
Trim	**⌘T**
Invert	**⌘[**
Fade In	**⌘/**
Fade Out	**⌘**
Normalize...	**⌘M**
Find Peak	**⌘K**
Change Gain...	**⌘G**
Compare Files...	**⌘=**
Smoothing	**⌘-**
✓ **Allow Edit Undo**	**⌘U**
Select All	**⌘A**
Show Clipboard	

Figure 17.46 The Edit menu.

something else first, you will blow out what you have just copied and will have to go back and do it all over again.

Paste

You can paste a copied section anywhere you want by tapping once on the "Line" window, going to where you want to insert the copied region, placing the line, and then opening the Edit menu and drawing down to "Paste" (or simply use "Apple"-keystroke "V")

Replace

If you wish to replace a section of track with something that you have just highlighted and copied, simply use the "line" to highlight the section of track you wish to swap out, then open the Edit menu and draw down to "Replace" (or simply use "Apple"-keystroke "Y").

Reverse

If you want to reverse the entire audio file, or maybe just a small highlighted section, simply highlight what you want to be reversed, open the Edit menu and draw down to "Reverse" (or use "Apple"-keystroke "]"). Very often I will want to have a reversed version of a particular sound event right next to the same sound playing forward. I simply highlight the sound event that I wish to also reverse ("Apple"-keystroke "C") to copy it, move the line just behind the forward version, tap the mouse to insert the line ("Apple"-keystroke "V") to paste a copy of the event, then highlight it and use"Apple"-keystroke "]" to reverse it.

Using this method when I am cutting an action scene means that I do not have to waste time stopping and making reverse copies of something that I have already anticipated I might need when I mastered the sound effect in the first place.

Silence

The Silence option allows you to mute parts of the audio file by highlighting the section of audio that you wish to be silent and using "Apple"-keystroke "E". Remember that this is a permanent mute. That part of the audio track will disappear forever.

Trim

Trim is the inverse application of Cut. When using the Trim option you highlight a section that you want to keep, then open the Edit menu and draw down to "Trim" (or simply use "Apple"-keystroke "T"). The rest of the audio file will be cut away, leaving only what you had highlighted to keep. For obvious reasons I do not use this option very often.

Invert

If you need to flop your sine wave so that you do not run into signal-cancellation issues, you can highlight one side of your stereo pair and open the Edit window, then draw down to "Invert" (or simply use "Apple"-keystroke "["). This will flip the waveform.

Fade-Ins and Fade-Outs

Two of the most used options are Fade In ("Apple"-keystroke "/") and Fade Out ("Apple"-keystroke "\"). Simply highlight the desired portion of your audio track and choose either the Fade In or Fade Out option. If you apply a fade once, it will equate to a 45-degree angle fade, as you saw in Chapter 13 (Figure 13.11). If you repeat the fade-in or fade-out application, the intensity of the fade-in or fade-out slope will change, moving to a more concave slope (as in Figure 13.11). And if you continue to apply the fade-in or fade-out option, the severity of the fade slope will increase accordingly.

Normalize

Normalize is one of my favorite options, as you can " kick butt" with the dynamics of sound design by utilizing it. The difference is, in this software I can apply it to only a highlighted area as needed, each one being of varying intensity. Highlight the section of audio you wish to affect in some way, such as dramatically increasing a face punch or a other kind of momentary audio event, then open the Edit menu and draw down to "Normalize" (or simply use "Apple"-keystroke "M"). A small window will appear for you to set how many decibels from maximum you wish the strongest point to be.

Personally, I never like to "Normalize" more than −3 dB of maximum. I choose what setting I wish and press the "Normalize" button. The software scans the highlighted area to be affected, looking for the loudest peak sample. Once it has found it, it will place it at the setting I choose—say, at −3 dB of peak meter maximum. The rest of the highlighted sine wave will increase in volume according to the decibel difference of where the peak sample point was as compared with the −3 dB position it is increased to.

This kind of audio track manipulation will make for a vast amount of fun sound-design opportunities, and I guarantee that you will use it a lot!

Find Peak

Suppose you want to increase the entire audio file, or a highlighted section by steps in decibels using the option of Change Gain, discussed next. You are unsure about spike points, so you use the Find Peak option to scan the audio track and show you the loudest point.

Let's say you wish to increase a section by −6 dB, which should be easy, but when you try it, you have an error window showing that some samples have "maxed" out. Now you want to know what is keeping you from being able to accomplish a simple global gain increase, so you use Find Peak in order to look throughout the audio file to find little peaks that are unusually higher than the rest of your track.

Now that you have found them, you can either use the Digital Pencil to draw them down, or highlight and lower them by precise decibel steps, or knock them down using the Normalize option to decrease them.

Sometimes I will have to do this throughout a two- or three-minute background track to tame a few rogue spikes before I can successfully raise a track by a desired amount without having any samples max out.

Change Gain

Rather than using the Normalize option, maybe I want to raise or lower an audio file or a highlighted region by precise decibel steps. Change Gain is exactly what I want for that job. Highlight the desired region or select all ("Apple"-keystroke "A"), then open the Edit menu and draw down to "Change Gain . . ." (or simply use "Apple"-keystroke "G"). A menu window will appear. It will show a "Change" box where you can either type in the exact decibel change you want (e.g., 6.500 dB to raise or −8.000 dB to lower) or choose a value within any thousandth of a decibel. There is a vertical "Gain" fader slide that you can simply push up or draw down, and the plus or minus decibel counts will be displayed in the "Change" box accordingly.

Next, you press the "Gain Change" button at the lower right, and the software will process the change. When it is completed, the "Done" button, which heretofore has been faded, will show boldly, but do not jump to press it until you take note of the "Clipping:" counts. If all three lines show zeros, then you know that no samples were elevated beyond maximum and you need have no fear of clipping. If you see any numbers next to "Samples Clipped," you will want to go up to the Edit menu and draw down to "Undo" and revert your Gain Change to the way it was and start over.

Allow Edit Undo

Always set the Allow Edit Undo option. At some point you will surely try something that you do not like, or you will slip and inadvertently choose something you did not mean to choose, and then you will need this option.

THE DSP MENU WINDOW

Open the DSP menu window (Figure 17.47). The options you will be most interested in are as follows.

SR Convert

Refer to "Speed Changing," discussed further on. SR Convert is the window that will come up when you choose this option.

Frequency Analysis

You can render a detailed spectral map of the audio timeline that you have highlighted with the Frequency Analysis selector. This map can help you understand what is going on in the various frequency ranges.

Time Comp/Exp

Frankly, I do not care for the Time Compress/Expansion option in Sound Designer II. I think that you can slow down or speed up a track only so much before it starts to sound metallic and flangey. I recommend that if you are interested in clean and dramatic slowing down or speeding up of your audio track, refer to "Speed Changing," a little further on in this chapter.

Figure 17.47 The DSP menu window.

Figure 17.48 The Parametric Equalizer.

Parametric Equalization

For parametric equalization (Figure 17.48), highlight the entire audio track, or just a highlighted portion that you wish to equalize, then open the DSP menu and draw down to "Parametric EQ." The window shown in Figure 17.48 will appear. You will note that you can choose one of five peak or notch options. You can set the parameters of whether to boost or attenuate the signal by adjusting the +/– "Boost/Cut:" option near the bottom. You move your cursor to the little fader slide to the right of each number and push them up or down, or you can enter exactly what you want by highlighting and typing in the exact number.

You choose the "Band Width:" and the "Center Freq." settings in the same way. The rectangular box to the right will instantly show you a variation graph of what kind of settings you are making. But your greatest meter, of course, is your own ears.

Graphic Equalization

The graphic equalization (Figure 17.49) on the Sound Designer II is useful for most easy tasks, but if you want real control, you may want to think about using an outboard equalizer prior to recording the material into your session—such as the thirty-band Klark-Technic. With the Sound Designer II, as shown in Figure 17.49, you have only ten equalization bands, and that is only if the audio track is monaural. On many softwares, when you are using the graphic equalizer option on a stereo audio file the ten-band graphic is cut in half to five bands. It does not allow you nearly as much maneuvering room for precise equalization as an outboard analog unit like the Klark-Technic would, with its thirty bands of stereo equalization at the ready.

Highlight the area you wish to equalize, or choose "Select All" for the entire file. Open the DSP menu and draw down to "Graphic EQ." Press the "Preview" button on the lower

Figure 17.49 The ten-band graphic equalizer for monaural audio files.

left, and the first five or six seconds of your audio file will loop while you adjust the settings. You should be very careful not to overprocess. Remember what I advised earlier in this book: the art to good sound editorial preparation is to rough the diamond down so that you can really see it and know how it is going to come on, but do not over-polish it. If you over-process, you run the risk of painting your rerecording mixer into a corner where she or he has lost too much low end or too much high end and thus cannot restore a fullness that, at the time you equalized your audio file, you thought was there. Now, played back in a mixing stage environment along with dozens if not hundreds of other sound effects, dialog, and music, your processing has emasculated the heart and soul from your sound cue. Let the user beware.

THE DYNAMIC SETTINGS MENU

The Dynamics Settings menu (Figure 17.50) is where you will find your compression/expansion options. These can be configured to be a noise gate or an expander, or a compressor/limiter—it's all in how you set them up. First, choose which mode you wish to manipulate the audio signal. Then press the "Preview" button on the lower left of the menu screen. The audio cue will play and loop continuously as you set your adjustments prior to reprocessing.

Input

You can adjust the volume of the audio signal with Input, a vertical fader slide. Note the "–4 dB" data at the base of the "Input" slide showing that the audio signal has been reduced by –4 dB.

Figure 17.50 The Dynamic Settings menu.

Detect

The Detect option sets the strength, or sensitivity, necessary to detect the incoming signal by use of "Averaging" the frequencies volumes or by using the "Peak" of greatest amplitude.

Threshold

You can set the Threshold sensitivity to a −dB of maximum setting, thereby setting the bar at what level you wish to start affecting either compression or expansion.

Attack

For the Attack option, you set the leading edge of the change by milliseconds to determine how suddenly you wish the ramp-up to hit, much like the fade-in and fade-out slopes we talked about earlier in the Pro Tools edit mode. You can make the effect too obvious and harsh by setting the Attack too short. It is up to your ears and your common sense to decide.

Release

The Release mode is where the threshold that activated the compression or expansion has been completed and now you are returning to the normal playback. How fast or how slow to "normalcy" will be determined by how long a "Release" you set. In the same way that you could think of the Attack as the fade-in, so you can think of the Release as the fade-out. This is a far more gentle slope—notice that at the base, it says 1.35 seconds. You can slope the Release to as much as 20.0 seconds. Again, it all depends on the audio cue and how your ears perceive the desired application effect to work.

Figure 17.51 The Setup menu.

Ratio

The amount of force applied by its unit value times whatever the ratio setting is will influence the desired effect.

Output

Once you have set the Dynamic settings, you can then set the "Output" level.

THE SETUP MENU

If you open the Setup menu (Figure 17.51), you will notice that this is where you find the "Hardware Setup . . ." It works very much the same as the Pro Tools hardware window except that Sound Designer II software works off the Audiomedia III card.

There are times that you may not want the screen to scroll after you stop playing. In the two- to three-second window, the playback "line" usually is not within the window anyway, and if you are concentrating on a particular waveform scape [that you wish to work with and then you stop the playback, the screen will instantly change to where the playback ended. This can really make your body temperature skyrocket until you remember to turn the Scroll After Play option off.

PITCH SHIFTING

After you have highlighted either the entire audio file, or just the portion that you wish to change, open the DSP menu and draw down to "Pitch Shift." The window shown in

Figure 17.52 The Pitch Shift option.

Figure 17.52 will appear. You may alter the pitch of only a portion of any given audio file, if you wish—it is not an all-or-nothing proposition.

Press the "Preview" button on the lower right-hand side of the menu. The highlighted portion will play and loop continuously so that you can audition it as you change the pitch up or down. The "Course" vertical slider moves the pitch up by semitone steps while the vertical slider next to it can adjust in percentages within those steps.

If you check the Time Correction box, the software will try to keep the audio file "time accurate"—though I have not always found it to succeed at this.

Once you have the settings the way you want them, turn off the "Preview" option and press the "Process" button. The program will ask if you are sure—remember, this is a destructive program, and you will be able to "Undo" only once if you do not like a result.

This option is especially useful if you are designing sounds where you want little variations so that repetition of the same type or seemingly same type of sound is used frequently—such as a sword fight where you want the sword swishes to have a more dramatic shift in variation than just depending on the subtlety of the actual performance. With Pitch Shift, you can pitch the swishes up and down from one cue to the next. Using the Pitch Shift option on numerous repetitious sound cues makes it extremely easy to build in variation and thus make audio-event performances more interesting.

SPEED CHANGING

Speed changing is is one of my favorite ways to manipulate speed shifting in the digital audio world. Frankly, I do not like the DSP function options that nearly all digital audio platforms offer. If you slow or speed up the audio too much, it takes on a whole lot of funny-sounding flangey anomalies and does not sound at all satisfying.

The trick is to fool the computer by making the sound something that it is not in order to resample it the way you want it. To do this you have to access the Information window

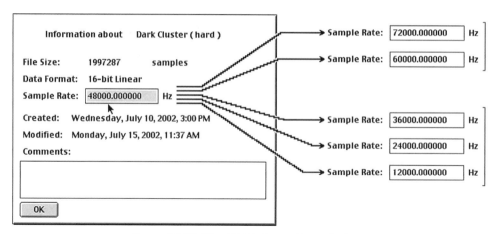

Figure 17.53 The SDII Information window.

that shows you the "Sample Rate" of the audio file. In the case of the Information window shown in Figure 17.53, the audio file is called "Dark Cluster (hard)."

You will note that it was recorded in as a 16-bit, 48 kHz (48,000) sample-rate audio file. Fine. Now suppose I wish to make a one-fourth-speed version of it. Note the sample-rate windows to the right. The two at the top show sample rates that I would enter instead of 48,000 if I wish to speed up the sound. In the case of 60,000, the sound would speed up 20 percent. In the case of 72,000, it would speed up 50 percent.

Notice the three sample rates to the lower right. These are three random choices that would slow the sound down. If I entered 36,000, it would slow the audio file by 75 percent of normal speed. If I entered 24,000, it would slow the audio file by half speed (50 percent). If I entered 12,000, it would slow the audio file by one-fourth of normal speed. It is all mathematical.

Once I enter the desired sample-rate change I will close the window and audition the sound by playing it. If I do not like the speed choice, I will reopen the window ("Apple"-keystroke "i") and change it again. Then I will close the window and audition the new speed choice. Once I have the new audio speed the way I want it, I will need to make a copy of it—resampling the audio file back to the 48 kHz (48,000) standard at which I am working.

My next step was to go up and open the "DSP" menu. I drew down to "SR Convert" (Sample Rate Convert). The Sample Rate Conversion menu appeared, as shown in Figure 17.54. In this case, the sample rate I had settled on was 12 kHz (12,000). I entered 48,000 in the "New Sample Rate" box and pressed the "Convert" button at the bottom. A new menu window appeared, as shown in Figure 17.55.

I was creating a new sound file, which is why I had to give it a new name. Never name the new sound file the same as the one you are making it from. Change just one letter, an extra space, an asterisk—or in this case I entered "-4" behind the world "hard," which was a signal to me that this is a one-fourth-speed version of the original.

On the lower group of choices you need to be consistent with the bit rate, so that is the same. In this case, it is a stereo audio file, so I left that, of course. However, I can have a stereo

Figure 17.54 Resampling the altered sound.

file made in one of two ways. I can have an interleaved single file that is stereo (which is the kind of file that you make to burn audio CD disks-provided, of course, that the sample rate is 44.1 kHz),or I can have them as split stereo files, which is how Pro Tools wants to see and work with stereo audio for editing purposes.

Just as you can choose other kinds of audio files to make when you create new ones (as discussed earlier under "Using the Recording Deck"), you need to make the same choices here. In the lower left-hand box, if you are making special outputs for non-Mac PC computers or for other applications, you can generate Sound Designer, Sound Designer II, Audio IFF [AIFF], System 7 Sound, Compressed, or WAV [PC] audio files. Make sure that you look at the drive window and highlight what folder in what drive you want your new copy to be placed.

Figure 17.55 This is where you give your new sound file a name and assign it to be placed somewhere.

ENOUGH TO GET STARTED

Although these are only highlights of the numerous digital tools and functions of the relevant software, they are important get-start techniques. Just remember not to let the computer take over and intimidate you. Digital technology has not reinvented the audio arts or established techniques and disciplines developed to achieve superior audio experiences. Digital technology provides excellent new tools to be used, not to dominate us.

Chapter 18
The Music Composer:
Audio Collaboration or
Mud and Destruction

"Music is nothing more than organized sound effects, and sound effects are nothing more than disorganized music."

David Lewis Yewdall, M.P.S.E., during a 1991 lecture at the Sibelius Academy, Helsinki, Finland

I remember, growing up, going to the local cinema to see the week's double feature. I sat transfixed, totally in awe of the epic spectacle of Charlton Heston dividing the Red Sea, painting the Sistine Chapel, driving the Moors out of Spain, protecting the foggy Norman bogs from raiders of the northlands, and defending the walls of Peking from the Boxer Rebellion. The majestic musical scores filled me with inspiration. Who are these musical dreamers that can create things that reach into my very soul and manipulate my emotions?

Names like Erich Wolfgang Korngold (*The Sea Hawk, Of Human Bondage, The Adventures of Robin Hood, Deception, Captain Blood*), Miklós Rózsa (*El Cid, Ben Hur, Ivanhoe, Men of the Fighting Lady, The Asphalt Jungle*), Dimitri Tiomkin (*Duel in the Sun, 55 Days in Peking, Giant, Big Country, The Guns of Navarone, Dial "M" for Murder*), Jerry Goldsmith (*Lilies of the Field, The Sand Pebbles, Planet of the Apes, Patton, Chinatown*), Elmer Bernstein (*To Kill a Mockingbird, The Hallelujah Trail, Hawaii, The Magnificent Seven, The Great Escape*), Alfred Newman (*The Robe, How the West Was Won, Airport, Demetrium and the Gladiators*), Maurice Jarre (*Lawrence of Arabia, Doctor Zhivago, The Train, Grand Prix*) thrilled me, lifted up and inspired me, made me want to come back and see it all over again and be bathed in the lush glory of it all.

There was Bernard Herrmann, a category unto himself. No one else had a style like him. Who would soon forget the haunting scores to pictures like *Citizen Kane, Jane Eyre, The Naked and the Dead*, and *The Day the Earth Stood Still*? Sometimes I wonder how successful

Alfred Hitchcock films would have been without Bernard handling the musical scores for *North by Northwest, Vertigo, The Man Who Knew Too Much,* and *Psycho*—and he even got to show off his flair for instrumental humor in *The Trouble with Harry.*

Other contemporaries wrote their own great works; Ennio Morricone, Brian May, Bill Conti, Lalo Schifrin, and Henry Mancini are just a few of the great music composers who added musical magic to dozens of major and well-loved motion pictures.

The filmography of music composers is truly a shelf of books unto themselves. Music is the most powerful and manipulative art form. It does not require translation for foreign sales; it does not require subtitles to explain itself or establishing shots to orient the listener. With a single note, music can reach into the heart and soul of the audience to set the mood, telegraph danger, or evoke romantic passions. Music whips up our emotions; reveals the guilty; sweeps us into the complex whirlpools of love, pain, anger, fear, patriotism, and joy, sometimes all at the same time.

So, if music is so powerful and omnipotent in films, why do we need dialog and sound effects? Many composers have asked that very question. Some would be perfectly content to return to the days of flickering images on the wall with insert cards for bits of dialog and story exposition while the only audio track would be their music.

CHALLENGES OF WRITING FOR THE SCREEN

An important lesson a music composer learns is that writing music for the screen is very different from writing music that is a total performance unto itself. When writing for the screen, the composer must understand that she or he is sharing the audio track with two other major concerns: spoken dialog and sound effects. These factors are working together as part of a collaborative trio, rather than each singing their own aria.

When I was preparing a film for the Sundance Film Festival, the director was scrambling to complete his project with the few dollars left. He could not afford an established music composer, but found a promising new music group who wanted to break into writing for the movies. The musicians delivered their music cues in two-channel stereo on DAT. They were so interested in the opportunity that they personally brought the tape to me.

I loaded the cues into the Pro Tools session and laced them up into sync, according to the director's notes. It was immediately evident that the music cues were unacceptable. From a technical point of view, the recordings had been overloaded—a common mistake of rock groups who think that volume is achieved by crashing the upper limits of the digital peak meter. At the very least, the cues needed to be transferred from the master and lowered by −6 dB.

The lead guitarist informed me they had no master; they performed straight to a DAT tape. I explained the virtues of recording to a multichannel master first, where one can record each element of the music group onto its own stereo pair of channels and then control the mix-down later. They were faced with having to reperform the cues over again. It was just as well, as I showed them where the levels had flattened out in what I call the "aircraft carrier effect," where they had run out of digital zeros and ones. Surely they did not want their music to suffer dynamic flatness and distortion.

That was only a technical problem, however. A deeper, more important issue was at hand. They had written the music as if they were performing a solo act at a rock concert—full out, with no regard for anything else happening on the screen. What did they expect would happen to their music when dialog was spoken? What did they expect would happen to their music when the comic and raucous car sound effects were played? They had not considered those things.

I took a piece of paper and drew a giant circle. I told them to think of this as the total amount of audio energy that can play on the screen at any given moment. It was like that peak meter where their music clashed. There just wasn't any more level to be had—the digital ones and zeros were all used up. This is the principle by which we mix any motion picture, whether in analog or digital form.

I drew pie slices out of the circle. In one pie slice, I wrote "MUSIC," in another I wrote "SOUND EFFECTS," in the last I wrote "DIALOG." Remember, the dialog track will always and must always play. On rare occasions, the filmmaker may decide to stylize particular moments of the film, in which case the dialog track shuts down, and either a combination of conceptual sound effects and music or simply music alone plays out. Such scenes can be extremely effective, but an entire motion picture cannot be made this way. Such moments are the exceptions, not the rule. For the majority of a film's sound track, the dialog track is dominant; therefore any music score that steps on a dialog line or makes it unintelligible is likely to be dropped or lowered so much that the composer will surely rewrite it rather than have it sound so squashed.

The smart composer knows this and carefully writes the music so it can expand, stretch, or envelop when not in competition with dialog cues; the composer also pulls back and writes music that complements or enhances the dialog in a collaborative fashion.

The same is true when it comes to sound effects, only with a different and competitive edge. Unlike the dialog track, which always plays, the sound effects track is not constantly heard. For decades, sound effects editors and music composers have been clashing and competing for dominance. Those on both sides have healthy creative egos and know their contribution is vital to a film's successful sound track. Some individual artists, however, such as the rock group mentioned earlier who had never written for the screen, are beset by ignorance. Almost all these difficulties can be eliminated by a collaborative effort between music and sound editorial far in advance of the rerecording stage. As we will discuss later, this process seems obviously necessary, yet is very seldom practiced, for a number of reasons.

One of the most common errors music composers make is that they often "sting" sound effect moments, probably the greatest contributor to sound effects and music colliding in competition on the dubbing stage. Stinging sound effect cues is what is done for silent movies, where no other sound-track elements exist other than music. A "stinger" is probably best described as a musical sound effect used as punctuation. It is the clash of a cymbal mixed with a blast of brass in dissonance—a short exclamation point. It is a sharp rip across the strings of violins and violas to the visual of the knife appearing suddenly above the victim. It is the crash of reverberating chords as the hero turns and suddenly confronts the killer. Stingers come in countless combinations, usually of very short duration to underscore, punctuate or shock the audience. By nature, they are usually robust in volume—but not always. Sometimes they can be a subtle low end thumb with a sustaining note or pitch shift variation. In the silent days, some of the major movie theatres had custom Wurlitzer organs with the capacity to generate a whole array of sound effects in addition to music. The organ could produce gunshots, booms, pealing bells, and even horse hooves for the inevitable chase.

Another sting-effect conflict occurs when explosions are planned in a sequence. Often, the temptation for the music composer is to sting the explosions. The result obviously leads to a clash between sound effects and music as they simultaneously attempt to share the same slice of that energy pie. Either music or sound effects, or both, suffer. The smart music composer recognizes that sound effects must work in sync with the event on the screen.

On the other hand, music does not need to be frame-accurate. Knowing this, the composer may write a stinger that hits just prior to, or just after, leaving a "hole," where the sound effect can properly live and play fully. This technique enhances not only the effect, but the musical emotion of the moment.

The intelligent composer also chooses the instruments according to what kind of timbre and frequency textures the sound effects possess. It makes no sense to compose a musical passage using bass violas with low-end dominance to play against the thunderous cascade of a volcanic eruption where rock and lava are flowing. Sound effects must work with low-end and mid-range music as a foundation. Wise instrument choices are those that get up out of the competitive regions—instruments that "cut" through the wall of sound effects surely produced by sound editorial, instruments that allow the music to survive and live alongside its sound effects track comrades.

Study the work of John Williams. He can write big, lush scores that still compete with big sound effects. This is accomplished not just because of his intelligent selection of when to push big and when to retract selective pieces, but also because of his experienced picks of which instruments fulfill the musical moment and best survive the rerecording mix without needing pull-back and emasculation.

Some modern composers use their own brand of sound effects, working them into the very musical score itself. Nagging incidents do occur when a music composer actually scores the picture in a deliberate attempt to torpedo the sound effects track, sometimes out of ego, other times out of ignorance or fear of collaboration. Some of these basic competitions are never overcome entirely. Nonetheless, we must continue to focus on what is good for the film, what serves the need of the film's sound track at each moment in time.

SET THE MUSIC COMPOSER EARLY

The smart producer sets a music composer far in advance of the actual work. This accomplishes two things. First, it assures the producer of the desired composer, rather than using one hired at the last minute because the initial choice was booked up and unavailable. Second, the producer can use what I call the "Debra Hill Logic." In the early 1980s, I was contracted to supervise the sound for *The Dead Zone,* directed by David Cronenberg and produced by Debra Hill. I had supervised the sound on several other projects Debra produced, and she knew how I worked. I received a call from her, saying she was going to fly me to Toronto so I could look at the director's cut of the picture. At the time, I thought it was a waste of money. The film would be coming down to my shop in just over a month anyway, so why spend the dollars?

Debra matter-of-factly replied that creativity does not happen instantly, that it takes time to ferment and percolate. Since she had a finite budget, she could put my subconscious to work, problem solving and creating at no cost until the film was turned over to me several weeks later. I never forgot that, or how true it is. By the time *The Dead Zone* was turned over, I was ready to hit the Moviola designing.

Setting the music composer as far in advance as possible, and submitting work-in-progress videotapes, allows the composer the same advantages to write a far more creative score than having to deliver the score overnight. A person asked to create instantaneously does not have time to develop new ideas; he or she simply falls back on the experiences of what was done before and creates variations to make it work. Hence, sometimes you hear a score written by a particular music composer with strains and elements that sound much like something written by the same person for a previous picture, or sounding incomplete since it was not possible to allot sufficient time for working out the details of instrument usage.

Listen to several of James Horner's scores. Though I enjoy the style of his music, you will quickly see how he recycles his own material. I often hear strains and/or passages of *Star Trek II: The Wrath of Khan* in many other scores he has written since. Listen to the opening music of *Millennium Man* and then play the opening score to *A Beautiful Mind*. It is the same music—simply remassaged. Many others who are guilty of repeating themselves this way, but these examples are particularly obvious.

BASIC MECHANICS

During the picture editing process, temp music is pulled from audio CDs or other tape sources to be cut in along the cut picture, to relate a scene's intent or a mood set by music. If a music composer is already set for a film, she or he is included in the preliminary process, discussing styles and possible temp pieces. During this time, the composer is already formulating certain concepts and ideas that will ultimately yield an interesting and successful musical score.

Most composers have a music editor with whom they are accustomed to working, and, in turn, the music editor is set for a film project as soon as the music composer is committed. The music editor handles and takes care of the management of the score, freeing the composer to focus on the singular and crucial task of creating the music itself.

One famous composer cannot even read music. He also is incapable of personally setting his themes to paper. As creative and wonderfully rich as his scores are, he either whistles or hums them to the orchestrater, who, in turn, sets them to paper. This is not to imply there is any deficiency in his work. On the contrary, his work is delightful and always in demand. It is just an additional hurdle he must overcome, along with the usual daily requirements that haunt all composers.

When the picture is locked and ready for turnover, the music composer and music editor have one or more music spotting sessions. The picture editor, director, and producer sit with the composer and music editor and run the film, discussing the kind of music required, the intent of the score, and its desired effect on the audience. Most music editors use a stopwatch to time the start and end points, making careful notes for the composer to review later. Other music editors take advantage of the computer that drives the Avid or Final Cut Pro, having the counter set to zero at the beginning of each cue point. Instead of feet and frames, the calibration is set for minutes and seconds. At the end of the session, the music editor has compiled the list of music cues and their running times. (This list immediately assists the composer in scheduling musicians and a scoring stage.)

Sometimes the music composer is involved in writing special cues for "source music" (music that comes from practical props in the film, such as radio, jukebox, TV, or Muzak in an elevator or waiting room). Such music often is licensed, broken down into a few parts based on how many seconds the piece is played in the film. Obviously, the cost of licensed music differs widely depending on the fame and importance of the piece or artist. We often hear "Bad to the Bone" used as temp music in a film, but rarely do we see it licensed for the actual sound track.

On major pictures, a composer may be contracted to produce a score electronically first (known as a "synth" score) so that studio executives can get a feel for the music and screen it with test audiences. With motion picture budgets soaring higher for the mega-blockbusters, and with the knowledge that a music score can make or break a picture, it does not seem unreasonable to have an electronic version produced first—as long as it is paid for in the budget. With digital emulators and synthesizers today, music scores sound extremely "real," and although they do not have the timbre and depth of a full orchestra, they bring the intent of the composer's design into a crisp focus. Once the studio approves and signs off on the "synth" score, arrangements are made for a scoring stage and musicians for a series of scoring sessions, where the music is rehearsed and recorded for final mastering.

Although music cues have nicknames or pet designations, for organizational reasons they are generally referred to by reel and position. For example, the fourth music cue in Reel 5 will be listed as 5-M-4.

BASIL POLEDOURIS

Basil Poledouris first trained to be a concert pianist, then studied opera because of its theatrical drama. He eventually discovered this thing called "film," which had all the theatricality of opera—the staging, the drama—plus close-ups! "It really excited me," remarks Basil. "Two of the most formative influences on the way I write music were Miklós Rózsa and Alfred Newman. I like the spectacle of it, the largeness—the scope. The sound of an acoustical orchestra, it is very thrilling!"

Figure 18.1 Music composer Basil Poledouris, in his studio in Venice, California, transposes his new theme concept via emulators and synthesizers into his 24-bit Pro Tools workstation for audition purposes. (Photo by David Yewdall)

Somehow it was more dramatic, more immediate. "All I've ever wanted to do is write film scores, and to this day that's all I have done. Oh, I've taken a couple of excursions outside of film, like the opening ceremonies for the Olympics, which is more like a ballet. It was really a dance with ancient Greek athletes sort of portraying it. The other outing was the *Conan: Sword and Sorcerer Show* that was at Universal Studios for years."

As only fitting, Basil had written the score for both *Conan the Barbarian* in 1980 and *Conan the Destroyer* in 1983. Some composers write a film score for the album and not for the movie, Basil considers his work of writing music for film an end unto itself. "There's no guarantee that you'll get an album out of the movie. You have to write for the film, otherwise you are not doing justice to the picture.

"The key to composing good music for the screen is to focus on the dramatic reinterpretation of the film itself. When I work on a picture, I try to interpret the story musically. There, by definition, I have to follow what is there, up on the screen. You can't tell a different story. Oh, you can tell it from a slightly different point of view, and that's often what I will end up doing, especially if the director has that intention, but you are still telling the same story."

Basil's personal style has served him well. He's written scores for *The Hunt for Red October, Free Willy, Les Misérables, Under Siege 2, Robocop, Wind, Big Wednesday, Quigley Down Under, Breakdown, Red Dawn,* and *Starship Troopers,* to name just a few. Each movie dictated a different style, demanding from Basil a fresh approach and precise awareness of the subject on screen.

"There is a very fine line between being aware of your work, without being self-conscious. We all walk that thin line, when we're in it. You don't want to be too aware of what you are doing, because then it becomes too intellectualized. You can overthink the process to the point that it becomes truly manipulative, because then you're thinking about how it's going to affect the audience—as opposed to how it affects you, as an artist, and then you are just retelling that affect."

Collaboration between music composer and sound effects team truly improves the final effort. "Of all the films to which we give the lip service—'Oh, yeah, we're gonna work closely with the sound effect editors'—*Wind* is the only picture that we really did [that on]. It takes two things to truly bring a music and effects collaborative effort together.

"First, it takes the willingness of both the music composer and the sound effects editing team to want to do this. To set up the communication lines—asking what the other side is doing in a particular sequence or even to ask if it might be possible to get a DAT layback of some of the key sounds that the sound effects editors are using so that a composer can listen to the frequencies and harmonics. It makes a tremendous difference in how I might handle a particular music cue, as well as what instruments I choose to use.

"Secondly, it takes time to collaborate. It was always difficult to encourage real collaboration when we worked back on film, let alone today with nonlinear technology and highly compressed post-production schedules. The lightning-speed delivery expectations have completely spun out of control.

"It is not unusual for the producer to call me up before breakfast, telling me they have a problem," Basil says with a sigh. "Another cue, either rewritten or new, is necessary and, by the way, they need it on the stage to mix into the film just after lunch. How can one possibly hope to exercise collaboration with sound effects like that? You can't. What has to happen is the producer and director have to continually be brought into the equation. They have to be made cognizant that they are the key to really encouraging and making intercollaboration work. If they understood how much positive impact it has on their sound-track, and therefore on their film, then more producers and directors would be making the collaboration concept a much higher priority."

After being contracted to score a new film, the music composer first must determine what it is about, not just as a filmmatic story, but as it translates to the needs of the music composition. "Sometimes it is very obvious," continues Basil. "When I write a score, I usually try to make a metaphor out of the movie. That is where I really start my work. Then I will sit and think it through, saying, 'What if it were this, instead of that? What if it were about something completely different? What if it were me in that situation? How would I feel or respond?' It's just a way to trigger, emotionally in me, something in my own experience that I relate to—such as bugs, from *Starship Troopers*. Bugs, in and of themselves, do not scare me, so I have to sit and transpose. What . . . really terrifies me is something like the Orwellian rats in 1984. Whatever it is, I find something within me from a personal experience.

"The very next step I will do is to sit at the piano and just free-associate, to think about a character, an event, or a philosophical concept in the film, and I then just start improvising. I don't even want to be held up by writing it down on paper or recording my improvisational sessions. Then there comes a time when I will know it is time to set it down, whether on tape or just start writing. It may come to me at two or three in the morning, and when it comes I have to get up and start working. Sometimes I will have fuller orchestration ideas, and I will fill it out earlier on with synthesizers."

The key is to capture the mood, the color of the sequence, for which you write. "Many times I find that I am actually scoring the director when I am writing the music. I have worked for the same director on more than one film, and I find that their personal themes and styles remain consistent. The material that they are attracted to is something that lives within them. I know what Paul Verhoeven's mind is like—I know his approach and take on how a particular scene will be, for the most part. That's not to say that [he doesn't] sometimes throw up some startling aspects, but Paul will usually go for the throat. You never need to be embarrassed about going over the top with Verhoeven. Rarely has he ever said that something is too much."

"Randal Kleiser (*Blue Lagoon*), on the other hand, wants a sort of gestalt between the audience and the film. Things are left . . . open. Not neutral, exactly. Just not so reinforced, musically, that the audience can only perceive it as one thing or the other.

"John Milius is another director who is very clear. He wants the music to speak very directly—mostly melodic. John is a romantic at heart. Bille August is another romantic director; it's just that he achieves his romanticism by keeping a restraint on it, a restraint that creates this kind of tension. On the other hand, Milius does not hold back, he just goes for it.

"John McTiernan is more interested in tension, on keeping the camera moving constantly, never letting the audience rest. On *The Hunt for Red October*, it was more than just developing a tension. John wanted the music to represent a culture. The whole Russian state was sort of poured into the building of the submarine *Red October*, which was the ultimate machine that they had been produced at that time."

During the filming of *The Hunt for Red October* the Soviet Union collapsed, which could not help but cause a change in inflection, a spin different than if that country had held her hard-line existence when the film was released to theaters.

Basil remembers the effect these historical developments had on his music for the film. "The Soviet Union's collapse did have an influence; how could it not have? I think it caused the producers to turn the film more into a mystery, rather than a straight-ahead defection. The book was very clear about the captain's actions in turning the submarine over to the Americans, and that, of course, is still there. But as the Soviet Union collapsed so suddenly, the producers wanted to slant it as more of a sympathetic mystery. The film had already been shot. We were deep in post-production when the Soviet Union ceased to exist politically. It was not a matter of reshooting anything, but through the editing and how the music would be scored, we could give the story a different slant, a different reality.

"Early on, we thought that the music would be more confrontational—there were the Russians, and there were the Americans. If I were to use role models of style, there would be Prokofiev and Aaron Copeland. Early on, Copelandesque parts went by the board, as it was really Ramius's story, and the action music was sort of rhythmic with a Russian choir. From the beginning, McTiernan had Russian choir elements in mind. He built it into his temp music tracks. Since the beginning of the film is rather lengthy, from the time that *Red October* leaves port, to the time we go to Washington and set up Jack Ryan and the metal fatigue issues, McTiernan did not want the audience to forget that there is a Russian submarine out there."

Basil asked McTiernan about *Red October's* Russian translation, which proved to have a tremendous influence on how Basil wrote the theme. The very lilt of the pronunciation of the words in Russian gave Basil the famous emphasis that underlined the theme.

"Latin does the same thing to me. We used a lot of Latin in *Conan the Barbarian*, which greatly influenced how I wrote it. The stress and the syllables. It scans differently than English, and it gives songs a melodic feel that says French, Italian, or Russian. It cannot help but influence how I write.

"For acoustic instruments, nothing sounds better than recording analog at 15ips with Dolby-SR. The richness of basses, cellos, the horns—there is a lushness that comes from saturation of the tape," explains Basil.

MUSIC EDITOR

After cutting music for the last thirty years, Ken Hall knows a thing or two about film music, whether for the big screen or television. Ken's original training was responsible for the foundation of his professionalism. "I was extremely lucky to break into music by learning my craft with the legendary music director, Lionel Newman. It was the greatest training ground in all of music editorial. You learned how to do bar breakdowns, how to do tie ins and tie outs. You learned cuing the Newman system. This kind of training was just unheard of in those days. You were taught how to subdivide bars. A guy could be in 7/8 or 5/8 flip-flop patterns. For instance, if you are in a 7/8 bar, there are seven eighth notes, but the composer may have written it in a quarter and a quarter and three-eighths—'daa, daa, da-da-da.' Or he might have written it 'da-da-da, daa, daa'—three eighths and two quarters, and so forth. You had to prepare the groundwork for the composer before we got to the scoring stage. That was the job of a music editor, and this kind of training was invaluable to anyone who expected to excel in this field."

Ken cut television music until theatrical composers became aware of his personal style and abilities. Shortly thereafter, Ken broke into working on theatrical films. Just prior to leaving 20th Century Fox, Ken handled the music cutting chores on the *Swiss Family Robinson* television series, as well as cutting theatrical work, such as *Silver Streak* with Henry

Mancini, and bringing Dino De Laurentiis's remake of *King Kong* into the studio with composer John Barry. Over the years, Ken has worked with top film music composers such as Lalo Schifrin, Jerry Goldsmith, John Williams, Bill Conti, and Henry Mancini—all names that at that time led Ken to believe he could break out on his own, offering his own independent music editorial service. It was a big gamble, but he knew he had to try. He sold his house to finance his independent music editorial service. The business succeeded, and he developed a reputation for excellence and dependable service. Years later, Ken met with Jerry Goldsmith about handling the music editing for *Poltergeist*. Near the end of the picture, John Williams called Ken Hall, informing him that Spielberg had another picture: *E.T. the Extra Terrestrial*.

"Steven Spielberg is probably one of the most articulate directors that I have ever worked with. He knows exactly what he wants, and, more importantly, he knows exactly how to communicate with his craftsmen the way he wants to achieve it. Those two pictures changed my career forever."

As for Jerry Goldsmith, a composer with whom Basil has worked on over seventy pictures, his output has anything but slowed down, with over 250 film scores on his résumé, film scores to pictures like *The Omen* (which earned Jerry an Academy Award), *Alien, Outland, First Blood, Explorers, Twilight Zone: The Movie, The Ghost and the Darkness, L.A. Confidential, Air Force One,* and *Mulan.* Goldsmith is fearless when it comes to working with unusual instruments, even going so far as to use bits of props in conjunction with traditional instruments, as well as fixing bits of wood and plastic chips to the strings of a piano to give an eerie and unusual sound.

Ken Hall knows that thorough note-taking is vital to successful, efficient development of a musical score. "After the spotting session, Jerry and I will talk briefly about the movie and a few preliminary ideas. I will write up formal notes based on the notes that I took during the spotting session. I will list the start and stop times of each cue throughout the picture, making any subnotes that the director has talked about—his intentions and personal thoughts. Jerry gives me a lot of latitude, allowing me to speak out during the spotting sessions. I try to give a tiny synopsis of the action of each scene alongside the notes for each particular music cue. Then I time the picture, using the Cue system. We use video now—it's faster than film—but I time the cues to a hundredth of a second. I list the cues in footage, not in time code.

"So many composers will get in and just start writing music. Jerry doesn't do that. He doesn't start writing cues until he is satisfied with the material. Jerry has banks of keyboards in his studio in Beverly Hills—he can create an entire orchestra. He'll have the director come over and run various cues. They always love it. Many times I'll get lucky and be invited over to experience the first musical themes or sometimes I'll just hear cues over the phone."

Preparations are crucial. The hourly cost of a scoring stage adds up; the cost of the musicians per session multiplies. "Jerry cannot be distracted by those kinds of things. I not only attend the recording sessions on the scoring stage, but I am present at the mix-down sessions later. Jerry might want to add something through the Auricle, so I'm still hooked up with the mixing board. Then we mix down to whatever format the producer requires from our forty-eight channels of digital.

"We usually mix down to five channels—1, 2, 3 across the front and split-surround. The rerecording mixer will often add a boom channel during the final mixing process. Jerry rarely shows up for the final rerecording process. It's my job to supervise the music mixing process during the final mix."

During the final mix of *Twilight Zone: The Motion Picture*, Ken and I had a heated discussion. Although I can't remember exactly which particular segment of film was in dispute, it certainly related to the theoretical dominance of music over sound effects, or of sound effects over music. As a final "dig," Ken Hall turned and snapped at all of us, "Well, when the audience leaves the theater, they certainly aren't whistling the sound effects, now are they?" That statement upset me for years, yet the more I wrestle with it, the more I have come to side with Ken. That's not to say that music and sound effects should not work harder to collaborate instead of creating "mud and destruction." The rerecording stage becomes a highly charged emotional battlefield. All parties present have spent weeks —some of them months, and a few even years—working on a project that is now focused on this final creative process, and motivations and protective instincts are in play.

THE DELICATE GAME OF INSIGHT

Often the composer finds that he or she must be especially insightful when scoring a picture. Sometimes the director tells the composer exactly what to do, and then, when the composer actually does the work as instructed, it gets rejected and thrown out. This sounds like an oxymoron, but many who have worked as supervising sound editors have seen this strange phenomenon. The composer and supervising sound editor must develop a sixth sense when working with a director, understanding that the director often gets scored rather than the film. Sometimes you must listen to the director's requests, agree completely with no hesitation or doubt, and then write (or design) what you know he or she really needs, not what was articulated.

For some reason, regardless of whether directors and producers know it, an unconscious atmosphere of "misspeak" develops. Many of us talk about it, but no one fully understands why it happens. When you realize it is present, trust your inner instincts and tastes, all the while with an outward appearance of following the director's or producer's request to the letter.

I have been on projects where the director made a very big deal about a particular item. He harped on it all through the spotting sessions, all through the weeks of cutting. We got to the dubbing stage, and suddenly he said, "Why'd you do that?"

"Because you asked for it," I insisted.

"That's not what I meant!" he defiantly exclaimed.

What do you do? In the case of one film I was working on, the producer fired the picture editor, and the director "retired" from the project. The producer hired a "film doctor" editor to complete the picture successfully. Usually, this does not happen. Usually, you are the one left holding the bag, working late into the nights, back-peddling to make the changes.

SIMILAR ISSUES AFFECTING THE CREATIVE EFFORT

One problem plaguing the post-production industry is the false notion that a shortened and accelerated schedule saves money. So many times we are presented with a post-production schedule and budget that looks good on paper (i.e., it appeals to business affairs at the studio or to the independent film company), but in application it falls apart. This truncated philosophy mostly stems from ignorance of how the process really works, not from the *perception* of how it works.

I became involved with several completion bond companies. My sound editorial firm had contracted to handle the post-sound services for film projects that were already over budget, with complete decision-making and financial dealings taken over by the completion bond company. More than once, a bond executive took me aside after a round-table discussion with the producer(s) and director, to ask what I really thought. Could I live up to a "chiseled-in-stone" contract now controlled by the completion bond company? Not one extra penny would be spent for "creative achievement," although they expected to get that, with the price tag they would authorize. I found it very interesting that, before bonding a picture, many completion bond executives flipped to the post-production part of a film budget to see how realistic the producer had been about allocated monies. If completion bond companies know what is realistic, though, why do we still have so many pictures run way over budget?

Resource assets of both sound editorial time and budget monies are diffused by the production of the plethora of temp material. Motion pictures have grown so expensive to make, the financial gamble so intense, that studios and executives want to take every possible step to ensure they make films with an eye focused on the audience, doing everything they can to broaden box office appeal.

This double-edged sword often spells doom for the outcome of the final sound track. Without anyone noticing, monies are drained by the development of temp music and sound effects for the temp dubs needed for test screenings—especially screenings for studio executives and distributors. Emphasis has shifted from making temp dubs in order to test the picture for an objective audience to selling the director's work to the studio to secure the next project. Many of us worked on pictures that exhausted their assets even before the real turnover for final preparation occurred.

Basil knows the scenario all too well. "Aside from the syndrome of this false sense of savings from compressed schedules, one of the biggest problems that we often face is a director who can not make up his or her mind, and the process just goes on and on and on, and there is a release date fast approaching. I think that digital technology has made a false promise that it will be quicker as well as cheaper. I have it here in my own studio. My place is loaded with digital equipment. It changes every two or three months. There is the latest this and the newest that, but when it comes down to it, the most important piece of equipment in my studio is me. Without a musical idea, the million dollar's worth of stuff in here to produce music is not worth a penny."

INDEX-LINKING FOREIGN SALES

With today's motion pictures costing nearly nine times the average budget of films made when I started in the industry, the studios understandably are concerned about making a profit. An important and proven way for them to hedge their bets is to develop ancillary sales through music. Music publication rights, sales of music scores on audiotape or CD, and licensing fees make a major contribution toward recouping a picture's budget.

No studio executive openly admits it. Many are not even aware of it. However, with the foreign box office share rising from 40 percent twenty years ago to well past 60 percent by the mid 1990s, a quiet understanding has arisen that the value of the licensing fee of a motion picture in foreign markets is directly index-linked to how much music is in the movie.

George Lucas made it fashionable to fit as many licensed songs into a film sound track as possible with his 1973 hit, *American Graffiti*. Others did the same with their coming-of-age films such as Rob Reiner's *Stand by Me* and other popular trash-the-dormitory films. It seems a movie cannot be made unless it has at least a dozen songs, either custom-written for the film (which the studio hopes will become hit singles in their own right) or oldies-but-goodies licensed to spruce up and flavor it.

Music composers are pressured to write increasingly more music for a picture than traditional artistic requirements anticipated. I know composers who felt that a music cue was not only unnecessary in a particular sequence, but actually inappropriate. The executive's insistence was nonetheless overruled, and the composer was compelled to write the music cue(s) anyway.

In one case a few years ago, I supervised the sound on a film that had 105 minutes of music in it. The film ran only 95 minutes in length! The producer and I had worked together on several previous pictures, so when I asked him why so much music, he was surprisingly open and candid with me. He admitted that in serving the index-linked issue for foreign territory sales, he feared the picture was too weak to make its money back on a domestic release alone.

Regardless of the reasons why there is so much music is in motion pictures today, whether the driving force is creative or purely related to dollars and cents, music is without question the greatest audio force that issues from the silver screen. It necessarily tells a story as much as breathing sustains life. Embrace it with a passion, as the art form itself can create great passions.

Chapter 19
The Rerecording Stage: Predubbing and the Final Mix

"Rolling the first rehearsal on a dubbing stage is weeks of blood, sweat, and tears followed by seconds of sheer terror!"

David Lewis Yewdall, M.P.S.E., commenting on Roger Corman's three-day mixing schedules

By the time Arnold Schwarzenegger had completed principal photography on *Predator*, he was well on his way to becoming a big-screen veteran of numerous action-adventure and fantasy motion pictures, most of which bristled with special effects and robust soundtracks (*Conan the Barbarian*, *Commando*, *Red Sonja*, and *The Running Man*). Inevitably, though, when he screened the finished pictures, they sounded nothing like he remembered during principal photography. Arnold soon realized that something very powerful and magical happened to a picture between the time shooting wrapped and the time of the cast-and-crew screening, and he was determined to figure out what that was—this thing called post-production.

Arnold followed *Predator* through the post-production process filled with cutting-edge CGI (computer-generated image) special effects as well as a high-energy soundtrack of music and dynamic sound effects. He thought that if he understood the magical contributions of post-production, he could select those future entertainment projects with the most potential. He would become empowered.

Indeed, several months later Arnold found himself on the Zanuck Stage at 20th Century Fox with the rerecording mixers as they painstakingly worked through the umpteenth predub of sound effects for the destruction of a rebel camp. The tail pop "bleeped," and the mixer leaned over and pressed the talk-back button to speak to the recordist in the machine room. He told him to take this predub down and to put up a fresh roll for the next dedicated sound effects pass. Knowing it would take the crew several minutes, the mixer pushed his chair back from the giant dubbing console and glanced at Schwarzenegger, who was taking in the entire mixing process. "Well, Arnold, whad'ya think of post-production now?"

Arnold considered the question, and then, in his Bavarian accent, replied, "Well, I'll tell you. I spent weeks in the jungle, hot and dirty and being eaten alive by insects—and now, here we are, for weeks going back and forth and back and forth on the console—I think I liked the jungle better."

RERECORDING

Rerecording is the process in which separate elements of various audio cues are mixed together in a combined format, then set down for preservation by either mechanical or electronic means in a form that allows reproduction. In simpler terms, rerecording, otherwise referred to as mixing or dubbing, is where you bring carefully prepared tracks from sound editorial and music and weave them together into a lush, seamless soundtrack.

With little variation, the basic layout of mixing stages are the same. The stage cavity, or the physical internal size of the stage itself, however, varies dramatically in height, width, and length, determining the spatial volume. Sound facilities that cater to theatrical release product generally have larger stages, duplicating the average size of the movie theatres where the film likely will be shown. Sound facilities that derive their business from television format product have smaller dubbing stages, as there is no need to duplicate the theatrical environment when mixing for home television presentation, whether for network, cable broadcast, or for direct-to-video product. In all cases, though, these rooms have been carefully acoustically engineered to deliver a true reproduction of the soundtrack without adding room colorization that does not exist in the actual track.

The mixing console (or the board) is situated approximately two-thirds the distance from the screen to the back wall of the dub stage. The size and prowess of the mixing console also reflect the kind of dub stage—theatrical or television. A theatrical stage has a powerful analog or digital console able to service one hundred to three hundred audio inputs at once. The console shown in Figure 19.1 is a Neve Logic 2 console on Stage "A" at Millennium Sound in Burbank, California. This particular console has 144 inputs with 68 outs. The board is not as long as traditional consoles, which can stretch thirty to forty feet. Digital consoles do not need to be as long, because they go down as well as side by side. Each fader module controls more than one audio input in a layered assignment configuration, allowing mixing consoles to be much bigger in their input capacity without being as wide as a football field.

This input expansion is not reserved only for digital consoles. International Recording, in Burbank, California, specializes in theatrical format projects. Its new expansion includes a custom-built analog console with a monster-size input capacity of just over 700 audio inputs! Such consoles can tackle any theatrical job, but are obviously not appropriate for television work.

I can tell how mindful a sound facility is to the needs of the supervising sound editor and the music editor by whether it has included supervisor desks on either end of the console. As a supervising sound editor, I want to be seated right next to the effects mixer, who is usually working on the right third of the console, so that I can talk to the head mixer and effects mixer in a quiet and unobtrusive manner. In this position, I also am able to maintain a constant eye on the proceedings and to make editorial update needs or channel assignment

Figure 19.1 Rerecording mixer John S. Boyd, twice nominated for an Academy Award for best sound on *Empire of the Sun* and *Who Framed Roger Rabbit*, works on a Neve Logic 2 console. (Photo by David Yewdall)

notations in my own paperwork without being disruptive. Supervising sound editor Greg Hedgepath has his sound effects session called up on one of the two Pro Tools stations on stage (Figure 19.2). This places him in an ideal position to communicate with the mixers as they mix the material, as well as to make any fixes or additions right on the spot. It also saves the effort of taking down a reel and sending it back to editorial for a quick fix that can be made in moments.

The same is true for the music editor. That person wants to sit next to the music mixer, who is usually situated on the left third of the console. From this position, the music editor not only can communicate with the music mixer quietly, but also can listen to the audio reproduction from the speakers in the same basic position as the music mixer.

Just behind the console is the credenza, a bank of rack-mounted gear and patch bays easily utilized by the mixers by just turning about in their chairs. When I walk onto an unfamiliar stage, I first glance at the console to see the platform used by the sound house, but I next study the credenza very closely. Here one can see what kind of extra "bells and whistles" gear the mixer has at command without resorting to equipment rentals from an outside supplier, which obviously affects the hourly stage-rental rate. Looking over the patch bay in the credenza, an experienced eye gets an immediate feel for the layout and prowess of the machine room as well as for the contemporary facets of the stage engineering.

THE CREDENZA

Fancy faceplates and "sexy" color schemes do not impress me. Many modern equipment manufacturers go to a great deal of trouble to give their equipment "sex appeal" through

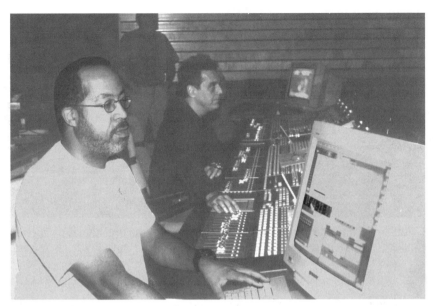

Figure 19.2 Head mixer André Perreault (center) helms the mixing chores of *The Wood* with his sound effects mixer Stan Kastner working the material on his left. Supervising sound editor Greg Hedgepath (foreground) checks over the channel assignments. (Photo by David Yewdall)

clever design or flashy image. The experienced craftsperson knows, however, that established names and precise tools are the mainstays of the outboard gear arsenal that produces the firepower for the mixer (Figure 19.3).

The mixing console is either hardwired to a patch bay in the stage credenza or hardwired to a patch bay up in the machine room. Either way, the patch bay is critical to giving full flexibility to the mixer or recordist when patching the signal path of any kind of playback equipment (whether film, tape, or digital hard drive) to the mixing console. The mixer can then assign "sends" and "returns" to and from other gear, whether internal or outboard, to enhance, harmonize, add echo, vocord, compress, dip filter, and perform many other functions not inherent in the fader slide assemblies of the console.

Once the signal path has passed through the fader assembly, the mixer assigns the signal to follow a specific "bus" back to the machine room, where the "mixed" signal is then recorded to a specific channel of film, tape, or a direct-to-disk digital drive.

IT CAN SEEM OVERWHELMING

The first time you approach a mixing console can be intimidating, especially if it is a feature film mixing stage, where you have a console with three mixers. Take a moment and look at the mixing console carefully. It is all about signal path, groupings, and routing. You see a desk with dozens of automated faders and a sea of tall, slender knobs for equalization. First of all, you can reduce the complexity down tremendously when you realize that the console

Figure 19.3 The credenza holds outboard signal-processing gear and signal-path patch bays just behind the mixing console in reach of the rerecording mixers. (Photo by David Yewdall)

is composed of dozens of fader/E.Q. components that are all the same. If you analyze and understand Channel 1, then you understand the majority of the rest of the board.

These fader/E.Q. components are long computer-board style assemblies that fasten into place by a couple of setscrews and can be removed and replaced in a few short minutes. The two basic components of the fader/E.Q. assembly are the fader (volume control) and the parametric equalizer.

The fader is a sliding volume control that moves forward (away from the rerecording mixer) to increase volume or back (toward the rerecording mixer) to reduce volume (Figure 19.4). Almost all fader controls today are automated—that is, they can be engaged to remember the rerecording mixer's moves and will play back those moves exactly the same way, unless the "ove" program data is updated by the mixer by using the computer software of the console to "rewrite" how he mixed the audio material.

You will note that the fader moves forward, or "up"—hence the cliché that you hear on the rerecording stage all the time: "Up is louder." This book will not attempt to judge whether that term, usually used in the heat of frustration, is meant as a sincere moment of instruction or an insult to the mixer's capacity to fulfill the client's soundtrack expectation.

In front of (or above) the fader is the equalization array. This is usually a classic GML parametric configuration such as the one shown in Figure 19.5. Some low-end parametric assemblies offer only three bands of influence. The one shown in Figure 19.5 is a four-band assembly; some have as many as five or six bands. Each area (low frequency, low-mid range, high-mid range and high end) has its own volume attenuation as well as a frequency selector, showing the apex of influence.

The next thing to understand is that a three-position console, supporting the music mixer (usually on the left side) the head mixer (usually in the center), and the effects mixer (usually on the right side), is really three consoles. For the majority of the time the three-position console works as three separate consoles that happen to be connected together as one console.

Each mixer is paying attention to his or her own assignments (dialog, music, and effects) and each mixer's designated audio signals are passing their own sections of the console on

Figure 19.4 Fader pot.

to either their own dedicated recorder or on to to their own dedicated channel assignments of a multitrack machine or nonlinear workstation. They just happen to be interlocked together and playing through the same speakers, giving the illusion that it is all one soundtrack, at least for the present.

After the supervising sound editor, editor, director, producer(s), executive producers, studio executives, and distribution executives have signed off on the Final Mix—only then will the Dolby, SDDS, and DTS techs be brought in to oversee the two-track print master and the various digital format masters. Only then will the soundtracks (dialog, music, and effects) truly reside together as a single theatrical soundtrack. And that will happen only after weeks of blood, sweat, and tears and other unmentionable spoken events, and sometimes even fisticuffs, have taken place.

For the record, though fisticuffs is never endorsed by any audio guild or technical manual, it has, from time to time, been the final argument for how a soundtrack has been conceived.

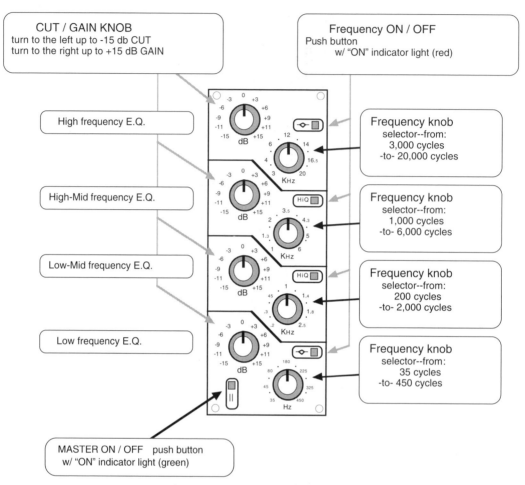

Figure 19.5 Parametric equalizer.

HEAD MIXER

With few exceptions, the head mixer is also the dialog mixer, usually running the stage from the center seat. This gives the head mixer ideal physical positioning in the dubbing stage cavity to listen to and evaluate the mix. Almost always, the head mixer is involved with each step of the predubbing process. Only with the mega soundtracks now being predubbed on two or more stages simultaneously is the head mixer not a part of each predubbing pass before the entire reel is mounted for a rehearsal for final mix.

During the final mix, the head mixer intercedes and instructs the music mixer and sound effects mixer to raise, lower, or tweak certain cues. Mixing teams often stay together for years because they reach a level of unspoken communication as they come to know each member's tastes and work habits. The head mixer has the last word in the balance and dynamic strategies of the final mix.

EFFECTS MIXER

Most sound effects mixers work from the right chair. During the predubbing process, they often work with the head mixer as a team. During the dialog predub, the effects mixer may help the dialog mixer with extra peripheral tracks if the cut dialog track preparation is unusually wide. By doing this, the dialog mixer can concentrate on the primary on-screen spoken words. On lower-budget projects, where stage time utilization is at a premium, the effects mixer may run backgrounds or even Foley as the dialog mixer predubs her or his dialog tracks. In this way, the dialog mixer knows how far to push the equalization or to change the level to clean the production tracks. He or she knows what to count on from backgrounds or Foley to bridge an awkward moment and make the audio action seamless.

When the dialog predubs are completed, the head mixer then assists the effects mixer in sound effects predubbing. At this point, the effects mixer runs the stage, as the sound effects predubs are his or her responsibility. The dialog (head) mixer helps the effects mixer in any way to make the most expeditious use of stage time, as only so much time is budgeted and the clock is ticking.

MUSIC MIXER

The music mixer rarely comes onto the stage during the predubbing process. The music mixer may be involved in music mix-downs, where an analog 2″ 24-track or a digital 1″ 48-track session master may need to be mixed down to a 35 mm six-channel for the music editor to cut into sync to picture. She or he may be asked to mix the music down to six- or eight-channel Pro Tools sessions. Many music mixers do not like mixing straight to a nonlinear platform, insisting instead on mixing down to a six-channel 35 mm fullcoat or six or eight channels of a 2″ 24-track tape, and then having the transfer department handle the transfer chores involved in a nonlinear audio format.

TIMES HAVE CHANGED

In the old days, the head mixer was God. Directors did not oversee the mixing process as they do today; the head of the sound department for the studio did that. The director would turn over the director's cut of the picture and move on to another project. He or she would see the finished film and mixed soundtrack several months later.

Head mixers dictated what kind of material went into a soundtrack and what would be left out. Often the supervising sound editor was an editorial extension of the will of the head mixer. When a head mixer did not like the material, it would be bounced off the stage, and the director would tell the sound editors to cut something different; sometimes the director would dictate the desired sound effects series. This is unheard of today. Not only do directors follow the process through to the end, often inclusive of the print master, but they have a great deal of say in the vision and texture of the soundtrack.

Supervising sound editors are no longer just an extension of the head mixer, but come onto the stage with a precise design and vision they already have been developing. From the Foley artist and sound designer on up through their sound editorial staff, they have taken a far more commanding role in the creative process.

Many film projects are brought to a particular stage and mixing team by the supervising sound editor, thereby making the mixing crew beholden to her or his design and concept wishes. This is a bad situation, although, in many instances, a greater degree of collaborative efforts does occur between sound editorial and rerecording mixers with an already established relationship. Many signal-processing tasks once strictly the domain of mixers are now being handled by sound designers and even sound editors, who are given rein to use their digital processing plug-ins.

Whole concepts now come to the stage virtually predubbed in effect-groupings. Whip-pans on lasers and ricos are just not cost effective to pan-pot on the rerecording stage by the sound effects mixer, and in some cases so many sound effects must move so fast that a mixer cannot pan-pot them properly in real time. These kinds of whip-pans are built in by the sound editor at the workstation level. (The lasers from *Starship Troopers* discussed in Chapter 13 are a case in point.)

As discussed in prior chapters, supervising sound editors and their sound designers handle more and more signal processing today, including equalization and filtering. Just a few years ago, these acts would have been grounds for union fines and grievances; now they take place every day in every sound facility. Some sound editorial services are even doing their own predubbing, bringing whole sections of predubbed material rather than hundreds of tracks of raw sound. Some of this is due to financial and schedule considerations, some due to sound-design conceptuality.

A VITAL COLLABORATION

And then, every once in a blue moon, you just find yourself working with a mixer who talks a good game, but when the chips are down he or she just "once-easy-overs" your stuff and basically mushes out any design hopes that you have built into your material. Or the mixer sometimes simply does not have the passion to go the extra distance to really make your soundtrack sing.

While supervising the sound editorial and mixing of *Near Dark,* Katherine Bigelow's first feature film as director, we were predubbing the dialog—which needed a lot of extra massaging with equalization and signal-processing gear. It takes a little work to make a silk purse out of sow's ear of mediocre location mish-mash. Katherine was a superb quick study, anxious to learn anything and everything she could to empower herself to be a better director.

I was becoming increasingly annoyed at the lack of assistance that the lead mixer was giving to help her out, both for the dialog track of her present film and to her personally for her future pictures.

I went out into the lobby and grabbed the phone and called my shop. I told my first assistant to build a bogus set of sound units, complete with intercut mag stripe (with no sound at all) and a full cue sheet advertising dozens of seemingly important cues.

The predub pass showed up at the stage by mid-afternoon, and with the usual setup time the machine-room crew mounted the units within twenty minutes. The head mixer got a full green-light status, so he rolled picture. The first cue passed through—with no audio being heard.

Standard procedure was to back up and try it again, checking the console to make sure that nothing was muted, turned off, or misrouted. The cue went through again—and, of course, with no audible result. The mixer turned to his credenza to make sure that the patch cords were firmly in place and in the right order. All of this takes time—precious time; the clock on a dubbing stage is always ticking, and every tick costs money.

The mixer rolled the projector again and the cue went by again, and again (of course) there was no audio. The mixer glanced at me. I shrugged innocently. He pressed the talk-back button to speak to his machine-room crew. "Is effects four in mag?"

The recordist had to get up out of his booth and walk around into the machine room to physically find "effects four" and see if the mag track was on over the playback head. Just by looking at the mag track itself, a recordist will assume that there is sound on it. Wouldn't you? So he walked all the way back into his booth to answer back, "Yes, it's in mag."

The mixer rolled the cue again, with the same silent results. He hit the talk-back button. "Bloop the track."

The recordist had to get up and walk around into the machine room, grab the "tone loop" off the hook, find "effects four," work the tone loop mag in between the mag track and the head, and pull it up and down to cause the tone to rub against the mag track. Loud "vrip-vrip-vrip" of tone modulation blasted out the speaker. That meant the patch cords were good, the routing was good, nothing was muted, and we were getting signal. The mixer shot a suspicious glance over at me. I shrugged. Standard procedure when you did not get a proper playback of a cue was to make a note and bring it back as a sweetener later, so I turned and scribbled a seemingly legitimate note to bring "effects four" as a sweetener later.

The mixer pushed on to the next cue. The next cue did not play. Again the mixer stopped to check the signal path for "effects five" as he had before. Again he ran the cue and again it played nothing. He shot me another suspicious scowl. I just gazed at him with an innocent expression.

Still again he had to have his recordist walk back and "bloop" the track, and again the "vrip-vrip-vrip" tone pounded the room. I shrugged and turned to write another bogus notation for a sweetener. The mixer rolled to the next cue, and once more it passed over the heads without any audio response. By now the mixer had had enough. He yanked back all of his faders with a smack and whirled around to me. "Okay, Yewdall—*what*?!"

I quietly put my pencil down and folded my hands while Katherine watched. My eyes met the mixer's enraged ones, and I quietly but firmly replied, "Let's understand one another. This is a collaborative effort. I am only as good as how you make my material sound, and you are only as good as the material I bring you. God blessed you with the arms of an orang-utan, and I would think that you could at least reach up to your parametrics and help the director achieve her vision."

The mixer leaped up and stomped off the stage to the head of the sound department, with the expectation that I would get my *#! chewed out and, he hoped, would be removed from the project. Instead I was called into the head of the sound department's office to watch the mixer get his *#! chewed out and be reminded of how the winds of post-production power have shifted.

The mixer and I walked back to the stage together to forge a working agreement on how we could both survive together and deliver the best soundtrack possible to a new rising director.

PREDUBS: TACTICAL FLOW

Predubbing is the art of keeping options open. You want to distill the hundreds of your prepared sound elements down into more polished (not final polish) groupings. By doing this,

Figure 19.6 The rerecording mixing flowchart.

you can put up all your basic elements, such as dialog, ADR, Group Walla, Foley, backgrounds, sound effects, and music, so that you can rehearse and "final" the reel as one complete soundtrack.

As shown in Figure 19.6, predubbing is broken into logical groupings. Because dialog is the most important component of a film soundtrack and must sound as smooth and seamless as possible, predub it first, especially if you have a limited amount of time in the schedule for predubbing. Ideally, we should always have enough time to predub all our cut material fully and properly, but rarely is this the case. Since I could write an entire book on mixing, encompassing budgeting, scheduling, and techniques, here I simply discuss one fairly common formula. Four-week dubbing schedules are normal for medium-budget feature films in Hollywood. Naturally, tactics differ, depending on whether you take the "single mixer" approach or the "mixer team" approach. This example is of a "mixer team" approach, using a two-mixer formula. Provided that sound editorial was not put into an insane schedule crunch and that the normal mixing protocol can be implemented, I generally find the following to be a safe tried-and-proven battle plan.

Four-Week Mixing Schedule

Dialog predubbing	allow 5 days (dialog w/backgrounds)
	allow 4 days (if dialog only)
Background predubbing	allow 2 days

Foley predubbing	allow 2 days
Sound effects predubbing	allow 3 days
Final mix	allow 7 days
Continuity playback and fixes	allow 1 day
Print master	allow 1 day
Foreign M&E	allow 1 day

Please note that this schedule does not allow for a digital sound mix and mastering process. This gets you through predubbing, final mix, continuity playback along with a conservative amount of fixes (if you have a greater list, add additional days to your mixing schedule), print master, and foreign M&E for the analog version.

This is a guide used over and over in generalities. The "what-ifs" factor a hundred variants, and no two motion pictures are ever the same. On one job you may have a mixer who prefers to predub dialog along with the Foley; on another, a mixer who wants backgrounds. And then you may have the "purist" mixer who wants it to be predubbed without anything camouflaging the material. (I endorse the purist philosophy, by the way.)

A client discusses the mixing schedule for his or her project with me. Naturally, this conversation is held months after the film has been scheduled and budgeted, so it is not a discussion about how to schedule the mixing process. Rather, it becomes a retrofit of, "This is all that we have budgeted for—how do you think we should utilize it?"

With this is mind, I always counsel that more time given to predubbing makes the final mixing process go much smoother and more quickly. You can adopt one of two tactics in deciding how to balance the number of days to predub, as opposed to how many days to final mix. First, you can take a fifteen-day mixing schedule and set aside five days for predubbing (at a lower per-hour rate) and have ten days to final mix (at a higher per-hour rate). The producer and director like the idea of having a full day per reel to final; that is how the big shows are done, so they want the same. This means much less material is predubbed, and during the final mix you stop more often to reset equalization or fix transitions between sound cues because not enough time was devoted to predubbing the material properly. With the stage cost at full rate, tensions on the stage quickly develop.

The second, more logical approach is to give a larger portion of the fifteen days to predubbing. I have often suggested that nine days be devoted to predubbing, meaning you must final two reels a day. This is often done. as the smart client knows, if the material was thoroughly predubbed, the final mixing goes much smoother and more quickly. As discussed in Chapter 4, the success or failure of a soundtrack is in your hands long before a postproduction sound craftsperson ever gets a chance to touch it.

But good soundtracks can be achieved in shorter schedules or for less budget dollars. *One False Move* is a perfect example. This picture had only nine days to mix, inclusive of predubbing. It looks like a much more expensive movie than its budget would suggest. Jeffrey Perkins at International Recording was set as the head rerecording mixer. He had recently won the Academy Award for Best Sound on *Dances with Wolves,* and both Carl Franklin (director) and Jesse Beaton (producer) of *One False Move* considered it a fabulous opportunity to have Jeffrey handle the mixing chores. The dubbing schedule happened to fall in the slow period during the Cannes Film Festival, which gave the added value of a lower hourly stage rate.

Even so, the schedule was only nine days, all inclusive. Jeffrey and I had not worked together before, and such a short schedule concerned him. I offered to go over to

International to talk with him about dubbing tactics. I grabbed the cue sheet envelope for Reel 7 on my way out the door, as I thought he would learn more about what to expect in sound editing preparation by seeing the cue sheets laid out.

I spread the cue sheets to Reel 7 across his dubbing console, starting with dialog and ADR, then Foley, then backgrounds, and finally sound effects. In moments he began to relax, seeing that I had not spread the sound assembly too wide should we have to forego some predubbing needs, hang the cut material, and final the reel from raw cut sound units.

The first thing we both agreed to was persuading the client to take one day from final mixing and use it for predubbing. We knew it would make for an easier and faster final mix. Jeffrey prioritized what he would predub—first, second, third. When we ran out of time and had to commence finals, at least the priority chores would be completed.

As it turned out, we did not need to compromise anything on the rerecording mix of *One False Move.* Although the mixing schedule was extremely tight, the client listened to our advice and counseling and, for the most part, took it. All the cut material ended up being predubbed. Nothing was left to hang raw. We set a methodical schedule for finals and, with very little exception, lived up to it. We predubbed, executed the final mix as well as shot the two-track print master, and made the M&E in nine days.

WHO REALLY RUNS THE MIX?

It never fails to amaze me who really has the last word on a dubbing stage. On the miniseries *Amerika,* Jim Troutman had to work on both Stages 2 and 3 of Ryder Sound simultaneously. His rerecording mixers down on Stage 3 were predubbing while another team of mixers made the final mix upstairs on Stage 2. Ray and Joe had just completed predubbing the action sequences on a particular reel and were about to play it back to check it when a tall gentleman in a business suit entered, patted Jim Troutman on the shoulder, and sat in a nearby makeup chair. The two mixers glanced at the executive-looking man with slight concern, then commenced the playback.

When lights came up at the end of the reel, Jim asked the businessman what he thought. He shrugged and was a little timid to give his opinion. With a little encouragement, he spoke his mind. "I thought the guns were a little low and mushy during the shoot-out."

Immediately, the mixers spun the reel down to the scene, took the safeties off the predub with the gun effects, and started remixing the weapon fire. That finished, they asked what else bothered him. Cue by cue, they coaxed him to give his ideas and concerns, immediately running down to each item and making appropriate fixes. After speaking his mind, he stood up and smiled, patted Jim on the shoulder again with appreciation for letting him sit in, then turned and left.

Once the door closed, the mixers turned to Jim. "Who was that?"

Jim smiled. "Who, John? Oh, he's my accountant." The two mixers sat frozen in disbelief—then started laughing in relief.

Not all "control" stories end with relief and humor. I supervised a science-fiction fantasy that was filled with politics and egocentric behavior. Reel 5 was a major special-effects-filled action reel. Everyone had arrived promptly to start rehearsals at

9:00 a.m., as it promised to be a long day. To stay on schedule, we would need to final Reel 5 and get at least halfway through Reel 6.

Everyone had arrived—everyone, that is, except for the producer. The mixing team had gotten right in and commenced rehearsing the reel. At the end of the first rehearsal pass, the head mixer glanced about, looking for the producer. He still had not arrived. The reel was spun back to heads, whereupon they commenced another rehearsal pass. By 11:00 a.m. the crew had completed four rehearsal passes of the reel, and still the producer was not there. The head mixer looked at me.

"We're starting to get stale," I said. "Let's make this reel. He'll be walkin' through the door any minute." The mixer pressed the talk-back button and informed his recordist to put the three Magna tech film recorders on the line and to remove the record safeties. We rolled.

Foot by foot, the mixers ground through the reel. The last shot flickered off the screen, and three feet later the tail pop beeped.

Suddenly the stage door burst open as the producer entered. "Hey, guys, what are we doing?"

"We've just finaled Reel 5 and are about to do a playback," the head mixer replied matter-of-factly.

The producer's demeanor dropped like a dark shroud. "Really? Well, let's hear this playback."

You could just feel it coming. The machine-room equipment wound down and stopped as the Academy leader passed by, then Reel 5 rolled. Almost every ten feet the producer had a grumbling comment to make. At first the head mixer was jotting down notes, but after the first 200 feet he set his pencil down.

As the reel finished, the lights came up. The producer engaged in a nonstop dissertation about how the mixing crew had completely missed the whole meaning and artistic depth of the reel. I studied the head mixer as he listened to the producer talk. Finally, the head mixer had had enough. He turned and hit the talk-back button, telling the recordist to rerack at Picture Start and prepare to refinal the reel—they would be starting over.

Satisfied that he was proving his command and control, the producer rose and headed out the side door to get a cup of coffee and a donut. I watched the head mixer as he quietly leaned over to the console mike. He pressed the talk-back button and whispered, "Take these three rolls down and put them aside. Put up three fresh rolls for the new take." He noticed me eavesdropping and winked.

We worked hard on the new final of Reel 5, slugging it out for the next two and a half days. We had given up any hope of keeping to the original dubbing schedule, as the issue of politics and egocentric behavior had gone way over the top. I knew the stage alone was costing $700 per hour. Over the course of the extra two and a half days, the overage bill for the stage would easily run close to $16,000.

Finally, the last scene flickered away, and the tail pop beeped. The producer rose from his makeup chair and strode toward the side door to get a fresh cup of coffee. "Awright guys, let's do a playback of that!"

I watched the head mixer as he leaned close to the console mike and alerted the recordist. "Take these three rolls off and put the other three rolls from the other day's backup. Thank you." He calmly turned to meet my gaze with a grin. The producer returned, and the lights lowered. For ten minutes, Reel 5 blazed across the screen, playing the original mix done three days before. The producer slapped the armrest of his chair. "Now that is how I wanted this reel to sound!"

ETIQUETTE AND PROTOCOL

Protocol is the code of correct conduct that should be observed by all who enter and spend any amount of time, either as visitor or client-user, on a rerecording stage. It is vitally important that you pay strict attention to the protocol and etiquette of the professional sound mixer's world. Just because you may be the director or producer does not mean you are suddenly an expert in how to mix sound. Clients often are on the stage during predubbing processes when they really should not be there. They speak up and make predubbing-level decisions without a true understanding of what goes into making the material and particularly what it takes to predub the material properly to achieve the desired effect.

One particular director who makes huge-budget pictures thinks he truly understands how good sound is made. I had spent weeks designing and cutting intricately interwoven sound effect cues that when mixed together would create the audio event that would make a sequence work. The sound effects mixer had never heard these sounds before, and I spread several layers of cue sheets across his console. One vehicle alone required forty-eight soundtracks to work together simultaneously. The mixer muted all but the first stereo pair, so that he could get a feel for the material. Instantly, the director jumped up. "That's not big enough; it needs more depth, more meat to it."

Knowing his reputation during the predubbing process from other sound editors, I turned to him. "This sequence is a symphony of sound. Our effects mixer has simply introduced himself to the first viola. Why don't you wait until he has tuned the entire orchestra before you start criticizing?" Booking the dubbing stage does not necessarily give the client the keys to the kingdom. On countless occasions the producer books a sound facility and then proceeds to push the dubbing crew to the brink of mutiny. The adage that "money talks" is not an excuse for disregarding protocol and etiquette.

I was dubbing a temp mix for a test-audience screening on a Wesley Snipes picture. It wasn't that the director and his committee of producers had nitpicked and noodled the temp mix to death. It wasn't that the schedule was grueling and demanding. All post-production professionals understand compressed schedules and high-expectation demands. It was the attitude of the three producers, the inflection and tone of their comments, that ate away at the head mixer.

During a reel-change break, I overheard the head mixer talking to the facility director in the hall. Once the temp mix was finished, the mixer would have nothing to do with any further temp dub or the final mix for this picture, regardless of its high profile. The facility director was not about to force his Academy Award–winning mixer to do something that he did not want to do, so he informed the client that the stage had just been block-booked by another studio, forcing the client to look elsewhere for sound facility services.

Usually the etiquette problem is much simpler than that. It boils down to who should speak up on a rerecording stage and who should remain quiet and watch politely, taking anything that must be said out to the hallway for private interaction with either the director or producer.

Teaching proper protocol and etiquette is extremely difficult because the handling of dubbing chores has changed so much that entire groups of young sound editors and sound designers are denied the rerecording-stage experience. A few years ago, before the advent of nonlinear sound editing, access to the rerecording stage was far more open, an arena in which to learn. You prepared your material, brought it to the stage, and watched the mixer run it through the console and work with it. You watched the mixer's style and technique. You learned why you should prepare material a certain way—what made it easier or harder for the mixer and what caused a breakdown in the collaborative process.

I always had the sound editor, who personally cut the material, come to the stage to sit with the mixers and me. After all, this was the person who knew the material best. We also would call back to the shop late in the afternoon for the entire crew to sit in on the playback of each reel on stage. The sound crew felt a part of the process, a process that today inhibits such togetherness. Somehow we must find a way to get editorial talent back on the dubbing stage and make the rerecording experience more available to up-and-coming audio craftspeople.

PRINT MASTERING

Upon completion of the final mix there are three 35 mm rolls of fullcoat per reel. The three basic elements of the mix—dialog, music, and sound effects—are on their own separate rolls. When you lace these three rolls together in sync and set the line-up tones so the outputs are level-matched, the combined playback of these three rolls produces a single continual sound-track. If not mixing to 35 mm film, you can mix to a 2″ 24-track tape, to DA-88s, or to a hard drive inside the mixing console system. Regardless of the medium, the rerecording mixers still want dialog, music, and effects in their own controlled channels.

Once the final mix is complete, the head mixer sets up the room for a playback of the entire picture. Many times, as you mix a film reel by reel, you feel you have a handle on the continuity flow and pace; however, only by having a continuity playback running of the entire film with the final mix will you truly know what you have. Much can be learned during a continuity playback, and you will often make notes to change certain cues or passages for various reasons.

Several days prior to completing the final mix, the producer arranges with either Dolby or Ultra*Stereo for a tech engineer to be on hand with a "matrixing" box and supervise the print mastering of the final mix. Although many theatrs can play digital stereo soundtracks such as Dolby SR-D, SDDS, or DTS, you should always have the analog stereo mix on the print.

Do not attempt to have discrete optical tracks for the component channels; Dolby and Ultra*Stereo offer a matrix process that encodes, combining the left, center, right, and split-surround channels of the final mix into two channels. When the film is projected in the theatre, this matrixed two-channel soundtrack is fed into a Dolby or Ultra*Stereo decoder box prior to the speaker amplification, where the two matrixed channels are decoded back out into the proper left, center, right, and surround channels. On many occasions a theatre that offers a digital sound presentation has a technical malfunction with the digital equipment for some reason. Sensors in the projection equipment detect the malfunction and automatically switch over to the analog two-track matrixed track.

The tech engineer sets up the matrix encoding equipment and sits with the head mixer, paying strict attention to peak levels on extremely loud passages. The analog soundtrack is an optical track and has a peak level that must be carefully adjusted—what used to be called "making optical."

There may be moments in the print-mastering process when the tech engineer will ask the mixer to back up and lower a particular cue or passage because it passed the maximum and clashed.

For some, the print-mastering phase is the last "authorship" of the soundtrack. Many a smart music composer who has not been on stage for the final mix always shows up for the print master; he or she knows that changes and level balances are still possible, and many films end up with a differently balanced soundtrack than that of the final mix. Hence, the supervising sound editor never considers the print-mastering process as "just a transfer job" to be left to others.

PULL-UPS

An overlooked finalizing task that must be done before the soundtrack can be shipped to the laboratory is having the "pull-ups" added. These are, technically, the first twenty-six frames of sound of the reel that has been attached to the end of a previous reel. Adding the pull-ups makes smoother changes in theatrical projection when one projector is finished and must "change over" to the next projector.

Because of electronic editing, pull-ups have become less precise than they used to be and sometimes downright sloppy. I see more and more mixers electronically "shooting" the pull-ups. This indicates laziness on the part of the supervising sound editor rather than being the fault of the rerecording mixer.

You do not need to put pull-ups on every reel, unless the show was mixed prebuilt in an A-B configuration. If the print master is in A-B configuration, then, of course, every reel needs to have a pull-up.

The mixer has the print master of the following reel mounted. The line-up tones are critical, and great pains are taken to ensure that the "X-Copy" transfer of the print master is an exact duplicate. The mixer includes the head pop and several feet of the opening shot. The recordist makes sure that each pull-up is carefully tagged to show from which reel it came. The supervising sound editor and assistant usually cut the pull-ups in the change room of the sound facility, as the print master should not be moved off-site for contract and insurance reasons. If the show was not mixed in A-B configuration, then the supervisor and assistant do so now.

Electronic editing has unfortunately made many editing services extremely sloppy in the head- and tail-pop disciplines. I have seen pops slurred in replication over several frames. The worst I have seen was a head pop that slurred eight frames, making it impossible to get a precise position for sync.

If you pay close, disciplined attention to the head and tail pops, you will have an easy time finding the precise perforations between which to cut. You can take satisfaction and ease in being 1/96th-of-a-second accurate, rather than trying to decide which frame "pop" to believe.

First, I take the roll of pull-ups the mixer transferred for me. I place it in a synchronizer and roll down until I pass a reel designation label; shortly thereafter are tones and then the head pop. I stop and carefully rock the film back and forth under the sound head, being absolutely assured of the leading edge of the pop. I use my black Sharpie to mark the leading edge, then count four perforations and mark the back edge. I rock the film back and forth gently to see if the back edge is truly four perforations long. I open the synchronizer gang and pick the film out, then roll the synchronizer so the "0" frame is at the top. I zero out the counter and then roll down to nine feet. I place the marked pop over the "0" frame, then roll down to 12+00. This is the exact leading edge of the soundtrack for this reel. Using the black

Sharpie, I mark the frame line. Just in front of the frame line, I write from which reel this piece of sound comes. I then cut off three or four feet of the incoming sound and hang it in the trim bin until I need it. After I prepare all my pull-up sections, I commence building the A-B rolls.

I always roll the picture in the first gang alongside the print master. This way I can physically see and verify the relationship of picture to soundtrack. I always locate the head pop first. I seat it exactly on the "0" of the synchronizer, with the footage counter at nine feet. I then roll backward toward the start mark. Head start marks are often one or two perforations out of sync. This is unconnected to how the recordist is doing his or her job. It is related to the way the film machines settle in when put "on the line." That is why the nine-foot head pop is critical, as its position is the only true sync start mark. From it, you can back up and correct the position of the start-mark label.

Once this is done, I roll down through the reel to the last frame of picture. Be sure you are using a 2000-foot split reel or 2000-foot projection reel on which to wind the reels. I mark the frame line with a black Sharpie and then mark past it with a wavy line to denote waste. I then take the next reel and seat the head pop at 9+00. I roll down to 12+00 and mark the top of the frame with a black Sharpie. Using a straight-edged (not an angle!) Rivas butt splicer, I cut the two frame lines, then splice the backside of the fullcoat with white 35 mm perforated splicing tape. Never use a splicer that punches its own holes in splicing tape during this procedure—never!

I then continue to roll down through the second reel, now attached to the first, until I reach the last frame of picture. I mark the bottom of the frame line of the last frame. I then pull the pull-up of the next reel and cut the frame line I had marked on it. I carefully make sure that the cuts are clean and without any burrs or lifts. I flip the film over and splice the back with white 35 mm splicing tape. It is only necessary to cut twenty-six frames of pull-up, but I have cut two feet, eight frames for over twenty years. I then cut in an eight-frame piece of blank fullcoat, which I took off the end of the roll, where it is truly blank and has not been touched by a recording head. The two and a half feet of pull-up and eight frames of blank equal three feet. The tail pop comes next. Now that the A-B configurations as well as the pull-ups have been built, you are ready to ship the print master to the optical house to shoot the optical master for the laboratory.

VARIOUS FORMATS: A WHO'S WHO

In theatrical presentation, basically two analog formats are used today: Dolby Stereo and Ultra*Stereo. Both processes are nearly identical in procedure and technical protocol.

Three basic digital formats dominate the American theatre. Dolby SR-D, SDDS, and DTS cover the majority of presentation formats. With the advent of digital stereo, the need to blow up 35 mm prints to 70 mm just to make bigger six-track stereo presentations became unnecessary.

Even though Sony will continue to support the SDDS product that is already out there, it will not offer SDDS as a digital audio matrix system. This leaves the field of theatrical presentation to Dolby and DTS.

DTS is now offering an opportunity to present a multichannel stereo soundtrack to 16 mm film. The proprietary DTS "time code-style" sync signal is placed on the 16 mm print,

35mm DIGITAL SOUND FORMATS

Figure 19.7 The various 35mm digital soundtrack formats: Dolby SR-D, digital DTS, and digital SDDS.

which in turns drives the outboard CD-style playback unit—much the same as their theatrical 35mm cousin.

Figure 19.7 shows where the various audio formats reside on a 35mm print. DTS does not have its digital track on the film; rather, it has a control track that sits just inside the optical two-track analog track and the picture mask. This control track maintains sync between the film and a CD that plays separately in a separate piece of gear nearby. The CD has the actual audio soundtrack of the movie.

Note that the SDDS digital tracks are on either side of the 35mm print, outside the perforations. The DTS time code control track lies snugly between the optical analog track in the traditional mask and picture, with the Dolby SR-D digital track between the perforations.

A few years ago New Line Cinema wanted to save money on the inventory of prints to maintain. Rather than shuttling around prints that had the correct digital soundtrack to service certain theatr venues, New Line decided to combine all the audio formats on a single

Figure 19.8 Actual image of various 35 mm digital sound formats on one print.

print. This idea caught on with many distributors. By using this combined-format technique, a distributor needed only one inventory of prints; no matter which print is sent to any theatre house projecting 35 mm film, one of the formats of sound will suit the presentation capabilities of that exhibitor.

FOREIGN M&E

Once the print master is complete, the next step is to satisfy the foreign market. You must produce a full and complete soundtrack without any holes or sound events missing—yet also without any track of English dialog. This mainly is why each component of dialog, music, and sound effects has been carefully kept on its own roll or separate channel. However, just keeping the components separated is not enough. This is where the cautious preparation of the dialog editor (discussed in Chapter 14) pays off. If he or she has done the work properly, the mixer need only mute the dialog track and make sure that the "P"-FX track, which the dialog editor so carefully prepared, is open and running so those production effects can be included in the foreign M&E.

PREPARING FOREIGN M&E

In preparing the foreign M&E (music and effects), the mixer laces the Foley backup, as he or she may need to use more, especially footsteps and cloth movement, than was used in the final domestic mix. When the English dialog is muted, more than just flapping lips go with it. Cloth rustle, footsteps, ambiance—an entire texture—goes with it. The only thing remaining from the dialog track is the "P"-FX that carefully were protected for the foreign M&E. Figure 19.9 shows an M&E dubbing chart.

We have a saying in post-production sound: if you can get it by Munich, then your M&E track is A-OK. The German film market is the toughest on quality-control approval of M&E tracks. One of the harshest lessons a producer ever has in the education of his soundtrack preparation is when she or he does not care about guaranteeing a quality M&E. When an M&E track is "bounced," with fault found in the craftsmanship, the foreign dis-

Figure 19.9 The Music and Effects (M&E) dubbing chart.

tributors must have it fixed by their own sound services, and the bill is paid by you, not them. It either comes out as a direct billing or is deducted from licensing fees.

The mixer combines the music and sound effects onto one mixed roll of film. The mixer makes a transfer of the dialog channel (called the "dialog stem") as a separate roll of film so that foreign territories can produce their own dialog channel to replace the English words, if desired.

Chapter 20
5.1 and Emerging
Audio Technologies

WHAT IS 5.1 (AND 6.1)?

Several years ago a young sound department trainee burst into my room. He was all excited as he announced that the decision had been made to mix the soundtrack we were working on in five-point-one. Wasn't that great?! I smiled at the news. He spun on his heels and disappeared down the hall to tell the rest of his friends.

My smile vanished as I sat stumped at the announcement. What the devil was five-point-one? All I knew was that this was the new breakthrough sound technology that everybody was talking about around town. Gee, I was going to have to learn a whole new way of doing things. I decided that I did not want to disclose my ignorance too blatantly, so I slipped down the hall and knocked on the door of our resident engineer.

"I hate to admit this, but I don't know what five-point-one is. Could you explain it to me?"

His eyebrows shot up. "Oh, you're going to love it! The sound comes out of the left speaker, the center speaker, the right speaker, as well as split-surrounds—and we have a subwoofer."

I waited for the shoe to drop. "Yeah . . . what else."

He shrugged. "Isn't that great?"

I studied his face suspiciously. "That's five-point-one?"

"Yeah."

I turned and paced back to my room. Geez-o-Pete! We've been doing that for the last thirty years! It's called theatrical format! What is so blamed new about this?! Well, of course what was so important about it was that it was an encode that would allow home consumers to have true dedicated audio signals assigned to the proper speakers in their home entertainment systems to replicate the theatre presentation with a compression that would allow

Figure 20.1 The theatrical speaker layout.

this enormous amount of audio information to take up less space on the DVD disk medium. It would mirror what we have been doing for cinema for the last three decades. Okay, that's a good thing. So let's just remove the idea that it is a new *sound system*; it is not. It is a new sound *delivery format*—a better way to bring the big theatrical sound to the consumer.

The first thing we should review is the speaker layout for theatrical presentation, as follows (Figure 20.1):

Center speaker—where all dialog (except for more recent mixing philosophy) emanates from.
Subwoofers—(also known as "baby booms") low-frequency speakers sit in between the left-and-center and center-and-right speakers. These speakers reproduce very low-frequency audio signals, some of them are subharmonic and are meant to be felt and not just heard.
Left speaker and right speaker—where the stereophonic presentation of sound effects and music lives (with occasional hard-left or hard-right placement of dialog).

Left surround and right surround speakers—where a growing taste in aggressive 360-degree sound experience is rapidly evolving. Both music and sound effects come from the surround speakers. Since the movie *Explorers* (1984), the surround speakers have been "dedicated left" and "dedicated right," allowing wonderful abilities to truly surround the audience and develop an ambianic envelope that the audience sits within to enjoy the full soundtrack experience.

The introduction of Dolby EX has allowed the placement of a dedicated speaker to the rear of the theatre. It is meant for the "hard" assignment of sound effects that will perform behind the audience—for further envelopment—as well as, I am sure, "pop-scare" effects and dramatic swoop from rear-to-front-aspect audio "events."

Everyone knows that the home theatre has skyrocketed both in technology as well as the ability, in many cases, to present the theatrical exprience more vibrantly (in the audio sense) than the hometown cinema can do. This tidal wave of home-entertainment theatre development has demanded an audio encoding system that can properly place the prescribed audio channels to the correct speakers and do it with as little fuss or muss (as well as technical understanding) on the part of the consumer as possible.

Many home systems use a separate speaker on either side of their big-screen television screens instead of the built-in speakers (Figure 20.2). The dialog is "phantomed" from the left and right speakers, making an illusion of a center channel. More and more consumers are now buying a special "center" channel speaker and placing it either on top or just below the television screen, thus having a dedicated dialog signal assignment. This makes for a much fuller and more natural front "dialog track" experience than the phantom technique.

For many years home systems have had a "surround" system wherein both the left and right rear speakers are fed by the same "surround speaker" signal—just like theatrical presentation was prior to the movie *Explorers.* But more and more consumers are taking advantage of the "split-surround" option and incorporating that into their home system as well.

The favorite of many consumers—especially those who love to irritate their neighbors—is the "subwoofer" speaker additive. It comes in all prices and sizes, even up to a 3000-watt subwoofer that can just about move walls. This full speaker system, for consumer venues, is what 5.1 is all about.

Now, with Dolby EX and DTS-ES, the 5.1 rises one more notch, allowing the consumer to place a dedicated rear-surround channel just as they experience in the theatre. Technically, this feature raises the encode designation to 6.1, rather than 5.1, though the term "6.1" has not officially taken hold at the time of this writing.

CHANNEL ASSIGNMENTS

The channel assignments are as follows:

Channel 1:	Center Speaker	(front)
Channel 2:	Left Speaker	(front)
Channel 3:	Right Speaker	(front)
Channel 4:	Left Surround Speaker(s)	(rear left)

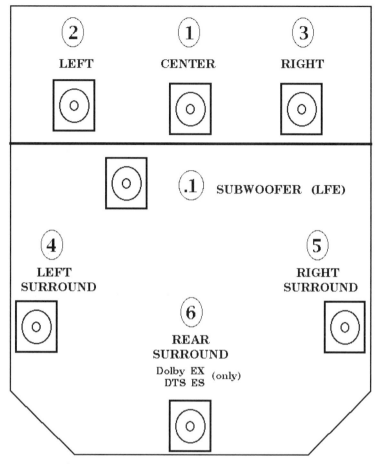

Figure 20.2 The basic consumer speaker layout.

Channel 5:	Right Surroud Speaker(s)	(rear right)
Channel 6:	Rear (Dolby EX) Speaker	(rear center)
Channel .1:	Subwoofer	(low-frequency effect)

QC—QUALITY CONTROL

One would not know it by looking at the sleek disk products coming into the market, but there are huge problems with quality control (QC).

All DVD authoring facilities have a "QC" department. but only a small percentage of DVD authoring is done with proper 5.1 playback-room environments. Some DVD authoring companies simply have their QC techs sit at a workstation and handle the QC evaluation by listening to the soundtrack through headsets! As incredibly stupid as this sounds, it is no joke. You obviously can't have someone listen to and properly evaluate a 5.1 soundtrack (review Figure 20.2) through a left-right set of headsets!

To add insult to injury, there is a general plus or minus four-frame sync acceptability! Ever wonder why those lips seem a little "rubbery" to you? Now you know. And I am not just talking about low-budget products. One major studio that subcontracted its DVD authoring to an independent firm discovered that the DVD had been mastered with the audio channel assignments directed to the wrong speakers. This was a huge-budget picture, by the way. The studio had to buy back all the DVDs and remaster, which cost them several million extra dollars.

Here is a little piece of warning for those who thought it was perfectly safe to watch DVDs on your computer. Much to the chagrin of a major (and I mean major) studio executive who watched a test DVD of a his $100-million-dollar-plus epic motion picture on his personal computer, he found out that the DVD authoring service had contracted a virus in its system, and that virus was transplanted onto the DVD—and as he watched the movie the virus transplanted itself into his own computer hard drive, eating away and destroying his computer files.

Unfortunately, the world of DVD authoring is so misunderstood that, like so many technical disciplines that are misunderstood, there are few in the business who really know their own business. The aforementioned studio put its foot down about the independent contractor that misassigned the audio channels of its major motion picture. The studio execs decided to build their own in-house state-of-the-art operation. Good idea, except for one problem: they did not hire the right person to head it up. Over time the work was outsourced to independent contractors, again because of mismanagement and technical ineptitude from the inside. A doctor may be a doctor by virtue of the initials M.D., but you do not hire a podiatrist when you need a brain surgeon.

This studio found itself back where it started. It was another example of quality and craftsmanship being destroyed as a result of throat-cutting low-ball bidding and decision makers who think they know how things should be done, but don't, and are guided by who-knows-who relationships and greed rather than respect for the art form.

TOTAL IMMERSION OPPORTUNITIES

In addition to the obvious soundtrack mastering of linear entertainment product—such as authoring DVD media of motion pictures, rock videos, and the like—the need for "sound-event designers and audio authoring" is rapidly expanding.

One of the most exciting emerging technologies for the future generation of entertainment venues is the "Total Immersion" experience. Total Immersion is the next quantum step, with photorealistic visuals fed to you via wraparound goggles, spherical-audio that is event-linked to visual action and touch/temperature sensations phantomed throughout your nervous system—all driven by complex algorithmic interdependent softwares that obey the laws of physics.

Interactive programs have evolved from very crude digital color block figures to mirroring reality. The technologies that drive the serious replication of such high-level audiovisual experiences require faster computers and mammoth amounts of high-speed access to compressed visual and audio files. With every passing week the computers get faster, and the drive storage medium gets bigger, faster, and cheaper.

Several serious developers, thanks to Department of Defense dollars, are emerging with almost unbelievably realistic audio—visual "scapes" that defy the boundaries of tomorrow's entertainment possibilities. The promises of 1980s *Brainstorm* and Isaac Asimov's remote viewing from *I Robot,* as well as countless science-fiction prognosticators of the last one hundred years, are finally coming to fruition.

An example of a software programs that has pushed the boundaries of realism is the "seascape" software that can replicate ocean waves as real as nature makes them. The operator simply fills in parameter requirements such as water temperature, wind direction, and speed, longitude and latitude, and the sea will act and react exactly as the laws of physics dictate. Another software can replicate any kind of ship. The operator enters parameters such as historic era, wood, metal, displacement, size, cargo weight, design, etc. The ship will replicate and ride the ocean-wave program, obeying the laws of physics as its size and displacement require.

New body-scanning platforms that can scan the human body down to a hair follicle and enter the images into the computer for action manipulation in "real time" are bringing forth a whole new area of opportunity. You can now create whole epic scene, limited only by the power of your own imagination and your understanding of how to enter parameters into the multitude of programs that will work in concert to create the future "vision" that you have in mind. Today's war cry is, "If you can think it, you can make it!"

There will be an exploding market for the new "Total Immersion" sound designer who will be hired, along with his or her team of sound creators—what we now call sound editors. These craftsmen and women will specialize in their own assignment audio events that once created and factored into the entire audio construct of the project, will work in concert with each other, all obeying the laws of physics along with the virtual real visual replications to create the brave new worlds. After we come home from a long day at the office, we can unwind by "jumping" into various "total immersion" entertainment scenarios.

Various new sensor-interactive technologies are currently being developed that will allow you to "feel" the visual realities. You are already able to turn your head and change the aspect of your view, turning to see a big oak tree with its leaves rustling in the warm afternoon breeze. Now with 360-degree "spherical-binaural" audio, you will be interlinked to visual events that will play for you the realistic sound of deciduous leaves fluttering in the breeze—while, through a device such as a wristband, embedded signals in the program will activate the sensation of a warm gust of wind washing across your body, with all the consequent sensations phantomed throughout your nervous system. You will feel pressure as well as temperature, in addition to seeing photorealistic visuals and spherical sound.

PRACTICAL APPLICATION FOR TRAINING PURPOSES

The armed forces believed that they could possibly save as many as 50 percent of their wounded if they could just train their combat personnel not fear the act of being shot or seriously inured in action. They had a scenario developed for total-immersion interactive software that would allow their soldiers to train in scenarios where they are ambushed by enemy forces. Realistic "spherical-audio" sells the distant weapon fire and the incoming flight of deadly bullet rounds. The wrist-wrap phantoms bullet strikes in the body, the first in the upper shoulder, the second in the left thigh. The sharp zip of other bullets fly past the trainee—striking and ricocheting off various surfaces (exactly linked and replicating the trainee's surroundings) around the soldier.

Now the wounded trainee has experienced as realistically as possible (short of really being shot) what it is like to be hit by incoming fire. Instead of reacting with the emotional side of our psyche—"Oh my God, I'm shot; therefore, I am going to die"—the trainee is now trained to think, "Damn it! I've been hit! Now I have to problem-solve how to survive!"

Mental attitude makes all the difference in the world. A self-disciplined "position" will hold back the emotional side and discard the primal fears and spur the will to live.

TOTAL IMMERSION ENTERTAINMENT

In the world of entertainment, one can just imagine the limitless applications to nervous system stimulation as triggered by "nervous system events" embedded in the Total Immersion program. It is hardly necessary to explain it.

New audio technologies are just now being perfected that will change everything. What if I could give you a microphone and tell you that you do not have to try to mimic Clark Gable or Cary Grant—all you have to do is perform the dialog line with that certain lilt and timing of pace and performance. Your spoken words would then be brought into a special audio software and processed through the "Clark Gable" plug-in or the "Cary Grant" plug-in, and out will come, voice-printable, Clark Gable or Cary Grant.

Science fiction? Not at all. In fact, as of the writing of this book, a number of first-step tests have already been accomplished. By the time this book is ready for its third edition I am sure that I will be updating this segment of the chapter to outline the specifics of the various software applications and how to use them.

Such technology will, of course, will change everything. Up to now, the visual "cut-paste" technique of integrating deceased celebrities into commercials and motion pictures (a la *Forrest Gump,* or beer commercials with John Wayne and Fred Astaire dancing with a vacuum cleaner) have been dependent on original footage. Yes, we have been able to "morph" an actor's face to look absolutely accurate for some time now—that is no trick at all. It is the human voice that has eluded us, and the use of voice mimics to impersonate the deceased actor has always been just detectable enough to make it useless for serious celebrity replication. With the advent of this new audio technology, however, the shutters will be thrown back on all of the projects that have wanted to enjoy bringing an actor back to life to perform in a project. We are on the eve of a new evolution of entertainment opportunities utilizing these new technological breakthroughs.

These new opportunities (and responsibilities) are staggering. By combining the technologies, one could create a Total Immersion entertainment venue whereby you could come home from a stressful day and decide that you want to put your Total Immersion gear on and activate a program that would give you a totally realistic experience of being in a Renaissance Faire on a nice spring afternoon, with, of course, a spherical-audio experience.

It only stands to reason that the more aggressive opportunists will develop programs where you can use Total Immersion to make passionate love to Marilyn Monroe or Tom Cruise or whoever else is on the menu.

Needless to say, there will be obvious exploitation of this new technology along with mind-blowing opportunities to do things we could not otherwise do, such as a space walk, or participating alongside Mel Gibson in the Battle of Sterling, or scuba diving amid the coral reefs. Imagine what it would be like to turn an otherwise boring afternoon (say that you are snowed in at home or maybe you are just grounded by your parents) into an educational adventure, sitting around in a toga in the Roman Senate or participating in the lively debates in the House of Lords during Cromwell's time. Or you could transport yourself aboard the frigate *Bonhomme Richard* under the command of John Paul Jones in the fierce night engagement with the *Serapis* off the Yorkshire coast at Flamborough Head. You are a member of the crew helping to man the cannons and then fight hand-to-hand combat in the grappling embrace of the two ships. Entertaining and extremely educational at the same time. What a concept!

All of this is going to need a new generation of sound craftsmen, developing and pushing the boundaries of how to design, develop, and bring to the consumer a myriad of amazing audio-event experiences.

CREATING AN AUDIO EVENT

In creating an audio event, the first thing you must do is to break the soundtrack down into its singular components. Unlike a movie or a music video that runs in a linear fashion, Total Immersion entertainment is not linear. There are not necessarily three minutes, fourteen seconds, and six frames of action to this bit of action. In Total Immersion you are capable of altering the action constantly—perhaps pausing and reflecting, perhaps speeding ahead to the next event. Who knows?

So we break the sound down into single audio events. It becomes instantly apparent that you do not think in terms of one sound event (audio file) at a time, or performing end-to-end, but rather as layers that perform onto their own cue "triggers," such as a pedal move by the operator or a switch being engaged or selector moved into position.

I often liken the experience to looking at a duck. You look at a duck and you see one fluid aquatic fowl in a single entity. But if you freeze that thought and move in closer and look at the duck's surface more closely, you see that it is composed of thousands of feathers, each with a certain unique difference, whether it be texture, colorization hue, or exact shape. Like a snowflake, no two feathers are exactly alike. Each feather fits under another feather and yet they are layered over one another. It is the blend of all these feathers as well as the musculature flexing during movement that create the physical ever evolving motion and reality of the body of the duck itself.

The same is true with the bundle of audio-event files that are linked to precise assignments of action or reaction—cause-and-effect creating a real-time illusion of reality. The more detailed your audio file designs are, and the more precise the degree of event breakdown, the more wonderful and natural the illusion will be.

For instance, the reality of getting into and driving a car requires a multitude of audio-event cues, each happening at precise assigned cause-and-effect points of action—either end-to-end, overlapping, cyclical or single performance, perhaps repeated action with the same audio file assignment fired as a random-access variation to thwart carbon-copy syndrome.

You open the car door, which triggers a CAR DOOR LATCH OPEN. This door latch is only half of the cue. The second half will not play until the operator pulls the door open and the mechanism passes the latch plate. That is the second click, and should not be part of the first audio cue, because what if the operator pulls on the car door handle but does not actually open the door, hesitating at that point? It would be inappropriate for the second part of the sound to be heard, as its action has not yet transpired.

When the door is opened to its widest point, a third audio cue, the CAR DOOR HINGE BOUNCE, will activate. This brief, but extremely real and satisfying sound sells the heft and reality of the door as it has reached the limit of the hinge swinging open. Depending on the depth and complexity of the design protocol, random variations can be used to give a different feel and texture to the hinge bounce. This, along with a little hinge squeak—or, if the car is old and beat up, WRENCHED CAR DOOR, in which the metal edges of the door crimp and wrench together because the fitting is no longer true—makes for a much richer, more realistic audio event.

Now the software reads the speed at which the operator closes the door, and it chooses from among three to five variations of door-closings, depending on the close velocity. Five examples are

GENTLE CAR DOOR CLOSE
SOFT CAR DOOR CLOSE
NORMAL CAR DOOR CLOSE
MED-STRONG CAR DOOR CLOSE
CAR DOOR SLAM CLOSE

You can take this even further. A car door opening and closing sounds different if the window is rolled up or rolled down. Does the client want you to factor these variations into the audio design?

As the car door is performing its cluster of cues, the operator has gotten into the car. One of my favorite effects is INTO CAR, which I recorded for *Christine* and which you hear in hundreds of television shows and motion pictures. I always make a cue of "body into car" movements—but here again, you need to develop several variations to be detected by the interactive software so it can choose the appropriate cue depending on the operator's movements. Three examples are

INTO CAR—SLOW/EASY
INTO CAR—NORMAL
INTO CAR—HURRY

Then you have KEY INTO IGNITION and a separate KEY TURN IN IGNITION. These are two separate cues because you have to anticipate that an operator may or may not turn the key once he or she has inserted the key. This interpretation of how an operator may or may not act or react to the scenario is exactly how you sit down and break down the audio cues into their protocol subroutines.

Everything you have learned from the previous chapters in this book and everything you have come to understand in breaking down action events in motion pictures in "A," "B," and "C" predub philosophy is focused now in your understanding of how to break down the single events and build them in performing layers so that the ongoing real-time random access of the software's audio library performs as if it were a linear reality of life. By the way, a KEY INTO IGNITION sounds different in a Cadillac than it does in a Toyota Landcruiser, as, of course, it would in a '49 Chevy pickup—so you need to factor in the reality of your vehicle.

A DEMONSTRATION

I made an attack helicopter series for an interactive training scenario. The client and his visual artists walked me through the various types of action and combinations of situations that they were planning to incorporate into the program. After noting all of the actions, including standard mechanicals such as canopy, engine cover, telemetry, and warning alarms, I also sketched out the twin General Electric engines start and warmup procedure, idle, lift-off, hover, flight, banking variations, various blade modes, maneuvers, land and power shutdown. In addition, I listed all modes of weapons, such as the *Hellfire* missile as fired from both port and starboard weapon racks as well as the classic 2.75 inch rockets from both port and starboard. Each needed its own unique aspect sound for launch and flights forward toward the acquired target.

In the days of crude visuals and even more simplistic synthetic audio, the forward 30 mm gun would have sounded like a raspy burst of upper low-end static hash. When the trainee would stop firing, the sound would just cut off—no over-ring, no tactile connection to reality in any sense of the word.

With today's interactive you would build in a long burst of 30mm fire, knowing that the gunner should not and cannot sustain too long a burst before barrel meltdown. That "full burst" audio file would be one cue linked to the "fire button" on the gunner's pistol grip. This sound file will play as long as the operator has the fire button engaged. When the operator lifts her or his finger to stop shooting, another audio file will be triggered to be the last 30mm shell fired along with the over-ring and mechanical movement, if any.

To get an idea of how this works, review cue #44 of the audio CD provided with this book to hear the first "full burst" of the Apache 30mm gun along with the second cue, or the "last shot and over-ring," followed by an example of how the gunfire might sound when the pilot trainee is actually shooting during simulation flight—yielding a very realistic illusion.

Audio CD Disc disclaimer: My apologies—the original attack helicopter cues (#44 through #46) were developed in 5.1, but for this book you will hear these audio examples only in left-right stereo. These audio mix-downs are only to reinforce your understanding of this chapter's text and to impart to you the philosophy of the subject and inspire you in developing your own material.

The helicopter's *Hellfire* missiles and 2.75" rocket pods must yield just as realistic a performance, whether fired from the port side weapons rack or from the starboard rack. Review cue #45 of the audio CD provided with this book to hear the *Hellfire* missile being fired from the port side and then the starboard rack, and then multiple 2.75 inch rockets being fired. Note that each rocket discharge would be a separate cue, but because the rockets could be fired very quickly, these cues will overlap as layered events. A good sound designer would build in slight variations into the rockets so that random-access selection by the interactive software would keep each rocket from sounding as if it were just a carbon copy.

It is like what one of my high school instructors said to me in a high school drafting class: "That line is the same as this line, only different." Well, the same holds true here. Each rocket firing is the same, except for a slight variation that makes each one unique and thus gives the textural differences that subtly separate them in our hearing. This slight variation keeps us from hearing each firing as just a repeat of the previous one and therefore lends a higher believability factor to the entire interactive scenario.

ENCODING THE AUDIO EVENT

In encoding the audio event, the first thing you want to do is make sure that you have all the stems to be encoded, organized and placed in their own "event" folders. This organization will, of course, make it extremely easy to access and point to each stem when you are in the encoding process.

Figure 20.3 shows the various audio-event folders in which you have carefully placed the various mixed "stems." Note the channel-assignment suffix extensions (.L, .C, .R, .Ls, .LR and .SUB or .LFE).

Figure 20.4 shows the various settings under the audio page that you need to review before you commit the audio encode. You need to choose whether you are making a generic AC3 file or whether you are making an audio track for film playback. In the example here

Figure 20.3 The attack helicopter series library.

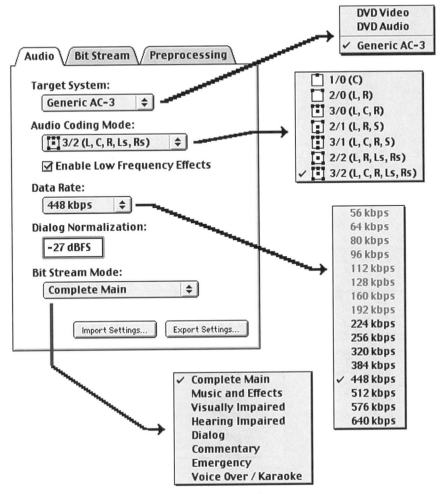

Figure 20.4 AC3 audio page.

we are making audio event AC3 files, so we are selecting "Generic AC-3," but if you were mastering a soundtrack for a video DVD transfer you would obviously choose "DVD Video."

You have numerous channel/speaker protocols to choose from. You need to choose the kilobyte-per-second rate, and 448 kbps is the high standard of today's DVD audio tracks for Dolby Digital. The software will default to this unless you choose to change it for some reason.

Most authoring houses today are using –27 dB for the "Dialog Normalization" setting for film soundtrack encoding. Some music DVD authoring houses are using –31 dB for non–feature film titles. You will need to research the delivery requirements of your client, usually supplied on an "AC-3 Audio Mastering" spec sheet for inventory delivery purposes. This step is critical, especially for foreign delivery requirements. Do not assume that the entire world operates under the same standards unless you want to do the work over again, at your own expense.

As you can see in Figure 20.5, you can choose numerous channel/speaker assignment configurations for encoding your audio files. Before you commit to a particular configuration you need to be diligent about meeting the end-user requirements so that you are not assuming to make one encode protocol instead of another. I know this last statement sounded a little obvious, but you would be surprised how many times AC3 encode files are rejected because they were improperly set up.

AUDIO ENCODE CONFIGURATIONS

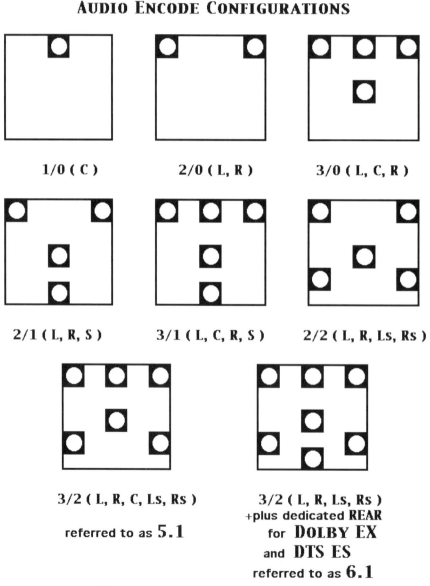

Figure 20.5 Audio encoding configurations.

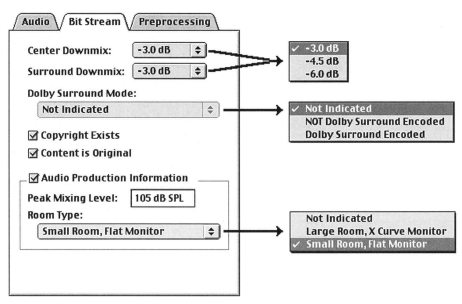

Figure 20.6

Figure 20.6 shows the various settings under the BIT page that you need to review before you commit the audio file group to the encoding process. When you boot up the A.Pack software, the software will default to a standard setting that should work for the majority of applications. You need to review them, being careful to double-check the spec sheet.

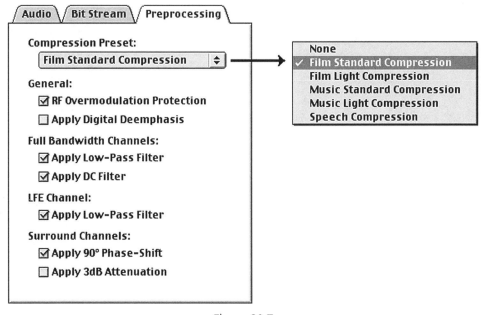

Figure 20.7

Some users opt to set the Peak Mixing Level at 85 dB, but the standard settings for today is 105 dB. For film soundtrack presentation you would choose "Large Room, X Curve Monitor;" after all, a very small percentage of the viewers are watching movies in their bathrooms. However, for the example here, where we are making interactive AC3 files for an interactive simulator, the playback proximity is close and small; therefore, we have chosen the "Small Room, Flat Monitor" option.

Figure 20.7 shows the various settings under the PROCESSING page that you need to review before encoding. "Film Standard Compression" is what you would obviously set if you are doing a film soundtrack master. Some authoring houses that specialize in music are opting to choose the "None" setting because they do not want any compression parameters to be utilized.

Figure 20.8 shows the A.Pack software booted up. Once you have pressed the left channel button, a dialog box appears for you to find and point to the group of audio file stems you wish to encode together into a 5.1 AC3 file. Take a moment to be sure that the correct stems are linked to the proper box assignments.

Figure 20.8

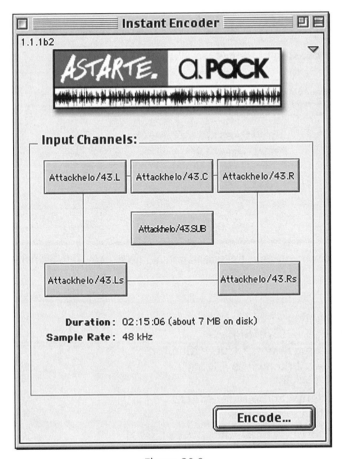

Figure 20.9

Figure 20.9 shows the A.Pack channel-assignment boxes filled with the stem names that they were linked to, each in its appropriate position.

Figure 20.10 shows the software encoding the six audio file stems into a single AC3 5.1 file. In this particular sound effect "event," the sum total of the Sound Designer II audio files that it took to create the six channels of sound consumed 87.6 megabytes of disk space. When the AC3 was completed, its net size was only 7.3 megabytes, or one-twelfth the size of the original audio file group.

Review cue #46 of the audio CD provided with this book to hear the attack helicopter's "Attack Maneuver."

STANDARD FILM SOUNDTRACK MASTERING SETTINGS

Following are examples of standard film soundtrack mastering settings:

Data Rate—448 kbps
Bit Stream Mode—"Complete Main"

Figure 20.10 The software encodes the six separate audio streams into a single AC3 matrixed audio file.

Dialog Normalization——27 dB
Peak Mixing Level—105 dB SPL
Room Type—"Large Room, X Curve Monitor"
Audio Coding—3/2 (known as 5.1)
Subwoofer (LFE)—"On"
Sample Rate (original audio file)—48 kHz
Center Down Mix Level——3 dB
Surround Down-Mix Level—3 dB
Dolby Surround Mode—"Not Indicated"
Apply Low-Pass Filter—"On"
Apply DC Filter—"On"
Surround Channels—"Apply 90-Degree Phase-Shift"

Chapter 21
The Venerable Nagra
IV-S (Analog)

The name of this book is *Practical Art of Motion Picture Sound*, and in this chapter we will discuss one of the most "practical" tools of all—the Nagra IV-S (analog). It is the highest-quality "bang-for-the-buck" audio recorder available today for production sound recording. In the heat of combat, when the production dollars are flowing as if through a sieve, when the proprietary DAT battery packs have taken a nosedive, when the extremes of high or low temperatures are turning your digital gear into inoperable lock-up, when the moisture of predawn dew or the blistering winds of Death Valley are turning all of your perfect preproduction plans of genius into just the mere desire to survive the day of shooting with any kind of track at all—*that* is when you stride back to your vehicle and pull out the Nagra. Forget the producer's or director's craving for techno-fads or their perception of cutting-edge digital promises. You *know* what the Nagra will deliver—under arduous conditions.

Nagras are tough, durable, and extremely forgiving. These remarkable recorders were invented by the Polish audio designer Stephan Kudelski and have been manufactured at the Kudelski/Nagra factory in Cheseaux, Switzerland, since the early 1960s. The Nagra audio recorder has attained legendary status, its name being synonymous with field audio recording for sync sound. Although DAT recorders have come into extremely wide use in the film industry, most professional sound mixers keep the Nagra close at hand as well anduse it in concert with digital recording equipment, thereby creating a greater collaborative alliance between the two technologies.

Figure 21.1 shows a Nagra IV-S with 7" reel expansion and oversize lid conversion that allows the use of standard 1/4" stock on 7" reels with the lid closed. Note that the width of the 7" reels is wider than the basic Nagra body. That is because originally the Nagra was designed to use the 5" reels. The manufacturer went on to design an adaptation kit that attaches to the unit with pulley belts so that the sound mixer can use 10" reels if desired (though this adaption is seldom used).

Figure 21.1 The Nagra IV-S overview.

This particular model in Figure 21.1 also has a slim pull-out time code panel that tucks neatly under the unit between the leg stumps.

There is rising interest in recording in analog on the Nagra again—no doubt due to comparison test recordings (such as cue #22 of the audio CD provided with this book) along with the recording mixers' evaluation of the quality of sound-versus-dollars-spent practicality. Some people are buying Nagras on ebay. Even though ebay is a great way to buy and sell goods directly from others, you should be aware of one very important fact about Nagras: they were built in two standards, CCIR and NAB. We all know what NAB is, the "western" standard for calibrations. CCIR, on the other hand, is the Eastern European equivalent, and those who do not remember to check whether the Nagra under consideration is NAB or CCIR may discover that they have a Nagra in beautiful condition that is unusable unless they convert it from CCIR to NAB.

Of course, CCIR models can be converted to NAB simply by sending them to a qualified tech maintenance service company. The cost of a conversion seems to be hovering around $1000 (as of this writing), which is not a bad price if you consider the overall value a used Nagra IV-S model in good shape, and reports are that many of these CCIR units are indeed in excellent shape. You can use a CCIR Nagra perfectly well *if* you transfer back from the same machine to whatever source, whether it be film mag or nonlinear digitization or whatever. But you cannot record with a CCIR model and ship the tape to any post-production facility without conversion to NAB.

THE BATTERY SUPPLY

One of the best engineering features of the Nagra is the practicality of its power. It does not run on a proprietary battery design like so many systems today. It runs on the classic D-cell battery (Figure 21.2), a standard power unit found everywhere. Unlike many new

Figure 21.2 D-cell batteries are used in the Nagra IV-S.

technology devices that work only an hour or two on their specially made batteries, the Nagra can work like a racehorse for days on one set of twelve D-cell batteries.

The designation chart in Figure 21.3 will help you through the rest of this chapter in identifying, by number, which part, switch, or selector procedure is being described. Look now at item 1 on the chart, the Power Source selector. When you change batteries, you need to flip the Power Source selector to EXT (external). Make sure that the Main Function selector (item 4) is turned to the OFF position, which is the horizontal, or nine o'clock, position. This will ensure that no power is flowing through the unit. Never change batteries when the Main Function selector is turned to TEST.

Make sure the lid of the unit is secured, and carefully turn it over. I like to use a hand towel as a protective surface, no matter where I am recording. On the underside you will see a rectangular stainless steel cover held in place on the back edge by two small stainless steel lips and locked down in front by two quarter-turn screws. Notice that the edge of the screws has a flattened side. It is a good idea to carry a coin in your pocket-to turn the two lock-down screws of the battery well cover. (They are designed perfectly for a nickel, though any coin will do. Place the coin in the screws and turn until the flattened edge of each screw is aligned with the edge of the battery well housing. Lift the lid up and out and place it to one side.

Always use Duracell batteries. No, I do not own any stock in in the company. I give you this advice from years of experience. With good operational procedure protocol your fresh change of Duracell batteries can last for days, even weeks if you use good power management. I had one set actually last six months.

Take a moment to check that the six spring-action contact terminals on the sides of the battery well are clean and free of any battery corrosive or fouling dirt or debris. On earlier Nagra models, the three positive-side contact terminals are spring-action fuses. You should take a moment to remove each one and closely inspect it. If they need to be changed, use 2.5 A 5 × 20 mm replacements. Be careful to insert them correctly or they could burn out. Of course, you will know very quickly that your fuse was replaced improperly when you turn the Nagra over and try to power it up again and nothing happens. Be sure you place the batteries into the trough guides facing the correct direction. If you do not place them all facing the correct direction, the power flow will be wrong.

Figure 21.3 Designation chart.

1. Power Selector Switch
2. Line & Phones Switch to Meter
3. Tape/Direct Switch to Headsets
4. Main Function Selector
5. Meter Light Button
6. Reference Oscillator Button
7. Potentiometer (Volume) Channel Control Knobs
8. Microphone/Line Input Selector Switch
9. NRS (Noise Reduction)/Normal Switch
10. Mono/Stereo Input Selector
11. Filter Selector
12. Meter Level Selector
13. modulometer
14. Pilot "Flag" Indicator
15. Speed/Power "Flag" Indicator
16. Headset 1/4" Connector (stereo)
17. Headset Volume Control
18. Headset Input Selector
19. Rewind/Fast Forward Switch
20. Tension Roller for the supply reel
21. Supply Reel (fresh 1/4" stock)
22. Erase Head
23. Lock-Down "Keeper" (supply reel side)
24. Stabilizer Roller (with a 50 or 60 Hz stroboscope)
25. Tape Speed Selector
26. Record Head (two channels)
27. Pilot Head
28. Playback Head (two channels)
29. Capstan
30. Pinch Roller Arm
31. Lock Down "Keeper" (take-up reel side)
32. Take-up Reel
33. Tension Roller for the take-up reel
34. Clutch Control Lever

Once you have properly inserted the new batteries, replace the stainless steel cover and, using your coin again, twist the lock-screws 90 degrees to secure it in place. Turn the unit over and flip the Power Source selector back to BATT (internal batteries). Turn the Main Function selector up to TEST, thereby powering up the Nagra electronics. Just off-center of the front control panel is the Level selector; rotate it to BATT. The modulometer needle should flip all the way over to the right side of the meter. If it does not, you need to go back and check your batteries and/or fuses.

If you use an older Nagra that has a "Volt/Cell" option on the Level selector, you can get an exact measurement of the battery power by turning the Level selector to this option. The modulometer needle should drop back to about midpoint on the meter. A fresh battery should read 1.5 volts or better. As the batteries diminish in strength you will notice that the voltage strength will drop bit by bit. It is unwise to use the batteries if their voltage strength has dropped under 1.2.

On the Nagra IV-S you do not have a "Volt/Cell" selection. That function is incorporated in the BATT position and shows up on the modulometer in the short third-level set of numbers to the right side. The same indication of voltage strength applies.

Remember that all batteries, no matter what make or model, are going to suffer in cold conditions, so it is a good idea to keep your batteries in a warm, temperature-protected spot. I include a packing blanket as part of my kit to wrap the Nagra in, leaving a blanket flap over it for easy access. When possible I also place two pair of battery-powered electrical socks under the Nagra to ensure stable battery power. Go to your favorite sporting goods store and think as if you were going duck hunting and need to keep warm—you will find a multitude of helpful devices.

SPEED AND EQUALIZATION SELECTOR

It is a good idea to decide the tape speed you want before you thread up a fresh roll of stock, since it is extremely difficult to get to this selector (item 25 in Figure 21.3) once you have threaded your tape stockphoto (see Figure 21.4).

The Nagra records at the following tape speeds:

3 3/4 ips = 9.525 centimeters per second
7 1/2 ips = 19.05 centimeters per second
15 ips = 38.1 centimeters per second

The Nagra IV-S also has a setting for 15 ips Nagra Master. This setting allows for an equalization curve as if you were recording at 7 1/2 ips, giving all the benefits of compensating for a high-frequency loss.

Note the "calibrated" sticker over the bias equalization adjustment, just to the lower left of the Speed selector. Unless you wish to be your own audio tech-engineer and recalibrate your equipment, you would be wise not to tinker with the machine's calibration. That kind of work should be handled by a professional audio engineer who does maintenance work on Nagras for a living. Your job is to go out and capture the audio recordings, so practice your art form and let the audio engineer do his or her job. Once you have decided on the tape speed you want, leave the setting there. It is a bad idea to change tape speeds during the recording process of a job.

Figure 21.4 The tape speed selector is nestled underneath and between the take-up reels.

TAPE THREAD PATH

The Nagra has to be the easiest tape path for loading (Figure 21.5). Open up the head/transport mechanism by grasping the clutch control lever (item 34 in Figure 21.3) and pulling it outwardly, toward yourself. This is a three-position lever. With it pulled all the way out, the head/transport mechanism will open up, allowing a clear path for the 1/4" tape stock to run from the far left tension roller across to the far right tension roller without obstruction.

Place your fresh roll of 1/4" tape stock on the left transport spindle (item 21) with the fresh roll of tape unwinding counterclockwise. You will see that there are three small stainless steel pins that the 1/4" hub must be seated on precisely for proper stability. Once the reel is seated correctly, screw down the lock-down keeper (item 23 in Figure 21.3). Mind that you do not misplace these little elusive jewels, as they are not cheap to replace. A clever trick

Figure 21.5 The tape path—clean and simple.

many mixers use is to slide the two keepers over the upright handle of the clutch control lever so that it acts as a hook to keep them from being misplaced.

Now pull the 1/4″ tape toward you. Pull it around the supply reel's tension roller (item 20 in Figure 21.3), then straight across, past the head stack and around the take-up reel's tension roller (item 33). As you pull the tape up and into the take-up reel, you will see a slot for inserting the head end of the tape. Be careful not to inadvertently flip the tape stock over, as it will cause the tape to wind onto the take-up reel with a half-twist. It is easier to load this incorrectly than you might think, so try it a few times to get the hang of it.

I recommendpulling the end of the stock into the slot and then spinning the take-up reel three or four turns to hold it in place. I keep either a razor blade or a small pair of scissors in my recording kit, which I then use to trim the head-end excess *flush* to the take-up reel hub. The reason you want to do this is so when you close the lid of the Nagra and begin recording, you will not have any excess 1/4″ stock sticking up and scraping on the underside of the lid, which can cause unwanted noise.

Once you are satisfied that the tape is securely loaded and the excess stock trimmed away, grasp the clutch control lever (item 33) and push it in toward the tension roller. The head/transport mechanism will rotate into place, properly pinching the 1/4″ tape against the capstan (item 29) and pinch roller lever (item 30). If your Nagra is equipped with a playback shield (which may cover the pilot and playback heads or just the playback head), be sure that it was flipped open when you loaded the tape. Believe it or not, I have seen several rolls of transfers where the mixer was listening directly from microphone and had no idea that he had loaded the tape *over* the playback shield, thereby causing a misalignment over the record head.

Now flip your playback shield up into position (if your Nagra is equipped with one). Note that when you roll tape (for Record or Playback), the tension rollers will undulate— that is, wobble back and forth—for a brief moment as they bring the feed and take-up transportation of the 1/4″ stock past the head stack array and capstan/pinch roller. They should settle down quickly, but sometimes they continue to vacillate. If so, turn your hands over and use your thumbnails to gently drag on the top of them to stop them from undulating. Most of the time undulation occurs only during the first rolling of the morning, perhaps because of temperature acclimation stiffness (who knows?). You must settle the tension rollers down or you will suffer major wow-and-flutter as they yank and slack out on the 1/4″ tape that is being pulled across the capstan.

If the tension rollers continue to undulate, your Nagra probably needs an adjustment by your audio tech contractor. But first check to make sure there is no foreign matter on the deck that is inhibiting smooth operation. You should keep a can of compressed air in your kit so you can place the nozzle extension under the bottom edge of the rollers and give each tension roller a blast. This simple procedure may just solve the problem.

REWIND SWITCH

Rewinding

This is a good time to comment about the rewind and fast-forward capabilities of the Nagra (Figure 21.6). If you need to rewind your tape to listen to a previous take, grasp the clutch control lever (item 34) and open up the head/transport mechanism. Turn the main function

Figure 21.6 The rewind/fast forward switch, located on the upper left-hand edge of the deck.

selector (item 4) up one click to "TEST." Doing this powers up the unit, allowing the motors to work in rewind mode if necessary.

It is best not to rewind with the Playback Shield in an upright position. Flip the shield back so the 1/4" tape will not rewind against the heads, which would effectively sandpaper the tape emulsion unnecessarily.

Keep your right index finger in place just to the side of the take-up reel, but not actually touching it, to guard against runaway tape when you stop rewinding. Now click the Rewind/Fast Forward Switch (item 19) to the left. The Nagra will instantly start rewinding.

I like to use my left thumb to guide the rewinding tape in close, but not actually touching the playback head. In this manner I can hear important audio points of reference as the tape rewinds. Also, this method makes it very easy to rewind virtually exactly where you want to be for playback.

When you wish to stop, simply click the Rewind/Fast Forward switch (item 19) straight up and the left motor will stop. This is where your right index finger comes in handy as a gentle brake. If you do not encourage the take-up reel (gently) to stop, it will unwind a bunch of recorded tape off the right side of the machine.

Close the clutch control lever (item 34), closing the head/transport mechanism. Flip the playback shield back up into position. Turn the Main Function selector (item 4) back down to the horizontal position. You can now play back the tape by turning the Main Function selector down to either of the two playback positions.

Fast-Forwarding

The Nagra does not fast-forward at the speed it can rewind. The idea of fast-forwarding is simply running twice as fast as normal speed. When you have the Nagra in playback mode, you can click the Rewind/Fast Forward switch to the right and the Nagra will accelerate the playback speed to some extent.

You have to understand that the Nagra is designed not to high-speed wind and rewind, but to record at a very high resolution and ship the reels "tails out" to the lab. It is just as simple and as practical as that.

HEAD STACK AND TRANSPORT

The head stack (Figure 21.7) is beautifully designed, with very easy access for cleaning the heads. Take a moment to inspect and clean the head stack before loading another roll of 1/4" tape. Do not use consumer cotton-tipped "ear" swabs, as they "fleece," leaving stringy cotton remnants on the heads. (Remember, it takes only the slightest speck of foreign matter to ruin your recording.) Use foam-tipped video cleaning swabs instead. In addition, a cotton-tipped cleaning stick, such as the Realistic brand at Radio Shack, works well. This cotton tip does not unravel and leave remnants.

Use denatured alcohol to clean the head stack. If you use isopropyl alcohol, you must wait a few moments for the heads to fully dry out before loading up a fresh roll of stock.

Make sure that you clean everything along the tape path. Look for grit and excess magnetic emulsion—an extremely fine dark shedding of the stock that occurs as a result of the physical rubbing across the heads.

The erase head (item 22) is on the far left of the photo in Figure 21.7. Do not depend on this head as a bulk degausser—it is meant to erase "field-strength." If you are using recycled 1/4" stock (which you should never use for important production dialog), you need to have those recycled tapes' bulk degaussed through a heavy-duty magnetic unit prior to recording.

STABILIZER ROLLER

The stabilizer roller (item 24) sits right next to the record head and serves two important functions. First, it guides the 1/4" tape around at the proper angle to seat against the record head for proper recording. Second, it has an interesting gearlike adornment on top, with either a "50" or a "60" (European 50 cycles or American 60 cycles) label. As the machine is running up to speed, you can lean over and look down at this spinning top, and under AC light (burning at either 50 cycles European or 60 cycles American), if you squint slightly, and

Figure 21.7 Transport assembly in "open" position.

if the machine is running at proper speed, the "gear" will appear to be holding still. If the machine is running fast or slow, the gear will appear to drift around. This is an indication that you should have your machine checked.

RECORD HEAD

The record head (item 26) records two channels of analog audio.

PILOT HEAD

The pilot head (item 27) records the sync signal down the center (in between the left and right audio channel).

PLAYBACK HEAD

The playback head (item 28) plays back the two channels of analog audio that is recorded by the record head. As stated before, most of the more recent machines are equipped with a hinged playback shield. Note that the photo in Figure 21.7 has the shield covering both the pilot and playback heads. Some machines have playback shields that cover only the playback head. These shields help guard against RF radio signal interference.

CAPSTAN AND PINCH ROLLER

The capstan (item 29) is extremely important. This little spinning metal post is the precise speed mechanism that literally drags your 1/4" tape across the heads at exactly the right speed. It is dependent on the pinch roller (item 30). When the clutch control lever is pushed forward into position, as it is in the photo in Figure 21.8, the pinch roller arm is rotated into position, with the roller (made out of a hard, rubberlike synthetic material) perfectly pressing a smooth and even surface firmly against the capstan. If you do not take great care in the delicate cleaning of this roller, making sure that there is no buildup of oxide, grit, or other foreign matter, the pinch roller will not properly track the 1/4" tape, resulting in improper tape speed. This problem can even cause the tape to "walk" up the capstan, causing the tape stock to ride out of alignment with the Rrcord, pilot, and playback heads.

Be extremely careful not to create any kind of dimple, nick, or scratch on the pinch roller. It is exactly these kinds of wounds that will lead to catastrophic performance problems.

On the far right of the photo in Figure 21.8, you can see the clutch control lever (item 34) in the "open" position.

Note the position of the stabilizer roller (item 24), also in Figure 21.8. When the clutch control lever is pushed in, the stabilizer roller moves forward, pressing in against the 1/4" tape to make it track in across the record head at just the right angle. Note the 90-degree rotation of the pinch roller arm up against the capstan. When the Nagra is not in motion, the

Figure 21.8 Transport assembly in "closed" position.

pinch roller "rests" slightly relaxed off the tape. It "pinches" in on the tape stock when in the Record or playback mode.

FRONT CONTROL PANEL

Figure 21.9 presents the full frontal view of the front control panel. On other Nagra models, certain controls and indicators are located differently. The IV-S model has its Pilot and Speed/Power flag indicators located to the left side of the modulometer rather than on the far right, just to the side of the Main Function selector. Some versions have their Tape/Direct, Line-&-Phones, and Power switch array to the left of the Main Function selector, whereas the IV-S has those switches to the right of the Main Function selector. These differences evolved over years of refining the sound mixer's eye-hand coordination efficiency with the machine.

Figure 21.9 Front control panel, full view.

Figure 21.10 Front control panel, right side.

Right Side of Front Control Panel

Power Selector Switch

The Power Selector switch (item 1) is shown in Figure 21.10. Since the Nagra can work on an external power converter power pack from an AC outlet, you need to tell the machine whether it is using the AC power pack or internal battery power. Up is AC power pack; down is internal batteries.

Tape/Direct Switch

Put your headsets on and flip the Tape/Direct switch (item 3) to the right (DIRECT) and you will be listening directly from the microphones. You will need to do this when the 1/4" tape is not in motion in either the record or playback mode. When you are monitoring for levels in standby (TEST) mode you will be able to hear only in the DIRECT position.

Once you have engaged the machine to record, you should flip the Tape/Direct switch to the left (TAPE), so you can hear what you are actually recording. Believe me, there are times, due to oxide buildup, incorrect threading of the machine, or some other problem, that you will hear your incoming signal just fine when in DIRECT mode even though you are not actually recording properly. You will not know this unless you are monitoring in playback mode, with the Tape/Direct switch flipped to TAPE position.

Most mixers will flip the switch back and forth during the recording to A-B the signal— in other words, to see if they are getting a true, or "transparent," replication from the microphones onto the tape oxide.

Line & Phones Switch

The Line & Phones switch (item 2) will allow you to A-B compare by use of the meter (item 13, the modulometer). This switch is a momentary contact switch, so when you let go of it, it will automatically return to the DIRECT position. I personally do not use this option very much, as my ears will tell me much more about the clarity and coloration of the A-B comparison using the Tape/Direct option instead. However, I can see where it would be useful if you are doing Line Input line-up tones and want to see how accurately your tape oxide is mirroring the incoming signal.

Main Function Selector Bar

When the Main Function selector (item 4) is in the horizontal position, as shown in the full view of the Nagra panel (refer again to Figure 21.9), all electrical power to the Nagra is turned off. There is no power running through any electronic components, and the batteries are not being drained.

Because it takes a few moments for the electronics to warm up to optimum capacity, you never want to just flip the selector bar straight up into a record mode from the OFF position. The first few seconds of the recording will sound dreadful—like a breaking-up distorted awakening. This is why recording mixers will anticipate the assistant director's call to make the shot. Most good mixers are already rolling when the assistant director calls out, "Roll sound"—usually because the mixer is also responsible for sounding the warning bell and turning on the red light. Once the assistant director calls for "light and bell," the mixer usually flips the warning on and rolls the recorder.

To anticipate this call by the assistant director, the recording mixer gets into a rhythm that starts with knowing when to warm up his Nagra by flipping the Main Function selector up to the TEST position. In a matter of four to six seconds you will hear the signal from your microphones well up, and the signal will become clear. From this moment on you can roll sound and record confidently.

Roll to RECORD

There are two record positions. The first position will record with a limiter that will compress the volume signal when it peaks too high, thereby guarding against distortion and spikes, explosive moments that oversaturate the stock. That is all well and good for documentary and other monitoring missions where you cannot ask for a second take because you peaked out. However, recording with a limiter also means you are going to have an audio track that may (and probably will) have periodic compressed areas that are not at all desirable in a theatrical film. That is why you have the second recording position: the twelve o'clock position, straight up. This is the NO LIMITER position, which turns off the compressing limiter option. Now you are on your own, but of course that is why you are the recording mixer and getting the big bucks, right?

Roll for PLAYBACK

To listen to recorded material in a playback mode, simply click the Main Function selector downward to either the first or second playback position. The difference between these two options is that the first position will give you playback signal through the headsets only. It is important to note that the internal resolver (to maintain sync speed) function is turned off during playback in this position.

To play back the audio signal with the internal resolver in an active mode, you need to turn the Main Function selector down to the second playback position (marked with a double "cone" icon). This second position will send the signal to the headsets and also to the built-in speaker that is mounted on the right flank of the unit. This speaker should not be expected to yield the full fidelity that you will hear through full-spectrum monitor speakers later, but it should let you know whether what you have done is clear and acceptable sound or whether you have distortion issues that you need to correct.

Light Button

Pressing the small LIGHT button (item 5) will turn on the light in the modulometer so you can read it under poorly lit conditions. This is a momentary button; when you take your finger off it, the light will shut off. If you wish to have the light remain on, push and pivot the button to the right. The meter light will remain on until you pivot the button back to the left. Try not to leave the light on too long, as it does accelerate the wear and tear on the batteries.

Reference Oscillator Button

The REFERENCE OSCILLATOR button is a momentary contact button (item 6). When you press it, the built-in Reference Tone Oscillator will activate. You will want to press and hold this button down for ten to twenty seconds to lay down the −8 dB reference line-up tone at the head of each roll of tape.

When the mixer ends each recorded take, he or she will press this button twice to leave two short beep-beeps to mark the end of each take. Later, in sound transfer, the transfer engineer can spin the tape at high speed, holding her or his thumb against the tape, nudging it partially in toward the playback head (without touching it). This reference-tone signal is strong enough to be heard as fleeting "blips" going by. The transfer engineer can count those blips as he or she looks at the sound report and counts down (or up, depending on winding direction) to quickly locate the precise take required.

Volume Control "Potentiometers"

The two volume control knobs, or "pots" (item 7), are what Nagra likes to call the "potentiometers." Channel 1 (left) has a small crescent latch built into it. If you move the latch down, you will unlock the two knobs so they can work independently. If you move the latch up, you will lock the two knobs together. In this manner, if you move one, the other will move in precisely linked calibration. This feature is very useful if you wish to have Channel 2 (right) record the same incoming signal as Channel 1 (known as two-track mono), but at a lower level (e.g., 10 dB).

Unlock the two knobs. Turn them both completely to the left until they are at OFF. Now move the crescent lock upward to link the two knobs together. If you feed an incoming line-up tone into the Nagra from your outboard mixer or from a portable reference generator, you can quickly calibrate an exact −dB setting. Turn Channel 1 up until the two needles on the meter (modulometer) read "0." Obviously Channel 2 has come up to the exact same position because the two pots are locked together. Now move the crescent lock down to unlock the two channels. Move the Channel 2 (right) knob to the left until the red needle (Channel 2) backs down to the −10 dB position on the meter. Now move the crescent lock up to lock the two volume pots back together again.

Now you have Channel 1 and Channel 2 locked together in precise relationship with each other, only −10 dB apart. This arrangement works wonders when you have sudden volume bursts, such as gunshots, screams, door slams, or other sudden concussionary sounds that will blow out and distort Channel 1. Later in the post-production phase, the dialog editor will take the Channel 2 transfer of the blown-out Channel 1 performance and integrate it into the dialog (or "P-FX" track) so as to utilize the undistorted version.

Linking the two channels is also mandatory for true stereophonic recordings, where the two channels have to be in precise left-right balance to effectively create the envelope of the audio "field" presence.

I like to simplify the signal path in recording. I feel that the more you run the audio signal through things, the more you are going to add noise and/or hiss. Be careful not to

Figure 21.11 Front control panel, center.

send a weak or artificially lowered signal into your Nagra if you are using an outboard mixer. Beginners often make the mistake of having too low a level feed into the mixer (using the LINE input mode), which compels them to turn the potentiometer volume pots up too high in order to boost the signal. By doing this you will dramatically increase "hiss" and excessive ground-noise rumble. That is why you want reference tones and known levels that can be read on meters and matched accordingly. If you are having to turn your volume controls over past the two o'clock position, you are risking unwanted hiss and noise—so beware.

Center Controls

Meter Selector

The Meter Selector (item 12) (see also Figure 21.11) tells the meter (modulometer) (item 13) what it is you wish to view. This selector is your gateway to check the performance of the machine and/or incoming or outgoing signals as read on the meter. Different models of Nagras have different variations on possibilities to meter. Some Nagras, for instance, have options to measure compression, volt/cell, and bias. The Nagra IV-S shown here has been greatly simplified, excluding the need for some settings found on older models.

Pilot Frequency

The PILOT FREQ (Pilot Frequency) setting is used in conjunction with the built-in QFMS frequency meter, between the pilot signal—recorded or played back on the pilot track and a 50 Hz or 60 Hz internal reference. The red needle may deviate as much as plus or minus 4 percent as it compares the pilot signal versus a 60 Hz crystal. The green needle will show on the dB scale the signal from the channel with the greatest amplitude.

Figure 21.12 Front control panel, left side.

This setting measures on a 0-to-100 percent scale the groove depth of a record made from recorded signals in accordance with NAB weighting; 100 percent corresponding to a 50 µm vertical deviation of the cutting stylus. The green needle, as with the Pilot Frequency setting, will show on the dB scale the signal from the channel with the greatest amplitude.

Level

ThE straight-up position, pointing at LEVEL, will allow you to monitor the two audio input levels of Channels 1 (left) and 2 (right). Note the top dB scale on the modulometer (Figure 21.12). The modulometer is a peak meter. Unlike its cousin, the VU meter, which shows an averaging of the signal, a peak meter shows the exact peaks of the loudest amplitude of the signal.

It is important to know that −8 dB on the Nagra's modulometer equals "0" level on a VU meter. The "0" level shown on the modulometer is therefore 8 dB hotter than on other tape recorders using the standard VU meter system. Therefore, a normal dialog recording should be bouncing around −5 dB to 10 dB (or around the straight-up area on the meter). This gives you a nice amount of head room for loud, sudden sounds, such as screams, door slams, crashes, and impacts, etc. If your dialog is recording as high as "0" dB on the modulometer, it will be far too hot when you transfer to the audio signal to another medium—for that would be equivalent to a peak of +8 dB to +10 dB, which is *really* hot!

You should reserve the need to record above "0" dB for exceptional situations, such as momentary sounds (e.g., gunshots or door-slam type sounds)—and *only* momentary sounds!

Battery

Flip the selector to the BATT position and you will be able to see how your batteries are doing. This is your "Battery Reserve" level, and is read in the bottom scale—the short one on the right side of the modulometer window. Remember, as discussed earlier under "The Battery Supply," a fresh battery array will read 1.5 volts or better. When the power drops down close to 1.2 volts, it is time to change to a fresh set.

TC/Pilot Playback

The TC/PILOT PLAYBACK selection will measure the sync signal on the tape. The strength will be read on the center scale (with PILOT above it) of the modulometer window. The red needle will read −4 to +4 percent on the scale, the frequency shift between the pilot signal recorded or played back on the pilot track and a 50 Hz or 60 Hz internal reference. The green needle will read on the 0-to-100 percent scale the level of the signals recorded or played back on the pilot track; 100 percent corresponds to a frequency deviation of ±40 percent. This setting is used more often by your tech maintenance person when your Nagra goes into the shop for its 3000-mile tire rotation.

M Setting

The M setting will read the current through the motor. The red needle will read on the 0-to-100 percent scale, in which 100 percent corresponds to 250 mA.

Filter Selector

The Filter Selector (item 11) is where you choose what kind of frequency attenuation you wish to record. On the Nagra IV-S most mixers will record at either FLAT (which is most of the time) or for exterior work they find a need to flip the filter selector down to S+LFA2 (Speech plus Low-Frequency Attenuation 2). This will help with some wind noise and low-end rumble issues. With today's microphone wind-abatement technologies, there is little need to resort to the second setting unless you hear a great deal of low-end rumble. When in doubt, record FLAT. Post-production may very well want the low-end frequencies that you rolled out of a recording. They can always remove them later, but they cannot reinstate them naturally if you canceled them out of the equation.

Flat

The FLAT setting is for the linear response curve.

Music

The MUSIC setting is for the high-pass filter, −3 dB at 40 Hz.

M+LFA

The M+LFA setting is for music and low-frequency attenuation, −7 dB at 40 Hz and −3 dB at 400 Hz.

Speech

The SPEECH setting is for the high-pass speech filter, −3 dB at 80 Hz.

S+LFA2

The S+LFA2 setting is for the speech filter and low-frequency attenuation, −7.5 dB at 80 Hz and −3 dB at 400 Hz.

Roll Off

The ROLL OFF setting is for strong low-frequency attenuation, −10 dB at 100 Hz and −3 dB at 400 Hz.

NOTE: Most older Nagras may show these filter settings as LFA1, LFA2, FLAT, HP1, HP1+LFA1, and HP2. Obviously, LFA stands for Low-Frequency Attenuation. Those Nagras that have LFA1 and LFA2 offer two roll-off variations. The same is true with HP—that is, High Pass. You need to listen through your headphones to the subtle differences and decide what "feels" best for your needs. Most mixers use two basic settings: FLAT for interior work and HP1+LFA1 (which is denoted with a box around it) for exterior work. These two settings will usually achieve a consistent response for your production track throughout the shoot.

Mikes/Line Selector Switch

Now look at the MIKES/Line Selector Switch (item 8) in Figure 21.11. If you are recording with microphones, you obviously will switch it up to MIKES. If you are recording with an outboard mixer or making a machine-to-machine transfer, you will need to flip this switch down to the LINE position. Remember that you should not plug LINE inputs into the XLR inputs on the left flank side of the Nagra. To do so will cause you to double-phantom your microphones, as your outboard mixing panel is sending a phantom power signal, and by going through the microphone, XLR inputs of the Nagra defaults through the phantom power supply, causing a distorted signal. This subject will be covered later when we talk about the Tushel in and out connectors and XLR microphone inputs.

Noise Reduction Switch

If you intend to utilize the internal noise reduction system (item 9), or if you intend to utilize an outboard noise reduction system (by coming into the left flank Tushel connector marked EXT.NRS), you need to flip the switch up to NRS. If you do not want to use NRS, simply flip the switch down to the NORMAL position.

Mono-Stereo Selector

Set the Mono-Strereo Selector (item 10) in the configuration that you wish to import your signal. In the MONO mode the two coupled inputs are connected to the two channels. In the STEREO mode each input is connected to the corresponding channel for dedicated control. In the ST.HS (Stereo High-Sensitivity) mode each input is connected to the corresponding channel as in the STEREO mode, but the sensitivity of the input signal is +6 dB higher. This gives you a little extra firepower if you need it without cranking the volume control potentiometers up too high and building up unwanted bias floor hiss. Of course it will add a little more extra bias hiss. More volume cannot help but do that, but it is better than just cranking up the volume controls to maximum. This is especially useful for subtle stereophonic backgrounds and non-close proximity audio events.

Left Side of Front Control Panel

Headphone Jack and Headphone Controls

The lower left-hand corner of the Nagra has a 1/4" stereo phono jack for your headsets. Just above it and to the right is the volume control setting—you simply turn the flattened-edged screw using the 0-to-7 level calibration. Older Nagra models have the volume control located just below and to the right of the phono plug input, right next to the modulometer. Other Nagra models use the upper left-hand corner selector switch as a volume control selector with a 0-to-5 level setting.

In the model shown in Figure 21.12 the upper-left selector is the Headset Input selector. You can turn your headsets off by clicking the selector all the way to the left. Click it to the right one stop for the CUE option. Click it one more stop to the right to hear LEFT channel only. Click it one more stop to the right to listen to RIGHT channel only. Click it one more stop to the right to listen to full STEREO. If you wish to listen in flat monaural through both ears, click the selector to the far right to MONO.

If you are recording STEREO, or two separate microphones as monaural feeds, and you are concerned about phasing issues, you can click the selector to the right to the MONO position and the two channels will be "folded down" together. If you have phasing issues, you will immediately experience a fully swimming quality to the signal, indicating that you need to make an adjustment. Some Nagra models have been outfitted with a very convenient momentary contact switch. You merely press it and both channels are automatically folded down so that you can easily A-B compare between discrete two-channel and folded mono. Both procedures accomplish the same result.

Pilot Flag Indicator

The pilot flag (item 14) shows completely black when the unit is at rest. When you roll in the record mode, two little white flags will flip open and hold steady when while it reads the incoming sync signal. As you record, these two flags hold perfectly still until you shut down. If they flicker, it means you are getting a bad sync signal and you will probably not be able to warrant good lip sync. If you are using an external sync source, check the jumper cable—it might be loose, or the contact might not be not clean.

Speed and Power Indicator

The speed and power indicator (item 15) works just like the pilot indicator. When you roll this, the flag indicator will flip on and hold steady. It tells you that your speed is constant and that your power is good. If the flag flickers or goes out, you know that you are not going to have proper lip sync. Naughty, naughty—you have not kept good account of your battery power and it has dipped below the safe level that we talked about earlier in this chapter. Check your batteries by flipping the meter selector to BATT. If your batteries are croaking—well, you know what to do! If, on the other hand, your batteries are fine and the flags continue to flicker—cease using the machine. Get your backup unit out and send your Nagra immediately to maintenance tech to be checked out.

Modulometer

We have spoken enough about the modulometer in the preceding paragraphs that you should know all about it by now. Enough said.

The Left Flank INPUT Panel

Figure 21.13 shows the left flank side of the Nagra, or the inputs side. Notice that the outboard LINE inputs and outputs use Tushel (pronounced "Too•shell") connectors and are located on the left side of the panel. The microphone inputs, using XLR female input connectors along with their counterpart phantom power settings, are on the right side of the panel.

Figure 21.13 Left flank "INPUT" panel.

Tushel In and Out Connectors

LINE INPUTS (Tushel 7-Pin Connector)

Figure 21.14 shows a closer view of the left side of the Tuschel inputs. If you are transferring from another machine or using an outboard mixer to control your microphones and slating chores, you will patch into the Nagra using a Tushel 7-pin connector. If you need to make a Tushel connector cable, or have one made, look at the schematic of the pin assignment configuration in Figure 21.15.

Remember, when you use the Tushel connection for an outboard mixer or input from another machine, you must go to the front panel of the Nagra and flip the MIKE/LINE Switch (item 8) down to LINE.

EXT.NRS (Tushel 7-Pin Connector)

If you are utilizing an outboard noise reduction system, you will connect the system via the Tushel 7-pin connector into this screw socket. You must then go to the front panel of the

Figure 21.14 Closer view of the Tushel inputs.

Figure 21.15 Tushel 7-pin connector.

Nagra (item 9) and flip the switch up to NRS. This will send the signal out to the outboard noise reduction gear and then return it back into the Nagra after the noise reduction encode is effected.

Line Outputs (Tushel 7-Pin Connector)

If you are using the Nagra as a transfer machine, you can output the signal either through the Tushel 7-pin connector on the far left of the left-side panel or from the banana plug options on the right-side panel that we will talk about a little later.

Nagra Wiring Assignment Specifications

Nagra wiring assignment specifications are listed here in case you should need to custom-fabricate your own connector cables. The illustration of the Tushel connector in Figure 21.15 shows the external view of chassis connector or plug from the soldering side.

OUTPUTS—Tushel Connector:
1. Channel 2 (right) output: output voltage is 1 V at '0'dB, minimum impedance load 500 Ω.
2. −10G: −10 V stabilized voltage output, maximum current 100 mA for all −10 V terminals.
3. Channel 1 output (left) identical to #1 in this list.
4. Vunstab: unstabilized power supply voltage.
5. −10 R: −10 V stabilized voltage output available on record only, maximum current 100 mA for all −10 V terminals.
6. STOP: input for the motor stop control (connect to −10 V to stop).
7. Ground.

EXT. NRS (Noise Reduction System)—Tushel Connector:
1. External noise reduction system output Channel 2 (right).
2. −10G: −10 V stabilized voltage output, maximum current 100 mA for all −10 V terminals.
3. External system output, Channel 1 (left).
4. External system input, Channel 1 (left) minimum input impedance 47 Ω.
5. External system input, Channel 2 (right) minimum input impedance 47 Ω.
6. Ground (common).

XLR connector

CCIR   NAB

Figure 21.16 The wiring assignment schemeatic for the XLR microphone inputs.

INPUTS—Tushel Connector:
1. Channel 2 (right) input, impedance variable from 0 to 5 k Ω when switch 11 is on ST. HS, current drive with minimum source impedance 47 k Ω; current to obtain 0 dB at maximum sensitivity 7.8 μA.
2. –10 G: –10 V stabilized voltage output, maximum current 100 mA for all –10 V terminals.
3. Channel 1 (left) input, identical to #1 in this list.
4. Ground for input signals.

Microphone XLR Connector

The first thing you will want to take note of in regard to the microphone XLR connector is the difference between the NAB wiring scheme and the CCIR scheme. Again, Nagra wiring assignment specifications are given here in case you should need to custom-fabricate your own connector cables. The illustration of the XLR connector in Figure 21.16 shows the two standard wiring schemes as external views of the chassis connector or plug from the soldering side.

Microphone XLR Inputs

The two microphone XLR inputs (Figure 21.17), unlike previous monaural models, record on two dedicated channels. I know that seems very obvious, but you have to remember that the previous Nagras were, in fact, *monaural* machines, because even though they had two microphone inputs, they combined both signals into a single channel. Now that this seemingly obvious statement is set aside, let us move on. LEFT is Channel 1 and RIGHT is Channel 2 (industry standard configuration).

Phantom Power Selectors

Nagra includes a six-option Phantom Power supply for each input as follows:

1. **DYN 50**—if you are using a dynamic microphone with an impedance of 50 Ω. 0.1 mV/μbar sensitivity.
2. **DYN 200**—if you are using a dynamic microphone with an impedance of 200 Ω. 0.2 mV/μbar sensitivity.
3. **+12**—if you are using a condenser microphone that has a 0.1 mV/μbar sensitivity and requires +12 volt phantom powering.

Figure 21.17 Close view of microphone XLR inputs and Phantom Power selectors.

4. **+48**—if you are using a condenser microphone that has a 0.1 mV/μbar sensitivity and requires +48 volt phantom powering.
5. **−12**—if you are using a condenser microphone that has a 0.1 mV/μbar sensitivity and requires −12 volt phantom powering.
6. **"T"**—if you are using a condenser microphone that has a 3 mV/μbar sensitivity and requires +12 volt T-powering (Tonaderspeisung).

PHASE Selector

Occasionally you may have microphones that do not have matching wiring schematics, and you may need to invert the phase of one mike to properly record against another one. If you flip the screw slot switch (located between the two Phantom Power selectors) to the right, you will invert the phase of Channel 1 (left).

The OUTPUT Panel

Figure 21.18 shows the right flank side of the Nagra, or the outputs side. Notice that the grill on the left part is where the built-in loudspeaker is. This speaker works only when the Main Function selector is turned all the way down to the second playback position, the one with the double cone icon. On the Nagra IV-S the speaker volume is controlled by the volume potentiometers. On older Nagra models there is a volume control screw, sometimes located on the left flank side of the Nagra just below the Phantom Power selector, and other models have it just to the left of the loudspeaker up near the shoulder strap bolt.

External Power Pack—(6-Pin Tushel)

The Nagra can work off a 50 Hz or 60 Hz AC power adapter (that comes with the Nagra package). The power pack (Figure 21.19) uses a 6-pin Tushel connector to attach rigidly into the screw socket to feed the machine. You must go to the front panel of the Nagra and flip the power switch (item 1) up to EXTERNAL.

Figure 21.18 Right flank OUPUT panel.

You will find that most mixers are very reluctant to try to use the power pack out in the field, feeding from an unknown or suspect power source. The power pack works fine for interior and stage work where known power feeds are dependable.

Line Outputs (via Banana Jacks)

Output transfers can be efficiently made using banana jacks, feeding from the left and right banana ports just below and to either side of the 5-pin Lemo Time Code connector. The "ground" banana-jack ports are located below and to either side of the CUE 7-pin Tushel connector (discussed next).

Cue—(7-Pin Tushel Connector)

The CUE 7-pin Tushel connector is for recording and playback on the pilot track. The illustration of the Tushel connector in Figure 21.20 shows the external view of the chassis connector or plug from the soldering side. Following are the specifications:

1. Modulation signal input.
2. −10 V stabilized voltage output, maximum current 100 mA for all −10 V terminals.

Figure 21.19 Close on OUTPUT panel.

Figure 21.20 CUE Tushel 7-pin connector.

3. Pilot signal input.
4. −10 V stabilized voltage available on record only, maximum current 100 mA for all −10 V terminals.
5. Voltage terminal to activate the FM modulator.
6. Signal output (direct or recorded).
7. Ground.

Pilot—(4-Pin Tushel Connector)

The PILOT 4-pin Tushel connector receives signal input for the pilot track. The illustration of the Tushel connector in Figure 21.21 shows the external view of the chassis connector or plug from the soldering side. Following are the specifications

1. Ground.
2. CLAPPER: reference oscillator or crystal pilot generator control input.
3. Xtal: 50 Hz or 60 Hz internal crystal pilot generator OUTPUT.
4. PILOT IN: pilot signal INPUT.

Time Code In/Out

The 5-pin Lemo connector (TIME CODE IN/OUT in Figure 21.19) can either import an external time code signal or output the time code signal generated from the internal generator.

Time Code Option

Some Nagra models, including the one featured in this chapter, are equipped with a pancake-thin time code panel (Figure 21.22) that slides forward from the underside—tucked neatly between the two front stumpy feet on a scissor fold-out mechanism.

Figure 21.21 PILOT 4-pin Tushel connector.

Figure 21.22 Time Code panel.

The Nagra can accept an external time code signal (via the TIME CODE connector on the right flank panel) or it will default to using its own generated time code signal.

When using a Smart Slate, plug the time code wireless transmitter into the TIME CODE IN/OUT connector on the right side "output" panel. The Smart Slate will display whatever time code the Nagra is generating for visual reference by the camera when the clapper assistant holds out the slate to snap sync. The illuminated red numbers make it easy for the assistant picture editor to sync the dailies later in picture editorial.

Now look at the illustration in Figure 21.23. If you want to check the time code status, press the STATUS/7 button. Unless you *want* to record in a "Drop Frame" mode, there should *not* be the little marker under where "Drop Frame" is shown on the far left-hand side of the display. If there is a marker, it indicates that you are recording "Drop Frame Time Code"—which is not what you want if you are recording for film projects.

Press the NEXT ST/8 button to check the frame rate. It should read "30 Fr," since 30 fps NDF (non-drop frame) is the industry standard for film cameras running 24 fps or 30 fps.

To clear the time code panel of previous programming, press the following buttons in this order: SHIFT, STATUS/7, NUM/0, →/2, NUM/0, NUM/0, SHIFT, NUM/0. (Or, if you wish to read the words under the buttons: SHIFT, ENTER, EXECUTE, INT TC, EXECUTE, EXECUTE, SHIFT, EXECUTE.)

To program the user bits for use in the date format, press NUM/0, ←/1, NUM/0, DISP UB/6, SHIFT, EXECUTE.

To enter the time of day, press these buttons: DISP TC/5, NUM/0, then the HOUR, HOUR, MINUTE, MINUTE, and then NUM/0, NUM/0, NUM/0, NUM/0, SHIFT, ENTER.

To enter the date, press these buttons: DISP UB/6, NUM/0, then the DAY, DAY, MONTH, MONTH, YEAR, YEAR, and then NUM/0, NUM/0, SHIFT, ENTER.

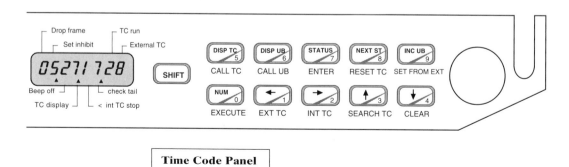

Figure 21.23 Pull-out time code panel.

To display this new time code, press the DISP TC/5 button.

To program the Nagra for RECORD RUN time code (or code that advances only while the machine is in record mode), press SHIFT, ENTER, NUM/0, ←/1, NUM/0, NUM/0, SHIFT, EXECUTE.

Note that this last feature is only on machines with software version 1.95 or above. To check what software version is on your Nagra, press the button STATUS/7, and then repeat pressing the button NEXT ST/8. To return the machine to a regular time code mode, follow the instructions for clearing the time code panel and setting the time of day again.

AUDIO TECH MAINTENANCE

Here are the authorized Nagra IV-S sound service centers that render outstanding services in the United States.

CALIFORNIA

Alternative Audio Services
5750 Camelia Avenue
North Hollywood, CA 91601
  (818) 764-5164

Location Sound Services
10639 Riverside Drive
North Hollywood, CA 91602
  (818) 980-9891

Dan Dugan Sound Design
290 Napoleon Street
San Francisco, CA 94124
  (415) 821-9776

The Sound Check
5435 Cahuenga Blvd.
North Hollywood, CA 91601
  (818) 766-2920

MARYLAND

Vark Audio
8101 MacArthur Blvd.
Cabin John, Maryland 20818
  (301) 229-0288

NEW YORK

Audio Services
353 West 48th Street
New York, New York 10036
  (212) 977-5151

Professional Sound Sevices
311 West 43rd Street
New York, New York 10036
  (212) 586-1033

TENNESSEE

Trew Audio
240 Great Circle Road
Nashville, Tennessee 37228
  (615) 256-3542

NAGRA USA, Inc.

Nashville, Tennessee
Nancy Belt, General Manager
  (615) 726-5191

Chapter 22
The Digital Nagra V—
Direct to Disk

Before examining the direct-to-hard-disk digital Nagra V, let's consider the three most important things that you want to know when you are considering a recording tool:

1. How much engineering experience does the manufacturer have in the field of production sound?
2. How sturdy is the unit? The last thing you want is a unit that appears to work fine in a controlled studio environment but cannot stand up to the rigors of on-location temperature and humidity shifts. Also, is the device truly portable, or is it bound to a sound cart with a bunch of other gear to make it operate?
3. Do you have electrical power to run the recording device?

Suppose you are out in "Poe-dunk-nowhere" and the special dedicated rechargeable batteries that came with the unit are down. You need power and you need it now. You have no access to an AC outlet, and you have to function—no excuses. The lonely gas station just down the road probably has D-cell batteries, but will your recording run on common D-cell power?

Now let's apply these issues to the direct-to-disk digital Nagra V.

ENGINEERING EXPERIENCE

Stephan Kudelski's sixty years of audio engineering experience has brought forth several of the world's premier field sound recorders for film and television production. And, as in any field of discipline, decades of experience is a priceless commodity. The digital Nagra V is a product of Kudelski's experience.

STURDINESS

Nagras have a reputation for being able to take a great deal of punishment, both in transportability and vibration, field temperature and humidity conditions, as well as just plain abuse. Many recorders work fine in the showroom or controlled studio environment but are not engineered to handle the demands and hardships of location sound work. The Nagra machines, on the other hand, have excelled in this regard.

ELECTRICAL POWER

Like its cousins, the analog Nagras, the Nagra V can operate on eight D-cell batteries, available everywhere in the world, (using the NA-BB8B #701911000 unit). It can also run off an AC power outlet. In addition, it can operate using a lithium ion pack (NV-LISET #2098260 000), which yields 65 Wh of power. The recharge time is seven hours. Remember that lithium ion cells do not like to be charged rapidly the way nickel cadmium cells can be charged. If you use the battery charger to run the machine from an AC source, the battery pack can be recharging simultaneously, as well as the traditional AC power adaptor.

One of the more interesting attractions of the Nagra-V is its warranty policy. In the past Nagras have had a one-year warranty on their equipment, but the manufacturer is so confident of its new direct-to-disk digital recorder that it is including a three-year warranty with it.

INPUT CAPABILITIES

The Nagra-V is capable of four analog inputs, two using the traditional XLR microphone input connectors and being controlled by the left and right potentiometers on the front panel in classic Nagra protocol. Using the Aux. In & Line Out potentiometer (with the menu mode set to AUX IN) two additional Line Input signals (such as radio mikes) can be serviced using a 15-pin D-type connector using the EXTENSION pin socket on the left Input-side panel.

DIRECT-TO-DISK RECORDING

In today's highly accelerated, demanding world of post-production schedules and shortcuts, the Nagra-V sets out to service the key issues of being able to record "direct to disk" in an audio file format that is universally suited for the sample rates and bit depths for today's recording expectations as well as delivering the high standards of recording quality that Nagras are famous for. A WAV (Broadcast Wave) audio file will be created as it records either in 44.1 or 48 kHz. Using the NV-HSF (High Sampling Frequency) option, you can record at either 88.2 or 96 kHz sampling rate. The Nagra-V also offers both the 16- and 24-bit depths.

One can see the classic Nagra organization protocol of controls and flow in this sleek, efficient unit (Figure 22.1). With very few exceptions, those who have enjoyed the use of the analog Nagra units will find that working with the Nagra V is like slipping on an old comfortable pair of shoes—you feel right at home.

Figure 22.1 Front view of the Nagra V. (Photo courtesy of Glen Trew of Trew Audio, Nashville)

In Figure 22.2, note the hard-drive enclosure. As of this writing, Nagra is offering a 20 gig and 40 gigabit removable hard drive. These drives are G-force-rated so that you need not be concerned about carrying the unit around while you are recording.

The left Inputs-side panel of the Nagra V (Figure 22.3) offers a traditional microphone (XLR) as well as a 15-pin EXTENSION connector for supplemental signal needs.

Figure 22.2 Front view with lid up. Note the removable Orb Drive for direct-to-disk digital recording. (Photo courtesy of Glen Trew of Trew Audio, Nashville)

Figure 22.3 View of the left-side inputs. (Photo courtesy of Glen Trew of Trew Audio, Nashville)

As with the traditional analog Nagra IV, the Nagra V offers two XLR inputs with a simplified microphone-powering selector. The sensitivity of the microphone inputs is selected on the front panel of the Nagra V, but the microphone-powering choices are just above the XLR inputs and are as follows:

+12V "T" power
Dynamic
Phantom +48V

A 15-pin EXTENSION D-type connector is positioned at the lower left side of the input panel. This input socket serves several purposes. It has a symmetrical transformerless "Line Input" (AUX). If you are using an outboard mixer, you would send your "Line Out" signal to this connector. You can also send a digital audio input using the AES input cable (#P/N 7031 140 000) that is required. Should you wish to use a noise reduction system, the In/Out access is also served by the 15-pin EXTENSION. Here is the correct pinning of the connector:

Pin Number	Connection
1	Ground
2	Not presently used
3	Not presently used
4	Not presently used
5	Start/Stop—connect this pin to ground to stop
6	Digital input (AES bus using a special cable P/N 7031 140 000 is required)
7	External NRS Right channel IN
8	AUX IN—Right channel High
9	External NRS Right channel OUT
10	AUX IN—Right channel Low

Figure 22.4 View of the right side outputs. (Photo courtesy of Glen Trew of Trew Audio, Nashville)

Pin Number	Connection
11	Ground
12	AUX IN—Left channel Low
13	External NRS Left channel OUT
14	AUX IN—Left channel High
15	External NRS Left channel IN

There is a 9-pin RS 422 symmetrical serial communication port for connection to the outside world. The factory uses this port to test the Nagra V unit. For remote controlling the Nagra V by a PC or laptop, this same 9-pin connector can be used using Nagra software.

The right Outputs-side panel of the Nagra V (Figure 22.4) offers several analog and digital signal "send" opportunities.

ANALOG AUDIO OUTPUTS

Two XLR 3-pin male output connectors are the traditional standard for two-channel stereo analog outputs.

DIGITAL AUDIO OUTPUTS

An XLR 3-pin male AES output connector services the digital audio output requirements. The resolution is of either 16 or 24 bits, depending on the output settings chosen. This, of course can be directly connected with any other digital equipment with an AES interface for direct-to-disk (D-to-D) transfer.

TELEPHONE OUTPUT

On the left side of the outputs panel are three banana-output connectors. These are for the telephone output, with a transformer that has an output impedance of 600—from 300 Hz to 5 kHz. If you connect to a standard switched telephone line, the output level of this connection can be selected in the TEL LEVEL of the menu mode to be either 1.55 V or 4.4 V. When in operation, the return feed from the telephone can be heard in the headphones or on the internal loudspeaker.

HEADSET OUTPUT

The headphone output is a standard 1/4″ stereo jack connector. The rotary volume control for the headsets is just to the right of the female connector.

CAMERA INPUT RETURN

The camera input return is a "mini" jack connector that can receive the audio signal from a video camera to the headphones (or speaker) of the Nagra V. This signal is not recorded on the hard drive, but simply used as a monitoring mechanism.

TIME CODE CONNECTOR

The 5-pin Lemo connector (located just to the right of the AES XLR output) is used for time code for the input and output. The pin connections correspond to those of the Nagra IV-S (Time Code unit), T-Audio (Time Code), and the Nagra D.

Pin Number	Connection
1	Ground
2	Time Code Input
3	Time Code Output

The time code system of the Nagra V can be set to record all the currently accepted standard time code frame rates, which are as follows:

24 fps—film applications
25 fps—PAL/SECAM Video & film to video applications
29.97 fps—NTSC black and white television

29.97 fps (drop frame)—NTSC colour television
30 fps—film applications (NTSC)
30 fps (drop frame)—film to video (NTSC)

In addition, the Nagra V can record any of these frame rates either accelerated or retarded by 0.1 percent in order to deal with all the possible anomalies of the NTSC "Pull-up" or "Pull-down" issues, as follows:

Frame Rate −0.1%	Actual Frame Rate	Frame Rate +0.1%
23.976	24	24.024
24.975	25	25.025
29.940	29.97	30
29.97	30	30.03

These frame rate choices are made in the REF.FREQ menu on the front panel.

It is important to note that when the reference frequency is set to master +0.1% (or −0.1%) the Nagra V will speed up (or slow down) when making the recording. This refers to the time code *and* the sampling frequency of the audio. For example, setting the machine to 29.97 at 48 kHz sampling rate, and then selecting MASTER +0.1% in the reference frequency menu means that the Nagra V will actually accelerate by 0.1% and the result will be a 30-frame time code at a sampling frequency of 48.048 kHz. The +0.1% will be stored in the memory of the Nagra V when the power is turned off and will remain accurate for one week.

Unlike previous time code Nagra recorders that recorded a continuous time code signal, the Nagra V simply records a time "stamp" at the start of each recording, and according to the selected frame rate and sampling frequency, the time code value of any given point after the stamp is calculated by counting the number of samples of the audio file. This time code information is readable by any computer device capable of reading an audio file—standard throughout the post-production industry.

VIDEO SYNC IN

If the Nagra V is fitted with the Internal Time Code option, then this is the connector where a video signal (NTSC, PAL, NTSC B/W, 75 ohms internally loaded) or an external work clock can be imported. The external sync input is yet another way to synchronize the internal clocks of the Nagra V. The advantage of this 5V logic input is that it can be used to control the VCXO (Voltage Controlled Crystal Oscillator) from an external source. The input can be 44.1 kHz, 48 kHz 88.2 kHz, or 96 kHz with a logic voltage level from minimum 0.5 V to 5.0 V. This signal can be fed to the machine through the BNC connector.

The front panel of the recorder (Figure 22.5) is a classic Nagra layout—the Modulometer and sensor metering to the left, volume control potentiometers in the center, the menu panel and transport controls to the right.

MODULOMETER

The Nagra V modulometer (Figure 22.6) uses a single needle rather than two as the analog Nagra IV-S does (one for microphone input #1 and one for microphone input #2). Note the

Figure 22.5 Full view of front panel of Nagra V. (Photo courtesy of Glen Trew of Trew Audio, Nashville)

two LEDs at either extreme of the scale. The one on the left is marked "L > R" and the one on the right is marked "R > L"—which will indicate the individual values of their corresponding channels when in the two-channel mode or indicates the highest of the channels when in stereo mode.

Note the thick green crescent area just below from −15 dB up to −6 dB. This is the area where the needle will move to when you are in the "BATT." position (the switch to the lower left under the modulometer). This will indicate the strength of your battery pack.

Remember that the Nagra V is a digital recorder, so even though at a cursory glance you may mistake this meter as the analog modulometer that you are accustomed to work with on analog Nagras, do not think that you have headroom after "0." the way you do on a VU meter. Like a digital peak meter, this modulometer ends at maximum, which is "0"—there is nothing after it. Your "headroom" is whatever you consider headroom lower than "0"—above what you decide to use as a "0" VU equivalent (such as −18 dB), as we have discussed in previous chapters.

Figure 22.6 Modulometer. (Photo courtesy of Glen Trew of Trew Audio, Nashville)

LIGHT/BATTERY SWITCH

The little cloud and sunshine icon just above the BATT designation on the lower left switch controls the backlighting of the meter for dark environments or bright situations.

MODULOMETER SWITCH

The MODULOMETER switch directly under the modulometer itself allows you to select whether you want to read Left (Channel 1) or Right (Channel 2) only. If you leave the switch in the center, or the MAX position, the needle will indicate the highest level obtained between the two channels and the LEDs will indicate which channel this corresponds to. Though it seems a bit odd not to have two needles for two channels, you will actually find it easy to get used to—and actually will find it very effective for stereo level adjustment, especially with the two green LEDs.

MEMORY/NORMAL/RESET SWITCH

The MEM/NORM/RESET switch, to the lower right of the modulometer, controls how you wish the meter to operate. If you leave the switch in the center NORM position, the modulometer will operate in a normal manner, according to the signal (whether input or output). If you flip the selector up to MEM, the needles will indicate the highest obtained level. You can reset the MEM mode by flipping the selector down to RESET. This is a snap-switch position, and it can be used at any time without affecting the recording. In stereo operation of the machine, the operation of this switch is, of course, linked to the Meter Selection switch.

POTENTIOMETERS

The two MIKE LEVEL potentiometers (Figure 22.7) are used for precise volume control of the Left (Channel 1) and Right (Channel 2) microphone inputs (the two analog XLR microphone inputs on the left-side input panel).

Figure 22.7 The volume controls. (Photo courtesy of Glen Trew of Trew Audio, Nashville)

CHANNEL ROTARY LOCK

Note the little stubby stumplike rotary lock seated just between the two MIKE LEVEL potentiometers. If the lock is turned upward toward the two small circle icons, it means that each channel can operate independently of the other; thus, the two will work as two separate monaural feeds. If the rotary lock is turned to the left to the nine o'clock position at the two circle icons that are joined, resembling a figure eight on its side, the two potentiometers are mechanically locked together, irrespective of their individual positions. To make the rotary lock move into the "interlock" position you must depress it in slightly, and then rotate.

SENSITIVITY SELECTORS

The two SENSITIVITY selectors just below the rotary lock are what you use to select the desired sensitivity for the two microphone inputs. There are three settings: 1 mV/hPa, 4 mV/hPa, and 0.2 mV/hpa.

EQUALIZATION SELECTOR

Just to the right of the sensitivity switches is the Equalization selector. The filters available are the same as those on other Nagra recorders and act on both the microphone and Line Inputs. These filters are LFA (Low-Frequency Attenuation), SPEECH, and FLAT.

REFERENCE TONE GENERATOR

The reference tone generator is the REF switch. Push this switch upward to activate the internal reference generator. As long as the switch is held in the "up" position, a sine wave of 1 kHz tone will be generated. The reference level is set at the factory at –18 dB. If the Nagra V is in the TEST position, the reference line-up tone will be generated and heard as an "output" only. To record the reference tone, the EE/TAPE/AUTO selector must be in AUTO and the Main Function Selector must, of course, be in either of the two RECORD selections.

AUXILIARY IN AND LINE OUT

The AUX. IN & LINE OUT potentiometer has two different functions, depending on which you make in the menu mode. If the menu is selected to LINE OUT, then the pot will adjust the Line output level of both channels simultaneously, as well as the headphone and loudspeaker level. Its position is memorized by the microprocessor inside the machine. If you change the menu to use the potentiometer to control the AUX IN input, then the initial output setting will be stored in the memory of the machine until accessed later. Once the menu is set to the AUX IN mode, the potentiometer serves to adjust the level of the Auxiliary Line Input coming from the 15-pin D-type EXTENSION connector on the left Inputs panel of the Nagra V. If you change back to LINE OUT in the menu mode, the AUX IN level will be stored in the memory until accessed later.

EE (ELECTIC-ELECTRIC)/TAPE/AUTO SELECTOR

The EE/AUTO/TAPE selector is situated just below and to the right of the AUX. IN & LINE OUT potentiometer. With the selector in the EE position, only the input signals will be available at the outputs.

The TAPE position simulates the behavior of a tape transport. The output signal signal is the recording from the hard-drive. It functions like a confidence (playback) head, playing what you are recording, not just listening to the input signal. You will also hear the sounds (as like a playback head) when you use the rewind option.

The AUTO position will automatically select the EE mode or TAPE mode depending on the status of the transport (using the Main Function Selector).

Note that if the CAM. RET (camera return) is selected (via the mini-plug on the right inputs panel), the camera return signal will be available for the speaker or headphones only when the EE/TAPE/AUTO selector is in the TAPE position. Switching between TAPE and AUTO is a fast way to select CAM. RET or LINE OUT as a monitoring source.

TRANSPORT CONTROLS AND MENU PANEL

Figure 22.8 shows the transport controls and menu panel.

Main Function Selector

The rotary Main Function Selector operates almost exactly like the one on its Nagra IV-S cousin. Let us review each of the positions.

Stop

In the horizontal STOP position, the machine is off. There is now power being fed to the electronics of the unit. When you turn the selector to this position, the machine will switch off after a few seconds if the POWER DELAY (in the menu option), MANUAL is not set.

Test

When you turn the selector up to TEST, all of the electronics are powered up, allowing the adjustment of levels and signal monitoring, (just as with the Nagra IV-S). This can be

Figure 22.8 Transport controls. (Photo courtesy of Glen Trew of Trew Audio, Nashville)

considered as a "Stand-By for RECORD" mode. All menu verification and settings can be made in this position.

If in the menu, the PREREC is set to "ON," the record LED will start blinking, meaning that the closed-loop recording (a revolving buffer) is activated.

The Nagra V has a pre-record buffer option. You can set the PREREC setting in the menu for as little as one second up through a maximum of twenty seconds. This means that before you turned the selector up to RECORD position, the audio file created would have the previous amount of time (up to twenty seconds) in the audio file. The pre-recording option is extremely handy for situations of confusion or hasty-start recordings where invaluable material was lost before the recording mixer could get his or her machine into the record mode.

Record

The Nagra V does not use a limiter. For the time being this position is not used.

NO A.L.C./LIM

When you turn the selector up to the NO A.L.C./LIM position, The Nagra V does not use a limiter. For the time being this position is not used.

STD. BY

When you turn the selector down to the STD.BY position, the five gray pushbuttons (Figure 22.9) under the LCD menu display will be activated to work as rewind, fast-forward,

Figure 22.9 Transport Control Menu Panel.

Figure 22.10 Transport Control Menu Panel for "Play" mode".

skip-to-next-cue-and-stop—whether moving forward or backward. Should you be in the middle of playing back a cue and suddenly find that the first assistant director has called to roll sound, you can instantly move into RECORD mode without fear of recording over any audio files, as the machine automatically moves to free space on the hard drive.

Play

When you turn the selector down to the PLAY position, the unit will play back audio files recorded on the removable hard drive. Once the PLAY mode has been selected, the five gray pushbuttons (Figure 22.10) under the LCD menu display become activated.

Menu Panel

LCD Display

The menu panel is a fourteen- segment eight-digit backlit LCD display, permitting alphanumeric indications of a large quantity of different information and allowing internal settings of the machine to be made while in the MENU MODE. In normal operation it will indicate the current take number and time from the beginning of the recording. It is also used to display the internal status of the machine, as well as the remaining disk space available on the removable hard drive for recording. The display will be illuminated if the LIGHT/BATT switch (just to the lower left of the modulometer) is flipped up to the cloud-icon position.

The LCD display can be used to display the following:

MENU TREE
Take Number and time from start of take
Remaining Time on the removable hard drive
    (related to bit and sampling rate)
Time Code
Error Codes

The FLAGS on the top of the display show:

Video—shows whether a valid video versus time code format is connected.
Tcext—shows whether an external time code is present.
Tcint—shows whether during playback the time code is accurate.
Lock—shows whether the machine is locked in chase mode.
PWER—shows if the BATT. or EXT. voltage drops below the limit.
Flag 1—shows if the SHIFT button was pressed twice (for menu lock).
Flag 2—not used as of this writing.
Flag 3—not used as of this writing.

SHIFT Button

The SHIFT button, located just to the right under the Main Function Selector, is how you navigate through the various menus on the LCD menu display (just under the Nagra emblem). When the SHIFT button is pressed, the five gray transport buttons just below the display will operate, using their "shifted" arrow features shown just above each gray button.

When you take your finger off the SHIFT button, the display will return to its main display screen. While you are in the menu mode, the STOP button (the one with EXE just above it) becomes the "Execute" function.

When the SHIFT button is pressed rapidly twice, the display will stay in the menu mode (Flag 1 on the display will be on). To remove the menu mode, press once again on the SHIFT button or move the Main Function Selector to another position.

Sync Mode

When the SHIFT button is pressed and held while moving the Main Function Selector to the PLAY position, the machine turns on the Synchronizer.

There are two different modes in which the internal synchronizer can operate. One is the VAR CLK (variable clock) mode and the other is the FIX CLK (fixed clock) mode.

In the FIX CLK mode the machine will always follow the external reference. Once the machine is in the LOCKED state, the internal synchronizer will no longer influence the transport and the playback speed will be controlled entirely by the reference frequency (REF FREQ menu). If, however, the synchronizer of the Nagra V sees an error of more than one frame, it will reengage itself to correct the synchronization error. This is the recommended operating mode. In this mode the maximum variation accepted is 100 ppm.

The VAR CLK mode is designed to allow the machine to follow an external reference that is not the same as the REF FREQ, using the internal synchronizer. This setting allows the internal synchronizer to modify the internal clocks in such a way as to follow this REF FREQ (for example, NTSC/NTSC 60). In this mode, the digital output is not available and the quality of the analog outputs may be slightly degraded. Also, in this mode variations of up to +4 percent in the reference signal will be tolerated.

The SYNC MODE will turn off when the Main Function Selector is turned out of the PLAY mode to any other position.

Power Delay

If the POW. DELAY menu is set to MANUAL, press and hold the SHIFT button while turning the Main Function Selector to the STOP position. Continue to keep the SHIFT button depressed for an additional two seconds until the machine powers off.

Speaker

Selecting ON, OFF, or AUTO for activating the speaker without going into the menus can be done by holding the SHIFT button in while pushing the LIGHT/BATT switch. Every time this function is executed, it will scroll on the display through the three options.

In/Out Pot

The In/Out pot gives access to the mode of operation of the third potentiometer (AUX IN & LINE OUT) in the case that in the menu, the line potentiometer of the Nagra- is set to the POT.SHIFT position. That means that the potentiometer will adjust the input signal if the SHIFT button is pressed in and held in place, and the potentiometer will adjust the output signal if the SHIFT button is not being pressed and held in place.

The Nagra V owner's manual provides a full description and schematic of the various menus.

Once you have wrapped the recording session, you can simply remove the hard-drive and either ship it to post-production editorial or make an archival backup (i.e., DVD-ROM) and ship either the backup or the original. You will soon develop your own techniques and protocols for what works best for you and your recording project.

Glossary

Acetate base—The transparent cellulose acetate plastic film that forms the foundation—that is, the base, or backing—for the magnetic medium that is placed on the tape or film by the manufacturer.

Acoustics—Science dealing with the production, effects, and transmission of sound waves; the transmission of sound waves through various media, including reflection, refraction, diffraction, absorption, and interference; the characteristics of auditoriums, theatres, and studio stages, as well as their design.

ADC (analog-to-digital converter)—Electronic device used at the input of digital audio equipment to convert analog electronic signals to digital values whose numbers represent the level and frequency information contained in the original analog signal.

AES—Audio Engineering Society.

Alignment—For film and tape recorders, refers to the correct adjustment of the Record and Playback head positions with respect to the exact positionof the film or tape path; also refers to the adjustment of the electronics for the ideal frequency response.

Ambiance—The distinctive acoustics of a given location being recorded; the environmental sounds that create a mood and a sense of "place." The resulting audio sources (i.e., fluorescent ballast hums, distant traffic, air-conditioning ducts, etc.) create relatively constant characteristics that reverberate off the walls, ceiling, pavement, etc.

Amplification—An increase in signal level, amplitude, or magnitude.

Analog signal—Electrical signal that continuously varies in strength; not *digital*. Magnetic and optical sound recording and playback systems are analog.

Articulation—A quantitative measurement of the intelligibility of human speech, where 100 percent is completely understandable. For the typical sound reinforcement or communications system no more than a 15 percent articulation loss is acceptable.

Asperity noise—Also called *hiss*; caused by minute imperfections in the surface of the recording tape. The cheaper the tape, the higher will be the degree of imperfections in the surface and the greater the danger of tape hiss.

Attenuate—To reduce a signal's strength. An attenuator is a device that reduces or weakens the amplitude of a signal. Attenuators are used on volume control; also called *faders*.

Audio analyzer—Test instrument used by motion picture theatresound engineers. The device contains terminations of various values capable of carrying up to 150 watts of audio power. Included is an AC voltmeter for measuring the frequency response of amplifiers, equalizers, filters, and the overall frequency response of the sound system.

Audio fatigue—Hearing weariness brought on by listening for a long time to a soundtrack that does not let up in intensity, either in volume or complex detailed makeup. The result is anoversaturation of the ears as well as the brain in its attempt to assimilate the audio material. First signs are tingling and "fuzzy" sensation in the ears, followed by a shutting down of brain attention.

Audio frequency—Any frequency within the range of normal audio sounds, in which sound waves undulate roughly 20 Hz to 20,000 Hz (Hz = cycles per second).

Backup—Term most commonly used to describe having a protection redundancy recorder to guard against accidental erasure or loss of material, as in a DAT backup recorder to the primary nonlinear ProTools recording session or 24-track or DA-88 recorder. Such protection can also be made after a recording or edit session, as in making a "backup" of the hard drive at the end of the day, or making a DVD-RAM "backup" from the Deva's internal hard drive to ship to editorial.

Balance stripe—Also known as *guide stripe* or *balance track*; a narrow stripe of magnetic material identical to the primary magnetic stripe that the audio signal will be recorded on and reproduced from. This balance stripe is not used for sound recording, but is used to maintain a level contact with the sound head.

Balanced cable—*See* Cable, balanced.

Balanced connectors—Microphone cable connections in which both conductors are electronically symmetrical with the case and cable shield (ground).

Bandwidth—Refers to the "space" in the frequency response of a device through which audio signals can pass (between lower and upper frequency limits, those points where the signal level has rolled off 3 dB).

Bias—Direct current (DC) or high-frequency alternating current (AC) signal fed to a magnetic recording head with the audio signal in order to minimize distortion. (AC bias ordinarily provides higher fidelity.)

Bit rate—The amount of the binary information code included in the audio file. The number of bits assigned to each sample (not the sampling rate) limits the dynamic range; for example, if you are working in a 16-bit system, you have 65,636 possible volume levels to work with in each sample of the recording. If you try to drive the signal to 65,637, you will experience clipping and distortion because no more ones and zeros are left to use. The volume-level saturation geometrically increases as you work at a higher bit rate. If you were working in a

20-bit system, you would have 1,048,576 choices; working in a 24-bit system would give you 16,777,216 for each sample.

Blooping ink—Opaque paintlike ink that an editor can apply over splices to protect the join in the optical track from making popping or snappin sounds when it runs over the optical reader head of the projector.

Boom (of microphone)—Telescopic arm to which a microphone and hanger are attached. The boom is held up over the head of the actors by the boom operator to place the microphone in an ideal out-of-camera position to record the action in the scene.

Boom operator—Person who operates an overhead microphone unit such as a microphone boom to place the microphone in the most desirable position to capture the best quality recording.

Bounce to disk—Process by which an editor can choose which channels of an edit session he or she wishes to combine in a mix-down, creating a new monaural or stereo audio file. This process is done inside the computer using the editorial software and does not involve the output of any audio signal outside the computer to achieve a new "mixed" combination.

Cable, balanced—Audio cable with three wires; two wires carry the signal, high (+) and low (−), and the third is a shield that is connected to the chassis or system ground. The signal leads are both of equal potential difference from the ground and are hence "balanced" with respect to the ground, which is sometimes referred to as "floating."

Cable, unbalanced—Audio cable with two wires. There is no third "shielding" and the cable is not grounded to the chassis or ground. The signal leads are therefore unbalanced.

Capstan—Rotating shaft used with a pinch roller that pulls magnetic tape stock through a tape deck mechanism at an exact rate of speed. This is necessary because, unlike film, there are no perforations to engage with sprockets.

Cardioid response—Heart-shaped microphone pickup, directional in various degrees of configuration; sound waves coming to the microphone's rear and sides are rejected, and those directly in front of it are received, giving it its directional qualities.

CCIR—Committee Consultatif Internationale Radiofusion. This French name means International Radio Consulting Committee. The CCIR sets the standard for central and eastern Europe in regard to equalization. Settings meeting CCIR standards will not play back correctly on NAB (Western Hemisphere) equipment.

Click track—In motion picture or television sound recordings, an electronic metronome is applied to the audio recording so that musicians can synchronize the musical tempo with the visual action or frame rate. The channel carrying the metronome signal is known as the click track.

Clipping—Occurs when the capabilities of an amplifier are exceeded. The result is a very audible distortion, also visible on an oscilloscope.

Colorization—Distortion of frequency response by resonances at particular frequencies.

Compander—The combination of a compressor and an expander used together to achieve noise reduction and/or increase the dynamic range capabilities of recorders or audio systems.

Compressor (compression)—Process whereby the dynamic range of the audio signal is reduced by making the louders part of the signal quieter or the quieter parts louder, as desired.

Condenser mike—Microphone in which sound strikes an electronically charged diaphragm that acts like a variable capacitor as it moves near a fixed plate of opposite polarity. Ultra-low-moving mass ensures extended frequency response. Condenser mikes require phantom power to operate.

Connector—Type of pin device at the end of a cable to either send (male) or receive (female) audio signals, power, sync pulse, etc. Examples are XLR, Tushel, phono jack, Lemo, etc.

Cross talk—Audible signal that spills over from one line to an adjacent line.

Cue control—Ddevice on the recording machine for finding a desired cue or audio-event selection while winding (or rewinding) at high speed.

DAT—Digital Audio Tape; Specifically, 4 mm high-density magnetic tape, loaded in a small cassette unit. Maximum length of DAT tapes is 120 minutes (at 48 kHz sampling rate).

Decibel (dB)—Measurement of relative intensity of power or voltage, based on an algorithmic scale.

Decoder—Device that reads the "encoded" signal or pulse and turns it into some form of control or usable information signal; for example, a two-track print master decoded in the theatre into its six-component signal streams).

Degauss—The process of erasing the recordings on magnetic tape by passing the tape stock either over or through a powerful electrical coil which can be turned on and off for the purpose of influencing the iron oxide molecules of the emulsion of the tape stock, thereby erasing or degaussing it. The film or tape roll must be moved in a rotating motion as it is moved into and out of the magnetic influence, thereby degaussing the magnetic stock properly and not causing spikes or uneven erased areas.

Digital—Advanced method of recording that involves a sequence of pulses or on-off signals rather than a continuous variable or analog signal.

Digital system—System wherein a continuously variable analog signal is sampled at regular intervals (usually 44,100 to 48,000 times a second). Each sample is assigned a numerical value, encoded into discrete binary bits (ones and zeros to represent quantities) that establish a mathematical model of the original sound.

Discrete—Single audio channel carrying a signal with no attachment or dependency on any other channel—not a matrixed multichannel signal.

Distortion—Undesired qualities in the sound signal, usually introduced by electrically generated devices or changes in the relative levels of the different frequencies involved, overloading the saturation maximums allowable for clear audio recording.

Distortion while recording means an audio signal from the microphone to the recorded medium (analog or DAT) is distorted because of either (1) overloading of the Record level beyond the capacity of the tape to accept the signal, or (2) the use of underqualified preamplification power or overamplification (i.e., double-phantom powering a microphone).

Distortion during playback means a modification of the original audio signal appearing in the output of audio equipment that was not present in the input during the recording process. The most common way of expressing distortion is by percentage of original signal, Total Harmonic Distortion (THC).

Drop frame—Drop-frame time code is so named because the counting sequence skips, or drops two frames, every minute except at the tens of minutes. (See Chapter 6.)

Dropout—Loss of a portion of the signal caused by lack of oxide on the portion of the tape, or by dirt or grease covering the portion of the tape, or by an interruption of the signal from the microphone to the record head. Dropout is a term also used when a nonlinear session is locked to time code and is either recording or is in playback mode when the time code reader (i.e., slave driver) loses the steady flow of time code data and suddenly stops because there is no time code stream to lock on to and follow.

DSP functions—Digital signal processing; refers to special algorithmic software plug-ins for audio signal-processing equipment and digital audio workstations for altering audio signals in a myriad of ways.

Dynamics—Term used to describe the intentional design of an audio event (or mix) to build in strategic quiet passages to help the perception of louder passages from being bigger than they otherwise may appear. Dynamics is involved in strategically designing high and low points into a soundtrack so that the audience will not suffer from audio fatigue. The result of good dynamics is to greatly increase the listening value, making an audio "rollercoaster ride."

Dynamics range—The way in which sound volume varies; the difference (in decibels) between the loudest and quietest portions of the audio signal, or between the maximum signal level of the audio performance and the noise floor of the electronic equipment.

Emulsion—Magnetic "batch" mixture coating that is adhered to the base stock of film or tape for eventual audio recording and playback purposes.

Encode (Encoder, Encoded)—An encoder is a device that brings in electronic signals and alters the character or superimposes other information onto it (e.g., multichannel matrix encoding or noise-reduction encoding, etc.)

Exciter lamp—Lamp housing in the optical head of a projector or Moviola whose light passes through the optical soundtrack image of the film and impinges on a photoelectric cell, causing current fluctuations that accurately reproduce the analog audio signal for playback.

Feedback—In a PA system, feedback is produced by a microphone, amplifier, and loudspeaker; it is the ringing or howling sound caused by amplified sound from the loudspeaker being picked up by the microphone and recycled through the system, reamplified and played through the speaker and being picked up by the microphone again, and so on.

Flutter—Rapid change in frequency of an audio or video signal as a result of variations in tape or disk speed. *Wow* is usually considered a lower-frequency speed variation. *See also* Wow.

Foley—Process whereby a "Foley artist" can perform custom sync-to-picture audio events by watching the projected image of action and simultaneously performing the desired sound event in sync. Originally developed by Jack Foley at Universal Studios and eventually named in his honor at Desilu Studios. Foley sound is usually associated with footsteps, prop movement unique to the film, and cloth movement.

Frequency—Number of times a signal vibrates each second—expressed as cycles per second (cps) or as hertz (Hz).

Frequency response (in audio and video systems)—The frequency range over which signals are reproduced within a specified amplitude range; generally expressed in dB versus Hz; example: 100–5000 Hz plus or minus 5 dB.

Fullcoat—Audio film stock in which the magnetic emulsion covers the entire surface of the film, from edge to edge over the perforations.

Gain—Amount of signal amplification.

Gain brain—Signal-processing device that can be adjusted to be less or more sensitive to the dynamics of an incoming audio signal and then lift and compress the volume of that signal according to the operator's need, both in preset decibel expansion as well as duration of sensitivity.

Generation loss—Decrease in quality that occurs every time an audio or video signal is copied, whether it is transferred from one medium to another or as one-to-one duplicate copies are made; more pronounced in analog form than in digital form. There is a myth that digital does not suffer from generation loss, but there is always some degradation when you make a copy of a signal.

Graphic equalizer—Multi-band fixed area of frequency influences that can be boosted or attenuated as needed. Thirty-band graphic equalizers are the most popular for post-production work, with plus or minus 6 dB shifts with 6 dB boosters to make them capable of 12 dB shifts per channel.

Head room—Amount of "safe recording" range above the established "0" VU (and whatever you have designated as equivalent on the digital peak meter—e.g., −18 dB to −22 dB) reserved for more robust audio-event moments where additional momentary increased volume is desired, but before you hit distortion or maximum.

Head stack—A rigidly fixed array of Erase, Record, and Playback heads (or Record, Pilot Sync, and Playback heads) that are aligned precisely together to appropriately write or read audio information. Head stacks are often modular and can be removed and replaced with other variations, such as the Magna-Tech multichannel combinations or the Stellavox interchangeable head-stack arrays.

Hertz (Hz)—Unit of measurement for frequency; 1 Hz is equal to one cycle per second.

Impedance—Resistance to the flow of an electrical current, expressed as high or low impedance—*Hi-Z* or *Low-Z*—measured in ohms. A lower value means you can run longer lengths of cable without loss of signal integrity.

Inputs—Program that enters a unit or system; also, a connector or receptacle into which a signal is fed.

Interlock—To sync up two or more recorders or playback machines, either by mechanical or electronic means, so that they will run in exact sync with each other.

Jam sync—Process of synchronizing a time code generator with time code being played on a tape, and then reentering that time code onto the tape. Done to extend code or to replace bad code dropouts without disturbing the continuous count of time code.

KEM—Flatbed picture editing machine. The film (both picture and sound) are mounted on cores and placed flat on aluminum plates that are synchronized together using sprocketed rollers that can interlock to run in sync or disengage to run each roll of film independently for ease of editing.

Kilohertz (kHz)—One thousand hertz (Hz).

Lay back—To transfer from one medium to another medium, usually in multichannel form and usually involving time code lock-up to maintain synchronization. This term is usually used when describing the transfer of a nonlinear edit session from the computer software with which the picture and/or sound edit session was created to another medium for presentation purposes (such as 24-track analog tape; multichannel perforated 35 mm film; 2-, 8-, 16-, 24-, 32-, or 48-channel digital tape; or to any kind of video medium). *See also* Output.

Limiter—Automatic control to reduce volume when the audio signal rises above a level that would introduce significant distortion.

Magna-Tech—A rugged rack-mounted film recording and playback machine that is extremely accurate and practical. It is one- to six-channels-capable, using mag-stripe (for mono) and fullcoat for multichannel; uses 60-cycle stepping motors for sync accuracy, push-button choice of American 24 fps or European 25 fps standards.

MIDI—Musical Instrument Digital Interface, a communication system between musical synthesizers.

Monaural (monophonic)—Single audio channel; not stereophonic.

Monitor (verb)—To watch, to listen—to oversee and be vigilant about quality control of something, as in "she monitored the digitization process."

Monitors (noun)—(1) Refers to one or more television monitors used to view visual images. These are specialized, highly calibrated television monitors designed for professional use to judge color values and quality control. (2) A pair (or set, as in 5.1 audio imaging field) of audio speakers of high-quality standard to accurately reproduce an audio signal for professional use.

Moviola—Upright picture and sound editing machine used during the 1920s through the middle 1990s. Ultimately replaced by nonlinear digital workstations, except in rare cases.

NAB—National Association of Broadcasters.

Noise cancellation—Microphone designed to cancel ambient noise so that it will not be recorded. The housing of the microphone allows noise to reach both sides of the diaphragm simultaneously, thereby canceling each other out.

Noise gate—Signal-processing device that can be adjusted to various calibrated sensitivities to compress or cut out noise peaks that are stronger than some specific desired maximums of the desired signal, thus limiting unwanted audio anomalies from the audio track.

Nondrop—Unlike "drop-frame" time code that skips, or drops two frames, every minute, nondrop time code does not drop or skip anything.

Ohm—Unit of measure of electrical resistance or impedance.

OMF—Open Media Framework, a file format technology designed to allow media-handling applications to communicate in a platform-independent manner—that is, to speak a common language. The goal of OMF is to allow any OMF-compatible application that handles audio, video, picture, or other media to communicate with any other OMF-compatible application. It is most often used to convert a Final Cut Pro or Avid picture edited session into a ProTools session. OMF translates simple single, continuous time code. It translates any number of audio tracks, and it translates clip names (region names) sample-accurate (precision sync).

Omnidirectional—Picking up signal equally from all directions.

Optical head—*See* Exciter lamp.

Output—Signal delivered from any audio or video device; also, a jack, connector, or circuit that feeds the signal to another device such as a speaker or headset.

Overtones—Individual component frequencies in a sound that when added to the fundamental signal help to define its spatial quality (e.g., cathedral expanse).

Pan-pot—Multichannel volume controller. The pan-pot does not control how loud the signal will be, as it usually rides in line with the volume fader control, but it controls the spatial placement of the sound—that is, whether it will favor the left or right speaker. If hooked up to the surround speakers, the pan-pot can literally "fly" sounds around the room by the placement of the joystick during the performance of the audio cue. *See also* Phantom imaging.

Parametric equalizer—Unlike the graphic equalizer, which hasbands that are precisely fixed to control exact sectors, a mixing console parametric equalizer has three or more (usually four or five) ranges of influence: Low-frequency, Lower Mid-Range, Upper Mid-Range, High-End. Each influence can be adjusted in attenuation or amplification by decible steps or by fractions of decibels. Each influence can also be adjusted according to how broad of a frequency range in that influence the user may want to affect. The user may want it to be quite broad or may want to narrow the swath for fine surgical work. The usual attenuation/amplification can be as much as plus or minus 24 dB.

Peak meter—Unlike the VU meter, which shows an average of the modulation volume, a peak meter shows the maximum amplitude hits, moment to moment. Some meters will hold that level for a fraction of a second for easier reading, unless superseded by a louder level.

Phantom imaging—Sound that is reproduced through two or more speakers in a varying percentage balance so that it is "imaged" in a part of the listening envelope where there is no speaker. For example, right and left channels phantom a center channel by causing certain parts of the signal program to have identical elements that will result in perceived central derivation.

Phantom power—Method of remotely powering the preamplifier or impedance converter that is built into many condenser microphones by sending voltage along the audio cable. Phantom power is usually from 6 to 48 volts DC and is run along the same conductors that carry the audio signal. The electrical power is separated from the audio by using capacitors and special transformers.

Phase—Timing relationship between two signals.

Phasing—Recording with two identical audio signals (from two separate microphone input sources) that cancel each other out. Phasing is most often noticed in two microphones that are placed in a non-X-Y pattern. The two-microphone diaphragm capsules are separated too much, and as a moving sound source, such as a car passing by, changes from the source, striking the first diaphragm a millisecond before striking the second diaphragm, or vice versa, the signal is in a moment of transition and "winks" out.

Phase-matching—Playback in which a "swimming" sensation is produced when two identical audio signals are lined up *almost* identically. This result tells the dialog editor that his replacement reprint of production audio is perfectly in sync with the work track.

Pick-up pattern—Directions from which a microphone is sensitive to sound waves. Pick-up patterns vary with each mic element and mic design. The two most common patterns are omnidirectional and unidirectional.

Pink noise—Electronic signal that has equal energy levels at all frequencies across the range from 20 Hz to 20 kHz.

PNO (Program Number)—Term used on DAT recording machines that can lay down a tape location reference, using 1 to 99 for the number of countable cues.

Polar pattern—Graph of a transducer's directional characteristics measured in a 360-degree pattern, and usually at several different frequencies. Speaker polar patterns indicate relative output level, whereas microphone polar patterns indicate relative sensitivity.

Pop—(1) One frame of 1 kHz tone placed at the "2" frame of an Academy Leader at the top of the reel (six seconds from the PICTURE START frame). This 1/24th of a second "pop" or "beep" is used as head line-up for sync relative to a unit of sound or a mixed predub or final mixed track. One frame of "pop" is also placed two seconds (or three feet in 35 mm terms) from the last frame of picture (also known as LFOP). (2) A thump or explosive breathy impact produced when a puff of air from the actor strikes the microphone diaphragm. This most often occurs with the "P," "T," and "B" consonants of speech.

Pop filter—(1) A foam or cloth shield placed over a microphone to avoid popping consonant sounds from suddenly impacting the microphone diaphragm. Stretched nylon hose over a metal ring (such as a bent wire clothes hanger) can make a very effective pop filter in a pinch. (2) An electronic filter than can attenuate low frequencies where the "popping" sound exists (a high-pass filter with its cutoff at approximately 70 Hz to 100 Hz).

PostConform—Nonlinear picture editing software in which you use the EDL (edit decision list) it generates with transfer equipment that will automatically ask for certain production audio tapes (whether analog or digital), then have the time code driven audio deck automatically spin down to and transfer only the sections of the tape required (along with prescribed pre and post roll "handles"). These sections are transferred into perfect sync in a nonlinear sound editing software session. This procedure is used if (1) the picture editor's audio material is not trustworthy enough to warrant using the OMF method, or (2) if the original production audiotapes used time code as a sync reference, thereby having the time code signal on the tapes to follow. Often this procedure is used with video transfer tapes that are made at the laboratory during the original telecine process—but it is not much good to use PostConform with a medium that is already in question, as it is not the original material and thus is already suffering from generation loss.

Preamplifier (Preamp)—Amplifier that strengthens weak signals such as those from a microphone, magnetic playback head, photo cell, or a phonograph pick-up to a level sufficient to drive a power amplifier.

Presence peak—Increase in microphone output in the "presence" frequency range of 2 kHz to 10 kHz. A presence peak increases clarity, articulation, and apparent closeness.

Print-thru—Occurs as the analog tape passes over the head stack and the recorded audio signal is laid on. The tape continues around the tension roller and winds onto the take-up reel. If the recorded audio was very loud, the highly saturated recorded molecules on the tape, because of the very loud signals that registered in the upper maximums of the head room on the peak meter, are vibrating much more strongly than quieter passages. As the take-up reel revolves and winds yet other layers of tape over these highly agitated passages, the excited magnetic molecules will affect the layers on either side of itself, both prior and following, causing influences of phantom audio imaging known as *print-thru*. This gives you a faint reproduction of that sound approximately one second between each phantom prior to and following the actual recording.

Quadraphonic—Describes the result of four cardioid microphone capsules aligned at precise 90-degree angles to each other, so that when reproduced in a listening environment, with four audio speakers in proper spatial positioning, the signal will produce a realistic 360-degree envelope that replicates the original environmental reality.

Response—The sensitivity, frequency, and polar characteristics of a microphone.

Reverberation—The sum of many reflections of a sound in an enclosed recording environment.

Rivas tape splicer—Precision film tape splicer (either 16 mm or 35 mm) that uses pre-perforated splicing tape for exact alignment. Clear tape is used for the picture, and white base perforated tape is used for the sound. Rivas is the name of a particular manufacturer.

Sample rate—The number of measured moments during every second of a digital sound file where number data represents the volume level and frequency information that models the audio signal. The two basic industry standards for sample rates are 44.1 kHz (44,100) and 48 kHz (48,000) times per second. Played in real time, these "moments" render a recreation of the sound. Look for the sample rate standards to rise to 96 kHz and possibly as high as 182 kHz within a decade.

Session—(1) A scheduled, continuous length of time during which a group assembles to perform and/or record; may include the picture or sound editor, the director, or other participants. (2) In nonlinear terms, a software icon that contains all of the edit decision data that the picture or sound editor has worked with to create either a picture or sound reel of action. This icon session can tell through the editor's "input" access where in the computer hard drives all of the digitized media material resides.

Shotgun mike—Slang term for a highly directional tubelike Cardioid microphone.

Sibilance—In speech, the overemphasis of "s" and "ch" sounds, causing undesirable sharp and shrilly spikes.

Signal cancellation—Occurs when one audio signal is combined with another audio signal that has a varying degree of identical information in it (being recorded at the exact same time) and thus cancels out its counterpart in the first signal. This is like taking a positive image and aligning it with its identical image in negative form—the two cancel each other out and become nothing. The audio signal material from the first source that does not have a counterpart in the second signal will be all that remains.

Signal-to-noise ratio—Ratio of audio information of a signal that has unwanted hiss, rumble, hum, and other unwanted background noises in balance to the desired signal; measured in decibels.

Sine wave (sinusoidal)—Signal wave signature that has a magnitude that varies as the sine of an independent variable. (See Chapter 6, Figure 6.8.)

Slate—Slang term is *sticks*; rectangular surface (either black background or white) on which the slate assistant can write data information for the camera to see just prior to snapping sync. Information such as production title, company, date, camera roll, sound roll, director's name, cameraman's name as well as the scene number, angle designation, and take number can clearly be seen. At the top of the slate is a hinged bar, usually painted with alternating black and white angled stripes for ease in designating the exact frame of sync when the slate assistant is told to "Mark it." After marking it, the slate assistant claps the hinged bar down onto the slate, causing an audible snap for the microphone to hear.

Smart slate—Works identically to the conventional slate, in that data information is handwritten onto the white slate surface, but the "smart slate" has a wireless receiver that reads the running time code transmitted from the audio recorder and displays it in large red LED numbers. These numbers run until the slate assistant claps the hinged bar down onto the slate, causing the two electrical contacts on the inside surfaces to touch and freeze the time code. The frozen time codes help the picture assistant sync dailies back at picture editorial.

SMPTE—Society of Motion Picture and Television Engineers.

Square wave—Signal wave signature that is periodic and equal to one constant on one half of the period and a different constant (which may be zero) on the other half. (See Chapter 6, Figure 6.8.)

SRT—Standard reference tape.

Stereo—Results when audio signals are recorded using two discrete channels in parallel. The playback yields a spatial presence with a balanced left and right signal. Movement of audio-generating sources within the program will appear to move from left to right or right to left as the two microphones were set up to record them. *See also* Quadraphonic.

Supervising sound editor—The individual who is responsible for working with the post-production sound editorial team and various audio facility services to bring together a polished production dialog track, sound design, and custom-performed and edited Foley and stereo backgrounds. She or he also oversees the mixing of the final rerecording process with the cut music sessions. The supervising sound editor is solely responsible to the director and producer and often is the contractor of the post-sound edit process.

Sync (synch)—The exact alignment of the audio event to the corresponding frame of visual action.

Sync generator—A pulse generator producing the sync signals necessary to integrate the functioning of various pieces of sound, camera, or video equipment in relationship to each other.

Synchronizer—Also known as a *sync-block*. When working with picture and sound 16mm and 35mm film, the most accurate synchronization device is the synchronizer, which is composed of up to six side-by-side sprocketed wheels (known as *gangs*) that are coupled to each other with a solid metal rod. When one wheel turns, the others turn at exactly the same rate because they are physically coupled together. Each full rotation equals one foot of film. These wheels have sprocket teeth on the perimeter edge, precisely engaging into the perforated holes of the film stock, forcing the film to remain in rigid synchronization due to locking arms that are lowered and clicked into place. Each locking arm has two rollers with grooved glides that allow the sprocket wheel teeth to pass through; yet the roller holds the film against the wheel, so that the film does not slip and slide out of sync with the picture or the other mag-stripe strand of film.

Magnetic heads can be lowered down onto the magnetic film strands so that the sound can be heard. The heads feed the signal into a tabletop amplifier.

The synchronizer does two things. First, it keeps the picture and parallel tracks of sound in sync. Second, the synchronizer keeps track of the position of the film by means of a precision foot-and-frame counter. This counter can be "zeroed-out" by the editor when he or she has locked the strands of film into the synchronizer in the desired line-up positions (usually using a start-mark or frame-designation marking). Even in today's nonlinear digital domain editing environment, going back to film—whether by negative cutting or use in the post-sound mixing process—and using the film synchronizer is ultimately the most accurate way to guarantee sync in the film industry. (See Chapter 13, Figure 13.8.)

Time code—"Electronic perforations"; a numbering system developed by SMPTE that assigns a number to each frame. The time code is the "frame address" denoted by hours, minutes, seconds and frames. There is a visual time code for visual reference as well as an audio time code (sounds like a constipated electronic cricket on steroids) that matches its visual reference.

Transducer—Device that converts one form of energy to another form. A microphone transducer converts acoustical sound energy into electrical signal energy.

Transfer bay—An array of equipment (usually in a dedicated room) that can transfer audio or video media material from one source to another source. Such transfer bays have calibration tools and meters so that accurate and precise one-to-one copies can be made to the closest tolerances.

VITC—Vertical Interval Time Code (pronounced "Vit-See"). This time code reference is recorded in the video frame line vertical interval. Computers can read this time code very accurately.

VU meter—Volume unit meter; used in most American equipment for measuring audio signal levels. It averages the sound, showing a percentage modulation, and is not linear in decibels theway the peak meter is.

Watt—Unit of measure for electrical or acoustical power.

Wavelength—Provided that the wave is perfectly regular (such as a sine wave), this is the distance between successive peaks.

Wow—A cyclic fluctuation in pitch resulting from mechanical malfunction (usually in the tension rollers) or a disruption of theconstant speed of the transport capstan—as in wow-and-flutter.

XLR—Professional connector (having three or more conductor pins) with an outer shell that shields the connection and makes a solid male/female lock. Most commonly used for balanced audio signals for microphone and line feeds. The XLR-type connector is sometimes called a *canon* connector, so named for the original manufacturer.

X-Y pattern—A pair of Cardioid microphones or mic elements aimed at crossed directions, with the two microphone diaphragms as close together as possible, putting the two signals in phase.

The Audio CD

an audio companion to *Practical Art of Motion Picture Sound*

narrated by: Lisa Howes Yewdall

program #		program description
1.	4:06	Taping into the "Theatre-of-the-Mind."
2.	:35	1 kHz line-up tone at –18 db on digital peak meter which would equal '0' dB on the V.U. meter (sine wave)
3.	:34	1 kHz line-up tone at –18 db from the left speaker only
4.	:34	1 kHz line-up tone at –18 db from the right speaker only
5.	:34	10 kHz—high end tone at –18 db line-up
6.	:34	40 Hz—low end tone at –18 db line-up
7.	:34	Pink noise at –18 db line-up
8.	:33	1 kHz (square wave) at –18 db line-up

Scene 36—an exercise in the evolution of a sound track

Cues 9-thru-12 follow the evolution of the sound from the original location shoot—through the Picture Editor's "Cut," filled with temp voices and temp sound effects—through the Dialog Editor's "Cut," where the track has been recut, filled and smoothed—and then through the Final Mix with sound effects. A copy of the script is supplied at the end of this audio CD cue listing, should you wish to follow along.

9.	8:37	Scene 36—The production "dailies" the master shot—Scene 36 takes 1 & 2 medium angle of Frank—Scene 36 "A" takes 1 & 2 medium angle of Vikki—Scene 36 "B" takes 1 & 2
10.	2:12	Scene 36—the PICTURE Editor's "cut"
11.	2:13	Scene 36—recut and smoothed by the DIALOG Editor
12.	2:08	Scene 36—the FINAL mixed scene with Effects and Foley
13.	:54	"PHASING" tracks as a technique to identify and match exact sync
14.	:24	Digital Ticks—Chapter 11

15.   1:44   Cleaning up sound effect cues—Chapter 11

16.   1:11   Cleaning up distortion and over modulation from a recording of rolling a piano around Chapter 11

Custom Recording Vehicles—Chapter 10

17.   1:19   Car recording: Start & IDLE—two angles, then REVs

18.   :27   Car recording: Start & AWAY

19.   :20   Car recording: In & STOP

20.   1:07   Car recording: BYs—slow, medium & fast

21.   1:43   Car recording: MANEUVERS—slow, medium & fast

22.   1:45   COMPARISON RECORDINGS: ".308 assault rifle shots" and "glass bottle breaks" as recorded both analog and digitally. Recording medium formats:
    audio cassette at 1 7/8 ips
    Nagra 1/4" recorder at 7 1/2 ips
    Nagra 1/4" recorder at 15 ips
    Digital Audio Tape recorder (DAT)
    DEVA recorder (digital—straight to hard disk)
Each recorder used identical microphones mounted together for identical perspectives. These are flat responses. No audio processing or equalization has been employed in any way.

23.   :34   Machine-gun "AUTO BULLET BYs"—from Chapter 10

24.   1:25   A Steerman 220 AIRPLANE start, rev and "sputter BY"

25.   3:14   Layering BACKGROUNDS.
In each BACKGROUND example group, a new layer will be added every four seconds, underlining the unlimited creative combinations possible in BACKGROUND ambiances to create a fuller and more dramatic soundtrack.

26.   1:14   How to create PSEUDO STEREO backgrounds. Each background will play for four seconds in its original monaural configuration. Then it will expand to a "pseudo stereo" format. To completely appreciate the expansion potential, listen to this cue through stereo headsets for the most dramatic representation.

27.   1:40   Editing: creating theatrical CANNONS—from Chapter 13

28.   :24   Editing: LASERS—from Chapter 13

29.   :52   Editing: CAR START & AWAY—from Chapter 13
Building a performance from individual bits and pieces to create a new reality.

30.   :50   Creating a theatrical rifle shot—from Chapter 12

31.   :33   The descending Huey helicopter—from Chapter 12

32.   :46   Mushrooming Flames from Wood Flames Using an analog 30 band graphic equalizer to create extremely dramatic fireballs.

33.   2:11   Vocal Effect creations—Choral Winds, an Alien Ship and other vocal poltergeists.

34.   :29   The distant cry of the Mokele Mobembe. Recorded on the Lake of the Congo, Africa. This sound is not processed or treated in any way whatsoever. It has, however, been repeated six times so that you can begin to detect the mournful cry of the Mokele, estimated to be about half a mile away. Recording courtesy of Dr. Herman Regusters.

35.	:52	Lisa explains the A.D.R. Practice sessions as described in Chapter 15. Each cue is repeated six times to assist you in getting used to the beeps and practicing repeating the lines to be revoiced. This series of exercises is a must for first time actors who have never worked on an A.D.R. Stage before.
36.	:51	A.D.R. Practice Line #1 "I don't know how to get to him—you tell me!"
37.	:41	A.D.R. Practice Line #2 "This ain't what I pay you for, Sam—so don't give me no excuses, awright?!"
38.	:52	A.D.R. Practice Line #3 "I don't give excuses—I just give headaches to knumb skulls like you."
39.	:39	various BODYFALLS
40.	2:49	various FOOTSTEPS for temp Foley
41.	1:34	FOLEY—John Post does "Autopsy"
42.	1:22	various Fight sound effects
43.	1:47	a demonstration of NORMALIZATION and VARI-SPEED
44.	0:33	Attack Helicopter—30 mm Chin-Gun
45.	1:05	Attack Helicopter—Hellfire Missiles and 2.75 inch Rocket Pods.
46.	1:00	Attack Helicopter—Attack Maneuvering cue
47.	3:50	Attack Helicopter—As it might sound on a typical interactive flight run.
48.	:35	The Final Challenge—your creative power of sound is limited only by your own imagination.

SCENE 36—FOLLOW-ALONG SCRIPT COMPANION

— The Cast —

Frank Young	Dwayne Avery
Vikki Landaker	Alexandra Di Vecchio-Taylor
Taylor	Rodney Reuben
Police Officer	Kip Silverman

36. EXT. CRIME SCENE—BUSY CITY SUBURB (afternoon) **36.**

Frank Young and Vikki Landaker drive up to the crime scene and park.

They get out and make their way through the crowd of curious onlookers and uniformed police officers who are standing by during the investigation.

Frank and Vikki walk around the side of the old ramshackle house toward the back door where Vikki spots fresh footprints in the flower garden.

> VIKKI
> Frank—look here. Footprints.
> Mature male—expensive dress shoes.

> FRANK
> I doubt he was out gardening.

> VIKKI
> I also doubt they belong to the
> victim. Make sure Rodney gets
> photos before the lab boys touch 'em.

> FRANK
> Hey, take a look at this.

> VIKKI
> What?

> FRANK
> Looks like little sprinkles of sand.

> VIKKI
> Yeah, so?

> FRANK
> It doesn't look like it belongs here.
>   (beat)
> Look at this—there's even some sand
> on these protruding sweet pea nails on
> the side of the garage.

> VIKKI
> Here's a bag, better take some samples.
>   (beat)
> Careful where you step.

Rodney approaches with his camera equipment.

> RODNEY
> Anyone interested in some pictures?

> FRANK
> Let's get some shots of it first.
>   (to Rodney)
> Get some shots of these nails on the
> wall—we're interested in the sand.

> VIKKI
> We're going to need a compaction analysis.
> We need to know how heavy this guy is.

> FRANK
> One thing bothers me.

> VIKKI
> Yeah, what's that?

> FRANK
> I see footsteps going into the house. But
> I don't see any coming back out.

> VIKKI
> Suspect fled out the front door.

> FRANK
> No, couldn't have. Front door is wrenched
> shut. Neighbors said Ricky always used
> the back door. Besides, you can see the
> front porch hasn't been swept in ages.

> VIKKI
> Let's check the side windows.

> FRANK
>   (to Rodney)
> Make sure you get full coverage of the
> footprints before they plaster them.

> RODNEY
> No problem, I got it covered.

Frank & Vikki walk around the side of the house as Rodney starts taking pictures of the crime scene.

- - - - o O o - - - -

Index

WARRANTY AND DISCLAIMER OF LIABILITY

PRESS AND ANYONE ELSE WHO HAS BEEN INVOLVED IN THE CREATION PRODUCTION OF THE ACCOMPANYING CODE ("THE PRODUCT") CANNOT DO NOT WARRANT THE PERFORMANCE OR RESULTS THAT MAY BE TAINED BY USING THE PRODUCT. THE PRODUCT IS SOLD "AS IS" WITHOUT WARRANTY OF ANY KIND (EXCEPT AS HEREAFTER DESCRIBED), EITHER EXPRESSED OR IMPLIED, INCLUDING, BUT NOT LIMITED TO, ANY WARRANTY OF PERFORMANCE OR ANY IMPLIED WARRANTY OF MERCHANTABILITY OR FITNESS FOR ANY PARTICULAR PURPOSE. FOCAL PRESS WARRANTS ONLY THAT THE MAGNETIC CD-ROM(S) ON WHICH THE CODE IS RECORDED IS FREE FROM DEFECTS IN MATERIAL AND FAULTY WORKMANSHIP UNDER THE NORMAL USE AND SERVICE FOR A PERIOD OF NINETY (90) DAYS FROM THE DATE THE PRODUCT IS DELIVERED. THE PURCHASER'S SOLE AND EXCLUSIVE REMEDY IN THE EVENT OF A DEFECT IS EXPRESSLY LIMITED TO EITHER REPLACEMENT OF THE CD-ROM(S) OR REFUND OF THE PURCHASE PRICE, AT FOCAL PRESS'S SOLE DISCRETION.

IN NO EVENT, WHETHER AS A RESULT OF BREACH OF CONTRACT, WARRANTY OR TORT (INCLUDING NEGLIGENCE), WILL FOCAL PRESS OR ANYONE WHO HAS BEEN INVOLVED IN THE CREATION OR PRODUCTION OF THE PRODUCT BE LIABLE TO PURCHASER FOR ANY DAMAGES, INCLUDING ANY LOST PROFITS, LOST SAVINGS OR OTHER INCIDENTAL OR CONSEQUENTIAL DAMAGES ARISING OUT OF THE USE OR INABILITY TO USE THE PRODUCT OR ANY MODIFICATIONS THEREOF, OR DUE TO THE CONTENTS OF THE CODE, EVEN IF FOCAL PRESS HAS BEEN ADVISED OF THE POSSIBILITY OF SUCH DAMAGES, OR FOR ANY CLAIM BY ANY OTHER PARTY.

ANY REQUEST FOR REPLACEMENT OF A DEFECTIVE CD-ROM MUST BE POSTAGE PREPAID AND MUST BE ACCOMPANIED BY THE ORIGINAL DEFECTIVE CD-ROM, YOUR MAILING ADDRESS AND TELEPHONE NUMBER, AND PROOF OF DATE OF PURCHASE AND PURCHASE PRICE. SEND SUCH REQUESTS, STATING THE NATURE OF THE PROBLEM, TO ELSEVIER SCIENCE CUSTOMER SERVICE, 6277 SEA HARBOR DRIVE, ORLANDO, FL 32887, 1-800-321-5068. FOCAL PRESS SHALL HAVE NO OBLIGATION TO REFUND THE PURCHASE PRICE OR TO REPLACE A CD-ROM BASED ON CLAIMS OF DEFECTS IN THE NATURE OR OPERATION OF THE PRODUCT.

SOME STATES DO NOT ALLOW LIMITATION ON HOW LONG AN IMPLIED WARRANTY LASTS, NOR EXCLUSIONS OR LIMITATIONS OF INCIDENTAL OR CONSEQUENTIAL DAMAGE, SO THE ABOVE LIMITATIONS AND EXCLUSIONS MAY NOT APPLY TO YOU. THIS WARRANTY GIVES YOU SPECIFIC LEGAL RIGHTS, AND YOU MAY ALSO HAVE OTHER RIGHTS THAT VARY FROM JURISDICTION TO JURISDICTION.

THE RE-EXPORT OF UNITED STATES ORIGIN SOFTWARE IS SUBJECT TO THE UNITED STATES LAWS UNDER THE EXPORT ADMINISTRATION ACT OF 1969 AS AMENDED. ANY FURTHER SALE OF THE PRODUCT SHALL BE IN COMPLIANCE WITH THE UNITED STATES DEPARTMENT OF COMMERCE ADMINISTRATION REGULATIONS. COMPLIANCE WITH SUCH REGULATIONS IS YOUR RESPONSIBILITY AND NOT THE RESPONSIBILITY OF FOCAL PRESS.